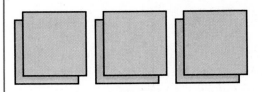

PASCAL

A New Introduction
to Computer Science

Terrence W. Pratt

Department of Computer Science
University of Virginia

PRENTICE HALL, Englewood Cliffs, New Jersey 07632

Library of Congress Cataloging-in-Publication Data

Pratt, Terrence W.
   PASCAL: a new introduction to computer science / Terrence W. Pratt.
   p. cm.
   ISBN 0-13-654286-7
   1. Pascal (Computer program language)   I. Title.
QA76.73.P2P725 1990   89-16385
005.13′3—dc20   CIP

Editorial/production supervision: *bookworks*
Interior design: **Maureen Eide**
Cover design: **Bruce Kenselaar**
Cover Art: ***Thomas Jefferson Papers, Special Collection Department,***
Manuscripts Division, University of Virginia Library
Manufacturing buyer: **Mary Noonan**

 © 1990 by Prentice-Hall, Inc.
A Division of Simon & Schuster
Englewood Cliffs, New Jersey 07632

Printed in the United States of America

10 9 8 7 6 5 4 3 2 1

ISBN 0-13-654286-7

Prentice-Hall International (UK) Limited, *London*
Prentice-Hall of Australia Pty. Limited, *Sydney*
Prentice-Hall Canada Inc., *Toronto*
Prentice-Hall Hispanoamericana, S.A., *Mexico*
Prentice-Hall of India Private Limited, *New Delhi*
Prentice-Hall of Japan, Inc., *Tokyo*
Simon & Schuster Asia Pte. Ltd., *Singapore*
Editora Prentice-Hall do Brasil, Ltda., *Rio de Janeiro*

DEDICATION

To my brother Dennis
(1937 – 1986)

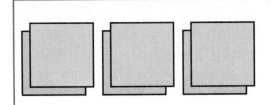

Contents

☐ 6

Choosing a Data Representation   258

☐ 7

Implementing Procedures and Functions   314

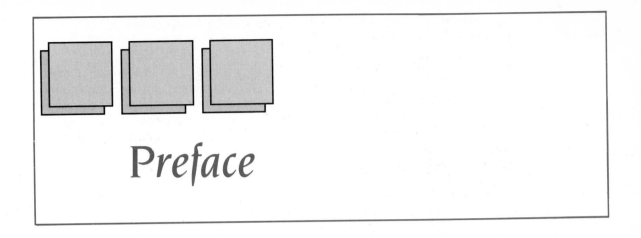

Preface

Welcome to the fascinating world of computers, computer programming, and computer science. *PASCAL: A NEW INTRODUCTION TO COMPUTER SCIENCE* represents a fresh look at how to approach these subjects in a first course. Instead of the traditional approach that treats computer programming as "problem solving" and that emphasizes the details of coding in a particular programming language, this book has developed from a more modern view of computer programming and computer science.

Representative of this view is the new definition of the subject given by the ACM Task Force on the Core of Computer Science (published in the *Communications of the ACM*, January, 1989). Slightly paraphrased, their definition is:

> *Computer science* is the systematic study of algorithmic processes that describe and transform information: their theory, analysis, design, efficiency, implementation, and application. The fundamental question underlying all of computer science is, "What can be (efficiently) automated?"

The ACM report suggests an approach to computer science that is based on understanding computers as *information processing machines* and on understanding computer programming as the activity of *automating an information processing task.* The basic concerns of computer science are those listed in the definition: the theory, analysis, design, efficiency, implementation, and application of algorithmic processes (in the form of algorithms and computer programs). The same report also points to the importance of the rich history of ideas, concepts, and principles that underlie and support our current understanding of the basic subject areas of a first course—algorithms, data structures, and programming methods. It is these threads that form the fabric for the organization and content of *PASCAL*.

□ □ □
TO THE STUDENT

This book is intended for a person who knows nothing of computers and computer programming. It is primarily about computers, programming, and the fundamentals of computer science. For the implementation of computer programs, it uses the Pascal programming language. If you know something about computers and programming but not about Pascal, you should find the language parts of the book interesting. If you already know the Pascal language, you should still find much here that is new. The book provides an introduction to many important concepts in computer programming and computer science.

For background, nothing is expected of you except some basic familiarity with high school algebra. No previous experience with computers is required.

□ □ □
TO THE INSTRUCTOR

This book is intended for a one semester course with a title such as "Introduction to Computer Science" or "Introduction to Computer Programming." If you have taught such a course before, you will find that the *content* of *PASCAL* is largely familiar—most of the same basic topics about Pascal and programming are here—but the *treatment* of this content is strikingly different. Because the content is largely the same, the starting and ending points of a course based on *PASCAL* are almost identical with those of a traditional CS1 course, *Introduction to Programming Methodology,* as described in the Curriculum '84 recommendations of the ACM The content is also suitable for the first part of a secondary school Advanced Placement course.

In the section below, the key points of difference between *PASCAL* and the traditional introduction to computer programming and computer science are described. On the surface, the differences might be described as bringing "modern software engineering practices" into the first course, but those words have often meant something quite different from what is attempted here. *PASCAL* provides a *foundation* on which to build modern software engineering practices in later courses, but it is not itself a course in software engineering.

□ □ □
WHAT IS NEW, AND WHY?

Here is a brief summary of the key items that differentiate *PASCAL* from texts that use a more traditional approach.

□ □
Abstraction is First and Fundamental

Abstraction is central to modern software engineering, in the form of data type and subprogram definitions. Mastering the use of abstraction in programming is the key to learning to program. To use abstraction effectively, the student must learn to identify when a new data type or subprogram is needed, and how to define and use it, before deciding how it should be implemented. To help the student learn to use abstraction effectively, Chapter 5 separates the definition and use of abstractions from questions of their implementation. Definition of both data types and subprograms are treated in this chapter. Chapter 6 looks at issues in the choice of the representation of new data types; Chapter 7 does the same for subprograms. From the beginning, students are taught that defining data types to represent the objects in their programming world and defining subprograms to represent the operations on those objects are fundamental programming activities.

Data Representation Comes Early

In place of the traditional sequence of topics that defers discussion of data representation issues, especially records and arrays, until late in the course, *PASCAL* begins discussion of these issues much earlier. By the end of Chapter 6 the student has been introduced to the major elements of data representation in Pascal: the scalar types, including subranges and enumerations, records, linear arrays, and strings. These concepts provide all that is required for building good representations of fairly complex real world data. The fundamental importance of good data representation is emphasized and exemplified throughout.

Design is a Separate Activity from Coding

A fundamental teaching problem in the first course is to separate program *design* from *coding in Pascal*. Three methods are used in this text to emphasize this separation to the student:

1. A separate *design vocabulary* is used throughout, which speaks of "algorithms," "data objects," "states," and "actions" during the design phase; a distinct *coding vocabulary* of "programs," "variables," and "statements" is used when discussing Pascal.
2. A chapter on basic program design methods (Chapter 3) provides the chance to practice designing complete algorithms before seeing how to code an algorithm in Pascal in the following chapter.
3. A new *design pseudo-code* is used throughout, developed expressly for this text, which provides an explicit language for developing *complete* program designs.

The Concept of "Program State" is Central

Woven through every part of the book, beginning in Chapter 3, is the fundamental concept of *program state*—meaning the "state of affairs" in the computation at some point during program execution—the current values of all the program's variables, what is displayed on the screen, where the files are positioned, and the like. *Program state* is the dual to the concept of *program action*. Actions are represented by assignments, I/O, procedure calls, and control structures—the things we see in the program body. But the goal of each action is to *change the program state*. During execution, actions and states alternate, beginning in an initial state and terminating in a final state, with each action leading from the current state to a next state.

In solving problems in the real world, we often make use of the state/action duality. A problem is often described in terms of a starting state and a goal state. We may see a sequence of actions leading from here to there, or, equally likely, we may see a sequence of intermediate states that lead from here to there. But always between each pair of actions there is a state, and between each pair of states there is an action. Terms like "means-ends analysis," "divide and conquer," "stepwise refinement," and even the venerable "top-down decomposition" are as much methods for defining a sequence of states as they are methods for defining a sequence of actions.

From the central concept of program state flow many benefits in understanding other parts of the programming process. Program *design* may now include the design of program states as well as program actions. Program *verification* may be seen as primarily a process of verifying the properties of program states. For example, assertions, loop invariants, preconditions, and postconditions are all statements about properties of program states. Program *testing* may be understood as the process of determining if the program reaches the correct intermediate and final states.

□ □

Analysis Skills are as Important as Synthesis Skills

The traditional introductory course is almost entirely a course in program *synthesis*—you learn how to *write* programs, not *analyze* them. Program analysis, outside of finding syntax errors, enters only in two minor topics, if at all: analysis of algorithm efficiency (Big Oh analysis) and formal program verification using axiomatic "proof of correctness" concepts.

A practicing programmer probably spends more time analyzing programs than writing them. Program analysis is the major skill needed for *debugging:* if the output is wrong, find the error. Program analysis is the major skill needed for informal *verification:* show that the procedure implements its specifications. Program analysis is an essential part of *modification:* show that you can make these modifications safely, without introducing new errors. And, in fact, program analysis naturally goes hand in hand with program synthesis, because at each step in designing and coding a program, you need to analyze what has been designed or coded.

PASCAL introduces an explicit set of program analysis concepts and skills centered on three basic forms of analysis:

1. *Control flow analysis.* Determine the possible execution paths through the program statements. Which statements are on each path? Which tests determine the path? Under what conditions will a path be taken during execution?

2. *Data flow analysis.* Analyze the flow of data values through the computation. Where is each value defined, where is it used, and where is it lost? Which statements and variables participate in defining it? In a procedure or program segment, what data values are coming in and what values are going out?

3. *Precondition/postcondition analysis.* Identify actions whose correct execution depends on assumptions about the data values used in the action. What are those assumptions? How can those assumptions be guaranteed, regardless of the control path?

These fundamental analysis methods are used in three major ways in the text: for informal *verification* of the correctness of an algorithm, for *debugging* a program quickly, and for checking that *modification* is done safely. Analysis skills provide a strong foundation for later work in computer science or professional programming.

Common Programming Patterns are Presented Rather than Invented

The traditional course instructs primarily at the level of language features. Larger patterns that involve the coordinated use of several language features are left to the student to invent or else they appear in examples without being pulled out and abstracted into learnable "chunks." The student spends considerable time and intellectual energy inventing versions of common programming patterns.

These common patterns should be part of the repertoire of every programmer. *PASCAL* identifies many such standard patterns and presents them explicitly as separate, learnable chunks. The student is encouraged to use the standard patterns when programming "in the small" (within a single procedure or segment) and to concentrate on larger design issues rather than reinventing well-known patterns.

Software Engineering Topics are Emphasized

Several additional topics from modern practice in software engineering are emphasized:

1. Written program requirements, before design begins.
2. Data abstraction and information hiding.
3. Testing strategy, developed along with the program design.
4. Comments and good style, used to capture the program design in the code.
5. Efficiency achieved through a wise choice of data representations and algorithms, not coding tricks.

ORGANIZATION

The fifteen chapters fall into three major groups: introduction, programming fundamentals, and optional topics. The book uses a spiral approach. Important topics are introduced in a simple form in the early chapters and then are revisited in greater depth in later chapters. Interactive programming is emphasized throughout.

Chapters 1–2: Introduction to Computer Science and Systems

These chapters provide introduction, historical background, an overview of computer hardware and software, and motivation for the remainder of the book. They are intended to be read while the student is being introduced to an actual computer system and Pascal implementation in the laboratory.

Chapters 3–10: Programming Fundamentals

These chapters are the core of the book. Chapter 3 introduces the basics of program requirements and design. Chapter 4 follows with the basics of Pascal coding, compiling, and testing. Chapter 5 is the central chapter on *abstraction:* data types, subprograms, and constants. Chapter 6 looks at the choice of *data representations* for new data types, and Chapter 7 explains the issues in implementing *subprograms.* Chapter 8 is the central discussion of program *analysis.* Chapters 9 and 10 provide more depth on the design and analysis of conditionals and loops.

Chapters 11–15: Optional Topics

The last five chapters may be covered in any order, or omitted. These topics are usually treated in greater depth in a second course. Chapter 11 treats *data files* and the associated input/output concepts. Chapter 12 introduces *recursion,* and Chapter 13 discusses *abstract data types, modules,* and the proper use of *global variables* in Pascal. Chapter 14 discusses program *performance* and algorithm *efficiency,* using the setting of *tables* and *sorting* and *searching* algorithms. Chapter 15 covers *multidimensional arrays, matrix/vector operations,* and the problems associated with computing with *real numbers.*

A suggested pace is to assign Chapters 1 and 2 for introductory reading during the first week. Then cover about a chapter per week through Chapter 10, and as many of the last five chapters as time allows. Assignments should develop skills in both program analysis and program synthesis.

Learning Aids

All chapters begin with a list of *Chapter Goals* and end with a list of *Review Questions.* Each chapter that introduces new pseudo-code or Pascal elements also ends with a *Pseudo-code and Pascal Summary* section that provides a brief syntax/semantics reference for the student. Programming examples, case studies, exercises and larger problems are provided throughout. Because of the early introduction of data structures and subprograms, interesting examples and problems can be used immediately.

□ □ □ ABOUT PASCAL

PASCAL provides more emphasis on fundamental programming concepts and less emphasis on the details of the Pascal language itself than traditional texts. Most of the major elements of the standard Pascal language are treated, but no attempt is made to provide complete coverage of all features of the standard language or of the many extensions that are widely used.

The Pascal design dates from the late 1960s and some features are no longer considered appropriate in modern software engineering. Several Pascal features are intentionally not covered (e.g., GOTO statements, WITH statements, and anonymous data types) and others are used only in tightly controlled circumstances (e.g., global variables and VAR parameters).

□ □ □ ACKNOWLEDGMENTS

The final form of this book has benefited from the suggestions of many individuals during the four years of its development. My thanks to the following individuals for their thoughtful comments:

- Michael A. Covington (University of Georgia)
- Dan Drew (Texas A&M University)
- Eileen B. Entin (Wentworth Institute of Technology)
- Henry A. Etlinger (Rochester Institute of Technology)
- Frank T. Gergelyi (New Jersey Institute of Technology)
- Terry A. Gill (Carnegie-Mellon University)
- Michael G. Gonzales (Gwynedd-Mercy College)
- Barbara Harris (DeVry Institute of Technology)
- Elmer K. Hayashi (Wake Forest University)
- Patricia Hurst (Editor, *Deadline* Newsletter)
- Leon Levine (University of California, Los Angeles)
- John M. Lloyd (Montgomery College)
- Keith B. Olson (Montana Tech)

Stephen P. Wartik (Software Productivity Consortium), my former colleague on the faculty at the University of Virginia, made a class test of the first version under difficult circumstances. I am indebted to him for his patience and for his thoughtful suggestions on the first and second versions. The students in that CS 180R class, Spring semester, 1986, also provided many useful suggestions.

Marcia Horton, my editor at Prentice Hall, was uniformly helpful and extraordinarily patient throughout this one-year project that stretched into a four-year project. Lisa Garboski and the production team have done an outstanding job of producing the book on a tight schedule.

Finally, thanks to Pat, Kirsten, Randy, Laurie, Josie, and Jessica for being part of my life during this (not always easy) time.

□ □ □
COMMENTS AND SUGGESTIONS

The approach taken in *PASCAL* is, quite obviously, experimental. Comments, criticisms, and suggestions for improvement are welcome (from both students and instructors). Mail them to the author at:

Department of Computer Science
Thornton Hall
University of Virginia
Charlottesville, VA 22901

or via electronic mail:

twp@virginia.edu

T.W.P

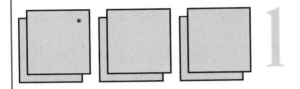

Computers and Computer Science

CHAPTER GOALS

When you have mastered the content of this chapter you should be able to:

- Explain what a *computer* does.
- Define what *computer science* is, and list the major sub-areas of computer science.
- Briefly describe the historical development of computers and computer science.
- Describe a *Turing machine* and what it can do.
- Define what *computer programming* is, and explain the four phases involved in constructing a computer program.
- Explain the difference between programming *methods*, programming *languages*, and programming *tools*.
- Describe three types of *limits* on what tasks can be automated using computers.
- Explain why *complexity* is the central problem in constructing a program.
- Tell what *abstraction* means, and why abstraction is our main solution to the problem of complexity in programming.

The modern computer has greatly changed the world we live in. In the period since 1950, we have come to depend on computers for help in handling many complicated information processing tasks. Computer science is a new discipline that has developed out of the need for a systematic understanding of computers, what they can do, and how they are used.

□□□ **1.1**
WHO USES COMPUTERS?

A travel agent listens as a customer describes the vacation trip she has planned. With a few keystrokes, he brings into view on his computer terminal the flight options for the customer. After a few minutes of discussion, the agent has made all the required reservations, printed the tickets, and even printed boarding passes with seat assignments. A computer program handled all the transactions.

The successful movie producer, with a long string of science fiction hits, is watching scenes from her latest production. A space ship glides low over the surface of an alien planet. The ship and the planet are marvelously realistic. The entire scene is generated by a computer program from specifications provided by the producer and her co-workers.

An architect is walking through the multimillion dollar shopping mall that he has designed. He sees how the design looks from the inside on each of the various levels. He climbs the stairs and rides the escalators. But the mall has not yet been built—the entire scene is generated directly from the architect's drawings by a computer program, which displays the scene on a computer terminal in the architect's office.

The test pilot climbs to 60,000 feet in a new experimental jet. The airplane's wings are extremely thin and sweep forward rather than backward. The plane is more maneuverable than any existing jet, but it is so unstable that it would break apart in less than a second without continuous attention to the slightest change in the flex of the wings or tail. The test pilot cannot provide this attention—her reflexes are too slow. A computer program reads the sensors attached to the wings and tail and makes minute adjustments in the position of the jet's control surfaces continuously during the test flight.

Who uses computers? Almost everyone in our modern world. What is it that computers do? A computer is an *information processing machine*. The travel agent, the movie producer, the architect, and the test pilot are all using computers to perform *information processing tasks*. These tasks are not new—producing movies, de-

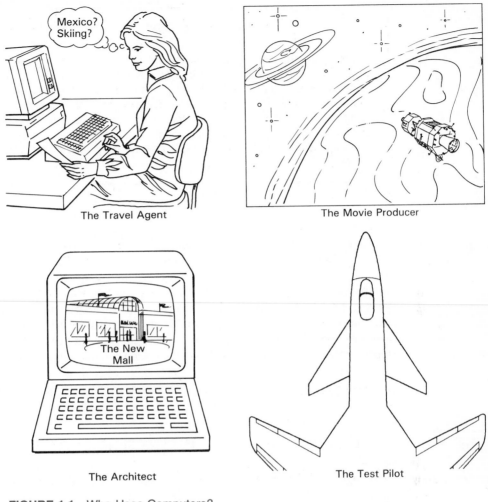

FIGURE 1.1 Who Uses Computers?

signing buildings, making travel reservations, piloting airplanes—these tasks were done before the invention of computers and can still be done today without computers. But computers allow people to perform larger and more complex information processing tasks and perform them more easily and accurately. In short, a computer is a *useful tool* for information processing.

Inventing tools and other mechanical aids to make difficult, tedious, or dangerous tasks easier is a universal human response. To travel faster and further than our legs can manage, we invent bicycles, motorcycles, automobiles, and airplanes. To dig holes deeper and more quickly than our arms and hands can manage, we invent pickaxes, bulldozers, and steam shovels. It is no surprise that we also seek mechanical aids and tools to allow us to manage larger and more complex information processing tasks. The term *computer* is the name for any one of a large and varied class of information processing machines that we have invented.

This book is about computers. But more importantly, it is about *information processing tasks*—how to recognize and define them, how to find *algorithms* to perform them, and how to represent those algorithms as *computer programs* so that a computer can be used to aid in performing them repeatedly, quickly, and accurately.

This book assumes that you know nothing about computers, computer programming, or computer science. Its goal is to introduce you to the fundamental issues and concepts of computer science, through the experience of creating computer programs to perform a variety of information processing tasks. Along the way, you will develop into a reasonably skillful programmer, but skill in programming is not our central goal. If you already have some programming experience, whether in Pascal, BASIC, Ada, or any other programming language, read on—you should find some interesting and exciting new ideas here, regardless of your previous experience.

□□□ **1.2**
THE ROOTS OF COMPUTERS AND COMPUTER SCIENCE

Although computer science is a new discipline, its roots lie deep in the history of science, engineering, and mathematics. We can trace several threads as they develop over the history of human civilization which ultimately lead to the invention of the modern electronic computer and to the development of the discipline of computer science.

□

Automating Complex, Repetitive Calculations.   Calculation has been a central need since the beginnings of mathematics, science, and engineering. From mathematical formulas that model various real world phenomena, such as the shape of parcels of land, the costs and prices in commercial transactions, the strength of dams and bridges, and the trajectories of the moon and planets, we use calculations to determine numbers on which we base our future actions. How much land in the parcel, how much gain from the commercial transaction, how high to make the dam, how strong to make the bridge, and when to expect the tides and the next eclipse? These questions can be answered by calculations based on mathematical formulas.

Most calculations are tedious, repetitive, and error-prone information processing tasks. Tools to automate some of the effort involved in calculation have been invented throughout history. In 500 B.C., the *abacus* originated in Egypt. This simple calculation aid is still used in some parts of the world today.

In the Middle Ages and during the Renaissance, many devices were invented to aid in surveying land and navigating the oceans. These devices not only allowed more accurate measurements of position, but they also simplified the calculations involved.

In 1622, William Oughtred (English) invented the *slide rule,* which became the basic tool for scientific and engineering calculation until it was largely supplanted by the handheld calculator (an offspring of the electronic computer) in the 1970s. In 1642, Blaise Pascal (French) constructed the first *mechanical calculator*. (The Pascal programming language is named in his honor.)

A nineteenth century precursor to the modern computer lies in the work of Charles Babbage (English) in the 1830s. He devised a machine called the *difference engine* that could mechanically perform complex calculations involving logarithms, trigonometric functions, and arithmetic for applications such as computing the tables of numbers needed for the accurate firing of cannons. A second Babbage design, the *analytical engine,* was a more general calculating device that was guided by a "program" similar to that used in modern computers. Babbage's assistant, Ada Lovelace, through her development of programs for the analytical engine, is regarded as the first computer programmer. (The Ada programming language is named in her honor.)

The development of theories of electricity and electronics during the late 1800s and early 1900s led to the rapid development of more sophisticated calculating machines in the 1920s and 1930s, constructed from electromechanical switches. The stage was set for the entry of the fully electronic computer (no moving parts) in the 1940s. Full automation of complex, repetitive calculations was finally possible.

□

Automating Large, Simple Tabulating/Counting Tasks.   Another thread of development lies in attempts to automate a different class of information processing tasks—those that involve relatively simple but very large tasks in tabulating and counting. Examples include counting of populations in a given area (the problem of the census taker) and the maintenance of business and government tax and accounting records. This thread also begins with the *abacus* and similar counting devices.

In 1890, the problem of counting and tabulating information from the U.S. census spurred Herman Hollerith (American) to invent the *punched card tabulating machine.* The idea of using punched cards as a means to control machinery had first been introduced in 1801 by Joseph-Marie Jacquard (French) as a means to control the patterns woven by mechanical weaving looms.

Hollerith's work led directly to the development of a large variety of electromechanical machines for counting, tabulating, sorting, and simple accounting during the first half of the twentieth century. These machines were based on the use of punched cards to represent the information to be processed. By the 1940s, many large businesses were automating an increasing number of their accounting tasks by using punched card tabulating machines.

□

Advances in Electronics.   A third thread, the rapid advances in electronic circuitry during the period 1900–1950, was fundamental in allowing the construction of the first electronic computers. Many different types of switching devices were developed during this period. It was shown that groups of switches could be wired together into *switching networks* that were capable of performing arithmetic operations like addition and multiplication. For example, an electronic *adder* would have two sets of wires coming in and one set going out. If signals were sent down the incoming wires that represented two numbers to be added, then the signals that appeared on the outgoing wires would represent the sum of the two numbers.

By the 1940s it was well understood how all of the basic operations of arithmetic and many more complex operations (for example, the square root, sine, and cosine functions) could be represented by electronic switching networks. The switches themselves, which had originally been partly electronic and partly mechanical ("throwing" the switch meant physically moving a part of the switch) now could be constructed entirely electronically by using the *vacuum tube* as a switching device. ("Throwing" the switch now meant electronically changing the voltage in a wire.)

□

Mathematical Foundations.   A fourth thread that formed the intellectual basis for modern computers is found in developments in mathematics and mathematical logic. In 1854, George Boole (English) invented a logical calculus that used only *true/false* values and basic operations such as *and, or,* and *not* to combine *true/false* values. This calculus (later named *Boolean algebra*) could be used to easily calculate

---

FIGURE 1.2   Threads in the Development of the Modern Electronic Computer

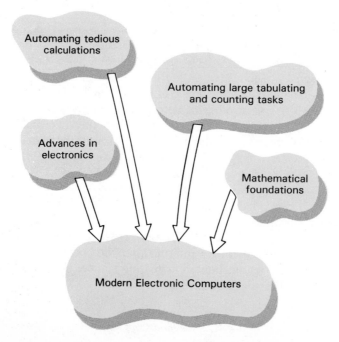

6

the truth or falsity of complicated logical arguments. It also could be used to represent switching networks, by replacing *true/false* by the *on/off* positions of a switch and *and, or,* and *not* by simple electronic circuits.

Boole's work also supported attempts to formalize larger areas of mathematical argument during the last half of the nineteenth and early twentieth century, culminating in the attempt by Bertrand Russell and Alfred North Whitehead to formalize much of mathematics in the 1920s. This field came to be known as *mathematical logic.*

During this same period, mathematical logicians began to try to formalize the concept of an *effective procedure* for computing some quantity, meaning a procedure that could be carried out by a person (or machine) that would always lead to the desired result in a finite number of steps. Clearly, we knew of effective procedures for computing the sum, difference, product, square root, and many other quantities defined in mathematics, but were there other more complex mathematical functions which could never be computed by any effective procedure?

□ □

Turing's Remarkable Machine

Although there were several attempts by logicians to define the concept of "effective procedure" during this period, the most striking results were obtained by Alan Turing (English) in the 1930s. His simple mathematical "machine," later named the *Turing machine,* is shown in Figure 1.3. It bears some important similarities in organization to the modern electronic computer.

FIGURE 1.3 Turing's Remarkable "Machine"

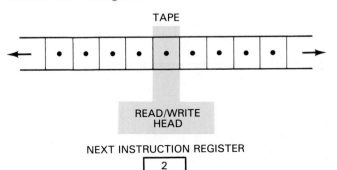

TAPE

READ/WRITE HEAD

NEXT INSTRUCTION REGISTER

2

PROGRAM

Instruction number	Symbol read	→ Symbol to write	Direction to move	Next instruction
1	•	•	•	•
2	•	•	•	•
•	•	•	•	•
•				
•				

The Turing machine consists of a simple *tape,* divided into squares, and extending as far as needed in both directions. Each square on the tape contains a single symbol, such as a letter or digit. Squares that are unused contain a space.

The machine also has a *read/write head* positioned over some square of the tape. The read/write head moves back and forth on the tape as the Turing machine performs its actions.

The third element of the machine is a *next instruction register* that indicates the next action to be taken. This storage register simply contains the number of the next instruction to be executed by the machine.

The actions of a Turing machine are determined by a simple *program,* which consists of a table of *instructions,* numbered in sequence. Each instruction chooses what the machine should do next depending on what symbol on the tape happens to be positioned beneath the read/write head. Depending on the symbol read, a particular sequence of three actions is taken:

1. A new symbol (or a space) is written on the tape underneath the read/write head, replacing the symbol read,
2. The read/write head is moved one square left or right, and
3. The number of the next instruction is stored in the next instruction register. If the machine is to stop (because the computation is complete), then the next instruction number is replaced by "HALT".

Figure 1.4 shows a program for a Turing machine. This program describes an "effective procedure" for adding one to any positive decimal number, where the number is initially written on the tape in the form:

$$\langle \text{whole number part} \rangle . \langle \text{fraction} \rangle$$

Let's see how the Turing machine carries out the instructions in its program.

□ □

How a Turing Machine Works

The computation of a Turing machine takes place in the following fashion.

□

Initial State.   The *data* required for the computation is placed initially on the tape, using one square of the tape for each symbol, and the read/write head is positioned over the leftmost symbol. The number of the first instruction in the program is stored in the next instruction register. We term this starting situation the *initial state* of the Turing machine.

□

Instruction Execution Cycle.   The machine then begins to execute the instructions of its program, by repeating the cycle:

PROGRAM

Instruction number	Symbol read		Symbol to write	Direction to move	Next instruction
1	0 – 9	→	same	R	1
	space	→	same	R	1
	.	→	same	L	2
2	0	→	1	L	HALT
	1	→	2	L	HALT
	2	→	3	L	HALT
	3	→	4	L	HALT
	4	→	5	L	HALT
	5	→	6	L	HALT
	6	→	7	L	HALT
	7	→	8	L	HALT
	8	→	9	L	HALT
	9	→	0	L	2
	space	→	1	L	HALT

FIGURE 1.4 A Turing Machine Program to "Add One"
("L" = left; "R" = right)
("same" means "write the same symbol that was read")

1. Read the symbol on the tape that is currently positioned under the read/write head and fetch the instruction number stored in the next instruction register. Let's call the symbol, A and the instruction number, K.

2. In the program, find the instruction numbered K and the line for the symbol A in that instruction. Write the designated new symbol on the tape under the read/write head (replacing symbol A), move the read/write head one square in the specified direction, and store the specified next instruction number in the next instruction register (replacing number K).

3. If the next instruction is HALT, then stop, otherwise repeat the cycle, starting with step 1 again.

□

Final State.   If the Turing machine ever reaches HALT and stops, then the final contents of the tape represent the result of the computation. We term this the *final state* of the machine.

Possibly the Turing machine may reach a cycle of instructions that never leads to a HALT and a final state. In this case the Turing machine runs forever, without halting and producing an answer (because as it runs, the contents of the tape will keep changing).

Look again at the program in Figure 1.4. To use this program with a Turing machine, you would write a decimal number on the tape, say the number

5177199.2213

and position the Turing machine's read/write head over the leftmost digit, 5. Then you start the Turing machine running. When the machine halts, the tape will contain a number one greater than the original:

5177200.2213

If you watched the actions of the Turing machine while executing the instructions of this program, you would see its read/write head sweep down the tape to the right, looking for the decimal point in your number (see Figure 1.5). When it finds the decimal point, it moves back left to the ones digit. If the ones digit is not a "9", then it replaces that digit by a new digit that is one greater than the original, such as replacing a "2" by a "3". Then it halts. If the original digit happens to be a "9", then it writes a "0" and moves left to propagate the carry to the tens digit. It continues this process until there is no further carry to make.

You can play "Turing machine" by executing the instructions of the program by hand. Choose any positive decimal number and try following through the actions of a Turing machine when it is given your number on its tape and the program of Figure 1.4.

Note that if you forget to include a decimal point in the number you write on the tape originally, then this Turing machine program never reaches a final state. The Turing machine will continue to move to the right forever, looking for a decimal point on the blank part of its tape to the right of the number.

□ □

Turing's Thesis: What can a Turing Machine Compute?

Turing's goal was to convince other mathematicians of his day of two things. The first is easy to accept, but the second is surprising:

Point 1: Any Turing machine program represents an "effective procedure." If a Turing machine can compute some quantity, then the instructions of its program represent an effective procedure for making that computation. There is nothing "intelligent" or "creative" about the actions of a Turing machine.

Point 2 (Turing's thesis): Any "effective procedure" for computing any quantity can be represented as a program for a Turing machine! That is, if you think up an effective procedure for computing some quantity, using whatever means you choose, there would always be a Turing machine program that could compute the same quantity. Your method might allow you to perform the computation faster and more easily than with a Turing machine, but ultimately any effective procedure could be expressed as a program for a Turing machine.

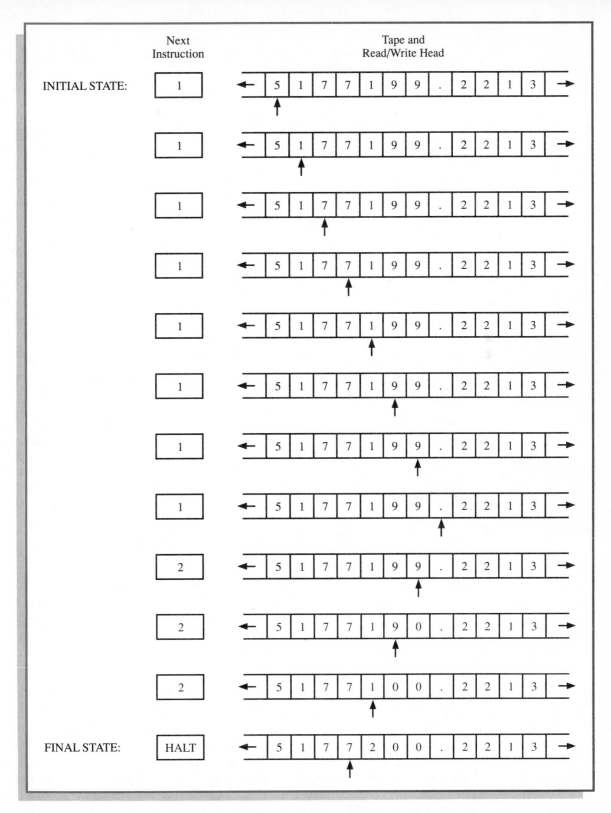

FIGURE 1.5 The Turing Machine at Work
(executing the instructions of the program in Figure 1.4)

Point 2 has become known as *Turing's thesis*. It is not something that can ever be "proved" mathematically (because we can always invent new ways of computing things), but it has stood up under repeated questioning and is now widely accepted. Mathematicians and computer scientists have invented dozens of other ways of representing effective procedures, many of them entirely different in concept from the Turing machine, and they have all been shown to be no more powerful than the Turing machine in what they could compute.

Turing's thesis is interesting to mathematicians, but it also forms one of the central foundations for understanding modern computers and computer programs. Translated into terms relevant to today's computers, it says that *no computer that exists today, or that might ever be invented in the future, could possibly be programmed to perform a computation that would be impossible with a Turing machine.* In this sense, the simple Turing machine is equivalent in computing ability to the most powerful supercomputer that might ever be built. Keep Turing's thesis in mind as you study the rest of this book.

□ □

The Birth of Electronic Computers

By the 1940s, the need for large-scale automated aids for calculation and other information processing tasks was evident. The demands of World War II, the advent of atomic weapons, and the increasing complexity and amount of information required by government and industry provided the need. Developments in electronics and punched card accounting and tabulating equipment provided the necessary engineering base. And developments in mathematics provided the concepts that set the stage.

In 1939, John Atanasoff (American) constructed a small prototype machine that is regarded as the first *electronic digital computer*. The first large-scale electronic computer, the ENIAC, was completed in 1946 by J. Presper Eckert and John Mauchley (American). While these machines could perform calculations entirely electronically, the "program" that controlled them was not easy to change—each change in the program required rewiring parts of the machine.

A mathematician, John von Neumann (American), provided the concepts needed to complete the picture. Von Neumann suggested three principles to guide the design of a fully electronic computer:

1. Encode both program and data as binary numbers (sequences of 0's and 1's),
2. *Store the program* along with the data electronically in a set of switches (the computer *memory*), and
3. Provide a *central processing unit* that could not only perform calculations but also fetch, decode, and execute the instructions contained in the program.

With these three principles, von Neumann saw that it would be possible to construct an electronic computer that could perform large complex information processing tasks entirely without human intervention, once the necessary program and data were stored in the computer's "memory." And to make such a computer perform a different computation, you would simply store a different program in the computer's memory. No rewiring would be needed.

Von Neumann's concept of the *stored program, binary, electronic computer* marks the beginning of the modern computer era. Todays computers are still largely based on von Neumann's concepts. In the late 1940s and early 1950s, dozens of stored program electronic computers were constructed in many countries and the automation of information processing tasks became possible on a scale that was impossible a generation before.

EXERCISES

1.1 Modify the Turing machine program in Figure 1.4 so that the machine will add 2 to the number originally on the tape.

1.2 Modify the Turing machine program in Figure 1.4 so that the machine will *subtract* one from the number originally on the tape. The original number must be greater than one. For example, if the tape originally contains 100.221 then in the final state the tape should contain the result 99.221. Here is the hard part: The whole number part of the result should never have a *leading zero* unless the whole number part is itself zero. Thus, the result must be 99.221, not 099.221, but if the initial number is 1.221 then the result should be 0.221.

1.3 Modify the Turing machine program in Figure 1.4 so that the machine will always HALT eventually. If there is no decimal point in the number on the tape, then have the machine assume the decimal point is at the right end of the number. For example, if the tape originally contains 217999 then in the final state the tape should contain 218000. Assume that there are no spaces within the original number.

□□□ 1.3
THE DEVELOPMENT OF MODERN COMPUTER SYSTEMS

A computer system consists of both *hardware* and *software:*

□ **Hardware**

The *hardware* of a computer system consists of its physical components, such as the various electronic circuits, printers, keyboards, display screens, and the cables that connect them.

□ **Software**

The *software* of a computer system consists of the programs that are available to be run on that computer to perform various information processing tasks.

In the next chapter, we look closely at both the hardware and software that form a modern computer system, but to complete our short history here, let's briefly follow the development of computer hardware and software from the early beginnings in the 1950s up to today.

□ □

The Development of Computer Hardware

The electronic switches at the core of an electronic computer are the key to the speed and size of the overall computer system. The computers of the 1950s used *vacuum tubes* as switches (you may have seen vacuum tubes in old radios or other early electronic equipment). Computers based on vacuum tubes are today called *first generation computers*. By todays standards, these computers were slow, unreliable, and very large. (What would fill a large room in the 1950s fits in a briefcase today.)

In 1947, a much faster and smaller electronic switch, the transistor, was invented. By 1960, *second generation computers,* using transistors as switches, were replacing the vacuum tube machines of the 1950s. These machines were physically smaller but could store more information and process it more quickly and with greater reliability.

Because both programs and data must be stored in the memory of a computer, large numbers of switches are required to construct a computer memory. The invention of *magnetic core memory* in 1950 provided a way to build large, inexpensive, fast and reliable computer memories. The second generation computers of the 1960s used magnetic core memories almost exclusively. Even today a computer's memory is often referred to as "core."

But even as second generation computers were being introduced, further advances in electronics were making them obsolete. In 1959, *integrated circuits* were invented—tiny chips of silicon that contained many transistors. This began a rapid period of development in electronics that allowed ever more complex switching circuits to be constructed on single chips of silicon.

Some of these silicon chips were designed to store information—they became the *electronic memory chips* of the modern computer. Others were designed to make calculations and process information—they became the *microprocessor chips* of the modern computer. The typical computer of today, at its electronic heart, is constructed by wiring together a relatively small number of silicon chips, each containing 10,000 to 1,000,000 microscopic electronic switches.

The development of microprocessor chips provided the electronic base for many familiar devices such as *handheld calculators, video games, automatic teller machines,* and *VCR's.* These devices are not computers, but they utilize some of the same developments in electronics.

A modern computer system consists of many devices working together, such as keyboards, CRT's (television screens), and printers, as well as the basic *processors* and *memories* that form the center of the system.

Early computers used *punched cards* adapted from the punched card tabulating equipment of the 1940s and 1950s to provide a means to enter programs and data into the system. Punched cards were also used to store the result of the computation. To prepare the punched cards containing the program and data, the programmer used a separate device called a *keypunch,* whose only purpose was to punch the necessary holes in the cards to represent each letter or digit typed on the keyboard. To translate the holes in a punched card back into readable letters and digits, a separate *line printer* was used. The printer "read" the holes in the cards and printed the equivalent information on paper. For storing larger quantities of information, early computers used *magnetic tape*.

In the late 1960s and 1970s these early computer system components were rapidly replaced by newer devices. In place of punched cards, *computer terminals* were developed that consisted of a TV-like display screen and a typewriter-like keyboard. These terminals could be directly connected to the computer system, and the user then could type in the required programs and data on the keyboard and receive the results directly on the display screen. There was no longer any need to use punched cards. The development of the *magnetic disk* in the 1960s provided a faster and more reliable means of storing large amounts of information than the magnetic tape.

During the late 1970s and 1980s, another major change in computer systems occurred—the advent of the *personal computer,* based on the new microprocessor chips. The personal computer provided a small, inexpensive desktop computer which allowed each user to have a private system. Previously, to use a computer, you had to have access to a large, expensive machine; now you could buy your own. The result was predictable—an explosion in the availability and use of computers for new purposes.

During the 1980s, *networks* of computers became important. These networks connect different computers together, often dozens or hundreds of them, and provide a means for one person using a computer terminal or personal computer to access the network. Once the network has been accessed, the person may use any of the various computers connected to it.

The Development of Computer Software

During the period from the 1950s to today, developments in computer software kept pace with developments in hardware. One major thread is seen in the development of *programming languages*—notations for writing instructions for a computer. The earliest computers required that instructions be encoded as binary numbers, and this difficult encoding process led to many errors. Beginning in the mid-1950s, "languages" that were more like familiar notations from algebra or English were developed and "implemented" on computers. These programming languages allowed large, complex computer programs to be constructed more easily.

In the early 1960s, another type of software became important—an *operating system*. An operating system is a collection of computer programs that control and monitor the operation of the hardware of a computer system. The operating system software decides which users get to use the system, what they are allowed to do, and when they are allowed to do it. The operating system also keeps accounting records, so that each user can be charged a fair amount for using the computer system. The development of operating systems made it feasible to allow many users to simultaneously use the different parts of a computer system without interfering with each other.

As personal computers and computer networks were developed, operating systems were extended to take account of these new hardware organizations. For a personal computer, a greatly simplified operating system was all that was needed. For a computer network, the operating system software on each computer had to take on new duties in order to allow users access to other computers in the network.

Software in the form of *applications programs* has been important throughout the development of computers, because it is these programs that actually perform the tasks whose results are of interest to people. In the 1950s, most applications of computers were confined to scientific, engineering, and military uses. During the 1960s and 1970s, however, software for applications in almost every aspect of our lives became available, from computer games and toys to education, banking, business, government, entertainment and politics.

□□□ 1.4
WHAT IS COMPUTER SCIENCE?

Computer science is the systematic study of algorithmic processes that describe and transform information: their theory, analysis, design, efficiency, implementation, and application. The fundamental question underlying all of computer science is *"What information processing tasks can be (efficiently) automated?"*

ACM Task Force on the Core of Computer Science

The field of computer science (also called *informatics* or *information science* in various parts of the world) developed as a separate discipline of study in the period

1950–1965. It grew out of the same developments in mathematics, engineering, and science that led to the development of the modern electronic computer. Its development was spurred by the increasing complexity of information processing tasks in the modern world—tasks that require a more disciplined, scientific approach to their automation. During the 1960s most major universities formed departments for research and teaching in computer science. A large and diverse research literature began to develop, and courses in computer science at both the graduate and undergraduate level became widespread.

Several major sub-areas of the discipline emerged as relatively cohesive subjects. (See Figure 1.6.) One recent definition of the discipline divides the subject into nine major sub-areas. As with any discipline of study, these areas overlap and interact in many ways, so the divisions are not precise. The nine sub-areas are:

1. *Algorithms and data structures*. The study of methods for performing various general classes of information processing tasks—how best to represent the information to be processed, and how best to choose the steps to be performed to accomplish the task.

2. *Programming languages*. The study of notations ("languages") for representing the algorithms and data structures involved in information processing tasks. These languages must both be easy for people to use and be easy to translate automatically into detailed sequences of instructions and data for a broad range of different computer systems.

3. *Computer architecture*. The study of how to organize the various hardware components of a computer system into an efficient, reliable, useful whole.

4. *Operating systems*. The study of how to organize the programs that monitor and control the overall operation of a computer system.

5. *Software engineering*. The study of how best to construct programs to automate large and complex information processing tasks so that the resulting programs are correct, reliable, efficient, and easy to use.

6. *Numerical and symbolic computation*. The study of how to automate the task of constructing mathematical models of complex real world phenomena, such as the flight of an airplane or the movement of ocean currents, and how to calculate solutions to these mathematical models that predict the behavior of the system being modeled. The calculations may be "numeric"—using actual numbers as the data in the formulas—or "symbolic"—using algebraic manipulation of the formulas themselves.

7. *Database and information retrieval systems*. The study of how to organize and process large sets of data, such as are found in tabulating and accounting problems in business and government, large and complex manufacturing processes, and large scientific and engineering problems. Both the storage and processing of the data must be efficient, reliable, and secure.

8. *Artificial intelligence*. The study of how to automate tasks that humans perform using "intelligent" methods that are difficult to describe and characterize

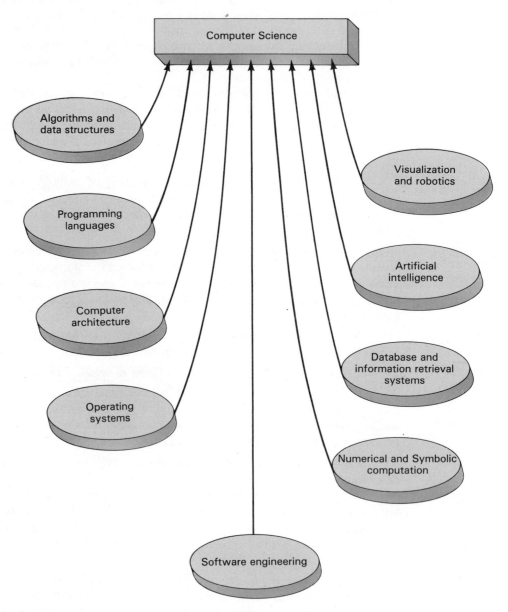

FIGURE 1.6 The Major Sub-areas of Computer Science

precisely, such as understanding language, learning how to do a task better, creation of new mathematics, science, art, and music, and evaluating and responding to complex situations such as are found in medical diagnoses or games like chess.

9. *Visualization and robotics.* The study of how to generate and process pictorial images, understand what is seen and heard, and determine an appropriate response to an external situation in terms of the actions of a robot or robot-like device.

□ □
Beginning the Study of Computer Science

In this book, we enter the field of computer science through a study of core concepts in three of the major sub-areas listed above: algorithms and data structures, programming languages, and software engineering. We look briefly at computer architecture and operating systems in the next chapter. The other areas provide a base of interesting tasks to automate in later chapters, but we do not attempt a deeper study of these areas in this first course. However, even attempting to automate simple versions of everyday information processing tasks is a fascinating study, and you will probably learn to appreciate more fully the marvelous abilities of the human mind in processing complex information.

The study of computer science also provides some additional practical benefits. By learning how to identify, define, and automate an information processing task using a computer, you will have the basic knowledge needed to construct a useful computer program for any one of the hundreds of types of computer systems in use, and using any of the hundreds of programming languages available. You can automate tasks by writing computer programs just for your benefit, or for the benefit of someone you work for or with.

Of course, you can *use* a computer without ever knowing how to write computer programs—just by using the programs that are already stored in a computer system. You can buy programs, written by someone else for your use, to perform many kinds of information processing tasks. But understanding the general principles behind the construction of such programs will give you a deeper understanding of their organization and their often frustrating quirks and inadequacies.

□ □ □ **1.5**
WHAT IS COMPUTER PROGRAMMING?

A *computer program* is a specification that describes how to automate a particular information processing task. It has to be written in a form that can be systematically translated into a detailed list of instructions for a computer. The instructions can then be executed by a computer to perform the desired task as often as required. To allow a program to be systematically translated into instructions for a computer, the program must be written using a specialized notation provided by a *programming language,* such as the Pascal language used in this book.

For example, a computer program might be written to automate the task of assigning students to classes during the registration period for a college. Before the program could be used to allow a computer to perform the task, two steps are required:

1. The program must be expressed using the notation of a programming language, such as the Pascal language.
2. The computer must be used to translate the Pascal form of the program into a detailed list of instructions for the computer to execute. This translation is carried out by another program called a *compiler*. The detailed list of instructions is then saved in a "file" within the computer system.

The college registration program would be written to specify how the task would be performed for any chosen semester, any list of courses and instructors, and any list of students. Each semester, during the student registration period, a college employee would use the computer to execute the detailed list of instructions saved in the file (called *running the program*). The person running the program would also provide the *input data* required by the program—the particular lists of courses, instructors, and students to be used by the program for this semester. The *output data* produced by the program would be the desired results—lists of which students were assigned to which classes. Running the program would allow the course registration task to be accomplished more quickly, easily, and reliably than would be possible by hand.

□ □

Programming Tools, Languages, and Methods

Programming is the activity of designing, constructing, testing, or modifying a computer program that automates an information processing task. Programming involves use of programming *tools,* programming *languages,* and programming *methods:*

□

Programming Tools.   Many parts of the task of constructing a program that can be run on a computer have already been automated. That is, there already exist computers and computer programs that automate large parts of the task of programming. We call these *programming tools*—they are the tools we use in programming, to make it possible to produce new programs more quickly, easily, and reliably. Some of these tools form the *hardware* of the computer system. Other tools are part of the *software* of the computer system—programs that we use, such as the *operating system, compiler,* and *editor* programs. In order to construct and run a new program, you need to know how to use these programming tools.

□

Programming Languages.   The notation provided by a programming language represents the interface between the parts of the programming task that have and have not been automated. If we can express how to perform an information processing task in the special notation of a programming language, then the rest of the work of translating the program into instructions for a computer is already automated. To construct a new program, you need to know how a program is expressed in the notation of the programming language that you intend to use.

☐

Programming Methods.   The construction of a computer program to automate a complex information processing task remains a difficult and error-prone activity. To be successful in constructing a program, you need to use programming methods that allow the construction to proceed quickly, easily, and reliably, regardless of the programming language that will be used ultimately to express the final program. Methods for designing the program, verifying its correctness, and testing it are among the methods used in constructing a new program.

Writing a computer program is somewhat like writing the script for a play. A script contains instructions to the actors telling exactly what actions to take, what to say to each other and to the audience, and so forth. A script also contains a list of the props and sets that will be used by the actors during the course of the play. Similarly a computer program contains a list of actions for the computer to take and a list of the "data objects" that will be needed for storing items of information during these actions.

The computer is like the group of actors in the play (the computer plays all the "parts" in your program). Just as the actors read the script and follow the instructions given there, the computer follows the instructions given in your program. And just as the actors rely on the "objects" (props and sets) provided on the stage, the computer uses the data objects specified in your program to store information while it is carrying out your instructions. However, unlike a good actor, a computer is unable to truly understand your *intention* in the program and correct for any minor errors you may have made in writing it. The computer does *exactly* what you specify—even if it's nonsense.

A computer program also has an "audience," just as a play does. The audience for a program consists of the people who *use* the program after it is written. To use the program, a person just requests the computer to execute again the instructions in the program. An audience for a play does not need a copy of the script in order to understand the play. Similarly, the user of a program does not need to know exactly what was specified in the program "script" in order to use the program.

☐ ☐

Programming and Mathematics

What are the skills required for computer programming? In particular, do you need to know a lot about mathematics? Mathematics and programming are related, but only in an indirect way: both use (and help develop) skill at logical analysis of a problem and careful attention to detail. If you have a strong background in mathematics, you probably have already become skilled at analyzing problems, developing ways of solving those problems, and handling the details involved in the solution. Those same skills will serve you well in programming. But you do not need to know many particular *mathematical facts* to be good at computer programming. For many types of programming, a basic knowledge of the facts of arithmetic and algebra is all that is required.

Mathematics may be important in a computer program because the particular information processing task performed by the program requires the use of mathematical methods, but not because programming itself requires the use of mathematics. For example, if a program is automating the calculation of "how much concrete is required for this particular kind of highway bridge," it requires some sophisticated mathematical formulas to calculate the answer, even if you compute the answer by hand. The program just uses the same mathematical formulas, but makes the computation more quickly and reliably than you could do it by hand.

□ □
Computer Science and Mathematics

While programming does not rely on mathematical facts or skills, mathematics is central to many aspects of computer science, where a more disciplined study of algorithms and computers is the goal. In computer science, we often build and analyze mathematical models of different kinds of algorithms, programming languages, and computer systems. These mathematical models allow us to probe deeply into the characteristics of particular ways of performing information processing tasks. From the results of this probing we learn how to construct better algorithms, programming languages, and computer systems.

□ □
The Limits of Computation

Although many information processing tasks have been successfully automated through the use of computers, there remain many that have not. In some cases, the limit lies simply in the size and power of current computers. We may know *how* to automate such tasks, but we may be unable to complete the required computations on existing computers in a reasonable amount of time. For example, it is possible to use existing mathematical models of weather patterns to provide better and more detailed global weather predictions than are currently available, but the computational task is so enormous that it is impractical on current computers.

Other information processing tasks have not been automated because we simply do not understand enough about the processes involved to be able to design and implement the required computer programs. For example, the remarkable abilities of the human mind to understand written and spoken language are still not understood in detail. It is well beyond our programming abilities to automate a broad range of tasks that involve understanding English, French, German, or any other language.

Finally, there are some information processing tasks that are *inherently* beyond the capabilities of any computer that could ever be constructed, not simply because they are too large or complex, but because the very attempt to define a method to solve the problem leads to a contradiction. The *halting problem* is such a task: can we write a program that will always be able to determine if another program will eventually halt when applied to some particular set of data? Surprisingly, the answer is *no*—not if the program has to solve the halting problem for *any possible program*.

The reasoning leading to the conclusion that the halting program is "unsolvable" (regardless of how you construct the program or what computer or programming language you use) is based on a mathematical argument. We won't try to give the argument here, but it is based on a standard type of mathematical reasoning called *proof by contradiction*. You assume you could write such a program, and then prove that the assumption leads to a contradiction—if you could write it, then you can show that it could not possibly work correctly. So you conclude that you cannot possibly write such a program.

EXERCISES

1.4 Programming and playwriting are similar in that the creator who writes the script, the actor who carries out the instructions in the script, and the viewer who observes the actions are distinct. In programming, one person creates the program. A machine carries out the instructions in the program to produce the desired result. Another person serves as an audience to receive the results and evaluate whether the results are really correct/useful or not. Name two other kinds of creative activity that involve a similar arrangement between creator/performer/audience.

1.5 If you are intrigued by the "halting problem," you might be interested to know about other "unsolvable" problems. The book *Computation: Finite and Infinite Machines* by Marvin Minsky (Prentice Hall, 1967) provides a fascinating introduction to these questions.

□□□ **1.6**
PROGRAMMING IS A FOUR-PHASE ACTIVITY

Let's examine in more detail what is involved in programming. Constructing a useful computer program involves four distinct phases, each of which includes several kinds of tasks:

1. *Determine the requirements that the program must meet.*
2. *Design an algorithm and verify that it satisfies the program's requirements.*
3. *Code a program from the algorithm, enter it into a "file" in the computer, and verify that it correctly represents the algorithm.*
4. *Compile, test and debug the program.*

We look briefly at these phases in this section. In the next section, we look at two examples of complete programs. In later chapters we discuss each phase again in more depth.

□ □

Phase 1: Determine Requirements

As you begin a programming project, you need to analyze the problem and determine the *requirements* that the program must meet. What information processing task must the program be able to perform? The program's requirements specify the

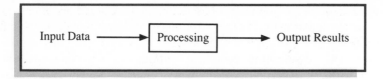

FIGURE 1.7   Requirements Specify What the Program Must Do

input data, processing, and *output results* of the program—what data goes into the program to be processed, what processing of this data is required, and what results come out, as shown in Figure 1.7. The requirements also describe any special assumptions about how the program will be used.

Analyzing the problem is important, because often you find that a computer program is of *no* help in automating part of the task. Usually a person has to get involved in collecting and preparing the data for the program to process, and a person has to analyze and evaluate the results produced by the program. Sometimes you find that the task cannot be done by a computer at all—because you cannot specify the required input data and output results of the program well enough. For example, you might want a computer program that could "write a good short story"—but what would you specify as the requirements for such a program?

□ □
Phase 2: Design an Algorithm and Verify that It Satisfies the Requirements

The requirements specify *what* the program must be able to do, but not *how* it should do it. For *how* you need an algorithm:

> □ **Algorithm**
>
> An *algorithm* is a specification of (1) the *sequence of steps* required to perform a particular information processing task and (2) the *data objects* used in performing each step.

Each step in an algorithm must have a clearly defined and unambiguous meaning, and the sequence of steps must perform the desired task and halt.

An algorithm is basically a program without many of the details, or, perhaps more accurately, a computer program is an algorithm that includes additional information required to allow its translation into instructions for a computer.

Designing an algorithm involves two major activities:

1. *Determine a sequence of steps for performing the task.* What sequence of steps are needed to perform the information processing task? Each step consists of one or more actions. The actions must lead from an *initial state,* where nothing has been done, to a *final state* where all the required results have been computed and displayed for the user.

2. *Choose a representation for the data.* How should each piece of data be represented within the program? You must decide what *data objects* are needed and what the *data types* of the objects should be.

The design phase is a paper and pencil activity. Often you start by thinking about how you would perform the task without a computer, by hand. Then you work out the details of a similar algorithm appropriate for a computer program.

After you have designed an algorithm, you stop and verify that the algorithm satisfies all the requirements that you identified in the first phase. Does the algorithm correctly specify how to automate the task? If not, you stop and revise the algorithm until all the requirements are fully satisfied.

□ □
Phase 3: Code, Enter, and Verify the Program

Once the algorithm is designed and verified, you proceed to *code* the algorithm as a computer program, following the rules of the Pascal language (or some other programming language). Your coded Pascal program also must be typed in ("entered") and stored in a "file" in the computer system you are using. This is the first step that involves actually using the computer. Before leaving this phase, you usually have the computer print a listing of exactly what you have typed in, which you use to verify that you have correctly coded and entered the program.

The code, enter, and verify phase is where you are involved with all the details of the Pascal programming language. Each part of your algorithm must be correctly coded according to the rules of the Pascal programming language. There are lots of "picky" details here—spelling, punctuation—it all has to be exactly right.

□ □
Phase 4: Compile, Test, and Debug

In the final phase, you use the computer twice. First, you use it to translate your program into a detailed sequence of computer instructions, and then you use the computer again to carry out these instructions, in order to test whether your program works as desired. There are two main activities in this phase:

1. *Compile the program and correct syntax errors.* A program called a *compiler* is used to translate your Pascal program into the detailed instructions required by the computer. If any errors are detected by the compiler (called *syntax* errors), you change the program to repair them and try again to compile the program, continuing until all syntax errors have been corrected. These errors are usually caused by minor typing mistakes while entering the program (that you overlooked during the previous phase) or by minor misunderstandings of some detail of the Pascal language, like proper punctuation of the program.

2. *Run the program and test it on some sample input data.* Finally you are ready to begin testing the program to be sure that it works as you expected. You ask the computer to execute your *compiled program* (the result of compiling the program in the last step). You provide the program with some test input data, representing a task to be performed, and retrieve the results produced by executing the program. You decide if the results are correct. If not, then the program contains a *bug*—an error—and you have to engage in some "debugging." You go back and determine what caused the error, change the program to correct the error, compile it again, and test it again. When the program successfully passes all your tests, it is ready for use.

□□□ **1.7**
TWO EXAMPLE PROGRAMS

Let's begin with two simple information processing tasks and follow through the development of programs that allow a computer to perform these tasks. For illustration, each step is discussed in detail, even though the actual programs are extremely simple.

EXAMPLE 1 *Greetings from George*

George wants to send a greeting to his instructor, Mr. Jones, by writing a program that will display a message on the display screen of a computer. He then plans to give a copy of the program to his instructor. Whenever Mr. Jones wants a cheery greeting from George, he can run George's program, and the greeting will be displayed on his computer's display screen, as shown in Figure 1.8. It is a simple task. Let's look at the steps involved in developing the program.

1. DETERMINE REQUIREMENTS.

George can state the requirements for this program easily:

> INPUT: none
> PROCESSING: none
> OUTPUT: Display the greeting.
> ASSUMPTIONS: Used only by Mr. Jones.

To complete the requirements, George has to decide on the exact text of the greeting. He chooses to have the program output the two lines:

```
Hi, Mr. Jones! Let's Compute!
              -from George
```

2. DESIGN AND VERIFY THE ALGORITHM.

George's algorithm consists of two steps in sequence:

FIGURE 1.8 Mr. Jones Running George's Greetings Program

Step 1: DISPLAY THE FIRST LINE:

"Hi, Mr. Jones! Let's compute!"

Step 2: DISPLAY THE SECOND LINE:

"—from George"

The algorithm uses no data objects because it does not need to store any information during these two steps. To verify the algorithm, George only needs to check that the two lines displayed match those required.

3. CODE THE ALGORITHM IN PASCAL, ENTER, AND VERIFY IT.

Figure 1.9 shows how George codes this algorithm in the Pascal programming language. The line numbers are just provided for the explanation that follows; they are not part of the program. George uses a personal computer to enter his program and

LINE NUMBER	PASCAL PROGRAM
1	PROGRAM Greetings (OUTPUT);
2	PROCEDURE DisplayTwoLines;
3	BEGIN
4	writeln ('Hi, Mr. Jones! Let''s Compute!':50);
5	writeln ('- from George':45);
6	END;
7	BEGIN
8	DisplayTwoLines;
9	END.

FIGURE 1.9 George's Greetings Program in Pascal
(The line numbers are only for the discussion in the text;
they are not part of George's program.)

store it in a file on a diskette (a "floppy disk"). After he enters it, George has the computer print a listing of his program, and he checks the program again to verify that it correctly represents his algorithm.

Here is a line by line explanation of how the Pascal program represents George's two-step algorithm. As you can see, there is a lot of detail in the program that does not appear in the algorithm. Let's follow the program through in its *logical* order, not in the order that it is written in Pascal:

Lines 7–9. Logically, the program starts at the BEGIN in line 7. The first action taken by the program is that in line 8: "DisplayTwoLines". The "END." in line 9 indicates that there are no further actions to be taken by the program. The task is complete.

Lines 2–6. These lines define what the action "DisplayTwoLines" means. In Pascal terms, such an action is called a *procedure*. Line 2 is the heading that indicates that a definition for the procedure "DisplayTwoLines" follows. The BEGIN in line 3 and the matching END in line 6 delimit the list of actions that make up the procedure.

Lines 4 and 5 represent the two actions in George's algorithm. Line 4 specifies in Pascal terms the action: Display the line "Hi, Mr. Jones! Let's compute!" on the computer's display screen. The word *writeln* means "write (display) a line". The characters within single quotes specify the message that is to be displayed. The "50" specifies that the message should be displayed so that it ends in the 50th character position, counting across the display screen from the left-hand margin. Line 5 specifies in similar terms the second action in George's algorithm.

Line 1. This line names the program ("Greetings") and lists the Pascal name of the display screen ("OUTPUT").

Notice the many details of the Pascal program that have little to do with the basic algorithm that George designed for this task. In coding the algorithm into Pascal, George has to worry with details of program form, such as punctuation, headings, BEGIN-END delimiters, and so forth. He also has to deal with minor details of program meaning, such as specifying the position of the end of each line he wants displayed. In line 4, he even had to use a special Pascal "trick" to allow the apostrophe in "Let's" to be displayed (he wrote the apostrophe twice to distinguish it from the single quotation marks that begin and end the entire line).

4. COMPILE, TEST, AND DEBUG.

After George has entered the program into a file and checked the listing for errors, he uses the Pascal compiler to translate the Pascal program into a detailed sequence of instructions for the computer. The compiler stores the translated program in another file in the computer system. During this translation, the compiler finds no errors in his program (so George has no syntax errors to correct). Finally George tests the compiled program by running it (commanding the computer to execute the instructions produced by the compiler). When the program runs, George sees displayed on his display screen:

```
Hi, Mr. Jones! Let's Compute!
    -from George
```

George is pleased—*it works*! Because the task performed by the program is so simple, only one test run is needed to ensure that George has made no mistakes in his programming. George can now give a copy of the program to his instructor as his "Greetings." ■

EXAMPLE 2 *Nancy's Temperature Conversion Program*

Let's try a program that is slightly more challenging. Here is the setting.

Nancy is in charge of writing some simple demonstration programs for her high school science fair. The school expects a large crowd for the fair, and the students want some programs available for people to try on the schools's new computer equipment. Nancy chooses a very simple task for her first program: automate the task of converting a temperature value from Fahrenheit degrees to Celsius degrees. Here is how she develops the program:

1. DETERMINE REQUIREMENTS.

Nancy explains the program's requirements: "The program should ask the user to type in a temperature in degrees Fahrenheit. Then I'll have the program convert it to degrees Celsius and display the result. I can describe the program's requirements as:

INPUT: A temperature value in degrees Fahrenheit.

PROCESSING: Compute the Celsius temperature equivalent to the input temperature.

OUTPUT: Display both the Fahrenheit and Celsius temperatures.

ASSUMPTIONS: This program will be used on a personal computer at the science fair.

"To complete the requirements, I need to decide on exactly what dialogue should take place between the program and the person using it. This is the sort of dialogue that I want:

DIALOGUE

PROGRAM: Please type a temperature value (degrees F):

USER: 68 (or some other temperature value)

PROGRAM: 68 degrees F = 20 degrees C

2. DESIGN AN ALGORITHM AND VERIFY IT.

"The algorithm for this program is straightforward, but I will need to know the formula for converting degrees Fahrenheit to degrees Celsius. I look the formula up in my science book:

$$\text{degrees } C = 5/9 \times (\text{degrees } F - 32)$$

"The program will need two data objects, one to store the Fahrenheit temperature value that the user types in and a second to store the equivalent Celsius temperature value computed using the formula. I'll name these two data objects *DegreesF* and *DegreesC*. Because these data objects will store numbers that may have fractional parts, I'll define their data type as *Real number*. Now I can write down the steps in the algorithm and make up my list of data objects. Because the algorithm is so simple, I'll just show the actions required for each step."

ALGORITHM

Step 1: DISPLAY: "Please type a temperature value (degrees F)."

READ: DegreesF   (store the value typed by the user)

Step 2: Use the formula to compute the equivalent Celsius value and store the value in DegreesC:

DegreesC := (5/9) * (DegreesF − 32)

Step 3: DISPLAY: "⟨DegreesF⟩ degrees Fahrenheit = ⟨DegreesC⟩ degrees Celsius"

DATA OBJECTS

NAME	DATA TYPE	PURPOSE
DegreesF:	Real number.	The temperature value typed in by the user.
DegreesC:	Real number.	The equivalent Celsius temperature value.

3. CODE, ENTER, AND VERIFY.

Nancy continues, "From this design it is easy to code the Pascal program (see Figure 1.10). I just fill in the details according to the rules of the Pascal language. The overall program consists of just a single action which I have named "ConvertAndDisplay".

"Each of the data objects in my list becomes a *variable* in the Pascal program. The variables are listed in the section that begins with VAR. The actions of the algorithm are coded as Pascal *statements*. The purpose of each step of the algorithm is included as a Pascal *comment*, enclosed in braces. These comments help to make the program readable by a person, but they are meaningless to the computer itself. A comment at the start of the program describes the overall purpose of the program, its author, and the date it was written.

"To enter the program I have to go down to school and use one of the school's computers. I use an *editor* program on the computer to help me as I type in the program, correct typing errors, and store the program in a computer file for later use. I choose the name CONVERTPROG for the file that stores the program. After I have entered the program, I request the editor program to print a listing of the program, exactly as it is stored in file CONVERTPROG. I check the printed listing to verify that I have done everything correctly.

4. COMPILE, TEST, AND DEBUG.

Nancy continues, "Now I run the Pascal compiler program to translate the program in file CONVERTPROG into the detailed instructions to be executed by the computer. I choose the name COMPILEDPROG for the file to contain these instructions.

"If there are no errors detected during the compilation of the program, I am ready to start testing the program. I command the computer to execute the instructions stored in file COMPILEDPROG. As the program begins to run, I see it display on the terminal screen:

```
    Please type a temperature value (degrees F):
  ?
```

```
PROGRAM TempConversion (INPUT, OUTPUT);

  {PURPOSE: This program reads a temperature value in degrees F.,
    converts it to degrees C., and displays the result.
   AUTHOR: Nancy NewJersey.
   DATE WRITTEN: October 1989.}

PROCEDURE ConvertAndDisplay;

  VAR
    DegreesF: Real;      {Temperature in degrees F.}
    DegreesC: Real;      {Temperature in degrees C.}

  BEGIN
          {Ask the user to type a Fahrenheit temperature value,
          read it in and store it in DegreesF.}

    writeln ('Please type a temperature value (degrees F):');
    readln (DegreesF);

          {Compute the equivalent Celsius temperature}

    DegreesC := 5/9 * (DegreesF - 32);

          {Display both temperature values.}

    writeln (DegreesF:6:1, ' degrees F = ',
           DegreesC:6:1, ' degrees C');

  END;

BEGIN

  ConvertAndDisplay;

END.
```

FIGURE 1.10 Nancy's Temperature Conversion Program

"I type in a test value. I've chosen 50 because I know that 50 degrees F should be converted to 10 degrees C. So the display screen now looks like:

```
    Please type a temperature value (degrees F):
  ? 50
```

"As soon as I hit the RETURN key after typing 50, a new line appears on the screen, as I planned in my program design:

```
    Please type a temperature value (degrees F):
?  50
        50.0 degrees F = 10.0 degrees C
```

IT WORKS!

"I run the program in COMPILEDPROG a second time, try typing another test value, and check the result. For this test I choose 212 as the input data value, which should be converted to a Celsius temperature of 100 degrees:

```
    Please type a temperature value (degrees F):
?  212
        212.0 degrees F = 100.0 degrees C
```

CORRECT!

"I run the program in COMPILEDPROG several more times with several more test cases and check that the conversions are correct in all my test cases. When I am satisfied that the program is working correctly, then I am finished. The program is ready to be used by visitors during the science fair.

"If the program had not worked correctly—either displaying the lines improperly or converting the temperature value incorrectly—then the program would have had a *bug*. I would stop testing and use my printed listing of the program to determine the cause of the error—find the bug. Then I would use the editor program to make whatever changes were required in the original program in file CONVERT-PROG.

"After making the changes, I would again run the Pascal compiler program to produce a new compiled version of the corrected program and store it again in file COMPILEDPROG (the old compiled program would be deleted by this action). Then I start testing again. I continue testing and debugging the program until it is performing exactly as the requirements specified it should." ■

Many computer programs solve a problem using steps that mimic the steps you would take to solve the same problem by hand, without a computer. Nancy's program is like that. You could do almost the same thing the program does with only paper and pencil:

1. Ask a friend to give you a temperature in degrees Fahrenheit.
2. He says "68".

3. You write 68 down on a piece of scratch paper, use the formula to convert it to degrees Celsius, and announce the result: "68 degrees F = 20 degrees C".

When you use a computer to perform an information processing task, the computer speeds up the work. The computer also can make the results look better—in the same way that a typed report looks better than a handwritten one. However, if you could not solve the problem with paper and pencil (given enough time), you will not be able to write a computer program to do it—the computer provides no magic answers to hard problems.

□ □

Programming It is not Always Easier than Doing It by Hand

In some ways, using a computer to do an information processing task is *more difficult* than doing it by hand. To use the computer you must be much more precise in deciding exactly what input data you need, how the data should be represented, exactly what actions are required to process the data, and so forth. Thus there is much more work to do at the beginning, when you are setting up the task as a computer program.

Another way that using a computer is more difficult: a person easily deals with special cases and unexpected situations as they arise in performing a task. A computer must be instructed in advance (when the program is written) what to do for every situation that may arise. In writing a program, you often spend a lot of time trying to anticipate what odd situations might arise and planning what the program should do in each of them.

□ □ □ **1.8**
COMPLEXITY AND ABSTRACTION

The two programs above are very small ones. Programs that automate important information processing tasks can be large, extremely complex, and very difficult to construct. Because they are used by many different people and may be used for many years on many different types of computers, they must be extremely reliable. Large programming projects often involve dozens or hundreds of programmers and continue for several years before a working program is delivered. What is a *large program?* Table 1.1 gives a general picture of what is involved in programming projects of various sizes.

Large computer programs are among mankind's most complicated creations. Yet most of these programs are written in programming languages like Pascal, using a few simple constructs over and over. That is why the listings of large programs are often as long as a large book—and those of the largest programs rival the size of an encyclopedia! When you consider that every single part of such a program must be

TABLE 1.1 Program Sizes

Size of Program	Length of Program Listing	Time to Construct	Number of Programmers
Trivial	10–200 lines	1 week or less	1
Small	500–2000 lines	1–4 months	1
Medium	5000–20,000 lines	6–12 months	1–3
Large	50,000–500,000 lines	2–3 years	5–30
Huge	Over 1,000,000 lines	Over 5 years	Over 50

correct if the program is to correctly perform the task it was written to automate, then you begin to understand the difficulties involved in programming.

The problems involved in constructing large programs can be summed up in a single word: *complexity*. The complexity of a large program makes it difficult to design and code, difficult to verify and test, and difficult, in many cases, even to use correctly. Complexity makes it doubly difficult to modify a program, because you usually do not fully understand all its details. And complexity leads to errors.

Our brain is limited in the amount of information it can actively work with at one time. The number of "chunks" that you can remember temporarily, while you are actively using the information, is usually less than ten (for example, the number of items in a list that you can remember without going to a special effort to memorize them—see Figure 1.11).

This limit comes into play strongly when you are programming. In trying to understand a program there are often many more than ten things that you need to

---

COMPUTER HORROR STORIES: THE NEVER-CORRECT OPERATING SYSTEM

Most large programs contain errors, even after many years of use. One classic story illustrates the problem. An operating system (a very large and complex program) for the computers manufactured by a major computer company was in widespread use for about ten years. As it was used, if a user found an error, an error report would be sent to the company. Once or twice a year, when about 1000 errors had been reported, some of the company's best programmers would prepare a new version of the operating system which corrected all the reported errors. This new version would then be sent to all users, installed on their computer systems, and another cycle of error reporting would begin.

Unfortunately, because of the complexity of this program, the changes made to correct the current 1000 errors might introduce new errors. Indeed, in the next cycle, another 1000 errors would be reported—including errors in parts of the program that used to be correct! Even though the operating system was used for many years, it never got any closer to being entirely error-free.

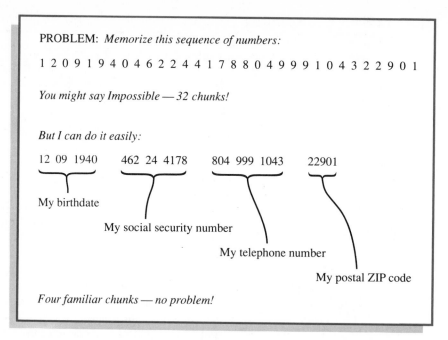

PROBLEM: *Memorize this sequence of numbers:*

1 2 0 9 1 9 4 0 4 6 2 2 4 4 1 7 8 8 0 4 9 9 9 1 0 4 3 2 2 9 0 1

You might say Impossible — 32 chunks!

But I can do it easily:

12 09 1940   462 24 4178   804 999 1043   22901

My birthdate

My social security number

My telephone number

My postal ZIP code

Four familiar chunks — no problem!

FIGURE 1.11 Your Brain Is Limited to Remembering a Few 'Chunks' at a Time

remember at one time. When you reach your brain's temporary storage limit you begin to forget how the parts of the program fit together, and you start to make errors.

If *complexity* is the central problem in programming, then there is also a single word for the solution to the problem: *abstraction*. Abstraction is the process of hiding details. It is the way that we take a complex set of facts and group them into a unit that can be remembered as a single chunk. A good abstraction hides in its internal structure the details, and presents to the user of the abstraction a much simpler chunk of information, such as the abstract chunks "birthdate," "telephone number," and so forth in Figure 1.11.

□ □

Procedural Abstraction and Data Abstraction

Abstraction is the programmer's shield against complexity. Two major kinds of abstraction are seen in programming:

Procedural abstraction is the grouping of a complex sequence of actions into a single unit, a single "chunk." The group of actions forms a "procedure" within a program, such as the procedure named *DisplayTwoLines* in George's program. We can think of the procedure as providing a single action and ignore the fact that the single action may actually require many smaller steps to complete. For example, we might have a single procedural abstraction called "ComputeIncomeTax" that represents the entire computation of an employee's income tax. There would be many steps involved in making the computation, but our procedure would hide them within a single abstract action.

Data abstraction is the grouping of a complex set of data items into a single unit, a single "chunk." We can then work with the larger chunk of data and ignore the fact that it is actually made up of a number of smaller data items. For example, we might define a "date" as a data abstraction composed of three parts, a "day," a "month," and a "year."

As you master the basic skills of programming, your effort increasingly becomes the *design of new abstractions* appropriate for each new program. You try to invent procedural and data abstractions that provide a natural way of expressing what is to be done and that at the same time keep the complexity of the program within the reach of your limited human brain power. Often you find that an abstraction you used in a previous program can be put to good use in a new one. Understanding how to develop and use abstractions in programming is one of the central themes of this book.

■ ■ ■
REVIEW QUESTIONS

1.1   A computer is a tool that helps people perform certain kinds of tasks better. What kinds of tasks can a computer perform? In what ways does using a computer help a person with those tasks?

1.2   Complex, repetitive calculations and large, simple tabulating/counting tasks provide two kinds of tasks that motivated the development of computers. Give an example of each type of task and explain why such tasks are difficult for people to perform without mechanical aids.

1.3   What are the four main parts of a *Turing machine?*

1.4   A *program* for a Turing machine consists of a table of *instructions*. What are the parts of an instruction?

1.5   A Turing machine begins a computation in an *initial state* and executes instructions until it reaches a *final state*. What is the initial state of a Turing machine? What is the final state?

1.6   Does a Turing machine have to reach a final state during its computation? Why or why not?

1.7   State *Turing's thesis* and explain its significance.

1.8   John von Neumann suggested three key principles on which to build a completely electronic computer. What were they?

1.9   What is computer *hardware*? What is computer *software*?

1.10   *First generation* computers and *second generation* computers are distinguished from each other and from later computers by the type of electronic *switch* used in the hardware. Name the devices used as switches in first generation computers. In second generation computers. In later computers.

1.11   Give a brief explanation of what is studied in the field of *computer science*.

1.12   Name nine major sub-areas of computer science.

1.13 What is a *computer program*? What is *computer programming*?

1.14 Constructing a computer program involves the use of specialized *tools, languages,* and *methods*. Explain the distinction between programming tools, languages, and methods.

1.15 Explain the relationship between computer programming and *mathematics*. Between computer science and mathematics.

1.16 Not all information processing tasks can be automated by using computers. Explain three different kinds of *limits* on what tasks can be successfully automated, and give an example of a task that is currently limited in that way.

1.17 Constructing a computer program involves four different "phases" of activity. Name the four phases and briefly explain what activities are part of each phase.

1.18 What is an *algorithm*? What distinguishes an algorithm from a *computer program*?

1.19 Give two reasons why using a computer to perform a task can sometimes be *more difficult* than doing it by hand.

1.20 Suppose you were put in charge of a project to build a "large" computer program. Give an estimate of the size of a "large" program (number of lines in its printed listing), how long it might take to construct, and about how many programmers might be needed.

1.21 What is the word that best sums up the problems involved in constructing a large computer program? What is the word that describes our best method for solving these problems?

1.22 Name the two main kinds of *abstraction* used in programming. Each is used to *group certain kinds of things together into a single chunk* in a program. Explain what kinds of things are grouped in each type of abstraction.

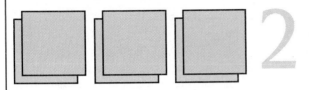

Computer Systems

CHAPTER GOALS

When you have mastered the content of this chapter you should be able to:

- Name the five major *hardware parts* of a computer system.
- Tell what a *time-shared* computer system is.
- Explain three different ways of *gaining access* to a time-shared computer system, and explain what happens during *login* and *logout*.
- Describe the major functions of the computer's *operating system*.
- Define the purpose of the *editor* and *compiler*.
- Distinguish between a *source program* and an *object program*.
- Explain what an *integrated programming environment* does.
- Explain the difference between the *syntax* and *semantics* of a programming language.
- Distinguish between the *definition* and the *implementation* of a programming language.
- Describe how a language is implemented with a *compiler* and with an *interpreter*.
- Name several *standard programming languages*.
- Explain four features of computer hardware that make it a useful information processing tool.
- Explain the *Principle of Binary Encoding*.
- Describe briefly how characters, integers, and real numbers might be encoded in bits.
- Explain the overall organization of a *computer memory,* including the use of *bytes* and *words*.
- Name and describe briefly the major types of *secondary storage devices* used in computer systems.
- List some typical *input devices* and *output devices* used in computer systems.
- Name the major components of the computer's *processor*.
- List and define the *prefixes* for very small and very large quantities that are commonly used in describing a computer system.
- Distinguish the major types of computer systems.

A computer system consists of both hardware, the physical components of the system, and software, the programs that are available to be run by the hardware. In this chapter we look in more depth at the organization of modern computer systems, to provide a background for our study of computer programming in the following chapters.

□□□ 2.1
HARDWARE BASICS: THE PARTS OF A COMPUTER SYSTEM

A *microcomputer* (or *personal computer*) is just a small, relatively inexpensive computer system used by only one person at a time—typically one that is small enough to fit on top of a desk. Microcomputers are seen in many homes, schools, and offices. Figure 2.1 shows the major parts of the *microcomputer* used by Nancy in Chapter 1 for her science fair program.

Although Nancy's microcomputer is a small one, it has the same major hardware components as any computer system, whether large or small:

FIGURE 2.1   The Major Parts of Nancy's Microcomputer

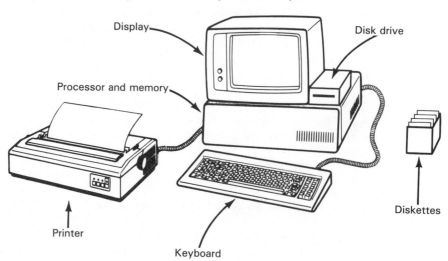

1. *Memory* (also called the *primary storage* or *store* of the computer)—used to store programs and data while they are being used by the computer. The memory of Nancy's microcomputer consists of a set of electronic circuits etched on silicon "chips" inside the central box of the system in Figure 2.1. While Nancy is entering, compiling, or running a Pascal program, the program (and the data it is processing when it is running) will be stored in the computer's memory.

2. *Processor*—used to execute the instructions of a program. The processor is also a set of electronic circuits etched on silicon chips inside the central box in Figure 2.1. When Nancy runs a Pascal program, the processor performs the actions specified in the program.

3. *Secondary storage*—used to store copies of programs and data that are not currently in use by the computer. The secondary storage on Nancy's computer is composed of a set of *diskettes* (or *floppy disks*). The *disk drive* is a device that can transfer programs and data back and forth from the computer memory to a diskette. The disk drive is shown as a separate box in Figure 2.1. The information on each diskette is organized into a set of named *files,* each of which can store a program or some data. Nancy stores all her Pascal programs in files on diskettes when she is not actually working with them.

4. *Input devices*—used to transfer programs and data into the computer from the outside world. On Nancy's microcomputer, the main input device is the *keyboard,* which is like an ordinary typewriter keyboard with some additional keys.

5. *Output devices*—used to transfer programs and data from the computer to the outside world. Nancy's microcomputer has two output devices, the *display*—the television-like device on top of the main computer box—and the *printer,* a separate component connected by a cable to the main computer box. Since the memory, secondary storage, and the processor work entirely electronically, without any visible results that Nancy can see, these output devices provide the only means for Nancy to determine what processing is going on inside the computer.

COMPUTER MEMORY—DOES A COMPUTER "REMEMBER"?

Computer jargon is sometimes confusing because common words, like *memory,* are given specialized meanings. Because a computer is often likened to a "mechanical brain," the term "memory" used for the storage component of a computer suggests that a computer "remembers" in the same way that a person "remembers."

Actually a computer memory "remembers" in the same sense that a piece of paper "remembers" what you write on it. You can store information in a computer memory, just as you can store information by writing it on a piece of paper. You can also "read," "erase," and "write over" what is stored in a computer memory, in a manner similar to how you use a piece of paper as a "memory."

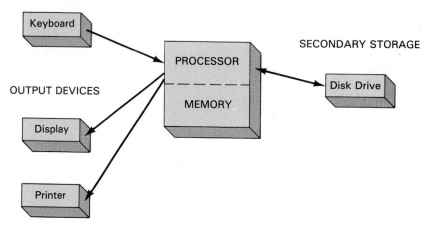

INPUT DEVICE

Keyboard

OUTPUT DEVICES

Display

Printer

PROCESSOR

MEMORY

SECONDARY STORAGE

Disk Drive

FIGURE 2.2 Logical Organization of Nancy's Microcomputer

Figure 2.2 shows the logical organization of the components of Nancy's microcomputer system. The arrows show the direction of information flow between the various components.

□ □
Time-shared Computer Systems

A microcomputer is among the simplest of computer systems—a self-contained system for a single person to use. To gain access to such a system, you have to work directly at the keyboard and display that are attached to the system.

As a computer system gets larger and more powerful (and more expensive), the number of each kind of hardware component will increase. For example, a large computer system may have several processors and several memories, dozens of disk drives for secondary storage, and hundreds of input and output devices. Obviously a larger computer system cannot be restricted to a single user at a time—many people have to be able to use the system simultaneously. Such a computer system is called a *time-shared* system:

□ **Time-shared Computer System**

A *time-shared* computer system allows many users to simultaneously access and use the system.

To access a time-shared computer system, you do not need to go to where the computer is located. Instead you access the computer through a *computer terminal,* composed of a display screen and a keyboard, as shown in Figure 2.3. The terminal may have no processor, memory, or secondary storage of its own, in which case it is

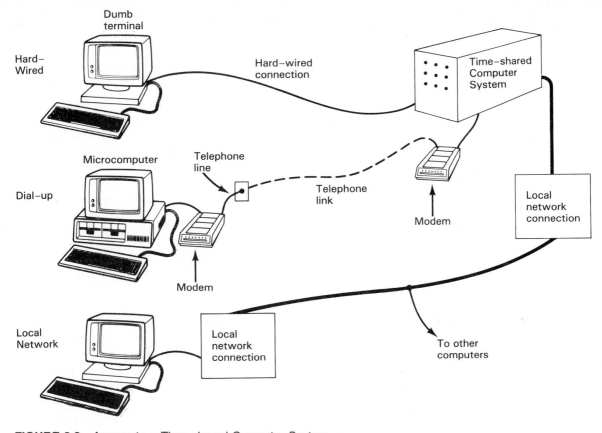

FIGURE 2.3 Access to a Time-shared Computer System

called a *dumb terminal*. A dumb terminal serves strictly as an input/output device for a time-shared computer system.

A microcomputer can also be used as a computer terminal, by using special software that makes the microcomputer act like a dumb terminal. The software allows you to switch back and forth between using a microcomputer as a dumb terminal to access a larger time-shared computer and using it as a self-contained computer system (with its own processor, memory, and secondary storage)—the best of both worlds.

The terminal that you use to access a time-shared computer system may be connected to the computer in various ways, as shown in Figure 2.3:

1. *Hard-wired connection.* A time-shared computer system may have terminals connected to it directly via wires—called *hard-wired connections*. To access the computer, you simply find a free terminal and turn it on.

2. *Dial-up connection.* A time-shared computer system may allow access via an ordinary telephone line. The computer will have a *telephone number*. You use a terminal connected to a device called a *modem* (short for "modulator-demodulator"). The modem allows you to connect the terminal to a telephone line and then dial the computer's phone number. When the phone rings, the computer answers (electronically, of course) and sends the appropriate startup messages to your terminal. You then use the computer just as you would with a hard-wired connection.

3. *Connection through a local computer network.* A local computer network is a group of separate computers that are linked together with a network of cables to which user terminals may be attached. The network may spread across several buildings, so that terminals are found in various offices and laboratories. Terminals may be hard-wired to the network, and dial-up access may also be provided. To use the network, you find an available terminal, turn it on, and type a command to specify which of the various computers you want to use. Each computer will have a name that identifies it to network users. Then you are connected through the network to that computer, and from there on, you use the computer just as you would if you had been connected directly to that computer in the first place.

□ □

Login and Logout

Time-shared computers are protected so that unauthorized users cannot gain access to them and run programs without permission. The usual form of protection is to provide each authorized user with an "account" that is identified by a special *user identification name* (*user-id*) and a *password*. From a terminal you may be able to access many different computers, but you are only able to use those on which you have an authorized account.

When you access a computer system that you want to use, you must first establish that you have an authorized account on that system. This process is called *logging in* to the computer system. A time-shared computer system is always "listening" for terminals that are trying to access the system, regardless of whether the access is through a hard-wired connection, a dial-up connection, or a computer network connection. When the computer notices a terminal that is trying to access the system, it sends a message to that terminal that says (approximately):

        PLEASE LOGIN:

You, the person using the terminal, then login by typing your personal *user-id* and *password* to identify yourself to the system. The computer checks that you have an authorized account with that user-id, and that you have given the correct password. Then you are free to begin your working session with the computer. Many other people may be logged in to the same computer at the same time on other terminals.

When you are finished using a time-shared computer system, you *logout*, usually by just typing a "logout" command. This tells the computer system that your work is complete. Usually the connection established from your terminal to the computer system is electronically switched off when you logout. You do not need to physically switch off the terminal to break the connection.

HACKERS: PART 1

There are two definitions of the term *hacker* in wide use in the computer world. The first definition is the one used most commonly in newspaper and magazine stories about "computer break-ins":

A *hacker* is a person who uses illegal or devious means to make use of a computer system on which he has no authorized account.

Almost anyone with a microcomputer or computer terminal can gain access to many different computers through dial-up telephone numbers and computer networks. But a person cannot login to those computers and make use of them without an authorized account. A hacker uses various tricks to bypass the usual login sequence, often by fooling the computer system into thinking he is an authorized user.

(For the second definition of *hacker,* you have to wait until Chapter 3.)

EXERCISES

2.1 For a microcomputer you have access to, determine where the memory, processor, secondary storage, input devices, and output devices are located in that computer system.

2.2 Repeat Exercise 2.1 for a larger computer system you have access to. List the number and type of each component of the larger system.

2.3 For the computer system that you will be using, determine your options for access to the system. Is it a single-user system or a time-shared system? Are hard-wired terminal connections available? Can you use a dial-up connection? Is the computer accessed through a computer network?

□ □ □ **2.2**
COMPUTER SOFTWARE ORGANIZATION

The software of a computer system fills the gap between what the computer hardware provides and what an ordinary computer programmer or computer user would like to have available. The hardware of a computer system is extremely complex and difficult to use. The details of processors, memories, and the rest are overwhelming, even to experienced programmers.

In the early days of computers, every programmer had to deal directly with the details of the hardware organization. Today, computer software has developed to the point where the details of the hardware are entirely hidden by layers of software, as shown in Figure 2.4. The software simplifies by *abstraction*—underlying details are hidden and a much simpler structure is provided to the computer user.

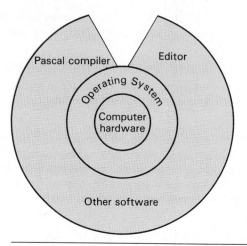

FIGURE 2.4 Software Layers
Hide Hardware Details

Only a few parts of the software of a computer system are relevant to learning how to program in Pascal. Let's go back to Nancy's Pascal programming in Chapter 1 and look more closely at the software that she uses as she enters one of her programs, compiles it, and then runs it several times with test data.

Nancy uses three major pieces of software, the *operating system*, the *editor*, and the *Pascal compiler*. The editor and compiler themselves make use of the operating system software. Thus they form an "outer layer" of software, built on top of the layer provided by the operating system, as shown in Figure 2.4.

The Operating System

The *operating system* is the program that controls the overall operation of a computer system. Its two main functions are (1) control of the *file system* and (2) control of *execution of user commands*.

On a time-shared computer system, the operating system also (3) *controls access* to the system, through the user login-logout procedure, (4) *controls the switching of the processor among users,* so that each gets a fair "time-slice" of use of the processor, and (5) *maintains accounting data* to track the amount of use of the system by the various users.

Controlling the File System

At the heart of a computer system is its file system—the set of all the files of programs, data, documents, and other information available to the computer user. In a single-user microcomputer, like Nancy's system, most of the files will be stored on diskettes. When a file is needed, the diskette that stores the file is inserted into the disk drive of the computer and, on the user's command, the operating system then copies the required file from the diskette to the computer's memory. In a larger computer system, files will be saved permanently on the secondary storage part of the system, where they can be copied into the computer's memory by the operating system whenever they are needed by a user.

The operating system keeps track of all the files that are stored on secondary storage in the computer system—the user-id of the owner of each file, its size, and its location in secondary storage. In a time-shared system, each user has *private files* that cannot be accessed by other users. There are also *public files* that can be accessed by any user.

Files are usually organized into *directories,* which are themselves a type of file containing information about other files. A diskette will have a directory showing all of the files currently stored in that diskette. In the secondary storage for a larger computer system, there will be directories showing the private files for each user and directories showing the public files that are available to all users.

□ □

Command Execution

The second major function of the operating system is to execute commands given by the user. Nancy may command the operating system to run a program, like an editor, the Pascal compiler, or one of her own programs. She may command the operating system to print a file on a printer or display the file on her terminal screen. Or she may command the operating system to simply display the names of the files that are listed in a certain directory.

The operating system usually has hundreds of different commands that it can execute. The user chooses a command, the operating system executes the command, and the cycle repeats until the user chooses the command "logout" (or, on a microcomputer, until the computer is turned off).

Two different methods are commonly used for specifying commands to be executed by the operating system:

1. *Menu.* A *menu* is a list of commands displayed on a terminal screen. You simply choose the command you want executed by "pointing" to it in some way—either by using a *mouse* to move an arrow on the screen to touch the chosen command name or by typing the number or first letter of the command.
2. *Typed command.* Alternatively, you may have to know the name of the command you want and type it on the keyboard when the appropriate "type command" prompt is displayed by the operating system.

□ □

Programming Environments: The Editor and Compiler

The *programming environment* consists of the software of the computer system that you use while you are actually constructing, compiling, and testing a new program. The programming environment provides tools that automate various parts of the process of program construction. In the programming environment, the two main tools are the *editor* and the *compiler*. Let's look at these first.

□ □
The Editor

The *editor* is the program that aids you in typing in your program, storing the program in a file, and making changes in the program once you have typed it in (see Figure 2.5). When you are ready to enter your program, you run the editor program. While the editor is running, you can use various "editor commands" to specify the actions that you want taken, such as inserting or deleting words or lines in your program file.

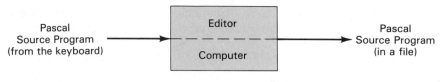

FIGURE 2.5 Entering a Pascal Program

You can use the editor to create and edit files containing any form of written information, including letters, term papers, and data for a program to process. In using the editor, whether a file represents a program or some other type of information makes no difference. The editor is simply concerned with the text in the file, which is made up of lines of characters.

Editor programs vary widely in the types of commands allowed. You will need to learn the details of the editor program available on your computer system before beginning to program in Pascal.

□ □
The Pascal Compiler

The program that you, the programmer, type in and store in a file (using the editor) is termed a *source program*. A source program, written in Pascal or any other programming language, is just a document, like a letter or term paper, that has been typed in as a sequence of characters.

The *compiler* is the program that is used to translate a source program into a detailed sequence of instructions and data that can be executed by the computer. The result of the translation performed by the compiler is termed an *object program*. A source program can be read and understood by a person, but an object program is intended only to be used by the computer's processor.

When you run the compiler program, you provide the name of the file that

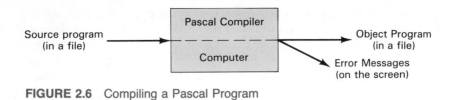

FIGURE 2.6 Compiling a Pascal Program

contains the source program that you want translated. The compiler program will copy the source program from the file into computer memory, translate it into an object program, and copy the object program into a second file, termed the *object program file,* as shown in Figure 2.6.

While the compiler performs this translation, you simply wait at the terminal. If the compiler detects an error in the way you have written the source program (for example, a misspelled word or missing punctuation mark), then it will display an error message on the screen. You then have to modify the source program file, using the editor, and run the compiler again. If the compiler finds no errors in your source program, then it will simply perform the translation you requested and leave the result in the object program file.

Notice that the compiler *does not change* the source program. If an error is detected by the compiler, you, the programmer, are responsible for determining how to correct the error. You have to use the editor to make the correction. Thus you are continually going back and forth between the editor and compiler until the time that the compiler finds no further errors in your source program.

□ □
Testing a New Program

Once a source program has been successfully compiled to produce an object program, you are ready to test the new program. During testing, you command the operating system to run the object program repeatedly as you try it out with different test data values, until you feel certain that it is working correctly for every case (see Figure 2.7). The source program is not involved when you are testing—only the object program is used.

FIGURE 2.7 Executing a Pascal Object Program

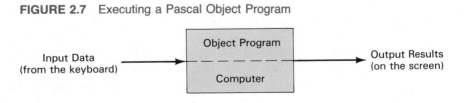

During testing you may discover that the program does not work correctly, or that you do not like the way the results of the program are displayed on the screen (even though the results are correct). If so, then you go back to the *source program* (you cannot change the object program). You determine the appropriate set of changes in the source program and use the editor program to make the changes in the source program file. Then you compile the modified program to produce a new object program, and resume your testing with the modified program.

□ □

Integrated Programming Environments

As you can see, when you are entering, compiling, and testing a program, you are constantly going back and forth between the three steps of *edit, compile,* and *run*. An *integrated programming environment* is a programming environment that automates the transfer between these three steps, so that you can go back and forth more easily. In a typical integrated environment, the programmer is given a menu that includes the options:

- *Name* the source program file.
- *Edit* the source program file.
- *Compile* the source program file to produce an object program file.
- *Run* the object program file.
- *Exit* the programming environment.

The transfer back and forth between the edit, compile, and run phases is automatic in an integrated environment. For example, when you type C (for "Compile"), the compiler is run with your designated source program file. If you have forgotten to name the source program file, then you are prompted for the name of the file. If the compiler detects an error in the source program, then the compiler quits and the editor program starts up automatically—usually with the exact point of the error in the source file displayed on the screen. You simply make the appropriate correction, terminate the editor to return to the menu, and type "C" again to rerun the compiler.

An integrated programming environment provides a convenient way to construct programs. The environment may also provide additional menu options that allow you to use other automatic tools that aid in program construction and testing.

□ □

Making a Program Available for Others to Use

After testing of the program is complete, the object program represents a *new piece of software* for your computer system. If you want to make the program available to others to use, you simply make the file that contains the object program available

USING OTHER SOFTWARE

Most computer systems have a wide variety of software available for any user. Here are some other types of programs that you may want to learn how to use (in addition to the operating system, editor, and Pascal compiler):

Electronic mail

A program that allows you to type in a message and have it "mailed" to another user. The mail is stored in a file and when the other user logs in, the operating system displays a message "YOU HAVE MAIL" to that user, who can then run the MAIL program to retrieve and display the mail on the screen, and send you a reply.

Word processor

A program that allows you to type in a term paper, letter, or any other written document and store it in a file. The word processor is like an editor program, except that the word processor knows about things like paragraphs, numbered lists, centered lines, page margins, and footnotes.

Spreadsheet

A program that allows you to easily compute and display tables of figures, such as business sales figures, loan payments, or basic statistics. Simple commands allow you to recompute the table over and over to answer "what if" questions, such as "what would be the final payment date if the interest rate goes down one percent on this loan?"

Games

Programs that play a variety of games, from chess to tic-tac-toe, are available on most computer systems.

"publicly" (often you have to copy the object program into a file in a "public" directory). Any other user of the computer system can then run your program to perform whatever information processing task your program automates.

If you were a professional writing programs for general use, then you might copy the program onto a diskette file and sell it to interested users. If you sold a copy of the object program, then they could only use the program on exactly the same type of computer system that you used when you were testing the program. However, if you sold them a copy of the source program, then they could make whatever minor changes were required for their computer system (possibly a completely different brand of computer), and then compile and run the modified program on their system.

EXERCISES

2.4 Determine the name of the operating system on the computer you are using.

2.5 If your computer system is a time-sharing system, determine what accounting information, if any, your operating system maintains about your use of the computer. Are there limits on your computer use? What are the limits?

2.6 If your computer system is a time-shared system, get an "account" on the system, and:

    a. Determine how to login and logout, and do it.

    b. Determine how to display the names of the files in a directory, and do it for a "public" directory to which you have access.

2.7 Find out the name of the editor program and the name of the Pascal compiler that you will be using. Are the editor and Pascal compiler part of an integrated programming environment, or are they separate programs invoked by different operating system commands?

2.8 For each of the two example programs in Chapter 1 (Figures 1.9 and 1.10), use the programming environment of your computer system to enter the program into a file, compile it to produce an object program, and test the object program by running it to see if it works correctly. If any errors occur because you have typed in the program incorrectly, use the editor to repair them and then recompile and retest the program until it works correctly.

2.9 Revise Nancy's program so that it uses an incorrect formula for converting degrees F to degrees C (for example, multiply by 9/5 instead of by 5/9). Now compile and run the modified program. Does it appear to work correctly? How can you tell that the answers are wrong? Explain why it would be easy to think that any results produced by a computer are correct, when in fact they are not.

2.10 Determine where to go to find out detailed information about other software that is available on your computer system.

□ □ □ **2.3**
MORE ABOUT PROGRAMMING LANGUAGES AND ENVIRONMENTS

Pascal is only one of many programming languages available on modern computer systems. To complete our picture of computer software, let's look in more depth at programming languages and environments for programming.

□ **Programming Language**

A *programming language* is a notation for writing programs to be executed by a computer.

□ □
Syntax and Semantics

The notation of a programming language gives a precise set of rules for the *form* of what you can write down in your program (termed the *syntax* of the language), and for exactly what each thing you write *means* in terms of actions by the computer (termed the *semantics* of the language).

Language Definition and Implementation

When a new programming language is developed, its syntax and semantics are first *defined,* that is, all the details of the form and meaning of the new notation are specified. New languages are sometimes developed by individuals or small research groups. For example, the definition of the Pascal language is largely the work of the Swiss computer scientist, Niklaus Wirth, and his research group. In other cases, new languages have been developed by national or international committees.

A particular programming language is said to be *implemented* on a particular type of computer system when there is a way to execute programs written in that language on that computer system. The two most common ways to implement a programming language are either to use a *compiler* or to use an *interpreter*. Each is a particular kind of program that runs on the computer system. Once a programming language has been defined, it can be implemented on almost any computer system.

Compilers

A *compiler* is a program that can translate programs written in a "high-level" programming language such as Pascal into instructions that can be directly executed by a computer. We looked at some details of the Pascal compiler in the preceding section. Figures 2.6 and 2.7 show how a compiler is used to translate a source program into an object program, which then can be run on the computer to process the input data and produce the desired results.

Interpreters

An alternative way to implement a programming language on a computer is to construct an "interpreter." An *interpreter* is a program that takes a source program written in a programming language like Pascal and directly performs the actions specified by the source program, without ever constructing an object program. The interpreter program reads in the source program and then "interprets" each line in the program to decide what action that line says to perform. As each line is interpreted, the interpreter program *immediately performs the action*. The interpreter then goes on to the next line of the source program, "interprets" it, and performs its actions, and so forth. Figure 2.8 illustrates the inputs and outputs of an interpreter. Note that the interpreter does *not* translate the source program into an object program at all—it simply executes the source program directly and produces the desired results.

Implementing a programming language with an interpreter rather than a compiler is often done for languages like BASIC (and, less often, Pascal) when they are used primarily for teaching programming to beginners. For small student programs, an interpreter is useful because you immediately see the result of each action as the source program is executed.

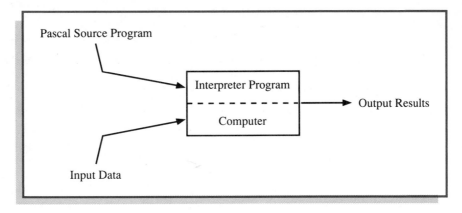

FIGURE 2.8 Executing a Pascal Program with an Interpreter

Executing a source program with an interpreter is slow compared to executing a compiled object program derived from the same source program. For large programs that are to be used over and over again, it is better to compile the program before execution if possible. Because student programs are seldom run more than a few times, however, using an interpreter is appropriate. Don't be surprised to find that a computer system, possibly even the one you are using, has *two* implementations of Pascal—a compiler and an interpreter.

□ □
Standard Programming Languages

There are hundreds of different programming languages and hundreds of different types of computer systems. A compiler or interpreter for a programming language is itself a large and complex program that often takes several programmers a year or more to construct. Thus only the most popular programming languages are implemented on most types of computer systems. One of the key questions you ask when buying a computer is: *what programming languages are implemented on this computer?* You can buy a computer system and you can write programs in your favorite programming language to specify what you want that computer system to do, but unless that programming language has been implemented on that computer system (and you have a copy of the compiler or interpreter program), you cannot run your programs on that computer.

Having *standard programming languages,* such as Pascal, that are implemented on almost every type of computer system is important. To develop a standard programming language, a committee of programming language experts is formed to write down a complete definition of the syntax and semantics of the language (often based on an earlier version of the language as developed by an individual or research group). The standard definition is critiqued and revised by other experts until a finished definition is reached. This definition is published as the *standard definition of the language*. Then, about every ten years, the standard definition is revised and

TABLE 2.1 Some Widely Used Standard Programming Languages
(Year = when the language was first defined)

Fortran (1954) Used primarily for scientific, engineering, and statistical applications requiring extensive mathematical calculations.

Lisp (1958) Used primarily for programs written to solve complex "intelligent" tasks, such as chess-playing programs and programs that can understand written or spoken English.

COBOL (1959) Used primarily for business programs, such as payroll, inventory control, and banking.

PL/I (1964) Used primarily as a general purpose language on large computers.

BASIC (1965) Used primarily as a general purpose language on small computers and for teaching elementary programming.

Pascal (1971) Used primarily for teaching programming and as a general purpose language.

C (1973) Used primarily for building operating systems, compilers, and other "system software."

Ada (1980) Used primarily for programming computers "embedded" as parts of larger machines, such as airplanes, ships, and satellites; also as a general purpose language.

---

updated by a new committee to reflect advances in computer use and computer science. Table 2.1 lists some of the major standard programming languages.

Each implementation of a standard language has to follow the standard definition in every detail. A program written in the standard language then can be run without change (or with only minor changes) on any computer that has an implementation of the standard language. We say that such a program is *portable* to different computer systems. Most important programs are written in standard programming languages so that they will be portable.

□ □
Extensions to a Language

When a standard language is implemented on a computer system, the programmers that construct the compiler or interpreter often include some additional *extensions* to the standard language—new features and capabilities that are not part of the standard language. You will probably find some of these extensions in whatever implementation of Pascal you happen to be using.

Such extensions are both good and bad—good because they often make it easier to do things in your programs, but bad because the extensions are peculiar to one implementation of the language, and thus any program that uses the extensions is not portable to other computer systems without change (unless you happen to find an implementation on the other computer that has the same extensions).

EXERCISES

2.11 For the computer system you are using:

a. List the programming languages that are implemented on that system.

b. Determine if each language is implemented with a compiler or interpreter (or both).

2.12 For the Pascal implementation that you will be using, find out what extensions to the standard Pascal language are provided by that implementation. Find out what features of standard Pascal are *not* provided by that implementation, if any. (The *User's Manual* for your Pascal implementation will provide this information.)

□□□ **2.4**
MORE ABOUT COMPUTER HARDWARE ORGANIZATION

This section provides additional background on how information is stored and manipulated within the various parts of a computer system. Although not required for programming in Pascal, this additional background will help you to understand more fully how the computer hardware is able to perform information processing tasks effectively.

What is surprising about computer hardware is not that it does so much, but that *it does so little*! That is, the basic operations that a computer can perform, such as the addition, multiplication, or comparison of two numbers are exceedingly simple. But in spite of the simplicity of its basic operations, a computer does have some characteristics that make it a useful information processing tool. Four characteristics in particular are important:

1. *Large storage capacity*. A computer can store a large amount of information in a very small space and access it very quickly. An average sized computer system might have *tens of millions* of pieces of information stored in its memory and secondary storage, with each piece accessible in a tiny fraction of a second.

2. *Fast processing speed*. Even a small computer can perform *hundreds of thousands* of operations on the data it has stored each second that it is running.

3. *Control by a stored program*. Unlike a hand calculator, which usually pauses between each operation to await the next command from the user (entered by pushing one or several buttons), a computer is guided by programs that are stored along with the data in its memory and secondary storage. These stored programs allow us to make effective use of the fast processing speed of the computer, since no human interaction is required between each instruction of a program. Also, the same computer can be made to perform many different information processing tasks simply by changing its stored program.

4. *Reliable hardware*. A computer is an extremely reliable information processing machine, in that it will reliably perform exactly the instructions that are in its stored program. If the program instructs it to add ten thousand numbers stored in its memory, it will add those numbers reliably, as often as instructed. A typical computer will run for days or weeks and execute billions of instructions without an error.

□ □

Bits and Binary Encoding

To understand how a computer processes information, let's look first at how information is represented inside a computer system. If you removed the outer cases from the various computer hardware components shown in Figure 2.1 and looked inside each box, you would find almost nothing that indicated how the components worked. The major parts of a computer operate entirely electronically; there are few moving parts.

Electronically, information is represented in many different ways in a computer, but logically there is a single basic principle:

□ **The Principle of Binary Encoding**

Any piece of information may be represented by encoding it as a sequence of bits (binary digits).

Bit is short for *binary digit*—one of the digits 0 or 1. Restated, the principle of binary encoding simply says that we can take any piece of information (such as you could write down on a sheet of paper) and encode it as a long sequence of 0's and 1's in some way. When Nancy hits a key on her microcomputer keyboard, that "keystroke" is encoded and sent to the computer as a sequence of bits. Suppose Nancy types "V"; what is transmitted to the computer is a bit sequence like "01010110". When Nancy's printer is instructed to print the letter "V" at the next position on the current line, the instruction to "print" and the letter "V" to be printed are sent to the printer electronically as a sequence of bits ("V" again may be transmitted as "01010110").

Any information stored in the memory of a computer is stored as a sequence of bits. In most parts of a computer system it makes no difference what the bits represent—they are just bits, their "meaning" in terms of the information they encode does not matter to the operation of the hardware. Thus "bits" are what come in from input devices; "bits" are sent out to output devices; "bits" are stored in memory; "bits" are stored on secondary storage; and "bits" are what the processor manipulates.

□ □
Why Bits?

Why do computers use bits and a binary encoding of information rather than the letters, decimal numbers, and other symbols with which we are familiar? That's simple—a single bit can be represented electronically by a two-state device—for example, a switch that is either "on" or "off". We can think of the "on" state as representing the bit "1" and the "off" state as representing the bit "0". A row of ten such switches can represent a sequence of ten bits; a thousand switches can represent a thousand bits, etc. Electronically, there are dozens of different ways to construct a two-state device. Figure 2.9 illustrates some of the possibilities. We can pack millions of such two-state devices into very small spaces, and operate them electronically at very high speeds. The storage capacity and speed of a computer come primarily from this ability to store and manipulate bits electronically.

□ □
Binary Representation of Data

Any sort of information, including numbers, letters, pictures, sounds, and even instructions for the computer's processor to execute, can be encoded as sequences of bits. The details of how different kinds of information are encoded vary among different computer systems, and they are of little direct concern to the programmer. Briefly summarized, here are some typical methods:

FIGURE 2.9   A bit can be represented by many different two-state devices

A *switch*
 can be "on" (1) or "off" (0).

The *voltage in a wire* during one clock tick
 can be "high" (1) or "low" (0).

A *spot on a disk or tape*
 can be "magnetized" (1) or "not magnetized" (0).

□

Characters.   Each individual letter, digit, space, or special character (such as punctuation, parentheses, and so forth) is encoded as a sequence of bits of some fixed length. Eight bits for each character is typical. There is an international standard encoding that is widely used, called ASCII (American Standard Code for Information Interchange). In ASCII, the letter A is encoded as "01000001" and the digit 9 is encoded as "00111001". Similar binary codes are assigned to every other character on a computer terminal keyboard. If you are interested, Appendix A shows the entire set of ASCII codes for all the characters used in Pascal.

□

Integers.   Each integer (positive or negative whole number) is encoded as a *fixed-length binary number*. The same number of bits are used for each number (for example, 31 bits), regardless of the size of the number. Leading zeros are added as needed to make every integer use exactly the same number of bits. An additional bit on the left is used to represent the sign of the integer (1 = plus, 0 = minus). For example, using this encoding:

$$9 = 0 \ 0000000000000000000000000001001$$
$$-7 = 1 \ 0000000000000000000000000000111$$

sign bit

Note that the integer 9 is not encoded in the same way as the digit "9" (a character). Each digit in a decimal number is equivalent to about 3.3 bits in a binary number, so it takes about 30 bits in a computer to represent a decimal number with nine digits.

□

Real Numbers.   Numbers with fractional parts (*real numbers* in computer jargon) are encoded using a form of scientific notation called *binary floating point notation*. Remember that in ordinary scientific notation, you write a number with an explicit power of 10 to control the decimal point position. For example, 9.5 can be written as 9.5×10^0 or 0.95×10^1 (or 95×10^{-1}, etc.); -7 can be written as -7×10^0 or -0.7×10^1, etc. Notice how scientific notation allows the decimal point to "float" to different positions by changing the exponent (the power of 10).

In binary floating point notation, you encode the number in a similar way, but you represent the number's value and the exponent as binary numbers, and make the exponent a power of 2 rather than 10. You also need two extra bits, one to encode the sign of the number and one for the sign of the exponent. The encoded number might also use 32 bits, just as for an integer, but the bits would be used differently to encode the four parts of the number. For example, 9.5 and -7 might be encoded:

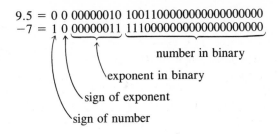

$$9.5 = 0\ 0\ 00000010\ 10011000000000000000000$$
$$-7 = 1\ 0\ 00000011\ 11100000000000000000000$$

number in binary

exponent in binary

sign of exponent

sign of number

□

Pictures and Sounds.

Pictures and sounds can be encoded as sequences of bits by sampling the light or sound level at a large number of distinct points and encoding each sampled value as an integer. The process is called *digitizing* the picture or sound. For music, the familiar *compact disk* (CD) uses such a binary encoding, which can be "read" and converted back into sound by a laser in the CD player.

□

Instructions.

The instructions that control the operation of the computer are also encoded as sequences of bits. For example, an instruction like "ADD X to Y and store the result in Z" might be encoded (using 32 bits):

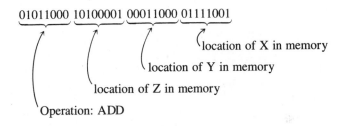

01011000 10100001 00011000 01111001

location of X in memory

location of Y in memory

location of Z in memory

Operation: ADD

□ □

Bytes and Words: Computer Memory Organization

Let's look at the organization of a typical computer memory. Because all instructions and data are encoded in a binary representation, logically we can think of a computer memory as simply a place to store sequences of bits. Within the memory, each bit is represented by a separate electronic switch. If the switch is ON, then the switch represents the bit 1, if OFF, then it represents the bit 0.

Larger units of storage in a computer memory are called *bytes* and *words*. The exact number of bits in each of these larger units varies among different types of computer systems. Here is a simple rule for remembering the distinctions:

Bit: One binary digit (0 or 1).

Byte: Can store one character of data. A byte can be 6-9 bits, depending on the computer system. 8 bits = one byte is standard.

Word: Can store one integer or real number (or an instruction). A word might consist of 2–8 bytes, depending on the computer system.

□

A Typical Memory.   Figure 2.10 shows a typical computer memory organization. In this memory, the bits are formed into 8-bit bytes, which in turn are formed into 4-byte (32-bit) words. The words are numbered in sequence, starting with zero. Each number is called the *memory address* of the corresponding memory word.

The number of bits in a computer memory does not change as we use the computer. When a program is stored in part of the computer's memory, the settings of the switches in that part of the memory are set to represent the bits for the encoded instructions and data that we are using. Some bits will represent instructions, some will represent data, and some will just be bits that are not currently in use and represent nothing of interest. As different programs are executed, the various bits of the memory are used for different purposes. For example, bits that represented useful

FIGURE 2.10   Typical Computer Memory Organization

Memory Address   Memory Words

Address		Memory Words		
0	11110101	01000100	00101010	11100000
1	00001101	01000011	11111111	11111100
2	11110000	00000011	10101001	01001011
3	00000000	00000000	00000000	00000000
4	11111111	11111000	00000000	01111000
•			•	
•			•	
•			•	
127999	00000000	00000000	00000000	00001110

byte   byte   byte   byte

data a second ago while one program was running may now represent the instructions for the program that is currently running.

Fetch/Store Operations.   Bits are transferred into and out of the computer memory by the processor of the computer, when it executes each instruction of the program. In computer jargon, we say the processor *stores* bits into the memory and *fetches* bits from the memory.

Storing a sequence of bits in a memory word means only that the electronic switches that represent the bits of the memory word are each set to a new position (0 or 1) to "store" each incoming bit appropriately. Thus storing bits in a memory word erases the existing settings of the bits there, just as you would have to erase something on a piece of paper before you could write something else in the same place.

On the other hand, *fetching* the bits in a word means that a copy of the bit settings is made somewhere else (wherever the bits fetched are to be stored). Fetching does not change the bit settings in the word, so a program can fetch the same data from a word as many times as needed (just as you can read the information on a piece of paper as often as you want).

To specify which word is to be the target of a fetch or store operation, the memory address of the word is used. Because any word "chosen at random" can be used without affecting any other word, a computer memory is sometimes called a *random access memory* or *RAM*.

A computer memory is not suited for long-term permanent storage. Because memory is more expensive than secondary storage, the memory of a computer system is usually only large enough to store programs and data that are in current use. Also when the computer system power is turned off, the contents of the memory are lost.

☐ ☐

Secondary Storage: Disks and Tapes

Secondary storage devices provide permanent storage for programs and data. The two most common secondary storage devices are *magnetic disks* with their associated *disk drives,* and *magnetic tapes* with their associated *tape drives*.

☐

Disk Storage.   A *magnetic disk* is shaped like a phonograph or CD record, but it may be much smaller or larger. It is usually plastic, with a surface coating that can be magnetized easily. A single bit is represented by a particular spot on this surface coating that is magnetized (1) or not magnetized (0).

The *disk drive* is the device used to store bits on a magnetic disk and later fetch them. Instead of the terms "fetch" and "store," we use the term *read* for the action of copying into memory the settings of some of the bits on a disk and the term *write* for the action of setting some bits on a disk to particular values.

A disk drive has one or several *read/write* heads (similar to the needle on a stereo turntable arm but not physically touching the disk surface). Each head can electronically read and write the bit positions on the disk. The disk drive spins the disk fast and continuously beneath the read/write heads. The arms that hold the heads can be moved in and out to position each head over a particular point on the disk, so that any portion of the storage area on the disk can be read or written very quickly.

□

Fixed and Removable Disks.   Nancy's microcomputer had a disk drive with *removable* diskettes (also called *floppy disks*). She keeps the diskettes in a small rack next to her computer and simply inserts the one with the proper programs or data into the disk drive when that information is needed by the computer. Her computer might also come with a *fixed disk* (or *hard disk*), which is more reliable and has a much greater storage capacity but which cannot be removed. Larger computer systems usually have several disk drives, including both fixed and removable types.

Removable disks can be used to transfer programs and data between computer systems. For example, programs that Nancy could buy to use on her microcomputer would ordinarily be sold in the form of one or several diskettes. The manufacturer writes the information on the diskettes using a computer at the factory, and then Nancy uses her computer to read the information off the diskettes at school.

□

Magnetic Tapes and Tape Units.   The *magnetic tapes* used in computer systems are similar to the tapes used for recording music—a plastic tape with a surface coating that can be magnetized. When a particular spot on the tape is magnetized, it is storing the bit 1. If the same spot is not magnetized, it is storing the bit 0. The *tape drive* is the device that reads and writes bits on a tape.

Compared to removable disks, tapes are usually cheaper (per bit of storage) and have larger storage capacity, but they are not as reliable. They are often used to carry data and programs from one system to another. The major disadvantage of a tape is that it cannot be read or written as quickly as a disk. A tape drive must "fast forward" down the tape to get to the right information (just as you must fast forward through a music tape to find a particular song). This positioning may take several minutes (a very long time at computer speeds). Thus information on a tape is usually transferred to a disk before it is processed in a modern computer system.

□ □

Input Devices

An *input device* for a computer is a device that *encodes* some sort of information into bits and *transmits* the bits to the computer. The information could be the characters that you type on a keyboard, a picture, music, spoken words, the reading on a thermometer, the speed of an airplane, the amount of gas in your car, etc. The principle is the same: take the information to be input, break it down into pieces in some way, encode each piece as a sequence of bits, and transmit the bits to the computer. Figure 2.11 shows some typical input devices. For learning to program using Pascal,

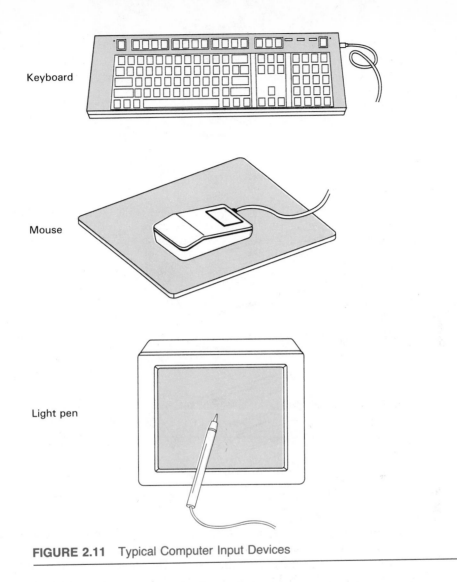

Keyboard

Mouse

Light pen

FIGURE 2.11 Typical Computer Input Devices

you will probably be concerned only with the input of character data, usually from the keyboard of your computer terminal.

□ □
Output Devices

An *output device* for a computer system is any device that can *receive* a sequence of bits from a computer and *decode* the bits to produce information usable by a person. One common output device is a *printer*, which receives bytes representing characters from the computer, decodes each byte to determine what character to print, and then activates its print mechanism to print the character on the paper. A second

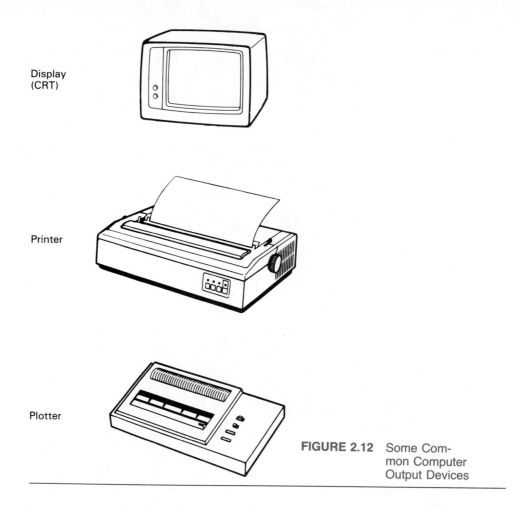

Display
(CRT)

Printer

Plotter

FIGURE 2.12 Some Common Computer Output Devices

common output device is the *display* or *CRT* (*cathode ray tube*), which can receive sequences of bytes representing characters from a computer, decode them, and display the specified characters on the screen. The bits transmitted from a computer can be sent to many other kinds of output devices—to produce drawings, sound, or to control motors, valves, or other mechanical apparatus. Figure 2.12 shows some common computer output devices.

□□

The Processor

The *processor* (*central processing unit* or *CPU*) is the part of the computer system that controls the overall activity of the computer by executing the instructions stored in programs in the memory. A processor has two main parts, traditionally called the *control unit* (*CU*) and the *arithmetic/logic unit* (*ALU*). It also has a small amount of internal memory, termed the *registers*. Figure 2.13 illustrates this organization.

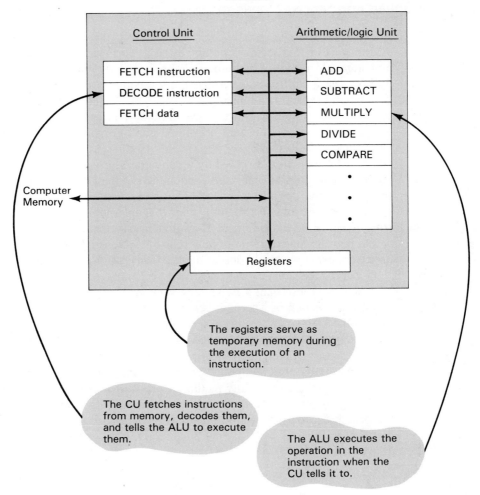

FIGURE 2.13 Organization of the Computer's Processor

□
Control Unit (CU).   The purpose of the control unit is to fetch instructions from memory, decode them to determine what operation to perform and what data to use, fetch the data, and then request the ALU to execute the designated operation with the specified data.

□
Arithmetic/Logic Unit (ALU).   The arithmetic/logic unit can be thought of as a set of separate circuits, each capable of performing one of the basic operations of the computer. For example, one circuit is used to add two numbers, one to multiply two numbers, one to compare two numbers for equality, and so forth.

At the start of this section, we noted the importance of the great processing speed and storage capacity of a computer. The basic speed of the processor is determined by how fast it can repeat its instruction execution cycle—the cycle of fetching, decoding, and executing an instruction. We term this the *instruction execution speed* of the processor. Execution speeds are commonly measured in *millions of instructions executed per second* (termed *mips*). A small computer might run at 0.1 mips; a larger one at 2–20 mips.

Each instruction executed by a computer's processor is extremely simple, so it takes the execution of many instructions to get the computer to perform any action that you would consider useful. For example, it would require execution of thousands of instructions just to run Nancy's simple "temperature conversion" program from Chapter 1. Execution of a million instructions to perform some minor task would be routine; execution of hundreds of millions of instructions to perform some larger computation would not be the least surprising.

A processor that executes instructions at a rate of 20 mips can execute a *billion* instructions in less than a minute. A very large computation, such as computing a detailed prediction of where oil is most likely to be found in a large oil drilling area, might take 15 hours to complete on a processor that runs at 20 mips. That adds up to over a *trillion* instructions executed. You see why a computer needs to be fast!

Because it takes many instructions to specify useful computations in a computer, programs often contain tens of thousands of instructions. The data that the program is processing usually requires more storage than the program. Thus, the total storage requirements for one program and its data, while it is being executed by the processor, routinely run to hundreds of thousands of bytes, and storage requirements of millions of bytes are not uncommon. You see why a computer system needs a large memory!

EXERCISES

2.13 For your computer system:
a. Name the manufacturer and model number.
b. Determine the number of processors.
c. Determine the number of disk and tape drives attached, and for each disk drive, whether the disk(s) is fixed or removable.
d. List the input devices attached.
e. List the output devices attached.

2.14 The International Morse Code is another way of encoding characters as sequences of bits, but in Morse Code the bits are called "dots" and "dashes" instead of zeros and ones. Morse code was invented before computers, as a way for people to communicate using a telegraph, blinking lights, or even flag positions. In an encyclopedia or other source, look up the International Morse Code and compare it with the ASCII code in Appendix A. What are the similarities and differences between the two?

MICROCOMPUTERS TO SUPERCOMPUTERS

Now that we have looked at the basics of computer hardware and software, let's look at computer systems as a whole. What are the different types of computer systems? And how do you measure how "big" or "small" a computer system is?

□ □

The Large and Small of It—Units of Measure

In measuring the size and speed of computers, the numbers seldom seem to come in everyday sizes. In your daily life, a simple task may take a few minutes if you're "slow," a few seconds if you're "fast," but a slow computer may do a simple task in a few *millionths* of a second and a fast computer may take only a few *billionths* of a second. In your daily life, a "long" list may have 50 or 100 items, and a "short" one 5 or 10, but in a computer a "long" list might have 50 to 100 *thousand* items and a "short" one 500 to 1000.

To measure the very large and very small quantities involved in working with computers, we need a set of prefixes for units of measure that are seldom needed in everyday life. You probably have used the prefixes *centi-* (meaning "one hundredth of," as in *centi*meter—one hundredth of a meter) and *kilo-* (meaning "one thousand," as in *kilo*gram—one thousand grams). We need the prefixes for much larger and smaller units in computing. Table 2.2 shows the prefixes that you need to know.

TABLE 2.2 Prefixes for Large and Small Units of Measure

Large Units		
Prefix	*Meaning*	*Example*
kilo-	one thousand	2 kilobits = 2 thousand bits
mega-	one million	8 megabytes = 8 million bytes
giga-	one billion	5 gigabytes = 5 billion bytes
tera-	one trillion	1 terabit = 1 trillion bits

Small Units		
Prefix	*Meaning*	*Example*
milli-	one thousandth of	4 milliseconds = 4 thousandths of a second = 0.004 seconds
micro-	one millionth of	3 microseconds = 3 millionths of a second = 0.000003 seconds
nano-	one billionth of	7 nanoseconds = 7 billionths of a second = 0.000000007 seconds
pico-	one trillionth of	725 picoseconds = 725 trillionths of a second = 0.000000000725 seconds

Measuring the Size and Power of a Computer System

A few numbers are usually enough to give an idea of the relative size and power of different computer systems:

1. *Memory size.* The approximate number of bytes of storage in the memory of the computer, usually measured in kilobytes (*Kbyte* or *Kb*) or megabytes (*Mbyte* or *Mb*).

2. *Processor speed.* The approximate number of instructions that the processor can execute each second, usually measured in millions of instructions executed per second (*mips*).

3. *Secondary storage capacity.* The approximate total amount of secondary storage available at each instant while the computer is running—the storage capacity of each fixed disk drive in the system plus the capacity of each removable disk available on a disk drive. Tape storage capacity is ignored because tapes are used primarily for very long-term storage in current systems. Secondary storage capacity is usually measured in megabytes or gigabytes (*Gbyte* or *Gb*).

4. *Maximum number of simultaneous users.* The number of users that can be using the computer system at the same time, using separate terminals connected to the system.

5. *Price.* How much does the complete system cost?

Note that physical size is not on our list—the largest computers are not a great deal larger physically than the smallest ones, although larger computers have many more *peripheral devices* like disk and tape drives, printers, and so forth, attached to them.

Types of Computer Systems

Computer systems are often categorized into a few different major types. You will hear these terms often, so it helps to be familiar with them:

□ **Microcomputer**

The simplest type of computer system, for a single user. Also called a *home computer* or *personal computer*.

Typical system: A single processor and memory, one or two small disk drives (removable diskettes), possibly a larger fixed disk drive, a keyboard, display, and printer.

Typical users: Home use, schools for instruction, textbook authors, small businesses.

□ **Workstation**

A system for one or a few users with more computational power and memory than a microcomputer.

Typical system: Two processors, one for computations and one to handle input and output, each with its own memory, a medium-sized fixed disk drive, a small tape drive, a keyboard, mouse, high quality display, and printer. Also usually connected to a larger computer system through a network.

Typical users: Engineers and scientists, software developers.

☐ Minicomputer

A medium-sized computer system capable of handling several dozen simultaneous users.

Typical system: A single fairly fast processor and medium-sized memory, several medium-sized disk drives, a tape drive, several dozen (20–50) terminals with display and keyboard, several printers.

Typical users: Small to medium-sized businesses, small colleges, single departments in universities, small government agencies.

☐ Mainframe

A large computer system capable of handling several dozen to several hundred simultaneous users, with storage for all their programs and data.

Typical system: One or two fast processors to handle computations and several smaller processors to handle input and output and traffic to secondary storage. A large central memory and several smaller memories; 4–20 disk and tape drives; dozens to hundreds of user terminals; several printers and a variety of other input/output devices.

Typical users: Large businesses, universities as a central computing facility, large government agencies.

☐ Supercomputer

The largest and fastest type of computer available, usually reserved for very large computations that cannot be performed on smaller computers.

Typical system: 4–8 extremely fast processors for the main computations, 10–20 slower processors to handle transfers to secondary storage. A very large central memory and several smaller memories. Several dozen large disk and tape drives. User terminals, printers, and other input/output devices are usually not connected directly to the supercomputer but instead are connected to a minicomputer or mainframe that handles user commmands, editing, and smaller user needs. When a program is to be run on the supercomputer, the mainframe sends the appropriate program and data files to the supercomputer. The supercomputer runs the program and leaves the results in files on one of the disks, where the mainframe can retrieve them for printing or display.

Typical users: Research laboratories, large corporations.

Advances in computer hardware technology have allowed computer systems to become faster, with larger memories and secondary storage systems, at ever lower prices. The numbers change almost yearly. Table 2.3 shows a snapshot of the dimensions of a typical system of each type, circa 1988.

TABLE 2.3 Major Types of Computer Systems

Type	Memory Size	Processor Speed	Secondary Storage	Simultaneous Users (maximum)	Price (U.S. dollars)
Microcomputer	0.25–1 Mbyte	0.025–0.1 mips	2–40 Mbytes	1	$1–6,000
Workstation	2–8 Mbytes	0.2–0.8 mips	20–160 Mbytes	1–4	$8–35,000
Minicomputer	4–16 Mbytes	0.5–2 mips	200–800 Mbytes	15–40	$100–500,000
Mainframe	8–60 Mbytes	4–30 mips	2–20 Gbytes	25–200	$1–6,000,000
Supercomputer	60 Mbytes– 4 Gbytes	200–2000 mips	50 Gbytes– 2 terabytes	**	$8–20,000,000

** Users not directly connected.

EXERCISES

2.15 For each of the following amounts, restate it using the most appropriate prefix:

a. Two billion bits.

b. One trillionth of a meter.

c. One millionth of a gram.

d. One thousandth of an inch.

e. Three million dollars.

f. A trillion meters.

2.16 For each of the following amounts, write it as a decimal number of seconds, bytes, bits, or grams, as appropriate:

a. 17.5 microseconds.

b. 12 teraseconds.

c. 64 kilobits.

d. 3 gigabytes.

e. 2.4 nanograms.

2.17 For the computer you will be using, determine:

a. The general type of computer it is (microcomputer, workstation, etc.).

b. The memory size, in bytes.

c. The processor speed, in mips.

d. The capacity of each disk storage unit.

e. The maximum number of simultaneous users.

f. The price.

■ ■ ■
REVIEW QUESTIONS

2.1 Name the five *major hardware parts* in a computer system and explain briefly the purpose of each.

2.2 What is a *time-shared* computer system?

2.3 Explain three common ways to *access* a time-shared system.

2.4 What is the purpose of *login* and *logout* procedures?

2.5 Name the three major pieces of *software* used by the programmer.

2.6 List and explain briefly the two major functions of a computer's *operating system*. List and explain three important additional functions of the operating system on a time-shared computer.

2.7 What is the difference between a *directory*, a *public file*, and a *private file* in a computer system?

2.8 Name and explain briefly two methods for choosing *commands* for the operating system to execute.

2.9 Explain how a Pascal programmer might use an *editor*.

2.10 What service does the Pascal *compiler* provide for the Pascal programmer?

2.11 Explain the difference between a *source program* and an *object program*.

2.12 What is an *integrated programming environment*?

2.13 Define the term *programming language*.

2.14 What is the difference between the *syntax* of a programming language and its *semantics*?

2.15 Explain the distinction between the *definition* and the *implementation* of a programming language.

2.16 Name and explain briefly the two major methods of *implementing* a programming language.

2.17 What is a *standard programming language*? Name five standard languages.

2.18 What is an *extension* to a standard programming language?

2.19 Name and explain briefly four reasons why a modern computer is such a *useful* information processing machine.

2.20 What does the term *stored program* mean?

2.21 State the *Principle of Binary Encoding*.

2.22 What is a *bit*?

2.23 Why are bits and binary encoding used as the basis of modern computers?

2.24 Explain briefly how each of the following types of data can be encoded in binary:

characters
integers
real numbers (numbers with fractional parts)
instructions

2.25 What is the *ASCII code*?

2.26 Describe the organization of a typical *computer memory*, including bytes, words, and addresses.

2.27 Name and explain briefly the two *basic operations* used with a computer memory.

2.28 Explain how *disks* and *tapes* are used for secondary storage in a computer.

2.29 What is the difference between a *fixed* and *removable* disk?

2.30 List three *input devices* and three *output devices* used with computers.

2.31 Name the two parts of the computer's *processor* and explain the basic function of each part. Explain the purpose of the registers in the processor.

2.32 Explain how the speed of a processor is measured.

2.33 Define *four prefixes* for words that name *large units* of measure. Define four prefixes for *small units* of measure.

2.34 List and explain briefly five measures that can be used to compare the relative *size and power* of two computer systems.

2.35 Rank, in order of increasing size and power, computers in the categories: *mainframe, microcomputer, minicomputer, supercomputer, workstation*.

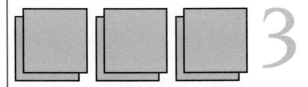

3

Program Design: Requirements and Algorithms

CHAPTER GOALS

When you have mastered the content of this chapter you should be able to:

- Define the *requirements* for a program.
- Explain how to describe a line of text in *Backus-Naur Form* (BNF).
- Use BNF to specify the required *dialogue* between computer and user for an interactive program.
- Describe the parts of an *algorithm.*
- Distinguish between *data objects*, *data values*, and *data types* in an algorithm.
- Describe a *program state.*
- Use *assertions* to describe properties of program states.
- Explain how *actions* change the program state.
- Describe how execution of a program leads from an *initial state* through a sequence of *intermediate states* to a *final state.*
- Express the design of an algorithm in *pseudo-code.*
- *Hand trace* the execution of an algorithm.
- Explain what a *control path* is.
- Use *control flow analysis* to verify that an algorithm is correct.

Programming methods allow us to control the complexity of a program as it is constructed. Although programming methods are important during all the phases of program construction, they are first evident during the early phases where we are determining the program's requirements and developing an algorithm for performing the specified task.

In this chapter, we develop the basic concepts and methods used in determining requirements and designing algorithms for simple programming problems. By the end of the chapter, you will be designing your own algorithms for automating simple information processing tasks.

□□□3.1
PROGRAMMING AND HACKING

In Chapter 1, we listed the major steps in building a program to solve a problem:

1. Determine the requirements that the program must meet,
2. Design an algorithm and verify that it satisfies the program's requirements,
3. Code a Pascal program from the algorithm, enter and verify it, and,
4. Compile, test, and debug the program.

Figure 3.1 illustrates these activities in more detail. Notice how you begin at the top with a real world problem and work down toward the actual running Pascal program. The result of each phase is a written specification, which gets progressively more detailed as you continue. First there is just a vaguely stated problem or task to be automated. Next, there is a detailed specification of the program's requirements—*what* the program must do. Then there is a detailed algorithm for performing the task—*how* the program actually accomplishes the task. Finally there is the fully coded Pascal program, which can be automatically translated into detailed machine instructions by the Pascal compiler.

□□
Hacking and How to Avoid It

It's time for our second definition of the term *hacker* (the first was given in Chapter 2):

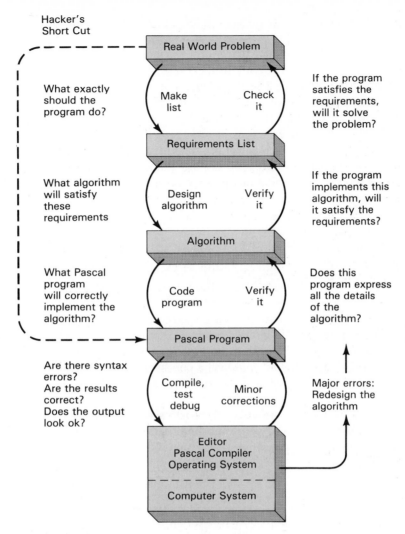

FIGURE 3.1 Steps in Building a Program

Notice the Hacker's Short Cut in Figure 3.1? A hacker never bothers to really analyze the problem and write down the requirements or an algorithm. Instead the hacker typically sits down at a terminal and starts writing Pascal code. He or she gets the program written, tests it a few times "until it works," and considers the job done.

Many programmers that are programming today started out as hackers, and some of them still are. Only in the 1970s did it become generally understood how carefully the design and implementation of computer programs must be controlled if the inherent complexity of the task is not to overwhelm the abilities of the programmer. Even the best intentioned programmer can produce a "hack program" when the programmer's skill in managing the complexity of design and coding is overwhelmed by the number of program parts and their interactions. When that happens, we say that the programmer has lost *intellectual control* of the programming task. Good programming methods are the key to maintaining intellectual control of a programming task.

Designing Programs: DEFINE, then REFINE

Constructing a computer program is like constructing a house—you need to *design* it before you start to *build* it. You need to carefully consider all the details of its construction and have a written "blueprint" that specifies exactly what you plan to build. *Requirements* and *algorithms* form the blueprint for a program. They detail exactly what you plan to build into the program. Notice that these are precisely the steps that the hacker skips in his rush to start building a program. If you built a house without a careful blueprint, you would get a poorly constructed shack; a program built without attention to the foundation—requirements and algorithms—is the programming equivalent of a shack.

In developing a program, there is a useful general method that we use at every stage: First define *what* you want the program to do, then fill in the details of *how* the program will do it. This idea is captured in the phrase:

> DEFINE, then REFINE

DEFINE *what* you want done, then REFINE that definition to fill in the details of *how* to do it. We will see this method in action in developing both the requirements and the algorithm for a program later in this chapter.

The terms *top-down design* and *stepwise refinement* are other names for this general principle. *Top-down design* means that you start at the "top"—with the big picture of what task the entire program must accomplish. Then you fill in the major steps involved in *how* the program will accomplish that task. Each step then is viewed as a smaller task to be accomplished—a new *what* that needs to be done. You fill in the details of *how* each of these sub-tasks is to be accomplished, by defining still lower level, simpler tasks. Finally you reach a level of sub-task that is so simple that it requires no further sub-tasks to be defined. In top-down design, you have used the principle of "DEFINE, then REFINE" to work from the largest view of the entire program down to the smallest details.

Stepwise refinement is another term for the same general principle. You begin with *what* the program is to do, and divide that task into a sequence of steps that accomplish the desired result. Then you refine each step by filling in the details. It's the same "DEFINE, then REFINE" principle.

EXERCISE

3.1 Many real world situations can get "out of control" for you if the complexity of the parts and their interactions overwhelm your abilities to manage the complexity. The result is usually embarrassing. Describe a social or physical activity or situation that might get "out of control" in this way. What means would you use to ensure that you kept the situation "under control"?

□□□ **3.2**
REQUIREMENTS: WHAT SHOULD THE PROGRAM DO?

The first step in developing a program is to determine its requirements: what should the program be able to do? There are two difficulties that you meet in determining the requirements:

1. *A program cannot do it all.* Determining a program's requirements involves first separating what a program can do in solving the problem from what a program *can't do*. For any real world information processing task you usually must have the intelligence of a person involved both before and after using a program—before to collect information and organize it and after to evaluate the results and put them to use. A computer program is an *aid* to its human users in automating the task, not a substitute for them. Some tasks may require that a person use several computer programs to help with different parts of the job.

2. *The problem is never clearly stated.* Once you have picked off a piece of a task that a computer program might be expected to handle, you face the second difficulty: descriptions of information processing tasks are almost always vague and incomplete. The purpose in writing down the requirements for the program is to clarify and complete the vague and incomplete information you start with. This step may include repeated conversations with the person or group that ultimately will use the program—what *exactly* do these future users want the program to do?

□□
Interactive and Batch-processing Programs

An *interactive program* is a program that carries on a dialogue with the user during its execution. Nancy's program in Chapter 1 is an interactive program—first it asks the user to type a temperature value, then it waits while the user types in the requested value, then it computes a new Celsius value from the input value, and finally it displays its results on the terminal screen. All this happens while the user is sitting at the computer terminal.

Not all programs are interactive programs. A program may simply read some data values from a "data file," process those values, and write its results into a second data file. The user of such a program does not have to wait at a terminal while the program runs. Such programs are called *batch-processing programs*—they process a "batch" of data, without interacting with the user.

For example, a program that computes the payroll for a small business might be a batch-processing program. Information about the employees (pay scale and hours worked) might be stored in one data file. The program would process this information to determine the paycheck amount and deductions for each employee and write the results in a second data file. At the end of each pay period, a payroll clerk would run the program. There would be no interaction between the program and the payroll clerk while the program was running.

For the next several chapters, we concentrate on interactive programs. In Chapter 11 we come back to batch-processing programs.

□ □
Writing Requirements for Interactive Programs

When you define the requirements for an interactive program, the "DEFINE, then REFINE" sequence has two parts:

1. *Basic requirements.* DEFINE the input data, processing, output data, and assumptions that form the program's basic requirements, and then
2. *Dialogue.* REFINE these requirements into a *dialogue* that the program should carry on as it interacts with the user. The *dialogue* provides a detailed specification of the input data and output data for an interactive program.

Let's look separately at these parts of a requirements specification.

□ □
Writing Basic Requirements

A program takes some *input data* and performs some *processing* of that data to produce some *output data,* as shown in Figure 3.2. Your basic requirements list should identify these three items, plus any *assumptions* that you are making about how the program will be used or any special properties it should have (outside of simply performing the task correctly).

In this book, we use a standard format for writing basic requirements. Four sections, titled INPUT, PROCESSING, OUTPUT, and ASSUMPTIONS, should suffice for simple programs:

- INPUT: What data must the user provide to the program?
- PROCESSING: What processing of the input data is required?
- OUTPUT: What data should be produced and displayed as a result of the processing?
- ASSUMPTIONS: What can be assumed about how the program will be used?

Larger, more complex programs may have several such sections and may include additional requirements about program performance (how fast it must respond to the user), reliability, security, and so forth.

ASSUMPTIONS: How will the program be used?

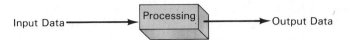

FIGURE 3.2 Basic Requirements View the Program in Terms of Input, Processing, Output, and Assumptions

In writing the requirements, concentrate on *what* processing is needed in the task, rather than *how* to perform that processing. At the same time you want to concentrate on *what* information is required as the input data and output data of the program, rather than on *how* that information is to be represented in the program.

When you are developing the basic requirements for a program, you often first understand the *output data* of the program; that is, you first write down the results that you want the program to produce. From these output data, you work backwards to determine what input data are required and what processing of the input data will be needed to produce the output data. And you often revise the requirements list several times as you more fully understand the problem. In programming, always be ready to revise and revise again what you have written. Even experienced hands seldom get it right the first time.

EXAMPLE

As a simple example, let's write out the full requirements for Nancy's temperature conversion program in Chapter 1:

INPUT: Temperature value in degrees Fahrenheit.
PROCESSING: Compute the equivalent Celsius value for the input temperature.
OUTPUT: Fahrenheit temperature ("echo" the input value).
Equivalent Celsius temperature.
ASSUMPTIONS: Program is to be used at a high school science fair.

From these basic requirements, Nancy can proceed to refine the INPUT and OUTPUT parts into a detailed specification of the dialogue between program and user, as she did in Chapter 1:

DIALOGUE

PROGRAM: Please type a temperature value (degrees F):
USER: 68
PROGRAM: 68 degrees F = 20 degrees C ∎

□ □
Writing an Interactive Dialogue

Designing the details of the dialogue between the user and your program is the RE-FINE step in writing requirements. Here you want to specify, as accurately as possible, what the program displays on the screen for the user to see, and what the user is expected to type in on the keyboard at various times. Thus the dialogue provides details for the INPUT and OUTPUT parts of the basic requirements.

The dialogue is simply a sequence of lines of information. Nancy used the simplest possible means to describe the dialogue: she simply wrote down an *example* of the dialogue, using the sample input data value "68". Using this sample data value leaves some key questions unanswered about the program's requirements. For example, 68 is one possible input value, but what is the range of allowed input values? Is minus 21 (-21) an allowed input value? What about 68.00001? Or 2,377,000?

To understand completely the requirements for Nancy's program, we must know what *range* of input temperature values are to be allowed. We also must know the *form* of the input and output temperature values. Will these values include commas (as in 2,377,000)? Can they be written in scientific notation (as in 6.8×10^2)?

Complexity has already reared its head. Specifying precisely what is possible in the dialogue between program and user can become rather complex. A programming method can help. We need a method for writing down descriptions of the lines of information that make up a dialogue between the user and the program. Our method uses a special notation called *Backus-Naur Form* (BNF).

□ □
BNF: A Method for Describing Lines of Text

Let's look at the problem more abstractly first. Suppose you want to describe just the *form* of a line of text, where the line may include:

1. Required items, like punctuation.
2. Optional items, like a + or − before a number. [ ]
3. Alternatives, such as two different ways of writing a number. |
4. Repeated items, such as the items in a list. { }
5. Choices—one item chosen from a set of possibilities. < >

For example, Nancy's output line:

    68 degrees F = 20 degrees C

has the form:

    [Fahrenheit temp] degrees F = [Celsius temp] degrees C

where the phrases "degrees F =" and "degrees C" are *required*—they must appear exactly as specified. Items that may be chosen from a set of possibilities are indicated by angle brackets enclosing the name of the set, such as ⟨Fahrenheit temp⟩ and ⟨Celsius temp⟩. In a separate set of definitions, we can define what is allowed for these sets of items.

Notice that we are describing the *form* of a line of text, *not its meaning*. For example, the line:

```
68 degrees F = 277 degrees C
```

has the *right form* according to the specification given above, but its meaning is wrong—68 degrees F does not equal 277 degrees C.

Our method for describing lines of text is based on these simple concepts. This method was invented early in the history of computing in the late 1950s by John Backus (American) and Peter Naur (Danish). They used it as a way of describing the syntax of statements in the programming language ALGOL 60. The notation they developed is now called *Backus-Naur Form* or *BNF*. We use BNF to describe the form of lines of text in a program-user dialogue and in a pseudo-code algorithm in this chapter. In later chapters, we use BNF to describe the form (syntax) of the various declarations and statements found in the Pascal language.

Our version of BNF is a variation on the original form used by Backus and Naur. The form of one or more lines of text is defined in our BNF as:

```
[name] ::=
    ... format of the line ...
```

The symbol "::=" means "is defined to have the form." The "name" is just a word or phrase that describes the purpose of the text, such as ⟨program-user dialogue⟩. The "format of the line" uses only the following elements:

1. *Literal strings*. If a line includes a "literal string" of characters (characters that are required to always appear exactly as written), the literal string is written exactly as it should appear. For example, the literal string "degrees F =" in Nancy's output line is written exactly as it should appear, spaces and all.

2. *Optional items*. If an item is optional (only sometimes included), it is written within square brackets, [...]:

```
[...optional item...]
```

3. *Alternative items*. If an item may have several alternative forms, the alternatives are listed in any order, separated by "¦" (meaning "or"):

```
...item format 1... ¦ ...item format 2... ¦ ...[
```

4. *Repeated items.* If an item can be repeated more than once or omitted altogether (repeated zero times), it is written in braces, {...}:

{...item to be omitted or repeated as needed...}

5. *Choice from a named set of items.* If an item should be chosen from a set of possible alternatives, the set is named by using a word or phrase enclosed in angle brackets, ⟨...⟩. Wherever the name of the set appears in a line of text, any item from the set may be inserted at that point. For example, when we wrote ⟨Celsius temp⟩ in Nancy's output line, we meant "insert a Celsius temperature value here."

To describe the sets of items named in angle brackets ⟨...⟩ more completely, we follow the overall BNF description by "WHERE" and a description of each item, as follows:

> **WHERE**
> ⟨item1⟩ ::= ...description of the allowed forms for this item...
> ⟨item2⟩ ::= ...description of the allowed forms for this item...

and so forth until each set of items has been defined. In making these descriptions, we can again use BNF to detail exactly the form of each item, which may lead to defining additional named sets of items whose definition must be included later in the list.

EXAMPLES

Here are two examples of how an informal description of an integer that might appear as part of a line of text can be described precisely (and concisely) in BNF:

1. Informal Description: Define an "integer" as a sequence of one or more decimal digits, with an optional plus or minus sign.

BNF description:

> ⟨integer⟩ ::=
> [+ ¦ −] ⟨digit⟩ {⟨digit⟩}
> **WHERE**
> ⟨digit⟩ ::= 0 ¦ 1 ¦ 2 ¦ 3 ¦ 4 ¦ 5 ¦ 6 ¦ 7 ¦ 8 ¦ 9

Examples: −12   277   +008   −9   −00   97653422211932

Discussion: The BNF description allows an ⟨integer⟩ to have leading zeros (or only zeros) and to contain as many digits as you want. No commas or decimal point are allowed.

2. Informal description: Define an "integer" as above, but do not allow leading zeros. Also require a comma between each triple of digits and allow an optional decimal point. Call this a "fancy integer."

BNF description:

$\langle$fancy-integer$\rangle$ ::=
$\quad$ [+ | −] $\langle$nonzero-digit$\rangle$ [$\langle$digit$\rangle$] [$\langle$digit$\rangle$]{, $\langle$digit-triple$\rangle$} [.]

WHERE
$\quad$ $\langle$digit-triple$\rangle$ :: $\langle$digit$\rangle\langle$digit$\rangle\langle$digit$\rangle$
$\quad$ $\langle$digit$\rangle$ :: 0 | $\langle$nonzero-digit$\rangle$
$\quad$ $\langle$nonzero-digit$\rangle$ :: 1 | 2 | 3 | 4 | 5 | 6 | 7 | 8 | 9

Examples: $\quad$ 2,310 $\quad$ −3. $\quad$ +500,000,000,000 $\quad$ 251

Discussion: This example shows how a more complex definition can be built from several BNF definitions of the parts. For example, a $\langle$digit-triple$\rangle$ is defined in terms of $\langle$digit$\rangle$, and $\langle$digit$\rangle$ in turn is defined in terms of $\langle$nonzero-digit$\rangle$. Note that the BNF definition does not allow us to write the integer zero—using this definition a plain "0" cannot be written as a $\langle$fancy-integer$\rangle$ (but the definition is easily extended, see Exercise 3.2). ∎

Describing Program-User Dialogues with BNF

BNF can be used to make very precise descriptions of lines of text, all the way down to the individual characters allowed in each item. However, in describing the requirements for the program-user dialogue, we are not usually interested in being quite so precise. Instead we want to use BNF to specify each line in the dialogue with only as much precision as required to ensure the requirement is unambiguous and understandable. When the definition of a set of items can be described more easily with words, we use words. If BNF is better, we use BNF.

Our form for describing a program-user dialogue is the following. We tag each line with "program" or "user" to indicate whether the program is expected to display the line or the user is expected to type the line. We use BNF to describe the details of each line as accurately as possible:

$\langle$Program-user Dialogue$\rangle$ ::=

DIALOGUE

$\quad$ PROGRAM: ...BNF description of program output line(s)...
$\quad$ USER: ...BNF description of what the user may type in...

PROGRAM: ...and continue describing the lines of the dialogue...
WHERE
...BNF or words to describe the form of each named set of items...

In describing numbers that the user is expected to type in, pay special attention to the form allowed for each number and the range of possible values for the number. If a computed number is being displayed by the program, then you may not know exactly the range for that number.

EXAMPLE: *Nancy's Dialogue*

Now we can use BNF to more completely describe the dialogue in Nancy's program:

DIALOGUE

PROGRAM: Please type a temperature value (degrees F):
USER: ⟨Fahrenheit temp⟩
PROGRAM: ⟨Fahrenheit temp⟩ degrees F = ⟨Celsius temp⟩ degrees C
WHERE
⟨Fahrenheit temp⟩ ::= ⟨number⟩ in the approximate range from
                            −100 to 200.
⟨Celsius temp⟩ ::= ⟨number⟩ in approximately same range of possible
                        values as ⟨Fahrenheit temp⟩.
⟨number⟩ ::=
    [−] ⟨digit⟩ {⟨digit⟩} [. ⟨digit⟩ {⟨digit⟩}]
    No spaces are allowed in a ⟨number⟩.

□
Note: Because the range of temperature values allowed in Nancy's program has not been specified before, we have chosen an appropriate range for the Fahrenheit value typed by the user. ■

A larger example will help to illustrate how to develop the requirements for a program. In the next sections, we continue with this same example, developing an algorithm that satisfies these requirements. Then in the next chapter, we code the algorithm into Pascal to produce a working program.

EXAMPLE: *Florida Joe's Gas Mileage*

Florida Joe has just come back from a long trip to the mountains. He wants to figure out what gas mileage he got on the trip. He wrote down the odometer reading before he left and after he got back, and as he traveled he kept track of the number of gallons required each time he filled up the tank. Today he wants to write a little program for his home computer that will compute gas mileage for this trip (and any later trips he takes). Joe writes down the requirements for his program:

INPUT: Before trip odometer reading.
After trip odometer reading.
Number of gallons bought at each fillup.

PROCESSING: Compute total miles traveled.
Compute total gallons used.
Compute miles per gallon for the whole trip.

OUTPUT: Before and after odometer readings.
Total miles and total gallons.
Miles per gallon for the trip.

ASSUMPTIONS: I'm the only one that will ever use this program. Keep it short and simple. No program checking of input data is required.

Joe now has DEFINE'd what the program should be able to do. Next he REFINE's the requirements into a detailed dialogue. The dialogue follows the general sequence of INPUT, PROCESSING and OUTPUT that he has specified:

DIALOGUE

PROGRAM: "Starting odometer reading?"

USER: ⟨StartMiles⟩

PROGRAM: "Ending odometer reading?"

USER: ⟨EndMiles⟩

PROGRAM: "List gallons in each fillup, one number per line."
"End the list with a zero value (on a separate line)."

USER: ⟨Gallons⟩
{⟨Gallons⟩}
0

PROGRAM: ODOMETER: Start of trip = ⟨StartMiles⟩
End of trip = ⟨EndMiles⟩

TOTAL MILES: ⟨TotalMiles⟩

TOTAL GALLONS: ⟨TotalGallons⟩

MILES/GALLON: ⟨MilesPerGallon⟩

WHERE
⟨StartMiles⟩ and ⟨EndMiles⟩ ::= ⟨digit⟩ {⟨digit⟩}
Range: 0 to 99999

⟨Gallons⟩ ::= gallons in one fillup, in the form:
⟨digit⟩ {⟨digit⟩} [. ⟨digit⟩ {⟨digit⟩}]
Range: 0 to 50

⟨TotalMiles⟩ ::= integer value; total miles traveled.
   Range: 0 to 99999.
⟨TotalGallons⟩ ::= total gallons used, to one decimal place.
⟨MilesPerGallon⟩ ::= miles per gallon over the trip, to one decimal
   place.

□

Discussion:

1. *Revise, revise, revise.* As Joe wrote down the program's requirements, he made several changes in this requirements list. He started out thinking about computing the miles per gallon, but then he thought it would be nice also to see the total miles traveled and the total number of gallons used, so he added those requirements. He also decided he would like to have a record of the before and after odometer readings given as input, so he added those as additional outputs. When writing requirements, expect to revise the requirements list repeatedly before you are happy with the result.

2. *Why mention assumptions about who will use a program? Wouldn't you write the program the same way regardless?* Any program has to be *correct:* given some allowed input values, it must compute correctly the output results. In a program written for your personal use, correctness is the main requirement. But a program written for other people usually has several additional requirements, such as a requirement that the output be neatly formatted so that it is easily understood or a requirement that the program check for bad input values and give appropriate error messages.

Also, when a program will be used by many people over a long period of time, it almost always will be modified and extended by other programmers (to accomplish additional tasks or variations of its original task). Designing a program so that it can be easily extended later is an important aspect of program design. If you know you will use a program only a few times without modification and then throw it away (as Florida Joe might do with his program), then you don't worry about extensions. ■

EXERCISES

3.2 Extend the BNF definition of a ⟨fancy-integer⟩ given above to allow the value zero to be written as "0". Example: 0. -100,000.

3.3 Choose an appropriate format and write a BNF description for the following text items or lines:
   a. A date (month, day, and year).
   b. A person's name.
   c. A person's home address.
   d. A weather report that includes the current temperature, wind speed and direction, type and amount of precipitation, and cloud cover.

3.4 Write the requirements for a program to perform each of the following tasks:

a. For a school science fair, write a demonstration program that will give a person's weight on the moon, Mars, Venus, and Jupiter, given that person's weight on earth.

b. For use by a high school math class, write a program to compute the roots of a quadratic equation, given the coefficients for the terms.

c. For a school science fair, write a program that will compute the area and perimeter of a rectangle or a right triangle, given the length of the base and height of the figure. The program should ask the user whether a rectangle or right triangle is to be used.

□□□ **3.3**
ALGORITHMS AND PSEUDO-CODE

Let's look at the next step: developing an algorithm to automate an information processing task, where the task is now defined by a requirements list. Think of the requirements list as defining the *outside view* of the program—what the program should appear to the user to be capable of doing. Think of the algorithm as the *inside view* of the program—what the program actually does to achieve what the user sees from outside. The "outside view—inside view" distinction is useful because often what goes on inside the program is quite different from what you might expect from the outside.

How do you think about and describe what is going on inside a program? A few concepts will help: *data objects, data values and data types, program states and assertions,* and *operations and actions.* These concepts form our "design vocabulary"—the terms we use to talk about the design of an algorithm.

These concepts are general concepts about programming; they are not peculiar to a particular programming language such as Pascal. But each corresponds to something in Pascal, so there is a natural translation back and forth between an algorithm expressed using these concepts and the final Pascal program that you want to write.

□□
Writing Algorithms in Pseudo-code

How do you develop an algorithm? The hacker's route is to simply dive into Pascal and start writing a program. But a programming language like Pascal is somewhat like a strait-jacket on your mind—all of its detailed rules and restrictions tend to hamper your thinking. While developing an algorithm, you want to be free to play with various solution strategies and ways of representing the data, until you find an overall algorithm that you like. It's like using an informal outline when you are writing a term paper instead of working directly with complete sentences, proper grammar, and full punctuation.

However, although freedom is nice, you cannot be too free in developing your algorithm, because when you get finished, you have to be able to code that algorithm into a Pascal program. So you cannot get too far away from what is "programmable" in Pascal.

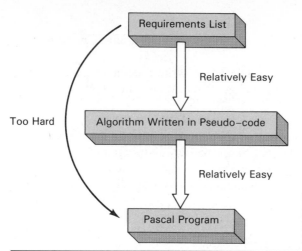

FIGURE 3.3 Pseudo-code Bridges the Gap Between Requirements and a Pascal Program

A good in between point lies in the use of a *pseudo-code* for designing an algorithm, as shown in Figure 3.3. The pseudo-code algorithm is to an actual Pascal program as an informal outline for a term paper is to the finished product.

> □ **Pseudo-code**
>
> Pseudo-code is an informal description of the design of a program, written so that each part is in approximate correspondence with a part of the final coded program.

The pseudo-code algorithm shows you the general structure of the Pascal program without the details of the Pascal syntax. In the pseudo-code algorithm you can be informal, describing the algorithm in terms appropriate to the task being automated rather than in terms of the Pascal language.

As we develop our concepts for designing algorithms in this section, we also develop a pseudo-code appropriate for writing down algorithms. This pseudo-code will be appropriate for simple algorithms. In later chapters, we extend our pseudo-code as we extend our knowledge of Pascal.

□ □
What is an Algorithm?

In Chapter 1 we defined:

> □ **Algorithm**
>
> An *algorithm* is a specification of (1) the *sequence of steps* required to perform a particular information processing task and (2) the *data objects* used in performing each step.

To write an algorithm in our pseudo-code we use two lists:

ALGORITHM

Step 1: PURPOSE: Ask the user to type a Fahrenheit temperature value and read it in.

GOAL STATE: DegreesF contains the temperature value typed by the user.

ACTIONS:
DISPLAY: "Please type a temperature value (degrees F)."
READ: DegreesF

Step 2: PURPOSE: Compute the equivalent Celsius temperature.

GOAL STATE: DegreesC contains the equivalent temperature.

ACTIONS:
DegreesC := (5/9) * (DegreesF − 32)

Step 3: PURPOSE: Display both temperature values.

GOAL STATE: Both values are displayed on the terminal screen.

ACTIONS:
DISPLAY: "⟨DegreesF⟩ degrees F = ⟨DegreesC⟩ degrees C"

DATA OBJECTS

NAME	DATA TYPE	PURPOSE
DegreesF:	Real number.	The temperature value typed in by the user.
DegreesC:	Real number.	The equivalent Celsius temperature value.

FIGURE 3.4 Nancy's Algorithm (from Chapter 1) in Pseudo-code

1. *Algorithm.* A list of the *steps* in the algorithm. Each step includes a purpose, goal state, and list of actions. We name this primary list the ALGORITHM.
2. *Data Objects.* A secondary list of the *data objects* used in the steps of the ALGORITHM part, and the *data type* and *purpose* for each data object.

Figure 3.4 shows Nancy's algorithm from Chapter 1 written out fully in pseudo-code. In the following sections we look at the various parts in more detail.

□□□3.4
DATA VALUES, DATA OBJECTS, AND DATA TYPES

A *data value* is a single piece of information used in an algorithm, such as a single number like 17 or 12.587 or a single character like "Z".

A *data object* is a named place where one or more data values can be stored, such as the data objects named DegreesF and DegreesC used in Nancy's algorithm.

Each of these data objects may be used to store a single number in Nancy's algorithm.

A *data type* is a name for a set of data values, such as the data type *Real* that Nancy used as the data type for her data objects DegreesF and DegreesC. The data type *Real* names the set of numbers that may have fractional parts.

In our algorithms these three concepts are connected as follows:

1. When a *data object* is defined, it is given a *name* and a *data type*.
2. When a *data value* is stored in a *data object,* the value must be one of the data values associated with the *data type* of the data object.
3. An action in the algorithm may change the *data value* stored in a data object, but the *data type* associated with a data object cannot be changed.

In this chapter we restrict our data objects to contain only a *single* data value at any given time. In later chapters, we expand our view to allow a data object to contain many data values at once.

□ □

The DATA OBJECTS List

When designing an algorithm, you may use as many different data objects as you need to store the data values used by the algorithm. The DATA OBJECTS list is simply a list of the data objects used, in the form:

⟨DATA OBJECTS list⟩ ::=

DATA OBJECTS

    ⟨data object name⟩: ⟨data type⟩ ⟨purpose of the data object⟩
    {⟨data object name⟩: ⟨data type⟩ ⟨purpose of the data object⟩}
    WHERE
      ⟨data object name⟩ ::=
        The name used to refer to the data object in the ALGORITHM part.
      ⟨data type⟩ ::= Real ¦ Integer ¦ Char ¦ Boolean
        (these types are discussed below)
      ⟨purpose of the data object⟩ ::=
        A brief description of what the data object represents in the program,
        including, for Real and Integer types, the *units of measure* and the *range of*
        possible values for the numbers stored in the data object.

In this chapter, we restrict the *data types* associated with our data objects to the four simple types that are defined in the Pascal language:

☐

Integer: the set of all positive and negative integers (whole numbers), including zero.

☐

Real: the set of all positive and negative numbers that may have fractional parts (including zero and all the integers).

☐

Char: the set of all single characters (such as can be typed with one keystroke on a computer terminal keyboard), including all the upper-case and lower-case letters, the digits 0 through 9, punctuation marks, the "space" character, and all the special characters.

☐

Boolean: the set composed of only the two values TRUE and FALSE. ("Boolean" is named for George Boole, who invented the logical calculus based on true/false values which is mentioned in Chapter 1.)

EXAMPLE With these new concepts, we can do a better job of writing Nancy's DATA OBJECTS list in pseudo-code (See Figure 3.4):

DATA OBJECTS

DegreesF: Real   Fahrenheit temperature value, range −100 to 200 (degrees F).
DegreesC: Real   Celsius temperature value, range approx. same as DegreesF (in degrees C).

EXERCISES

3.5 Write DATA OBJECTS list entries for the data objects you would use to store each of the data values needed in the following situations. Use as many data objects as you need for each situation:
  a. The price of your new sports car.
  b. A person's middle initial.
  c. The answer to the question "Did the employee buy life insurance?"
  d. The final score in a basketball game.
  e. The populations of each of the five largest cities in the world.
  f. Your birthday.
  g. The speed of the fastest snail in a snail race, in kilometers per hour.

☐☐☐ **3.5**
PROGRAM STATES

Data objects store data values. The *state* of a data object at some point during execution of a program just means the *data value that the data object contains* at that point. Thus in Nancy's program, you might ask: "What is the state of data object

DegreesC after the step in the algorithm that computes the Celsius value?" Nancy's answer might be: "After that step, DegreesC contains the newly computed Celsius temperature value." If you asked "What is the state of object DegreesC *before* this step?" the answer would be "The state of DegreesC is *uninitialized*," meaning that the value stored in DegreesC is unpredictable because no assignment of a value to the object has yet been made by the program.

The overall "state" of the program at some point during its execution is an important concept:

□ **Program State**

The program state at a particular point during program execution includes:

1. The *data state*, the state of each data object in the program at that point, and
2. The *display state*, what is displayed on the terminal screen at that point.

To ask "what is the program state after this step in the algorithm?" means "tell me what data value each of the data objects contains and what is displayed on the screen after this step?" If we want to ask only about the values stored in the data objects, we ask "what is the data state after this step?" If only the contents of the display screen are of interest, the question becomes "what is the display state after this step?"

To show a particular program state, we draw a box for each data object, showing its name and current value, and a box for the display screen, showing what is currently displayed. For example, Figure 3.5 shows the final state of Nancy's program.

If a data object is uninitialized, we show its value as ??. For example, if DegreesC is uninitialized, the state diagram would contain:

DegreesC: ??

The term *program state* here means something similar to "state of affairs" in ordinary conversation. If someone gets up in a meeting and summarizes the "state of affairs" of the group's activities, she would describe "how things stand right now" for each individual activity. Similarly, the "state of affairs" at some point during execution of a program is always summed up by looking at what data values have been computed and stored in the various data objects in the program, and what information is displayed on the screen at that point.

□ □
Initial States, Intermediate States, and Final States

As one action follows another during execution of a program, the program state changes repeatedly. The program begins execution in some *initial state*—that is, each data object contains something before the first action step is executed. In our

```
DegreesF:    [  68  ]

DegreesC:    [  20  ]

DISPLAY SCREEN:

    ┌─────────────────────────────────────────────────────┐
    │ Please type a temperature value (degrees F):          │
    │                                                       │
    │ 68                                                    │
    │ ──                                                    │
    │ 68 degrees F = 20 degrees C                           │
    └─────────────────────────────────────────────────────┘
```

FIGURE 3.5   A Program State

programs here, we assume the initial state is always the same: *in the initial state, all data objects are uninitialized and the display screen is blank.* "Uninitialized" means that the initial value stored in the data object is unpredictable. Only after the program explicitly assigns or reads a value into a data object the first time do you know its state. "The display screen is blank" means that this program has displayed no information on the screen yet. (However, the screen may still contain information from the user's previous activities.)

As actions of the program are executed, each action specifies a change in the state of one or more of the data objects or the display screen. After an action has been executed, the program is in some *intermediate state*. When the last action in the program has been executed, the program has reached its *final state*—all the data objects and the display screen contain their final values, and the program terminates. Figure 3.6 illustrates how states and actions are related during execution of a program.

Notice how the data objects and their values (the "data state") form the "inside world" of the program. The display state forms the "outside world" that is visible to the user.

Assertions About Program States

Often we are not interested in the entire program state (all the data objects and everything that is displayed on the screen). Instead, we want to focus on part of the state, so we restrict our discussion or diagrams to show only the data objects of interest, or perhaps to illustrate only the most recent lines displayed.

Equally as often we want to describe a program state more abstractly, in terms of properties of the values stored in the data objects or displayed, rather than in

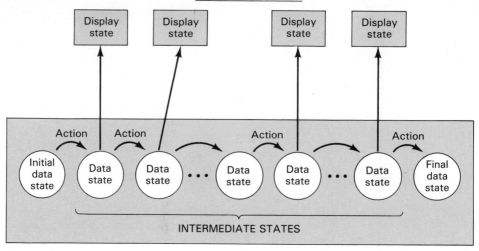

FIGURE 3.6   Program Actions and Program States

terms of particular data values (such as the values 20 and 68 in the state of Nancy's program). A statement that describes a property of a program state is called an *assertion:*

> ☐ **Assertion**
>
> An *assertion* is a statement about the data values contained in one or several data objects or the data values displayed on the screen in one or more states of a program.

For example, here are some typical assertions:

1. In this state, DegreesC contains the computed temperature value in Celsius degrees.
2. In this state, the values of X and Y are equal.
3. In this state and all following states, Total > 0.
4. In this state, the screen contains the prompt "Please type a Fahrenheit temperature value" and the program is waiting for the user to type a response.

An assertion may describe a property of a program state in one of several ways:

■ It may describe how the value of a data object in a state is related to the problem being solved, as in 1 above.

■ It may describe how the values in different data objects are related in a single state, as in 2 above.

■ It may describe a property of the value of a single data object in one state, many states, or all states, as in 3 above.

■ It may describe some aspect of what is displayed on the screen, as in 4 above.

In designing algorithms, we are continually using assertions to describe the various states that occur during execution.

EXERCISES

3.6 For each of the following statements, determine if it is an *assertion* according to the definition above. Explain why or why not:

   a. In this program state, the value of X is less than the sum of A, B, and C.

   b. In every state of this program after this action is executed, the value of OldStudent is unchanged.

   c. In this program state, the next action is to compute the new grade point average for the student.

   d. At this point during execution, the program is almost finished computing the table.

□□□ 3.6
WRITING THE ALGORITHM PART

Actions and states are the key elements during execution of the steps of an algorithm. A program may execute hundreds or thousands of actions and go through hundreds or thousands of different states during its execution. To describe an algorithm, we break the actions into larger *steps*, consisting of a sequence of several actions (usually 1-10 actions). Each step in the algorithm has a *purpose*—what the step is intended to accomplish—and a *goal state*—the state to be reached as a result of executing the actions associated with the step.

The ALGORITHM part describes the sequence of steps in the algorithm. In our pseudo-code, we write this part in the form:

⟨ALGORITHM PART⟩ ::=

   ALGORITHM

      INITIAL STATE: All data objects are uninitialized; screen is blank.

Step 1. PURPOSE: ⟨purpose⟩
      GOAL STATE: ⟨goal state⟩
      ACTIONS: ⟨action sequence⟩

{**Step k.** PURPOSE: ⟨purpose⟩   } Repeat this part for
      GOAL STATE: ⟨goal state⟩   } each additional step
      ACTIONS: ⟨action sequence⟩}   } in the algorithm.

      FINAL STATE: All actions complete; all data objects contain their final values; all results are displayed.

WHERE

⟨purpose⟩ ::=
A description of the purpose of the step—*what* the step accomplishes in terms of the overall task to be performed.

⟨goal state⟩ ::=
An assertion describing the goal state of the step—what should have changed in the program state as a result of executing this step (new values assigned to data objects or new lines displayed on the screen).

⟨action sequence⟩ ::=
A list of the actions required to reach the goal state.

Nancy's algorithm in Figure 3.5 shows a typical ALGORITHM part.

Operations and Actions: Changing the Program State

When we want to change the program state, by storing a new value in one of the data objects or by displaying another line of output on the screen, we use an *action*. An action is composed of the name of an *operation,* which tells what action to take, and the names of one or more *operands,* which tell what data objects should be used.

For this chapter, we restrict our attention to three basic operations:

1. *DISPLAY*. Display a new line of output on the terminal screen.
2. *READ*. As the user types a data value on the keyboard, "read" the typed value and store it in a specified data object.
3. *ASSIGN*. Assign a new value to a data object, replacing the value currently stored in the object.

Writing DISPLAY Actions

To write a DISPLAY action, use the syntax:

⟨DISPLAY action⟩ ::=
DISPLAY: "⟨line to be displayed⟩"

WHERE

⟨line to be displayed⟩ ::= A description of the form and content of the line to be displayed, preferably using BNF.

Meaning when Executed: The ⟨line to be displayed⟩ is displayed as the next line on the user's terminal screen.

EXAMPLES

1.   DISPLAY: "Please type a number between 1 and 100."

2. DISPLAY: "⟨DegreesF⟩ degrees F = ⟨DegreesC⟩ degrees C"
where "DegreesF" and "DegreesC" are the names of data objects in the DATA OBJECTS list.

Each DISPLAY action in an algorithm displays a line of output on the screen. Thus each DISPLAY action corresponds to a line in the DIALOGUE part of the program's requirements. The BNF description of that line should provide all the information that is needed to write the DISPLAY action. Where the BNF includes a value chosen from a set, ⟨...⟩, the DISPLAY action should be written to insert the value of an appropriate data object at that point.

The sequence in which DISPLAY actions appear in an algorithm must match the sequence in which the lines appear in the DIALOGUE. That is, you must display the lines from top to bottom on the screen. There is no way in our pseudo-code to display a line at the bottom of the screen and then go back later and display a line *above* that line on the screen.

Writing READ Actions

To write a READ action, use the syntax:

> ⟨READ action⟩ ::=
>   READ: ⟨data object⟩ {, ⟨data object⟩}
>
> **WHERE**
>
> ⟨data object⟩ ::= The name of the data object that is to be used to store the data value that the user types. List one data object to store each value that the user is expected to type.

Meaning when Executed: The computer waits until the user types one data value for each ⟨data object⟩ named in the READ action. Each data value typed is stored in the corresponding data object.

EXAMPLES

1. READ: DegreesF
   to read a number typed by the user and store it in data object DegreesF.
2. READ: Exam1, Exam2, Exam3
   to read three values typed by the user and store them in the three data objects named.

READ actions also correspond directly to lines in the DIALOGUE description. Each item of information typed by the user in the DIALOGUE must correspond to a READ action in the algorithm.

Writing ASSIGN Actions

To write an ASSIGN action, use the syntax:

⟨ASSIGN action⟩ ::=
⟨data object⟩ := ⟨value to be stored⟩

WHERE

⟨data object⟩ ::= Any data object name.
⟨value to be stored⟩ ::= The literal (actual) value to be stored, the name of another data object that contains the value, or a mathematical formula for computing the value. (These alternatives are discussed below.)

□

Meaning when Executed: The ⟨value to be stored⟩ is computed (if a mathematical formula is given) or a copy is made (if a literal value or the name of another data object is given) and the new value is stored in the named ⟨data object⟩, replacing the value currently stored in the ⟨data object⟩.

Our pseudo-code uses the symbol ":=" for the ASSIGN action (the same symbol used in Pascal). Each ASSIGN action assigns a new value to exactly one data object. If several data objects are to receive new values, a sequence of ASSIGN actions is used.

ASSIGN actions are used for several purposes. Some common patterns are the following:

1. *Assign a literal value.* If the value to be assigned is known when you write the algorithm, then that value can be written directly into the ASSIGN action. A value written directly in an action is termed a *literal value.* For example, to assign the literal value zero to data object Total, the ASSIGN action is:

Total := 0

2. *Assign a copy of the value stored in another data object.* If one data object contains the value, and a copy is to be stored in a second data object, the ASSIGN action is written:

⟨second data object⟩ := ⟨first data object⟩

For example, to assign data object NewMonth a copy of the value stored in TodaysMonth:

NewMonth := TodaysMonth

3. *Swap two values.* Suppose you want to *swap* the values of two data objects, that is, you want each data object to be assigned a copy of the current value of the other data object. If the data objects are named X and Y, you might first try the sequence:

X := Y
Y := X

but this does not work—both Y and X end up containing a copy of the original value of Y (explain why by showing the before and after data states). To make a "swap," you must use a third data object, say *Temp,* with the same data type as X and Y, and then write:

> Temp := Y   (save the old value of Y in Temp)
> Y := X   (copy the old value of X into Y)
> X := Temp   (copy the saved value of Y into X)

Using an additional data object, like Temp, to store a data value temporarily is a common pattern in programming.

4. *Counting.* Integer data objects (and less often, Real data objects) are often used as *counters* in programming. You assign the data object an initial value of zero and then add one to its value to count the occurrences of a particular event during the computation. The "count" action is written:

$$\langle \text{data object name} \rangle := \langle \text{same data object name} \rangle + 1$$

For example, a program might require counting the number of student grades above 60, using a data object named PassingGrades. To set the initial value of PassingGrades, the action:

$$\text{PassingGrades} := 0$$

would be used. Then the action to count another passing grade would be written:

$$\text{PassingGrades} := \text{PassingGrades} + 1$$

which means "fetch the current value of data object PassingGrades and add 1 to it; store the new value back in data object PassingGrades, replacing its current value."

5. *Use a mathematical formula.* A real or integer number may be computed using a mathematical formula, where the formula involves arithmetic operations like addition and subtraction, and standard mathematical functions like square root, sine, and cosine, using literal values or the values of data objects. For example, to convert a Fahrenheit temperature to Celsius, Nancy used the mathematical formula in an ASSIGN action:

$$\text{DegreesC} := 5/9 * (\text{DegreesF} - 32)$$

Table 3.1 gives a list of some of the mathematical operations and functions that are available in Pascal.

TABLE 3.1 Arithmetic Operations and Functions

OPERATIONS

Pascal Syntax	Meaning
+	addition
−	subtraction
*	multiplication
/	division producing a Real quotient
DIV	division of integers, producing an Integer quotient (no remainder)
MOD	Integer remainder after division of integers

FUNCTIONS

Pascal Syntax	Meaning
sqrt (...)	square root
sin (...)	sine
cos (...)	cosine
arctan (...)	arc tangent
exp (...)	exponential
ln (...)	natural logarithm (base e)
abs (...)	absolute value

---

6. *Test (compare) two or more values.* A TRUE/FALSE value (Boolean value) may be computed by testing whether two data values are equal, one is greater than the other, or a similar comparison. For example, to test if a Fahrenheit value is below freezing (32 degrees), we might use the ASSIGN action:

$$\text{BelowFreezing} := \text{DegreesF} < 32$$

which assigns BelowFreezing the value TRUE if the value of DegreesF is less than 32. Table 3.2 shows some of the operations that are available for tests in Pascal.

There are several additional operations and functions that are a standard part of the Pascal language, and each Pascal system may provide other non-standard operations and functions. We will look further at this part of Pascal in the next chapter. In pseudo-code, you should assume that you have available the operations and functions that you need for computing the data values required. If one of these operations or functions is not provided by your Pascal system, then you can define your own *function subprogram*. Once defined, such a function subprogram is used just as though it were one of the basic Pascal functions. We explain how to define function subprograms in Chapter 5.

TABLE 3.2 Relational Tests and Boolean Operations

RELATIONAL TESTS

Pascal Syntax	Meaning
=	equal?
<>	not equal?
<	less than?
<=	less than or equal?
>	greater than?
>=	greater than or equal?

BOOLEAN OPERATIONS

Pascal Syntax	Meaning
⟨test 1⟩ AND ⟨test 2⟩	both tests return TRUE?
⟨test 1⟩ OR ⟨test 2⟩	at least one test returns TRUE?
NOT ⟨test⟩	the test returns FALSE?

□ □
Straight-line Sequence of Actions

The operations of DISPLAY, READ, and ASSIGN can be combined to form larger actions in several ways. The simplest is a *straight-line* sequence, where the actions are listed in the ACTIONS part of a step in the order in which they are to be executed. In a straight-line sequence, each action is executed exactly once during execution of that step of the algorithm. No actions are skipped and no actions are repeated.

EXAMPLE

For an algorithm step described as:

PURPOSE: Initialize all totals and averages to zero.

GOAL STATE: SubTotal, GrandTotal, SalesAverage and WeeklyAverage all initialized to zero.

The actions might be the straight-line sequence:

ACTIONS:
    SubTotal := 0
    GrandTotal := 0
    SalesAverage := 0
    WeeklyAverage := 0

■

□ □
Conditional Choice of Action (IF)

Alternatively, a larger action may consist of a choice among several simpler actions, based on some property of the program state. Executing the larger action then consists of testing for the property of the state and choosing one of the simpler actions to execute based on the result of the test. We write such an action as an IF action:

⟨IF action⟩ ::=
   IF ⟨test 1⟩ THEN   —the first case
     ⟨actions for case 1⟩
   {ELSE IF ⟨test k⟩ THEN   } repeat if there
     ⟨actions for case k⟩}   } are several cases
   [ELSE
     ⟨actions if all tests return FALSE⟩] —the *default* case

WHERE

⟨test k⟩ ::=
   Any test on the values of the data objects in the program state, as described for the ASSIGN action above; the result must be a Boolean value (TRUE or FALSE).
⟨actions⟩ ::=
   A sequence of actions or sub-steps, which may include ASSIGN, DISPLAY, READ, WHILE and other IF's.

□

Meaning when Executed:

1. Evaluate ⟨test 1⟩, ⟨test 2⟩, ... in sequence until a test gives a TRUE value, using the values in the current state.
2. Execute the ⟨actions⟩ that follow the first ⟨test⟩ that gives a TRUE value.
3. If all the tests give a FALSE value, then execute the actions for the default case, if any; otherwise do nothing further.

Notice that you can use a sequence of tests and actions to distinguish as many cases as you need, and the final ELSE action is optional.

EXAMPLES   1.   If an algorithm step is:

PURPOSE: Display one of three possible messages depending on whether the temperature value in DegreesF is above, equal to, or below freezing.

GOAL STATE: The correct message is displayed.

then an IF action might be used:

ACTIONS:
  IF DegreesF < 32 THEN
    DISPLAY: "The temperature you typed is below freezing."
  ELSE IF DegreesF = 32 THEN
    DISPLAY: "The temperature you typed is exactly freezing."
  ELSE
    DISPLAY: "The temperature you typed is above freezing."

2. If the algorithm step is:

> PURPOSE: Test if NewValue is larger than the current maximum value, and if so, update the maximum value to the new value.
>
> GOAL STATE: CurrentMax contains the largest value so far.

then an IF action might be used:

> ACTIONS:
>   IF NewValue > CurrentMax THEN
>   CurrentMax := NewValue

□ □
Repeated Actions (WHILE Loop)

A larger action may also consist of repeating a simpler action a number of times. Each repetition begins with a test to determine whether to continue. If the test says to continue, then the simpler action is executed once and the test is repeated, continuing until the test says to stop. To write such an action, we use a *WHILE loop* in the form:

> ⟨WHILE-loop⟩ ::=
>   WHILE ⟨test to decide whether to continue⟩ DO
>   ⟨actions to be repeated⟩
>
> **WHERE**
>
> ⟨test to decide whether to continue⟩ ::=
>   Any test on the values of the data objects in the program state, as described for the ASSIGN action above; the result must be a Boolean value (TRUE or FALSE).
> ⟨actions to be repeated⟩ ::=
>   A sequence of actions and sub-steps, which may include DISPLAY, READ, ASSIGN, IF, and WHILE actions. These actions are termed the *loop body*.

□

Meaning when Executed: Perform the following steps:

1. Evaluate the ⟨test⟩, using the values of the data objects in the current state.
2. If the ⟨test⟩ = FALSE then do nothing further.
3. If the ⟨test⟩ = TRUE then execute the ⟨actions to be repeated⟩ and go back to step 1 above.

Notice that if the ⟨test⟩ returns FALSE the first time that it is evaluated, then the loop body is skipped entirely—the ⟨actions to be repeated⟩ are never executed at all. If the test never returns FALSE, then the loop body continues to be executed "forever."

1.   If the algorithm step is:

PURPOSE: Display the countdown sequence:

> 10 seconds to liftoff.
> 9 seconds to liftoff.
> ...
> 2 seconds to liftoff.
> 1 second to liftoff.
> LIFTOFF!

GOAL STATE: Countdown sequence displayed.

then a WHILE action might be used for displaying the first nine lines:

ACTIONS:

> Count := 10
> WHILE Count > 1 DO
>   DISPLAY: "⟨Count⟩ seconds to liftoff."
>   Count := Count − 1
> DISPLAY: "1 second to liftoff."
> DISPLAY: "LIFTOFF!"

2. If the algorithm step is:

PURPOSE: Read a list of numbers into data object Sales as the user types them in and compute the total of the numbers. Quit when a zero value is read.

GOAL STATE: TotalSales contains the total sales values.

then a WHILE action might be used:

ACTIONS:

> TotalSales := 0
> READ: Sales
> WHILE Sales < > 0 DO
>   TotalSales := TotalSales + Sales
>   READ: Sales

3. If the algorithm step is:

PURPOSE: Ask the user to type a temperature value that is above freezing, and then repeat the request until the user types an acceptable value.

GOAL STATE: DegreesF contains a temperature value > 32.

then the WHILE action might be used:

ACTIONS:

DISPLAY: "Please type a temperature that is above freezing."
READ: DegreesF
WHILE DegreesF <= 32 DO
  DISPLAY:
    "Try again. The value must be above 32 degrees F."
  READ: DegreesF   ■

□
Sub-steps in an IF or WHILE Action Occasionally the actions within an IF or WHILE action may be complicated enough that they really need to be broken into a sequence of *sub-steps,* each with a PURPOSE, GOAL STATE, and ACTIONS list, rather than a single sequence of actions. You can do this simply by numbering the sub-steps appropriately, using the same general form as in the main steps of the overall algorithm.

EXAMPLE Suppose one step in the algorithm uses a WHILE loop whose body contains a complicated sequence of actions. Then the body might be broken into sub-steps:

Step k. PURPOSE: ...

GOAL STATE: ...

ACTIONS:

WHILE ⟨TEST⟩ DO
  K.1 PURPOSE: ... PURPOSE OF SUB-STEP ...
    GOAL STATE: ...
    ACTIONS: ...
  K.2 PURPOSE: ... PURPOSE OF SUB-STEP ...
    GOAL STATE: ...
    ACTIONS: ...
  ...

EXERCISES

3.7 Suppose your program's DATA OBJECTS list includes the following data objects, of the type given:

Count: Integer   Grade1: Integer
Total: Integer   Grade2: Integer
FinalGrade: Char   Average: Real
IsComplete: Boolean

Write an ACTIONS list that will accomplish the PURPOSE and reach the GOAL STATE for each of the following:

a. PURPOSE: Sum and average Grade1 and Grade2.

GOAL STATE: Total contains the sum; Average contains the average.

b. PURPOSE: Ask the user to type two grade values in the range 0 to 100 and read them in.

GOAL STATE: Grade1 and Grade2 contain the two values typed.

c. PURPOSE: Display the names and values of data objects Total and Average.

GOAL STATE: A line with the names and values is displayed.

d. PURPOSE: Assign an "A" grade if Grade1 is larger than Grade2; otherwise assign a "B" grade.

GOAL STATE: FinalGrade contains the assigned grade.

e. PURPOSE: Determine if all ten assignments have been completed, by testing if Count = 10.

GOAL STATE: IsComplete contains the result of the test.

f. PURPOSE: Swap the values of Grade1 and Total, using Grade2 as temporary storage if needed.

GOAL STATE: Grade1 contains the original value of Total, and vice versa.

g. PURPOSE: Read a list of grades as the user types them in, until a zero grade is typed. As the grades are read, keep a running total in Total.

GOAL STATE: Total contains the total of all grades read.

h. PURPOSE: If Grade1 is larger than Grade2 then add Grade1 to Total, but if Grade1 is smaller than Grade2 then add Grade2 to Total. If the grades are equal, do nothing.

GOAL STATE: Total has been increased, unless Grade1 = Grade2.

i. PURPOSE: Ask the user to type an integer between 10 and 20. Read the number in and store it in Count. If the number is not between 10 and 20, ask the user to type a correct number. Continue until the user types a number that is in the correct range.

GOAL STATE: Count contains the number read in, and it is between 10 and 20.

3.8 Generalize the *swap* pattern to a sequence of assignment actions that "rotate" the values of three data objects, A, B, and C, so that A gets the value of B, B gets the value of C, and C gets the value of A. Do you still need an extra data object for temporary storage?

3.9 Suppose that the data state in a program is the following:

Total1: [15]   Total2: [20]

Count1: [2]   Count2: [6]

Show the new data state after execution of each of the following lists of ACTIONS:

a.
```
WHILE COUNT1 > 0 DO
      Total1 := Total1 + Count1
      Count1 := Count1 − 1
```

b.
```
IF Total2 > Total1 + Count2 THEN
      Count1 := Count1 − 1
ELSE
      Count2 := Count2 − 1
```

c.
```
Total1 := 0
WHILE Total2 > Total1 DO
      Total2 := Total2 − Count2
      Total1 := Total1 + Count1
      Count1 := Count1 + 1
```

□□□ **3.7**
HINTS FOR DEVELOPING ALGORITHMS

We now have a vocabulary of concepts and terms for talking about algorithms and a pseudo-code for writing them down. In an algorithm, we may define as many data objects as needed to build a program state; there are four basic data types, Integer, Real, Boolean, and Char, for these data objects. There are three basic operations, DISPLAY, READ, and ASSIGN, for building actions, and three ways to compose simple actions into larger actions: straight-line sequences, IF, and WHILE. We also have a general design principle: DEFINE, then REFINE.

In the next section, we will see Florida Joe design a complete algorithm for his "gas mileage" program. First, let's look at some general hints for approaching the design of an algorithm. Where do you start and how do you proceed?

□□
Design the PURPOSE and GOAL STATE of the Steps First

Our first suggestion is simply an application of the "DEFINE, then REFINE" principle: concentrate first on defining the algorithm's steps *without any actions*—just the PURPOSE and GOAL STATE of each step. The PURPOSE and GOAL STATE tell you *what* the step is to accomplish and what data objects need to be used. Go through all the steps to see if you can develop the PURPOSE and GOAL STATE of each step, so that the entire sequence of steps leads to a correct algorithm. If you can see how each step leads into the next, from the beginning to the end of the algorithm, then you have a plan for the overall algorithm and you are well on your way.

After you have DEFINE'd the PURPOSE and GOAL STATE for each step, go back and REFINE each step by filling in the ACTIONS list—*how* to accomplish the stated purpose and reach the goal state. You may find that a step is actually more complex than you thought, and that it needs to be divided into several smaller steps. Fine! At this stage it is easy to insert new steps or change old ones—that is what using pseudo-code for design is all about.

As you go along, when you use a new data object in stating the PURPOSE, GOAL STATE, or an ACTION for a step, add the name of the data object to your

DATA OBJECTS list. Include the data type and purpose for the data object at the same time.

How Precise Should the Pseudo-code Be?

Pseudo-code is meant to be somewhat informal, particularly when describing the PURPOSE and GOAL STATE of each step. You want to work out the overall structure of the algorithm, without being burdened with too many details initially. By concentrating on the PURPOSE and GOAL STATE of each step first, you can "rough in" the design. Then as you come back later to REFINE by filling in the ACTIONS list, you can also make the PURPOSE and GOAL STATE more precise.

When first learning to design algorithms, it is best to work out most of the details in pseudo-code. As you gain experience, you will know the sorts of details that are easily filled in when coding the program in Pascal. Then you can leave these details out of your pseudo-code. In our examples in this chapter, we try to show all the details in order to help you get started. In later chapters, our pseudo-code algorithms will also start to leave out details that can easily be filled in when the algorithm is coded into Pascal.

Combining the PURPOSE and GOAL STATE

When a particular step of an algorithm is straightforward, you may find the PURPOSE and GOAL STATE say almost the same thing. For example:

PURPOSE: Ask the user for a temperature value and read it in.

GOAL STATE: DegreesF contains the temperature value typed by the user.

The difference between these two statements is only that the PURPOSE says *what to do* but names no data objects, while the GOAL STATE *names the particular data object*, DegreesF, whose value will change. It is reasonable to combine these into a single statement to avoid saying similar things twice:

PURPOSE/GOAL STATE: Ask the user for a temperature value, read it in, and store it in DegreesF.

If you combine the PURPOSE and GOAL STATE in this way, be sure that you state both *what the step accomplishes* and *which data objects are affected*. Where the step is more complex, it is usually simpler to keep the PURPOSE and GOAL STATE separate.

Getting Started

The beginner is often overwhelmed with the seeming complexity of coming up with an algorithm to automate some information processing task. Where do you begin? Here are some useful tips that may help you in developing algorithms. Remember that finding an algorithm on which to base a computer program is very similar to solving any other sort of complex problem, so try your pet methods for tackling hard problems in other situations.

□

Hint 1: Use "Top Down Design"—Break the Task First into a Small Number of "Big" Steps.   To avoid getting lost in the details, force yourself to first divide the task into a few big steps (seven or fewer is a good rule of thumb). This top-level sequence of steps will give you the big picture of a possible algorithm. Once you have the big picture and are satisfied that your algorithm would work if you can fill in the details, then take each of the big steps you have identified as a separate sub-task and attack it in the same way. In this way, you can slowly work into the details of the algorithm. We call this *top-down design,* because you start at the top with the big picture and work your way down into the details.

□

Hint 2: Fill in the DISPLAY and READ Steps First, Using the DIALOGUE as a Guide.   The DIALOGUE part of the program's requirements directly corresponds to the DISPLAY and READ steps in the algorithm. Thus you can start by filling in these steps in the appropriate sequence first, and then fill in ASSIGN steps to compute the values displayed by each DISPLAY step. However, this hint will be of less help as you get to larger programs, because there will usually be many ASSIGN steps between each READ or DISPLAY.

□

Hint 3: Try Working Backwards From the Final State.   Sometimes it is obvious what state you want to reach—that is, you know what has to be computed by the program, so you know that you have to reach a state where all the needed values have been computed. Describe that final state. Now try working backwards: find an intermediate state that would be just one step backward from the final state. Describe that state and the actions that lead from there to the final state. Now try to move one step back from that intermediate state to an intermediate state two steps away from the final state, and so forth.

□

Hint 4: Use an Analogy—How Would You Perform the Task by Hand?   Think about how you would perform the task with just pencil and paper (and perhaps a hand calculator). Can you capture the method you would use? If you could describe your method to someone else, the same description might serve as an outline for your algorithm. However, look out for any "leaps of understanding" in how you perform the task by hand—your method has to be a straightforward sequence of steps that even a computer could perform. People routinely use methods that involve guessing, finding clues or hints with the eye or ear, or "intuition." These methods are very difficult to mimic in a computer algorithm.

□

Hint 5: Use Common Patterns.   As you gain experience, you will find that many common patterns appear over and over in different programs. Nancy's program used the simplest pattern:

- Read some data values that the user types.
- Compute some new data values.
- Display the computed data values.

Joe's program in the next section also uses a common pattern:

- Read some input values.
- WHILE a test says to keep going:
  - Compute some new values, using the input values.
  - Read some more input values.
- Display the computed values.

To get started, see if the task falls into any of these patterns, or others that you have used in previous programs. If so, then the pattern can provide a guide to the overall structure of the algorithm.

□

Hint 6: Revise, Revise, Revise.   Don't expect to get your algorithm right the first time. Keep revising the steps, actions, and states until you are satisfied with every part of the design.

□ □
What Makes a Good Algorithm?

Given the requirements for a program, there are usually many algorithms that might be used. How do you choose one algorithm over another? Here are some questions to use to help evaluate a possible design for an algorithm:

1. *Is it correct?* First and foremost, of course, the algorithm must be correct—it must satisfy the requirements.

2. *Is it straightforward and easy to understand?* Try to make your algorithm as simple and straightforward as the problem allows. Avoid "tricks." Compared to a tricky algorithm, a simple, straightforward algorithm is easier to get correct initially, easier to test, and easier to change later.

3. *Does it avoid unnecessary actions and data objects?* A good algorithm should not include unnecessary actions or data objects. Extra actions make the program run more slowly than necessary, and extra data objects use more of the computer's memory than is necessary to store the program's data. We say that a program that avoids unnecessary actions and data objects is an *efficient* program.

Often you may see a simple way to design part of an algorithm, but the simple design uses a few more actions or a few more data objects than a more complex design. You are faced with a dilemma—*simplicity* or *efficiency?* There is a simple answer: *always choose simplicity!* Simplicity should be your main design goal (after *correctness*, of course).

Efficiency is usually a secondary design goal. In most small programs, efficiency is not an important issue because a few extra actions or a few extra data objects will not have a noticeable effect when the program is executed. In larger programs, efficiency is usually a key issue in only a small part of the overall program. In Chapter 14, we discuss the efficiency of a program in more depth.

EXERCISES

3.10 In Exercise 3.4 you wrote the requirements for several programs. For each of these programs, "rough in" an algorithm by defining the PURPOSE and GOAL STATE of each step required to perform the task specified by the requirements.

3.11 Complete the algorithms begun in Exercise 3.10 by filling in the ACTIONS list for each step and the complete DATA OBJECTS list for each algorithm.

□□□ **3.8**
A CASE STUDY OF ALGORITHM DESIGN

Pseudo-code simplifies writing the design of an algorithm. Let's look at how Florida Joe uses pseudo-code to develop the algorithm needed to satisfy the program requirements from Section 3.2. In the next chapter, we code this algorithm as a Pascal program.

EXAMPLE: *Florida Joe's Gas Mileage*

Before looking at the pseudo-code below, go back to Section 3.2 and read again the REQUIREMENTS for Joe's program. Then compare the requirements against the algorithm that Joe develops.

ROUGHING IN THE ALGORITHM

Joe begins by defining the PURPOSE and GOAL STATE for each step. He "roughs in" the following algorithm:

> **ALGORITHM**
>
> INITIAL STATE: All data objects are uninitialized; screen is blank.

Step 1. PURPOSE/GOAL STATE: Ask the user for the starting and ending odometer readings and store in StartMiles and EndMiles, respectively.

Step 2. PURPOSE: Read and sum the list of gallons in each fillup.

GOAL STATE: TotalGallons contains the sum.

Step 3. PURPOSE/GOAL STATE: Compute total miles traveled and store in TotalMiles. Compute miles per gallon and store in MilesPerGallon.

Step 4. PURPOSE/GOAL STATE: Display odometer readings, total miles, total gallons, and miles per gallon.

FINAL STATE: All actions complete; all data objects contain their final values; all results are displayed.

DATA OBJECTS

StartMiles: Integer	Starting odometer reading.
EndMiles: Integer	Ending odometer reading.
TotalGallons: Real	Total gallons in all fillups.
TotalMiles: Integer	Total miles traveled.
MilesPerGallon: Real	Miles per gallon on the trip.

Discussion:

1. Joe finds all the steps easy to design except Step 2. The other steps simply follow the sequence of inputs and outputs specified by the DIALOGUE part of the requirements. For these simple steps, Joe combines the PURPOSE and GOAL STATE parts of each step.

2. Step 2 is more complicated for Joe. The DIALOGUE specifies that the user can type in a sequence of numbers, representing the gallons in each fillup during the trip. Joe wants the program to keep a "running sum," adding in each new number as it is read in. He is not sure about the details of how to do this, but he can see the GOAL STATE that he wants the program to reach: a state where a data object (he names it "TotalGallons") contains the sum of the entire list of numbers read in. For this step, he chooses to write the PURPOSE and GOAL STATE separately, expecting that he may want to add more detail in the final algorithm.

DEVELOPING THE FINAL ALGORITHM

After Joe is satisfied that his "roughed in" algorithm meets the program requirements, he proceeds to REFINE the steps by filling in the ACTIONS lists. He also determines the range of possible values for his data objects. His final ALGORITHM and DATA OBJECTS lists are as follows:

ALGORITHM

INITIAL STATE: All data objects are uninitialized; screen is blank.

Step 1. PURPOSE/GOAL STATE: Ask the user for the starting and ending odometer readings and store in StartMiles and EndMiles, respectively.

ACTIONS:

    1.1 DISPLAY: "Starting odometer reading?"
    1.2 READ: StartMiles
    1.3 DISPLAY: "Ending odometer reading?"
    1.4 READ: EndMiles

Step 2. PURPOSE: Display the instructions for typing the list of gallons. Read and sum the list of gallons in each fillup.

GOAL STATE: TotalGallons contains the sum.

ACTIONS:

    2.1 DISPLAY:
        "List gallons in each fillup, one number per line."
        "End the list with a zero value (on a separate line)."
    2.2 TotalGallons := 0
    2.3 READ: Gallons
    2.4 WHILE Gallons <> 0 DO
        TotalGallons := TotalGallons + Gallons
        READ: Gallons

Step 3. PURPOSE/GOAL STATE: Compute total miles traveled and store in TotalMiles. Compute miles per gallon and store in MilesPerGallon.

ACTIONS:

    3.1 TotalMiles := EndMiles − StartMiles
    3.2 IF TotalGallons <> 0 THEN
        MilesPerGallon := TotalMiles / TotalGallons
        ELSE
        DISPLAY:
          "ERROR: No gallons amounts were entered."
        MilesPerGallon := 0

Step 4. PURPOSE/GOAL STATE: Display odometer readings, total miles, total gallons, and miles per gallon.

ACTIONS:

    4.1 DISPLAY:
        "ODOMETER: Start of trip = ⟨StartMiles⟩
                  End of trip = ⟨EndMiles⟩
        TOTAL MILES: ⟨TotalMiles⟩
        TOTAL GALLONS: ⟨TotalGallons⟩
        MILES/GALLON: ⟨MilesPerGallon⟩"

FINAL STATE: All actions complete; all data objects contain their final values; all results are displayed.

DATA OBJECTS

StartMiles: Integer	Starting odometer reading; range 0–99,999
EndMiles: Integer	Ending odometer reading; range 0–99,999
Gallons: Real	Gallons in one fillup; range 0–20
TotalGallons: Real	Total gallons in all fillups; must be greater than 0
TotalMiles: Integer	Total miles traveled; range 0–99,999
MilesPerGallon: Real	Miles per gallon on the trip; must be 0 or larger

Discussion:

1. As Joe fills in the ACTIONS for Step 2, he uses a common pattern—a WHILE loop that keeps a running sum of a list of input data values. The pattern looks like this:

> ASSIGN zero as the initial value of the data object containing the running sum.
> READ the first data value.
> WHILE the data value is part of the list DO
> > Add the value to the running sum.
> > READ the next data value.

Because Joe has used the same pattern in several previous programs, he finds it easy to adapt the pattern to this situation. The requirement that the user type a zero value to indicate the end of the list of fillup values is the key to making this pattern work—you must have a simple way to decide when the WHILE loop can stop repeating its actions.

2. As Joe designs the ACTIONS in Step 3, he sees a problem. It is possible that the value stored in TotalGallons could be zero (if he, by mistake, types zero as the first value in the list of gallons when he is using the program). To compute miles per gallon, the program has to divide by TotalGallons, which might lead to a division by zero, which would make the program *crash*. To be sure that the program does not try to divide by zero, Joe puts in action 3.2—an IF that tests for the case where TotalGallons = 0. If it does happen to be zero, then Joe has to choose an alternative action. He decides to display an error message to alert the user (himself) and then set MilesPerGallon to zero in this case. If he makes this mistake when using the program, he will have to rerun the program and type the list of fillup amounts correctly.

3. Joe discovers a serious error in his design as he checks it over. On Joe's old car, the odometer can only record mileage up to 99999 miles, and then it "turns over" and the next value is 00000. What does the algorithm do if his odometer goes past 99,999 during the trip? Trace through the actions and see what happens. Exercise 3.12 corrects this error in Joe's algorithm. ■

EXERCISES

3.12 Modify Florida Joe's algorithm so that it works correctly without any change in the original requirements except a new assumption that the trip is never longer than 99,999 miles total. The user gives the two odometer readings, and if the EndMiles value is smaller than the StartMiles value then the program determines that the odometer went past 99,999 during the trip and it still computes the value of TotalMiles correctly. *IF EndMiles > StartMiles then 100,000 − StartMiles + EndMiles*

3.13 Modify Florida Joe's algorithm so that it counts the number of fillup amounts that are entered by the user and then displays this count on the same line as the miles per gallon.

□□□ 3.9
ANALYZING AND VERIFYING AN ALGORITHM

Verification is a central part of programming—verifying that all or part of an algorithm or Pascal program is correct. Verification is based on *analysis*—determining exactly what the algorithm or program does in a certain situation. When an algorithm contains an error, it is called a *logic error*. Our first analysis and verification methods are used to check for logic errors in an algorithm in pseudocode, before the algorithm becomes a Pascal program.

Logic errors are much easier to find and repair before you start coding the algorithm in Pascal. As you code the program, you can make mistakes in the way that you write the actual Pascal declarations and statements. These errors can mask a logic error and make it difficult to find when you are testing the final Pascal program. And fixing a logic error in the final coded program is harder and takes more time than fixing the error in the original algorithm. Thus making sure that your algorithm is correct before you start coding it into Pascal can save you a lot of time and energy later.

In this chapter we look at two simple analysis methods: *hand tracing* and *control flow analysis*. Both methods are useful for checking either an entire algorithm or just part of it (such as several key steps).

□□
"Hand Tracing" Program Execution

Hand tracing (or *playing computer*) is our first method for analyzing the steps in an algorithm. You actually execute the steps in the algorithm by hand, using test input data values. During hand tracing, you begin with the first step in the algorithm and go through each action in turn, keeping track on a sheet of paper of the program state. As you come to READ actions, you use your test input values, just as though a user had typed them in. As you come to DISPLAY actions, you see if the correct output values are being displayed (to match the program's requirements). As ASSIGN and READ actions change the data values stored in certain objects, you note the new values on your paper. As you reach IF or WHILE actions, you use the current data values in the program state (from your paper) to determine whether an action is executed repeatedly, executed once, or skipped altogether.

During hand tracing, you verify that the program state shown on your paper at the end of each step of the algorithm correctly matches the GOAL STATE of the step. If the actual program state reached does not match the desired goal state, then there is a logic error in that step of the algorithm.

EXAMPLE

Let's hand trace Florida Joe's gas mileage algorithm. To stay in the available space on the page, we show the value of each variable in the data state but not the content of the display screen. For this trace, let's use input data values that bring to light the logic error that Joe discovered. Let's suppose that Joe took a 450 mile trip during which the odometer reading went past 99,999. For test data, let's assume the odometer read 99800 before the start of his trip and 00250 after. For fillup amounts, we use 9.1 and 10.1. We do the arithmetic with paper and pencil (or use a hand calculator) to compute the new value when an ASSIGN action involves a mathematical formula. The hand trace is shown in Table 3.3. The step numbers are those from the algorithm in the last section. Remember that the value "??" means the data object is uninitialized (its value is unpredictable).

The logic error in Joe's algorithm shows up in the hand trace in step 3.1: a negative value is assigned to TotalMiles (obviously Joe did not travel negative miles on his trip). When we see that the goal state for this step has not been reached cor-

TABLE 3.3 Hand Trace of Florida Joe's Algorithm

| | | \multicolumn{6}{c}{PROGRAM DATA STATE} |
Step	Action	Start Miles	End Miles	Gallons	Total Gallons	Total Miles	MilesPer Gallon
INITIAL STATE:		??	??	??	??	??	??
1.1	DISPLAY. . .	??	??	??	??	??	??
1.2	READ. . .	99800	??	??	??	??	??
1.3	DISPLAY. . .	99800	??	??	??	??	??
1.4	READ. . .	99800	250	??	??	??	??
2.1	DISPLAY. . .	99800	250	??	??	??	??
2.2	ASSIGN. . .	99800	250	??	0	??	??
2.3	READ. . .	99800	250	9.1	0	??	??
2.4	WHILE. . .	99800	250	9.1	0	??	??
	ASSIGN. . .	99800	250	9.1	9.1	??	??
	READ. . .	99800	250	10.1	9.1	??	??
2.4	WHILE. . .	99800	250	10.1	9.1	??	??
	ASSIGN. . .	99800	250	10.1	19.2	??	??
	READ. . .	99800	250	0	19.2	??	??
2.4	WHILE. . .	99800	250	0	19.2	??	??
3.1	ASSIGN. . .	99800	250	0	19.2	−99550	??
3.2	IF. . .	99800	250	0	19.2	−99550	??
	ASSIGN. . .	99800	250	0	19.2	−99550	−5184.89
4.1	DISPLAY. . .	99800	250	0	19.2	−99550	−5184.89
FINAL STATE:		99800	250	0	19.2	−99550	−5184.89

rectly, we stop and analyze that step of the algorithm to find the logic error. But what is the logic error in the ASSIGN action for Step 3.1? Here is the action:

3.1 TotalMiles := EndMiles − StartMiles

Think about it for a minute before you read the next paragraph.

The formula for computing TotalMiles is correct, *provided that EndMiles is greater than StartMiles*. Thus Joe's algorithm uses a formula that works correctly only if the data values stored in EndMiles and StartMiles satisfy a certain condition when the formula is used. We call such a condition a *precondition* on the ASSIGN action. (Preconditions are a major source of logic errors. We meet them again and again in the following chapters.)

Notice how the value of MilesPerGallon is also incorrect when it is computed in step 3.2 because its value is computed using the incorrect value of TotalMiles. However there is no logic error in the computation of MilesPerGallon—the error is only in the computation of TotalMiles. As a rule, once a logic error causes one incorrect value to be computed, then any later computations that use the bad value will also produce bad values. ∎

Hand tracing is a useful way to analyze the actions of an algorithm in cases where the input data values might cause the algorithm to fail, such as where input numbers might be zero or negative. In the example above, we used an unusual combination of input values to identify an error. The test data values that you use in hand tracing are the same sorts of "test data cases" that you will want to use to test the final Pascal program; hand tracing just allows you to find errors before coding begins.

□ □
Hand Tracing Part of an Algorithm

It is not necessary to hand trace every step of an algorithm from beginning to end; you can start at any point and only trace through a part of the algorithm. Choose some step in the algorithm as a starting point. Write down the program state that you want to use in checking that part of the algorithm—the values of the data objects and what is currently displayed on the screen when you reach that step. Now begin hand tracing from that point, using that state.

But there is a catch: *Be sure that the program state you started from is a state that can actually be reached by the program.* That is, be sure that the earlier part of the program (the part you skipped in the hand tracing) can actually produce the state from which you started hand tracing.

For example, we do not have to trace Joe's algorithm from the first step to the last as we did in Table 3.3. Instead we could just skip the DISPLAY and READ actions in steps 1.1 through 2.1 and start at 2.2 with the first ASSIGN action, assuming that the program state contains our test values for StartMiles and EndMiles. From this starting state we could trace through to step 3.1, where the logic error shows up in the computation of TotalMiles.

□ □
Disadvantages of Hand Tracing

Hand tracing is a useful method for checking the correctness of all or part of an algorithm, but it has two disadvantages:

1. *Specific data values*. Because it uses actual input data values and keeps track of the actual value stored in each data object, it checks the algorithm for a *specific* set of input data values. But the requirements usually allow a range of possible input values, possibly in several different combinations, and each combination may lead to a slightly different sequence of program actions. Checking with a particular set of input values can show you that the algorithm works for that set of input values, but it does not show that the algorithm is correct for *all possible* input values.

2. *Tedious*. Hand tracing can be tedious, because you have to actually carry out by hand all the calculations made in ASSIGN actions and in the tests of IF and WHILE actions, using the actual values stored in the program state.

□ □
Control Flow Analysis

Control flow analysis is a more powerful way of checking an algorithm. It is less tedious than hand tracing, and it also avoids working with particular data values. Control flow analysis is a good example of the power of *abstraction*—by looking at an algorithm somewhat more abstractly, we get an analysis method that is more powerful, more general, and simpler to use.

Control flow analysis consists of checking the *control paths* in the algorithm:

□ **Control Path**

A *control path* in a program consists of one of the possible sequences in which the actions can be executed when the program is run.

A control path represents one *logical sequence* in which the actions of the program can be executed. When a control path includes an IF, then some actions of the algorithm may be skipped; when it includes a WHILE, then some actions may be repeated. Thus the logical sequence of actions is not necessarily the same as the sequence in which the actions are written in the algorithm (the "textual sequence" of actions)

In control flow analysis of an algorithm, we raise three questions:

1. What are the control paths in the algorithm?
2. Under what conditions will each control path be chosen for execution?
3. For each control path, if it is chosen for execution, will it perform the correct computation according to the program's requirements?

By looking at each control path separately, and verifying its correctness, we have a better chance of detecting a logic error. If there is a logic error, it must occur on at least one control path, but it may not occur on others. That is, if we execute the actions in one sequence, we may not see the error, but if we execute them in a different sequence, the error may appear.

□ □
Writing Control Path Descriptions

To write down a description of a control path, write down the following elements, in the sequence executed or evaluated:

1. Each DISPLAY, READ, and ASSIGN action encountered along the path.
2. For an IF, write down the *test* and its outcome (TRUE or FALSE). If there are additional "ELSE IF" cases, write down each test whose outcome is FALSE, until you reach the first test whose outcome is TRUE. Follow the first TRUE test with the actions for that alternative.
3. For a WHILE loop, write down the *test* and its outcome. If the outcome is TRUE, then follow with the actions inside the loop and write the WHILE test again. Continue until the WHILE test gives FALSE.

EXAMPLE

In Florida Joe's algorithm, here are the three shortest control paths. The comment in parentheses gives an informal description of the path. For simplicity, we only indicate the number of each action and its type rather than writing out the entire action. The *tests* in IF and WHILE actions are important in determining the control path, so we do write them out:

■ *Path 1:* (Zero trips through the loop, and take the FALSE branch of the IF)

    1.1 DISPLAY...
    1.2 READ...
    1.3 DISPLAY...
    1.4 READ...

    2.1 DISPLAY...
    2.2 ASSIGN...
    2.3 READ...
    2.4 WHILE (Gallons <> 0) = FALSE

3.1 ASSIGN...
3.2 IF (TotalGallons <> 0) = FALSE
    DISPLAY...
    ASSIGN...
4.1 DISPLAY...

■ *Path 2:* (One trip through the loop, and take the TRUE branch of the IF)

1.1 DISPLAY...
1.2 READ...
1.3 DISPLAY...
1.4 READ...

2.1 DISPLAY...
2.2 ASSIGN...
2.3 READ...
2.4 WHILE (Gallons <> 0) = TRUE
    ASSIGN...
    READ...
2.4 WHILE (Gallons <> 0) = FALSE

3.1 ASSIGN...
3.2 IF (TotalGallons <> 0) = TRUE
    ASSIGN...
4.1 DISPLAY...

■ *Path 3:* (Two trips through the loop, and take the TRUE branch of the IF)

1.1 DISPLAY...
1.2 READ...
1.3 DISPLAY...
1.4 READ...

2.1 DISPLAY...
2.2 ASSIGN...
2.3 READ...
2.4 WHILE (Gallons <> 0) = TRUE
    ASSIGN...
    READ...
2.4 WHILE (Gallons <> 0) = TRUE
    ASSIGN...
    READ...
2.4 WHILE (Gallons <> 0) = FALSE

3.1 ASSIGN...
3.2 IF (TotalGallons <> 0) = TRUE
    ASSIGN...
4.1 DISPLAY...

Path 3 is the control path that we followed during hand tracing (Table 3.3). ■

The comments in the examples above show how to informally describe a control path. For each WHILE loop, tell how many times the loop is repeated, and for each IF, tell whether the TRUE or FALSE part is executed.

Straight-line, Branching, and Looping Programs

A program that contains no IF or WHILE actions is called a *straight-line* program because it has only one control path—straight through the actions from first to last. In a straight-line program no actions are ever skipped and no actions are ever repeated.

A program that contains an IF is called a *branching program* because the IF causes a "branch" in the control path—one control path splits into two possible paths. On each execution of the program, some actions are skipped (those on the path not taken). In a branching program, each IF introduces a new control path.

A program that contains a WHILE is a *looping program* because the WHILE introduces a "loop" that allows an action to appear repeatedly in a single control path. A looping program has many control paths, one for each possible number of repetitions of the loop.

Figure 3.7 illustrates the control paths in straight-line, branching and looping programs. Most programs contain both looping and branching, giving a number of different control paths to be analyzed.

FIGURE 3.7 Control Paths in Straight-line, Branching, and Looping Programs

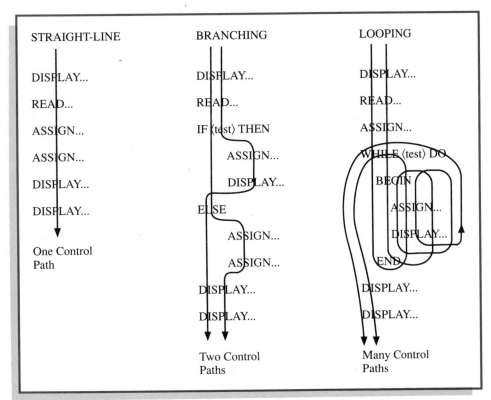

In a looping program, you often cannot hope to analyze every possible control path through every loop. One simple approach is to look only at three key paths in each loop:

1. *Zero trips*. Check the path that never enters the loop at all (test = FALSE when the WHILE statement is reached the first time),
2. *One trip*. Check the path that makes exactly *one trip* through the loop (test = TRUE the first time and test = FALSE the second time), and
3. *Two trips*. Check the path that makes exactly two trips through the loop (test = TRUE twice and test = FALSE the third time).

These paths usually are adequate to identify any errors in the loop action. In Chapters 8 and 10 we will look at more sophisticated ways of analyzing loops.

As with hand tracing, control flow analysis can also be used to check a part of an algorithm instead of the whole. Where there are a large number of possible control paths, it may be necessary to analyze individual steps or groups of steps in the algorithm, rather than the whole.

□ □

Verifying the Correctness of Control Paths

Knowing the different control paths allows you to analyze and verify the correctness of your algorithm. Look at the individual control paths. For each control path, ask two questions:

□

Question 1:   *Under what conditions will this control path be chosen for execution, and are those the right conditions?* To answer this question, concentrate on the *tests* in the control path and their outcomes (TRUE or FALSE). Trace through the actions that lead up to each test and analyze how each value used in each test is computed. From this analysis you can determine the conditions (the *range* of possible values of the data objects used in the tests) that will cause that path to be chosen for execution. Now verify that those conditions represent exactly the cases where that particular control path should be chosen for execution.

EXAMPLE   Florida Joe wants to analyze the control path that leads to the error message in the ELSE branch of the IF in step 3.2 of his algorithm:

Step 3.2.

```
IF TotalGallons <> 0 THEN
    MilesPerGallon := TotalMiles / TotalGallons
ELSE
    DISPLAY: "ERROR: No gallons amounts were entered."
    MilesPerGallon := 0
```

The error message should be displayed only if, when he is using the program, he types "0" as the number of gallons in the first fillup. Is this the only condition under which this DISPLAY action will ever be executed?

To decide, Joe looks at the *test* in the IF:

IF TOTALGALLONS <> 0 THEN...

Because the test has to be FALSE if the ELSE branch of the IF is executed, Joe knows that TotalGallons = 0 if the error message DISPLAY action is executed. So he focuses his attention on how the value of TotalGallons is determined.

The value of TotalGallons is computed in step 2, earlier in the control path:

Step 2.

    2.1 DISPLAY...
    2.2 TotalGallons := 0
    2.3 READ: Gallons
    2.4 WHILE Gallons <> 0 DO
          TotalGallons := TotalGallons + Gallons
          READ: Gallons

Joe looks at the possible control paths through these actions. The path he is interested in is when the READ in step 2.3 reads a zero value—meaning the *first* fillup amount is typed as zero. He follows the control path forward from step 2.3. Because Gallons = 0, the WHILE test at 2.4 gives FALSE, so the loop is skipped. TotalGallons was initialized to zero in step 2.2, so it is still zero. OK! The right condition (first fillup amount is zero) causes execution of the control path that leads to the DISPLAY of the error message.

Joe makes a second analysis: Are there *any other control paths* that include the display of the error message? What if the loop actions in step 2.4 are executed once or several times? Joe checks the conditions for execution of these paths. The first fillup amount typed by the user has to be non-zero in order for the loop actions to be executed the first time, and that fillup amount is immediately added to TotalGallons. So TotalGallons could not be zero if the control path leads through the loop once. Then, if the second fillup amount typed is zero, the path leads on to step 3 with TotalGallons <> 0. OK! On that path the error message would *not* be displayed.

What if the control path leads through the loop actions *twice?* Could TotalGallons = 0? Yes—but only if the user typed a *negative number* for the fillup amount. OK! A negative fillup amount would make no sense. If the second fillup amount is any positive number of gallons, then TotalGallons must be greater than zero. No matter how many times the loop is repeated, TotalGallons is always greater than zero. OK! Any control path that goes through the loop at least once will leave Total-Gallons > 0 so that in step 3 the error message DISPLAY action will never be executed.

In this example, Joe has used control flow analysis to check the conditions under which certain control paths are taken. By his analysis, he has verified that each path is chosen for execution in the correct circumstances. ∎

□

Question 2: *Assuming this control path is chosen for execution, will the actions on the path correctly compute and display the required output values (according to the program's requirements)?* To answer this question, focus on the *actions* in the control path and ignore the *tests*. Check that the actions taken along the path lead to the correct computation, and that the display of the output results occurs in the correct sequence (as specified by the DIALOGUE of the requirements.)

EXAMPLE

Joe wants to check the computation of the miles/gallon amount in his algorithm, assuming that the control path uses the formula in the THEN branch of the IF in step 3.2:

$$\text{MilesPerGallon} := \text{TotalMiles} / \text{TotalGallons}$$

Joe decides to check the computation when the control path leads *once* through the actions in the WHILE loop in step 2.4. The control path involves the following actions (Joe ignores the tests and the DISPLAY actions in the path):

```
1.2  READ: StartMiles
1.4  READ: EndMiles
2.2  TotalGallons :=0
2.3  READ:Gallons
2.4  WHILE...
        TotalGallons :=TotalGallons + Gallons
        READ...
3.1  TotalMiles :=EndMiles − StartMiles
3.2  IF...
        MilesPerGallon :=TotalMiles / TotalGallons
```

Joe looks at how TotalMiles and TotalGallons are computed on this control path. In the formula used to compute MilesPerGallon, he fills in the actual formulas used to compute TotalMiles and TotalGallons on this particular control path, giving the formula:

$$\text{MilesPerGallon} := \frac{\text{EndMiles} - \text{StartMiles}}{0 + \text{Gallons}}$$

which, Joe concludes, is the right formula for computing miles/gallon, given the values for EndMiles, StartMiles, and Gallons typed in by the user on this control path.

Joe asks: What about control paths that lead more than once through the WHILE loop? Is the computation still correct? Joe observes that each additional repetition of the loop causes another fillup amount to be read in and added to TotalGallons, so the computation of MilesPerGallon is only changed slightly on these control paths:

$$\text{MilesPerGallon} := \frac{\text{EndMiles} - \text{StartMiles}}{0 + \text{Gallons}_1 + \text{Gallons}_2 + \ldots}$$

where the values for Gallons are the fillup amounts typed by the user. OK! The computation of MilesPerGallon looks correct for each of these possible control paths. ∎

Combining Control Flow Analysis and Hand Tracing

Control flow analysis and hand tracing can be used together in checking an algorithm. For example, if the actions on a particular control path involve some complicated mathematical formulas, you might want to choose particular values for the data objects involved and hand trace through the actual execution of the actions, including evaluation of the formulas, to see if the resulting values are what the requirements specify.

If You Find a Logic Error in the Algorithm

Logic errors can be of two varieties, corresponding to our two questions about each control path:

1. An error in an IF or WHILE test can cause the *wrong control path* to be chosen for execution, or
2. An error in a READ, DISPLAY, or ASSIGN action can cause the action to make the *wrong change in the program state*.

An error in a READ, DISPLAY, or ASSIGN action can sometimes cause a later IF or WHILE test to choose the wrong control path, so watch out! Be sure you know which kind of error you have found before making a change in the algorithm. Looking at the whole control path that contains the error, before deciding how to repair it, will help you to pinpoint the first error in the path. Because the first error may cause later actions to work incorrectly, even though they are correct, fixing the first error may be all that is necessary to correct the algorithm.

Once you have modified the algorithm to repair the error, recheck the control paths that are affected by the change. Are they still correct? A major problem in repairing errors in a program is that a change to correct an error in one control path can often *introduce a new error in another control path*.

EXERCISES

3.14   Given the following steps of an algorithm (only the ACTIONS are shown):

Step 1.   ACTIONS:

    1.1 DISPLAY: "Type a list of positive and negative numbers. End the list with a zero."
    1.2 Count := 0

Step 2.   ACTIONS:

    2.1 READ: Number
    2.2 WHILE Number <> 0
        Total :=Total + Number
        Count :=Count + 1
        READ: Number

Step 3.   ACTIONS:

    3.1 Average :=Total / Count
    3.2 DISPLAY: "The average of the numbers is ⟨Average⟩"

    a. Hand trace the data state during execution of this algorithm, assuming the data state before Step 1 is:

Total: 7   Count: 2

Number: 3   Average: 0

and that the user types the following sequence of numbers:

$$2 \quad -4 \quad 3 \quad 12 \quad 0$$

What is the error identified by this hand trace?

    b. Hand trace the data state during execution of this algorithm, assuming the starting state is:

Total: 0   Count: 5

Number: 7   Average: 20

and that the user types only the number zero. What is the error identified by this hand trace?

c. List the control paths through this algorithm, including only paths that execute the loop body less than three times.

d. Which control paths contain the error identified in (a)? Is it an error in how the path is chosen or an error in the actions taken on the path?

e. Which control paths contain the error identified in (b)? Is it an error in how the path is chosen or an error in the actions taken on the path?

f. Modify the algorithm to repair both errors. Then repeat steps (a) and (b) with the corrected algorithm.

3.15 The *factorial* of a positive integer X (written X!) is the product of all the positive integers less than or equal to X. For example, 5! = 5 * 4 * 3 * 2 * 1. Given the following steps of an algorithm for computing the factorial of X (only the actions of interest are shown):

Step 2. ACTIONS:

    2.1 Count := 0
    2.1 Factorial := 1

Step 3. ACTIONS:

    3.1 WHILE Count <= X DO
        Count := Count + 1
        Factorial := Factorial * Count

a. Hand trace the data state during execution of this part of the algorithm, assuming the data state before Step 2 is:

X: | 5 | Count: | 2 | Factorial: | 251 |

What is the error identified by this hand trace?

b. Which control paths contain the error identified in (a)? Is it an error in how the path is chosen or an error in the actions taken on the path?

c. Write down the control path that is chosen for execution when X = 2 in the starting state. Write down the control path that *should be chosen* for execution in this case.

d. What is the *shortest* control path possible in this algorithm, assuming X > 0?

e. Modify the algorithm to repair the error. Then repeat (a) to check the correction.

3.16 Here is a mystery algorithm called *McCarthy's 91 function:*

Step 1. ACTIONS:

    1.1 DISPLAY: "Type an integer between 1 and 100."
    1.2 READ: MysteryNumber
    1.3 Count := 1

Step 2. ACTIONS:

> 2.1 WHILE MysteryNumber <= 100
> OR (MysteryNumber > 100 AND Count <> 1) DO
> IF MysteryNumber <= 100 THEN
> MysteryNumber := MysteryNumber + 11
> Count := Count + 1
> ELSE
> MysteryNumber := MysteryNumber − 10
> Count :=Count − 1

Step 3. ACTIONS:

> 3.1 Result := MysteryNumber − 10
> 3.2 DISPLAY: "The result = ⟨Result⟩"

a. Hand trace the data state during execution of this algorithm, assuming that the user types the input value 100.

b. Hand trace the data state assuming that the user types the input value 98.

c. State an assertion about the result displayed by this algorithm, for any value that the user types between 1 and 100.

d. Verify your assertion for the control path taken when the user types the value 99, by writing out the ASSIGN actions executed on that path and showing that these actions compute a result that satisfies your assertion.

e. Show that *any control path* taken when the user types a value between 1 and 100 must compute a result that satisfies your assertion.

f. Show that the assertion "The result displayed = ten less than the number typed" is always true if the user disregards the instructions and types an integer *greater than 100*. *Hint:* Start by writing out the control path executed in this case.

□□□ **3.10**
REQUIREMENTS AND PSEUDO-CODE SUMMARY

For later reference as you develop your own algorithms, here is a summary of the form of the requirements list and pseudo-code developed in this chapter.

□ □
Requirements

Requirements for an interactive program include a DEFINE phase where you specify:

- INPUT: What data must the user provide to the program?
- PROCESSING: What processing of the input data is required?
- OUTPUT: What data should be produced and displayed as a result of the processing?
- ASSUMPTIONS: What can be assumed about how the program will be used?

In the REFINE phase, you fill in the details of the INPUT and OUTPUT parts of the requirements as an interactive dialogue between the program and user, in the form:

⟨program-user dialogue⟩ ::=

DIALOGUE

PROGRAM: ...BNF description of program output line(s)...
USER: ...BNF description of what the user may type in...
PROGRAM: ...and continue describing the lines of the dialogue...

WHERE
...BNF or words to describe the form of each named set of items...

□ □
An Algorithm in Pseudo-code

An algorithm is defined by the two parts:

ALGORITHM: a sequence of steps that satisfy the program's requirements.

DATA OBJECTS: name, data type, and purpose of each of the data objects used in the ALGORITHM part.

□ □
The ALGORITHM Part

Write the ALGORITHM part in the form:

⟨ALGORITHM part⟩ ::=

ALGORITHM

INITIAL STATE: All data objects are uninitialized; screen is blank.

Step 1. PURPOSE: ⟨purpose⟩
GOAL STATE: ⟨goal state⟩
ACTIONS: ⟨action sequence⟩

{Step k. PURPOSE: ⟨purpose⟩   Repeat this part for
GOAL STATE: ⟨goal state⟩   each additional step
ACTIONS: ⟨action sequence⟩}   in the algorithm.

FINAL STATE: All actions complete; all data objects contain their final values; all results are displayed.

WHERE

⟨purpose⟩ ::=

A description of the purpose of the step—*what* the step accomplishes in terms of the overall task to be performed.

⟨goal state⟩ ::=

An *assertion* describing the goal state of the step—what should have changed in the program state as a result of executing this step (new values assigned to data objects or new lines displayed on the screen).

⟨action sequence⟩ ::=

A list of the actions required to reach the goal state.

□ □

DISPLAY, READ and ASSIGN

Write these actions in the form:

⟨DISPLAY action⟩ ::=
 DISPLAY: "⟨line to be displayed⟩"
WHERE
 ⟨line to be displayed⟩ ::=
 A description of the form and content of the line to be displayed, preferably using BNF.

⟨READ action⟩ ::=
 READ: ⟨data object⟩ {, ⟨data object⟩}
WHERE
 ⟨data object⟩ ::=
 The name of the data object that is to be used to store the data value that the user types. List one data object to store each value that the user is expected to type.

⟨ASSIGN action⟩ ::=
 ⟨data object⟩ := ⟨value to be stored⟩
 WHERE
⟨data object⟩ ::= Any data object name.
⟨value to be stored⟩ ::=
 The literal (actual) value to be stored, the name of another data object that contains the value, or a mathematical formula or test for computing the value.

□ □

IF and WHILE

Write these actions in the form:

⟨IF action⟩ ::=
 IF ⟨test⟩ THEN   —the first case
  ⟨actions⟩
 {ELSE IF ⟨test⟩ THEN   ⎫repeat if there
  ⟨actions⟩}   ⎭are several cases

 {ELSE
  ⟨actions if all tests return FALSE⟩   —the *default* case

$\langle$ WHILE-loop $\rangle$ ::=
    WHILE $\langle$ test to decide whether to continue $\rangle$ DO
      $\langle$ actions $\rangle$
WHERE
  $\langle$ test $\rangle$ ::=
    Any test on the values of the data objects in the program state; the result must be a Boolean value (TRUE or FALSE).
  $\langle$ actions $\rangle$ ::=
    A sequence of actions or sub-steps, which may include ASSIGN, DISPLAY, READ, WHILE and IF.

□ □
The DATA OBJECTS List

Write the DATA OBJECTS list in the form:

$\langle$ DATA OBJECTS list $\rangle$ ::=

DATA OBJECTS

  $\langle$ data object name $\rangle$: $\langle$ data type $\rangle$ $\langle$ purpose of the data object $\rangle$
  $\{\langle$ data object name $\rangle$: $\langle$ data type $\rangle$ $\langle$ purpose of the data object $\rangle\}$
WHERE
  $\langle$ data object name $\rangle$ ::=
    The name used to refer to the data object in the ALGORITHM part.
  $\langle$ data type $\rangle$ ::= Real | Integer | Char | Boolean
  $\langle$ purpose of the data object $\rangle$ ::=
    A brief description of what the data object represents in the program, including, for Real and Integer types, the *units of measure* and the *range of possible values* for the numbers stored in the data object.

■ ■ ■
REVIEW QUESTIONS

3.1 Name the two major programming phases that are concerned with the *design* of the program.

3.2 The phrase "DEFINE, then REFINE" describes a general design principle useful in designing both the requirements and the algorithm for a program. Explain how the principle applies to these phases of programming.

3.3 Explain the terms *top-down design* and *stepwise refinement*.

3.4 Name two difficulties encountered in determining a program's requirements.

3.5 What is the difference between an *interactive* program and a *batch-processing* program?

3.6 Explain the four items that should be included in defining the *basic requirements* of a program.

3.7 *Backus-Naur Form (BNF)* provides a useful method for doing what?

3.8 Show, by examples, how BNF describes each of the following: literal strings, named sets of items, optional items, alternative items, and repeated items.

3.9 Explain how BNF may be used to help describe the *dialogue* part of a program's requirements.

3.10 "Requirements represent the *outside view* and an algorithm represents the *inside view* of a program." Explain what this statement means.

3.11 What is *pseudo-code*? Why design an algorithm in pseudo-code rather than directly in a programming language like Pascal?

3.12 Define *algorithm.*

3.13 Explain the distinctions between a *data object,* a *data value,* and a *data type.*

3.14 Describe the *DATA OBJECTS list* in pseudo-code: its purpose and contents.

3.15 What is a *program state?*

3.16 Describe the *execution* of an algorithm in terms of *states* and *actions.* Identify the *initial state, final state,* and *intermediate states* during execution.

3.17 What is an *assertion?*

3.18 Name and explain briefly the three parts of each *step* of a pseudo-code algorithm.

3.19 Describe the *ALGORITHM* part in pseudo-code: its purpose and content.

3.20 What is the relationship between *operations, operands,* and *actions* in an algorithm?

3.21 Explain the general purpose and the meaning when executed of the DISPLAY, READ, and ASSIGN operations.

3.22 Name and explain briefly the three ways in which groups of DISPLAY, READ, and ASSIGN actions may be combined to form larger actions.

3.23 In designing an algorithm, is it better to design the *actions* before the *purpose* and *goal state* of each step, or vice versa? Why?

3.24 Give *five hints* about how to get started in finding the sequence of steps required for an algorithm.

3.25 List, in decreasing order of importance, three criteria for deciding whether one version of an algorithm is *better* than another.

3.26 What is a *logic error?*

3.27 Name two *analysis methods* that can help in finding logic errors in an algorithm.

3.28 Explain how to *hand trace* the execution of all or part of an algorithm.

3.29 What is a *control path?*

3.30 Distinguish between a *straight-line* program, a *branching* program, and a *looping* program. How many control paths are possible in each type of program?

3.31 Given an algorithm in pseudo-code, explain how to write down a description of one of its *possible control paths.*

3.32 What is *control flow analysis?*

3.33 Explain how control flow analysis can be used to find logic errors or to verify the correctness of an algorithm.

3.34 Given a control path, what *two questions* should be asked (and answered) to decide whether the path is correct?

3.35 After you have repaired a logic error in a program, what should you *recheck* about the program? Why?

■ ■ ■
PROGRAMMING PROBLEMS

Develop the requirements and an algorithm for a program to automate each of the following information processing tasks.

3.1 *Computing Tuition.* In many state colleges in the U.S., the cost of tuition is based on the number of credit hours a student takes, multiplied by a cost per credit-hour. The cost per credit-hour is determined by whether the student lives in-state or out-of-state. Design a program for use by a clerk in the college business office. The program should ask the clerk for the number of credit hours a student is taking and whether the student lives in-state or out-of-state. Then it should compute the tuition charge for that student. For the cost per credit-hour, use $50.00 for in-state students and $250.00 for out-of-state students.

3.2 *Balancing a Checkbook.* Design a program for use by an individual in balancing her checkbook. The program asks the user for the checkbook balance from her checkbook and the account balance as given on the bank statement. The program then asks for a list of the deposit and check amounts that are entered in her checkbook but that are not listed on the bank statement. After the last deposit or check amount is entered, the program determines whether the checkbook and bank statement agree as to the account balance (adjusted for the items not yet received by the bank).

3.3 *Clem, the Carpet Man.* Clem's Carpets needs a program to compute the total area and perimeter of the rooms in a house (so Clem can know approximately the number of square yards of carpet required and the number of yards of "tack strip" needed at the base of the walls). The program should ask Clem for the length and width of the first room and of each connecting room or hall to be carpeted. After Clem has typed in the size of each room in the group, the program should display the total area and perimeter of the group of rooms.

3.4 *Euclid's GCD Algorithm.* Algorithms for computing useful numbers have been developed throughout history (such as the algorithms that we use for addition, subtraction, multiplication, and division of decimal numbers using paper and pencil). One of the earliest recorded algorithms was given by Euclid (Greek, 300 B.C.) for computing the *greatest common divisor* (GCD) of two positive integers. The GCD is the largest integer that divides both numbers evenly. The GCD algorithm can be stated informally as follows:
  a. Divide A, the larger of the two numbers, by B, the smaller, and get the remainder R (where $0 <= R < B$). If R = 0 then B is the GCD.
  b. If R is not 0, then go back and repeat step (a), but using B as the new larger number, A, and R as the new smaller number, B.

Design a demonstration program for a school science fair that asks the user for two positive integers, A and B, and which then uses Euclid's algorithm to compute the GCD. As the program repeats the division step (a) each time, it should display for the user what it is doing, so that the user can see how the steps in the algorithm work toward finding the correct GCD.

3.5 *Table of Loan Amounts.* You have taken out a bank installment loan in order to buy a car. You know how much you borrowed, the interest rate, and your monthly payment amount. But you would like to have a table that shows, for each month, how much of the payment is interest, how much goes toward reducing the principal (the amount borrowed), and what the balance owed on the principal is at the end of the month. For example:

Table of Monthly Payments
Original Principal: 4000.00   Interest Rate: 12.0%
Monthly Payment Amount: 130.00

MONTH	INTEREST	PRINCIPAL PAYMENT	BALANCE
1	40.00	90.00	3910.00
2	39.10	90.90	3819.10
...	...	...	...

Assume that the loan is computed using *simple interest*. The formulas that you need are:

```
<Interest each month> =
  <Loan balance at start of month> × <Interest rate/month>
<Principal payment each month>=
  <Monthly payment amount> - <Interest for that month>
<Balance each month> =
  <Balance last month> - <Principal payment this month>
```

Design a program that asks the user for the principal, interest rate, and monthly payment amounts and then computes and displays the table of monthly payments.

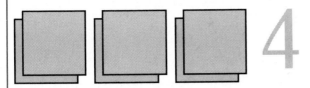

Program Coding, Compiling, and Testing

CHAPTER GOALS

When you have mastered the content of this chapter you should be able to:

- Describe the overall form of a *Pascal program.*
- Explain the basic rules of Pascal *syntax,* including identifiers, reserved words, punctuation, and comments.
- Code a DATA OBJECTS list as a group of Pascal *variable declarations.*
- Explain the limits on the size of Pascal integer and real numbers.
- Code an ALGORITHM part as a sequence of Pascal *statements,* including properly coded IF and WHILE statements.
- Explain the rules for writing and evaluating Pascal *expressions.*
- Code ASSIGN actions as Pascal *assignment* statements.
- Code DISPLAY actions as Pascal *writeln* and *write* statements.
- Code READ actions as Pascal *readln* and *read* statements.
- Explain how to detect and correct *syntax errors* when compiling a Pascal program.
- Explain the role of *program testing* in determining whether a program is correct.
- Describe how to prepare for testing a program, including the choice of *test data.*
- State and explain the *Cardinal Rule of Debugging.*
- Use debug WRITE statements to display important program states during debugging.
- Explain the importance of good *coding style* in programming.

The Pascal language represents a particular notation for coding algorithms for a computer. The pseudo-code that we developed in Chapter 3 is intended to be easy to code into Pascal. In the next sections we look at the details of how to code an algorithm into Pascal, in preparation for compiling and testing the program.

You will notice that as we code an algorithm into Pascal, we also change to a different *vocabulary*—terms that are particular to coding in Pascal. For example, the *data objects* of an algorithm in pseudo-code are coded as *variables* in the Pascal language, and the *actions* are coded as Pascal *statements*.

□□□4.1
CODING PROGRAMS IN PASCAL: BASIC PRINCIPLES

The overall form of a Pascal program is shown in Figure 4.1. Notice the parts that represent the ALGORITHM part and DATA OBJECTS list of an algorithm. For this chapter our program always consists of a single Pascal *procedure,* called the *main procedure.* The overall program form shown in Figure 4.1 should be taken as a standard pattern for coding a Pascal program.

The elements in angle brackets, ⟨. . .⟩, are the elements to be chosen by the programmer in coding the algorithm. The ⟨program-name⟩ and ⟨main-procedure-name⟩ are Pascal *identifiers* used to name the program and its main procedure. The ⟨program-header-comment⟩ and ⟨procedure-header-comment⟩ are *comments* used to provide information for the *human reader* of the program.

Coding a Pascal program from a pseudo-code algorithm is primarily a process of filling in details and forming each part into a syntactically correct Pascal declaration or statement. As you become more familiar with the details of Pascal, this process will become straightforward, although it can be difficult when you are just beginning.

□□
Names and Identifiers

While programming, you must choose *names* for many of the elements of your program, such as the data objects in the DATA OBJECTS list and the ⟨program-name⟩ and ⟨main-procedure-name⟩ in Figure 4.1. When you code the algorithm in Pascal, these names must be coded as Pascal *identifiers:*

```
⟨PASCAL-program⟩ ::=

    PROGRAM ⟨program-name⟩ (INPUT, OUTPUT);

        ⟨program-header-comment⟩

    PROCEDURE ⟨main-procedure-name⟩;

        ⟨procedure-header-comment⟩                Algorithm

      VAR

          ⟨variable-declarations⟩   ◄——— DATA OBJECTS list

      BEGIN

          ⟨statements⟩              ◄——— ALGORITHM part

      END;

    BEGIN

        ⟨main-procedure-name⟩;

    END.
```

The blue indicates the outer "shell" used with every program.
The black indicates the "main procedure" of the program.

FIGURE 4.1 Overall Form of a Pascal Program

□ **Identifier**

A Pascal identifier is a name chosen according to these rules. The identifier:

1. Must begin with a letter, and
2. Must consist of only letters (capital A–Z and lower-case a–z) and digits (0–9).

EXAMPLES

VALID IDENTIFIERS	INVALID IDENTIFIERS
ReportFor87	Report_for_87 Report.87 87Report
X2 x2Yz	X+2 2X X-2 X 2

The difference between capital letters (upper-case) and lower-case letters in a Pascal identifier is not significant to the Pascal compiler. Thus, for example, the identifiers:

```
DegreesF    degreesF    DEGREESF    dEGrEEsf
```

are all treated as equivalent by "standard" Pascal systems.

Why these strict rules for Pascal identifiers? Because it is only these forms of identifiers which can be recognized automatically by all Pascal compilers (these forms are part of the *standard Pascal language*). The particular Pascal compiler you are using may allow other characters to appear in identifiers, such as underscores, " ". Such an extension to standard Pascal would make it easier to choose readable identifiers, but your program might not be recognized as valid if you try to use a Pascal compiler on another computer system.

Many Pascal systems also consider only the first eight or ten characters of an identifier as significant, so that two identifiers must differ in at least one "significant" character in order to be considered different. For example, in many Pascal systems, the two identifiers:

```
TableOfLoanPayments    and    TableOfLoanResiduals
```

might be considered equivalent because the identifiers have the same first eight characters, "TableOfL. . .". Check the rules for your Pascal system before you begin coding a Pascal program.

Well-chosen names for the elements of your Pascal program are important to make the program easy for a *person* to read and understand. For example, when you choose the ⟨program-name⟩ and ⟨main-procedure-name⟩ as you code your Pascal program, choose names that indicate the purpose and the main action of the program.

The Pascal compiler, of course, does not care whether a name is meaningful in the "real world." Inside the computer each name (identifier) is simply a sequence of characters. The compiler decides if two identifiers are the same (and thus refer to the same thing) by matching the significant portion of the two identifiers character-by-character. If the characters are the same (under the rules discussed above), then the two identifiers are the same. If any character differs, then the identifiers are considered different by the compiler. This means that you have to spell each identifier correctly each time you write it. For example, the ⟨main-procedure-name⟩ is written in two places in the program of Figure 4.1. It must be spelled exactly the same in both places. If not, the compiler will be unable to recognize that the names are the same, and it will display an error message and may stop compiling the program.

Reserved Words and Punctuation

A *reserved word* is an identifier like PROGRAM, WHILE, or PROCEDURE that has a special meaning in Pascal. As the term implies, these identifiers are "reserved" and cannot be used by a programmer to name things in a program. Here is the list of reserved words in standard Pascal (your Pascal system may have a few more—check your *Pascal User's Manual*):

AND	DO	FORWARD	MOD	PROCEDURE	TO
ARRAY	DOWNTO	FUNCTION	NIL	PROGRAM	TYPE
BEGIN	ELSE	GOTO	NOT	RECORD	UNTIL
CASE	END	IF	OF	REPEAT	VAR
CONST	FILE	IN	OR	SET	WHILE
DIV	FOR	LABEL	PACKED	THEN	WITH

Punctuation is critical in Pascal. Watch carefully how each type of declaration and statement is punctuated as we discuss the rules below. To the Pascal compiler, reserved words and punctuation are the only means it has to distinguish where one declaration or statement ends and the next begins. The visual aspects that a person sees, such as the way a statement is indented on a line, or the place where one line ends, have no significance to the Pascal compiler. Thus what appears to be correct to a person is often incorrect to the compiler because of some seemingly minor error in punctuation.

Blank Lines and Spacing

To make a Pascal program more readable, you may use blank lines to separate groups of program elements. You also may space program elements on each line to make the individual line more readable. Indenting lines appropriately is important for readability. If a line becomes too long, you may continue it on the next and suc-ceeding lines as needed, using as much indentation as you want.

Comments in Pascal Programs

Comments are an essential part of coding a program in Pascal. A comment is delimited by braces, {. . .}, or by the equivalent markers, (*. . .*). For example:

```
{This is a Pascal comment}
```

and

```
(* This is also a Pascal comment *)
```

You may use either form of comment. Whatever is written within the comment delimiters is ignored by the Pascal compiler, so a comment has no effect on whether your program works correctly.

In coding a Pascal program, you might think of yourself as writing the program for two different readers—the *compiler* and the *human reader*. The compiler "reads" the Pascal statements and declarations and ignores the comments. The human reader, however, reads the comments to understand the design of the program. Without an understanding of the design, a human reader quickly gets lost in the details of Pascal code.

Documenting a program means providing the information necessary to make your program readable and understandable by another person. Comments can be used to clarify your design for a later human reader (often yourself a few weeks after writing the program). Because a human must read the program in order to repair errors and make changes later, capturing the program design in the comments is vital if the program is to be used for any length of time.

We say a program is *well-documented* if it is easy for a human reader to understand its design well enough to make changes and repair errors. A well-documented program may often contain about as many lines of comments as it does of Pascal declarations and statements. The key to good documentation of a program is to use comments to explain *what* each part of the program is intended to accomplish, while leaving the Pascal statements (and declarations) to show *how* that part is accomplished.

Two *header comments* should appear in every Pascal program, as shown in Figure 4.1:

1. *Program header comment*. At the beginning of every program, immediately following the PROGRAM line, place a *program header comment* that contains at least the following information:
   a. PURPOSE of the program—brief description of the task performed by the program.
   b. AUTHOR of the program—your name, if it's your program.
   c. DATE WRITTEN—when the program was coded in Pascal. For example, a header comment for Nancy's program in Chapter 1 might be:

   > {PURPOSE: Convert a Fahrenheit temperature value provided by the user to an equivalent Celsius value.
   > AUTHOR: Nancy NewJersey
   > DATE WRITTEN: August 20, 1988}

2. *Main procedure header comment*. A Pascal program will usually contain many procedures. The *main procedure* in Figure 4.1 is the "top-level" procedure—the procedure that controls the overall execution of the program by executing the main actions in the algorithm's ALGORITHM part. Each procedure in the program, including the main procedure, should include a *header comment* that describes at least:
   a. PURPOSE of the procedure—what task the procedure performs.

b. AUTHOR, DATE WRITTEN—if different from the author and date of the whole program.

For example, Nancy's main procedure might have the header comment:

{PURPOSE: Main procedure—controls overall execution of the program}

She omits the AUTHOR and DATE WRITTEN because they are the same as the AUTHOR and DATE WRITTEN in the program header comment.

□ □

Syntactic and Semantic Errors

Coding an algorithm into Pascal can introduce two new kinds of errors:

1. *Syntactic errors.* A *syntactic error* (or *syntax error*) is a mistake in the *form* of something you write in Pascal, such as a punctuation error, a misspelling of a Pascal keyword, or the wrong order of the elements of some statement or declaration.

2. *Semantic errors.* A *semantic error* is a mistake in the *meaning* of something you write in Pascal. You write a Pascal statement or declaration that means something other than what you intend. For example, if you forget to put a BEGIN. . .END around the statements in the body of a WHILE loop, only the first statement will be included in the loop, and the others will be executed only after the loop is finished. You know what you wanted to say, but what you wrote means something else in Pascal.

The beginner is often plagued by syntactic and semantic errors while learning a new programming language. Most syntax errors and a few semantic errors will be detected by the Pascal compiler. But the error messages produced by the compiler are often hard to understand, for reasons we discuss in Section 4.8. Thus, even when the compiler detects an error, you may still have a lot of work left to pinpoint exactly what is wrong with your understanding of Pascal.

Errors that the Pascal compiler does not detect are more troublesome. Since the compiler does not complain, you are lulled into thinking that your Pascal code is correct. Later, during testing of the program, you find the program does not work correctly, but you do not know if there is a semantic error (or sometimes a syntactic error) in your coding or a logic error in your algorithm design. You can spend hours or days tracking down such errors.

The moral: before you use a Pascal construct in your program, be sure that you understand *exactly* what it means in terms of actions taken or data objects/types defined. That is, be sure that what you are *writing* in Pascal *means* what you want to say.

EXERCISES

4.1   Which of the following are valid Pascal identifiers? If not, why not?

27May1988   May271988   X-YCoordinate

OnProbation?   2Timer   RosieO'Grady

□□□ 4.2
CODING THE DATA OBJECTS LIST IN PASCAL

The DATA OBJECTS list of your algorithm is coded as the first section of the main procedure in Figure 4.1, following the keyword VAR (for "variable"). In Pascal the data objects of a program are called *variables*.

Each variable used in a program must be *declared*, by listing its name and data type in the VAR section. The syntax is:

⟨variable-declarations-section⟩ ::=

```
VAR
    ⟨variable-name⟩: ⟨data-type-name⟩;   ⟨purpose⟩
    {⟨variable-name⟩: ⟨data-type-name⟩;   ⟨purpose⟩}
```

WHERE
⟨variable-name⟩ ::=
Name used for the data object in the DATA OBJECTS list
(modified if necessary to make it a valid Pascal identifier).
⟨data-type-name⟩ ::=
Data type from the DATA OBJECTS list—for now, one of the types Real, Integer, Boolean, or Char.
⟨purpose⟩ ::=
A Pascal comment that describes the *purpose*, *range of possible values*, and *units of measure* of the variable (again taken from the DATA OBJECTS list).

The order in which the variables are declared in the VAR section makes no difference. Choose an order that makes the program easiest to read.

EXAMPLES

```
VAR
    StudentAge:  Integer;     {Age of this student}
    TodaysHigh:  Real;        {High temperature, range -50..120,
                               degrees F}
    ExamGrade:  Char;         {Letter grade on final exam,
                              range A-F}
    OnProbation: Boolean;     {TRUE if student is on probation}
    PassingGrades:  Integer;  {Count of passing grades in
                              class, range 0..500}
```

□ □
Punctuation in the VAR Section

Each declaration of a variable in the VAR section includes a colon after the variable name and a semicolon after the data type name. The remainder of each declaration is a comment, so it is enclosed in braces, {...}, or alternatively, (*...*). Be sure to follow this punctuation carefully.

□ □
What About Units?

Before we go any further, let's look at the question of how a Pascal program handles *units of measure*. In real life, the numbers we use are often measuring something, like the length, size, weight, or distance of some object. Such measurements have to be in terms of a unit of measure—inches, centimeters, pounds, liters, light-years, and so forth. If we are going to add two numbers, we always have to be careful that the units are the same—as the old saying goes, "you can't add apples and oranges."

You might expect that computers would work the same way, because the numbers that we use in computers are often measuring something in the real world in terms of these same units of measure—such as Nancy's variables DegreesF and DegreesC that stored temperature values in units of degrees Fahrenheit and degrees Celsius.

Unhappily, the Pascal language, and computers in general, take no notice of units of measure. For example, Nancy knows that her variables DegreesF and DegreesC contain values that represent temperatures in two different units of measure. It would make no sense to add two such temperature values together without first converting both values to the same units—for instance, convert both to degrees C. But in Pascal, both variables DegreesF and DegreesC are declared as type Real. The Pascal language will allow Nancy to add DegreesF + DegreesC without complaint—any two Real values in Pascal can be added together.

You might think that a data value could be entered from the terminal keyboard with the right unit of measure attached, for example by typing: "50 degrees F" instead of just "50" or "$21.75" instead of just "21.75". Unfortunately, attaching a unit of measure to an input data value is not allowed in a computer. If the program action is "READ: DollarAmount", where DollarAmount is a data object of type Real, and you type "$21.75" as the input data value, the Pascal system will reject your input data value. Either execution of the program will be terminated with an error message about "illegal data value" or the Pascal system will ask you to reenter a correct value *without the unit of measure*. In Pascal, a number is just a number. You cannot attach a unit of measure to it as you type it in.

The moral of this story is: *you can add apples and oranges in a computer*. The result will be meaningless, as we all know, but the computer does not care—the result is just a number to the computer. You, the programmer, are entirely responsible for keeping track of the units of measure for each number that you use—the Pascal language and the computer provide no help in keeping separate your "apples" and "oranges."

□ □

The Range of Integer and Real Values

The *range of possible values* for an Integer or Real data object must also be considered when coding the DATA OBJECTS list into the VAR section of a Pascal program. Integer values, in particular, are a common source of problems.

□

MAXINT—the Largest Integer.   Because of the fixed length of the binary representation of integers (for example, using exactly 32 bits to represent each integer), every computer has a limit on the size of integer numbers that it can store conveniently. This limit varies from computer to computer. In Pascal, the largest positive integer is represented by a special predefined value, MAXINT. MAXINT is a *defined constant*—an idea we discuss further in the next chapter. For now, just think of MAXINT as the largest positive integer value you are allowed to use in Pascal on your computer system. Conversely, −MAXINT (minus MAXINT) is the largest *negative* integer value allowed (some computers use −MAXINT−1 as the largest negative integer value; we assume it is −MAXINT here). On some microcomputers, MAXINT is 32,767—not a large value in computer terms. On other computers, MAXINT is much larger.

Suppose that in your DATA OBJECTS list, the range of values for an Integer data object includes numbers larger than MAXINT. For example, suppose you are working with the populations of various countries, and you want to use the range 0 to 5 billion for a data object named TotalPopulation. If MAXINT is 32,767 in your Pascal system, then you cannot use the Pascal Integer data type for variable Total-Population. To represent numbers larger than MAXINT or smaller than −MAXINT, you must use the Pascal type Real, even though the numbers will never have fractional parts.

□

The Range of Real Values. As with integers, each computer has a maximum positive real data value that it can store, but in Pascal, there is no predefined constant like MAXINT that gives you that value. The largest positive Real number, however, is always very large—larger than you will be likely to need in any ordinary computations. Similarly the largest negative Real value is also very large. In more advanced calculations, these limits become important. For now we ignore them and take up the subject again in Chapter 15.

There is also a limit on the *precision* of a Real value—the number of digits you can use in a real number. For example, your computer can probably store the real value 1.5 but not the real value 1.500000000000000000000043. The second value will be rounded off (or truncated—chopped off) before it is stored, so that the actual stored value is just 1.5. For our purposes, most computers provide enough precision in storing Real values, but in more advanced calculations the limit on precision becomes important. We also ignore this limit for now.

□ □

Program States in Pascal

In a Pascal program, we talk about the *state* of the program at some point during its execution, just as we do with an algorithm in pseudo-code. The variables listed in the VAR section define the data objects in the program state. To describe a program's data state, we must show the current value of each variable. To describe its display state, we show what is displayed on the display screen at that point.

The *initial state* of a Pascal program matches that assumed for an algorithm in pseudo-code: each variable is *uninitialized* (its value is unpredictable), and the display screen is "blank" (the program has not yet displayed any information on it). Some Pascal systems will actually initialize each Real or Integer variable to a zero value in the initial state, but such initial values are not standard in Pascal and should never be assumed when programming. If you want a variable to start out with a particular initial value, you must use an ASSIGN action to explicitly assign the initial value after the program begins execution.

□ □

Variables in the Computer's Memory

Each variable that is declared in your Pascal program causes a location in the computer's memory to be reserved for storing the value of the variable. The details of how this is done are unimportant for Pascal programming; just remember that variables represent storage locations in the computer's memory.

In pictures, we often draw a variable as a rectangle, with the variable's name on the left and the current value of the variable inside the rectangle. For example:

StudentAge: | 22 |

Note that we write the values as they are represented in Pascal, even though the actual values are encoded in a binary representation in the computer's memory, as discussed in Chapter 2.

EXERCISES

4.2 Determine the value of MAXINT on your Pascal system. *Hint:* Write and run a program that displays MAXINT.

4.3 Assuming MAXINT = 32,767 on your computer system, code each of the following data objects lists into Pascal:

a. **DATA OBJECTS**

TodaysHigh: Integer	Today's high temperature, range −20 to 110 degrees F.
Precipitation: Real	Measured precipitation, range 0 to 10 inches.
WindDirection: Char	One of the characters N,S,E,W.
WindVelocity: Integer	Range 0 to 180 mph.

b. **DATA OBJECTS**

Size: Integer	City size, range 1 to 500 square miles.
Population: Integer	City population, range 1 to 30 million.
AverageIncome: Integer	Average personal income, range $1000–$50,000

□□□ **4.3**
CODING THE ALGORITHM PART IN PASCAL

In a Pascal program, the ALGORITHM part is coded as the "body" of the main procedure, bracketed by the reserved words BEGIN. . .END, as shown in Figure 4.1. The steps of the algorithm are coded as groups of Pascal *statements* and comments, which follow the same order as the steps of the algorithm in pseudo-code.

Each step in the algorithm is coded as follows:

1. The PURPOSE and GOAL STATE sections of the step are copied into *comments* in the corresponding position in the Pascal code.
2. The ACTIONS list is coded as a sequence of Pascal statements.

It is a good idea to place a blank line between each step in the coded program, for readability. Indent the PURPOSE and GOAL STATE comments so that it is easy to see the statements that represent the ACTIONS of each step. The numbering of steps and actions in the pseudo-code algorithm is omitted in the Pascal program.

Punctuation

The Pascal rules for punctuation of statements are complicated. Rather than worry about the details, we adopt a simple rule: *end each Pascal statement with a semicolon.* We discuss the complete punctuation rules in Chapter 9.

IF and WHILE Actions

The Pascal rules for punctuating IF and WHILE actions are also somewhat complicated. Again we adopt a simple rule: place BEGIN. . .END around each group of actions within an IF or WHILE. The syntax for a Pascal IF statement is then:

```
⟨IF-statement⟩ ::=
        IF ⟨test⟩ THEN
          BEGIN
              ⟨sequence of Pascal statements⟩
          END
        {ELSE IF ⟨test⟩ THEN
          BEGIN
              ⟨sequence of Pascal statements⟩
          END}
        [ELSE
          BEGIN
              ⟨sequence of Pascal statements⟩
          END];
```

The syntax for a WHILE statement is:

```
⟨WHILE-statement⟩ ::=
        WHILE ⟨test⟩ DO
          BEGIN
              ⟨sequence of Pascal statements⟩
          END;
```

Remember that *indentation* is meaningless to the Pascal compiler, so the punctuation and BEGIN-END pairs are essential in the Pascal code. In pseudo-code, we can use indentation to indicate the actions that form the body of a WHILE loop or that form the different cases of an IF, so we do not have to include these elements in the pseudo-code (although, of course, you can include them if you wish).

EXERCISES

4.4 Code the following ALGORITHM steps in Pascal (the ASSIGN actions are correct as written):

a. PURPOSE/GOAL STATE: Set LargestScore to the larger of Score1 or Score2 and set Found = TRUE if Score2 is the larger. Otherwise set Found = FALSE.

ACTIONS:

```
IF Score1 < Score2 THEN
    LargestScore := Score2 ;
    Found := TRUE ;
ELSE
    LargestScore := Score1 ;
    Found := FALSE ;
```

b. PURPOSE: Sum the integers from 1 to MaxCount.

GOAL STATE: Total contains the sum.

ACTIONS:

```
Count := 1 ;
Total := 0 ;
WHILE Count <= MaxCount DO
    Total := Total + Count ;
    Count := Count + 1 ;
```

□□□ 4.4
CODING ASSIGN ACTIONS IN PASCAL

In pseudo-code an ASSIGN action has the general form:

⟨data object⟩ := ⟨formula defining new value to be assigned⟩

The Pascal *assignment statement*, which is used to code an ASSIGN action, has a similar form:

```
⟨ASSIGNMENT-statement⟩ ::=
        ⟨variable-name⟩ := ⟨expression⟩
   WHERE
      ⟨variable-name⟩ ::= Pascal name of the data object.
      ⟨expression⟩ ::= Pascal form of the pseudo-code formula.
```

□

Meaning: Evaluate the ⟨expression⟩ on the right side of the assignment symbol (which results in a single data value being computed) and store the resulting data value in the variable named on the left side of the assignment symbol.

□ □
Data Types in Assignment Statements

In a Pascal assignment statement, you must be sure that the *data type* of the ⟨variable-name⟩ that appears on the left-hand side of the assignment statement corresponds to the data type of the *data value* produced by the ⟨expression⟩ on the right-hand side. In general, the Pascal rules allow the following assignments:

⟨Integer-variable⟩ := ⟨Integer-valued expression⟩
⟨Real-variable⟩ := ⟨Real-valued or Integer-valued expression⟩
⟨Boolean-variable⟩ := ⟨Boolean-valued expression⟩
⟨Char-variable⟩ := ⟨Char-valued expression⟩

Thus the general rule is that the ⟨expression⟩ on the right-hand side must produce a value of the same data type as the declared data type of the ⟨variable⟩ on the left-hand side. The only exception is that an *Integer* value may be assigned to a *Real* variable (which means that the integer value is first changed into the equivalent Real value before it is stored in the variable).

The data type of the variable is given in the VAR section of the procedure, but sometimes it is tricky to determine the data type of the ⟨expression⟩ on the right-hand side. Let's look at how expressions are formed and at the rules for determining the data type of an expression.

□ □
Writing Literal Values in Pascal

The simplest ⟨expression⟩ consists of a single literal data value. The Pascal rules for writing literal values of the four basic data types are as follows:

□

Integer Literal Values.   Written as a sequence of decimal digits. Negative numbers are preceded by a minus sign (the hyphen key), positive numbers by a plus sign or by no sign. No commas, spaces, or decimal point are allowed. In BNF:

⟨Integer-literal-value⟩ ::=

$$[+ \;|\; -] \; \langle\texttt{digit}\rangle \; \{\langle\texttt{digit}\rangle\}$$

WHERE
⟨digit⟩ ::= 0 | 1 | 2 | 3 | 4 | 5 | 6 | 7 | 8 | 9

EXAMPLES

VALID INTEGERS			INVALID INTEGERS		
2	-57	34522	2.0	-57.	24,522

□
Real Literal Values.   Written in one of two forms:

(Form 1). As an ordinary decimal number with a whole number part and a fractional part separated by a decimal point. At least one digit must appear on both sides of the decimal point—thus 0.1 is a valid real number but .1 is not. Negative numbers have a preceding minus sign; positive numbers are unsigned or preceded by a plus sign. No commas or spaces are allowed. In BNF:

⟨Real-literal-value⟩ ::=

$$[+ \;|\; -] \; \langle\texttt{digit}\rangle \; \{\langle\texttt{digit}\rangle\}.\langle\texttt{digit}\rangle \; \{\langle\texttt{digit}\rangle\}$$

EXAMPLES

VALID REAL NUMBERS			INVALID REAL NUMBERS	
273.98	-5.01	0.0003	.0001	-202.
+223456.0	0.0			

(Form 2). As a decimal number in a Pascal form of *scientific notation*. In ordinary scientific notation you write the number times some power of ten. For example, 1500 is written as 1.5×10^3 and 3.2 million is written as 3.2×10^6. Scientific notation is particularly useful for writing numbers that are very large or very small. For example, 500 million can be written as 5×10^8 (or 50×10^7, 500×10^6, etc.) and 1/1000 can be written 1×10^{-3}. In Pascal you can write a real number literal in the same way, but you replace the "$\times 10$" with the letter "E" (for "exponent") followed immediately by the power of ten written as an integer. In this Pascal scientific notation you do not have to include a decimal point and fraction part. In BNF:

⟨Real-literal-value⟩ ::=

$$[+ \;|\; -] \; \langle\texttt{digits}\rangle \; [.\langle\texttt{digits}\rangle] \; E \; [+ \;|\; -] \; \langle\texttt{digits}\rangle$$

WHERE

1.5E3	(= 1500)
3.2E6	(= 3,200,000)
5E8	(= 500,000,000)
1E-3	(= 0.001)
-4.666E-2	(= -0.04666)

□

Boolean Literal Values. There are only two Boolean values, TRUE and FALSE. In BNF:

⟨Boolean-literal-value⟩ ::=

TRUE | FALSE

□

Character Literal Values. A single character may be written as a literal value by enclosing it in single quotes: '⟨character⟩'. For example, 'A', represents the literal character capital A. Any character can be quoted as a literal, including spaces, digits, and punctuation marks. A single quote character must be written twice (and enclosed in quotes) as a literal value, ''''. In BNF:

⟨Char-literal-value⟩ ::=

'⟨character⟩' | ''''

WHERE

⟨character⟩ ::= Any character on the keyboard,
except ' (single quote).

```
FinalGrade := 'A';
MaritalStatus := 'S';
PunctuationMark := '.';
SingleSpace := ' ';
SingleQuote := '''';
```

□

Similar Literals of Different Data Types. Be careful not to confuse these similar literals:

2 = the Integer value 2
2.0 = the Real value 2
'2' = the Char value 2 (a single decimal digit)

Any integer can be written as both a Pascal Integer literal or a Pascal Real literal—the difference lies only in whether you include a *decimal point* or *exponent* when you write the number. Any integer that has only a single digit (like 2 above) can be written either as a Pascal Integer, a Real, or a Char literal.

□ □
Copying the Value of Another Variable

If you name another variable on the right-hand side of a Pascal assignment statement, such as:

```
NewGrade := OldGrade;
```

the meaning is "make a copy of the value of the variable named on the right-hand side and store the *copy* in the variable named on the left-hand side."

The same rules about corresponding data types apply: both variables must have the same data types, except that the assignment:

```
⟨Real-variable⟩ := ⟨Integer-variable⟩
```

is allowed. For example, if DollarAmount is type Real and WholeDollars is type Integer, then the assignment:

```
DollarAmount := WholeDollars;
```

converts the current Integer value of WholeDollars to the equivalent Real value, with a fractional part of zero, and stores the Real value in DollarAmount. Thus, if WholeDollars contains 21, then DollarAmount contains 21.0 after the assignment.

□ □
Evaluating a Mathematical Formula

Frequently it is necessary to evaluate a mathematical formula to compute a new Real or Integer value, which then is stored in some data object. The pseudo-code for such an ASSIGN action would take the form:

```
⟨data object⟩ := ⟨mathematical formula⟩
```

The Pascal code uses an assignment statement:

```
⟨variable name⟩ := ⟨Pascal version of mathematical formula⟩
```

where the variable is declared as type Real or Integer.

In most cases you will find that a mathematical formula that involves just the basic arithmetic operations like addition and subtraction and the elementary mathematical functions like square root, sine, and cosine can be translated into an equivalent Pascal expression relatively easily. There are a few subtleties, however, in learning how to write a formula in a single line, rather than displayed across several lines in standard mathematical fashion.

EXAMPLES
    1. *Pseudo-code ASSIGN action*:

        PURPOSE/GOAL STATE: Average Max and Min and store result in Average.

$$Average := \frac{Max\ +\ Min}{2}$$

    Pascal:

```
Average := (Max + Min) / 2;
```

    2. *Pseudo-code ASSIGN action:*

        PURPOSE/GOAL STATE: Compute Root1 using the quadratic formula with values of coefficients A, B, and C.

$$Root\ 1 := \frac{-B\ +\ \sqrt{B^2 - 4 \times A \times C}}{2 \times A}$$

    Pascal:

```
Root1 := (-B + sqrt (B*B - 4*A*C)) / (2*A);
```

  ■

□ □
Expressions and Their Evaluation

Expression is the general name in Pascal for what is written on the right side of an assignment statement. Thus when coding a mathematical formula, we must code it as a Pascal expression. We say an expression is *evaluated* to produce a resulting data value when an assignment statement is executed. Expressions are used in many different places in Pascal, not just in assignment statements; so, it is important to understand how expressions are written and evaluated in Pascal, whatever the context of their use.

To understand expressions and their evaluation, you need to understand several things:

    1. *Syntax*. How an expression is written.

2. *Semantics of each part.* The meaning of each individual part of an expression when the expression is evaluated.
3. *Evaluation order.* The order in which the parts of an expression are evaluated.
4. *Data type of result.* How the data type of the result of the expression is determined.

□ □
Syntax for Expressions

A Pascal expression that evaluates to give a Real or Integer value is restricted to the following elements:

1. Integer or Real literal values.
2. Variables names, where the variable is of type Integer or Real.
3. Arithmetic operations:

    +   (addition)
    −   (subtraction)
    *   (multiplication)
    /   (division producing a Real quotient)
    DIV   (division of integers, producing an Integer quotient)
    MOD   (Integer remainder after division of two integers)

4. Calls on predefined functions that return Integer or Real values.
5. Calls on functions that you define that return Integer or Real values (discussed in Chapter 5).
6. Parentheses surrounding any sub-expression (for readability or to control the order of evaluation).

□ □
DIV, MOD, and the Predefined Functions

Most of the parts of an expression have familiar meanings from mathematics, but three need further explanation:

□
The DIV operation.   The DIV symbol represents *Integer division,* in contrast to the "/" symbol which represents *Real division.* Both of the operands of DIV must be of Integer type, and the second operand cannot be zero. The result is the whole number quotient from dividing the first operand by the second; any remainder is lost. The result is *not* rounded.

EXAMPLES

        7 DIV 2   ⟶   3
      10 DIV 5   ⟶   2

$$5 \text{ DIV } 10 \longrightarrow 0$$
$$-7 \text{ DIV } 2 \longrightarrow -3$$
$$-7 \text{ DIV } -2 \longrightarrow 3$$

■

☐

The MOD operation. The MOD symbol represents the "modulus" operation—the *remainder* after division of two integers. Both of its operands must be of Integer type, and the second operand cannot be zero or negative. The result is the remainder from dividing the first operand by the second.

EXAMPLES

$$7 \text{ MOD } 2 \longrightarrow 1$$
$$10 \text{ MOD } 5 \longrightarrow 0$$
$$-7 \text{ MOD } 2 \longrightarrow 1$$
$$9 \text{ MOD } 6 \longrightarrow 3$$

■

The MOD operation is surprisingly useful in programming. One common use is in counting, where you want to count from zero up to some limit and then begin again at zero.

EXAMPLE

Suppose you have a counter variable, Count, to which you want to add one each time a certain event happens within a WHILE loop. Count starts at zero and when it reaches some limit, say 20, you want to restart the count at zero (so that Count never actually has a value of 20). Without using MOD, you would have to write something like this in pseudo-code:

```
Count := 0              —initialize the count
. . .
WHILE . . . DO          —a loop that is doing the counting.
. . .
    IF Count < 19 THEN    —increment Count
        Count := Count + 1
    ELSE
        Count := 0
    . . .
```

Using MOD, you can replace the four line IF action by the single line:

$$\text{Count} := (\text{Count} + 1) \text{ MOD } 20$$

In this assignment, if the value of Count = 19, then Count+1 = 20, which gives a remainder of zero when divided by 20. Thus Count is assigned a new value of zero in this case. But if the value of Count is in the range 0 to 18, then Count+1 is in the range 1 to 19, and the remainder when divided by 20 is just exactly the same value. Thus, Count is assigned a new value of Count+1 in these cases, exactly as in the longer IF action. ∎

□

Predefined Mathematical Functions. Many standard mathematical functions are predefined in Pascal and can be used within any Pascal expression. The predefined functions correspond to the functions that you often find in hand calculators, such as square root, square, sine, cosine, and so forth. The usual predefined functions are listed in Table 4.1 (many Pascal systems extend this list). If you do not find the function you need in the predefined list, you often can define your own without much difficulty, as discussed in Chapter 5.

To invoke one of the predefined functions, you write a *function call,* using the syntax:

$$\langle \text{function name} \rangle \ (\langle \text{argument} \rangle)$$

The function returns a data value, which may then be stored in a variable or used as part of a larger expression. For example, to compute the square root of the value of variable X and store the square root in variable RootOfX, you would write the assignment:

$$\text{RootOfX} := \text{sqrt} \ (\text{X});$$

In specifying an argument for a function, you can use any Pascal *expression* that gives a value of the proper data type—that is, anything you can write as an ex-

TABLE 4.1 Pascal Predefined Functions

I = Integer R = Real

Function Name and Argument Type	Result Type	Function Computed
abs(R)	⟶ R	absolute value
abs(I)	⟶ I	absolute value
sqr(R)	⟶ R	square
sqr(I)	⟶ I	square
sqrt(R or I)	⟶ R	square root
sin(R)	⟶ R	sin (argument in radians)
cos(R)	⟶ R	cosine (argument in radians)
arctan(R)	⟶ R	arc tangent (argument in radians)
exp(R or I)	⟶ R	exponential
ln(R or I)	⟶ R	natural logarithm (base e)
round(R)	⟶ I	round to nearest integer
trunc(R)	⟶ I	truncate fraction part

pression on the right-side of an assignment can be written as an argument for a function call. All of the predefined functions just have a single argument, but functions that you define yourself may have more than one.

1. Compute Average as the average of the square roots of Max and Min:

```
Average := (sqrt(Max) + sqrt(Min)) / 2;
```

2. Compute RootOfAverage as the square root of the average of New and Old:

```
RootOfAverage := sqrt ((New + Old) / 2);
```

3. Round the value of RootOfAverage to the nearest integer and store the result in IntegerRoot:

```
IntegerRoot := round (RootOfAverage);
```

□ □

Order of Evaluation of Parts of an Expression

An arithmetic expression that represents a mathematical formula may contain several different operations and function calls. To figure out the value of such an expression for given values of the variables involved, you need to know the *order* in which the various operations are evaluated. For example, in the expression

$$3 * 4 + 2$$

you need to know whether the add operation or the multiply operation is evaluated first. Is it $(3 * 4) + 2$, which evaluates to 14, or $3 * (4 + 2)$, which evaluates to 18?

The rules for determining the order of evaluation of the operations in a Pascal expression generally match the familiar rules of algebra:

1. *Function calls first*. Any function calls within an expression are evaluated before the larger expression. This requires that the *argument* to the function be evaluated before the function call—and the argument may itself be an expression. For example, in evaluating the assignment:

```
Average : = (sqrt(Max) + sqrt(Min)) / 2;
```

the first step is to compute *sqrt* (Max) and then *sqrt* (Min), before evaluating the rest of the expression.

2. *Parenthesized subexpressions next.* Any subexpression in parentheses is evaluated before the larger expression. If there are several levels of nested parentheses, then you work outward from the innermost level. For example, in evaluating the assignment:

$$Root := (-B + 2*A*C) / (2*A);$$

the two parenthesized sub-expressions are evaluated first, before the division, "/", is performed.

3. *Multiplication and division precede addition and subtraction.* If several arithmetic operations appear with no parentheses to indicate the order of evaluation, then the order of evaluation is:

Multiplication and division first (*, /, DIV, MOD)
Addition and subtraction last (+, -)

Thus the expression 3 * 4 + 2 is grouped as if it were written:

$$(3 * 4) + 2 \longrightarrow 14$$

Likewise:

$$2 + 3 * 4 \longrightarrow 14$$

This ordering is called the *precedence order* of the arithmetic operations—it specifies which operation precedes another in an expression when no parentheses are used. Table 4.2 shows the precedence order for all the Pascal operations.

4. *Left-to-right associativity of operations of the same precedence.* If several multiplication and division operations appear with no parentheses to indicate the order of evaluation, they are evaluated moving across the expression from left to right.

TABLE 4.2 Precedence Order for Pascal Operations

Highest precedence:	NOT
↓	* / DIV MOD AND
	+ - OR
Lowest precedence:	= <> < > <= >= IN

The same rule applies if several addition and subtraction operations appear with no parentheses.

Expression		Evaluation order		Result
8 - 2 - 4	$\longrightarrow$	(8 - 2) - 4	$\longrightarrow$	2
10 DIV 5 * 2	$\longrightarrow$	(10 DIV 5) * 2	$\longrightarrow$	4

■

Because parenthesized sub-expressions are always evaluated before sub-expressions without parentheses, you can always use extra parentheses to get the exact order of evaluation that you want. So a good rule to follow is: *when in doubt about the order of evaluation, use extra parentheses to show the order that you want*. Parentheses also can be used to make an expression more readable when the expression is complicated.

□ □
Data Type of the Result of an Expression

You need to be able to determine the type of data value that results when an expression is evaluated—is the result of type Integer or Real (or Boolean or Char)? To determine the type of the result, use the following rules:

1. *Literal value.* A Real value always has a decimal point or an exponent; an Integer value has neither.
2. *Variable name.* The data type is its declared type.
3. *Arithmetic operation.* The data type of the result depends on the types of the operands, as given in Table 4.3. Notice in particular that "/" always gives a Real result, even if both operands are type Integer.
4. *Call on a predefined function.* The data type of the result depends on the type of its argument, as given in Table 4.1.

TABLE 4.3 Data Type of Result of an Arithmetic Operation
I = Integer   R = Real

Left Operand	Operation	Right Operand		Result Type
I	+ - * DIV MOD	I	$\longrightarrow$	I
I	/	I	$\longrightarrow$	R
R or I	+ - * /	R	$\longrightarrow$	R
R	+ - * /	R or I	$\longrightarrow$	R
R or I	DIV MOD	R	$\longrightarrow$	illegal
R	DIV MOD	R or I	$\longrightarrow$	illegal

Assume your variables are declared as follows:

```
VAR
    A, B, C: Real;
    I, J, K: Integer;
```

Each of the following expressions gives a result of the following data type:

```
I + J * K        ⟶ Integer result
A + B * C        ⟶ Real result
round(A) * K     ⟶ Integer result
A + abs(J)       ⟶ Real result
```

□ □
Testing Properties of Values

Tests that produce TRUE/FALSE values are another type of Pascal *expression*. Such tests appear in IF or WHILE actions, and they can also appear in ASSIGN actions, where the value is assigned to a Boolean variable. The operations involved in such tests are the *relational operations* and the *Boolean operations*:

Relational Operations

Pascal Syntax	Meaning
=	equal?
<>	not equal?
<	less than?
<=	less than or equal?
>	greater than?
>=	greater than or equal?

Boolean Operations

Pascal Syntax	Meaning
⟨test 1⟩ AND ⟨test 2⟩	Do both tests return TRUE?
⟨test 1⟩ OR ⟨test 2⟩	Does at least one test return TRUE?
NOT ⟨test⟩	Does the test return FALSE?

□ □
Precedence Order for Boolean Operations

When you write an expression that uses the Boolean operations AND and OR, it is best to always use parentheses to explicitly enclose the operands of the operations. Pascal provides a precedence order (Table 4.2) for the Boolean operations that applies when you do not use parentheses, but the order is peculiar and gives some surprising results. For example, in the *range test* pattern (see the box), a common error is to translate the mathematical expression "1 < X < N" into the Pascal expression:

$$X > 1 \text{ AND } X < N$$

Because of the precedence rules, this Pascal code means:

$$X > (1 \text{ AND } X) < N$$

The unexpected grouping leads to a compiler syntax error because the sub-expression "1 AND X" is invalid. Using parentheses explicitly will give the expected result:

$$(X > 1) \text{ AND } (X < N)$$

□ □
Flag Variables

In programming, a Boolean variable is often called a *flag* (because it is used to "signal" that some particular event has taken place or that a particular fact is true). When the variable is assigned a TRUE/FALSE value resulting from a test, we say

---

THE RANGE TEST PATTERN

Suppose you wish to determine if the value of a variable is within a given range. In mathematics, such a *range test* is usually written in the form:

$$\text{Min} \leq \text{Variable} \leq \text{Max}$$

where Min and Max are the limits of the allowed range.

Expressed in Pascal, a range test must be written as the AND of two separate tests:

```
(Variable >= Min) AND (Variable <= Max)
```

The parentheses are important and must be included. For example, the range test "$1 \leq \text{Count} \leq 150$" is coded in Pascal:

```
(Count >= 1) AND (Count <= 150)
```

---

that we *set the flag*. When we later use the value of the variable, perhaps in an IF statement, we say that we *test the flag*.

For example, suppose that we wish to determine whether the value of a variable, Income, is in the range 5,000 to 10,000. We might use a flag variable named "IsPovertyRange" to indicate an income in this range. After reading in a value for Income, the assignment statement:

```
IsPovertyRange := (Income >= 5000) AND (Income <= 10000);
```

can be used to "set the flag." Then later, when we needed to take different actions depending on whether the value of Income is in this range, we just test this flag in an IF statement:

```
IF IsPovertyRange THEN ...
```

By using the flag variable, we avoid having to repeatedly write the range test on the value of Income. The program also is made more readable.

□ □
The Ordering of Char Values

Data values of type Char can be compared by using the same relational operations used for numbers: =, < >, <, <=, > and >=. The "less than" and "greater than" tests, <, <=, > and >= depend on the ordering of Char values defined for the character codes used in your Pascal system, such as the ASCII character code sequence (Appendix A). Each Char value has a corresponding Integer value that represents its position in this ordering, with the first character in the sequence numbered 0, the second numbered 1, and so forth. Thus, for example, "A" has value 65 in the ordering defined for the ASCII codes, because it is the 66th character in the ASCII sequence.

The ordering for digits is as expected: '0' is less than '1', which is less than '2', and so forth. For example, the Boolean-valued expression:

```
(NewCh >= '0') AND (NewCh <= '9')
```

tests if the value of Char variable NewCh is a decimal digit.

The ordering for letters is more complicated. You can count on the capital letters being ordered in the sequence A, B, . . . , Z and on the lower-case letters also being ordered in the sequence a, b, . . . , z. However, because the lower-case and capital letters are represented by different character codes, A and a, B and b, etc., are different characters, so that either A > a or a > A, depending on the character codes used in your Pascal system (in ASCII, a > A). Also, in Pascal systems that do not use the ASCII character codes, the character codes may include other non-letters between A and Z or between a and z. Thus, to test if Char variable NewCh is a capital letter, the test:

$$(\text{NewCh} \geq \text{'A'}) \quad \text{AND} \quad (\text{NewCh} \leq \text{'Z'})$$

works correctly with ASCII character codes but may be incorrect with Pascal systems that use other character codes.

□ □
The ORD, CHR, PRED, and SUCC Functions

Four predefined functions make use of the ordering defined for Char values. These functions are listed in Table 4.4. Function *ord* gives you the Integer value representing the position of a Char value in the ASCII ordering. Function *chr* goes the other way, from an Integer representing a position to the Char value at that position. Functions *succ* and *pred* allow you to move forward or backward to the succeeding or preceding character value in the ordering.

Functions *ord* and *chr* provide a convenient means to convert a decimal digit stored as a Char value to the corresponding Integer value, and vice versa (for example, to convert the Char digit '7' to the Integer value 7, or Integer value 7 to Char '7'). You do not have to know anything about the ordering of the ASCII character codes, except that the characters '0', '1', . . . , '9' appear in sequence in the ordering, but you have to know the trick. The box on the next page shows the pattern to learn.

EXAMPLE   Georgia is writing a program that will be used by children in elementary school. At one point she wants the child to type in a single digit number between 1 and 9. But she knows that many children will make mistakes and hit some other key, so the program must read in a character value (whatever the child types), check that it is in fact a single digit between 1 and 9, and then convert the digit to an Integer value for use in the rest of the program.

TABLE 4.4   Predefined Functions for Char Values

C = Char   I = Integer

Function Name and Argument Type	Result Type	Function Computed
ord(C)	⟶ I	Position in ordering of values
chr(I)	⟶ C	Char value for given position in ordering of values
succ(C or I)	⟶ C or I	Succeeding value in ordering, undefined for last value
pred(C or I)	⟶ C or I	Preceding value in ordering, undefined for first value

```
┌─────────────────────────────────────────────────────────────────────┐
│              CHAR DIGIT ↔ INTEGER DIGIT CONVERSION PATTERNS           │
│                    Char digit ⟶ Integer digit:                       │
│                                                                       │
│  Suppose variable Ch (type Char) contains one of the characters '0'–'9'. To convert │
│  the value of Ch to the corresponding Integer value 0–9 and store the result in vari- │
│  able Int (type Integer), use the assignment:                         │
│                                                                       │
│      Int := ord (Ch) - ord ('0');                                     │
│                                                                       │
│                    Integer digit ⟶ Char digit:                       │
│                                                                       │
│  Suppose variable Int (type Integer) contains a value in the range 0–9. To convert │
│  the value of Int to the corresponding Char digit '0'–'9' and store the result in vari- │
│  able Ch (type Char), use the assignment:                             │
│                                                                       │
│      Ch := chr (ord ('0') + Int);                                     │
│                                                                       │
└─────────────────────────────────────────────────────────────────────┘
```

In her program she uses the data object CharTyped (type Char) to store the character value typed in and the data object IntegerValue (type Integer) to store the result of converting the character value to an integer. Her pseudo-code actions are as follows. Notice how the last assignment converts the character to an integer value after she is sure that the child has typed the value correctly:

> DISPLAY: "Now type a number between 1 and 9,
>   using the keys at the top of the keyboard."
> READ: CharTyped
> WHILE (CharTyped > '9') OR (CharTyped < '1') DO
>   DISPLAY: "Try again; you hit the wrong key.
>   Type any number between 1 and 9."
>   READ: CharTyped
> IntegerValue := ord (CharTyped) − ord ('0')

The IN Test

A common need is to test if the value of a variable is one of a set of Char values. A convenient way to write this test is to use the Pascal IN test:

⟨variable⟩ IN [⟨list of literal values⟩]

The literal values are separated by commas in the list. The data type of the variable must match the data type of the literal values in the list.

For example, to test if the value of variable NewCh (type Char) is one of the arithmetic operation symbols, +, −, *, or /, you can write:

```
IF NewCh IN ['+', '-', '*', '/'] THEN ...
```

To simplify testing for a range of Char values, you can use the Pascal *subrange* notation:

```
⟨first value⟩..⟨last value⟩
```

to specify a sequence of literal values. For example, to test if the value of variable NewCh is an upper-case or lower-case letter, you might write:

```
IF NewCh IN ['A'..'Z', 'a'..'z'] THEN ...
```

The IN test is another form of Boolean-valued expression. You can combine IN tests with other Boolean-valued tests by using AND, OR, and NOT. For example:

```
IF (Count = 1) AND (NewCh IN ['0'..'9']) THEN ...
```

□ □
Preconditions of Expressions

An *expression* in a Pascal program defines how to compute a particular data value. Each time the expression is evaluated, the current values of the variables in the program state determine the value computed by the expression. Suppose that there are circumstances (particular program states) in which a given expression, when evaluated, will *fail to compute a correct value*. In such a case, we say that the expression has a "precondition":

□ **Precondition of an Expression**

A *precondition* of an expression is an assertion stating *restrictions* or *constraints* on the values of the variables that appear in the expression. The meaning of a precondition P of an expression E is:

1. If the constraints stated in P are TRUE of the values of the variables when the expression E is evaluated, then E is *guaranteed to compute its value correctly,* and
2. If the constraints stated in P are FALSE when E is evaluated, then E *might compute an incorrect value* or E *might fail to compute any value at all,* by causing a run-time error that terminates execution of the entire program.

Preconditions of expressions arise from several sources:

1. *Constraints on division operations.* Pascal has three division operations, "/", "DIV", and "MOD". The denominator for any division operation must not be zero or the operation will fail, and the denominator for MOD cannot be negative. *Precondition:* Values of the variables used in the denominator must not lead to a zero denominator or a negative denominator for MOD.

2. *Constraints on arguments for predefined functions.* For example, you cannot take the square root of a negative number, so the argument to *sqrt* cannot be negative. You cannot apply *chr* to a negative number or *pred* to the first character in the ASCII ordering. *Precondition:* Values of the variables used in the argument for a predefined function must lead to a valid argument for that function.

3. *Constraints on when a particular formula is valid.* A formula used to compute a value may only be valid in certain cases, such as when some of the variables have non-zero or positive values. If these constraints are not met then the value computed may be meaningless. *Precondition:* Values of variables used in the formula must be within the ranges for which the formula is valid.

EXAMPLES

1. If Week1 = total sales for the first week in the month, and TotalSales = total sales for the month, then the percentage of monthly sales made in the first week is given by the expression:

$$(Week1 \ / \ TotalSales) \ * \ 100$$

But the formula causes division by zero if TotalSales = 0. Hence the expression has a precondition:

$$PRECONDITION: \ TotalSales \ <> \ 0$$

2. The quadratic formula:

$$(-B \ + \ sqrt \ (B*B \ - \ 4*A*C)) \ / \ (2*A)$$

determines one root of the quadratic equation $A*X^2 + B*X + C$, provided that (i) the denominator for the division is not zero and (ii) the argument for *sqrt* is not negative. If not, then an attempt to evaluate this expression will cause a run-time error and termination of program execution. Hence the expression has:

$$PRECONDITIONS: \ (A \ <> \ 0) \ AND \ (B*B \ >= \ 4*A*C)$$

3. The formula for converting a decimal digit in Char form to the equivalent Integer value:

$$Int \ := \ ord \ (Ch) \ - \ ord \ ('0')$$

assumes that variable Ch (type Char) contains a digit—one of the characters '0', '1', ..., '9'. If not, then an attempt to evaluate the formula will compute a meaningless value. Hence:

PRECONDITION: Ch IN ['0'..'9'] ∎

As we noted above, Pascal Integer and Real values also have restrictions on their range (largest and smallest allowed values). These restrictions can also cause expressions to have preconditions. However, to simplify the discussion, we ignore these restrictions until Chapter 15.

Preconditions of expressions are an important source of programming errors. Every time you use an expression in an ASSIGN, IF, WHILE, or DISPLAY action (or the equivalent Pascal statement) check whether the expression has any preconditions. The question may be stated conveniently in the form:

Will this expression work correctly for any possible values of the variables involved? If the answer is NO, then the expression has preconditions. Check whether you should modify the program to ensure that the preconditions are satisfied each time the expression is evaluated.

EXERCISES

4.5 Given the declared types for the variables:

```
A,B,C: Real;   I,J,K: Integer;
```

Determine which of the following are valid Pascal expressions. If valid, determine the data type of the result of the expression.

a. A * B * J

b. 22(J + K)

c. I DIV abs (J)

d. (I/J) MOD K

e. trunc (A) * round (B)

f. 5A - 6B

g. A*B - C*C / sqrt (J)

h. abs (trunc (A/K) + 2)

4.6 For the following data state:

I: 4   J: 6   K: 0   L: 1   M: 10

evaluate each of the following expressions:

a. I + J * L - M

b. (I + K) DIV (M - J)

c. (J + (M - L * (J+I)) - M) + 5

d. I - J + 5 - L + M

e. 3 * J MOD M - I

f. J * J - I - I

4.7 Write each of the following assignment sequences as a single assignment to the last variable in the sequence:

a. B := B + 1;
   C := 2;
   D := B + A;
   E := 2 * C - D;

b. X := sqrt (U + V);
   Y := U - W;
   Z := 21 * X - Y;

4.8 Translate the following pseudo-code ASSIGN actions into single Pascal assignment statements:

a. $Y := \dfrac{\sqrt{(A + B)(A - B)}}{A^2 - 1}$

b. $Z := \dfrac{3X^3 + 7X^2 - 15X + 3}{X + \dfrac{1}{X^3 - 2}}$

4.9 Code each of the following pseudo-code actions as a single Pascal assignment to a Boolean variable (do not use IF):

a. Set IsPassing to the result of the test "Is GradeValue in the range 60–100?"

b. Set IsBit = TRUE if Char variable Ch contains one of the characters '0' or '1'.

4.10 Suppose your program has the following declarations:

```
VAR
    NewCh: Char;
    IntValue: Integer;
    IsReady: Boolean;
```

Give the result of evaluating each of the following Pascal expressions in the data state:

NewCh: `'3'`   IntValue: `7`   IsReady: `FALSE`

a. (IntValue > 10) OR IsReady
b. NewCh IN ['0'..'9']
c. ord (NewCh) - ord ('0')
d. NOT IsReady OR (Newch = 'A')
e. chr (ord ('0') + IntValue)
f. pred (IntValue)
g. succ (NewCh)

4.11 Char variables OnesDigit, TensDigit, and HundredsDigit represent a three digit decimal number, with OnesDigit = 1's digit, TensDigit = 10's digit, HundredsDigit = 100's digit. For example, the number "607" would be represented:

OnesDigit: `'7'`   TensDigit: `'0'`   HundredsDigit: `'6'`

Write a sequence of assignment statements that convert the number from its character form to a Pascal integer and that store the value in variable NewInteger (type Integer). Do not use any other variables. Use three assignments to NewInteger to progressively construct the desired integer value. For example, given the state above, the final value of NewInteger should be the *integer* value 607.

4.12 For each of the following expressions, determine the preconditions, if any, of each of the expressions:

a. A / B

b. sqrt (D + 1)

c. (E + F) MOD G

d. To convert an Integer value to a single decimal digit in Char form:

$$Ch := \underline{chr} \ (\underline{ord} \ ('0') + Int);$$

e. To use the Pythagorean theorem to compute the length of the hypotenuse, C, of a right triangle from the lengths of the other two sides, A and B:

$$C := sqrt \ (A*A + B*B);$$

CODING DISPLAY ACTIONS IN PASCAL

Each DISPLAY action in an algorithm is coded as one or more Pascal *write* or *writeln* statements. The DISPLAY action gives you the general format of the line or lines to be displayed. During coding into Pascal, you must consider the fine points of exactly how each part of each line of text will be formatted and positioned on the screen. First, let's understand exactly what an "output line" means in Pascal.

□ □
What is an Output Line?

An *output line* is simply a single line that can be displayed. In Pascal, each output line begins at the left margin of the display. A line consists of zero or more characters, followed by a special *end-of-line* character. The end-of-line character is designated ⟨EOLN⟩ in our examples. It is a special non-printing character code in ASCII that serves as a signal to the display terminal to advance the cursor down the screen to the beginning of the next line.

An output line can be of any length. The shortest line just contains an ⟨EOLN⟩. When displayed, it just moves the cursor down the screen one line, leaving a blank line. Most display screens can accommodate up to 80 characters in a line. Output lines longer than the screen can actually display on a single line are usually automatically "wrapped-around" to be displayed on the next line on the screen, starting at the left margin.

In Pascal programming there is no concept of a "right margin" or "center" of an output line. Every line begins at the left margin and continues to the ⟨EOLN⟩. Lines advance down the screen continuously, with no breaks at "page" boundaries.

WRITELN Statements

The *writeln* statement has the form:

⟨WRITELN-statement⟩ ::=

```
writeln [(⟨output item⟩ {, ⟨output item⟩})]
```

> **WHERE**
> ⟨output-item⟩ ::= ⟨literal-string⟩ | ⟨expression⟩
> ⟨literal-string⟩ ::= '. . .any sequence of characters. . .'
> ⟨expression⟩ ::=
> Any Pascal "expression" (as allowed for the right-hand side of an
> assignment statement).

Each *writeln* statement in your program will display a complete output line each time it is executed. You just list the expressions whose values are to be displayed, separating the expressions by commas, and also include any literal strings that you want displayed to identify the values. Each literal string will be displayed exactly as written (without the quotes). Each expression will be evaluated, using the current values of the variables in the program state. The values will be displayed starting at the left margin of the screen and continuing across the screen until all values have been displayed in the order specified in the statement. The *writeln* puts an ⟨EOLN⟩ at the end of the line, to advance the display or printer to the next line. Figure 4.2 shows examples of typical *writeln* statements and the results of executing them in a particular program state.

□ □
Blank Lines

Executing the statement:

```
writeln;
```

will end the current line and advance the cursor to the beginning of a new one. If the cursor is already positioned at the beginning of a line when the statement is executed, then the effect of this *writeln* is to display a blank line.

□ □
WRITE Statements

A *write* statement has the same form as a *writeln* statement, replacing the identifier *writeln* with *write*. Executing a *write* statement just extends the current line, without ending it (no ⟨EOLN⟩ is put in the line to end it). Thus several *write* statements exe-

Suppose the program state is the following:

VARIABLE NAME	VALUE	DATA TYPE
Age:	22	Integer
BirthDay:	12	Integer
BirthMonth:	11	Integer
BirthYear:	1966	Integer
Salary:	785.90	Real
FinalGrade:	'C'	Char
Married:	TRUE	Boolean

Executing the WRITE segment:	*Produces the output line:* *(the ⟨EOLN⟩ will not be displayed)*
writeln (Age, BirthYear)	_____22_____1966⟨EOLN⟩
writeln ('Grade = ', FinalGrade)	Grade_=_C⟨EOLN⟩
writeln (Salary)	__7.85900000000E+002⟨EOLN⟩
writeln (Married)	true⟨EOLN⟩
writeln (Age, Salary)	_____22__7.85900000000E+002⟨EOLN⟩
writeln ('Age is ', Age, ' years.')	Age_is_____22_years.⟨EOLN⟩
write ('Age is '); write (Age); writeln (' years.')	Age_is_____22_years.⟨EOLN⟩
writeln (' Month Day Year'); writeln; write (BirthMonth); write (BirthDay); writeln (BirthYear);	_____Month_____Day_____Year⟨EOLN⟩ ⟨EOLN⟩ _____11_____12_____1966⟨EOLN⟩

FIGURE 4.2 WRITELN and WRITE Examples (_ indicates a blank space)

cuted in sequence can be used to build up a long output line. To end the line, a *writeln* must be executed to insert the ⟨EOLN⟩. In all other ways, a *write* statement looks and works just like a *writeln* (see Figure 4.2).

□ □
Output Fields and the Default Format

In general, you want your program's output to be nicely formatted on the screen (or printed page). Using *writeln* and *write* statements as we have above gives your output a *default format* ("default" means "what you get if you do not specify what you want"). Often the default format is adequate, but in many cases you want better control of exactly where values are positioned on each line. For example, you may want to center something on a line or to align the columns of a table underneath the column headings. Pascal provides *field-width* and *fraction-size* specifications to allow detailed control of line format.

Let's look at the format of a single line first, as produced by a *writeln* (using the default format). Each output value or string listed in the *writeln* statement is printed in a *print field*—a certain number of character positions wide. The *width* of the print field is the number of character positions it takes up. The width depends on the type of data value being printed and is set locally by each Pascal system. Other details of the default format may vary locally. Here is a typical list of how values of each basic data type are printed:

DEFAULT FORMATS

□
Integer value:

- Field width: 10 character positions.
- Printed in decimal, with a minus sign if negative.
- Value is right-justified in the field, with spaces on the left to fill out the field.

Examples (variables declared as type Integer):

Program State		Value When Printed
Age:	27	--------27
LowTemp:	−185	------−185

□
Real value:

- Field width: 22 character positions.
- Printed as a decimal number in scientific notation, with an exponent, right justified in the field.

Examples (variables declared as type Real):

Program State		Value When Printed
Salary:	1250.75	_1.250750000000E+003
LowAverage:	−56.2	_5.620000000000E+001
NearZero:	0.0003	_3.000000000000E−004

□
Char value:

- Field width: 1 character position.
- Printed as a single character, without quotes.

Examples (variables declared as type Char):

Program State		Value When Printed
Size:	'M'	M
Grade:	'B'	B
Symbol:	'+'	+

□
Boolean value:

- Field width: 4 or 5 character positions.
- Printed as "true" or "false".

Examples (variables declared as type Boolean):

Program State		Value When Printed
IsHot:	TRUE	true
RaceStarted:	FALSE	false

□

Quoted string of characters:

- Field width: number of characters in the string.
- All characters between the quotes are printed.

If there are several output items listed in the *writeln* or *write* statement, the output field for each item is printed left to right across the page, with each value *right-justified* in its field.

The default field widths give nice printed columns if you are printing numbers (all integers or reals, but not mixed). Since numbers are printed as far to the right in each field as possible, the columns will be aligned vertically. For example, executing the two statements:

```
writeln (12, -277, 3);
writeln (23456, 1033333, -5678);
```

gives the output:

```
    12        -277           3
 23456     1033333       -5678
```

The default widths for printing characters and strings also give you the output you expect when you don't mix them with numbers.

When you mix data types in an output line, however, the default widths can make things look peculiar. For example, executing the statement:

```
writeln ('Temperature', 212, 'F. is', 100.0, 'degrees C.')
```

displays the output line:

```
Temperature_____212F._is_1.000000000000E+002degrees_C.
```

The spaces before the Integer value 212 are inserted because of the default field width of 10 used for Integer values. The Real value 100.0 appears in scientific notation because that is the default format in Pascal. The last two literal strings are jammed up next to the numbers, with no spaces, because the default format for strings includes no extra spaces. The line is not very readable in this format.

If you do not like the default spacing of the values in a particular output line, you can associate a *field width specification* with one or more of the items in the *writeln* or *write* statement to adjust the spacing.

> □ **Field Width Specification**
>
> A positive integer used in a *writeln* or *write* statement to specify the field width to be used in spacing a particular output value.

You write a field width specification as follows:

```
writeln (⟨variable or string⟩ : ⟨field width specification⟩, ...)
```

For example:

```
writeln ('TABLE OF PRICES':50)
```

specifies a field width of 50 character positions for displaying the string "TABLE OF PRICES". Since the string is printed at the right of the field (right-justified), the output line looks as follows:

```
_____TABLE_OF_PRICES⟨EOLN⟩
```

You can place a field width specification with any or all of the items in the *writeln* or *write* statement. The number you specify is used as the field width for that particular output item, replacing the default field width, whenever the statement is executed.

In choosing a field width, keep two rules in mind:

□
Rule 1.   Regardless of the size you specify for the field width, the value will be printed *right-justified* in the field.

□
Rule 2.   If you specify a field width that is too *small* for the value to be printed, the field will be expanded to be just large enough to hold the characters that need to be printed.

Rule 1 means that you can always line up columns of integers or reals easily, and use the field width specification to space the columns apart. For example, executing the statements:

```
writeln (12:20, -277:20, 3:20);
writeln (23456:20, 1033333:20, -5678:20);
```

gives the output:

```
          12                -277                   3
       23456             1033333               -5678
```

which is the same table that we saw above, except with different column spacing.

Rule 2 means that you can mix data types in the same line by setting the field width for numbers to 1, which means they will be printed with no extra spaces. You then explicitly include the spaces you want using literal character strings. For example, the statement above can be written as follows. The underscores show where explicit spaces are included in quoted strings:

<u>writeln</u> ('The_temperature_', 212:1, '_F._is_', 100.0:1, '_degrees_C.')

which gives the output line:

The_temperature_212_F._is_1.000000000000E+002_degrees C. ⟨EOLN⟩

which spaces both numbers nicely (although the Real value is still displayed in scientific notation).

□ □
Fraction Size Specifications

A *fraction size* specification allows a Real data value to be printed as an ordinary decimal fraction rather than in Pascal scientific notation (in the example, as 100.0, instead of as 1.000000000000E+002). The fraction size specification is a positive integer that indicates the *number of digits after the decimal point* that you wish displayed. The syntax is:

⟨expression⟩:⟨field width⟩:⟨fraction size⟩

where the expression item must give a value of type Real.

For example, with a fraction size in the above example, the statement:

<u>writeln</u> ('The_temperature_', 212:1, '_F._is_', 100.0:1:2, '_degrees_C.')

displays the output line:

The_temperature_212_F._is_100.00_degrees C. ⟨EOLN⟩

which spaces both numbers nicely. Figure 4.3 shows some additional examples of format specifications in WRITE segments.

178   □ Chap. 4 *Program Coding, Compiling, and Testing*

Suppose the program state is the same as in Figure 4.2:

VARIABLE NAME	VALUE	DATA TYPE
Age:	22	Integer
BirthDay:	12	Integer
BirthMonth:	11	Integer
BirthYear:	1966	Integer
Salary:	785.90	Real
FinalGrade:	'C'	Char
Married:	TRUE	Boolean

Executing the WRITE segment:	*Produces the output line:* *(the ⟨EOLN⟩ will not be displayed)*
writeln (Age:4, BirthYear:5)	__22_1966⟨EOLN⟩
writeln ('Grade =':15, FinalGrade:4)	_____Grade_=___C⟨EOLN⟩
writeln (Salary:8:2)	__785.90⟨EOLN⟩
writeln (Married:10)	_____true⟨EOLN⟩
writeln (Age:1, Salary:1:2)	22_785.90⟨EOLN⟩
writeln ('Age is ', Age:1, ' years.')	Age_is__22_years.⟨EOLN⟩
write ('Age is '); write (Age:1); writeln (' years.')	Age_is__22_years.⟨EOLN⟩
writeln ('Month Day Year'); writeln; write (BirthMonth:5); write (BirthDay:5); writeln (BirthYear:5);	Month__Day__Year⟨EOLN⟩ ⟨EOLN⟩ ___11___12_1966⟨EOLN⟩
writeln ('*':Age);	_____*

FIGURE 4.3 Examples of WRITE Segments with Format Specifications

When a fraction size is specified, only the number of digits indicated for the fraction are displayed. The last digit is rounded, and any digits after the decimal point beyond the specified fraction size are not displayed.

EXERCISES

4.13 Suppose the program state contains Integer variables A, B and Sum. You want to display a line with the format:

⟨value of A⟩ + ⟨value of B⟩ = ⟨value of Sum⟩

Give a *writeln* statement that will produce this output line.

4.14 Suppose the program state contains a Boolean variable, Answer. You want to display a line with the format:

And the answer to your question is ⟨value of Answer⟩!

Give a *writeln* statement that will produce this output line. Don't forget the exclamation point!

4.15 Using the program state shown in Figure 4.3, give one or more *write* or *writeln* statements to accomplish each of the following tasks:

a. Use the values of BirthDay, BirthMonth and BirthYear to display the line:

Linda's birthday is mm/dd/yy.

Don't forget the "/" between each number and the "." at the end.

b. Display the character "*" in the kth character position on the next output line, where k is the value of variable BirthMonth. (For the state in Figure 4.3, this would display an asterisk in the 11th character position on the line.)

c. Display the line:

⟨value of FinalGrade⟩ is your final course grade.

with the grade value displayed in the 10th character position on the line.

4.16 Construct DISPLAY actions, coded in Pascal, to satisfy the following design specifications:

a. Display the column headings:

PRINCIPAL   INTEREST

Then display the numbers 33.3 and 22.2 in the column under the PRINCIPAL heading and the numbers 5.55 and 4.44 in the column under the INTEREST heading (use three *writeln* statements).

b. Display your name and address at the left margin of the screen, as though you were writing the return address on an envelope.

c. Display your name and address as in (b), but indented 10 character positions and double-spaced.

d. Display a "tic-tac-toe" board, with the first "X" already placed in the center square. Center the board on the screen (from left to right, not top to bottom):

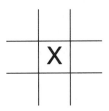

□□□ 4.6
CODING READ ACTIONS IN PASCAL

Each READ action in a pseudo-code algorithm is coded as a Pascal *readln* or *read* statement. Both *readln* (read a line) and *read* (read part of a line) statements work in the same way when your program is reading a single data value from the terminal. (There are slight differences if you are reading several values at once.) The statement has the form:

⟨READ-statement⟩ ::=

       <u>readln</u> (⟨variable-name⟩ {, ⟨variable-name⟩})
    | <u>read</u> (⟨variable-name⟩ {, ⟨variable-name⟩})

  WHERE
    ⟨variable-name⟩ ::=
      Any declared variable of the right data type for the value typed by the user.

□

Meaning: When the *readln* or *read* statement is executed, the computer pauses and waits for the user to type the desired value followed by a RETURN (the ENTER or 'end-of-line' key). The value is taken into the computer's memory, converted to the appropriate binary encoding, and stored in the variable named in the statement. If the user types a value that is of the wrong data type (a type that cannot be assigned to the ⟨variable⟩), then an error message is displayed and execution of the program may be terminated (the details depend on your Pascal system).

□□
What Can the User Type?

When a *read* or *readln* is executed, the user must respond by typing a literal value of the appropriate type and then hitting the RETURN key. What kind of value is acceptable depends on the data type of the variable named in the statement. Here are the general rules and some funny restrictions that the Pascal language imposes:

1. *If the variable is type Integer.* The user must type a Pascal Integer literal value—a sequence of decimal digits, possibly with a sign, but with no spaces, commas, or decimal point. Leading spaces are allowed, but once the number begins then the first non-digit character, including a space or RETURN, ends the number. Some Pascal systems insist that a space or RETURN be used to end the number.

2. *If the variable is type Real.* The user can type either an integer (as above) or a number with a fractional part. The number can be typed as an ordinary decimal number or in Pascal scientific notation, using the syntax for Pascal Real literal values. Again leading spaces are allowed, but after the number begins the first space or RETURN (or any character not allowed in a Real literal value) ends the number. Some Pascal systems insist that a space or RETURN be used to end the number.

3. *If the variable is type Char.* The first character the user types is taken as the value for the variable, including a space (but not a RETURN).

4. *If the variable is type Boolean. Not allowed!* If you name a variable of Boolean type in a *readln* or *read* statement, the compiler will point out your error and refuse to compile your program.

□ □
Is a Prompt Necessary?

Reading in a value is a separate operation in the computer from displaying a message on the screen. If you don't explicitly include a *writeln* or *write* statement to display a prompt that tells the user what to type, the user will see only whatever "prompt" is automatically provided by the computer system (usually something like "?"; on some systems, nothing at all). Thus unless you write the program so that it explicitly displays a prompt, the user will not know what input value your program is waiting to read.

□ □
How Long Will the Computer Wait?

Notice that the execution of a *read* or *readln* statement causes the computer to *wait* until the user has typed in a value and hit the RETURN key. Suppose you are using a program, and a friend comes by to talk. You forget to notice that the program has displayed a prompt and is waiting for you to type an input value. How long will the program wait? Forever! (Not always—on some systems, the operating system may terminate the program and log out the user after a few minutes.) The computer system will not continue to execute your program until the requested input value is typed. That's another reason that displaying a prompt is critical—the prompt alerts the user that some action is required on her part in order for execution to continue.

Reading Several Values with a Single READ Statement

If you want to read several values into different variables, you can list them all in the same *read* or *readln* statement:

readln (⟨variable⟩, ⟨variable⟩, . . .);
or read (⟨variable⟩, ⟨variable⟩, . . .);

When such a statement is executed, the program waits until the user types in *all* of the required values, following the last by a RETURN. The rules are the same as for a single value, except that the user can type the values all on the same line, with numbers separated by spaces, or on separate lines, or in some combination of the two. If separate lines are used, each is ended by a RETURN. When several values are read at once, be sure that the prompt tells the user exactly what is expected. Otherwise, the program may still be waiting for a value when the user thinks all the values required have been typed.

□ □

What If the User Makes a Typing Error?

Suppose your program asks the user to "Type a temperature value (degrees F)", and then tries to read an Integer value. The user types "NO!" or "Baloney" or −3.052 or something else that is not an integer. What happens? The computer system will notice such an error and issue a *run-time error message* that will be displayed on the user's terminal screen. Sometimes the system will allow the user to try again, but usually execution of the program is abruptly terminated. In general, whenever the user types something that is of the wrong *data type* for the variable named in the *read* or *readln* statement, an error message will appear on the terminal screen.

□ □

The Difference Between READ and READLN

When reading input data values from the user's terminal, your program may use either *readln* or *read* statements. The only difference lies in what happens to an input line typed by the user *when the line contains extra characters beyond the end of the last data value*. Suppose the user types:

⟨value⟩ . . . extra typing . . . RETURN

and the *read* or *readln* statement contains a single variable name. The first value typed will be stored in the variable as usual. Then one of two things happens, depending on whether you have used a *read* or a *readln*:

1. READLN: the extra typing (everything after the data value) is discarded by the Pascal system. The next *read* or *readln* executed will take values from the next line the user types.
2. READ: the extra typing is *saved* by the Pascal system. The next *read* or *readln* executed will take values starting with the first character of the extra typing.

□ □

Prompt and Response on the Same Display Line

Sometimes you would like to construct a "prompt-and-read" so that the prompt appears, and then the cursor is left positioned *on the same line*. When the user types an input value in response, the response continues on the same display line. For example, Florida Joe's first "prompt-and-read" is:

DISPLAY: Starting odometer reading?
READ: StartMiles

In coding this action, suppose Joe wants the prompt-and-read to appear:

```
Starting odometer reading?
                              ^
```

where the ^ indicates the cursor position. Then if the user types "27350", the display appears:

```
Starting odometer reading? 27350
```

with both the prompt and the user's response on the same line.

The secret is to use a *write* instead of a *writeln* to display the prompt. Because *write* does not end the line with an ⟨EOLN⟩, the cursor is left positioned on the same line. Either a *read* or a *readln* can be used to read the user's response, and the response will be displayed on the same line. For example, if Joe's code is:

```
write ('Starting odometer reading? ');
readln (StartMiles);
```

then he gets the display shown above, but if his code is:

```
writeln ('Starting odometer reading? ');
readln (StartMiles);
```

then he gets the display:

```
Starting odometer reading?
27350
```

EXERCISES

4.17 Construct "prompt-and-read" actions, coded in Pascal, to accomplish the following tasks:

a. Ask the user to type the number of the month, the sales for that month, and the total sales for the year, typing all three values on the same line. Read the month into SalesMonth, the sales into MonthlySales and the total sales into Annual-Sales. Use a separate *read* or *readln* statement to read each value.

b. Ask the user to type today's date in the form:

```
mm/dd/yy
```

Read in the data and store integer mm in DateMonth, dd in DateDay, and yy in DateYear. All three variables are of type Integer. *Hint:* Use an extra variable, Junk, of type Char, to read past each "/".

c. Ask the user to type a three letter name, and then display the response:

```
Hi ⟨name⟩! Let's compute!
```

Have both the prompt and the user's response appear on the same display line, followed by the line above. For example, the dialogue might be:

```
Please type your name or initials (3 letters only): Sam
Hi Sam! Let's Compute!
```

□□□ **4.7**
AN EXAMPLE OF PASCAL CODING

In the preceding sections we have explained the various Pascal declarations and statements required for coding simple programs. Let's take the algorithm that Florida Joe developed for his gas mileage program in Chapter 3 and code it as a complete Pascal program. Because of our careful attention to developing the pseudocode for the algorithm in Chapter 3, the actual work involved in the Pascal coding is small.

Figure 4.4 shows the algorithm that Joe developed. Figure 4.5 shows the Pascal program coded from this algorithm. Notice how the DATA OBJECTS list of the algorithm is coded as the VAR section of the Pascal main procedure and the AL-

ALGORITHM

INITIAL STATE: All data objects are uninitialized; screen is blank.

Step 1. PURPOSE/GOAL STATE: Ask the user for the starting and ending odometer readings and store in StartMiles and EndMiles, respectively.

ACTIONS:
1.1 DISPLAY: "Starting odometer reading?"
1.2 READ: StartMiles
1.3 DISPLAY: "Ending odometer reading?"
1.4 READ: EndMiles

Step 2. PURPOSE: Display the instructions for typing the list of gallons. Read and sum the list of gallons in each fillup.

GOAL STATE: TotalGallons contains the sum.

ACTIONS:
2.1 DISPLAY: "List gallons in each fillup, one number per line.
                     End the list with a zero value (on a separate line)."
2.2 TotalGallons : =0
2.3 READ: Gallons
2.4 WHILE Gallons <> 0 DO
            BEGIN
                TotalGallons := TotalGallons + Gallons
                READ: Gallons
            END

Step 3. PURPOSE/GOAL STATE: Compute total miles traveled and store in TotalMiles. Compute miles per gallon and store in MilesPerGallon.

ACTIONS:
3.1 TotalMiles := EndMiles − StartMiles
3.2 IF TotalGallons <> 0 THEN
            MilesPerGallon := TotalMiles / TotalGallons
      ELSE
            DISPLAY:
                "ERROR; No gallons amounts were entered."
            MilesPerGallon := 0

Step 4. PURPOSE/GOAL STATE: Display odometer readings, total miles, total gallons, and miles per gallon.

ACTIONS:
4.1 DISPLAY:
      "ODOMETER: Start of trip = ⟨StartMiles⟩
                     End of trip = ⟨EndMiles⟩
        TOTAL MILES: ⟨TotalMiles⟩
        TOTAL GALLONS: ⟨TotalGallons⟩
        MILES/GALLON: ⟨MilesPerGallon⟩"

FINAL STATE: All actions complete; all data objects contain their final values; all results are displayed.

FIGURE 4.4 Florida Joe's Gas Mileage Algorithm in Pseudo-code

DATA OBJECTS

StartMiles: Integer	Starting odometer reading; range 0–99,999
EndMiles: Integer	Ending odometer reading; range 0–99,999
Gallons: Real	Gallons in one fillup; range 0–20
TotalGallons: Real	Total gallons in all fillups; must be greater than 0
TotalMiles: Integer	Total miles traveled; range 0–99,999
MilesPerGallon: Real	Miles per gallon on the trip; must be 0 or larger

FIGURE 4.4   (continued)

```pascal
PROGRAM GasMileage (INPUT, OUTPUT);

     {PURPOSE: Computes gas mileage and total miles and gallons
          for a trip by car.
      AUTHOR: Florida Joe
      DATE WRITTEN: October 1989}

PROCEDURE ComputeMileage;

     {PURPOSE: Main program procedure -- controls overall
          execution of the program. }

  VAR
     StartMiles: Integer;     {Starting odometer reading; range
                                   0-99,999}
     EndMiles: Integer;       {Ending odometer reading; range
                                   0-99,999}
     Gallons: Real;           {Gallons in one fillup; range 0-20}
     TotalGallons: Real;      {Total gallons in all fillups; must
                                   be greater than 0}
     TotalMiles: Integer;     {Total miles traveled; range
                                   0-99,999}
     MilesPerGallon: Real;    {Miles per gallon on the trip; must
                                   be 0 or larger}
  BEGIN
          {PURPOSE/GOAL STATE: Ask the user for the starting and
          ending odometer readings and store in StartMiles and
          EndMiles, respectively. }

     write ('Starting odometer reading?');
     readln (StartMiles);
     write ('Ending odometer reading?');
     readln (EndMiles);
```

FIGURE 4.5   Pascal Program for the Gas Mileage Algorithm

```pascal
      {PURPOSE: Display the instructions for typing the list
      of gallons. Read and sum the list of gallons in each
      fillup.
      GOAL STATE: TotalGallons contains the sum.}

  writeln ('List gallons in each fillup,',
          ' one number per line.');
  writeln ('End the list with a zero value',
          ' (on a separate line).');
  TotalGallons := 0;
  readln (Gallons);
  WHILE Gallons <> 0 DO
     BEGIN
        TotalGallons := TotalGallons + Gallons;
        readln (Gallons);
     END;

      {PURPOSE/GOAL STATE: Compute total miles traveled and
      store in TotalMiles. Compute miles per gallon and
      store in MilesPerGallon.}

  TotalMiles := EndMiles - StartMiles;
  IF TotalGallons <> 0 THEN
     BEGIN
        MilesPerGallon := Total Miles / TotalGallons;
     END
  ELSE
     BEGIN
        writeln ('ERROR: No gallons amounts were entered.');
        MilesPerGallon := 0;
     END;

      {PURPOSE: Display odometer readings, total miles,
      total gallons, and miles per gallon.}

  writeln ('ODOMETER: Start of trip = ', StartMiles);
  writeln ('          End of trip = ', EndMiles);
  writeln;
  writeln ('TOTAL Miles: ', TotalMiles);
  writeln;
  writeln ('TOTAL GALLONS: ', TotalGallons:1:2);
  writeln;
  writeln ('MILES/GALLON: ', MilesPerGallon:1:2);

  END:   {procedure ComputeMileage}

BEGIN
    ComputeMileage;
END.
```

FIGURE 4.5 (continued)

GORITHM part of the algorithm is coded as the sequence of statements in the Pascal main procedure body. The important parts of the algorithm that are not directly coded into Pascal are retained as comments in the Pascal code, to aid the human reader.

EXERCISES

4.18 By looking at Joe's coded program, see if you can correctly predict what the format of the display lines will be when Joe's program is executed. Then run the program and check your answer.

□□□ **4.8**
COMPILERS AND SYNTAX ERRORS

Ordinarily the program is entered into a file in the computer, using the editor program, as you complete the coding step. Once the program is entered, it is important to check it over for typing errors. You can either display the program on your terminal screen or get a printed listing to use during this checking. Then you are ready to use the Pascal compiler to compile this "source program" to get an object program that can actually be executed by the computer. By this point, you should be familiar with your local Pascal compiler and how to use it.

□□
What the Compiler Does

Let's look a little more deeply at your interactions with the compiler. A Pascal compiler is a large and complex program. Its basic tasks are to read in your Pascal source program, line by line, to check each line for syntax errors, and to generate and write into the object program file the detailed "machine language" instructions that the computer will execute when you run your program.

A key point to remember when using most Pascal compilers is this: *the compiler scans your program once, from first line to last, and when it produces an error message that refers to a certain line it usually has not looked at any following line in your program.* It is as though someone were uncovering each line of your program one by one, and asking you, as each new line is uncovered, whether there is an error in the program.

As the compiler proceeds through your program, errors that seem minor to you can easily cause the compiler to "get confused" (because the algorithm used in the compiler program is not designed to anticipate all the errors that might occur in a source program). For example, if you forget a semicolon at the end of a statement (a minor matter to you), the compiler scans forward to the next statement in the next line as though it were a continuation of the statement in the previous line. Then the structure of the new statement does not match what the compiler algorithm anticipated would come next. The compiler "gets confused"—it can't make any sense out of the characters in the new line. When the compiler gets confused by an error in your source program, it often reports non-existent errors in the following parts of your program. These are called *spurious error messages,* and they are a major source of confusion for beginners.

What happens when the compiler finds a syntax error depends on the particular Pascal compiler that you happen to be using. Two typical reactions to a syntax error are:

1. *Integrated programming environment.* If you are using an integrated Pascal programming environment, the compiler immediately stops compiling the program and reports the error with a message on the screen. You are switched back to the editor program. The part of your program where the compiler detected the error will be displayed, with the cursor positioned at the point of the error. However, be careful here—the error message and cursor position indicate where the compiler first "got confused," but the actual error may be in an earlier line of the program, often in the immediately preceding line.

2. *Separate Pascal compiler.* If the compiler is a separate program that you invoke by a command to the operating system, then the compiler usually will *not* stop at the first syntax error. Instead, it is designed to report the error (by displaying an error message) and then try to continue compiling the program. Sometimes the attempt to continue is successful, and the compiler may detect further syntax errors at later points in your program, so that a single attempt to compile the program gives you information about almost all the errors that you need to repair. However, sometimes the attempt to continue fails—the compiler remains "confused" and reports non-existent errors in many later parts of the program. It is not unusual for one small error early in your program to cause a Pascal compiler to generate a cascade of *dozens* of spurious error messages reporting errors in parts of your program that are entirely correct. You may think your program is a complete disaster when there is really only one minor spelling or punctuation error!

EXAMPLE In Florida Joe's program in Figure 4.5, suppose Joe misspells the word "Integer" in the first variable declaration and forgets the semicolon, so that the line reads:

```
VAR
    StartMiles: Intereger          {Starting odometer. . .}
    EndMiles: Integer;             {Ending odometer. . .}
```

The compiler ignores comments, indentation, and spacing, so the compiler sees these lines as:

```
VAR StartMiles: Intereger EndMiles: Integer; . . .
```

The compiler "gets confused" because this syntax is not that of a valid Pascal declaration.

Suppose the compiler tries to continue by skipping to the semicolon at the end of the second declaration, in the process skipping the declarations for StartMiles and EndMiles (because they do not appear to be valid Pascal). Then *every later statement* that refers to either StartMiles or EndMiles will be marked with a spurious error message: "Undeclared variable." There are six such statements, so Joe's minor error in the first declaration causes a cascade of six spurious error messages in later parts of the program that are entirely correct. ∎

□ □
Types of Syntax Errors

Here are some common types of syntax errors that may cause a compiler to get confused and report spurious errors:

1. *Misspelled or missing reserved word.* For example, writing "BGIN" instead of "BEGIN". A compiler has no concept of "almost right" in spelling—every character must be correct.

2. *Incorrect or missing punctuation.* For example, using "=" instead of ":" in a variable declaration, or forgetting a semicolon. Indentation and line breaks are meaningless to the compiler; only precisely correct punctuation counts.

3. *Misspelled variable name in a declaration.* For example, typing "Zotal" instead of "Total" in a declaration. The compiler will detect every use of the variable "Total" in a later statement as an "undeclared variable" error.

4. *Missing ending brace, "}", on a comment.* This error causes very mysterious error messages, because the compiler *skips everything until it finds the next ending brace,* which is usually at the end of the next comment several lines further down in your program. All the statements or declarations in between the two comments have been ignored by the compiler—effectively they have disappeared from your program!

5. *Missing END in a BEGIN. . .END pair.* When you forget an END, the compiler sometimes only will discover that BEGIN's and END's are not properly paired when it reaches the final END of your program body. In between it may be very confused about your program's structure.

□ □
Finding and Correcting Syntax Errors

A good rule of thumb in analyzing syntax error messages produced by the Pascal compiler is this: *assume that the first message indicates the point where the compiler first got confused—there is probably an error at that point or immediately before that point.* Beware, however, of "fixing" a correct statement or declaration simply because the compiler indicates an error. Be sure you have identified the actual error before you make a change in the program.

EXERCISES

4.19 Take a Pascal program that you have available and intentionally introduce one of the syntax errors described above. Then compile the program. Does the compiler generate spurious error messages?

□□□ 4.9
TESTING AND DEBUGGING

When you have successfully compiled your program without errors, the next step is program testing.

□□ What is Program Testing?

Program testing means using the program to determine if the program correctly implements its design and satisfies its requirements. During testing you try out the program, just as if you were a user of the finished product. You provide some test input data values for the program and observe the results that are displayed or printed. Does the program work correctly? Do you like the way the program output looks? Is it confusing or difficult to use for some reason?

If the program is not acceptable to you as user, then you have to make corrections. For minor corrections, you change the Pascal code. More difficult cases may require redesigning the algorithm and recoding part of the program. You may even discover that some element in the original requirements needs correction, introducing a related set of changes in several parts of the program.

After you have made the required changes and have verified that you made them correctly, you compile the program again to get a new object program file. Then you continue your testing with the modified program.

□□ Debugging

A *bug* is an error in your program that causes the program results to be incorrect. The process of finding and correcting these errors is *debugging*. If the program results are wrong then you know the program contains a "bug"—but *where*? Finding out where is the central problem of debugging.

Testing can be fun—if your program works the way you expected. You finally are seeing the results you envisioned on the computer screen! However, testing can also be difficult and tedious if your program does not work the way you wanted it to, and you have to find and correct several bugs.

□□ How Much Time Should Testing Take?

A rule of thumb in large projects is that testing and debugging the program will take roughly *one-third* of the total time and effort for the project. Think about it—you have finished all the design and coding, and you have compiled the whole program without error—and you are only two-thirds done!

Thorough testing of a complex program takes a long time, even if no errors are detected. But each error can take a long time to track down and repair—*hours* for a simple error, *days* for a more subtle error. Every experienced programmer can tell you horror stories about subtle bugs in programs that took many days of detective work to pinpoint and repair.

Errors can be introduced at any point during the development of a program. The requirements can be incorrect; the algorithm can be incorrect; the Pascal code can be incorrect. An error introduced at an early stage in development tends to enlarge in its impact as development proceeds. For example, a small error in stating the requirements for the program may cause you to develop several parts of the algorithm incorrectly, which can lead to dozens of lines of Pascal code that are incorrect. When such an error is detected during testing, it requires a lot of time and effort to correct. On the other hand, an error introduced late in program development, such as an error in coding a Pascal statement, is usually easily repaired.

These facts lead to a simple rule that can save you many hours of time in the development of any program:

The earlier an error is found during the development
of a program, the faster and easier it is to correct.

Experienced programmers make a point of carefully verifying the requirements before they proceed to the design of the program. Then they carefully verify the program design before they proceed to coding. And they check the coding before they proceed to testing. They want to get each stage correct before they proceed to the next. Their goal is to *make it run correctly from the first test*. Testing proceeds quickly and smoothly when there are no bugs to track down. Debugging is what takes most of the time during testing.

□ □
What Can Go Wrong?

One of the reasons program debugging is difficult is that during testing the program is like a *black box*—its internal data state is hidden. During testing you run the program, you give it some input data values, and it produces some results (usually). But you cannot see what is going on inside the program as it executes—its data states or its actions. All you see is what is displayed on the screen. From that you have to deduce whether the program is operating correctly, and if it isn't, you have to deduce exactly what went wrong.

Here are some ways that you might see a program behave during testing if it contains an error:

1. *Incorrect results are displayed.* Most obviously, the program might run as expected, but display the wrong answer for the test input data that you provided. Easy to spot, right? *Wrong!* To know the answer is wrong, you have to know what the *right* answer is. But if the program is doing something complicated, you may not be sure what the answer should be. You may have to sit down with a calculator and figure out by hand what the right answer is, just to be able to tell if the program has computed the right answer.

2. *Confusing or garbled output results or requests for input data are displayed.* These obvious errors involve minor details of displaying output results or

prompting for input data values. Such errors are usually easy to find and fix because the error can immediately be associated with a particular DISPLAY or READ action.

3. *The program "hangs"*. These errors are among the most frustrating. The program seems to work correctly for a while, perhaps producing some of the expected output results, and then it seems to get stuck and proceed no further. We say the program *hangs* at some point. It does not stop, it does not ask for more input, it does not do anything further that is visible to you. You sit and wait, but nothing further happens. You may have to "kill" the program (by hitting a special key sequence to signal the operating system to stop the program). The most common cause of this problem is when an error in the program leads to an *infinite loop*—the program enters a WHILE loop and keeps repeating the loop over-and-over "forever." If the loop contains no WRITE or READ statement, then the program continues to run with no change visible on the display screen.

4. *An infinite WRITE loop or READ loop occurs*. In an infinite WRITE loop, the program enters an infinite WHILE loop that contains a WRITE statement, and it then proceeds to produce a cascade of output—often page after page of useless information. You feel like the Sorcerer's Apprentice—you've created a program monster! An infinite READ loop is similar: the program asks for some input data, you type it in, the program asks again, you type it again, and so on until you figure out that the program is hanging in an infinite WHILE loop that contains a READ statement.

5. *A Pascal run-time error message is displayed and program execution terminates*. If your program attempts an action that is clearly incorrect for *any* program to try, such as attempting to read an Integer value that is larger than MAXINT, attempting to divide by zero, or attempting to take the square root of a negative number, the error will be detected by the Pascal system. An error message, such as "ATTEMPTED DIVISION BY ZERO" will usually be displayed and execution of the program will be terminated immediately. Every Pascal system is different in exactly what run-time errors are detected and what happens when one is detected. Check your *Pascal User's Manual* for details about your system.

□ □
Preparing for Testing

Before you start testing a program, prepare for testing in four ways:

1. *Have a program listing in hand*. During testing you will need to look at a listing of your source program, in order to trace through the program statements that are being executed and determine if the results on the screen match what you intended. Get a printed listing of your source program before you start testing.

2. *Know how to stop and start the display*. If your program displays more than a few lines of results, you may find that the first results "scroll" off the top of the screen before you have a chance to read them, to make room for new lines being displayed at the bottom. Most systems have a way to stop the display of new lines temporarily, so that you can read what is already on the screen. Then you can restart the display and let it continue as before. Learn how to stop and restart the display of results on the screen before you start testing. One widely used method is to type CTRL-s (hold down the CTRL key and type "s") to stop the display and then type CTRL-q to restart it, but your system may use a different method.

3. *Know how to "kill" a running program.* Before you start testing your program, be sure that you know how to *kill* (or *abort*) a running program, that is, how to terminate its execution prematurely. As you can see from the list above, several bad things might happen when the program starts to run, and you might have to kill it without completing the test run.

Remember that the operating system of your computer is always in overall control. The operating system can terminate execution of your program if you request it. A common way to kill a running program is to hit a particular key (or key sequence) on the terminal. This keystroke signals the operating system to kill the program. However, every operating system is different. Find out how yours works before you start program testing.

4. *Have a testing strategy.* A *testing strategy* is a plan for how to test a program. Professionals usually develop a testing strategy during the design of the program—as they design, they also plan how to test each part of the resulting program. Testing large programs is done in phases: first the parts are tested individually, and then in larger groups, until finally all the parts are put together and the whole program is tested. For simpler programs, a testing strategy involves two elements:

a. *Choose test input data.* Before you start testing, decide what input data values you will use to test the program, and determine what the correct results should be for each set of test data values.

b. *Decide what additional "debug" output you need to tell if each test run worked properly.* Decide if you need to insert extra *debug WRITE statements* to provide additional information about the data state of the program during a test run.

Let's look at these two parts of a testing strategy in more detail.

Choosing Test Data

The source of test data is the *requirements* for the program. The requirements tell you the *range* of allowed input values for each input data item. The primary goal of testing is to exercise the program through the full range of input data allowed by its requirements. However, even a simple program is likely to allow a large range of possible input values, larger than you can reasonably test completely. You have to be smart about choosing test data to get the "most bang for the buck"—the most thorough testing with the fewest test cases.

Take the requirements for the program and choose your test data based on these rules of thumb:

1. *Easy: Test one or more simple "standard cases."* The first tests should always be of very simple cases, to test that the program has no major errors that will affect every test run.

2. *Moderate: Test the input data for each requirement separately, while keeping the other input data invariant.* The next set of tests should keep most of the input data of one of the simple tests the same, but vary *one input data item.* For the item that is varying, test the different cases allowed by the requirements, particularly the *extremes* of its range (such as zero values, negative values, or very large values). If an error results then you know the bug is probably in the actions related to the varying value.

3. *Hard: Test combinations of input values.* A final set of tests should be the hardest ones you can think up. Choose combinations of input values that you think are the most likely to cause the program to fail. Pay particular attention to combinations of extreme values that are allowed by the requirements but that are unlikely to come up in ordinary use of the program.

□ □

Can You Break It?

When you have just completed developing a program and are ready to start testing, the natural inclination is to choose test data that will show how well your program performs. So you choose tests that will demonstrate your good work—the "easy" and "moderate" tests discussed above—but you hesitate to go any further in testing. That attitude is exactly *wrong* for testing a program!

To test a program, you have to change hats: no longer are you the programmer building a correct, elegant program; now you are the mean-spirited *program breaker*—and your job is not to show that the program works, but to show that it *doesn't work*! After your "easy" and "moderate" tests have shown that the program appears to be working correctly, you want to enter the final stage of testing where you choose test data that intentionally tries to *break the program*—that is, you try to make it fail (Figure 4.6). If your program holds up under the hardest tests you can invent, then you are a successful programmer.

THE "BLACK TEAM"

One of the earliest and best known testing teams in the computer industry was a group formed by a major computer manufacturer back in the early 1960s—a group that became known as the *Black Team.* This group was given responsibility for the final testing of major programs before they were delivered to the customers. This testing team took the "can you break it?" attitude to the limit. They enjoyed devising fiendish tests for each new piece of software that the company's programmers produced.

As the group developed, they took increasing delight in their role as program breakers. They began to dress in black (hence the "Black Team" name), grew long wicked mustaches, and cackled with delight when they found a bug in some program—to the chagrin of any development programmers who happened to be watching. The Black Team was a huge success—at testing!

PROGRAMMMER

I'll show you how nicely my program works!

PROGRAM TESTER

Just give me a chance to break it! I'll find those bugs!

FIGURE 4.6   Program Testing: Be a Program BREAKER!

Professional programming teams often divide into two groups. One group is responsible for developing the program. The second group is responsible for testing it. The first group tries to make the program *unbreakable* (no errors). The second group tries to break it.

□ □

Path Testing

Program testing is closely related to the ideas of *control paths* and *control flow analysis* used to verify the correctness of an algorithm. Remember the two verification questions from Chapter 3:

1. Under what conditions will this control path be chosen for execution, and are those the right conditions?
2. Assuming this control path is chosen for execution, will the actions on the path correctly compute and display the required output values (according to the program's requirements)?

Each choice of test data for the program determines what control path will be taken during program execution. The actions along that control path determine whether the correct results are computed and displayed.

In choosing test data, it does little good to "exercise" the same control path repeatedly because the same statements will be executed in the same sequence on each test run. Instead you want to exercise as many *different control paths* as you can, to test *different statements* and *different sequences of statements*. In these tests, you are asking:

1. Do the test data values cause the *correct execution path to be chosen,* and
2. Does the computation on that path cause the *correct results to be computed and displayed?*

Path testing is the name used for testing based on knowledge of the control paths in the program, testing that tries to exercise as many different control paths as possible. Path testing is used by many professionals as a testing strategy because it provides thorough testing with a minimum number of test runs—you can avoid the wasted effort of testing the same control path repeatedly.

Consider how our easy, moderate, and hard test cases correspond to control paths in your program:

1. *Easy:* You are testing the simplest, shortest control paths in the program, such as paths that go only once around each loop and that take the "usual" branch in each IF.
2. *Moderate:* You are taking an easy control path and making only a small change, such as including zero trips or multiple trips through one of the loops or taking the "unusual" branch of an IF.
3. *Hard:* You are combining moderate control paths into the most complex and unlikely combinations.

Path testing is a good testing strategy for programs that you have written. Because you are already familiar with the control paths in your program, you can easily choose test data to exercise the different paths. When testing a program written by someone else, working from the program's requirements without looking at the internal structure of the program is usually the simpler strategy.

□ □
Robust Programs

We say a program is *robust* if it always "fails gracefully" when given *incorrect* input data. If a program is not robust, even a minor error in the input data may cause the program to hang or terminate abruptly with no error message (or a meaningless one). Worse, the program may simply compute with the erroneous input data and produce results that are wrong but appear to be correct. When the input data is incorrect, you expect the program to fail, but it should *fail gracefully*—for example, by displaying a meaningful error message and terminating. The most robust program design is one that displays an error message and then allows the user to *reenter* the incorrect data correctly.

Testing should also include runs using incorrect test data, representing errors that the user might be expected to make when using the program. With these runs you are testing how robust the program is. If the program does not fail gracefully, consider whether there is a simple way to have the program check for that error and display a meaningful error message.

Finding Bugs: The Cardinal Rule of Debugging

Remember that a bug is the error in the program that *causes* things to go wrong. Simply knowing a bug exists may not tell you much about where to find the bug. How do you start debugging a program that has an error?

There is a simple, general strategy for debugging a program with an error:

□ **The Cardinal Rule of Debugging**

To find a bug in a program, first find two program states:

1. A *correct state,* where no error has yet occurred, and
2. An *incorrect state following the correct state,* where the error has already occurred.

The bug must be in one of the actions on the control path taken to get from the first state to the second. Analyze that control path to find the error.

To apply this debugging rule, you need two kinds of information about the execution of the program: (1) what *sequence of states* the program went through during its execution, so that you can pin down a correct state preceding the later incorrect one, and (2) what *control path* led from the correct state to the incorrect one. How do you get this information?

The *program listing* is essential to show you the possible control paths in the program. You look at the listing and find the WRITE statements that display the output from the *correct* program state. Then you trace through the control path that leads from there to the WRITE statements that display the results from the *incorrect* program state. The "Cardinal Rule" says that the bug must be somewhere in the statements and tests on that control path.

Debug WRITE Statements

Often the DISPLAY actions in the program do not provide enough information about intermediate program states during the program's execution. To apply the "Cardinal Rule," you need detailed information about whether the intermediate states are correct.

There is an easy way to find out more about the intermediate states that the

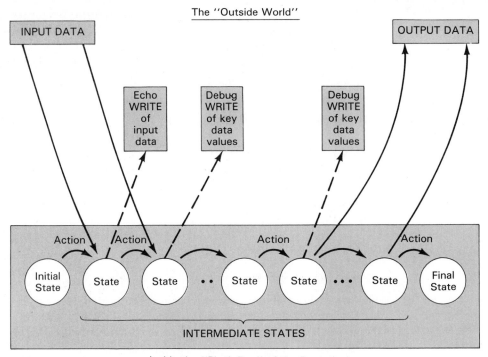

FIGURE 4.7 Debug WRITE Statements Penetrate the Black Box

program went through during its execution: In your program, put extra WRITE (*writeln* or *write*) statements in at key points to display the data state. Then when your program runs, it will display these intermediate states for you as it proceeds. You can check each one, and when you see a correct state displayed followed by an incorrect state, you are in position to apply the "Cardinal Rule."

WRITE statements used in this way during program testing and debugging are called *debug WRITE statements*. Note that they have nothing to do with the WRITE statements that display the regular output of the program—they are just used while testing and debugging the program. Figure 4.7 illustrates what debug WRITE statements do for you.

Consider using debug WRITE statements in the following places in any program:

1. *"Echo" all input data values.* A common source of bugs lies in failure to correctly READ input data values. If you use a debug WRITE statement to immediately display input values after they are read (called *echoing* the input data), then you will know whether the program begins the main part of its computation with a correct data state.

2. *Display the key data values after each major step in the algorithm.* It is unreasonable to display every data value after every action. But you need to be able to check that after each major step, the key values in the data state are still correct. Use debug WRITE statements to display these values after each major step.

After testing is complete, you can remove debug WRITE statements before you make the program available for others to use. However, a better method is to leave the debug WRITE statements in the final program, protected by an IF statement that tests a "debugging flag":

```
IF DEBUGGING THEN
    BEGIN
        〈debug WRITE statements〉
    END
```

If the DEBUGGING flag is TRUE, then the debug WRITE's are executed; otherwise they are skipped. The advantage of this method comes if you modify the program and then need to retest it. In the next chapter, after we have the Pascal concepts we need, we come back to the details of how to create and use a "debugging flag."

Tracing Program Execution

Many Pascal systems provide a useful alternative to debug WRITE statements— *automatic tracing facilities*. Remember the idea of *hand tracing* program execution—"playing computer" and executing each program action by hand? Many Pascal systems have automatic tracing facilities that allow you to display information about the states that the program has reached during its execution and about the statements executed by the program, without changing the program itself.

Usually you have to "turn on" the tracing facilities when you compile the program. Then when it runs, information about the program's execution will be automatically displayed for you. Exactly what information is available from such a trace depends on your Pascal system, but typically you may be able to find out which statements were executed and the values of certain variables at key points. Read your local *Pascal User's Manual* to find out what automatic tracing facilities are available on your system—they can save you hours of debugging time.

Fixing Bugs

Once you have pinned down the section of the program that is causing the error, analyze that section carefully to find exactly what is wrong and to determine a strategy for fixing it.

The problem with any change to a program is that it may introduce new errors—one bug is fixed, but a new bug (or several) has been introduced. The more complex the change, the more likely you are to introduce new bugs. Analysis skills, such as control flow analysis and others introduced in later chapters, provide the basic skills needed to find an error quickly and make a repair to the program safely.

□ □
Errors Caused by System Malfunctions

Is it possible that an error during execution of your program was caused by some malfunction of the computer system itself—by an error in the hardware or the Pascal system software? When faced with a bug that seems unexplainable, the beginner usually suspects "a computer error." However, it seldom is the computer hardware or software that has failed. Of course, both hardware and software are constructed by people, who can (and do) make errors, and some parts of the hardware may actually wear out and cause errors. However, you usually can easily detect a hardware or software failure because something rather drastic happens—such as your terminal display suddenly goes blank, or the keyboard on the display no longer responds when you type. In 99.99999 percent of cases, an error that you find during testing will be caused by your own "programmer error."

□ □
What Does Testing Prove?

Testing helps you to detect errors; but no reasonable amount of testing can guarantee the *absence* of all errors. Put another way: *Testing can show a program is wrong, but it can never show the program is completely right.*

To completely test a program you would have to try it out with every possible input data set that the program requirements allow—usually far too many to test. For example, if the program simply added two numbers and displayed the result, complete testing would require that you try all possible pairs of input numbers.

If you have tested a program reasonably well, with a variety of test data sets, then you know "for sure" only that the program works correctly when run with those input values. You cannot be entirely sure what the program will do with any other input data. Frustrating, isn't it? Not only is testing tedious and time-consuming, but when you are finished you still have no guarantee that the program will work correctly in all cases.

If you put testing together with analyzing and verifying that the algorithm and program code are correct, you have a much more powerful combination than with either one alone. The advantage of testing is that the program is actually being executed by the computer, just as if it were being used. If you have misunderstood some part of the Pascal language or some aspect of the computer system that affects the correctness of your program, then testing will probably uncover the error (and analysis and verification probably will not). On the other hand, if there is a logic error in your design, then analysis and verification are more likely to uncover the error, and uncover it earlier, during design or coding, where it is easily repaired.

EXERCISES

4.20 Take a Pascal program and intentionally insert a statement that divides by zero. Compile and run the program. What happens on your Pascal system when the division by zero is executed?

4.21 For Florida Joe's program in Figure 4.5, determine two key points where debug WRITE statements might be used effectively to display intermediate data states. Which values in the state would you choose to display at each point?

4.22 Determine if your Pascal system provides any automatic *tracing* facilities that can be used to trace the execution of a program. Determine how to use these facilities for your programs.

4.23 For Florida Joe's program in Figure 4.5, make a list of the test input data that you would choose to be most likely to *break* the program. First, work only from the program's requirements—don't look at the internal structure of the Pascal code. Then try looking at the *control paths* in the program and choose test data to exercise each control path. Are the resulting test data sets the same? Which is likely to be the most effective? Which is easier to generate?

□□□ **4.10**
DOCUMENTING A PROGRAM

Testing is complete, and your program is working correctly. You now have a new piece of computer software! You can keep the program for your own personal use, or you can make it available to other users of your computer system. To make it available to others, all that is usually required is to copy the object program into a public file that others can access. Another user can then run the program simply by knowing the right file name. (Of course, no one else is likely to want to use the programs you write while you are learning, but you can look forward to the day when you begin to write programs "for real.")

□□
The User's Manual

Other users need to know how to use any new piece of software. The *User's Manual* provides the information. At a minimum, the *User's Manual* explains the purpose of the program, how to run it, and generally what it expects as input data and what it produces as results. For a simple program, the *User's Manual* may just be a page or less in length. For a more complex program like a compiler or an editor it may run to the length of a small book.

□□
Internal Program Documentation

Any piece of software that will be used by others needs *internal documentation* that describes the algorithms on which the program is based and other elements of the program design. If you have developed your program from a pseudo-code algorithm, then most of this information will already be captured in comments within the Pascal program itself. Your original requirements specification also provides useful documentation that should be retained.

□ □
Program "Maintenance"

Who uses this internal program documentation? Almost every program requires changes at some point after it has been used for a while. There may be errors to be fixed that escaped detection during testing, and often there are new features that users want added to the program to make it more useful. These activities are termed *maintenance* of the program. Some programmer will have to make these changes to the program. The internal documentation provides the information needed for that programmer to do the work successfully.

□ □ □ 4.11
PROGRAM IT WITH STYLE!

Program style refers to the choices that an individual programmer makes in coding a program—choices that have no effect on how *correct* the program is, but choices that greatly affect how *readable* and *understandable* the program is to another person (including yourself when you come back to it a few weeks later). In this section we gather together some tidbits about good programming style.

□ □
The Basic Rule: Capture the Design in the Code

The most critical element of good style is to "capture the design in the code." As you code your algorithm from its pseudo-code description, include (as comments in the code):

1. The PURPOSE, AUTHOR, and DATE WRITTEN as a header comment for the overall program and the main procedure.
2. The PURPOSE of each data object, including the *units of measure* and *range of allowed values* where appropriate.
3. The PURPOSE and GOAL STATE of each step in the algorithm.

Your goal is to use comments in the code to capture the overall design of the algorithm, so that a person reading the code can see the larger picture of the algorithm's structure. Do *not* use comments to describe in detail *how* individual actions or steps work—for that information the Pascal statements should "speak for themselves."

□ □
Meaningful Identifiers are Important

Individual Pascal statements are made readable when the names for data objects (variables) are carefully chosen to reflect what the data object represents. Hackers often use cryptic, abbreviated names (identifiers) because they are simpler to *write*. For example, a hacker might choose "Var1" as the name for our data object "TotalMiles" in Florida Joe's program. It is shorter and easier to write, but meaningless to the reader. The extra effort to find a meaningful name is one of the key elements in a good programming style. A noun or short noun phrase makes the best name for most data objects. For Boolean variables that serve as "flags," try a phrase that begins with a form of the verb "to be", for example, "IsOnProbation" or "IsExempt". To help make an identifier readable, capitalize each individual word within it, as we do in all our examples.

□ □
Use Blank Lines, Spacing, and Indentation

Use plenty of "white space" to make the program more readable by visually setting apart the important elements. Some style guidelines for white space are:

1. Use a blank line between steps in the algorithm.
2. Never put more than one variable declaration or statement per line.
3. Indent each declaration and statement from the VAR or BEGIN that begins the section of code.
4. Within an IF or WHILE, indent statements within each BEGIN. . .END pair.
5. Within an ASSIGN, put spaces on either side of ":=". Use spaces to set off the major operations in a formula (lowest precedence) from the minor ones (highest precedence). For example, instead of writing:

```
Average:=(Exam1*0.6+Exam2*0.4)/2
```

use spaces to make it more readable:

```
Average := (Exam1*0.6 + Exam2*0.4) / 2
```

Some programmers like to use tabs to align the ":=" in a sequence of assignment statements to improve readability. For example:

```
ReportDay     := 1;
ReportMonth   := 1;
ReportYear    := 1980;
```

6. In a variable declaration, use tabs to align vertically the beginning of the PURPOSE comment for each variable.

□ □
Coding READ/WRITE Statements

Inside your program, when coding the details of READ and WRITE statements:

1.   Remember that WRITE statements are often long and rather complex. If a WRITE statement must extend to more than one line in your program body, break it at a comma (between two output items) or some other natural point, rather than just

whenever you hit the edge of the terminal screen. Then indent the second line beyond the start of the first line, so that it is obvious that the second line is just a continuation of the first and not a separate statement.

    2. Keep the WRITE statements that prompt the user for input together with the READ statements that read the input values, to make a "prompt-and-read" sequence.

□ □
Style in Designing the User Interface

There is another aspect to good programming style: attention to the details of how information appears on the display screen. The *user interface* of a program is the term used to refer to the overall characteristics of how the program interacts with a user of the program—is the program easy to use without a lot of training?, is it clear what the output means?, and so forth. A program can be completely correct and satisfy all its requirements, but still have a poor user interface because it is hard to use.

    In designing the user interface, put yourself "in the user's shoes." Some things to think about:

1. Make your output self-explanatory, by including enough extra information so that the user can tell immediately what each output value represents. Joe's output is a good example—each output number is accompanied by a phrase showing what it represents.

2. Use format specifications in WRITE statements to position the output data on each line so it is easy to read.

3. When prompting the user for an input value, include in the prompt the *meaning* of the value, the *format* of the value, and the *unit of measure* for the value, if appropriate. For example, suppose your program needs to prompt the user to type the "month". If you use the prompt:

```
        Please type the month.
```

then the user might type "March", "MAR", or 3. If you expect only an integer in the range 1–12, a better prompt is:

```
        Please type the month (1-12).
```

4. Expect that the user will sometimes make typing errors when entering an input value. As soon as your program reads an input value, try to *validate* that the input value is a reasonable value, for example, by checking whether the value is within the allowed range for that data item. If there is an error, give the user another chance to reenter the value correctly if possible.

□ □ □ **4.12**
PASCAL SUMMARY

This section serves as a convenient reference for the main points of Pascal covered in this chapter.

□□ Overall Form of a Pascal Program

⟨PASCAL-program⟩ ::=

```
PROGRAM ⟨program-name⟩ (INPUT, OUTPUT);
    ⟨program-header-comment⟩
PROCEDURE ⟨main-procedure-name⟩;
    ⟨procedure-header-comment⟩          Algorithm
  VAR
      ⟨variable-declarations⟩    ⟵── DATA OBJECTS list
  BEGIN
      ⟨statements⟩               ⟵── ALGORITHM part
  END;
BEGIN
    ⟨main-procedure-name⟩;
END.
```

□□ Identifiers

An *identifier*:

1. Must begin with a letter, and
2. May contain only letters and digits.

□□ Comments

A *comment* is any text enclosed by {. . .} or (*. . .*). A *header comment* should begin the main program and each procedure. At a minimum the header comment should specify:

- PURPOSE—a brief description of the task performed by the program or procedure.
- AUTHOR—the programmer's name.
- DATE WRITTEN—when the program or procedure was coded.

□□ The VAR Section of the Main Procedure

A DATA OBJECTS list is coded as the VAR section of the main procedure:

⟨variable-declarations-section⟩ ::=

```
VAR
   ⟨variable-name⟩: ⟨data-type-name⟩; ⟨purpose⟩
 {⟨variable-name⟩: ⟨data-type-name⟩; ⟨purpose⟩}
```

WHERE

⟨variable-name⟩ ::=
    Name used for the data object in the DATA OBJECTS list (modified if
    necessary to make it a valid Pascal identifier).

⟨data-type-name⟩ ::=
    Data type from the DATA OBJECTS list—for now, one of the types Real,
    Integer, Boolean, or Char.

⟨purpose⟩ ::=
    A Pascal comment that describes the *purpose, range of possible values,* and
    units of measure of the variable (again taken from the DATA OBJECTS
    list).

□ □
The Body of the Main Procedure

The ALGORITHM part of the algorithm is coded as the body of the main procedure:

⟨procedure-body⟩ ::=

```
BEGIN
        ⟨sequence of Pascal statements⟩
END;
```

Each statement ends with a semicolon (simplified Pascal punctuation rule).

□ □
IF and WHILE Statements

These control statements have the form:

```
⟨IF-statement⟩ ::=

    IF ⟨test⟩ THEN
      BEGIN
        ⟨sequence of Pascal statements⟩
      END
    {ELSE IF ⟨test⟩ THEN
      BEGIN
        ⟨sequence of Pascal statements⟩
      END}
    [ELSE
      BEGIN
        ⟨sequence of Pascal statements⟩
      END];

⟨WHILE-statement⟩ ::=
    WHILE ⟨test⟩ DO
      BEGIN
        ⟨sequence of Pascal statements⟩
      END;
```

□□ Assignment Statements

The general form is:

⟨ASSIGNMENT-statement⟩ ::=

⟨variable-name⟩ := ⟨expression⟩

WHERE
⟨variable-name⟩ ::= Pascal name of the data object.
⟨expression⟩ ::= Pascal form of the pseudo-code formula.

□□ Literal Values

The syntax for writing literal values of the basic data types is:

⟨Integer-literal-value⟩ ::=

[+ | -] ⟨digits⟩

⟨Real-literal-value⟩ ::=

[+ | -] ⟨digits⟩.⟨digits⟩
| [+ | -] ⟨digits⟩ [.⟨digits⟩] E [+ | -] ⟨digits⟩

⟨Boolean-literal-value⟩ ::=

TRUE | FALSE

⟨Char-literal-value⟩ ::=

'⟨character⟩' | ''''

WHERE
⟨digits⟩ ::= ⟨digit⟩ {⟨digit⟩}
⟨digit⟩ ::= 0 | 1 | 2 | 3 | 4 | 5 | 6 | 7 | 8 | 9
⟨character⟩ ::=
    Any character on the keyboard, except ' (single quote).

□ □ Predefined Operations

■ ARITHMETIC:

- \+   (addition)
- \–   (subtraction)
- *   (multiplication)
- /   (division producing a REAL result)
- DIV   (division of integers, producing an Integer quotient)
- MOD   (Integer remainder after division of two integers)

■ RELATIONAL:

- =   (equal?)
- <>   (not equal?)
- <   (less than?)
- <=   (less than or equal?)
- >   (greater than?)
- >=   (greater than or equal?)

■ BOOLEAN:

- AND   (Are both tests TRUE?)
- OR   (Is at least one test TRUE?)
- NOT   (Is the test FALSE?)

■ IN (set membership):

⟨variable⟩ IN [⟨list of literal values⟩]

□ □ Order of Evaluation of Expressions

1. Function calls.
2. Parenthesized subexpressions.
3. Operations in order of precedence:

```
NOT
*   /   DIV   MOD   AND
+   -   OR
=  <>   <   >   <=  >=   IN
```

4. Left to right order for operations of equal precedence.

□ □ WRITE Statements

⟨WRITE-statements⟩ ::=

<u>writeln</u> [(⟨output item⟩ {, ⟨output item⟩})]
| <u>write</u> [(⟨output item⟩ {, ⟨output item⟩})]

WHERE
⟨output-item⟩ ::=
⟨literal-string⟩

| ⟨expression⟩[:⟨field-width⟩[:⟨fraction-size⟩]]
⟨literal-string⟩ ::= '. . .any sequence of characters. . .'
⟨expression⟩ ::= Any Pascal expression.
⟨field-width⟩ ::=
An Integer-valued Pascal expression with a value in the range 1 to the
width of the terminal screen or page, usually 80 for a screen.
⟨fraction-size⟩ ::=
An Integer-valued Pascal expression with a value in the range 1 to the
maximum number of digits allowed to the right of the decimal point in
the particular Pascal system, usually less than 20.

□ □
READ Statements

⟨READ-statement⟩ ::=

readln (⟨variable-name⟩ {, ⟨variable-name⟩})
| read (⟨variable-name⟩ {, ⟨variable-name⟩})

WHERE
⟨variable-name⟩ ::=
Any declared variable of the right data type for the value typed by the user.

■ ■ ■
REVIEW QUESTIONS

4.1 Show the *overall form* of a Pascal program—the elements that appear in every
program.

4.2 Define the rules for constructing a valid Pascal *identifier*.

4.3 What is a *reserved word* in Pascal?

4.4 Give two ways of delimiting a Pascal *comment*.

4.5 What elements should appear in a *header comment* for a program or procedure?

4.6 Distinguish between a *syntactic error*, a *semantic error*, and a *logic error* in a
program.

4.7 Explain how a DATA OBJECTS list is coded in Pascal.

4.8 The numbers used in a program may represent data using different *units of measure*.
Explain who is responsible for keeping track of units of measure in a program, and why?

4.9 What is the allowed *range* for Integer values in Pascal? Name the *two kinds of
limits on Real values* in Pascal.

4.10 Explain how to code an ALGORITHM part into a sequence of Pascal statements, including the coding of IF and WHILE actions.

4.11 Give the rules for writing *literal values* in Pascal, for the basic Integer, Real,
Boolean, and Char types.

4.12 Give the basic form of a Pascal *assignment statement*. Explain the rules governing the *data type* of the value assigned and the data type of the receiving variable.

4.13 Show how to code a *mathematical formula* as a Pascal *expression,* including the rules for coding of the basic arithmetic operations and mathematical functions, the use of parentheses, the order of evaluation, and the data type of the result.

4.14 Explain how to code a *test* as a Pascal Boolean-valued expression, using *relational operations, Boolean operations,* and the *IN test* correctly.

4.15 What is a *flag variable?*

4.16 Explain how the *ordering of Char values* is determined.

4.17 Give the patterns for coding (a) a *range test,* (b) converting a *Char digit* to an *Integer value,* and vice versa.

4.18 What is a *precondition* of an expression? Give three examples of types of preconditions that arise in Pascal expressions.

4.19 Describe the form of a Pascal *output line.*

4.20 Show how to code DISPLAY actions as Pascal *writeln* and *write* statements, including the use of *blank lines, field width specifications,* and *fraction size specifications* to give a desired format to the output lines.

4.21 What is a *default format?* Explain the default formats in Pascal for display of the four basic types of data values.

4.22 Show how to code READ actions as Pascal *readln* and *read* statements. Explain what the user is allowed to type in response to a READ using variables of the four basic data types.

4.23 What information should a *prompt* give the user before a READ statement is executed?

4.24 Explain how to get a prompt and a response *on the same line.*

4.25 List five types of *syntax errors* that the Pascal compiler will usually detect.

4.26 Explain why the *error message* produced by the compiler in response to a syntax error may not identify the actual error. Explain why a compiler may generate *spurious error messages* in response to some errors.

4.27 Give a good rule of thumb for *locating* a syntax error when the compiler produces one or more error messages.

4.28 What is *program testing?* What is a *bug?*

4.29 In a large programming project, about how much effort might be devoted to testing, relative to other parts of the project?

4.30 List and explain briefly *five types of behavior* during a test run that might indicate the program contains a bug.

4.31 Name four ways that you should *prepare for testing* before running your first test.

4.32 Explain how to use the *program requirements* to *choose test data.*

4.33 What is *path testing?* How do you choose test data if your goal is path testing?

4.34 Why should testing try to *break the program?*

4.35 What is a *robust program?* How does testing to determine whether a program is *robust* differ from testing to determine if a program is *correct?*

4.36   State and explain the *Cardinal Rule of Debugging*.

4.37   What is a *debug WRITE statement*? Describe how to use debug WRITE statements to display the data states during a test run. Give two useful rules for determining what data values to display with debug WRITE statements.

4.38   What are *automatic tracing facilities*?

4.39   Is it likely that a bug is caused by a *system malfunction*? Why or why not?

4.40   What does testing prove about the *correctness* of a program?

4.41   When a program is ready to be put into use, what two pieces of *documentation* need to be provided?

4.42   What is program *maintenance*?

4.43   What is *programming style*? State and explain the *basic rule of good style*.

4.44   State and explain rules for good style in the following areas: (a) choice of identifiers, (b) use of "white space," especially in assignment statements, and (c) coding READ and WRITE statements.

4.45   What is the *user interface* of a program? List four things to consider to improve the user interface of any program.

■ ■ ■
PROGRAMMING PROBLEMS

4.1   For each of the programming problems at the end of Chapter 3, code the algorithm in Pascal and compile and test it on your computer system.

4.2   *Displaying a Rectangle.* Programs that display geometric figures of various sizes and shapes present interesting programming difficulties. Rectangles are the simplest. Suppose that you want a program that will display a rectangle of a given size on the screen. The program should ask the user for two integer values, a Height in the range 1 to 24 and a Width in the range 1 to 80. Then it should display a rectangle, composed of asterisks (or another character of your choice), that is Width characters wide and Height lines long. The rectangle should be approximately centered in the screen. For example, if Height = 8 and Width = 20, the program would display the rectangle:

```
********************
*                  *
*                  *
*                  *
*                  *
*                  *
*                  *
********************
```

Determine the detailed requirements for this program, and then design and verify it, code it in Pascal, and test it. The program should check its input data values to be sure they are in the allowed ranges. If not acceptable, the program should ask the user to enter acceptable values.

4.3   *Table of Square Roots, Squares, and Cubes.* Develop a program that will display a table of the following form:

TABLE OF VALUES

Number	Square Root	Square	Cube
.	.	.	.
.	.	.	.
.	.	.	.

The program should ask the user to enter three integer values:

- The starting number for the table (row 1, column 1).
- The number of rows in the table.
- The "step size" between rows of the table.

The step size indicates how much to add to the starting number to get the number for the second row, how much to add to that number to get the number for the third row, and so forth. The square root, square, and cube columns give these computed values for the number in the first column of each row.

SPECIAL REQUIREMENTS:

1. In order to keep the table displayed on the display screen, limit the number of rows to 20.
2. Allow a *negative* starting value or a *negative* step size. If the number for a row is negative, do not attempt to compute the square root for that row. Instead print "NOT COMPUTABLE" in the square root column for that row.

Write the detailed requirements for this program, then design it, code it, and test it thoroughly.

4.4 *Checking and Converting a Character String to an Integer Value.* Users of a program often type unexpected characters when asked to enter a number. If you read what the user types as an Integer or Real value, any extra characters will cause the Pascal system to reject the value. To make a program more "user friendly", it is often necessary to read a number as a sequence of characters, and then compute the equivalent Integer or Real value inside the program after any extra characters have been removed.

Design, code, and test a program that will read a sequence of characters that are supposed to represent an integer value, delete any characters that are not digits, and convert the digits to a Pascal Integer value. The integer value should be displayed as the result. For example, you might see:

```
Program: Type an integer value.
User:   +2,345
Program: The value is:   2345
```

Allow the user to start the number with a minus sign to indicate a negative number, but otherwise ignore characters that are not digits. Let the first space terminate the number.

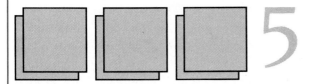

5

Abstraction: Defining Constants, Data Types, and Operations

CHAPTER GOALS

When you have mastered the content of this chapter you should be able to:

- Explain how *abstractions* are defined and used in programming.
- Identify the need for a *defined constant* in a program.
- Define and use defined constants in an algorithm and in a Pascal program.
- Identify the need for a new *data type* in a program.
- Define and use a new data type in an algorithm and in a Pascal program.
- Identify the need for a new abstract *operation* in a program and decide whether to use a *function* or a *procedure* subprogram to represent it.
- Define the meaning of the terms *subprogram call, actual parameter,* and *formal parameter.*
- Define and use a new subprogram in an algorithm and in a Pascal program.
- Explain how abstractions such as new data types, subprograms, and defined constants can simplify a program.

The predefined data types, Integer, Real, Boolean, and Char, and their associated operations, such as the arithmetic operations and predefined functions, suffice to construct small programs. For most programs, however, these simple data types and operations are not enough. More complex data types and operations are needed that more closely approximate the "real world"objects and operations of the information processing task that the program automates.

For example, a program that performs some of the record-keeping tasks associated with the student records of a university might use data types such as "student," "instructor," "grade," "transcript," and "course." The operations used in the program might include "list the grades for all the students in a course," "compute the current grade point average of a student," and "list the courses taught by a given instructor this year."

These more complex data types and operations are not provided directly in the programming language. Instead the programming language provides facilities that allow you, the programmer, to *define* new data types and operations that are appropriate for the program being constructed.

In this chapter, we focus on how to define and use new data types and operations in a program. In Chapters 6 and 7, we discuss how to fill in the details of the definitions of new types and operations to get a complete program.

□□□5.1
DEFINING AND USING ABSTRACTIONS

Defining new data types and new operations is the main form of *abstraction* in programming. You introduce new data types and operations in order to control the overall complexity of the program. There is a third type of abstraction that is simpler, but still useful: the *defined constant*. Let's look at the overall process of defining and using abstractions before we look at the details of these three kinds of abstractions.

Recall our fundamental design principle: DEFINE, then REFINE. Suppose you are developing an algorithm to automate some information processing task. As you design the steps and data objects of the algorithm, you try to identify new data types, operations, and constants that would simplify the algorithm. Then you DEFINE just *what* you need to know about the data type, operation, or constant in order to be able to use it. For a new data type or constant, this step is simple: just name it and describe its purpose. For a new operation, slightly more must be defined, but not much.

Once defined, you continue to develop the algorithm, using the new data type, operation, or constant as required. Then later you come back and REFINE the definition to fill in the details of *how* the data type, operation, or constant is to be represented in the program.

For example, you might be developing an algorithm in which calendar dates are used frequently. You identify the data type "date" as a useful abstraction for this program. To DEFINE this data type, it suffices simply to name it, say using the name "Date". You do not know yet exactly what you want a "Date" to consist of—that is the REFINE step, which comes later. But without knowing how a "Date" is represented, you begin to *use* this new data type in your program. Each time you need a data object to store a date, you specify that data object as type "Date" in your DATA OBJECTS list. For example:

DATA OBJECTS

Today: Date   The date to use on the report.
GameDay: Date   The date of the next game.

Defining and using this new data type has already simplified your work in designing the algorithm.

Continuing with your algorithm, as you design actions in the program you identify new *operations* that you need for working with "dates," such as an operation "MonthOf" that gives the "month" stored in a particular data object of type Date. You DEFINE the operation MonthOf as a new *function*:

FUNCTION MonthOf
    (D: Date)   IN
    FUNCTION VALUE: Month
    PURPOSE: Returns the month part of date D.

In defining this new operation, you identify another new data type that you need—the type "Month", which is the data type of the result of the function. Having named this type, you can now use it as the data type for other new data objects. For example, you might define a data object:

ReportMonth: Month   The month of the sales report.

The new MonthOf function can be used just like the predefined functions *sqrt* or *sin*. That is, just as you can write the ASSIGN action:

$$Z := sqrt\ (X)$$

to assign the square root of X to Z, you can now write:

$$ReportMonth := MonthOf\ (Today)$$

to assign the "month" part of the date stored in Today to the data object Report-Month.

Of course, eventually you have to come back and REFINE the definitions of the data types "Date" and "Month" and the new operation "MonthOf" by choosing exactly how the data type and the operation are to be represented in terms of the basic data types like Integer, Real, Boolean, and Char and the basic operations like ASSIGN, READ, and DISPLAY. But the REFINE step is done later, so it does not interfere with your development of the basic algorithm.

□ □

IDENTIFY, DEFINE, USE, then REFINE

The process of defining new abstractions—new data types, operations, and constants—has introduced two changes in our DEFINE, then REFINE principle:

1. *IDENTIFY first.* Defining an abstraction begins when you *identify* the need for a new abstraction. Most commonly, you identify a needed abstraction when you are designing part of an algorithm and you notice the part becoming too complicated. A new data type, operation, or constant can reduce the complexity of that part so that you can proceed without losing *intellectual control* of the design.

2. *USE before REFINING.* After a new data type, operation, or constant is defined, you *use* the abstraction, continuing with the development of the part of the algorithm that you were working on when you first identified the need for the abstraction. Only later, as a separate REFINE step, do you come back to fill in the details of the abstraction.

□ □

Three New Lists in Pseudo-code

From this point on, every algorithm you develop is likely to include definitions of new data types, operations, and constants. In pseudo-code, we put these definitions on three new lists:

- DATA TYPES—new data types you have defined.
- SUBPROGRAMS—new operations you have defined.
- DEFINED CONSTANTS—new constants you have defined.

The term *subprogram* is the usual programming term for an operation defined by the programmer, so we use this name for our list of defined operations.

Each of these forms of abstraction is supported by features of the Pascal programming language. Thus we can easily move from our pseudo-code into Pascal.

□ □ □ **5.2**
DEFINED CONSTANTS

Defined constants are a simple, but extremely useful, form of abstraction.

</...>

What is a Defined Constant?

A *defined constant* is an abstraction of a *literal value* in a program. Each defined constant is simply a name (a Pascal identifier) that stands for a particular literal data value. For example, the name PI might be used to stand for the literal value 3.1416.

Literal values might not appear to be a source of complexity in a program, but they can be. For example, suppose your program is computing the tuition for a student in your college, and you write an ASSIGN action as:

TotalTuition := CreditHours ∗ 29.50

where $29.50 is the tuition charge per credit hour. The literal value "29.50" makes the program more complex in two ways:

1. *Less readable*. Someone reading the program will find the literal "29.50" hard to understand. What does it represent?

2. *Harder to change*. Next year, when the tuition cost changes to $35.00 per credit hour, the program will be hard to modify. Which ASSIGN action uses that literal value? Are there several places where that literal value is used?

As a program gets larger, the use of particular literal values becomes more and more of a problem because the literal values appear in more places. The program becomes increasingly less readable and harder to change.

IDENTIFYING the Need for a Defined Constant

When you are designing an algorithm, look at each literal value that is used in the actions of the algorithm, such as the tuition rate value above. Use a defined constant instead of the actual literal value:

1. If the literal value is *likely to change* at some later time, such as the tuition rate,
2. If the literal value represents a *mathematical constant,* such as pi, or
3. If the literal value is used in *several different places* in the program.

Simple numeric literal values like 0, 1, and 2 do not need to be replaced by defined constants, but most other literal values are candidates.

DEFINING and USING Defined Constants

Defining and using a defined constant is straightforward:

1. Define a *name* for the defined constant, such as the name TUITIONRATE.

2. Write the algorithm using the name of the defined constant instead of the particular literal value. A defined constant name can be used anywhere in an algorithm where a literal value is allowed. For example, in the ASSIGN action, write:

$$\text{TotalTuition} := \text{CreditHours} * \text{TUITIONRATE}$$

or in a DISPLAY action:

$$\text{DISPLAY: "The tuition rate per credit hour is} \langle \text{TUITIONRATE} \rangle$$

or in the test of an IF or WHILE:

$$\text{IF CreditHours} * \text{TUITIONRATE} < \text{ScholarshipAmount THEN} \ldots$$

3. As you design the algorithm, keep track of the names of the defined constants on a DEFINED CONSTANTS list:

$\langle \text{DEFINED CONSTANTS list} \rangle ::=$

DEFINED CONSTANTS

$$\langle \text{name} \rangle = ? \qquad \langle \text{purpose} \rangle$$
$$\{\langle \text{name} \rangle = ? \qquad \langle \text{purpose} \rangle\}$$

WHERE
$\langle \text{name} \rangle ::=$
   Name for the abstract literal value (a Pascal identifier, preferably all upper-case letters).
$\langle \text{purpose} \rangle ::=$
   Describe what the value represents in the program.

The "?" in the definition indicates that the particular literal value to be used for the defined constant has not yet been chosen.

EXAMPLES

DEFINED CONSTANTS

TUITIONRATE = ?	In-state tuition rate.
OUTOFSTATERATE = ?	Out-of-state tuition rate.
PI = ?	Value of pi.
ABSOLUTEZERO = ?	Value of absolute zero, in degrees Celsius.
MAXGRADE = ?	Highest allowed exam grade.

REFINING a Defined Constant

The REFINE step for a defined constant consists of choosing the particular literal data value that the constant name represents. The algorithm itself should not depend on what particular literal value is used for a defined constant, so you can delay this REFINE step as late as when you actually code the program in Pascal. If the defined constant represents a mathematical or scientific constant like PI or ABSOLUTE-ZERO, then you may need to look up the actual literal value in a textbook or encyclopedia. If the defined constant represents a value that may change later, such as TUITIONRATE, then you have to find out the appropriate value to use "today" in the program.

Pascal Coding: The CONST Section

In your Pascal program, all the defined constants are listed at the beginning of the program, immediately following the PROGRAM line and the header comment for the program, in a section that begins with the keyword CONST:

⟨defined constant section⟩ ::=

       CONST
           ⟨constant name⟩ = ⟨literal value⟩; ⟨purpose⟩
           {⟨constant name⟩ = ⟨literal value⟩; ⟨purpose⟩}

       WHERE
           ⟨constant name⟩ ::= A Pascal identifier.
           ⟨literal value⟩ ::=
               A Pascal Integer, Real, Char, or Boolean literal value, or a character string
               enclosed in single quotes.
           ⟨purpose⟩ ::=
               A Pascal comment describing what the constant represents in the program.

Notice that an *equals* separates the constant name from its definition and that each constant definition ends with a *semicolon*. Also note that a quoted string of characters may be a defined constant.

EXAMPLES
```
CONST
    TUITIONRATE = 29.50;       {In-state tuition rate}
    OUTOFSTATERATE = 150.00;   {Out-of-state tuition rate}
    PI = 3.14159265;           {Value of pi}
    ABSOLUTEZERO = -273.15;    {Value of absolute zero, in degrees Celsius}
    MAXGRADE = 'A';            {Highest allowed exam grade}
    DATELINE = 'Version 1.2, October 1989';
                               {Line displayed on program startup}
```

The Data Type of a Defined Constant

The identifiers used for defined constants, such as TUITIONRATE or PI, are *not* declared in the VAR section, so their data type is determined by the data type of the *literal value* that is given as their defined value in the CONST section. For example, because TUITIONRATE in the example above is given the value 29.50 and 29.50 is a Real literal value, TUITIONRATE has data type Real. You can use TUITIONRATE at any place in the program that it would be valid to use a Real literal value. If TUITIONRATE had been defined to have the Integer value 29, then TUITIONRATE would have data type Integer and it could be used anywhere an Integer literal value is allowed.

Because defined constants represent *literal values* in the program, they cannot be used in places where a *variable* is required. For example, they cannot appear on the left side of an assignment statement. Thus, the value of a defined constant is truly a constant—it cannot be changed during program execution. To change the value of a defined constant, you have to change its definition in the CONST section and then recompile the program.

Example: Using a Defined Constant as a DEBUGGING Flag

When you are testing a program, you often want to include debug WRITE actions to display the values of the key data objects at various points during program execution. However, after the program has been tested and is ready to use, you no longer want these debug WRITE statements executed. Rather than remove the debug WRITE statements, it is a good idea to leave them in the program, so that if you later modify the program and want to retest it, you do not have to insert the debug WRITE statements a second time. Thus rather than actually *removing* the debug WRITE statements when you finish testing, you often want only to *turn them off*, so that they are no longer being executed.

A defined constant can be put to good use in this situation as follows:

□
Step 1.   Define a constant named DEBUGGING. This constant is your *debugging flag*. Its value will be either TRUE or FALSE.

```
CONST
     DEBUGGING = ?                    {Debugging flag}
```

□
Step 2.   Whenever you insert a debug WRITE statement in your program, "guard" it with an IF that first tests if the debugging flag is set to the value TRUE. For example:

```
IF DEBUGGING THEN
    BEGIN
        writeln ('DEBUG: Value of X = ', X, 'Value of Sum = ',Sum);
    END;
```

□

Step 3.   Before testing your program, set the value of the debugging flag to TRUE:

```
CONST
    DEBUGGING = TRUE;                    {Debugging flag}
```

and then compile the program. Use this compiled program for testing. All your debug WRITE statements will be executed because the debugging flag is set to TRUE.

□

Step 4.   After testing is complete, set the value of the debugging flag to FALSE:

```
CONST
    DEBUGGING = FALSE;                   {Debugging flag}
```

and compile the program again. Make this compiled program the one that is made available for other people to use. When this program is executed none of your debug WRITE statements will be executed because the debugging flag is FALSE.

□

Step 5.   If you modify the program and want to retest it, set the value of the debugging flag back to TRUE, recompile the program and test it. Now all your debug WRITE statements will again be executed.

EXERCISES

5.1   Write constant definitions in pseudo-code appropriate for each of the following situations:

a.   Several formulas used in ASSIGN actions use the value of 2^{10} (1024).

b.   In a program to compute grades for a university class, you anticipate a maximum class size of 200 students, with each student having at most three exam grades and ten homework assignments.

5.2   Code your constant definitions from Exercise 5.1 as a Pascal program CONST section.

5.3   In one of the programs that you designed and coded in Chapters 3 and 4, introduce a debugging flag and "guard" each of your debug WRITE statements with an IF that tests the flag.

IDENTIFYING, DEFINING, AND USING A NEW DATA TYPE

Defining new data types is a fundamental form of abstraction in programming. A data type has two parts:

1. The *name* of the type, and
2. The *representation* of the type.

The *name* is what you specify when you DEFINE a new data type. The *representation* is what you specify when you REFINE the definition of a data type. Obviously, defining a name for a data type is easy. The hard part comes later, when you have to choose a particular representation for the data type.

In the next chapter we look at the basic options available in Pascal for choosing a representation for a data type. The representation of the type specifies how many data values each data object of that type can store, how the data values are organized, and the data type of each individual data value. Here is a preview of the Pascal options:

1. *Records—lists of named attributes*. The data type might be represented as a list of named attributes (called a *record* in Pascal), such as "name," "address," "birthdate," "height," "weight," and so forth. Each attribute in the list is itself a data object of a simpler type, such as an Integer, Char, or another data type you have defined.

2. *Arrays—lists of numbered items*. The data type might be represented as a list of numbered items (called an *array* in Pascal), such as a numbered list of all the students in a class. Each item in the list is itself a data object of a simpler type.

3. *Strings—sequences of characters*. The data type might be represented as a single sequence of characters (called a *string* in Pascal), such as the characters in a person's name.

4. *Subranges—restricted ranges of Integers or Chars*. The data type might simply be a restriction of the predefined Integer or Char data types to a smaller set of possible values (called a *subrange* in Pascal), such as the representation of a "month" by the subrange composed of the integers 1 to 12.

5. *Enumerations—sets of words*. The data type might consist of a set of words (Pascal identifiers) enumerating the possible values of an attribute (called an *enumeration* in Pascal), such as a set of possible "hair colors" enumerated by the words RED, BROWN, BLACK, BLOND, and GRAY.

□□

Identifying When a New Data Type is Needed

The data types used in a program should mirror the way that you think about the data objects in the algorithm as you design it. If you think of a particular data object as storing a "date," then "Date" probably should be its data type. If you think of another data object as storing a "list of students in the class," then "ListOfStudents" probably should be its data type.

When a data object is very simple, it may be natural to use one of the predefined types (Integer, Real, Char, or Boolean). But if you can see that a data object will need to store more than a single value, or if you are not sure what kind of value a data object will store, then it is best to define an appropriate data type for it and worry later about the details. Later, if you determine that an object will store only a single data value and one of the predefined data types can be used, you can define your new type name to be equivalent to the predefined type.

For example, a program that is computing the payroll for a small business might naturally have data objects that store information about "employees," "tax deductions," "fringe benefits," "hours worked," and "sick leave." The data types in the program usually would mirror this structure, using types named "Employee," "TaxDeduction," and the like. If later, during the REFINE step, you find that one of these types, say the type "HoursWorked," is best represented as a single integer value, then you may define type HoursWorked as equivalent to the predefined type Integer.

□□

Pseudo-code: The DATA TYPES List

As you begin the design of an algorithm in pseudo-code, start a DATA TYPES list, using the syntax:

⟨DATA TYPES list⟩ ::=

    DATA TYPES

       ⟨data type name⟩ = ?   ⟨purpose⟩
      {⟨data type name⟩ = ?   ⟨purpose⟩}
    WHERE
      ⟨data type name⟩ ::=
        A Pascal identifier used to name the new data type.
      ⟨purpose⟩ ::=
        A description of what data objects of this type are intended to represent.

The "?" indicates that you have not yet chosen the representation for the data type.

EXAMPLE   In an algorithm for working with student grades, your DATA TYPES list might contain the following types:

    DATA TYPES

    LISTOFGRADES = ?   Grades list for one class.
    QUIZGRADERANGE = ?   Allowed grade range for a quiz.

HomeworkGradeRange = ?   Allowed grade range for homework.
StudentRecord = ?   All grades for one student.   ■

Each time you identify a new data type that your program needs, name the type, and add its name and a description of its purpose to your DATA TYPES list.

□□

Using a Defined Data Type

Using a defined data type means declaring data objects to be of the new type. Sometimes the program may have many data objects of a particular new type. In other situations, there may be only a single data object of a particular new type. For example, in a program to compute the payroll for a small business, there might be many data objects of type "Employee" but only a single data object of type "MasterListOfCurrentEmployees" to contain the list of all current employees of the company.

□□

Pascal Coding: The TYPE Section

In your Pascal program, all the defined data types are listed at the beginning of the program in a section beginning with the keyword TYPE, which immediately follows the CONST section. The syntax is:

⟨TYPE section⟩ ::=

```
TYPE
 ⟨data type name⟩ = ⟨representation⟩;   ⟨purpose⟩
{⟨data type name⟩ = ⟨representation⟩;   ⟨purpose⟩}
```

WHERE
   ⟨data type name⟩ ::=
      The Pascal identifier used to name the new data type.
   ⟨representation⟩ ::=
      The Pascal definition of the representation of the new type (discussed in the next chapter).
   ⟨purpose⟩ ::=
      A Pascal comment—the description of what data objects of this type are intended to represent.

Notice that an *equals* separates the type name from its representation and that each type definition ends with a *semicolon*.

EXAMPLE   The DATA TYPES list in the preceding example would be coded in Pascal as the TYPE section:

```
TYPE
    ListOfGrades = ?           {Grades list for one class}
    QuizGradeRange = ?         {Allowed grade range for a quiz}
    HomeworkGradeRange = ?     {Allowed grade range for homework}
    StudentRecord = ?          {All grades for one student}
```

Each of the "?" unknowns must be replaced by the definition of the representation for the type before the program can be compiled and executed. ■

EXERCISES

5.4 For each of the following programs, make a list of five of the data types that might be among the "natural" data types of the objects involved:

a. A program to play the game of chess.

b. A program to read in and display the local weather report for your city.

c. A program to record and average the grades for the students in a university course.

□□□ **5.4**
IDENTIFYING AND DEFINING SUBPROGRAMS

A data type, by itself, is not very useful. You need new *operations* on data objects of the type in order to construct actions in an algorithm. For example, operations such as "MonthOf", "DayOf", "YearOf", "AdvanceToNextDay", "ReadDate", and "DisplayDate" are what really make a "Date" data type into a useful abstraction in a program.

When a new data type is defined, you typically need operations of the following sorts to make the type useful:

□

Creation operations: Operations that "create" a data object of the type by storing appropriate initial values in it, such as a "SetDate" operation that stores a particular month, day, and year in a data object of type Date.

□

Retrieval operations: Operations that retrieve the various data values stored in a data object of the new type, such as "MonthOf", "DayOf", and "YearOf" operations to retrieve the month, day, and year parts of a Date data object.

□

Update operations: Operations that modify or update a data object of the new type, such as an "AdvanceToNextDay" operation to update a Date data object.

□

Comparison/test operations: Operations that compare two objects of a new data type or that test an object of the type for a particular property, such as operations "IsBefore" or "IsLastDayOfMonth" that compare or test Date data objects.

□ Sec. 5.4 *Identifying and Defining Subprograms*   **227**

□

Read/display operations: Operations that read in or display values for data objects of a new data type, such as operations "ReadDate" or "DisplayDate" on Date data objects.

□ □

Pseudo-code: the SUBPROGRAMS List

New operations in a Pascal program are defined as either *functions* or *procedures*. The term *subprogram* means "either a procedure or function." During the DEFINE step, you only specify the *heading* of a subprogram definition. The heading provides all the information needed to be able to use the subprogram. During the REFINE step you define the *body* of the subprogram—the actions, states and data objects used to accomplish the operation. In this chapter, we are only concerned with defining the subprogram heading. In Chapter 7, we explain how to design the subprogram body.

The term "subprogram" is appropriate for describing procedures and functions because each can be understood as a "program" in miniature—it has a set of data objects that form its private "local state," and it has a private algorithm that specifies how it carries out its operation using data from this local state.

In pseudo-code, new operations are defined on a SUBPROGRAMS list. As you identify a new operation to be defined as a subprogram, enter the appropriate *function heading* or *procedure heading* in the list:

⟨⟨SUBPROGRAMS list⟩ ::=

SUBPROGRAMS

⟨subprogram heading⟩
{⟨subprogram heading⟩}
WHERE
⟨subprogram heading⟩ ::
⟨function heading⟩ | ⟨procedure heading⟩

The form of these headings is defined below.

Because new data types and new operations on those data types are closely connected, you usually find yourself putting several new operations on the SUBPROGRAMS list at about the same time you are putting a new data type on the DATA TYPES list. Later, when you come back to REFINE the definition of a new data type, by choosing its representation, you also REFINE the definitions of the operations for that data type, by choosing the algorithm that each operation uses.

□ □

Subprogram Call: Who "Uses" a Subprogram?

When a subprogram is used as an operation, we say that the subprogram is *called*. What we write in the algorithm at that point is termed a *procedure call* or a *function call*. The part of the program that executes the call is termed the *caller* of the subprogram. For example, the MonthOf function described above is used through a function call in the assignment:

$$ReportMonth := MonthOf \ (Today)$$

If this assignment appears in the main procedure of the program, then we say "the main procedure calls function MonthOf." While the "user" of a *program* is a person, the "user" of a *subprogram* is the caller of that subprogram—another part of the same program. The details of the states and actions within a subprogram are hidden from its user, just as the details of the inner workings of a program are hidden from the user of the program.

□ □
What is a Procedure?

A *procedure* is a subprogram that *changes the program state,* either by changing the state of one or more data objects or by changing the state of the display screen. Operations that create new data objects, update or modify the values stored in existing data objects, or display or read values stored in data objects would ordinarily be defined as procedures.

The data objects and data values made available to the procedure when it is called are termed the *actual parameters* of the call. Each time the procedure is called, a different set of actual parameters may be given. For example, a procedure named SetDate might be used to store a particular month, day, and year value in a Date data object. The actual parameters for SetDate would consist of the three values for the month, day, and year and the name of the Date data object whose state was to be set to the new values. Each time SetDate is called, the actual parameters may be a different month, day, and year value and a different Date data object.

The procedure is defined in terms of its effect on data objects called *formal parameters* that correspond to the actual parameters given in each call of the procedure. The formal parameters "stand for" the actual parameters within the procedure definition. For example, procedure SetDate might have formal parameters named NewDay, NewMonth, NewYear to stand for the month, day, and year actual parameters and a formal parameter named NewDate to stand for the Date actual parameter whose state will be set to the new values.

□ □
The Elements of a Procedure Heading

To DEFINE a procedure, you define only its heading, which consists of:

1. The *name* of the procedure (a Pascal identifier).
2. The name, data type, and purpose of each of the *formal parameters.* Each *name* is a Pascal identifier and the *data type* may be any Pascal data type, either a predefined type or one that you have defined. The *purpose* indicates the purpose served by the parameter within the procedure. Sometimes the purpose is omitted if the parameter name effectively states the purpose.

3. The PURPOSE and GOAL STATE of the procedure, described using only the names of the formal parameters as data objects. The PURPOSE and GOAL STATE describe the action performed by the procedure when it is called—what changes are made in the values stored in some of the formal parameters by using the values stored in the other formal parameters.

4. A classification of each formal parameter as IN, OUT, or IN/OUT. This classification indicates whether the parameter carries a data value IN to be used in the procedure, OUT as a result of the procedure's actions, or both IN and OUT.

5. (Optional) *Preconditions* on the values of the formal parameters that must be satisfied if the procedure is to work correctly.

Figure 5.1 shows these elements in the heading for procedure SetDate.

□ □

Procedure Headings in Pseudo-code

In pseudo-code, our form for a procedure heading is the following:

⟨PROCEDURE-heading⟩ ::=

      PROCEDURE ⟨procedure name⟩
          (⟨formal parameter name⟩: ⟨data type⟩ ⟨description⟩
          {⟨formal parameter name⟩: ⟨data type⟩ ⟨description⟩})

FIGURE 5.1   Elements of a Procedure Heading in Pseudo-code

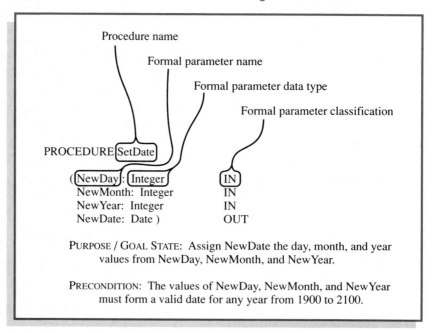

PURPOSE: ⟨purpose of the procedure⟩
GOAL STATE: ⟨desired goal state⟩
[PRECONDITION: ⟨list of preconditions⟩]

WHERE
⟨procedure name⟩ ::= Pascal identifier.
⟨formal parameter name⟩ ::= Pascal identifier.
⟨data type⟩ ::=
   Data type of the formal parameter—a predefined type or one defined on the
   DATA TYPES list.
⟨description⟩ ::=
   The IN, OUT, or IN/OUT specification for the parameter and a brief
   description of what the parameter represents.
⟨purpose of the procedure⟩ ::=
   A brief description of *what* the procedure does—what operation it performs
   when executed, expressed in terms of its effect on its OUT and IN/OUT
   parameters, given the values of its IN and IN/OUT parameters.
⟨desired goal state⟩ ::=
   A brief description of what the final states of the OUT and IN/OUT
   parameters should be when execution of the procedure is complete—what
   values they should contain.
⟨list of preconditions⟩ ::=
   A list of properties of the values of the IN and IN/OUT parameters that
   must be true before the procedure is called if the procedure is to perform its
   operation correctly.

EXAMPLES OF PSEUDO-CODE PROCEDURE HEADINGS

1. A procedure to build a sorted list of student grades:

PROCEDURE BuildSortedList

   (InitialList: GradesList   IN: Unsorted list.
   SortedList: GradesList)   OUT

   PURPOSE: Construct a copy of the list of grades in InitialList, sorted into descend-
      ing order, largest first.
   GOAL STATE: SortedList contains the sorted list of grades.
   PRECONDITION: InitialList contains at least one grade.

2. A procedure to choose and make the next move in a chess game:

PROCEDURE ChooseMove

   (BoardPosition: ChessBoard) IN/OUT

   PURPOSE: Make a good next move, given the current board position in
      BoardPosition.
   GOAL STATE: BoardPosition contains the new board position.

What is a Function?

A *function* is a subprogram that *returns a single data value* to its caller. A function should *not* change the program state. Operations that retrieve a data value from a data object, that test or compare data values stored in data objects, or that compute the value of a mathematical formula using values stored in several data objects are ordinarily defined as functions.

A function is called with a list of *actual parameters,* just as when calling a procedure. However, the actual parameters of a function are always IN parameters—they provide data values that the function can use, but the state of the actual parameter data objects is not changed by the action of the function.

□ □

The Elements of a Function Heading

To DEFINE a function, you define its heading, similar to a procedure heading, which consists of:

1. The *name* of the function (a Pascal identifier).
2. The name, data type, and purpose of each of the *formal parameters.*
3. The data type of the *function value,* and what the value represents.
4. The PURPOSE of the function—what the function does, described in terms of the values of the formal parameters.
5. (Optional) *Preconditions* on the values of the formal parameters that must be satisfied if the function is to work correctly.

□ □

Function Headings in Pseudo-code

In pseudo-code, a function heading is written as follows—notice the FUNCTION VALUE line:

⟨FUNCTION-heading⟩ ::=

    FUNCTION ⟨function name⟩
      (⟨formal parameter name⟩: ⟨data type⟩ IN: ⟨description⟩
      {⟨formal parameter name⟩: ⟨data type⟩ IN: ⟨description⟩})

    FUNCTION VALUE: ⟨data type of value⟩   ⟨value description⟩
    PURPOSE: ⟨purpose of the function⟩
    [PRECONDITION: ⟨list of preconditions⟩]

    WHERE
      ⟨function name⟩ ::= Pascal identifier.
      ⟨formal parameter name⟩ ::= Pascal identifier.

⟨data type⟩ ::=
  Data type of the formal parameter—a predefined type or one defined on the
  DATA TYPES list.
⟨description⟩ ::=
  A brief description of what the formal parameter represents.
⟨data type of value⟩ ::=
  Integer | Real | Boolean | Char
  or a defined type that represents a *single data value*.
⟨value description⟩ ::=
  Brief description of what the value represents.
⟨purpose of the function⟩ ::=
  A brief description of what the function does—what operation it performs
  when executed, expressed in terms of the function value returned, given the
  values of its formal parameters.
⟨list of preconditions⟩ ::=
  A list of properties of the values of the parameters that must be true before
  the function is called if the function is to perform its operation correctly.

EXAMPLES OF PSEUDO-CODE FUNCTION HEADINGS

1. A function that returns the largest value in a list of grades:

FUNCTION FindMaxGrade

  (Grades: GradesList   IN: List of exam grades.
  NumGrades: Integer)   IN: Number of grades in the list.

  FUNCTION VALUE: Real   Largest grade in the list.
  PURPOSE: Returns value of largest grade in the list Grades.
  PRECONDITION: Grades must contain at least one grade.

2. A function that tests if a Date is the last day of a month:

FUNCTION IsLastOfMonth

  (TestDate: Date)   IN: date to be tested.

  FUNCTION VALUE: Boolean   Result of the test.
  PURPOSE: Returns TRUE if the date in TestDate is the last day of a month;
       FALSE otherwise.

□ □
Summary: Choosing Between a Procedure and a Function

When choosing whether a new operation should be defined as a procedure or as a
function, the basic rule is:

1. If you want the operation to *change the program state* or to *compute and
return more than a single data value*, use a *procedure*, but

2. If you simply want the operation to *retrieve a single value from the state, compute a single new value,* or *test some property of the state,* use a *function.* A function subprogram should never make changes in the program state (including what is displayed on the screen).

Suppose that your algorithm uses a data type, Date, that represents a day of the year:

☐

Functions: Use functions such as "DayOf", "MonthOf", and "YearOf" to retrieve the day, month, and year values stored in a Date. Use functions such as "IsLastDayOfMonth", "IsBefore", and "IsLeapYear" to test for properties of Date values.

☐

Procedures: Use procedures to create or modify a Date value (change the state of a Date data object), such as "AdvanceDay" to advance a Date to the next day of the month, and "SetDate" to set a Date to a particular day/month/year combination. Also use procedures to display or read Date values. ■

☐ ☐

Identifying When a New Subprogram is Needed

Whenever a particular step in an algorithm becomes complex, all or part of that step should be considered as a candidate for being represented by a subprogram. Your goal is to identify abstract operations that you can define clearly and succinctly and then use immediately, by replacing complicated parts of the algorithm with subprogram calls. In that way you can put off worrying with the details of a complicated step or action and continue developing the larger structure of the algorithm.

Steps (or shorter sequences of actions) that make good candidates for becoming subprograms include:

1. *Complex steps.* Any step that appears to be rather large and complex is a candidate for becoming a subprogram. (As a rule of thumb, "large and complex" means a step that probably cannot be coded in less than ten Pascal statements.) You want to hide the details of the actions of such a step within a subprogram.

Suppose you are writing a program to play the game of chess. One step of your algorithm is described as:

PURPOSE: Choose a good move to make next.

GOAL STATE: Modify the Board to include the new move.

You see that the part of the algorithm that determines what is a "good move" will be large and complex. You define a subprogram, ChooseMove, to hide the details. ■

2. *Steps that work with complex data objects.* Any step or action that depends on exactly how a complex data object is *represented* is a candidate for becoming a subprogram. You want to hide the details of the representation of complex data objects within subprograms.

EXAMPLE

In your chess playing program, the "chess board" is likely to be a data object with a complex representation. Suppose one step of your algorithm is described as:

> PURPOSE: Initialize the chess board for the start of the game.
> GOAL STATE: ChessBoard contains the pieces in their proper starting positions.

You define a subprogram, InitializeBoard, that hides the details of how the chess board is represented and initialized, even though the actions are likely to be straightforward. ∎

3. *Similar steps that appear repeatedly*. A step that appears in several places in the program, either in exactly the same way or in very similar ways, is a candidate for becoming a subprogram. You want to avoid coding similar steps over and over again.

EXAMPLE

Suppose your algorithm for processing student grade records uses the action "find the average of a list of grades" in several different places, for several different lists. You define a subprogram, ComputeAverageGrade, for performing this action in order to avoid coding the details repeatedly. ∎

As you design your program, some steps or sequences of actions will be obvious candidates for becoming subprograms the first time you encounter them. Others may become candidates after you have used several very similar steps in different parts of your design, and you see that a single abstract operation could serve in all the situations you have encountered.

□ □

Designing Subprograms: Two Basic Principles

Once having identified that a subprogram is needed, you are ready to DEFINE the subprogram. Usually there will be several different ways that you might break up a sequence of steps, a single step, or an individual action or sequence of actions into one or more subprograms. Two basic principles should guide your choice:

□

Principle 1: *A subprogram should have only a SINGLE PURPOSE*. A subprogram should only represent *one* abstract operation, not several. The operation can be very large and complex, but you should be able to describe *what* it does with a simple, succinct PURPOSE/GOAL STATE statement. Combining several operations into a single subprogram, so that the subprogram tries to serve several purposes, leads to subprograms that are complicated to understand and difficult to use.

CHESS PLAYING PROGRAM:

Single Purpose (Good Design):

1. ChooseMove: Choose the next move in the game.
2. IsWinningMove: Test if a given move wins the game.
3. IsLegalMove: Test if a given move is allowed in this board position according to the rules of chess.

Not Single Purpose (Poor Design):

4. ChooseMoveAndCheckWin: Choose the next move and test to see if it wins the game.
5. TestIfLegalAndMakeMove: Test if a given move is allowed in this board position, and if so, change the board position to "make" the move. If not legal, return a "NOTLEGAL" value.

PROGRAM USING DATES:

Single Purpose (Good Design):

1. SetDate: Set a Date data object to a given month/day/year value.
2. AdvanceDay: Advance the date stored in a Date data object to the next day of the year.
3. IsBefore: Given two Date data objects, test if the first date comes before the second.

Not Single Purpose (Poor Design):

4. CopyAndAdvanceDate: Copy a Date data object into a second Date data object and then advance the second date to the next day of the year.
5. TestBeforeAndAdvanceDay: Given two Date data objects, if the first comes before the second, advance the first to the next day of the year, otherwise, return a NOTBEFORE value. ■

□

Principle 2:   *A subprogram should represent a COMPLETE OPERATION.* When you read the definition of a subprogram, you should be able to understand the complete abstract operation that the subprogram represents. All the parts of the operation should be included in the subprogram.

If the subprogram represents only part of an operation, then the caller will be expected to fill in the missing parts. For example, the caller may be expected to begin the operation, then the subprogram provides the main part, and then the caller completes the operation. Such a subprogram is hard to understand and difficult to use. If the caller does not fill in the missing parts of the operation, the program will have a bug.

STUDENT GRADES PROGRAM:

Complete Operation (Good Design):

1. AverageGrades: Compute the average of all the grades in a grades list. The list is assumed to contain at least one grade.
2. DisplayTopStudents: Display the name of the top student in the class. If a tie, display all top student names.

Incomplete Operation (Poor Design):

3. AverageLongList: Average a list of grades, provided the list has at least two grades in it. (The caller must provide a separate action if the list has only a single entry.)
4. DisplayTopStudentIfNoTie: Display the name of the top student in the class, provided only one student qualifies. (The caller must handle separately the case of a tie.)

PROGRAM USING DATES:

Complete Operation (Good Design):

1. SetDate: Set a Date data object to a given month/day/year value.
2. AdvanceDay: Advance the date stored in a Date data object to the next day of the year.

Incomplete Operation (Poor Design):

3. AdvanceDayIfNotLastDay: Advance the date stored in a Date data object to the next day of the year, provided the date is not the last day of the month. (The caller must test and take an alternative action if the date is the last day of the month.)
4. SetMonthAndYear: Set the month and year of a Date data object to particular values. (The caller must provide whatever action is needed to set the day value; if the caller forgets, the day value may become an "uninitialized value" bug.) ■

EXERCISES

5.5 For each of the following informally described operations, define an appropriate subprogram heading in pseudo-code. If you need any new data types for the parameters of the operation, define those data types as well.

    a. An operation that computes the average of a list of exam grades, given the list and a count of the number of grades in the list.

    b. An operation that displays a graph of the monthly sales in a grocery store, given a table of the total sales amounts for each month.

c. An operation that determines if a given date is in the first, second, third, or fourth quarter of the year.

d. An operation that finds the highest and lowest grades in a list of grades, given the list and a count of the number of grades in the list.

e. An operation that converts a temperature value from Celsius degrees to Fahrenheit degrees.

f. An operation that alphabetizes the names in a given list of names.

g. An operation that computes the sales tax on a television set, given the price of the set and the state in the U.S. where the set was purchased.

□□□ **5.5**
CALLING PROCEDURES AND FUNCTIONS

You use a subprogram by inserting a *call* on the subprogram at the point in your algorithm where you want the action of the subprogram to take place. A procedure is called as a separate action. A function is called within an *expression* as part of some other action, such as an ASSIGN or IF.

A procedure or function call includes two parts:

1. The *name* of the procedure or function to be called, and
2. A list of *actual parameters*, specifying the data objects and data values to be used during the execution of the procedure or function.

In pseudo-code, we write a procedure call in the form:

⟨procedure-call⟩ ::=

    CALL ⟨procedure name⟩ (⟨actual parameter⟩ {, ⟨actual parameter⟩})

      WHERE
       ⟨procedure name⟩ ::= Name used in the SUBPROGRAMS list.
       ⟨actual parameter⟩ ::=
         ⟨expression⟩ —corresponding to an IN parameter
         ⟨data object name⟩ —corresponding to an OUT or IN/OUT parameter

and a function call in the form:

⟨function-call⟩ ::=

      ⟨function name⟩ (⟨expression⟩ {, ⟨expression⟩})

      WHERE
       ⟨function name⟩ ::= Name used in the SUBPROGRAMS list.
       ⟨expression⟩ ::= Any Pascal expression.

EXAMPLES OF PROCEDURE CALLS Using the procedures BuildSortedList, SetDate, and ChooseMove whose headings are defined in the preceding section, here is how the following algorithm steps might be designed:

1. PURPOSE/GOAL STATE: Sort the list of grades in PsychologyClass into descending order and store the result in NewList.
   ACTIONS:

   CALL BuildSortedList (PsychologyClass, NewList)

2. PURPOSE/GOAL STATE: Set the date StartOfFiscalYear to July 1, 1989.
   ACTIONS:

   CALL SetDate (1, 7, 1989, StartOfFiscalYear)

3. PURPOSE/GOAL STATE: Make the next move in the chess game by modifying the board position stored in CurrentBoardPosition.
   ACTIONS:

   CALL ChooseMove (CurrentBoardPosition)   ■

EXAMPLES OF FUNCTION CALLS

Using the functions FindMaxGrade and IsLastOfMonth whose headings are defined in the preceding section, here is how the following algorithm steps might be designed:

1. PURPOSE/GOAL STATE: Find the largest grade value in the grades list stored in EconomicsClass and store it in TopGrade. The number of grades in the list is given by defined constant CLASSSIZE.
   ACTIONS:

   TopGrade := MaxGrade (EconomicsClass, CLASSSIZE)

2. PURPOSE/GOAL STATE: Compute and store in Average the average of the largest grades for two different classes, where the grades are stored in Class1 and Class2; Class1 has 50 grades and Class2 has 100.
   ACTIONS:

   Average : = (MaxGrade (Class1, 50) + MaxGrade (Class2, 100)) / 2

3. PURPOSE: Test whether the date stored in TodaysDate is the last day of the month and take different actions in each case.
   ACTIONS:

   IF IsLastOfMonth (TodaysDate) THEN
       . . . actions for last day of the month . . .
   ELSE
       . . . actions for other days of the month . . .   ■

□ □

Correspondence of Actual and Formal Parameters

In a procedure or function call, the list of actual parameters must correspond to the list of formal parameters given in the subprogram heading in the following ways:

1. *Same number of actual and formal parameters.* There must be exactly as many actual parameters listed in the call as there are formal parameters listed in the subprogram heading.

2. *Same order of actual and formal parameters.* The order in which the formal parameters are listed in the subprogram heading determines the order in which the actual parameters must be listed in the call—the first actual parameter listed in the call corresponds to the first formal parameter listed in the heading, the second actual parameter corresponds to the second formal parameter, and so forth.

3. *For an OUT or IN/OUT formal parameter, the corresponding actual parameter (a) must be the name of a data object and (b) must have the data type specified for the formal parameter.* The actual parameter corresponding to an OUT or IN/OUT formal parameter is used to return results from the subprogram to the calling program. The subprogram assigns a new value to the actual parameter during its execution, so the actual parameter must be the name of a data object whose value can be modified. The actual parameter's data type must match that specified in the subprogram heading for the formal parameter.

4. *For an IN formal parameter, the corresponding actual parameter may be any expression whose value is of a data type that can be assigned to the formal parameter.* The actual parameter corresponding to an IN parameter provides a *data value* for the subprogram to assign as the value of the corresponding formal parameter. Thus the actual parameter can be any expression that returns a value of a data type that can be assigned to the formal parameter. In particular, if the formal parameter is type Real, then the actual parameter can be an Integer value.

EXAMPLES   Suppose the SetDate procedure has the heading:

PROCEDURE SetDate

(NewDay: Integer	IN
NewMonth: Integer	IN
NewYear: Integer	IN
NewDate: Date)	OUT

PURPOSE/GOAL STATE: Assign NewDate the day, month, and year values from NewDay, NewMonth, and NewYear.

PRECONDITION: The values of NewDay, NewMonth, and NewYear must form a valid date for any year from 1900 to 2100.

EXAMPLE CALLS OF SETDATE:

CALL SetDate (1, ThisMonth + 1, NextYear, NewReportDate)
> VALID, provided NewReportDate is of type Date and ThisMonth and NextYear are of type Integer and contain values in the appropriate ranges.

CALL SetDate (2, 1980, NewReportDate)
> INVALID—wrong number of parameters.

CALL SetDate (NewReportDate, 1, 2, 1991)
> INVALID—wrong order of parameters.

CALL SetDate (1, 2, 1991, NewDate + 1)
> INVALID—OUT parameter is not a data object name.

CALL SetDate (1, 2, 1991, GradeList)
> INVALID—4th actual parameter is not of same data type as corresponding formal parameter.

CALL SetDate (1, 2, 1199, NewDate)
> INVALID—preconditions on 3rd parameter are not satisfied. ∎

There is no connection between the *names* used for the formal parameters and those used for the actual parameters. It is only the *position* of each actual parameter in the list, and its data type, that matters.

□ □
The Meaning of a Subprogram Call

When a subprogram call is made, the call causes the actions in progress in the caller to be temporarily interrupted while the actions defined for the subprogram are executed. If the subprogram is a procedure, then the states of the OUT and IN/OUT actual parameters change during the call. If the subprogram is a function, then a single value is computed and returned to the caller. From the caller's viewpoint, all that happens is that there is an interruption, the subprogram takes its action, and then the caller continues with its execution, using the function value or the new contents of the OUT and IN/OUT actual parameters. None of the details of what happens within the procedure or function are visible to the caller.

From the viewpoint of the caller, the *effect* of a call, as defined by the procedure or function heading, is all that you need to know. Thus, we use these newly defined procedures and functions in exactly the same way that we use procedures and functions that are *predefined* in the language, such as *readln* and *sqrt*. In Chapter 7, when we define the details of the *body* of a subprogram, we will look at a subprogram call from "the other side of the fence"— from the viewpoint of the subprogram that is *being called*.

Multiple Calls of the Same Subprogram

Any procedure or function may be called repeatedly, as many times as needed within the steps of an algorithm. On different calls you may use different data objects and data values as actual parameters, or the same data objects and values, or some mix of the two. Each call is entirely independent of any previous or following call of the same subprogram.

□ □
Watch Out for Preconditions

If there are any preconditions attached to a procedure or function in its heading, then the values of the actual parameters in a call must satisfy these preconditions at the time the call is executed. If the preconditions are not met, then execution of the subprogram may fail to produce correct results.

□ □
Coding Procedure and Function Calls in Pascal

Moving from pseudo-code subprogram calls to Pascal code is straightforward:

- PROCEDURE calls: Delete the word "CALL" and put a semicolon at the end.
- FUNCTION calls: Use as written in pseudo-code.

EXAMPLES   **PSEUDO-CODE:**

```
CALL BuildSortedList (PsychologyClass, NewList)
CALL SetDate (1, 7, 1989, StartOfFiscalYear)
TopGrade := MaxGrade (EconomicsClass. CLASSSIZE)
Average := (MaxGrade (Class1, 50) + MaxGrade (Class2, 100)) / 2
IF IsLastOfMonth (TodaysDate) THEN . . .
```

PASCAL:

```
BuildSortedList (PsychologyClass, NewList);
SetDate (1, 7, 1989, StartOfFiscalYear);
TopGrade := MaxGrade (EconomicsClass, CLASSSIZE);
Average := (MaxGrade (Class1, 50) + MaxGrade (Class2, 100)) / 2;
IF IsLastOfMonth (TodaysDate) THEN . . .
```

The coding of subprogram headings and the SUBPROGRAMS list in Pascal is discussed in Chapter 7, after we have added the "body" to each subprogram definition.

EXERCISES

5.6 For each procedure or function defined in Exercise 5.5, write one *valid* call on that subprogram and one *invalid* one. Explain why each invalid call is invalid.

□□□ **5.6**
DESIGNING WITH DATA TYPES AND SUBPROGRAMS: A CASE STUDY

Let's look at an example of the use of abstraction in building a program.

□□
Example: Nancy's "Compute Your Age" Program

Nancy NewJersey is writing another demonstration program for the science fair. This time she decides to write a program that will compute someone's age, given their birthdate and today's date. Let's look at how she uses new data types and subprograms to simplify the design of this program.

□□
Requirements Phase

Nancy's basic requirements for the program are these:

REQUIREMENTS

- INPUT: The user's birthdate.
    Today's date.
- PROCESSING: Compare the two input dates to determine the user's age. Also check for two special situations: (1) birthday is today, and (2) birthday is in the future (if the user tries to fool the program by typing a birthdate in the future).
- OUTPUT: The user's age and a special message if either of the two special situations is detected.

Nancy refines the INPUT and OUTPUT parts of the requirements into a detailed dialogue:

DIALOGUE

> *Program:* I can compute your age.
> Please tell me your birthdate.
> Month (1–12)?
> *User:* ⟨BirthdayMonth⟩
> *Program:* Day (1–31)?

User: ⟨BirthdayDay⟩
Program: Year?
User: ⟨BirthdayYear⟩
Program: Now tell me today's date.
       Month (1–12)?
User: ⟨TodayMonth⟩
Program: Day (1–31)?
User: ⟨TodayDay⟩
Program: Year?
User: ⟨TodayYear⟩
Program: You are ⟨Age⟩ years old on this day.

For the two special situations, the last line of the dialogue would become:

1. If today's date is the user's birthdate:

Program: Your birthday is today. ⟨Age⟩ years old.
       HAPPY BIRTHDAY!

2. If today's date is before the user's birthdate:

Program: Wait a minute! You haven't been born yet!

□ □
Design Phase

Next Nancy develops the steps in an algorithm for this task. Her "roughed in" algorithm (without the detailed actions) has three steps and uses three data objects. Two of the data objects are of a new type, "Date":

ALGORITHM

Step 1. PURPOSE/GOAL STATE: Read in the user's birthdate and store it in Birthdate.

Step 2. PURPOSE/GOAL STATE: Read in today's date and store it in Today.

Step 3. PURPOSE: Test if the birthdate is in the future and, if so, display the "future" message. If not, then:
Compute the age and store in Age.
If the birthday is today, display the "birthday" message, otherwise display the regular message.
GOAL STATE: Correct message and age displayed.

DATA OBJECTS

Birthdate: Date   The user's birthday, as given by the user.
Today: Date   Today's date, as given by the user.
Age: Integer   Computed age, in years.

DATA TYPES

Date = ?   A day of the year, not B.C.

Nancy now completes the program by using the "power of abstraction"— she leaves the details of the representation of a Date unspecified and simply defines a set of useful abstract operations on dates that allow her to fill in the details of the ACTIONS of each step of her algorithm.

She chooses as her operations a procedure, ReadDate, and four functions, IsAfter, YearsBetween, MonthOf, and DayOf. The headings for the operations go on her SUBPROGRAMS list; she will fill in the details later, after she chooses the representation for a "Date":

ALGORITHM

Step 1. PURPOSE/GOAL STATE: Read in the user's birthdate and store it in Birthdate.
ACTIONS:

DISPLAY: "Please tell me your birthdate."
CALL ReadDate (Birthdate)

Step 2. PURPOSE/GOAL STATE: Read in today's date and store it in Today.
ACTIONS:

DISPLAY: "Please tell me today's date."
CALL ReadDate (Today)

Step 3. PURPOSE: Test if the birthdate is in the future and, if so, display the "future" message. If not, then:
Compute the age and store in Age.
If the birthday is today, display the "birthday" message, otherwise display the regular message.
GOAL STATE: Correct message and age displayed.

ACTIONS:

IF IsAfter (Birthdate, Today) THEN
    DISPLAY: "Wait a minute!
              You haven't been born yet!"
ELSE
    Age := YearsBetween (Birthdate, Today)
    IF (MonthOf (Today) = MonthOf (Birthdate))
        AND (DayOf (Today) = DayOf (Birthdate)) THEN
    DISPLAY:
        "Your birthday is today. ⟨Age⟩ years old.
         HAPPY BIRTHDAY!"
    ELSE
        DISPLAY: "You are ⟨Age⟩ years old on this day."

DATA OBJECTS

Birthdate: Date	The user's birthdate, as given by the user.
Today: Date	Today's date, as given by the user.
Age: Integer	Computed age, in years.

DATA TYPES

Date = ?	A day of the year, not B.C.

SUBPROGRAMS

PROCEDURE ReadDate
    (NewDate: Date)   OUT: Date typed by user.
    PURPOSE: Prompt the user and read in a date.
    GOAL STATE: NewDate contains the date typed by the user.

FUNCTION IsAfter
    (Date1: Date   IN
    Date2: Date)   IN
    FUNCTION VALUE: Boolean
    PURPOSE: Return TRUE if Date1 comes after Date2; FALSE otherwise.

FUNCTION YearsBetween
    (Date1: Date   IN
    Date2: Date)   IN
    FUNCTION VALUE: Integer   Years between the two dates.
    PURPOSE: Compute the number of complete years from Date1 to Date2.
    PRECONDITION: Date1 must come before or be equal to Date2.

FUNCTION MonthOf
    (GivenDate: Date)   IN
    FUNCTION VALUE: Integer   Month part of GivenDate.
    PURPOSE: Retrieve the month part of a date.

```
FUNCTION DayOf
   (GivenDate: Date)        IN
   FUNCTION VALUE: Integer   Day part of GivenDate.
   PURPOSE: Retrieve the day part of a date.
```

□

Discussion: Nancy did not create this algorithm design on the first try. First she
played with some other alternatives, such as computing the Age value first, and allowing it to be a negative value if the user had given a birthdate in the future. She
decided that a "negative age"would be hard for a person reading the program to understand, so she redesigned the algorithm. The algorithm above is the one that she
decided was the most straightforward and easy to understand.

   To complete the program, Nancy has to choose a representation for the new
data type Date and then choose the algorithms for her five subprograms, based on
this representation. Then she will stop to verify the correctness of the different parts
of the algorithm. The final step will be to code the complete algorithm in Pascal,
enter it, and test it.

EXERCISES

5.7   Modify Nancy's ComputeYourAge algorithm so that it also tests for the
case of a user trying to trick the program by entering a birthdate that gives an Age
of zero years. Let the modified program print an appropriate message, such as:

```
"My, my -- just a few months old and already using the computer!"
```

□□□ **5.7**
ABSTRACTION IN LARGER PROGRAMS

If written without using abstractions such as subprograms, defined data types, and
defined constants, a program with even a few hundred actions would be overwhelming in its complexity. But by using abstractions appropriately, a programmer can
easily manage the complexity of programs with thousands or tens of thousands of
actions. Abstraction works almost like a "magic wand" that a programmer can wave
over a program to make complexity vanish. Besides controlling complexity during
the design of a program, abstractions also make programs easier to verify, test, and
modify.

   Let's look at the major advantages that subprograms, defined data types, and
defined constants provide:

   1.   *Information hiding*. These abstractions allow you to hide the details of
how a complex action is performed, how a data object is represented, or what literal
value a constant has. The abstraction can be used by another part of the program

without the other part knowing these details. The term *information hiding* is used to characterize this advantage of using abstractions. A subprogram may hide two different kinds of information in a program:

a. It may hide the details of *how a complicated action is accomplished*. Hiding this sort of detail is the basis of *procedural abstraction*.

b. It may hide the details of *how a complicated data object is represented*. Hiding this sort of detail is the basis of *data abstraction*.

2. *Reusability*. A subprogram need only be defined once, but it can be used repeatedly in other parts of the program, simply by calling it in the appropriate place. Similarly, a defined data type or constant can be defined in a single place but used repeatedly throughout the program.

Good abstractions can also be used in other programs, by copying the definitions into each program that requires them or by including them in *libraries* available to other programmers.

3. *Replaceability*. A subprogram that uses one algorithm may be easily replaced by a subprogram that represents the same operation but which uses a different algorithm. Other parts of the program are not affected by this substitution, provided that the subprogram heading is unchanged. Similarly, the representation of a defined data type or the value of a defined constant can be changed without affecting the parts of the program that use these abstractions.

4. *Reliability*. Verifying and testing a program that uses abstractions is made simpler because the abstractions can be analyzed and tested separately, before including them in the overall program. Thus, programs that use abstractions are made reliable more easily.

5. *Hierarchical program organization*. Subprograms and defined data types allow the overall program to be organized hierarchically. The main procedure and the data types of the data objects it uses are at the top of the hierarchy. The main procedure controls and coordinates the overall steps of the computation. It calls a few "second-level" subprograms, which perform the major actions in the computation. Each of these second-level subprograms may operate on data objects of various "second-level" data types and may call lower level subprograms, which represent the major actions at lower levels of the computation. Each of these lower-level subprograms may call yet lower-level subprograms, and so forth. The hierarchical program organization is simple to understand at each level, and, because of the information hiding of the lower-level subprograms and data types, each level can be understood without knowing the details of the levels below or above.

6. *Delayed definition*. Abstractions can save *time* during program design, by allowing you to delay defining the details of an operation or data type until you are sure what you want the operation to do or how you want the data type to be represented. Often, as you design the program you find that an operation or data type you thought was needed is unnecessary or can be made much simpler than you thought at first. By defining only the subprogram heading or data type name first and delaying the details of the full definition, you often save yourself a lot of work.

7. *Partitioned programming effort.* Defined data types and subprograms make it easy for a team of programmers to divide the programming task into separate parts. Each programmer may take one or a few related data types and subprograms to design, code, and test separately, and then the results can be combined to make the finished program. The subprogram headings and data type names are all that the other team members need to use these abstractions, so the team members can work relatively independently on their parts.

□ □
Modularity

The term *modularity* is often used to describe in more general terms the advantages of using abstractions. Each abstraction or group of abstractions represents a replaceable, reusable *module* that can be used to build a program. This modularity makes a program easy to understand, test, debug, and modify.

EXERCISES

5.8 Organizing a complex system into a hierarchy of replaceable, reusable modules is common method for structuring many real world systems that have nothing to do with computers. For each of the following kinds of complex systems, describe how this organizational method is used and the advantages that are gained by using it:
  a. An automobile.
  b. A public library.
  c. A stereo music system.

□ □ □ **5.8**
PROGRAM IT WITH STYLE!

Here are some style tidbits to consider when designing new types, operations, and defined constants:

1. *Choose meaningful names.* The names that you choose for the abstractions in your program are a central element in making it easy to understand for another person. A data type name should be a *noun phrase*—the name of the type of thing that is represented by the type, such as ListOfGrades or EmployeeTaxRecord. A subprogram name should be a *verb phrase* (verb and direct object) reflecting the operation performed by the subprogram, such as BuildSortedList or ComputeRoots. The names chosen for the formal parameters of a subprogram should be nouns that reflect the purpose of each parameter in the subprogram.

2. *Use all capital letters for names of defined constants.* When reading a program, it is helpful to know if a name used in an expression is the name of a variable

or the name of a defined constant. Because variables are declared in the VAR section of a procedure and constants are declared in the CONST section of the main program, you may have to search in two places for the definition of a name unless you make it obvious when a name refers to a defined constant. A simple way to do this is to write names of constants using *all capital letters,* as in PI or TUITIONRATE. Then the reader knows immediately where to go to find the definition of the name.

    3. *Choose a "natural" order for the parameters of a procedure or function.* The order in which the actual parameters are listed in a procedure or function call is determined by the order in which you list the corresponding formal parameters in the subprogram heading. If the order is a "natural" one, it will be easier to understand the meaning of each call on the subprogram. To choose a natural order, think about how you would tell a friend about what a procedure does. For example, if you described a BuildSortedList procedure, "This procedure takes a list of grades and the length of the list, and it returns a new list of the grades in descending order with duplicate grades removed; it also returns the length of the new list," then one natural order for the parameters would be:

```
PROCEDURE BuildSortedList
    (InitialList,
    LengthOfInitialList,
    SortedList,
    LengthOfSortedList)
```

If instead you chose this order:

```
PROCEDURE BuildSortedList
    (InitialList,
    LengthOfSortedList,
    SortedList,
    LengthOfInitialList)
```

then the procedure would be difficult to understand and use correctly. Putting the IN parameters first is often a good rule of thumb, but it's only a start.

□□□ **5.9**
PSEUDO-CODE AND PASCAL SUMMARY

Three new pseudo-code lists have been introduced in this chapter—DEFINED CONSTANTS, DATA TYPES, and SUBPROGRAMS. The Pascal CONST and TYPE sections corresponding to the DEFINED CONSTANTS and DATA TYPES lists have also been described. The Pascal form of the SUBPROGRAMS list is discussed in Chapter 7.

The Defined Constants List in Pseudo-code

⟨DEFINED CONSTANTS list⟩ ::=

DEFINED CONSTANTS

⟨name⟩ = ?   ⟨purpose⟩
{⟨name⟩ = ?   ⟨purpose⟩}

WHERE
  ⟨name⟩ ::=
    Name for the abstract literal value (a Pascal identifier, preferably all upper-case letters).
  ⟨purpose⟩ ::=
    Describe what the value represents in the program.

The "?" in the definition indicates that the particular literal value to be used for the defined constant has not yet been chosen.

The CONST Section of a Pascal Program

The DEFINED CONSTANTS list is coded in Pascal as the CONST section, which immediately follows the PROGRAM line and the program header comment:

⟨defined constant section⟩ ::=

```
CONST
  ⟨constant name⟩ = ⟨literal value⟩;   ⟨purpose⟩
{⟨constant name⟩ = ⟨literal value⟩;   ⟨purpose⟩}
```

WHERE
  ⟨constant name⟩ ::= A Pascal identifier.
  ⟨literal value⟩ ::=
    A Pascal literal value of type Integer, Real, Char, or Boolean, or a character string enclosed in single quotes.
  ⟨purpose⟩ ::=
    A Pascal comment describing what the constant represents in the program.

The DATA TYPES List in Pseudo-code

New data types are defined on this list:

⟨DATA TYPES list⟩ ::=

$$\langle \text{data type name} \rangle \ = \ ? \qquad \langle \text{purpose} \rangle$$
$$\{\langle \text{data type name} \rangle \ = \ ? \qquad \langle \text{purpose} \rangle\}$$

WHERE
$\langle$data type name$\rangle$ ::=
  A Pascal identifier used to name the new data type.
$\langle$purpose$\rangle$ ::=
  A description of what data objects of this type are intended to represent.

The "?" indicates that you have not yet chosen the representation for the data type.

□ □

The TYPE Section of a Pascal Program

The DATA TYPES list is coded in Pascal as the TYPE section, which immediately follows the CONST section:

$\langle$TYPE section$\rangle$ ::=

TYPE
  $\langle$data type name$\rangle$ = $\langle$representation$\rangle$; $\langle$purpose$\rangle$
  $\{\langle$data type name$\rangle$ = $\langle$representation$\rangle$; $\langle$purpose$\rangle\}$

WHERE
$\langle$data type name$\rangle$ ::=
  The Pascal identifier used to name the new data type.
$\langle$representation$\rangle$ ::=
  The Pascal definition of the representation of the new type (discussed in the next chapter).
$\langle$purpose$\rangle$ ::=
  A Pascal comment—the description of what data objects of this type are intended to represent.

□ □

The SUBPROGRAMS List in Pseudo-code

In pseudo-code, new subprograms are defined in a SUBPROGRAMS list:

$\langle$SUBPROGRAMS list$\rangle$ ::=

SUBPROGRAMS

$\langle$subprogram heading$\rangle$
$\{\langle$subprogram heading$\rangle\}$
WHERE
$\langle$subprogram heading$\rangle$ ::=
  $\langle$function heading$\rangle$ | $\langle$procedure heading$\rangle$

□ □

Procedure Headings in Pseudo-code

A procedure heading in pseudo-code has the form:

⟨procedure heading⟩ ::=

>PROCEDURE ⟨procedure name⟩
>(⟨formal parameter name⟩: ⟨data type⟩ ⟨description⟩
>{⟨formal parameter name⟩: ⟨data type⟩ ⟨description⟩})

>PURPOSE: ⟨purpose of the procedure⟩
>GOAL STATE: ⟨desired goal state⟩
>[PRECONDITION: ⟨list of preconditions⟩]

>**WHERE**
>⟨procedure name⟩ ::= Pascal identifier.
>⟨formal parameter name⟩ ::= Pascal identifier.
>⟨data type⟩ ::=
>Data type of the formal parameter—a predefined type or one defined on the DATA TYPES list.
>⟨description⟩ ::=
>The IN, OUT, or IN/OUT specification for the parameter, and a brief description of what the parameter represents.
>⟨purpose of the procedure⟩ ::=
>A brief description of *what* the procedure does—what operation it performs when executed, expressed in terms of its effect on its OUT and IN/OUT parameters, given the values of its IN and IN/OUT parameters.
>⟨desired goal state⟩ ::=
>A brief description of what the final states of the OUT and IN/OUT parameters should be when execution of the procedure is complete—what values they should contain.
>⟨list of preconditions⟩ ::=
>A list of properties of the values of the IN and IN/OUT parameters that *must be true before the procedure is called* if the procedure is to perform its operation correctly.

□ □

Function Headings in Pseudo-code

A function heading in pseudo-code has the form:

⟨function heading⟩ ::=

>FUNCTION ⟨function name⟩
>(⟨formal parameter name⟩: ⟨data type⟩ IN: ⟨description⟩
>{⟨formal parameter name⟩: ⟨data type⟩ IN: ⟨description⟩})

>FUNCTION VALUE: ⟨data type of value⟩ ⟨value description⟩
>PURPOSE: ⟨purpose of the function⟩
>[PRECONDITION: ⟨list of preconditions⟩]

WHERE
⟨function name⟩ ::= Pascal identifier.
⟨formal parameter name⟩ ::= Pascal identifier.
⟨data type⟩ ::=
　　Data type of the formal parameter—a predefined type or one defined on the
　　DATA TYPES list.
⟨description⟩ ::=
　　A brief description of what the formal parameter represents.
⟨data type of value⟩ ::=
　　Integer ¦ Real ¦ Boolean ¦ Char
　　or a defined type that represents a single data value.
⟨value description⟩ ::=
　　Brief description of what the value represents.
⟨purpose of the function⟩ ::=
　　A brief description of what the function does—what operation it performs
　　when executed, expressed in terms of the function value returned, given the
　　values of its IN parameters.
⟨list of preconditions⟩ ::=
　　A list of properties of the values of the parameters that *must be true before
　　the function is called* if the function is to perform its operation correctly.

□ □

Function and Procedure Calls in Pseudo-code and Pascal

In pseudo-code, a procedure call is written:

⟨procedure-call⟩ ::=

　　　　CALL ⟨procedure name⟩ (⟨actual parameter⟩ {, ⟨actual parameter⟩})

WHERE
⟨procedure name⟩ ::= Name used in the SUBPROGRAMS list.
⟨actual parameter⟩ ::=
　　⟨expression⟩ —corresponding to an IN parameter
　　| ⟨data object name⟩ —corresponding to an OUT or IN/OUT parameter

and a function call is:

⟨function-call⟩ ::=

　　　　⟨function name⟩ (⟨expression⟩ {, ⟨expression⟩})

WHERE
⟨function name⟩ ::= Name used in the SUBPROGRAMS list.
⟨expression⟩ ::= Any Pascal expression.

To code a subprogram call in Pascal:

PROCEDURE CALLS: Delete the word "CALL" and put a semicolon at the end.

FUNCTION CALLS: Use as written in pseudo-code.

REVIEW QUESTIONS

5.1 Name three forms of *abstraction* used in Pascal programming.

5.2 Name and explain briefly the four steps in the process of defining a new abstraction in a program.

5.3 What is a *defined constant*?

5.4 Explain two ways that *literal values* make a program more complex when used in program declarations and statements.

5.5 Name two types of literal values that should usually be abstracted by using defined constants in a program.

5.6 Explain how to define and use a defined constant in a Pascal program.

5.7 Describe how to use a defined constant as a *debugging flag* in a program.

5.8 What are the two parts of a *data type* definition? Which part is needed to be able to USE the data type to declare a data object?

5.9 What are the two main parts of a *subprogram* definition? Which part is needed to be able to USE the subprogram in another part of the program?

5.10 Name the two kinds of subprograms in Pascal.

5.11 Give the basic rules for determining whether an abstract operation should be represented as a *procedure* or as a *function*.

5.12 Describe the main parts of a *procedure heading*. Of a *function heading*.

5.13 Explain the distinction between IN, OUT, and IN/OUT parameters of a procedure.

5.14 What is a *precondition* of a subprogram?

5.15 What is a *subprogram call*? What are the two parts of a subprogram *call*?

5.16 List and explain the rules for the correct *correspondence* between actual parameters in a subprogram call and formal parameters in a subprogram heading.

5.17 Explain three situations where a step or action in an algorithm would be a good candidate for being represented by a subprogram.

5.18 Define and explain briefly two basic principles for deciding how to break up a step or action into one or more subprograms.

5.19 List seven advantages of using abstractions, such as subprograms, data types, and defined constants, in constructing larger programs.

5.20 Distinguish between *procedural abstraction* and *data abstraction*.

5.21 What is *modularity* in a program?

■ ■ ■
PROGRAMMING PROBLEMS

The goal in the following problems is to identify and define appropriate data types, operations, and defined constants to allow a straightforward algorithm for the information processing task to be constructed. Your answer should consist of the five lists in pseudo-code,

ALGORITHM, DATA OBJECTS, DATA TYPES, SUBPROGRAMS, and DEFINED CONSTANTS, needed to form a complete program design. The abstractions on the DATA TYPES, SUBPROGRAMS, and DEFINED CONSTANTS lists should be *defined* but not *refined*, as described in this chapter. Try to use abstractions to hide most of the details of the program.

5.1 *Graph of Golf Tournament Scores.* Write a program to display a bar graph of the winning scores in a golf tournament. The tournament is expected to have about 50 golfers, and their scores are expected to each be in the range from 60 to 90. The bar graph is to run from left to right across the screen, in approximately the form:

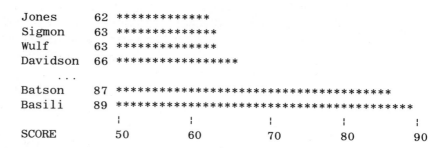

```
                        TOURNAMENT SCORES


    Jones      62 *************
    Sigmon     63 **************
    Wulf       63 **************
    Davidson   66 ****************

        . . .

    Batson     87 *************************************
    Basili     89 ***************************************
                  ¦        ¦         ¦         ¦        ¦
    SCORE         50       60        70        80       90
```

The program's requirements are:

a. As each player finishes, the player's name and score are typed in. No attempt is made to type the scores in ascending order.

b. The graph of the scores is displayed with the scores in ascending order, with the winner's score first (lowest score).

5.2 *Analysis of a Grades List.* Write a program that allows the user to obtain answers to a set of simple questions about a list of the exam grades for the students in a course. The program first asks the user to type in the list of exam grades. It then displays a *menu* of the questions that it can answer about the grades:

```
                      MENU OF QUESTIONS


    1.   How many grades are listed?
    2.   What are the lowest and highest grades?
    3.   What is the average grade?
    4.   What is the median grade?
    5.   How many grades are in a given range?
    6.   List the grades in a given range.
    Please type the number of your choice
    or 0 to exit the program:
```

The program should answer the indicated question for the user, and then display the menu again, continuing until the user enters a zero.

5.3 *Managing a Board Game*. Write a program to "manage" the board in a two-person board game such as chess, checkers, tic-tac-toe or any other board game in which two players alternate moves until one player wins, one player quits, or the game is declared a draw. The program should *not* depend on what game is being played. The program must be able to do the following:

a. Display the board with the positions of all the pieces before each move.

b. Ask the players alternately to type in their move or QUIT if they are quitting.

c. Determine if each move is legal and ask for a different choice of move, if not legal.

d. Determine if a move wins the game and display an appropriate message.

e. Determine if the game is a "draw" and display an appropriate message.

f. Continue to request moves alternately from each player until the game ends.

5.4 *Simulating an Automatic Teller Machine*. An automatic teller machine (ATM) is a machine at a bank that dispenses cash and accepts deposits at the request of a user with a valid bank identification card. The user inserts the card and then types in a personal identification number that serves as a password. Once the user is approved for access, a menu is displayed with the following options:

TRANSACTION OPTIONS

1. Receive cash from checking account.
2. Receive cash from savings account.
3. Make a deposit to checking account.
4. Make a deposit to savings account.
5. Display current account balance.
6. Return card and QUIT.

The user types the number of the desired option. Each option may lead to additional questions such as "amount to withdraw?" After each transaction request is completed, the menu is re-displayed and the cycle repeated.

Write a program that "simulates" the actions of an ATM, as described above. Among your operations should be an "accept card" operation, a "return card" operation, and a "dispense cash" operation. Because the program, obviously, cannot actually carry out these operations on your computer system, we say that it is *simulating* the operations performed by a real ATM.

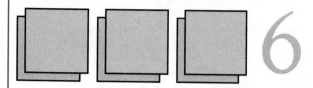

Choosing a Data Representation

6

CHAPTER GOALS

When you have mastered the content of this chapter you should be able to:

- Explain the meaning of the term *data representation*.
- Explain the *Fundamental Principle of Data Representation*.
- Use the Fundamental Principle in choosing a good representation for a data type in a program.
- Tell how to define and when to use a *subrange* type or an *enumerated* type as a data representation.
- Explain how to define and when to use a *record* type as a data representation.
- Use *dot notation* to select a particular field of a *record data object*.
- Explain how to define and when to use an *array* type as a data representation.
- Use a *subscript expression* to select a particular element of an *array data object*.
- Tell what a *subscript range error* is.
- Use an array to represent a *list* or a *simple table*.
- Describe how a *character string* may be represented.

Choosing a "representation" for a particular type of data is a common problem in the real world as well as in programming. Even something as simple as a "date" has a variety of possible representations. Abstractly we know that a "date" consists of a day, month, and year. But there are several common choices for representing each part. The month might be represented by an integer between 1 and 12, or by its name, such as "July," or by a three letter abbreviation of its name, such as "JUL." The year might be represented by an integer followed by A.D. or B.C., or it might be restricted to the range 1900–1999 and represented just by the last two digits, for example, "61" for 1961 A.D. The day might be an integer between 1 and 31, or it might be designated by "the third Thursday" or "the first Monday." Each of these representations is used at different times in the real world. And of course there are entirely different calendars that represent dates in other ways.

Choosing a good representation for the data objects used in a program is a fundamental programming skill. Let's get a definition of the term as it is used in programming:

□ **Data Representation**

The term *data representation* means the particular choice, from among the available alternatives, of the number of data values, their data types, and the organization of the data values stored in a data object.

This chapter is about some of the alternatives that you have available in Pascal for choosing a data representation for each particular type of data object. The predefined Pascal types, Integer, Real, Boolean, and Char, provide four choices for representing a single data value. Two other choices, *subranges* and *enumerations*, provide new alternatives for representing single data values. Three of the choices, *records, arrays,* and *strings,* provide ways of representing data objects that contain more than one data value—sometimes hundreds or thousands of values in a single data object.

□□□ 6.1 THE FUNDAMENTAL PRINCIPLE OF DATA REPRESENTATION

During the design of an algorithm, new data types and subprograms are identified and defined in the DATA TYPES and SUBPROGRAMS lists. Now it is time to begin choosing the particular representation for each new data type. How do you choose? There is a simple basic principle to remember:

> ☐ **The Fundamental Principle of Data Representation**
>
> To choose a good representation for a new data type in a program, first determine what *operations* will need to be performed with data objects of that type, and then choose the data representation in order to make the algorithms for performing those operations as simple and straightforward as possible.

For example, suppose you are choosing the representation for a "Date" data type in a program. The Fundamental Principle says that before choosing the representation, look at all the *operations* that the program performs on "dates." Then choose a representation for the Date data type that makes the algorithms for performing these operations as simple as possible.

As each new possibility for choosing a data representation is explained in the remainder of this chapter, remember that the art of choosing *when* to use one kind of representation instead of another is tied to this fundamental principle. By thinking about how you would perform each required operation if you chose one particular representation for a data type, you can evaluate whether that representation is a good choice. Sometimes a data type will have an obvious representation, but in many cases, the right choice might not be the one that you would think of first. The best programmers are often those who think through several different representations before making a choice, because they know that the right choice can make it easy to define the subprograms that operate on objects of that type, and the wrong choice can make the subprograms extremely complicated.

☐ ☐

Pseudo-code and Pascal Coding

The representations of the various data types in a program are REFINED during program design by replacing the "?" in each type definition in the DATA TYPES list with a particular choice of data representation. At the same time the definition of the body for each subprogram that operates on each type of data should be completed based on the representation chosen. This approach allows you to revise the data representation easily if you find that one or more of the operations could be made simpler by choosing a different representation.

In Pascal there are always some predefined operations available automatically for each choice of data representation. In the sections that follow, as each new option for data representation is explained, we also explain the predefined operations provided by Pascal.

EXERCISES

6.1 For each of the following situations in the real world, a representation for one or more items of information is given. Give two alternative ways of representing the same information:

- **a.** "The day after tomorrow."
- **b.** "Your twentieth birthday."
- **c.** "The last day of the twentieth century."
- **d.** "The number 27."
- **e.** "The first five presidents of the United States."
- **f.** "My jeans have waist size 32, length 30, and they cost $25.95."
- **g.** "In this school you are classified as either full-time, part-time, suspended, or on probation."

□□□ 6.2
SUBRANGE DATA TYPES

A *simple data object* (or in Pascal, a *simple variable*) is a data object that stores only a *single data value*. Let's begin our study of data representation by keeping the focus on simple data objects. Other than the predefined types, Integer, Real, Char, and Boolean, what are the alternatives for representing the type of a single data value? One option is to use a *subrange* data type.

□□
What is a Subrange Data Type?

A *subrange* is simply a *restriction* of an existing data type, such as Integer or Char, to a smaller set of possible values. For example, a data object, ReportMonth, that represents the month for a report, might have only the integers in the range 1 to 12 as possible values. We call the range 1–12 a "subrange" of the possible Integer values. Similarly, a data object named FinalGrade might have only the letters 'A'–'F' as possible values. The letters A–F form a "subrange" of the possible Char values.

A subrange data type consists of all the values in a single specified range—from the "smallest" value in the range through the "largest." You can only include one range of values, not several distinct ranges and not individual data values that do not form an ordered sequence.

In Pascal, subranges may only be defined of Integer or Char values or values from an "enumerated" type as described in the next section (termed *ordinal types* in Pascal). Subranges of Real values are not allowed.

□□
Defining a Subrange Data Type

To represent a data type as a subrange, you simply define the limits of the range of values to be allowed. The syntax for such a definition in pseudo-code is:

⟨subrange-type-definition⟩ ::=

⟨type-name⟩ = ⟨smallest-value⟩ ..⟨largest-value⟩

WHERE
⟨type-name⟩ ::=
   Pascal identifier used to name the data type.
⟨smallest-value⟩ ::=
   Integer or Char literal value or defined constant; the smallest value in the subrange.
⟨largest-value⟩ ::=
   Integer or Char literal value or defined constant; the largest value in the subrange.

In our pseudo-code for defining subranges, we are using the same syntax used in Pascal. Notice, in particular, that a *double period,* "..", separates the smallest and largest values in the defined subrange.

EXAMPLE

Dᴀᴛᴀ Tʏᴘᴇs

Month = 1..12   Allowed month values.
LetterGrade = 'A'..'F'   Allowed letter grade values.

In defining a subrange of type Char, the ordering of Char values in your Pascal system (such as the ASCII ordering shown in Appendix A) determines what values are included between the first and last characters that you specify for the subrange. Thus, you have to be careful to follow the defined ordering. For example, the subrange:

DecimalDigit = '0'..'9'

includes all the expected digits, but the subrange:

DecimalDigit = '9'..'0'

is nonsense because '9' *follows* '0' in the definition of type Char.

□ □

Coding a Subrange Data Type

The Pascal code for a subrange uses the same syntax, with the addition of a *semicolon* at the end of each type definition. The purpose of each type is made into a Pascal comment.

EXAMPLE

In Pascal the two subrange type definitions above would be coded in the TYPE section at the start of the main program:

```
TYPE
    Month = 1..12;              {Allowed month values}
    LetterGrade = 'A'..'F';     {Allowed letter grade values}   ■
```

Predefined Operations on Subrange Data Objects

A value of a subrange data type is considered a value of the "base type" of the subrange—Integer or Char. Thus any operation that can be used with an Integer or Char value can also be used with a subrange value. For example, you can do arithmetic with Integer subrange values, DISPLAY and READ them, compare them to other Integer values, and so forth.

The only difference between a subrange value and a value of Integer or Char type comes when you try to ASSIGN or READ a value into a subrange data object. The subrange restriction is checked at the time the ASSIGN or READ action is taken, and if the data value to be stored is outside the defined subrange, then the Pascal system terminates execution of your program and displays a run-time error message that says something like:

SUBRANGE VALUE OUT OF RANGE

CAUTION: In many Pascal systems, checking a subrange restriction at the time of an ASSIGN or READ action only occurs if you specify when the program is compiled that a special "subrange checking option" be used. This option tells the compiler to include instructions for subrange checking in the executable object program. Without these special instructions no checking is done, and any error that violates a subrange restriction will go undetected.

When to Choose a Subrange Representation

You gain two main advantages by using a subrange data type instead of simply using the predefined type Integer or Char:

1. *Automatic checking for subrange restrictions.* As described above, the Pascal system can automatically check the subrange restriction during execution of the program each time a new value is assigned to the variable. This automatic checking is helpful in tracking down errors during program testing.

2. *More readable programs.* Defined data types such as "Month" and "LetterGrade" make your program easier to read and to understand. The subrange definition specifies exactly what values are possible for a data object of that type. Using the predefined type Integer or Char conveys less information to the reader of the program.

□ □
The Limits of Subranges

Like most options for choosing data representations in a program, subranges are not perfect. The limitation to a *single range* of possible values means that you often have to choose a subrange that includes more values than you actually intend to use. For example, the subrange "LetterGrade" includes the possibility of a grade of "E" because the subrange is defined to include the Char values 'A'..'F'. There is no way in Pascal to define a data type that includes only the letters "A–D" and "F". When choosing the range of values for a subrange data type, you expect to choose a range that includes all the possible values that might be used, and in many cases that range may also include some values that will never be used.

EXERCISES

6.2   Write Pascal subrange type definitions appropriate for each of the following situations:

a.   You have defined a type TaxYear that allows as a value any year in the 20th century.

b.   You have defined a type WaterTemp that allows as a value any possible Celsius temperature for the water in a pond.

c.   You have defined a type ExamGrade to represent a student's numeric grades on the mid-term and final exam in a course.

d.   You have defined a type Initial to represent the middle initial in a person's name.

e.   You have defined a type TeamScore to represent the score of one team in a basketball game.

6.3   An Integer subrange cannot exceed the limits on Integervalues, −MAXINT..MAXINT. As an experiment, write a test program that contains a subrange type definition with a largest value larger than MAXINT. Try to compile and execute it. What happens?

□□□**6.3**
ENUMERATED DATA TYPES

Let's look at a second option for representing the data type of a simple data object (one that contains only a single value at any time). In the real world we often *classify* data into a small set of named categories. For example, in a program that plays a game with the user, you might classify the "game status" as either PLAYING, USER WIN, PROGRAM WIN, QUIT, or DRAW. To classify the cloud cover on a particular day, you might choose one of the phrases CLEAR, PARTLY CLOUDY, or OVERCAST. To classify the precipitation you might choose one of THUNDERSTORMS, SHOWERS, DRIZZLE, SLEET, SNOW or NONE. If you want to classify the status of a light in your bedroom, you might choose one of ON or OFF, or perhaps ON, OFF, or BROKEN. In Pascal programming, such classifications can be represented by an *enumerated* data type.

□ □

Defining and Coding an Enumerated Data Type

Suppose you have a data type that would be appropriately represented by a simple "enumeration" (a list) of the possible values, where each value is just a descriptive word. The definition of such an enumerated data type consists of a list of the words (Pascal identifiers) that represent possible values. The form for such a definition, in both pseudo-code and Pascal, is:

⟨enumerated-type-definition⟩ ::=

⟨type-name⟩ = (⟨word⟩ {, ⟨word⟩})

WHERE
⟨type-name⟩ ::=
Pascal identifier used to name the data type.
⟨word⟩ ::=
Pascal identifier used as one of the possible "literal" values for the data type; preferably an identifier that contains only capital letters and digits.

EXAMPLES   DATA TYPES

StatusValue = (PLAYING, DRAW, QUIT, USERWIN, PROGRAMWIN)
CloudCover = (CLEAR, PARTLYCLOUDY, OVERCAST)
Precipitation = (THUNDERSTORMS, SHOWERS, DRIZZLE, SLEET, SNOW, NONE)
LightStatus = (ON, OFF, BROKEN)

To code these definitions in Pascal, you simply add the usual *semicolon* at the end of each definition.

□ □

Predefined Operations on Data Objects of Enumerated Types

Three key facts are important about enumerated data types:

1. *The identifiers that name enumerated values become "literal data values."* You can use an enumerated value, such as the value OFF in the example above, wherever a literal data value is allowed in a program (except in READ and DISPLAY actions, see below). For example, if data object HouseLight is declared to have type LightStatus, then you can assign an enumerated value to it:

HouseLight := OFF

You can define a constant to represent a particular enumerated value:

```
CONST
    INITIALSTATUS = OFF;
```

You can compare the value of a data object to a particular enumerated value:

IF HouseLight = ON THEN ...

and so forth.

CAUTION: Do not confuse a value of an enumerated type, such as OFF, with a *character string literal value,* such as 'OFF'. Strings are written in quotes; enumerated type values are Pascal *identifiers* and are never quoted.

2. *READ and DISPLAY actions are not predefined for data objects of enumerated types.* You cannot name data objects or literal values of enumerated types in READ or DISPLAY actions. For example, you cannot use the action:

READ: HouseLight

If you code such actions in Pascal, the compiler will refuse to compile them (although some Pascal systems relax this restriction—check your local *Pascal User's Manual*). To read or display an enumerated value, you have to define your own subprogram to do the job.

3. *Enumerated values are "ordered" in the sequence that they appear in the type definition.* For any enumerated type, there is a "smallest value" (whatever value you happen to list first) and a "largest value" (whatever value you happen to list last). The predefined function *ord* gives the integer value designating the position of an enumerated value in the ordering. The smallest value is numbered 0, the second value 1, and so forth. For example, using the definition of LightStatus above:

LightStatus = (ON, OFF, BROKEN)

if HouseLight contains the value OFF, then "*ord* (HouseLight)" returns the Integer value 1.

The predefined functions *succ* and *pred* are defined to give you the next enumerated value in the ordering of an enumerated value (just as for the ordering of Integer or Char values). For example, if HouseLight contains the value OFF, then "*succ*(HouseLight)" returns the value BROKEN and "*pred* (HouseLight)" returns ON.

The ordering also allows subranges of enumerated values to be defined. For example, if you defined an enumeration that represented all the possible "status" values for an employee:

$$\text{EmployeeStatus} = \text{(HOURLY, SALARIED, PARTTIME, RETIRED,}$$
$$\text{DISABLED, SICKLEAVE, MATERNITYLEAVE,}$$
$$\text{EDUCATIONALLEAVE)}$$

then it might be helpful to define two subranges:

$$\text{ActiveEmployeeStatus} = \text{HOURLY..PARTTIME}$$
$$\text{InactiveEmployeeStatus} = \text{RETIRED..EDUCATIONALLEAVE}$$

The ActiveEmployeeStatus subrange includes only the first three status values; the InactiveEmployeeStatus subrange includes the last five values.

EXERCISES

6.4   Define enumerated types appropriate to represent the data in each of the following situations:
   a.   You have defined two types, HairColor and EyeColor, to represent the hair color and eye color of an applicant for a driver's license.
   b.   You have defined a type MaritalStatus to represent the marital status of an employee in a company (e.g., single and never married, divorced, . . .).
   c.   You have defined a type HomeworkStatus to represent the status of your homework for a math course (e.g., not yet started, already done, . . .).

6.5   Suppose your program contains the following definitions:

DATA TYPES

StatusValue = (READY, DISCONNECTED, BROKEN, INREPAIR)

DATA OBJECTS

OldStatus: StatusValue	Previous status of the printer.
NewStatus: StatusValue	Current status of the printer.

Give the result of evaluating each of the following Pascal expressions in a state where the variables have the values:

OldStatus: | BROKEN | NewStatus: | READY |

   a.   ord (NewStatus)
   b.   succ (NewStatus)
   c.   pred (OldStatus)

    d. pred (succ (OldStatus))

    e. ord (OldStatus) = 3

    f. NewStatus <> INREPAIR

6.6 As an experiment, write a test program that tries to DISPLAY a data value and READ a data value of an enumerated type. Try to compile and execute it on your Pascal system. What does your Pascal system do?

□□□ **6.4**
RECORDS: LISTS OF NAMED ATTRIBUTES

Simple data objects (ones that store only a single data value) allow you to get started in representing data in a program, but interesting programs routinely need to store hundreds of pieces of data. Using only simple data objects, such programs would be difficult or impossible to write and understand. Imagine trying to invent names and write declarations for hundreds of data objects!

A data object that stores more than one data value is termed a *data structure*. In a larger program, you will have many data structures, each containing from a few to several thousand data values. Designing and using data structures is an important programming skill. Let's begin with one of the simplest data structures in Pascal programming, the *record*.

□□

What is a Record?

Many kinds of real world objects are commonly represented in terms of a list of *attributes*. You name the "interesting" attributes of the object, and then fill in a particular value for each attribute. The list of attributes serves to describe the general class of objects—the object type. A particular object of that type is defined by giving a particular value for each of the attributes.

For example, suppose you are wearing a pair of jeans: describe them! Keep it simple—make a list of the important attributes of a pair of jeans, and then fill in the values for your jeans, such as:

LIST OF ATTRIBUTES	VALUE FOR MY JEANS
Waist	34
Length	31
Price	19.95
Color	BLUE
Condition	PATCHED

Notice how you naturally give names to the attributes that you are describing in the list, and then you use a value for that attribute that is of an appropriate type—sometimes an integer, sometimes a real number, sometimes a word from an "enumeration" of possibilities, and so forth.

In programming, we can describe the representation of a data type using this same style of definition. The representation of the data type consists of a list of the *names of the attributes* and the *data type* for each attribute. A particular data object of the new type contains a particular value for each of the specified attributes. Thus if there are ten attributes, then each data object of that type will contain ten data values, one for each of the attributes.

In Pascal, such a data type is called a *record data type*. Each attribute is called a *field* of the record. Each data object declared to be of the record type is called a *record* (or in Pascal, a *record variable*).

□ □

Defining and Coding Record Data Types

Defining the representation for a record data type is straightforward: you choose identifiers to name the fields (the "attributes") and specify the data type for the value to be stored in each field. The general form in pseudo-code for such a record data type definition is:

⟨record-type-definition⟩ ::=

    ⟨type-name⟩ =   ⟨purpose of the type⟩
      RECORD
        ⟨field-name⟩: ⟨data-type⟩   ⟨purpose⟩
        {⟨field-name⟩: ⟨data-type⟩ ⟨purpose⟩}
      END

  WHERE
    ⟨type-name⟩ ::=
      Pascal identifier used to name the data type.
    ⟨purpose of the type⟩ ::=
      A comment describing what objects of the type represent.
    ⟨field-name⟩ ::=
      Pascal identifier used to name the field (representing one of the "attributes").
    ⟨data-type⟩ ::=
      Pascal identifier naming the data type of the value stored in the field (a predefined type or a type that you have defined.)
    ⟨purpose⟩ ::=
      A comment describing the purpose of the field, including the range and units of measure, if appropriate.

□

Note: The comments describing the purpose of the type and the purpose of each field can be omitted if the type name and field names are self-explanatory.

To code the same type definition in Pascal, simply put a *semicolon* after the data type for each field and put the usual *semicolon* at the end of the entire definition, after "END".

EXAMPLE   Suppose you want to represent the class of "jeans" using a record data type, following the example above of a typical real world description. The field names could be the same as the attributes in our list: Waist, Length, Price, Color, and Condition.

What should be the data type for each of these fields? Let's represent the waist size and length as subranges of Integers:

WaistRange = 22..48   Waist size in inches.
LengthRange = 20..40   Inseam length in inches.

and the price as type Real (for a dollars and cents amount). For the color and condition, let's define enumerations:

JeansColor = (BLUE, BLACK, BROWN, WHITE)
JeansCondition = (NEW, FADED, TORN, PATCHED)

Now the Jeans data type can be written in pseudo-code:

DATA TYPES

WaistRange = 22..48   Waist size in inches.
LengthRange = 20..40   Inseam length in inches.
JeansColor = (BLUE, BLACK, BROWN, WHITE)
JeansCondition = (NEW, FADED, TORN, PATCHED)

Jeans =   Description of one pair of jeans.
     RECORD
          Waist : WaistRange
          Length : LengthRange
          Price : Real   In dollars/cents.
          Color : JeansColor
          Condition : JeansCondition
     END

Coding these definitions in Pascal, you would write:

```
TYPE
    WaistRange = 22..48;           {Waist size in inches}
    LengthRange = 20..40;          {Inseam length in inches}
    JeansColor = (BLUE, BLACK, BROWN, WHITE);
    JeansCondition = (NEW, FADED, TORN, PATCHED);
    Jeans =                    {Description of one pair of jeans}
        RECORD
            Waist : WaistRange;
            Length : LengthRange;
            Price : Real;          {In dollars/cents}
            Color : JeansColor;
            Condition : JeansCondition;
        END;
```

The data type of a field can be *any* data type, including another record type. For example, you might have a Date data type defined as a record type:

```
MonthRange = 1..12
DayRange = 1..31
YearRange = 1900..2100
Date =
    RECORD
        Month: MonthRange
        Day: DayRange
        Year: YearRange
    END
```

Then in your Jeans type definition, you might want to include a "PurchaseDate" field to represent the date of purchase of the jeans:

```
Jeans =
    RECORD
        . . . — other fields as above
        PurchaseDate: Date
    END
```

□ □

When Should a Record Data Type be Used?

Record data types are useful for representing a broad variety of data objects. The style of representation in a record—using a list of attributes and their values—is widely used in the real world. Think of almost any form that you have filled out recently, such as a tax form, an employment application, a school course registration form, or a driver's license application. The form asks for particular items of information—the "attributes" of interest. You provide the "values" for those attributes when you fill in the blanks in the form.

A record data type in a program is similar: the data type definition defines the structure of the "form"—what attributes are to be included, and what type of value is expected for each attribute. A particular data object of that record type is analogous to a form with your answers filled in—each field in the record data object stores a particular value for each "attribute." If a record data object is uninitialized (that is, no values have been stored in its fields), then that data object corresponds to a "blank form"—it has places to store the values for each attribute, but no particular values have yet been stored.

□ □

Selecting a Field of a Record

In using a record data object, the most important predefined operation is *selection*—selecting a particular field of the record to be used in some other operation. To select a field, you use the *dot notation*:

⟨record-data-object-name⟩.⟨field-name⟩

which names the record data object and the particular field that you want to select. Notice the dot (period) between the record name and the field name.

For example, if you declare a data object named MyJeans to have data type Jeans, then you can select the Length field of MyJeans by writing:

MyJeans.Length

Similarly, "MyJeans.Condition" selects the Condition field and "MyJeans.Price" selects the Price field.

Once having selected a field, you can use that field just as though it were itself a data object of the field's data type. For example, the Price field of the MyJeans record is itself of type Real. Thus you can use the selected field MyJeans.Price anywhere that you could use a data object of type Real. You can assign a new value to the field:

MyJeans.Price := 16.50

You can use the value stored in the field:

IF MyJeans.Price > MAXPRICE THEN . . .

or

NewPrice := MyJeans.Price + MARKUP

and you can refer to the field in a READ or DISPLAY action:

READ: MyJeans.Price

or

DISPLAY: "The price of the jeans is ⟨MyJeans.Price⟩"

If the field selected is itself a record, as in the example of the "PurchaseDate" field of type "Date" above, then a field of that record may be selected by appending:

.⟨field-name⟩

to the "⟨data-object-name⟩.⟨field-name⟩" that selected the original field. For example:

MyJeans.PurchaseDate.Month

selects the Month field of the PurchaseDate field of the MyJeans record.

□ □

Predefined Operations on Records

The operations that are predefined on a selected field of a record depend on the data type of the *field*. There is only one predefined operation on a record, taken as a whole: using an ASSIGN action to copy all the values in one record data object into another of the same record data type. For example, if MyJeans and YourJeans are two data objects of type Jeans, the assignment:

YourJeans := MyJeans

copies *all the data values* stored in MyJeans into record YourJeans. After the assignment, each field of YourJeans contains the same value as the corresponding field of MyJeans.

No other operations are predefined on whole records. Subprograms must be used to define operations such as "reading a record," "displaying a record," and the like. These subprograms would typically work with the individual fields of the record involved. For example, a subprogram to "read a Jeans record" might prompt the user with the names of the various items of information needed in a Jeans record and then store each item in the appropriate field of the record data object as it is typed in by the user.

□ □

Initial Values of Records

The initial values of the fields of a record variable in Pascal are unpredictable, just as with the initial values of simple variables. Thus each field of a record must be given an initial value through an ASSIGN or READ action before it can be used. Note a new twist, however: *some* fields of a record may contain useful values while others remain uninitialized. Often a record will have some fields that are assigned values early in the execution of the program, using values read in from the user, and other fields will only be assigned values much later, as new results are computed.

□ □

Record Variables in the Computer Memory

A Pascal record variable is represented in the computer memory by using a sequence of storage locations to store the individual fields of the record. For example, the variable MyJeans would appear as shown in Figure 6.1. The field names are not stored as part of the record; only the *values* of the fields are stored.

Record Variable   As Variable Appears in Memory

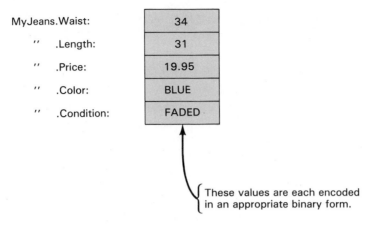

These values are each encoded in an appropriate binary form.

FIGURE 6.1   A Record Variable in Computer Memory

EXERCISES

6.7   Define appropriate record data types, declare the data objects needed, and write assignment statements to store the appropriate initial values for each of the following situations:

a.   You want to represent a person by using six items of information: age, height, weight, sex, hair color, and eye color. Your program uses a data object named StudentLeader of type Person. Assign StudentLeader your own age, height, and so forth.

b.   The current weather might be represented by five facts: air temperature, cloud cover, precipitation, wind speed, and wind direction. You want to represent the weather at the start and finish of a sailboat race (using two record data objects). As an initial setting, set the weather at the start to be represented as 50 degrees F, clear, with no wind. Do not set any initial values for the finish.

c.   A telephone number in the U.S. has a three-digit "area code," a three-digit "exchange" and a four-digit "local line designator," for example, 804–924–3777 is a number in area 804 with exchange 924. You want to represent several such telephone numbers in such a way that each of the three parts can be selected separately. The first data object of interest is named "LocalInformation." Its initial value should be the "information" number for your local area.   ■

□□□ 6.5
ARRAYS

Arrays are our second major type of data structure. The simplest use of an array is to represent data organized as a list of *numbered items*. Arrays are also used to represent other organizations of data, such as various kinds of tables. Whenever you need to store a list or table that contains more than a few data items, you would expect to use an array.

"Make a list of the grades of the students in this class on the last exam," Professor Harris tells her teaching assistant. The assistant's list might look like this:

STUDENT	GRADE VALUE
1	97
2	85
3	70
4	82
.	.
.	.
.	.

Such a list could be represented in a computer program by using an array. Suppose we define a GradeValue type as a subrange 0–100. Then to represent a list of up to 500 grades, we might define a GradesList data type as an array:

DATA TYPES

GradeValue = 0..100
GradesList = ARRAY [1..500] OF GradeValue

Each data object of type GradesList may then be used to store a separate list of grades.

□ □

What is an Array?

An array consists of a sequence of individual data items, the *elements* of the array, each of which is identified by a *subscript*. The elements are all of the same data type, which can be any type, including a predefined type or one that you have defined. The subscripts are usually a subrange of Integer values, but sometimes a subrange of Char or enumerated values are used as subscripts. The entire sequence of subscripts, from the first subscript to the last, is termed the *subscript range* of the array. For example, an array of type GradesList has a subscript range of 1 to 500.

Two things distinguish a list represented as an array from the list of attributes and values found in a record:

1. *In an array, the elements are ordered by the sequence of subscript values.* We order the elements in an array in sequence, rather than naming them as we did with the fields of a record. Thus, an array always has a first element and a last element, and we often use actions that step through the elements of the array from first to last.

2. *The elements are all of the same data type.* In an array, the elements do not vary in data type. In a record, each field may have a different data type.

□ □

Defining and Coding an Array Data Type

Defining the representation for an array data type requires that you choose two things: (1) the *subscript range* for the array and (2) the *data type of the elements* of the array. Our pseudo-code is:

⟨array-type-definition⟩ ::=

⟨type-name⟩ = ARRAY [⟨subscript-range⟩] OF ⟨element-type⟩

WHERE
⟨type-name⟩ ::=
Pascal identifier used to name the data type.
⟨element-type⟩ ::=
A data type, either predefined or one defined in the program.
⟨subscript-range⟩ ::= ⟨subrange-type-name⟩ | ⟨first-subscript⟩..⟨last-subscript⟩
⟨subrange-type-name⟩ ::=
The name of a subrange type that you have defined.
⟨first-subscript⟩ ::=
A literal value or defined constant representing the subscript of the first array element.
⟨last-subscript⟩ ::=
A literal value or defined constant representing the subscript of the last array element.

Notice that the subscript range is simply a subrange, either one that has already been defined and named or one that is specified directly in the array type definition. For example, the GradesList array type might be defined as:

GradesList = ARRAY [1..500] OF GradeValue

or, using a separate subrange definition:

StudentNumberRange = 1..500
GradesList = ARRAY [StudentNumberRange] OF GradeValue

Coding an array type definition in Pascal requires only appending the terminating semicolon to the definition. Thus, coded in Pascal, the definitions above would appear in the TYPE section as:

```
TYPE
    GradeValue = 0..100;
    StudentNumberRange = 1..500;
    GradesList = ARRAY [StudentNumberRange] OF GradeValue;
```

□ □ The Size of an Array

The *size* of an array is the number of elements in the array. For example, an array of type GradesList has size 500. If the subscripts of the array are integer values, then its size may be computed as:

$$\langle \text{array size} \rangle = \langle \text{last subscript value} \rangle - \langle \text{first subscript value} \rangle + 1$$

EXAMPLE   Suppose an array type is defined as:

TemperatureTable = ARRAY [−5..30] OF Real

The size of the array is:

$$30 - (-5) + 1 = 36 \text{ elements} \qquad \blacksquare$$

□ □ Selecting Elements of an Array

To select a particular element from an array, you write the name of the array data object followed by the subscript of the desired element in square brackets:

$$\langle \text{array-name} \rangle \; [\langle \text{subscript} \rangle]$$

(Note that the square brackets here are *not* the BNF "optional item" brackets.) For example, if data object CS101Grades is of type GradesList, then you can select the first element by writing:

CS101Grades [1]

The last element is selected by "CS101Grades [500]" and so forth.

Once selected, an array element can be used just as though it were itself a data object of the array element type. For example, the elements of array CS101Grades are of subrange type GradeValue. You can assign a new value to an element:

CS101Grades [2] := 98

You can use the value stored in an element:

Total := Total + CS101Grades [2]

or

IF CS101Grades [2] = MaxGrade THEN . . .

You can READ or DISPLAY an element:

READ: CS101Grades [5]

or

DISPLAY: "The first grade in the list is ⟨CS101Grades [1]⟩"

There is one important new concept here that we did not see with records: in selecting an array element, the subscript can be the value of an *expression*. Thus, the general form for selecting an array element is:

⟨array-element-selection⟩ ::=

⟨array-name⟩ [⟨subscript-expression⟩]
WHERE
⟨array-name⟩ ::=
A Pascal identifier naming an array data object.
⟨subscript-expression⟩ ::=
Any Pascal expression that gives a value in the subscript range defined for the array.

Notice that the subscript expression *must* compute a value within the subscript range defined for the array, and the value computed must be of the same *data type* as the subscript range for the array. Thus, if the array uses Integer subscripts, then the subscript expression must compute an Integer value equal to the subscript of one of the array elements.

EXAMPLES

1. Suppose data object CS101Grades is of type GradesList. Then the following are equivalent ways in Pascal of selecting the 10th grade in the list and assigning it the value 98:
   a. CS101Grades [10] := 98;
   b. StudentId = 10;
   CS101Grades [StudentId] := 98;
   c. StudentId = 2;
   CS101Grades [StudentId + 8] := 98;
2. Suppose that you want to initialize the array CS101Grades to contain all zero values. Using an Integer data object, I, and a WHILE loop in Pascal:

```
I := 1;
WHILE I <= 500 DO
   BEGIN
      CS101Grades [I] := 0;
      I := I + 1;
   END;
```

□ □
Predefined Operations on Arrays

There is only one predefined operation on a whole array in Pascal: using an ASSIGN action to copy all the values in one array data object into another of the same data type. Thus the assignment:

$$\langle \text{array name} \rangle := \langle \text{another array of the same data type} \rangle$$

means "copy all the values stored in the elements of the array named on the right side of the assignment into the corresponding elements of the array named on the left side."

EXAMPLE   Suppose data objects CS101Grades and OldGradesList are two arrays of type GradesList, then the assignment:

$$\text{OldGradesList} := \text{CS101Grades}$$

causes the entire list of 500 grades in CS101Grades to be copied and stored in Old-GradesList. ■

No other operations are predefined in Pascal on whole arrays, so subprograms must be used to build other operations.

□ □

Initial Values of Arrays

The initial values of the elements of an array are unpredictable, just as with other types of data objects. Thus each element must be assigned a value by the program before the value is used the first time. However, some elements of an array may remain uninitialized while other elements are being used. Not every array element must be used each time the program is executed.

□ □

Arrays in the Computer Memory

An array is represented in the computer memory as a sequence of storage locations, one for each array element, beginning with the first array element (the one with the smallest subscript). If an element is a single data item like an Integer or Real value, then each element requires a single word of storage. If an element is a record or some other type of data structure, the storage location for an element may consist of several words. The details are not important here—the Pascal *array* is an abstraction that hides the details of exactly how an array is organized in the computer memory.

In drawing an array as a data object in the program state, we draw a sequence of rectangles, one for each element, with the value of that element in the rectangle, as shown in Figure 6.2. Such a diagram corresponds approximately to the way an array is stored in the computer memory. Note that the subscripts are not stored as part of the array—only the values of the elements are stored.

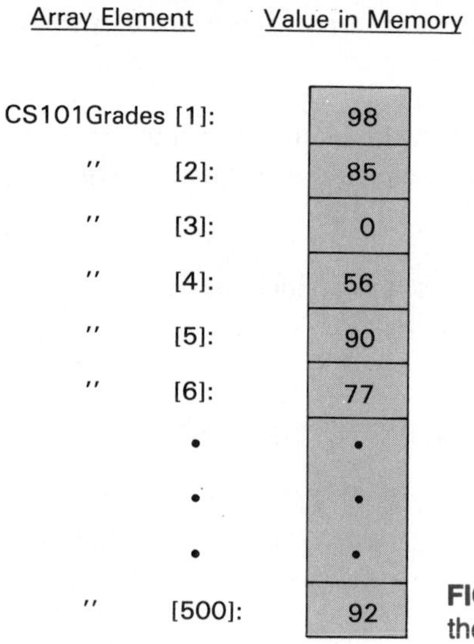

CS101Grades [1]:   98

    ''   [2]:   85

    ''   [3]:   0

    ''   [4]:   56

    ''   [5]:   90

    ''   [6]:   77

    •   •

    •   •

    •   •

    ''   [500]:   92

FIGURE 6.2 An Array in the Computer Memory

Subscript Range Errors

A *subscript range error* (or *subscript out-of-bounds* error) occurs when a program attempts to refer to an array element using a subscript value that is *outside the declared subscript range* for the array. For example, if array CS101Grades has subscript range 1..500 and your program refers to "CS101Grades [StudentId]" when variable StudentId happens to contain 506, then the program has a subscript range error. Subscript range errors are a common and troublesome source of program bugs, particularly in loops that process arrays.

When a subscript range error occurs during execution of a program, one of two things happens—and either is bad:

1. *The program CRASHES*. Your Pascal object program may contain special instructions, inserted by the compiler, that check the subscript used in each reference to an array element during program execution. If a subscript range error is detected, a run-time error message is displayed:

FATAL ERROR: SUBSCRIPT OUT OF RANGE

and execution of the program is terminated. The special instructions are usually inserted in your program only if you specifically request them when you compile the program (using a "subscript range check" option provided by the compiler). Your *Pascal User's Guide* will provide the details.

2. *The program doesn't CRASH.* Even worse is the alternative. If the compiler has not included the instructions to check for subscript range errors, then a subscript that is too large is used *as though the array were actually larger than it is*. The subscript value is computed and added to the memory address of the storage location where the array begins in the computer memory. This computation should give the memory address of the location that contains the desired element of the array. However, if this computation is performed with a subscript value that is too large, it still produces the memory address of a storage location, but the storage location is not part of the array. Figure 6.3 illustrates what happens.

If your program simply *uses* the value from this storage location, then the effect is just like using the value of an uninitialized variable—what you get is unpredictable. A much more serious problem occurs if your program *assigns* a new value to this storage location. Whatever was stored in this storage location is destroyed by the assignment. Because the storage location is not part of the array, the assign action destroys a piece of data or an instruction *entirely separate from the array you thought you were changing*. The subscript range error has caused a "random" change in some other part of your program. The effect of such a random change is unpredictable—the program could crash almost immediately, or it could crash in an unpredictable way later, or it could simply produce the wrong answers in some unpredictable way. As a result, subscript range errors are among the most difficult bugs to identify correctly.

□ □

Preconditions for Subscript Expressions

Whenever an action in a program uses a subscript expression rather than a literal value to specify the subscript of an array element, that action will have a *precondition* because of the possibility that the expression will return a subscript value that is outside the range of subscripts for the array. To guarantee that the subscript expression does not cause a subscript range error when the program is executed, you have to verify that the subscript value returned by the expression is always within the subscript range.

EXAMPLE   Q: What are the preconditions on the actions:

> DISPLAY: "Type the number of the grade you wish displayed."
> READ: SubscriptValue
> DISPLAY: "The grade is ⟨CS101Grades [⟨SubscriptValue⟩]"

A: The final DISPLAY action has a precondition:

> PRECONDITION: ⟨SubscriptValue⟩ must be in the range 1..500

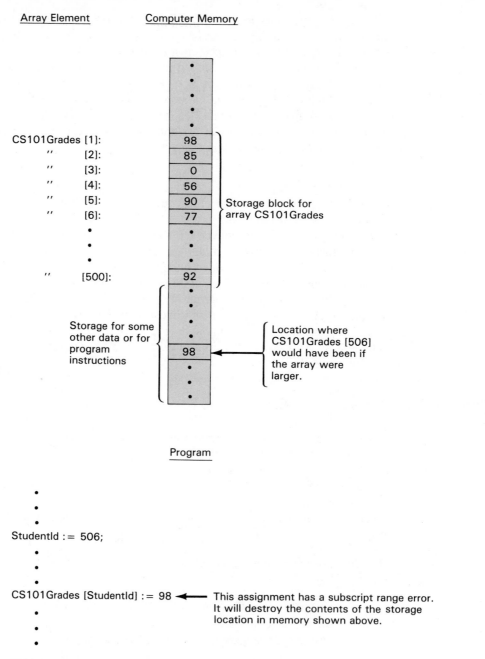

FIGURE 6.3 The Effect of a Subscript Range Error

If the precondition is not satisfied when this DISPLAY action is executed, the action will fail due to a subscript range error. ■

EXERCISES

6.8 Define array data types, declare array data objects, and write ASSIGN actions to give each array element an initial value appropriate to represent the data in each of the following situations:
   a. You want to represent a list of the powers of 3, from 3^0 to 3^6.
   b. You want to represent a list of the number of hours you worked, for each day in one week. Initially every entry should be zero.

6.9 As an experiment, write a program that uses an array and that deliberately executes a statement with a subscript range error. Does your Pascal system catch the error and display a run-time error message? If not, find out how you ask the compiler to include the extra instructions in your object program to check for subscript range errors. Recompile your test program using this option and rerun the test. What is the result now?

□□□ 6.6
USING ARRAYS TO REPRESENT LISTS AND TABLES

Let's look at how to use array data types to represent various kinds of lists and tables. We start with the simplest case: a list of numbered items, where you know the length of the list when you write the program. Then we look at simple tables where you want to use the subscript of the array element to represent the "key" used to look up entries in the table. Finally, we look at a harder case: a list whose length may vary from run to run of the program.

□□
Lists of Constant Known Length

Suppose you have a list of data to be stored, and you know exactly how long the list must be. For example, suppose you want to store the weekly sales totals for a grocery store, for each week in a year. There are 52 weeks in a year, so you know this list will always have exactly 52 items. We say that such a list is of *constant known length*, meaning you know *when you write the program* how long the list will be. Many kinds of lists are of constant known length, such as items listed by the hour, day, week, or month for a fixed period of time.

To represent such a list as an array is straightforward. The number of elements in the array equals the length of the list, so the subscript range runs from one to the length of the list. Each array element represents one item in the list.

EXAMPLE   **1.** To represent a list of weekly sales amounts, you might use the data type:

WeeklySalesList = ARRAY [1..52] OF Real

and then define the list as a data object of type WeeklySalesList:

SalesFor1989: WeeklySalesList

2. To represent a list of the hands in a four-person card game, you might use the data type:

HandsList = ARRAY [1..4] OF Hand

and then define the list as a data object of type HandsList:

NewHandsDealt: HandsList ■

The most common operations on a list are *create the list* and *select an item from the list*. Using the array representation, both operations are easily represented:

1. *Create the list*. Because the length of the list exactly equals the number of elements in the array, creating the list is accomplished by assigning an appropriate value to each element of the array. You might use a sequence of assignments, such as:

SalesFor1989 [1] := . . .
SalesFor1989 [2] := . . .
 . . .

or, more commonly, you might use a loop to read in the appropriate values:

DISPLAY: "Please type the weekly sales amounts for 1989."
         "Begin with week one and continue to week 52."
I := 1
WHILE I <= 52 DO
      READ: SalesFor1989 [I]
      I := I + 1

2. *Select an item from the list*. You can select an item at a given position in the list by using its subscript in the array representation. For example, to select the sales amount for the last week of 1989, you might use:

SalesFor1989 [52]

□ □
Simple Tables

A *table* is a common way of representing information in the real world. For example: a telephone directory is a table of telephone owners, a business might use a table of sales tax amounts, and Appendix A of this book is a table of ASCII character codes.

A table consists of a list of *entries*—the data items that we wish to use. The characteristic operation on a table is the *look up* operation (also called a *search* operation)—look up an entry in the table, given a "key" value. For example, given a name as the key value, you might look up in a telephone directory the telephone number and address associated with that name.

In the real world, we choose the representation of a table so that the look up operation is made easy for a given type of key value. For example, a telephone directory is organized so that it is easy to look up an entry using a person's name as the key. But if we want to use a telephone number as the key value, and look up the name and address of the person with a given telephone number, then a telephone directory is useless because of the way that its entries are organized.

Many programs also use tables of information. Representing tables and the look up operation in a computer program is an important programming topic. Most tables are represented using arrays in some way. We look at some simple tables that are easily represented by arrays here. In Chapter 14, we look at how to represent more complex tables.

The essential first step in choosing a representation for a table is to determine what *key values* will be used in the look up operation. The simplest tables, from a programming viewpoint, are those where the possible key values can be represented as a *subrange* data type. The subrange might be a subrange of Integer values, but it could also be a subrange of Char or enumerated values. If it is an Integer subrange, it may begin with a value other than one. For example, in a table of Fahrenheit to Celsius temperature conversions, the key values for the range of Fahrenheit temperatures might run from 32 degrees F. to 212 degrees F.

If the possible key values can be represented as a subrange, then the entire table can be represented as an array. You simply use the subrange as the subscript range for the array and represent the table entries as the elements of the array. The type definition for such a table has the form:

DATA TYPES

⟨table type⟩ = ARRAY [⟨key subrange⟩] OF ⟨entry type⟩

A data object of this type represents the actual table:

DATA OBJECTS

⟨table⟩: ⟨table type⟩   A particular table of the type.

The two operations of interest are *create the table* and *look up an entry*:

1. *Create the table*. To create the table initially, you might use a sequence of assignments to elements in the array, a READ loop to read in and assign the table entries in sequence, or a loop that computes and stores the table entries using a mathematical formula. The first two alternatives are similar to those for creating a list of constant known length. The third might be used where there is some regular mathematical relationship between the key value and the table entry. For example, to create a table named PowersOfTwo that stores the powers of two from 2^0 to 2^{15}, you might use the formulas:

$$2^0 = 1$$
$$2^{k+1} = 2^k * 2 \text{ for } k >= 0$$

and then use these formulas in the loop:

ACTIONS:

```
PowersOfTwo [0] := 1
I := 1
WHILE I <= 15 DO
        PowersOfTwo [I] := PowersOfTwo [I - 1] * 2
        I := I + 1
```

2. *Look up an entry, given a key value.* The look up operation for such a table is straightforward. Given the key value of the desired entry, you simply select the array element with that subscript. The array element represents the desired table entry. For example, to look up the value of 2^9 in the table PowersOfTwo, you might write:

PowersOfTwo [9]

as in:

DISPLAY: "The value of 2 to the 9th power = ⟨PowersOfTwo [9]⟩"

EXAMPLES

1. Suppose you want to create a table in a program to represent the following table of weather information for a particular city:

Record Low Temperatures (Degrees F.)

Month	Temperature
January	−12
February	−3
March	0
April	8
May	15
June	26
July	39
August	34
September	24
October	21
November	10
December	−2

For this table and a given month, the look up operation would return the record low temperature for that month. Thus, the months are used as the key values. Suppose that you choose to represent the months by the Integer subrange 1..12. Then the entire table could be represented:

Data Types

TemperatureValue = −100..120
TemperatureTable = ARRAY [1..12] OF TemperatureValue

Data Objects

RecordLows: TemperatureTable Table of record low temperatures.

To fill the table with the correct entries, use a sequence of assignments:

RecordLows [1] := −12
RecordLows [2] := −3
RecordLows [3] := 0

.
.
.

The final form of the table is shown in Figure 6.4.

To look up an entry, given the number of the desired month, write:

RecordLows [⟨month⟩]

2. One simple way to encode a written message is to systematically replace each letter in the message by another letter, using a table that specifies the encoding to use, such as shown in Figure 6.5. Suppose that the message is written entirely using the capital letters A–Z. These letters form the key values used in the look up operation, and the table entries are also chosen from this letter range. To represent

RecordLows [1]:	−12	
″ [2]:	−3	
″ [3]:	0	
″ [4]:	8	
″ [5]:	15	
″ [6]:	26	
″ [7]:	39	
″ [8]:	34	
″ [9]:	24	
″ [10]:	21	
″ [11]:	10	
″ [12]:	−2	

FIGURE 6.4 Table Represented by the RecordLows Array

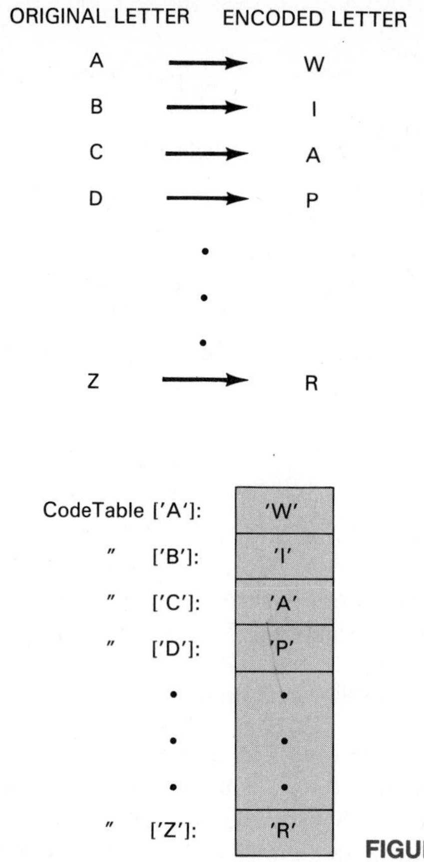

ORIGINAL LETTER   ENCODED LETTER

```
A  ──────▶  W
B  ──────▶  I
C  ──────▶  A
D  ──────▶  P
          •
          •
          •
Z  ──────▶  R
```

```
CodeTable ['A']:   │ 'W' │
     "    ['B']:    │ 'I' │
     "    ['C']:    │ 'A' │
     "    ['D']:    │ 'P' │
          •         │  •  │
          •         │  •  │
          •         │  •  │
     "    ['Z']:    │ 'R' │
```

FIGURE 6.5 A Code Table

such a table in a program, you can use the fact that the letters 'A' to 'Z' form a sub-range of type Char. The entire table could be represented:

DATA TYPES

LetterRange = 'A'..'Z'
CodeTableType = ARRAY [LetterRange] OF LetterRange

DATA OBJECTS

CodeTable: CodeTableType   Table of character encodings.

To fill the table with the correct entries, use a sequence of assignments:

CodeTable ['A'] := 'W'
CodeTable ['B'] := 'I'
CodeTable ['C'] := 'A'
    .
    .
    .

To read a character, encode it, and display the encoded character, you might use the actions:

```
READ: InChar
IF InChar IN ['A'..'Z'] THEN
    OutChar := CodeTable [InChar]
ELSE
    OutChar := InChar
DISPLAY: OutChar
```

Notice how the look up operation is represented by using the character read as the key value to select the array element that contains the replacement character value. ■

□ □
Lists of Varying Length

When you make a list, you often do not know how long the list will be when you start. The same is true when you represent a list as an array in a computer program. For example, suppose Florida Joe wants to store the "fillup" amounts in an array in his gas mileage program. How many elements should the array have? Each time he uses the program, Joe will probably have a different number of fillup amounts to enter. An array to store these amounts, then, will store different numbers of values on different runs of the program, maybe 25 fillup amounts on one run and only 17 on the next run. Such a list is termed a *list of varying length*.

A list of varying length has a *current length,* the number of items in the list at a particular time. In order to represent the list as an array, we must also choose a *maximum length* for the list, the largest number of items the list may ever contain at one time. The array is defined to have a subscript range from one to the maximum length of the list.

The maximum length for a particular list has to be chosen when the program is written, so that the subscript range for the array can be defined. In many cases, you may have to choose a number that you estimate to be considerably larger than will ordinarily be needed. That is, you *overallocate* elements in the array, just to take account of the rare situation when you may need to store a very long list.

During each run of the program, only some of the array elements will be used to store data values. The remaining elements are unused during that run. Occasionally the list of data values may actually require use of every array element, but that situation may be rare. An array that is usually only partially filled with data values during a run of the program is called a *partially filled array*. Figure 6.6 illustrates the concept of a partially filled array.

EXAMPLE   Florida Joe estimates that his gas mileage program will never need to store more than 50 fillup amounts, because he never expects to make a trip that would be long enough to require more than 50 fillups. Thus, he chooses to represent the list of fillup amounts as a partially filled array with a size of 50. His first try at choosing the representation is the type definition:

FillupList = ARRAY [1..50] OF Real

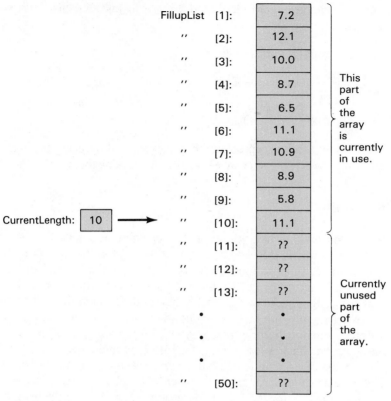

FIGURE 6.6 A Partially Filled Array

Each time the program is run, only the first portion of the array would actually be used—how many elements were used would depend on the length of the list of fillup amounts for that particular trip. ■

Several concepts are important in choosing the representation for a list of varying length:

1. *The maximum length of the list should be a defined constant.* Because the maximum length of the list is often a "best guess" at the time the program is written, abstract the maximum length as a defined constant. Then you can choose the exact length later, and change it easily if your initial choice turns out to be wrong.

For example, Florida Joe guessed "50" as the maximum list length he would need. But if he lives in Florida and takes a trip to Alaska next year, he might find his list of fillups is longer than 50. He will need to change the maximum length and recompile the program before he can use it with this longer list. Thus Joe decides to declare his array as:

FillupList = ARRAY [1..MAXFILLUPS] OF Real

and put the constant MAXFILLUPS on his DEFINED CONSTANTS list. He can pick the value 50 for MAXFILLUPS as he codes the program the first time:

```
CONST
     MAXFILLUPS = 50;      {maximum number of fillups allowed}
```

but after his trip to Alaska, he only has to change this constant definition to a larger value, say 100, recompile the program, and he can enter up to 100 fillup amounts to be stored in the array.

2. *The "current length" of the list must be stored separately.* For a list of varying length, you must keep track of its current length in a separate data object. Because the items in the list are numbered in sequence, the current length is also the subscript of the *last element in use* in the array. The array elements with subscripts from one up to the current length are in use, and the elements with subscripts greater than the current length are not in use.

3. *The list may be "empty."* If nothing has yet been stored in the list, then we say it is *empty,* meaning that none of the array elements are currently in use. In this case, we set the current length to zero.

4. *The list of items and its current length should be grouped into a record.* Rather than using two separate data objects to represent the items in the list and the current length of the list, it is better to group both into a single record with two fields:

DATA TYPES

⟨array type⟩ = ARRAY [1..⟨maximum length⟩] OF ⟨list item type⟩
⟨list length subrange⟩ = 0..⟨maximum length⟩
⟨list of varying length⟩ =
  RECORD
      ⟨list of items⟩: ⟨array type⟩
      ⟨current length⟩: ⟨list length subrange⟩
  END

EXAMPLE   Joe's list of fillup amounts might be represented:

DATA TYPES

ListType = ARRAY [1..MAXFILLUPS] OF Real
LengthRange = 0..MAXFILLUPS
FillupListType =
    RECORD
        List: ListType
        CurrentLength: LengthRange
    END

Notice that the LengthRange subrange includes the zero value representing an empty list. The list itself can then be defined:

DATA OBJECTS

FillupList = FillupListType   The list of fillup amounts.   ■

The characteristic operations on a list of varying length include:

1. *Create an empty list.* To create the list initially as an empty list, you set the current length to zero. For example, to create an empty list of fillup amounts, Joe might write:

$$\text{FillupList.CurrentLength} := 0$$

2. *Append a new item to the end of the list.* To append a new item, you increment the value of the current length to get the subscript of the next unused array element, and then assign the new item as the value of that element. But be careful! Always check that the array still has another unused element. For example, Joe's program might use the following actions to create the list of fillup amounts from the values typed by the user:

```
READ: Gallons
WHILE Gallons > 0 DO
    IF FillupList.CurrentLength < MAXFILLUPS THEN
        FillupList.CurrentLength :=
                FillupList.CurrentLength + 1
        FillupList.List [FillupList.CurrentLength] := Gallons
    ELSE
        DISPLAY:
            "ERROR: List exceeds maximum length of ⟨MAXFILLUPS⟩
            Please type a zero value to end the list."
    READ: Gallons
```

3. *Select an item from the list.* To select a particular item from the list, given the number of the item, use the number as a subscript to select the desired array element. For example, to select the second element of Joe's list, we might use:

$$\text{FillupList.List [2]}$$

However, this operation always has a *precondition*: the subscript value cannot be greater than the current length of the list. For example, if Joe's list is empty, then the attempt to select the second element above will fail to return a valid list item.

Notice that the error associated with this precondition is *not* a subscript-range error—the subscript is within the range of valid subscripts for the array, which runs from one to the maximum list length. But the subscript refers to an array element that is not within the part of the array that is currently in use. Thus the error is similar to an *uninitialized data object* error—the value returned will be unpredictable.

EXERCISES

6.10 For each of the following lists or tables, choose an appropriate data representation and write the necessary data type definitions in pseudo-code. Assume that the operations defined on tables are *create the table* and *look up an entry when given its key,* and the operations on lists are *create the list* and *select an item when given its position in the list*.

a. A table of the number of days in each month of the year, organized so that, when given the number of a month, it is easy to look up the number of days in that month.

b. A table of quarterly income amounts for a small business, using the number of the quarter as the key.

c. A list of the letter grades assigned to students in a physics class, for up to 300 students.

d. A grocery list—items to buy at the grocery store.

e. A table of Fahrenheit to Celsius temperature conversions, for temperatures in the range −60 to 130 degrees Fahrenheit. It should be easy to look up a given Fahrenheit temperature to find the equivalent Celsius temperature. Assume all the temperatures are rounded to the closest integer value.

f. A list showing the score at the end of each inning of a baseball game, including extra innings played (beyond the usual nine innings), if any.

6.11 In a list of varying length, you might sometimes want to *delete* an item from the list. In the array representation assume that you do not want to have "holes" in the list of elements in use, and assume that you do not care about the order of elements in the list. What actions would you use for each of the following operations?

a. Delete the *last item* in the list.

b. Delete an item that is not the last item.

□□□ 6.7
CHARACTER STRINGS

A sequence of characters is called a *character string* in computer jargon. Character strings are our third major type of data structure. Many programs process data that is best represented as a character string, such as a name, an address, or the words in a sentence. Thus, the representation of character strings and operations on character strings is an important issue in many programs.

□□
What is a Character String?

You have probably filled out a form that asked you to print your name within a sequence of small squares, like this:

Print your name, one letter per box:

B	E	U	L	A	H		P	E	A	B	O	D	Y	

Representing a character string as a data object in a computer program uses the same idea—the character string is viewed as a sequence of characters, including spaces and punctuation as needed. Each storage location for a character is termed a *character position*. The character positions in a character string are numbered from one up to the length of the string. Thus the character positions in the string above would be numbered from 1 to 15:

B	E	U	L	A	H		P	E	A	B	O	D	Y	
1	2	3	4	5	6	7	8	9	10	11	12	13	14	15

As you can see, the representation of a character string is similar to the representation of an ARRAY [1..⟨string length⟩] OF Char—an array in which each element is a Char value and the subscript range is from one to the length of the string. But there are two important differences in the way that we use data objects that contain character strings in a program:

1. The *length* of the strings being stored usually varies during execution of the program. For example, if a data object EmployeeName contains a person's name, then the length of the name (number of characters it contains) changes as different names are stored. Thus a data object that stores a string is similar to a *list of varying length*—some of the character positions may not be in use at any given time and the *current length* of the string must be stored along with the characters themselves.

2. The basic *operations* used on character strings differ from those ordinarily used with arrays. With an array, we usually work with one element at a time, selected with a subscript. With a character string, we more often want to work with a *substring* of characters rather than a single character, where the substring may be a word within a sentence, an item of input data within a line of input data, or the like. We often use operations that insert or delete a substring from a string, or that *concatenate* two or more strings together to form a longer string.

□ □

Character String Data Types in Pseudo-code

In pseudo-code, we define a character string data type using the syntax:

⟨character string type⟩ ::=
⟨type name⟩ = STRING [⟨maximum length⟩]

WHERE

⟨type name⟩ ::=
  Pascal identifier used to name the data type.
⟨maximum length⟩ ::=
  Integer literal value or defined constant giving the maximum number
  of characters that can be stored in a string of this type.

☐

Meaning: A data object of a STRING type may contain a character string of any
number of characters up to ⟨maximum length⟩. The *empty string* containing no
characters may also be stored.

EXAMPLES

DATA TYPES

MAX Length

EmployeeName = STRING [50]	Full name of employee.
MonthName = STRING [9]	Written month name.
DisplayLine = STRING [80]	Line to be displayed.

The maximum length defined for a string data type must be chosen to accommodate the longest string that might ever need to be stored in a data object of that
type. Thus, you usually *overallocate* storage space for strings, by choosing the maximum length to be longer than you would ordinarily expect to use, just as you overallocate storage in a partially filled array.

Unlike our pseudo-code for the other data types introduced in this chapter, our
pseudo-code for character strings does not resemble standard Pascal. Our STRING
pseudo-code provides for strings of *varying length,* up to the maximum declared
length for the type. Standard Pascal supports only strings of *constant length,* which
makes it difficult to define operations on strings. We describe the relevant features of
standard Pascal below.

Because of the limited utility of standard Pascal, we have chosen our pseudo-
code to resemble instead a common set of *extensions* to standard Pascal. These extensions provide a STRING type, similar to our pseudo-code STRING type, and a
set of predefined operations on string data objects that make it convenient to represent and manipulate strings in a program. Most Pascal programs that work with
strings use these extensions rather than the features of standard Pascal. We follow
the same pattern in our pseudo-code, and then describe how to code these pseudo-
code elements in both an extended Pascal and in standard Pascal.

☐ ☐
Character String Literals

A literal value of a STRING type is written as a quoted sequence of characters, exactly as you would write a quoted string in a DISPLAY action:

'. . .any sequence of characters. . .'

To include a single quote in the literal string, you write it twice, '', within the quoted string. The empty string is written as two single quotes, ''. A literal composed of a single character, such as 'A', is considered to be of type Char if assigned to a data object of type Char, or of a string type if assigned to a string data object.

□ □

Assignment to a String Data Object

The *length* of a string data value is the number of characters in the string. You can assign a string literal value directly to a string data object. For example, if NewEmployee has type STRING [15], then after the assignment:

$$\text{NewEmployee} := \text{'Clancy Cooper'}$$

the length of the string in NewEmployee is 13. After the assignment of the empty string to the same data object:

$$\text{NewEmployee} := \text{''}$$

the length is zero.

The length of the string stored in a data object can never exceed the maximum length defined for that data type. An attempt to assign a longer string results in the string being *truncated*—the extra characters are chopped off at the right end of the string. For example, the assignment:

$$\text{NewEmployee} := \text{'Major Major Major'}$$

results in NewEmployee containing the string 'Major Major Maj'—the last two characters have been truncated.

□ □

Predefined Operations on STRING Data Objects

For our pseudo-code, we assume the following operations are predefined for any string data object:

1. *READ and DISPLAY string values.* A READ action may specify a data object of a string type. The READ action reads characters that the user types and stores them in the data object until either (a) the maximum declared length for the string is reached or (b) the user types a RETURN (end-of-line). In case (b), the length of the string that is stored equals the number of characters read, not including the RETURN.

A DISPLAY action may specify the name of a string data object. Beginning at the current position in the output line, all the characters stored in the data object are displayed, up to the current length of the string.

EXAMPLE   Suppose StudentName is of STRING[10] type. Consider the actions:

DISPLAY: "Please type your name:"
READ: StudentName
DISPLAY: "Hi ⟨StudentName⟩! Let's compute!"

If the user types:

Oscar⟨RETURN⟩

then StudentName stores the string "Oscar" of length five and the second DISPLAY gives:

Hi Oscar!   Let's compute!

If the user types:

Captain Nemo⟨RETURN⟩

then StudentName stores the string "Captain_Ne" of (maximum) length ten and the second display gives:

Hi Captain Ne!   Let's compute!   ■

2. *Select a single character.* To select a single character value from a string, use a subscript expression to indicate the desired character position:

⟨string data object⟩ [⟨character position⟩]

EXAMPLE To select the second character of ReportMonth, write:

ReportMonth [2]

or use a subscript expression:

ReportMonth [FirstCharPosn + 1]

If the subscript value does not refer to a character position within the maximum length of the string, then you have a *subscript range error,* just as with an array.

3. *Select a substring.* To select a substring of a given length that begins at a given character position, use the predefined function Copy, defined as:

FUNCTION Copy

(String: ⟨any string type⟩	IN: The string data object.
Position: Integer	IN: Starting position of the desired substring.
Length: Integer)	IN: Length of the desired substring.

FUNCTION VALUE: ⟨string⟩   The specified substring.

PURPOSE: Returns a copy of the characters in String, beginning at character position Position and continuing for Length characters or until the end of the string in String is reached.

PRECONDITION: Position must be a character position within the string currently stored in String.

EXAMPLE   Suppose Name1, Name2, and Name3 are each of type STRING [10]. Then:

```
Name1 := 'Patricia'
Name2 := Copy (Name1, 3, 8)
Name3 := Copy (Name1, 4, 3)
```

assigns "tricia" to Name2 and "ric" to Name3.

4. *Find the length of a string.* To determine the length of the string currently stored in a string data object, use the predefined function:

FUNCTION Length
    (String: ⟨any string type⟩) IN: The character string.

FUNCTION VALUE: Integer in range 0 to maximum length for the type of String.

PURPOSE: Returns the length of the string currently stored in String.

EXAMPLE   Suppose Name1 is of type STRING [10]. Then:

```
Name1 := 'Patricia'
```

DISPLAY: "The name has ⟨Length (Name1)⟩ characters."

displays:

The name has 8 characters.

5. *Compare two strings.* To compare the values of two string data objects, use the tests = or <>. For example, the test:

$$\langle string1 \rangle = \langle string2 \rangle$$

returns TRUE if both strings have the same length and corresponding characters are identical.

To determine if one string comes "before" another, based on the ordering of the character values used in your Pascal system, use the tests <, >, <=, and >=. For example, the test:

$$\langle string1 \rangle < \langle string2 \rangle$$

returns TRUE if, when comparing the characters from left to right in the two strings, the first position where the strings differ finds the character in ⟨string1⟩ coming before that in ⟨string2⟩ in the character ordering. If the strings are identical up to the length of the shorter string, then the shorter string is less than the longer.

EXAMPLE

Assuming a Pascal system that uses the ASCII ordering (Appendix A), then after the actions:

```
Name1 := 'Billye'
Name2 := 'Billie'
Name3 := 'Bill
```

the tests:

```
Name1 = Name2   ⟶   returns FALSE
Name2 < Name1   ⟶   returns TRUE
Name1 = Name3   ⟶   returns FALSE
Name3 < Name1   ⟶   returns TRUE
```

6. *Locate the beginning of a substring.* To determine where a given substring begins within a longer string, use the predefined function Position, define as:

```
FUNCTION Position
        (String: ⟨any string type⟩        IN: The longer string.
        Substring: ⟨any string type⟩)     IN: The substring.
```

FUNCTION VALUE: Integer in range 0 to length of String.

PURPOSE: Returns the position of the first character of the leftmost occurrence of Substring within String. If Substring does not appear in String, a zero value is returned.

EXAMPLE   If Name1 is of type STRING[10] and Location1 and Location2 are of type Integer, then the actions:

```
Name1 := 'Billy_Bob'
Location1 := Position (Name1, '_')
Location2 := Position ('His name is Billy_Bob Williams', Name1)
```

assigns Location1 the value 6 and Location2 the value 13.   ■

7. *Concatenate two or more strings to form a longer string*. To concatenate several strings to form a longer string, use the predefined function Concat, defined as:

FUNCTION Concat
        (String1: ⟨any string type⟩   IN: The first string.
        String2: ⟨any string type⟩   IN: The second string.
        . . . ⟨as many additional strings as desired⟩ . . .)
      FUNCTION VALUE: The concatenation of the strings given as parameters.
      PURPOSE: Return a string composed of a copy of String1 followed by a copy of String2, followed by a copy of any additional strings, in the sequence listed in the call.

EXAMPLE   If Name1, Name2, and Name3 are of type STRING [20] then the actions:

```
Name1 := 'Green'
Name2 := 'Ham'
Name3 := Concat (Name1, ' Eggs and ', Name2)
```

leaves Name3 = 'Green Eggs and Ham'   ■

8. *Delete a substring from a string*. To delete a substring of a given length that begins at a given character position, use the predefined procedure Delete:

PROCEDURE Delete
        (String: ⟨any string type⟩   IN/OUT: The character string.
        Position: Integer   IN: Start of the substring.
        Length: Integer)   IN: Length of the substring.

      PURPOSE: Starting at character Position within String, delete the next Length characters, or as many as remain in String. Close the resulting gap, so that the characters in String after the deletion now immediately follow those before the deletion.

GOAL STATE: String contains the modified string value.

PRECONDITION: Position must select a character within the current string in String.

If Name1 and Name2 are of type STRING [20], then the actions:

```
Name1 := 'Harsh worry'
Name2 := 'Program error'
CALL Delete (Name1, 3, 6)
CALL Delete (Name2, 4, 99)
```

leave Name1 = 'Harry' and Name2 = 'Pro'

9. *Insert a substring into a string.* To insert a substring at a given position within a longer string, use the predefined procedure Insert:

PROCEDURE Insert
          (String: ⟨any string type⟩   IN/OUT: The longer string.
          Substring: ⟨any string type⟩   IN
          Position: Integer)   IN: Start of the insertion.

PURPOSE: Insert a copy of the characters in Substring into String, beginning immediately *before* the character currently at Position within String. If the resulting length of String exceeds the maximum length declared for the type of String, truncate the extra characters at the right end of the new value of String.

GOAL STATE: String contains the modified string.

PRECONDITION: Position must be a character position within the current value of String.

If Name1 is of type STRING [10], then the actions:

```
Name1 := 'Prom'
CALL Insert (Name1, 'gra', 4)
```

leaves Name1 = 'Program'

Initial Values of String Data Objects

As with other types of data objects, the initial value of a string data object is unpredictable. In particular, both the initial length and the initial contents are unpredictable—the initial length is *not* guaranteed to be zero.

□ □

Coding Strings and String Operations in Extended Pascal

We have chosen our pseudo-code to conform closely to the STRING extensions found in systems like Turbo Pascal. However, check your local *Pascal User's Manual* for the details of your Pascal system before coding a Pascal program from our pseudo-code. In particular, most Pascal systems impose a *limit* on the maximum length that can be used in a STRING type definition. For example, in Turbo Pascal and many other systems the limit is 255 characters—no string of any string type may be longer than 255 characters.

□ □

Coding Strings and String Operations in Standard Pascal

Our pseudo-code STRING types and the predefined operations on strings cannot be directly represented in standard Pascal. In standard Pascal a character string is represented as a PACKED ARRAY OF Char:

⟨string type⟩ = PACKED ARRAY [1..⟨maximum length⟩] OF Char;

("PACKED" means "pack the characters into storage locations in memory with no wasted space.") The PACKED ARRAY representation does not allow the length of the string stored in a PACKED ARRAY to vary—all strings must be filled out with spaces to *exactly* the declared maximum length before they are stored in a data object of the type.

Standard Pascal provides only a few predefined operations on strings that are represented as PACKED ARRAY OF Char:

1. *Assignment of literal strings to string variables.* The literal string must be exactly the right length, as mentioned above. For example, if StudentName is a data object of type:

PACKED ARRAY [1..15] OF Char;

then the assignment:

StudentName := 'Major_Major';

is *not allowed* because the literal string only contains 11 characters. To make the assignment valid, you must fill out the literal value to have exactly 15 characters:

StudentName := 'Major_Major____';

2. *Selection of individual characters.* Ordinary array subscripts may be used to select a particular character position in a string. For example:

```
StudentName [2]  : =  'T';
```

assigns 'T' as the second character in StudentName.

3. *Comparison of strings, using relational operations.* Two string variables of the same data type (same length) may be compared using the operations =, <>, <, <=, >, and >=. The less than, greater than comparisons use the ordering of the individual character codes, just as for comparisons of Char type values.

4. *WRITE of string type variables.* The *write* and *writeln* statements allow whole strings to be output, simply by listing the name of a string variable.

Although these predefined operations allow simple string manipulations to be programmed, they are inadequate for use in most programs that work with strings. For example, none of the following pseudo-code string operations are predefined in standard Pascal:

- READ of string values.
- Select a substring.
- Compare two strings of different lengths.
- Locate the beginning of a substring.
- Concatenate two or more strings.
- Insert or delete a substring.

Thus programs in standard Pascal that work with strings often require that subprograms to perform these basic operations be written.

EXERCISES

6.12 For each of the following situations, define an appropriate character string data type, declare the data objects that you need, and write assignment statements that store the desired string values in the data objects:

a. You want a data object that can store the name of a day of the week as a character string. Its initial value should be 'Monday'.

b. You want two data objects to store the name of the 'current month' and the 'next month', initially 'February' and 'March' respectively.

6.13 Use the predefined pseudo-code string operations defined in this section in short sequences of assignments that solve the following problems:

a. Suppose that Date1, Month1, Day1, and Year1 are of type STRING [20]. Date1 contains a string representing a date, written in the form:

dd mmm yyyy

where *dd* is a two-digit day (integer), *mmm* is a three-letter month abbreviation, and *yyyy* is a four-digit year between 1900 and 2100. For example, Date1 might contain:

03 JUL 1995

Use the predefined pseudo-code string operations of this section to break up the string in Date1 into its day, month, and year parts and assign each part to the appropriate string data object, Day1, Month1, or Year1. Your answer should be a sequence of ASSIGN actions. End your sequence with a DISPLAY action that displays the date, centered in the display line, in the form:

mmm dd, yyyy

For example:

JUL 03, 1995

Don't forget the comma.

b. Repeat (a), but assume that the day part may have one or two digits (but it ends with the first space in Date1) and the month part may have three to nine characters (but it begins after the first space and ends with the second space). Allow the year to have any number of digits and to optionally be followed by "B.C." or "A.D.". For example, initially Date1 might contain the string:

3 October 527 B.C.

□□□ **6.8**
CASE STUDY: DATA REPRESENTATION USING ARRAYS, RECORDS, AND STRINGS

Let's look at an example of a data type that requires a more complex data representation, one that includes arrays, records, and strings. Many programs need this sort of representation in order to represent in a natural way a type of "object" in the real world.

Consider a program that maintains information about the inventory of clothes sold in a clothes store. We focus on a simple list of the current inventory of jeans stocked by the store, in order to build on our earlier example of the record type

"Jeans". Our original Jeans type included fields named Waist, Length, Price, Color, and Condition. For the inventory list, we delete the Condition field and replace the Price field by two fields, Retail and Wholesale, that store the retail price and wholesale price for each pair of jeans. Also we add an InStock field to indicate the date when each pair of Jeans was received by the store. Finally, we add a new field, Brand, of a string type, BrandName, that contains the brand name of the jeans. This leaves our Jeans data type defined as follows:

DATA TYPES

```
MonthRange = 1..12
DayRange = 1..31
YearRange = 1900..2100
Date =
    RECORD
            Month: MonthRange
            Day: DayRange
            Year: YearRange
    END
WaistRange = 22..48          Waist size in inches.
LengthRange = 20..40         Inseam length in inches.
JeansColor = (BLUE, BLACK, BROWN, WHITE)
BrandName = STRING [25]
Jeans =          Description of one pair of jeans.
    RECORD
            Waist: WaistRange
            Length: LengthRange
            Retail: Real       Price in dollars/cents.
            Wholesale: Real    Price in dollars/cents.
            Color : JeansColor
            InStock: Date      Date shipment received.
            Brand: BrandName
    END
```

To complete the inventory list, we create a data type, JeansInventory, that consists of a list of the Jeans in stock represented as a list of varying length. The list itself is represented as an array with subscript range from one up to the largest inventory that we might ever expect—abstracted into a defined constant named MAXINVENTORY. We define the entire list as a record with two fields, the list itself, and the current length of the list. This gives the final data type definitions for this representation:

DATA TYPES

```
    . . . — as above
JeansList = ARRAY [1..MAXINVENTORY] OF Jeans
ListLength = 0..MAXINVENTORY
```

```
JeansInventory =                        Inventory for one store.
    RECORD
            Stock: JeansList            All the jeans in stock.
            Count: ListLength           Number of jeans in stock.
    END
```

Using these type definitions, we can define as many JeansInventory lists as needed. For example, there might be one such list for each branch of the store. Let's suppose that one such list is declared as follows:

DEFINED CONSTANTS

MAXINVENTORY = 2000   Maximum number of jeans in stock.

DATA OBJECTS

MallStore: JeansInventory   Stock at the mall store.

With this set of definitions, the data object MallStore can store the complete description of each pair of jeans in stock, for up to 2000 pairs.

Let's look at how some simple actions would use this representation of the inventory list to answer questions about the jeans in stock:

1. *What is the retail price of the first pair of jeans in the inventory list?*

ACTIONS:

```
Price := MallStore.Stock[1].Retail
DISPLAY: "The price is ⟨Price⟩"
```

□

Discussion: Notice how we work down through the representation of the data structure to select the particular field of the particular Jeans record that is needed. We begin with the "top-level structure," the record MallStore. Then we select the field Stock from that record. Because this field is itself an array, we use a subscript expression ("1" in this case) to select an element from that array. Because each element of that array is a record of type Jeans, we then select the particular field, Retail, from that record which contains the data value of interest.

2. *What is the brand name of the next to the last pair of jeans in the list?*

ACTIONS:

```
IF MallStore.Count > 1 THEN
        DesiredBrand :=
            MallStore.Stock [MallStore.Count − 1].Brand
        DISPLAY: "The brand name is ⟨DesiredBrand⟩"
ELSE
        DISPLAY: "Less than two pair of jeans are in stock."
```

□

Discussion: Notice how the IF checks the precondition for the ASSIGN action, to avoid a possible failure in case the list has no "next to the last" element.

3. *How many pairs of BLUE jeans are in stock?*

ACTIONS:

```
JeansCount := 0
I := 1
WHILE I <= MallStore.Count DO
        IF MallStore.Stock[I].Color = BLUE THEN
                JeansCount := JeansCount + 1
        I := I + 1
DISPLAY: "There are ⟨JeansCount⟩ blue jeans in stock."
```

EXERCISES

6.14   Write ACTIONS lists appropriate to answer each of the following questions about the information stored in the MallBranch inventory list defined above:

a.   In what month were the last jeans in the list entered into the inventory?

b.   How much is the mark up on the second pair of jeans in the list? (The mark up is the difference between the wholesale and retail prices.)

c.   How many jeans in the inventory have a retail price greater than 30 dollars?

d.   Are there any white jeans with waist size 30 and inseam length 28 in stock?

e.   How many jeans were received during May of last year?

□□□ **6.9**
PROGRAM IT WITH STYLE!

Here are a few suggestions for writing readable, understandable type definitions:

1.   *Use all capital letters for the names of the literal values in an enumerated type definition.* The reason is similar to the reason for writing a defined constant using all capital letters: the use of all capital letters allows the literal value to be easily identified as a literal value and not the name of a variable when it appears in a statement of the program. For example, if you use this style and a reader of the program sees the assignment:

```
DesiredColor := BLUE;
```

then the reader knows immediately that BLUE is defined as either a defined constant in the CONST section or in an enumerated type in the TYPE section. If you did not use this style and wrote:

```
DesiredColor := Blue;
```

then the reader would first look in the VAR section to find a data object named Blue. Very confusing!

2. *Choose short but meaningful names for the fields of a record.* In a complex data structure, such as the inventory list example above, it is often necessary to use several field names in sequence in order to select a particular data value needed from the data structure. If each field name itself is lengthy, then the sequence of field names becomes too long to read easily. Thus short field names are preferable, provided they still indicate the purpose of the field adequately.

3. *In a record type definition, put the words RECORD and END on separate lines and indent the field definitions.* Do *not* put the word RECORD after the "=" in the first line of the type definition because the entire record definition then is indented too far to the right. We have used this style throughout this chapter.

□□□ **6.10**
PSEUDO-CODE AND PASCAL SUMMARY

For later reference, here is a summary of the new pseudo-code and Pascal elements introduced in this chapter. For all except STRING types, the Pascal and pseudo-code forms are identical except for punctuation. We show the Pascal form with punctuation here.

□□
Subrange Data Types

⟨subrange-type-definition⟩ ::=

⟨type-name⟩ = ⟨smallest-value⟩..⟨largest-value⟩;

  WHERE
   ⟨type-name⟩ ::= Pascal identifier.
   ⟨smallest-value⟩ ::=
    Integer, Char, or enumerated literal value or defined constant; the
    smallest value in the subrange.
   ⟨largest-value⟩ ::=
    Integer, Char, or enumerated literal value or defined constant; the
    largest value in the subrange.

□□
Enumerated Data Types

⟨enumerated-type-definition⟩ ::=

⟨type-name⟩ = (⟨word⟩ {, ⟨word⟩});

WHERE
⟨type-name⟩ ::= Pascal identifier.
⟨word⟩ ::=
    Pascal identifier used as one of the possible "literal" values for the
    data type; preferably an identifier that contains only capital letters
    and digits.

Record Data Types

⟨record-type-definition⟩ ::=

⟨type-name⟩ =   ⟨purpose of the type⟩
    RECORD
        ⟨field-name⟩: ⟨data-type⟩;   ⟨purpose⟩
        {⟨field-name⟩: ⟨data-type⟩;   ⟨purpose⟩}
    END;

WHERE
⟨type-name⟩ ::= Pascal identifier.
⟨purpose of the type⟩ ::=
    A comment describing what objects of the type represent.
⟨field-name⟩ ::=
    Pascal identifier used to name the field (representing one of the
    "attributes").
⟨data-type⟩ ::=
    Pascal identifier naming the data type of the value stored in the field;
    a predefined type or a type that you have defined.
⟨purpose⟩ ::=
    A comment describing the purpose of the field,including the range
    and units of measure, if appropriate.

Note: The comments describing the purpose of the type and the purpose of each
field can be omitted if the type name and field names are self-explanatory.

Selecting a Field of a Record

⟨field selection⟩ ::=

⟨record data object name⟩ . ⟨field name⟩

WHERE
⟨record data object name⟩ ::= Pascal identifier.
⟨field name⟩ ::=
    Pascal identifier; a field name within the type definition for the record
    data object type.

Array Data Types

〈array-type-definition〉 ::=

〈`type-name`〉 = ARRAY "["〈`subscript-range`〉"]" OF 〈`element-type`〉;

WHERE
〈type-name〉 ::= Pascal identifier.
〈element-type〉 ::=
A data type name, either predefined or one defined in the program.
〈subscript-range〉 ::=   〈subrange-type-name〉
|〈first-subscript〉..last-subscript〉
〈subrange-type-name〉 ::=
The name of a subrange type that you have defined.
〈first-subscript〉 ::=
A literal value or defined constant representing the subscript of the
first array element.
〈last-subscript〉 ::=
A literal value or defined constant representing the subscript of the
last array element.

Selecting an Array Element

〈array-element-selection〉 ::=

〈`array-name`〉 "[" 〈`subscript-expression`〉 "]"

WHERE
〈array-name〉 ::= Pascal identifier.
〈subscript-expression〉 ::=
Any Pascal expression that gives a value in the subscript range
defined for the array.

Note: The brackets enclosing the subscript expression are quoted in the BNF
above to indicate that they are required punctuation; they are not the "optional element" brackets of BNF.

Character String Data Types in Pseudo-code

〈character-string-type-definition〉 ::=

〈type name〉 = STRING [〈maximum length〉]

WHERE
〈type name〉 ::= Pascal identifier.

⟨maximum length⟩ ::=
    Integer literal value or defined constant giving the maximum
    number of characters that can be stored in a string of this type.

□

Note: Check your local *Pascal User's Manual* for the details of coding STRING types in Pascal.

■ ■ ■
REVIEW QUESTIONS

6.1   What is *data representation* in a program?

6.2   State the *Fundamental Principle of Data Representation*.

6.3   What is a *subrange* data type? Show how to define a subrange type in pseudo-code.

6.4   Explain *two advantages* provided by representing a type as a subrange of integers instead of using the predefined Integer type.

6.5   Is it always possible to define a subrange type to restrict the possible values of a data object to exactly the values of interest? Why or why not?

6.6   What is an *enumerated* data type? Show how to define an enumerated type in pseudo-code.

6.7   What is a *literal value* of an enumerated type? What is a *subrange* of an enumerated type?

6.8   What is a *record* data type? Show how to define a record type in pseudo-code.

6.9   What are the *fields* of a record? Show how to *select* a particular field of a record to use in an action.

6.10   What is an *array* data type? Show how to define an array type in pseudo-code.

6.11   What are the *elements* of an array? Show how to select a particular element of an array to use in an action.

6.12   What is the only *operation* in Pascal that is predefined on an *entire record* or an *entire array*?

6.13   List two characteristics that distinguish the *elements of an array* from the *fields of a record*.

6.14   What is the *size* of an array?

6.15   What is a *subscript expression*?

6.16   What is a *subscript range error*? Describe two things that might happen when an action is executed that causes a subscript range error.

6.17   "Every subscript expression has a precondition." Explain the meaning of this statement.

6.18   Describe how to represent a *list of constant known length* in a program.

6.19   Describe how to represent a *table* in which the *key values* may be represented as a subrange. Show how the *look up operation* is represented for such a table.

6.20   What is a *partially filled array*?

6.21   Describe how to represent a *list of varying length* in a program, using a record in which one field is a partially filled array. Explain how an *empty list* appears in this representation. Explain how a list of several elements appears in this representation. Why is a *maximum length* for the list required in this representation?

6.22 What is a *character string* data type? Show how to define a character string type in pseudo-code.

6.23 Explain two reasons why a character string data type needs a different representation from an array in which the elements are of Char type.

6.24 What is the *length* of a character string value? Why does a STRING type require that a *maximum length* for the string be specified? What happens when a string is *assigned* to a data object and the length of the string is longer than the maximum length declared for the data object type?

6.25 What is a *string literal value*? How is the length of a string literal value determined?

6.26 Explain how to *select a single character* from a string value.

6.27 Explain the general principles behind the following pseudo-code operations on string values:
READ and DISPLAY string values.
Select a substring of a string.
Find the length of a string.
Compare two string values.
Locate the beginning of a substring.
Concatenate two or more strings.
Insert or delete a substring.

6.28 Explain the limitations of standard Pascal for defining the representation of character string data types and for defining operations on string data objects.

■ ■ ■
PROGRAMMING PROBLEMS

6.1 *Captain Nemo's Message Encoder*. Captain Nemo needs a program that will allow him to encode a message (that describes where the treasure is hidden, no doubt). The program must be able to read in a message that the user types, encode it, and display the original and encoded messages. For the encoding, use a table that shows for each letter of the alphabet the letter that should be substituted for it in the encoded message. The program should first allow the user to set up the desired encoding, as follows. Initially, set up the encoding table so that each letter is simply replaced by itself. Then allow the user to enter *changes* in the encoding for any letter. For example, allow the user to change the table so that "a" is encoded as "b", "b" is encoded as "c", and "c" is encoded as "a", while leaving all the other letters still encoded as themselves. Allow the user to display the encoding table at any point to check what the table currently contains.

Once the user is happy with the encoding table, proceed to the second stage, where the user enters a message to be encoded, the program encodes it, and both the original and encoded messages are displayed. Allow the user to enter and encode a sequence of messages, displaying the encoded form of each before proceeding to the next.

6.2 *Captain Nemo's Reverse Encoder*. Captain Nemo has found that the pirates can still read his messages, so he has a new idea: write the encoded message in *reverse order*, starting with the last letter instead of the first. Extend the program of Problem 6.1 so that the encoded message is displayed in reverse order. Limit any single message to 80 characters.

6.3 *Roger's Currency Exchange.* Roger runs the Currency Exchange booth at the River City International airport. Arriving international travelers can bring currency from almost any country and exchange it for U.S. dollars. Departing passengers can exchange U.S. dollars for the currency of their destination country. Roger's computer system runs a program that displays the correct exchange amount when given:

- Whether the exchange is to or from U.S. dollars.
- The country whose currency is being exchanged.
- The amount to be exchanged, in dollars if departing or in the foreign currency if arriving.

The currency exchange rates for each country change daily, so the program must maintain a table that stores the correct exchange rate for each country. Each morning, when Roger starts up his program, the program requests that he enter the exchange rate for each country in the table. After the table entries are made, the program continues to run throughout the day, handling each conversion calculation when given the three data items listed above. As each customer arrives at his booth, Roger asks for the information from the customer, keys it in to the program, and makes the exchange using the amount computed by the program.

Roger has to make some money off of each exchange in order to stay in business. Roger's method is to take a three percent cut of each exchange. Thus, for each dollar that a customer exchanges Roger keeps three cents and converts 97 cents to the foreign currency. Likewise, when converting from a foreign currency to dollars, Roger keeps three cents of each dollar and gives the customer 97 cents. Roger's program includes this computation, so that the program displays only the amount Roger should actually hand out to the customer.

Determine the requirements for Roger's program, design it, code it in Pascal, and test it. You can limit the program to six foreign currencies initially, but it should be easy to expand. Also, don't lock Roger in to a three percent profit—he may want to change his percentage if his competitors change their rates.

6.4 *Swim Meet Record Keeping.* In the Jefferson Swim League, each swim meet involves two teams of swimmers of various ages. There are 40 to 60 races during a meet. The important attributes of each race are:

- The distance (25, 50, 100, or 200 meters).
- The age group (the groups are named Mites, Midgets, Juniors, Intermediates, and Seniors).
- The type of race (freestyle, backstroke, breaststroke, butterfly, medley relay, freestyle relay).
- The number of lanes used (2 to 8 lanes).
- The time for each lane (in seconds).

At the meet, the record keeper runs a program on a microcomputer. The data values for each race are keyed in as the race takes place. After the meet is over, the program can display summary information about the meet, such as the number of races, the winning time in each race, the number of races of each type, and so forth. It also can display a complete listing of all the data for each race.

Determine the detailed requirements for this program, design it, code it in Pascal, and test it.

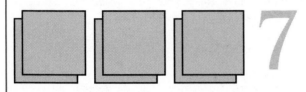

Implementing Procedures and Functions

Chapter Goals

When you have mastered the content of this chapter you should be able to:

- Design and code the *body* of a procedure or function.
- Explain how *parameter transmission* takes place when a subprogram is called.
- Build subprograms that work with data structures like records, arrays, and strings.
- Use a Pascal *FOR loop* in designing a subprogram that processes the elements of an array.
- *Hand trace* execution of a procedure or function call.
- Draw a *structure chart* for a program that uses several procedures and functions.
- Design a *test strategy* for a program that has several subprograms, including the use of *test drivers* and *stubs*.
- Explain how to use stubs to construct a program *prototype*.

Once the representation of a new data type has been chosen, it is time to REFINE into final form the definition of each new operation on objects of that type. The heading for each subprogram specifies *what* is to be done; during the REFINE step you construct the *subprogram body* that specifies *how* to accomplish the operation. Designing and coding the subprogram body is called *implementing* the subprogram.

There are slight differences between the way you design and code the bodies of procedures and functions, so we begin with procedures. The differences for functions are discussed in the following section.

□□□ 7.1
DESIGNING AND CODING A PROCEDURE BODY

The body of a procedure contains the algorithm giving the details of exactly how the procedure accomplishes its action. Each procedure has its own actions, data objects, and states that are largely separate from the rest of the program. Thus, each procedure body is defined using a separate ALGORITHM part and DATA OBJECTS list. In the ALGORITHM part, the actions of the procedure are specified in terms of the names of the *formal parameters* given in the procedure heading. The procedure may also have its own local data objects that are invisible to other parts of the program. These are listed in the DATA OBJECTS list for the procedure.

To complete the definition of a procedure, write the heading on a separate sheet of paper and then simply define the algorithm for the procedure (ALGORITHM and DATA OBJECTS lists) on the same sheet. In the ALGORITHM part, you can use ASSIGN, READ, and DISPLAY actions, IF and WHILE control actions, and call procedures and functions, exactly as you can in the ALGORITHM part of the main procedure.

As you develop the algorithm for a procedure body, you may discover that you need new abstractions to control the complexity of this part of the program (even though it is only a part of the overall program). If you need a new defined constant, data type, or subprogram, add its definition to the DEFINED CONSTANTS, DATA TYPES, or SUBPROGRAMS lists. Because these new abstractions may be useful throughout the program, put their definitions on the same lists used for the main procedure and other subprograms. Do *not* keep separate lists of abstractions for each subprogram.

Suppose you have defined a heading for a procedure AbsAverage in your SUBPRO-
GRAMS list:

PROCEDURE AbsAverage

    (X: Real   IN: first value to average.
     Y: Real   IN: second value to average.
     Average: Real)   OUT: the average.

    PURPOSE/GOAL STATE: Compute the average of the absolute values of X and
Y and store the result in Average.

To complete the definition of this procedure, you define the algorithm needed
to compute the average of the absolute values:

    ALGORITHM

    Initial state: X and Y contain the values to be averaged.

Step 1.   PURPOSE/GOAL STATE: Compute the average of the absolute values and
store in Average.
ACTIONS:

    Average := (abs (X) + abs (Y)) / 2

Final state: Average contains the computed average.

    DATA OBJECTS

    - none -

Notice that for this short procedure, the PURPOSE/GOAL STATE of the algorithm step is almost a repetition of the PURPOSE/GOAL STATE of the procedure
heading. Rather than repeat the information twice, we ordinarily omit the PUR-
POSE/GOAL state for the algorithm step to get the simpler definition:

PROCEDURE AbsAverage

    (X: Real   IN: first value to average.
     Y: Real   IN: second value to average.
     Average: Real)   OUT: the average.

    PURPOSE/GOAL STATE: Compute the average of the absolute values of X
and Y and store the result in Average.

ALGORITHM

Step 1. ACTIONS:

$$\text{Average} := (\text{abs} (X) + \text{abs} (Y)) / 2$$

DATA OBJECTS

- none -   ■

The Local State of a Procedure

The *local state* of a procedure contains only the formal parameters named in the procedure heading and any additional data objects listed in the DATA OBJECTS list for the procedure. During the development of the algorithm for a procedure, you can use as many additional data objects as you need—just name each one, specify its data type and purpose, and list it in the DATA OBJECTS list, exactly as you have been doing for data objects in the main procedure.

The actions in the ALGORITHM part of a procedure body may only refer to the data objects in the local state of the procedure. Thus, any data objects used in the main procedure or any other subprogram cannot be referenced by name within the procedure body—they are *invisible* within the procedure being defined.

Parameter Transmission

The key to understanding how a procedure works lies in understanding how the actual parameters provided by the caller are related to the formal parameters in the local state of the procedure body. The process of making this connection between actual parameters and formal parameters is termed *parameter transmission*.

Each time a procedure call is executed, two actions are performed automatically by the Pascal system:

1. An *initial local state* for the called procedure is created,
2. The actual parameters are *transmitted* to give the proper initial values for the formal parameters in the initial local state.

After these two steps, execution of the steps specified in the ALGORITHM part of the procedure takes place, exactly as for the ALGORITHM part of the main procedure. These actions make a sequence of changes in the local state until, after the last action is executed, a *final local state* is reached.

After the last action is complete, something surprising happens: *the final local state of the procedure is "thrown away."* That is, all the values stored in the local state are lost and are no longer available to be used. After throwing away the final local state, the Pascal system returns to the CALL statement, back in the calling program, and execution of the program continues from that point, with the statement following the CALL statement.

Each time a procedure is called, an entirely new local state is created just for that particular execution of the procedure. This new local state is used during the execution of the procedure and then thrown away. Because of this process, each particular call of a procedure is entirely independent of any preceding calls or any later calls of that same procedure. None of the local data objects used during one call are used again in any later call.

Of course the execution of a procedure has an effect on the values of the data objects provided as *actual parameters* by the caller, but this effect occurs entirely through actions in the procedure body using the corresponding formal parameters. Here are the details of how parameter transmission sets up this connection between actual and formal parameters. Suppose you consider a single actual parameter in a procedure CALL action:

1. *Transmitting IN Parameters.* If the corresponding formal parameter is an IN parameter, then remember that the actual parameter can be any Pascal *expression,* such as you might write on the right-hand side of an assignment. The actual parameter is "transmitted" by *evaluating the actual parameter expression, using the data objects of the caller, and then assigning the expression's value to the formal parameter.* It is just as though the ASSIGN action:

⟨formal parameter name⟩ := ⟨actual parameter expression⟩

were executed to assign an initial value to the formal parameter, except that the data objects named in the ⟨actual parameter expression⟩ are part of the local state of the caller, and the formal parameter is part of the local state of the called procedure.

EXAMPLE Suppose that procedure AbsAverage in the example above is called with the CALL action:

CALL AbsAverage (Score + 2, −4, Result)

in a state where Score = 12.

The first two actual parameters in this CALL correspond to the IN formal parameters X and Y in the heading for AbsAverage. The effect of parameter transmission is to assign the following initial values to formal parameters X and Y in the local state of AbsAverage:

X := 14   (14 = the value of the first actual parameter expression
                 "Score + 2")
Y := − 4   (− 4 = the value of the second actual parameter expression)

Parameter transmission is performed automatically at the time the procedure call is executed, so AbsAverage begins execution with its local state containing:

X: 14   Y: − 4   ■

2. *Transmitting IN/OUT and OUT Parameters.* If the formal parameter is an IN/OUT or OUT parameter, then remember that the actual parameter must be a *data object* of the same data type as declared for the formal parameter. The actual parameter is transmitted by storing a "pointer" to the actual parameter in place of the value of the formal parameter (the "pointer" is the memory address of the location of the actual parameter data object in the computer memory). The effect of this form of parameter transmission is: *the formal parameter name serves as another name for the actual parameter data object during execution of the procedure body.*

Because the formal parameter name refers to the actual parameter data object, any action in the procedure that uses the formal parameter, either to fetch its value or to assign it a new value, is in fact fetching the value of, or assigning a new value to, the actual parameter data object. Thus, during execution of the procedure, the value of the actual parameter data object back in the caller's state changes each time the procedure assigns a new value to the corresponding formal parameter. When execution of the procedure is complete, the local state of the procedure is thrown away, but the actual parameter's value has changed, and this change remains when the procedure call is complete.

EXAMPLE Using the same call of AbsAverage as in the example above:

CALL AbsAverage (Score + 2, −4, Result)

the third actual parameter, Result, corresponds to the OUT formal parameter, Average. Thus during this execution of AbsAverage, any reference to the formal parameter Average is in fact a reference to data object Result. Suppose the action:

Average := (abs (X) + abs (Y)) / 2

is executed when the local state is:

X: 14   Y: − 4

This action assigns the computed value, 9, to formal parameter Average, which in fact changes the value of data object Result back in the caller. Thus, after the procedure call is complete, the caller sees that its local state contains:

$$\text{Result:}\ \boxed{9}$$

regardless of what value Result had before the procedure call. ■

□□

Coding a Procedure in Pascal

Coding a procedure definition in Pascal, given its heading, ALGORITHM and DATA OBJECTS lists in pseudo-code, is straightforward. The Pascal syntax for a procedure definition is:

⟨PROCEDURE definition⟩ ::=

```
    PROCEDURE ⟨procedure name⟩
        ({ [VAR] ⟨formal parameter name⟩: ⟨data type⟩; ⟨purpose⟩}
         [VAR] ⟨formal parameter name⟩: ⟨data type⟩); ⟨purpose⟩
    ⟨purpose/goal state/preconditions⟩
    [VAR
        ⟨local variable declarations⟩]
     BEGIN
        ⟨statements⟩
     END;  ⟨end comment⟩
```

WHERE
> ⟨procedure name⟩ ::= Pascal identifier.
> ⟨formal parameter name⟩ ::= Pascal identifier.
> ⟨data type⟩ ::= Data type of the formal parameter.
> ⟨purpose⟩ ::=
>> A Pascal comment giving the IN, OUT, or IN/OUT classification and the purpose of the parameter.
> ⟨purpose/goal state/preconditions⟩ ::=
>> A Pascal comment giving the PURPOSE, GOAL STATE, and PRECONDITIONS, from the pseudo-code.
> ⟨local variable declarations⟩ ::=
>> The Pascal form of the DATA OBJECTS list from the pseudo-code, just as for the main procedure.
> ⟨statements⟩ ::=
>> The Pascal form of the ALGORITHM part from the pseudo-code, just as for the main procedure.
> ⟨end comment⟩ ::= A Pascal comment of the form:
>> {procedure ⟨procedure name⟩}
>> used to make the end of a procedure definition easily visible to a reader of the program.

□

Notes:

1. Use VAR in the procedure heading before the name of each OUT or IN/OUT parameter. Also use VAR before the name of any parameter of a data structure type—array, record, or string. Omit the VAR before the name of an IN parameter of a simple type.
2. If there are no local data objects on the DATA OBJECTS list, omit the entire list of ⟨local variable declarations⟩, including the preceding VAR.

Notice the punctuation: a *colon* between each formal parameter name and its data type, a *semicolon* after each data type name except the last, a *semicolon* after the closing right parenthesis of the formal parameter list, and a *semicolon* after the closing END of the procedure body.

EXAMPLE
In Pascal the AbsAverage procedure defined above would be coded:

```
PROCEDURE AbsAverage
     (X: Real;               {IN: first value to average}
      Y: Real;               {IN: second value to average}
      VAR Average: Real);    {OUT: the average}

     {PURPOSE/GOAL STATE: Compute the average of the
      absolute values of X and Y and store the result in
      Average.}

BEGIN
     Average := (abs (X) + abs (Y)) / 2;
END;   {procedure AbsAverage}
```

Notice that the reserved word VAR appears before the name of the OUT parameter Average but not before the IN parameter names X and Y.   ■

□ □

Pascal VAR and VALUE Parameters

In designing a subprogram, we use the IN, OUT, and IN/OUT classifications in pseudo-code to distinguish how the parameters are used to transmit data values back and forth between the subprogram and its caller.

In Pascal, you get a slightly different distinction:

1. *VAR parameters (also called "reference parameters")*. If you write the reserved word VAR before a formal parameter name in a Pascal subprogram heading, you get what is termed a *VAR parameter*. A VAR parameter is the Pascal equivalent of our OUT or IN/OUT parameter. A VAR parameter is transmitted by storing a

pointer to the actual parameter data object in the corresponding formal parameter in the local state of the subprogram. Within the body of the subprogram, the formal parameter serves as another name for the actual parameter data object.

2. *VALUE Parameters.* When you *omit* the reserved word VAR before a formal parameter name in a Pascal subprogram heading, you get what is termed a *VALUE parameter*. A VALUE parameter is the Pascal equivalent of our IN parameter. A VALUE parameter is transmitted by evaluating the actual parameter expression and assigning the resulting value as the initial value of the corresponding formal parameter in the local state of the subprogram. If a VALUE parameter is a data structure, all the values in the actual parameter are copied into the formal parameter data structure.

□ □

A Trouble Spot with Parameters

The design of Pascal makes it easy to blunder into a troublesome program bug: if you forget to write the keyword "VAR" in front of *each* OUT or IN/OUT formal parameter in a procedure heading, the Pascal compiler turns any parameter with a missing VAR into a VALUE parameter. A VALUE parameter is always treated as an IN parameter, regardless of how you code the procedure body.

A missing VAR before a formal parameter name cannot be detected by the Pascal compiler. The omission can have a disastrous effect on program execution. The procedure will be called and executed without error, but any new value assigned to the formal parameter (with the missing VAR) will be *lost* when control returns to the caller. After the procedure call is complete, the variable that is used as the actual parameter (corresponding to a formal parameter where you forgot the VAR) will still have its *old value,* regardless of what the procedure does during its execution. A confusing and subtle bug results!

The symptoms of this bug are worth remembering: you observe during testing that a procedure call which is supposed to change the values of one or more of its actual parameters appears to be "doing nothing." The procedure is called correctly, executes, and when control returns to the caller, it is as though nothing happened—no change has been made in the value of one or more of its OUT or IN/OUT actual parameters. If you see these symptoms, look for a missing VAR.

EXAMPLE   Suppose that in coding AbsAverage in Pascal, you forget the VAR on parameter Average:

```
PROCEDURE AbsAverage
      (X: Real;           {IN: first value to average}
       Y: Real;           {IN: second value to average}
 ⟶    Average: Real);     {OUT: the average}

      {PURPOSE/GOAL STATE:  Compute the average of the
        absolute values of X and Y and store the result in
        Average.}
```

322   □ Chap. 7 *Implementing Procedures and Functions*

```
BEGIN
      Average := (abs (X) + abs (Y)) / 2;
END;   {procedure AbsAverage}
```

Suppose that the program calls AbsAverage as follows:

```
AbsAverage (Score + 2, -4, Result);
```

when the state is:

Score: [12]   Result: [0]

You expect after the call to have Result = 9. Instead the value of Result after the call is still 0, even though the procedure computed the correct value, 9, and assigned it to the correct formal parameter, Average. Because of a missing VAR in the formal parameter list, the value of Result is never changed when the procedure is executed. ■

□ □

The "Main Procedure" Is a Procedure

Our "main procedure"—the DATA OBJECTS list and ALGORITHM part discussed in the preceding chapters—can now be understood as "just another procedure." The main procedure, like every other procedure, has its own algorithm and data objects. It is always called just once, to control the overall execution of the program. In the Pascal code, this procedure call occurs at the very end of the entire program, where we write:

```
BEGIN
      ⟨main procedure name⟩;        --call the main procedure
END.
```

□ □

Placement of Procedure and Function Definitions

Within the overall program, procedure and function definitions are placed just following the TYPE section of the main program. The order of the various subprogram definitions does not matter with one exception: if one procedure, say procedure B, calls another procedure, say procedure A, then the *definition* of procedure A must be placed *before* that of procedure B in the main program. Remember the rule: *In Pascal, a procedure's definition must appear in the program before the first call on that procedure.*

The Pascal rule for ordering subprogram definitions means that they usually appear in your final coded program in the *reverse order* from the order in which you defined them initially in your SUBPROGRAMS list. The definition of the main procedure must always be the *last procedure* defined in the program.

EXERCISES

7.1   Given the following pseudo-code procedure headings, design the body of each procedure and code the procedure definition in Pascal:

a.   PROCEDURE DivideIntegers

(X: Integer	IN: The dividend.
Y: Integer	IN: The divisor.
Quotient: Integer	OUT
Remainder: Integer)	OUT

PURPOSE/GOAL STATE: Compute the integer quotient and remainder of X/Y and store the results in Quotient and Remainder.

PRECONDITION: $Y > 0$

b.   PROCEDURE FindMaxMin

(Max: Real	IN/OUT
Min: Real)	IN/OUT

PURPOSE/GOAL STATE: Compare the values of Max and Min and set Max to the larger of the two original values and Min to the smaller.

c.   PROCEDURE MakeChange

(Amount: Integer	IN: Original amount, < 100.
Quarters: Integer	OUT: Number of quarters.
Dimes: Integer	OUT: Number of dimes.
Nickels: Integer	OUT: Number of nickels.
Pennies: Integer)	OUT: Number of pennies.

PURPOSE: Determine correct change for given Amount, using as few coins as possible.

GOAL STATE: Set Quarters, Dimes, Nickels, Pennies to correct number of each coin so that the total change equals the original value of Amount.

PRECONDITION: $0 < \text{Amount} < 100$

d.   PROCEDURE FindRoot

(B: Real	IN
C: Real	IN
Root: Real	OUT: Root of the equation, if any.
RootExists: Boolean)	OUT: TRUE if root exists; FALSE if equation has no root.

PURPOSE/GOAL STATE: Find the root of the linear equation B*X + C = 0. Store the root in Root and set RootExists = TRUE. If the equation has no root, set RootExists = FALSE and assign no value to Root.

PRECONDITION: The equation has at most one root.

7.2 Suppose that your Pascal system does not provide any means to display the value of a data object of an enumerated type directly. Thus, you must define your own display operations for values of enumerated types. In your program the enumerated type JeansCondition is defined as follows:

JeansCondition = (NEW, FADED, TORN, PATCHED)

Design and code the following procedure:

PROCEDURE DisplayJeansCondition

(Condition: JeansCondition)   IN

PURPOSE/GOAL STATE: Display the current value of Condition, as one of the words "NEW", "FADED", "TORN" or "PATCHED". The word should be displayed next on the current display line, using *write* so that the line is not ended. ∎

□□□ 7.2
DESIGNING AND CODING A FUNCTION BODY

To design the body of a function for which a heading appears in your SUBPROGRAMS list, use the same design methods as used for procedures. Write an ALGORITHM part and a DATA OBJECTS list for each individual function, and add any new data types, subprograms, or constants to the global DATA TYPES, SUBPROGRAMS, and DEFINED CONSTANTS lists.

Within the ALGORITHM part only one new concept is needed: how to specify which of the computed values is to be returned as the *value of the function*. Our pseudo-code uses an assignment of the form:

FUNCTION VALUE := ⟨expression⟩

to indicate that the value of the expression is to be returned as the value of the function.

EXAMPLE   Because the procedure AbsAverage used as an example in the preceding section computes only a single value that is returned to its caller, AbsAverage is more appropriately defined as a function. As a function, the heading and body in pseudo-code would be:

FUNCTION AbsAverage

    (X: Real   IN: first value to average.
     Y: Real)   IN: second value to average.

FUNCTION VALUE: Real   The average.

PURPOSE: Compute and return the average of the absolute values of X and Y.

ALGORITHM

Step 1. ACTIONS:

FUNCTION VALUE := (abs (X) + abs (Y)) / 2

DATA OBJECTS

- none -

Parameter Transmission

Each time a function is called, the same steps are taken automatically by the Pascal system as are taken during a procedure call:

1. An *initial local state* for the function is created.
2. The actual parameters are *transmitted* to give the initial values for the formal parameters in the initial local state of the function. Parameters are transmitted according to the same rules for functions as for procedures.

Function Value Return

Execution of a function value assignment:

$$\text{FUNCTION VALUE} := \langle \text{expression} \rangle$$

causes the value computed by the ⟨expression⟩ to be assigned to a "hidden" storage location within the local state for the function. If you execute a second function value assignment (within the same function), the new value replaces the first one in this hidden location. When execution of the function body is complete, the value stored in this hidden location is returned to the caller as the value of the function. The local state of the function is "thrown away" at the end of execution of the function, exactly as for execution of a procedure.

Execution of the function body must include execution of at least one function value assignment. If no such assignment is executed, then the hidden function value location remains uninitialized, and the value returned when execution of the function is complete will be unpredictable.

□ □

Coding Functions in Pascal

A function definition looks similar to a procedure definition except for the syntax of the heading:

⟨FUNCTION definition⟩ ::=

```
FUNCTION ⟨function-name⟩
    ({ [VAR] ⟨formal parameter name⟩: ⟨data type⟩;    ⟨purpose⟩}
     [VAR] ⟨formal parameter name⟩: ⟨data type⟩)    ⟨purpose⟩
     : ⟨data type of value returned⟩;    ⟨result returned⟩
    ⟨purpose/preconditions⟩
    [VAR
        ⟨local variable declarations⟩]
    BEGIN
        ⟨statements⟩
    END;    ⟨end comment⟩
```

WHERE
⟨function name⟩ ::= Pascal identifier.
⟨formal parameter name⟩ ::= Pascal identifier.
⟨data type⟩ ::= Data type of the formal parameter.
⟨purpose⟩ ::=
  A Pascal comment giving the IN classification and the purpose of the parameter.
⟨data type of value returned⟩ ::=
  Integer | Real | Char | Boolean
  or the name of a subrange or enumerated type.
⟨result returned⟩ ::=
  Pascal comment describing the result returned by the function, from the pseudo-code.
⟨purpose/preconditions⟩ ::=
  A Pascal comment giving the PURPOSE and PRECONDITIONS, if any, from the pseudo-code.
⟨local variable declarations⟩ ::=
  The Pascal form of the DATA OBJECTS list from the pseudo-code, just as for a procedure.
⟨statements⟩ ::=
  The Pascal form of the ALGORITHM part from the pseudo-code, just as for a procedure.
⟨end comment⟩ ::= A Pascal comment of the form:
            {function ⟨function name⟩}
  used to make the end of a function definition easily visible to a reader of the program.

□
Notes:

1. Notice the punctuation of the heading: the closing right parenthesis of the formal parameter list is *not* followed by a semicolon; instead the next line *begins with a colon* and a *semicolon* follows the data type of the result.
2. Use VAR in the heading before the name of a formal parameter of an array, record, or string type, to avoid having the actual parameter copied each time the function is called.
3. If there are no local data objects on the DATA OBJECTS list, omit the entire list of ⟨local variable declarations⟩, including the preceding VAR.

□ □
Function Value Assignment Statements

Within the function body, in place of the pseudo-code assignment:

$$\text{FUNCTION VALUE} := \langle\text{expression}\rangle$$

use the Pascal syntax:

```
⟨function-name⟩ := ⟨expression⟩;
```

That is, you "assign" the value to be returned as the function value to the *name of the function,* just as though the function name were the name of a variable. As described above, the effect of this assignment is to assign the value of the expression to the hidden function value location within the local state of the function, to be returned as the function value when execution of the function is complete.

A peculiar thing about the hidden location where the function value is stored is that you cannot *use* the value from this location during execution of the function—you can only *store* a new value in it (by using a function value assignment). Thus, the function name does *not* act like a true variable within the function body.

EXAMPLE

In Pascal the function version of AbsAverage defined above would be coded:

```
FUNCTION AbsAverage

    (X: Real;              {IN: first value to average}
     Y: Real)             {IN: second value to average}
      : Real;             {The average}

    {PURPOSE: Compute and return the average of the
    absolute values of X and Y.}

    BEGIN
      AbsAverage := (abs (X) + abs (Y)) / 2;
    END;   {function AbsAverage}
```

EXERCISES

7.3 Given the following pseudo-code function headings, design the body of each function and code the entire function definition in Pascal:

a. FUNCTION MaxOf3

(X: Real   IN
 Y: Real   IN
 Z: Real)   IN
FUNCTION VALUE: Real

PURPOSE: Return the largest of X, Y, or Z.

b. FUNCTION FindArea

(Diameter: Real)   IN

FUNCTION VALUE: Real

PURPOSE: Return the Area of the circle with the given diameter.

c. FUNCTION IsValidGrade

(Grade: Char)   IN: Grade to be tested.

FUNCTION VALUE: Boolean

PURPOSE: Return TRUE if Grade is one of the values A–D or F; return FALSE otherwise.

7.4 Suppose that the enumeration CharacterClass is defined as follows:

CharacterClass = (LETTER, DIGIT, SPACE, PAREN, ARITH, OTHER)

Given the following function heading, design the function body and code the entire function definition in Pascal:

FUNCTION ClassifyChar

(Ch: Char)   IN: Character to be classified.

FUNCTION VALUE: CharacterClass

PURPOSE: Classify Ch as a LETTER (upper or lower case), DIGIT (0–9), SPACE, PAREN (left or right parenthesis, square brackets, braces), ARITH (+, −, *, /, %), or OTHER (not one of the above), and return the classification as the function value.

□□□ 7.3
OPERATIONS ON RECORD DATA OBJECTS

In the next four sections, we build subprograms to implement operations that involve our three main data structures, records, arrays, and strings. These examples illustrate the interplay between the choice of data representation and the design of subprograms, and between the design of the heading for a subprogram and the design and coding of its body.

Nancy's "Compute Your Age" program in Chapter 5 provides a good case study. Her design uses a data type "Date" and several subprograms:

PROCEDURE ReadDate

FUNCTION IsAfter

FUNCTION YearsBetween

FUNCTION MonthOf

FUNCTION DayOf

Figure 7.1 shows the pseudo-code design for this program as Nancy defined it. Let's look at how Nancy proceeds with the design and implementation of her program.

FIGURE 7.1 Nancy's Pseudo-code Design for the "Compare Your Age" Program
Main Procedure

ALGORITHM

Step 1. PURPOSE/GOAL STATE: Read in the user's birthdate and store it in Birthdate.

ACTIONS:

DISPLAY: "Please tell me your birthdate."
CALL ReadDate (Birthdate)

Step 2. PURPOSE/GOAL STATE: Read in today's date and store it in Today.

ACTIONS:

DISPLAY: "Please tell me today's date."
CALL ReadDate (Today)

Step 3. PURPOSE: Test if the birthdate is in the future and, if so, display the "future" message. If not, then compute the age and store in Age. If the birthday is today, display the "birthday" message, otherwise display the regular message.

GOAL STATE: Correct message and age displayed.

ACTIONS:

IF IsAfter (Birthdate, Today) THEN
    DISPLAY: "Wait a minute!
                    You haven't been born yet!"
ELSE
    Age := YearsBetween (Birthdate, Today)
    IF (MonthOf (Today) = MonthOf (Birthdate))
        AND (DayOf (Today) = DayOf (Birthdate)) THEN
        DISPLAY:
                "Your birthday is today. ⟨Age⟩ years old.
                HAPPY BIRTHDAY!"

ELSE
DISPLAY: "You are ⟨Age⟩ years old on this day."

DATA OBJECTS

BIRTHDATE: Date	The user's birthdate, as given by the user.
TODAY: Date	Today's date, as given by the user.
AGE: Integer	Computed age, in years.

DATA TYPES

Date = ?   A day of the year, not B.C.

SUBPROGRAMS

PROCEDURE ReadDate

(NewDate: Date)   OUT: Date typed by user.

PURPOSE: Prompt the user and read in a date.

GOAL STATE: NewDate contains the date typed by the user.

FUNCTION IsAfter

(Date1: Date   IN
Date2: Date)   IN

FUNCTION VALUE: Boolean

PURPOSE: Return TRUE if Date1 comes after Date2; FALSE otherwise.

FUNCTION YearsBetween

(Date1: Date   IN
Date2: Date)   IN

FUNCTION VALUE: Integer   Years between the two dates.

PURPOSE: Compute the number of complete years from Date1 to Date2.

PRECONDITION: Date1 must come before or be equal to Date2.

FUNCTION MonthOf

(GivenDate: Date)   IN

FUNCTION VALUE: Integer   Month part of GivenDate.

PURPOSE: Retrieve the month part of a date.

FUNCTION DayOf

(GivenDate: Date)   IN

FUNCTION VALUE: Integer   Day part of GivenDate.

PURPOSE: Retrieve the day part of a date.

FIGURE 7.1 (continued)

Choosing the Data Representation

In completing the design, the first step is to choose an appropriate representation for the "Date" data type by following the Fundamental Principle of Data Representation. Let's look at how Nancy chooses this representation.

Nancy looks at the list of operations that are needed on Date's. She makes the following observations as she thinks about her choice of representation for the Date data type:

1. "I am asking myself whether to represent a date as three integers, for the month, day, and year, or as a single character string, such as 'July 9, 1975,' or in some combination of integers and character strings."

2. "The functions MonthOf and DayOf suggest a representation where the month and day parts of a date may be easily retrieved, so separate integers would make this easy."

3. "Function YearsBetween needs to find the number of years between two dates, which suggests that the year part of a date should be easy to retrieve, and that it should be represented as a number (not a character string) so I can subtract one year from another easily."

4. "Procedure ReadDate, on the other hand, would be simplest if a date could be stored directly as a character string, exactly as the user types it in."

5. "Function IsAfter requires that it should be easy to compare two dates, to decide which date comes first. This suggests integers for the month, day, and year."

Nancy's problem in choosing a representation for a Date is typical of most programs—the operations make conflicting demands on the representation, some would be simplest with one representation, some with another. The ReadDate procedure is a particular problem here, because it appears to be simplest with a character string representation, while the other operations are simpler with separate integers for the month, day and year. Nancy chooses the representation as three separate integers—ReadDate will have to be more complex in order to make the other operations simpler.

Separate month, day, and year parts of a date suggest the use of a RECORD for the representation with subranges for each of the parts:

DATA TYPES

```
MonthRange = 1..12
DayRange = 1..31
YearRange = 0..9999        A range sufficient for this program.

Date =
    RECORD
            Day: DayRange
            Month: MonthRange
            Year: YearRange
    END
```

Designing the Body of Each Subprogram

With this representation chosen, Nancy can now fill in the algorithms for the body of each of the five subprograms, as shown in Figure 7.2. Notice how each subprogram selects the particular fields of the record formal parameter that it needs, using the dot notation, "⟨formal parameter⟩.⟨field⟩".

FIGURE 7.2   Design for Nancy's Subprograms that Operate on Dates

---

SUBPROGRAMS

PROCEDURE ReadDate

(NewDate: Date)   OUT: Date typed by user.

PURPOSE: Prompt the user and read in a date.

GOAL STATE: NewDate contains the date typed by the user.

ALGORITHM

Step 1.   ACTIONS:

DISPLAY: "Type the month (1-12):"
READ: NewDate.Month

DISPLAY: "Type the day (1-31):"
READ: NewDate.Day

DISPLAY: "Type the year (not B.C.):"
READ: NewDate.Year

DATA OBJECTS

- none -

FUNCTION IsAfter

(Date 1: Date   IN
Date 2: Date)   IN

FUNCTION VALUE: Boolean

PURPOSE: Return TRUE if Date1 comes after Date2; FALSE otherwise.

ALGORITHM

Step 1.   PURPOSE/GOAL STATE: Compare year, month, and day values in sequence and set function value correctly.

ACTIONS:

```
IF Date1.Year > Date2.Year THEN
   FUNCTION VALUE := TRUE
ELSE IF (Date1.Year = Date2.Year)
        AND (Date1.Month > Date2.Month) THEN
   FUNCTION VALUE := TRUE
ELSE IF (Date1.Year = Date2.Year)
        AND (Date1.Month = Date2.Month)
        AND (Date1.Day > Date2.Day) THEN
   FUNCTION VALUE := TRUE
ELSE
   FUNCTION VALUE := FALSE
```

DATA OBJECTS

-none-

FUNCTION YearsBetween

(Date1: Date	IN
Date2: Date)	IN

FUNCTION VALUE: Integer   Years between the two date.

PURPOSE: Compute the number of complete years from Date1 to Date2.

PRECONDITION: Date1 must come before or be equal to Date2.

ALGORITHM

Step 1. PURPOSE/GOAL STATE: Compute the number of complete years by subtracting the years fields and then subtracting one additional year if the month/day in Date2 comes before the month/day of Date1. Store the result in Years.

ACTIONS:

```
Years := Date2.Year  −  Date1.Year

IF Date2.Month < Date1.Month THEN
   Years := Years  −  1
ELSE IF (Date2.Month = Date1.Month)
        AND (Date2.Day < Date1.Day) THEN
   Years := Years  −  1
```

Step 2. ACTIONS:
FUNCTION VALUE := Years

FIGURE 7.2 (continued)

Years: Integer   Computed years between the dates.

FUNCTION MonthOf

(GivenDate: Date)   IN

FUNCTION VALUE: Integer   Month part of GivenDate.
PURPOSE: Retrieve the month part of a date.

ALGORITHM

Step 1. ACTIONS:
FUNCTION VALUE := GivenDate.Month

DATA OBJECTS

- none -

FUNCTION DayOf

(GivenDate: Date)   IN

FUNCTION VALUE: Integer   Day part of GivenDate.
PURPOSE: Retrieve the day part of a date.

ALGORITHM

Step 1. ACTIONS:
FUNCTION VALUE := GivenDate.Day

DATA OBJECTS

- none -

FIGURE 7.2   (*continued*)

Nancy checks her pseudo-code design carefully and then codes her program in Pascal. Figure 7.3 shows the result. While testing the program, Nancy finds that she would like to have two additional blank lines displayed so that the output is more readable. She inserts the "*writeln*" statements where they are needed.

```
PROGRAM ComputeYourAge (INPUT, OUTPUT);

        {PURPOSE: A Science Fair demonstration program that
        determines the age of the user, given as input today's date
        and the birthdate of the user.
        AUTHOR: Nancy NewJersey.
        DATE: January 1990.}

TYPE
  MonthRange = 1..12;
  DayRange = 1..31;
  YearRange = 0..9999;        {A range sufficient for this program.}

  Date =
     RECORD
           Day: DayRange;
           Month: MonthRange;
           Year: YearRange;
     END;

PROCEDURE ReadDate
        (VAR NewDate: Date);        {OUT: Date typed by user}

        {PURPOSE: Prompt the user and read in a date.}
        {GOAL STATE: NewDate contains the date typed by the user.}

   BEGIN
      write ('Type the month (1-12):');
      readln (NewDate.Month);

      write ('Type the day (1-31):');
      readln (NewDate.Day);

      write ('Type the year (not B.C.):');
      readln (NewDate.Year);
   END; {procedure ReadDate}

FUNCTION IsAfter
        (Date1: Date;        {IN}
         Date2: Date)        {IN}
         : Boolean;          {Function value}

        {PURPOSE: Return TRUE if Date1 comes after Date2; FALSE
             otherwise.}
```

FIGURE 7.3   Nancy's "Compute Your Age" Program in Pascal

```
BEGIN
        {PURPOSE/GOAL STATE: Compare year, month, and day
        values in sequence and set function value correctly.}
    IF Date1.Year > Date2.Year THEN
      BEGIN
          IsAfter := TRUE;
      END

    ELSE IF (Date1.Year = Date2.Year)
            AND (Date1.Month > Date2.Month) THEN
      BEGIN
          IsAfter := TRUE;
      END

    ELSE IF (Date1.Year = Date2.Year)
            AND (Date1.Month = Date2.Month)
            AND (Date1.Day > Date2.Day) THEN
      BEGIN
          IsAfter := TRUE:
      END

    ELSE
      BEGIN
          IsAfter := FALSE;
      END;
  END;   {function IsAfter}

FUNCTION YearsBetween
      (Date1: Date;          {IN}
       Date2: Date)          {IN}
       : Integer;            {Years between the two dates.}

    {PURPOSE: Compute the number of complete years from Date1 to
        Date2.}
    {PRECONDITION: Date1 must come before or be equal to Date2.}

  VAR
     Years: Integer;              {Computed years between the dates.}

  BEGIN
        {PURPOSE/GOAL STATE:  Compute the number of complete
        years by subtracting the years fields and then
        subtracting one additional year if the month/day in
        Date2 comes before the month/day of Date1.  Store the
        result in Years.}
```

FIGURE 7.3 (*continued*)

```
            Years := Date2.Year - Date1.Year;

            IF Date2.Month < Date1.Month THEN
               BEGIN
                  Years := Years - 1;
               END

            ELSE IF (Date2.Month = Date1.Month)
                     AND (Date2.Day < Date1.Day) THEN
               BEGIN
                  Years := Years - 1;
               END;

            YearsBetween := Years;

         END;   {function YearsBetween}

      FUNCTION MonthOf
            (GivenDate: Date)          {IN}
            : Integer;                 {Month part of GivenDate.}

            {PURPOSE: Retrieve the month part of a date.}

         BEGIN

            MonthOf := GivenDate.Month;

         END;   {function MonthOf}

      FUNCTION DayOf
            (GivenDate: Date)          {IN}
            : Integer;                 {Day part of GivenDate.}

            {PURPOSE: Retrieve the day part of a date.}

         BEGIN

            DayOf := GivenDate.Day;

         END;   {function DayOf}

      PROCEDURE Main;

            {PURPOSE/GOAL STATE: Control the overall program actions.}

         VAR
            Birthdate: Date;     {The user's birthdate, as given by the
                                       user.}
            Today: Date;         {Today's date, as given by the user.}
            Age: Integer;        {Computed age, in years.}
```

FIGURE 7.3 *(continued)*

```
BEGIN
        {PURPOSE/GOAL STATE: Read in the user's birthdate and
        store it in Birthdate.}

    writeln ('Please tell me your birthdate.');
    ReadDate (Birthdate);
    writeln;

        {PURPOSE/GOAL STATE: Read in today's date and store it
        in Today.}

    writeln ('Please tell me today''s date.');
    ReadDate (Today);
    writeln;

        {PURPOSE: Test if the birthdate is in the future and,
        if so, display the "future message. If not, then
        compute the age and store in Age. If the birthday is
        today, display the "birthday" message, otherwise
        display the regular message.
        GOAL STATE: Correct message and age displayed.}

    IF IsAfter (Birthdate, Today) THEN
      BEGIN
        writeln ('Wait a minute! You haven''t been born yet!');
      END
    ELSE
      BEGIN
        Age := YearsBetween (Birthdate, Today);
        IF (MonthOf (Today) = MonthOf (Birthdate))
                 AND (DayOf (Today) = DayOf (Birthdate)) THEN
          BEGIN
            writeln ('Your birthday is today. ', Age:1,
                          ' years old.');
            writeln ('    HAPPY BIRTHDAY!');
          END
        ELSE
          BEGIN
            writeln ('You are ', Age:1,
                            ' years old on this day.');
          END;
      END;

  END;   {procedure Main}

BEGIN
    Main;
END.
```

FIGURE 7.3   (*continued*)

Transmitting Data Structures as VALUE Parameters

Nancy's first version of the Pascal code for her subprograms follows our guidelines for Pascal parameters exactly: each IN parameter is transmitted as a Pascal VALUE parameter and each IN/OUT or OUT parameter is transmitted as a Pascal VAR parameter. But where an IN parameter is a data structure like a record, array, or string, Pascal presents a difficulty.

In Pascal, as we saw in Sections 7.1 and 7.2 above, the transmission of a VALUE parameter is equivalent to executing the assignment:

⟨formal parameter name⟩ := ⟨actual parameter expression⟩

If the VALUE formal parameter is a *data structure,* such as the Date1 and Date2 parameters in Nancy's IsAfter function, then each time the subprogram is called, *all the values in the entire actual parameter data structure are copied and stored in the formal parameter data structure.* Thus, for example, each time function IsAfter is called, the month, day, and year fields in both actual parameters are copied and assigned to the corresponding fields of the formal parameters Date1 and Date2. Figure 7.4 shows the effect.

As you can see from Figure 7.4, copying each IN parameter can be costly when the parameters are data structures that might have many elements. Where a

---

FIGURE 7.4   Copying Actual Parameters when VALUE Transmission is Used

Function Call Being Executed

IF IsAfter (Today, Birthday) THEN ...

Caller's State

Today.Day:	27	Birthday.Day:	12
" .Month:	4	" .Month:	11
" .Year:	1994	" .Year:	1962

Local State of IsAfter Function After Parameter Transmission

Date1.Day:	27	Date2.Day:	12
" .Month:	4	" .Month:	11
" .Year:	1994	" .Year:	1962

Copies of values in corresponding fields of Today and Birthday.

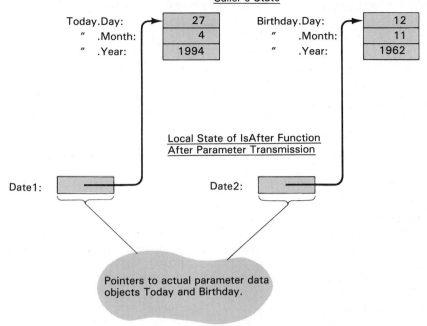

Function Call Being Executed

IF IsAfter (Today, Birthday) THEN ...

Caller's State

Today.Day: 27   Birthday.Day: 12
" .Month: 4   " .Month: 11
" .Year: 1994   " .Year: 1962

Local State of IsAfter Function
After Parameter Transmission

Date1:   Date2:

Pointers to actual parameter data objects Today and Birthday.

FIGURE 7.5 Transmitting a VAR Parameter (No Copying)

parameter is a large array, copying the entire array during parameter transmission can take much longer than the time it takes to execute all the actions in the subprogram body—kind of silly, don't you think?

The Pascal problem of copying IN parameters can be avoided when you code a subprogram into Pascal. Remember the following trick: *Transmit as a VAR parameter any formal parameter of a record, array, or string type.* That is, insert the reserved word VAR before the name of *any* formal parameter of a record, array, or string type, even if it is an IN parameter. Because a VAR parameter is transmitted by storing a pointer to the actual parameter data structure in the formal parameter, there is no copying of VAR parameters during parameter transmission. Figure 7.5 illustrates the effect. Figure 7.6 shows the improved coding of Nancy's IsAfter function.

EXERCISES

7.5 Compare the pseudo-code design of Nancy's program in Figure 7.2 with the final coded program in Figure 7.3. Note where each element of the pseudo-code design appears in the final Pascal program.

7.6 Suppose a Jeans data type is defined as in Chapter 6:

```
FUNCTION IsAfter
     (VAR Date1: Date;    {IN}            ⎤VAR parameters used to
      VAR Date2: Date)    {IN}            ⎦ avoid copying.
      : Boolean;               {Function value}

     {PURPOSE: Return TRUE if Date1 comes after Date2; FALSE
          otherwise.}
  BEGIN

     ... -- same as in Figure 7.3.

  END;   {function IsAfter}
```

FIGURE 7.6   Second (Improved) Version of Function Heading

```
TYPE
    WaistRange = 22..48;           {Waist size in inches}
    LengthRange = 20..40;          {Inseam length in inches}
    JeansColor = (BLUE, BLACK, BROWN, WHITE);
    JeansCondition = (NEW, FADED, TORN, PATCHED);

    Jeans =                        {Description of one pair of jeans}
        RECORD
            Waist : WaistRange;
            Length : LengthRange;
            Price : Real;          {In dollars/cents}
            Color : JeansColor;
            Condition : JeansCondition;
            PurchaseDate: Date;
        END;
```

where the type Date uses the same representation that Nancy's program used. Given each of the following subprogram headings, design the body of the subprogram and code the entire subprogram definition in Pascal:

a. FUNCTION CheckSize

(TestJeans: Jeans	IN
DesiredWaist: WaistRange	IN
DesiredLength: LengthRange)	IN

FUNCTION VALUE: Boolean

PURPOSE: Return TRUE if the waist and length fields of TestJeans match DesiredWaist and DesiredLength; FALSE otherwise.

b. PROCEDURE PutOnSale

(StockJeans: Jeans	IN/OUT
SalePrice: Real)	IN

PURPOSE/GOAL STATE: Change the price field of StockJeans to SalePrice.

c. FUNCTION IsNewer

(Jeans1: Jeans   IN
Jeans2: Jeans)   IN

FUNCTION VALUE: Boolean

PURPOSE: Return TRUE if the purchase date of Jeans1 is after or equal to the purchase date of Jeans2; FALSE otherwise.

□□□ 7.4
OPERATIONS ON ARRAY DATA OBJECTS: THE FOR LOOP

Let's turn our attention to subprograms that work with arrays. Sometimes an action in a subprogram may select an array element directly, using a literal subscript value, such as A [2] or B [23]. However, a typical array may have hundreds or thousands of elements. Clearly you cannot write separate ASSIGN, READ or DISPLAY actions for each element of an array. Instead, most operations on arrays are expressed with loops. You describe the action you want, expressed in terms of a "typical element," say the Ith element, and then embed that action within a loop so that the action is executed repeatedly, once for each of the elements of the array. For example, if array A can store a list of 1000 integers, using subscript range 1..1000, then you might express the action "store zero in the Ith element of A" using the assignment:

$$A \ [I] \ := \ 0;$$

Then to fill the entire array with zeros, you might embed the assignment in a WHILE loop:

```
I := 1;
WHILE I <= 1000 DO
  BEGIN
    A [I] := 0;           {Store zero in the Ith element}
    I := I + 1;
  END;
```

You can use a WHILE loop to express an operation on an array, but there is another Pascal loop, the FOR loop, that is exactly what you need for representing many operations on arrays. The FOR loop uses a subscript variable, like the variable I in the WHILE loop above, and combines the three steps of the WHILE:

1. Assign an initial value to the subscript variable:

$I := 1$

2. Test for the end of the subscript range:

Is $(I > 1000)$?

3. Increment the subscript variable:

$$I := I + 1$$

The FOR loop equivalent to the WHILE loop above has the form:

```
FOR I := 1 TO 1000 DO
   BEGIN
      A[I] := 0;                    {Store zero in the Ith element}
   END;
```

When a FOR loop is executed, the action specified is taken for each array element, using the subscript range specified in the FOR loop. Thus, the effect of executing the FOR loop above is the same as executing the sequence of assignment statements:

```
A[1] := 0;
A[2] := 0;
A[3] := 0;
A[4] := 0;
        .
        .
        .
A[1000] := 0;
```

or, alternatively, it is the same as executing the WHILE loop given originally. Notice that in a FOR loop, you do *not* have to include the action to increment the subscript variable, I, within the loop body. The FOR loop provides this action automatically at the end of each execution of the loop body.

□ □

The FOR Loop in Pseudo-code and Pascal

The Pascal FOR loop may be used for a variety of purposes, but its use in representing array operations is the most common one. In Chapter 10, we look at the FOR loop again when we discuss loops more generally.

Our pseudo-code follows the Pascal syntax:

⟨FOR loop⟩ ::=

```
FOR ⟨subscript variable⟩ := ⟨first subscript⟩ TO ⟨last subscript⟩ DO
   BEGIN
      ⟨loop body actions⟩
   END
```

WHERE
⟨subscript variable⟩ ::=
    A Pascal identifier, the name of the data object to be used to store the current subscript value on each iteration of the loop. The names I, J, and K are often used for subscript variables in Pascal FOR loops.

⟨first subscript⟩ ::=
> An ⟨expression⟩ whose value is the first subscript value to be assigned to ⟨subscript variable⟩, before the first execution of the actions in the loop body.

⟨last subscript⟩ ::=
> An ⟨expression⟩ whose value is the last subscript value to be assigned to ⟨subscript variable⟩, before the last execution of the actions in the loop body.

⟨loop body actions⟩ ::=
> A list of actions to be taken each time the loop is repeated.

□

Meaning of a FOR loop: The steps in executing a FOR loop are (see Figure 7.7):

1. Execute the ASSIGN action:

   ⟨subscript variable⟩ := ⟨first subscript⟩

2. Test if it is time to stop repeating the loop:

   IF ⟨subscript variable⟩ > ⟨last subscript⟩
       THEN execution of the FOR loop is complete.

3. Execute the ⟨loop body actions⟩.
4. Add one to the value of ⟨subscript variable⟩.
5. Repeat these steps again from step 2.

Let's look at some examples of operations on arrays that use FOR loops:

EXAMPLES OF PSEUDO-CODE OPERATIONS ON ARRAYS

Suppose that you want to represent a list of the weekly sales totals for a small business. During the define step you have specified:

DATA TYPES

Week: 1..52	Numbers of the weeks.
WeeklySalesList = ?	Total sales for each week.

SUBPROGRAMS

FUNCTION ComputeYearlySales

(Sales: WeeklySalesList)   IN: Sales for the year.

FUNCTION VALUE: Real   Total yearly sales.
PURPOSE: Sum the weekly sales and return the sum as the function value.

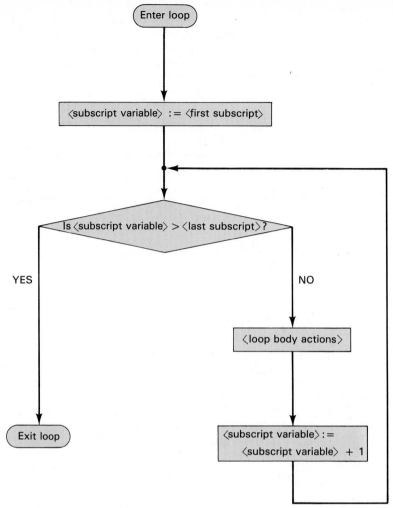

FIGURE 7.7 Execution of a FOR Loop

FUNCTION ComputePartialYearSales

    (Sales: WeeklySalesList   IN: Sales for the year.
     StartWeek: Week   IN: Starting week.
     EndWeek: Week)   IN: Ending week.

    FUNCTION VALUE: Real   Total sales for part of year.
    PURPOSE: Sum the weekly sales starting with StartWeek and ending with EndWeek and return the sum as the function value.
    PRECONDITION: $1 <=$ StartWeek $<=$ EndWeek $<= 52$

FUNCTION CountWeeksAboveMin

    (Sales: WeeklySalesList   IN: Sales for the year.
     Minimum: Real)   IN: Minimum sales level.

    FUNCTION VALUE: Integer   Number of weeks that sales exceeded Minimum.

PURPOSE: Count the number of weeks that sales exceeded the specified Minimum.

PROCEDURE FindBestWeek

(Sales: WeeklySalesList   IN: Sales for the year.
   BestWeek: Week   OUT: Number of best week.
   BestSales: Real)   OUT: Sales in best week.

PURPOSE: Find the week with the largest total sales. If several weeks tie, use the week latest in the year.

GOAL STATE: Store the number of the best week in BestWeek and the sales for that week in BestSales.

Suppose that during the REFINE step you choose the representation for WeeklySalesList, using an array:

DATA TYPES

Week: 1..52   Numbers of the weeks.
WeeklySalesList = ARRAY [Week] OF Real   Total sales for each week.

The subprogram bodies can now be defined in terms of this representation for WeeklySalesList. Note how the ComputeYearlySales function requires only a call on the ComputePartialYearSales function with the proper actual parameters:

SUBPROGRAMS

FUNCTION ComputeYearlySales

(Sales: WeeklySalesList)   IN: Sales for the year.

FUNCTION VALUE: Real   Total yearly sales.

PURPOSE: Sum the weekly sales and return as function value.

ALGORITHM

Step 1.   ACTIONS:

FUNCTION VALUE :=
        ComputePartialYearSales (Sales, 1, 52)

DATA OBJECTS

- none -

FUNCTION ComputePartialYearSales

    (Sales: WeeklySalesList   IN: Sales for the year.
     StartWeek: Week   IN: Starting week.
     EndWeek: Week)   IN: Ending week.

    FUNCTION VALUE: Real   Total sales for part of year.

    PURPOSE: Sum the weekly sales starting with StartWeek and ending with EndWeek and return the sum as the function value.

    PRECONDITION: StartWeek <= EndWeek

ALGORITHM

Step 1. ACTIONS:

```
TotalSales := 0
FOR I := StartWeek TO EndWeek DO
    BEGIN
        TotalSales := TotalSales + Sales [I]
    END
FUNCTION VALUE := TotalSales
```

DATA OBJECTS

I: Integer   FOR loop subscript variable.
TotalSales: Real   Running sum of weekly sales.

FUNCTION CountWeeksAboveMin

    (Sales: WeeklySalesList   IN: Sales for the year.
     Minimum: Real)   IN: Minimum sales level.

    FUNCTION VALUE: Integer   Number of weeks that sales exceeded Minimum.

    PURPOSE: Count the number of weeks that sales exceeded the specified Minimum.

ALGORITHM

Step 1. ACTIONS:

```
WeekCount := 0
FOR I := 1 TO 52 DO
    BEGIN
        IF Sales [I] > Minimum THEN
            WeekCount := WeekCount + 1
    END
FUNCTION VALUE := WeekCount
```

WeekCount: Integer   Count of weeks above minimum.
I: Integer   FOR loop subscript variable.

PROCEDURE FindBestWeek

(Sales: WeeklySalesList   IN: Sales for the year.
BestWeek: Week   OUT: Number of best week.
BestSales: Real)   OUT: Sales in best week.

PURPOSE: Find the week with the largest total sales. If several weeks tie, use the week latest in the year.

GOAL STATE: Store the number of the best week in BestWeek and the sales for that week in BestSales.

ALGORITHM

Step 1. PURPOSE: Assume the first week is the best week, and then compare all later weeks against the best week found so far.

GOAL STATE: Set BestWeek and BestSales to the last best week in the year.

ACTIONS:

```
BestSales := Sales [1]
Best Week := 1

FOR I := 2 TO 52 DO
    BEGIN
        IF Sales [I] >= BestSales THEN
                BestSales := Sales [I]
                BestWeek := I
    END
```

DATA OBJECTS

I: Integer   FOR loop subscript variable.   ■

□ □

Important Facts About FOR Loops

Note the following facts about Pascal FOR loops:

1. *The subscript variable must be declared.* The *subscript variable* is an ordinary variable, usually of type Integer or a subrange type. You must include a declaration for this variable in the subprogram, just as for any other variable. Traditionally the variable name I (and J, K . . . if you have other FOR loops nested within the body of one FOR) has been used in FOR loops as the subscript variable, so that the loop body describes the action on the typical "Ith" element of the array. However, you can use any variable name you want for the subscript variable, and sometimes other names make your intent clearer to the reader.

2. *Any subscript range may be used.* You do not have to perform the action on each element of the entire array. The "⟨first subscript⟩ TO ⟨last subscript⟩" part of the FOR loop can specify any subscript range—all or any part of the array.

3. *The loop body may never be executed at all.* The test:

⟨subscript variable⟩ > ⟨last subscript⟩ ?

is made before the loop body is executed the first time. If the result is TRUE, then the loop body is skipped entirely.

4. *The subscript variable may not be assigned a new value within the loop body.* Within the loop body, the value of the subscript variable may only be used, not modified. For example, you cannot end execution of a FOR loop prematurely by writing:

```
FOR I := 1 TO 1000 DO
   BEGIN
      IF A [I] = ⟨desired value⟩ THEN
         BEGIN
            I := 1001;        {This assignment is INVALID}
         END;
   END
```

5. *The final value of the subscript variable is unpredictable.* After execution of a FOR loop is complete, the value of the subscript variable is *unpredictable*—just as though the subscript variable had never been initialized. For example, after execution of the loop:

```
FOR I := 1 TO 1000 DO
   BEGIN
      A[I] := 0;             {Store zero in the Ith element}
   END
```

subscript variable I does NOT necessarily contain the value 1000 or 1001—I's value is unpredictable and may vary on different Pascal systems.

□ □
Pattern: DISPLAY an Array

A common FOR loop pattern arises when you want to display all the elements of an array, by displaying the same number of elements on each line (say, seven elements per line), and continuing until all elements are displayed. The loop involves a combination of *write* operations to display the elements and *writeln* operations to end the display lines after each group of elements has been displayed. This pattern is worth learning; you will find many uses for it.

Suppose that the number of elements to display per line is given by a defined constant, ELEMENTSPERLINE:

```
CONST
    ELEMENTSPERLINE = ⟨number of elements to display per line⟩;
```

The test for the end of an output line that contains ELEMENTSPERLINE values is coded as:

```
IF (⟨subscript variable⟩ MOD ELEMENTSPERLINE) = 0 THEN
                -- at end of an output line --
```

which uses the Pascal MOD operation to test if the subscript value is an exact multiple of the number of elements per line. If MOD returns a zero value (indicating a remainder of zero), then you are at the end of an output line. At the end of each line, an additional *writeln* is executed to end the line and advance to the next output line.

The pattern to display the elements of an array A [1..⟨last subscript⟩] is:

```
FOR I := 1 TO ⟨last subscript⟩ DO
  BEGIN
      write (A [I]);          {Begin or continue the current line}

      IF (I MOD ELEMENTSPERLINE) = 0 THEN
        BEGIN
            writeln;          {End the current line}
        END;
  END;

      {End a short last line if required}
IF (⟨last subscript⟩ MOD ELEMENTSPERLINE) <> 0 THEN
  BEGIN
      writeln;                {End the last line}
  END;
```

EXAMPLE

```
      {PURPOSE/GOAL STATE: Display the values in array
       GradesList [1..LastElement], seven values per line}

FOR I := 1 TO LastElement DO
  BEGIN
      write (GradesList [I]);
      IF (I MOD 7) = 0 THEN
        BEGIN
            writeln;
        END;
  END;
```

```
IF (LastElement MOD 7) <> 0 THEN
   BEGIN
      writeln;
   END;
```

□ □

WHILE Versus FOR Loops

Not every loop that involves the elements of an array can be represented as a FOR loop. Sometimes you have to use a WHILE loop. To decide which to use, ask the question:

```
┌─────────────────────────────────────────────────────────────────────────┐
│                                                                           │
│                            FOR or WHILE?                                  │
│                                                                           │
│  When the loop is reached during program execution, can the program      │
│  determine, before the loop body is executed the first time, exactly     │
│  the subscript range for the array elements that must be processed by     │
│  the loop? If the answer is YES, use a FOR loop. If NO, use a WHILE loop. │
│                                                                           │
└─────────────────────────────────────────────────────────────────────────┘
```

The two most common situations where a WHILE loop is needed are:

1. When the purpose of the loop is to *search* the elements of the array for an element that has a certain property, such as a search for the first zero element in the array. In such a loop, the search continues until the desired element is found, or until the end of the subscript range is reached. Before the loop is executed, you cannot determine exactly how many elements must be tested in the loop body, so the answer to the FOR versus WHILE question is NO—hence you need a WHILE loop.

2. When the purpose of the loop is to *read* a list of values into the elements of the array, terminating when a special value is read, such as zero or a negative number, or when the array is entirely filled. Before such a loop is executed, you do not know how many array elements will be filled, so the answer to the FOR versus WHILE question is NO—hence you need a WHILE loop.

EXAMPLE

Using the WeeklySalesList array representation above, consider the function:

FUNCTION FindFirstWeekAboveMin

    (Sales: WeeklySalesList   IN: Sales for the year.
     Minimum: Real)   IN: Minimum sales level.

    FUNCTION VALUE: Integer   Number of first week when sales exceeded Minimum.

    PURPOSE: Search for the first week where sales exceeded the specified Minimum. Return zero if no week exceeds Minimum.

ALGORITHM

Step 1.   ACTIONS:

```
FUNCTION VALUE := 0
Found := FALSE
I := 1
WHILE (I <= 52) AND (Found = FALSE) DO
      IF Sales [I] > Minimum THEN
            FUNCTION VALUE := I
            Found := TRUE
      ELSE
            I := I + 1
```

DATA OBJECTS

Found: Boolean   Flag: TRUE means Minimum has been exceeded; FALSE
                   means not exceeded so far.
I: Integer   WHILE loop subscript variable.

EXERCISES

7.7   Using the WeeklySalesList data type from the examples above and given each of the following subprogram headings, design the body of the subprogram and code the entire subprogram definition in Pascal. Your designs may use calls on the subprograms ComputeYearlySales, ComputePartialYearSales, CountWeeksAbove-Min, FindBestWeek, and FindFirstWeekAboveMin from the examples in this section, if appropriate.

a.   FUNCTION CountImprovedWeeks

(Year1Sales: WeeklySalesList   IN
  Year2Sales: WeeklySalesList)   IN

FUNCTION VALUE: Integer

PURPOSE: Return a count of the number of weeks in which sales in Year1Sales exceeded sales in Year2Sales.

b.   FUNCTION CountBestWeeks

(Sales: WeeklySalesList)   IN

FUNCTION VALUE: Integer

PURPOSE: Return a count of the number of weeks in which sales equal the sales for the best week of the year.

c.   PROCEDURE DisplaySalesList

(Sales: WeeklySalesList   IN
  ValuesPerLine: Integer)   IN: range 1-9.

PURPOSE/GOAL STATE: Display the weekly sales amounts in Sales, displaying the number of values per line given by ValuesPerLine.

d. PROCEDURE CreateSalesList

(Sales: WeeklySalesList)   OUT

PURPOSE/GOAL STATE: Prompt the user and read weekly sales amounts in sequence and store in the elements of Sales. Continue until 52 amounts have been read, or until the user types a negative amount. If a negative amount is read, do not store that amount; instead, fill the remaining elements of the Sales list with zero values.

7.8   Suppose data type WeeklySalesPercents is defined:

WeeklySalesPercents = ARRAY [Week] OF Real

Given the following subprogram heading, design the body of the subprogram and code the entire subprogram definition in Pascal:

PROCEDURE ComputeWeeklyPercents

(Sales: WeeklySalesList   IN
    Percents: WeeklySalesPercents)   OUT

PURPOSE: For each week of the year, determine what percentage of the total yearly sales were made in that week.

GOAL STATE: Store each weekly percentage in the appropriate element of array Percents.

□□□ 7.5
OPERATIONS ON STRING DATA OBJECTS

When an operation works with string data objects, its body would usually involve use of the predefined string functions and procedures described in Chapter 6. Table 7.1 gives a summary of these predefined operations.

Operations on strings are often used to break an input line typed by the user into parts and to assemble output lines from the parts. Using strings in this way allows a program greater flexibility in input and output than when only the standard Pascal READ and WRITE operations are used. Let's look at a few examples of subprograms that work with strings in this way.

EXAMPLES OF PSEUDO-CODE OPERATIONS ON STRINGS
Merrell is writing a program that works with "dates," just as Nancy's program did. However, Merrell decides to represent his dates entirely using character strings. In part of his program, he wants his program to read in a date typed by the user as a single character string. Then the program extracts the month, day, and year parts of the date as substrings. Later, these substrings are used to display the date in another format.

TABLE 7.1 Summary of Predefined Pseudo-code Operations on Strings

___

FUNCTION Copy (String, Position, Length)

PURPOSE: Returns a copy of the substring of Length characters that begins at Position within String.

FUNCTION Length (String)

PURPOSE: Returns the length of String.

FUNCTION Position (String, Substring)

PURPOSE: Returns the starting position of the first occurrence of Substring within String; zero if Substring does not appear in String.

FUNCTION Concat (String1, String2, . . .)

PURPOSE: Returns a string composed of a copy of String1 followed by a copy of String2, and so forth, for as many strings as are given as parameters.

PROCEDURE Delete (String, Position, Length)

PURPOSE: Deletes a substring of Length characters beginning at Position within String.

PROCEDURE Insert (String, Substring, Position)

PURPOSE: Inserts a copy of Substring beginning at Position within String.

___

Other Predefined Operations on Strings:

___

String [⟨character position⟩]	—Select a single character from a string.
READ: String	—Read to maximum string length or end of input line, whichever is reached first.
DISPLAY: ⟨String⟩	—Display all characters in String.
String := ⟨string-valued expression⟩	—Assign a string value to String.
String1 = String2	—Compare characters in String1 and String2. < >, <, >, <=, >= may also be used.

___

Merrell's program design includes the definitions:

DATA TYPES

InputLine: STRING [80]	A complete input line.
MonthString: STRING [9]	Name of a month.
DayString: STRING [2]	One- or two-digit day number.
YearString: STRING [4]	Four-digit year number.
StringDate =	A date, stored as three strings.

    RECORD

        Month: MonthString

        Day: DayString

        Year: YearString

    END

DateInputLine: InputLine	Complete date as typed by user.
TodaysDate: StringDate	Today's date in string form.

Suppose that Merrell's program asks the user to type in a date:

DISPLAY: "Please type today's date in the form:
⟨day⟩ ⟨month⟩ ⟨year⟩
Example: 21 July 1988"
READ: DateInputLine

The READ reads in whatever the user types, up to the RETURN at the end of the line, and stores it as a string in DateInputLine.

Merrell's subprograms list contains:

SUBPROGRAMS

PROCEDURE BuildDate

(Line: InputLine	IN: Date as typed by the user.
Date: StringDate)	OUT: Constructed date record.

PURPOSE/GOAL STATE: Break the Line into its day, month, and year substrings, and store them in Date. All spaces must be deleted from the strings in Date.

PRECONDITION: Line contains a valid date in the form:

⟨day⟩ ⟨month⟩ ⟨year⟩

with no spaces internal to the day, month, or year parts.

PROCEDURE DisplayDate

(Date: StringDate)	IN: Date to be displayed

PURPOSE/GOAL STATE: At the end of the current output line, display the date Date in the form: "⟨month⟩ ⟨day⟩, ⟨year⟩" and do not end the current output line.

Merrell is now ready to design the body of each procedure. His design looks as follows:

SUBPROGRAMS

PROCEDURE BuildDate

(Line: InputLine	IN: Date as typed by the user.
Date: StringDate)	OUT: Constructed date record.

PURPOSE/GOAL STATE: Break the Line into its day, month, and year sub-strings, and store them in Date. All spaces must be deleted from the strings in Date.

PRECONDITION: Line contains a valid date in the form:

$$\langle day \rangle \ \langle month \rangle \ \langle year \rangle$$

with no spaces internal to the day, month, or year parts.

ALGORITHM

Step 1. PURPOSE/GOAL STATE: Copy the input line into NewLine and delete any leading spaces in the copy.

ACTIONS:

NewLine := Line
CALL DeleteLeadingSpaces (NewLine)

Step 2. PURPOSE/GOAL STATE: Pick off the $\langle day \rangle$ part of NewLine, up to the first space, and store in Date.Day.

ACTIONS:

StringLength := Position (NewLine, ' ') $-$ 1
Date.Day := Copy (NewLine, 1, StringLength)

Step 3. PURPOSE/GOAL STATE: Delete the $\langle day \rangle$ part and any following spaces from NewLine.

ACTIONS:

CALL Delete (NewLine, 1, StringLength)
CALL DeleteLeadingSpaces (NewLine)

Step 4. PURPOSE/GOAL STATE: Pick off the $\langle month \rangle$ part of NewLine, up to the first remaining space, and store in Date.Month.

ACTIONS:

StringLength := Position (NewLine, ' ') $-$ 1
Date.Month := Copy (NewLine, 1, StringLength)

Step 5. PURPOSE/GOAL STATE: Delete the $\langle month \rangle$ part and any following spaces from NewLine.

ACTIONS:

CALL Delete (NewLine, 1, StringLength)
CALL DeleteLeadingSpaces (NewLine)

Step 6. PURPOSE/GOAL STATE: Pick off the ⟨year⟩ part of NewLine, up to the first remaining space or the end of the string, and store in Date.Year.

ACTIONS:

```
SpacePosn := Position (NewLine, ' ')
IF SpacePosn <> 0 THEN
        StringLength := SpacePosn  −  1
ELSE
        StringLength := Length (NewLine)
Date.Year := Copy (NewLine, 1, StringLength)
```

DATA OBJECTS

StringLength: Integer	Length of a substring.
NewLine: InputLine	Copy of actual parameter string.
SpacePosn: Integer	Position of space in a string.

and a new subprogram has been defined:

SUBPROGRAMS

PROCEDURE DeleteLeadingSpaces

    (Line: InputLine)   IN/OUT: string to be modified.

    PURPOSE/GOAL STATE: Delete any leading spaces from Line.

PROCEDURE DisplayDate

    (Date: StringDate)   IN: Date to be displayed

    PURPOSE/GOAL STATE: At the end of the current output line, display the date Date in the form: "⟨month⟩ ⟨day⟩, ⟨year⟩" and do not end the current output line.

ALGORITHM

Step 1. PURPOSE/GOAL STATE: For convenience, first build the output string in Out-String.

ACTIONS:

```
OutString := Concat (Date.Month, ' ',  Date.Day, ', ', Date.Year)
```

Step 2. PURPOSE/GOAL STATE: Display OutString at the end of the current output line:

ACTIONS:

```
DISPLAY using write: "⟨OutString⟩"
```

OutString: DisplayString   String to be displayed.

and a new data type:

DisplayString = STRING [20]

Merrell now completes the body of the new procedure DeleteLeadingSpaces, which is called in the body of BuildDate:

PROCEDURE DeleteLeadingSpaces
          (Line: InputLine)   IN/OUT: string to be modified.

PURPOSE/GOAL STATE: Delete any leading spaces from Line.

ALGORITHM

Step 1.   ACTIONS:

WHILE Line [1] = ' ' DO
          CALL Delete (Line, 1, 1)

DATA OBJECTS

- none -

EXERCISES

7.9 Code the three example subprograms of this section in Pascal. Then compile and test them.

7.10 Rewrite the body of the DisplayDate procedure so that it does not build OutString as a separate step, but instead it uses the Pascal *write* with five strings as parameters to create and display the output string as a single action. Which version do you find easier to understand?

7.11 Design, code, and test a procedure that converts Merrell's representation of a date into Nancy's representation of a date:

PROCEDURE ConvertStringDate
    (DateIn: StringDate   IN: Date in Merrell's format.
    DateOut: Date)   OUT: Date in Nancy's format.

PURPOSE/GOAL STATE: Convert DateIn to the equivalent date DateOut, represented as three integers instead of as three strings.

7.12 Suppose you have defined the representation of a person's name as a record:

DATA TYPES

InOutLine = STRING [80]
NameString = STRING [30]

NameRecord =	A person's name.
RECORD	
First: NameString	First name.
Middle: Char	Middle initial only
Last: NameString	Last name.
END	

Design, code and test the following procedures:

SUBPROGRAMS

PROCEDURE BuildNameRecord
       (Line: InOutLine)   IN; Contains the typed name.
       Name: NameRecord)   OUT: Constructed name record.

PURPOSE/GOAL STATE: Break Line into its first name, middle initial, and last name parts and store in the fields of Name. The fields of Name should include no spaces.

PRECONDITION: Line must contain a name in the form:

⟨first name⟩ ⟨initial⟩. ⟨last name⟩

with at least one space between each of the three parts and a period after the middle initial. ⟨first name⟩ and ⟨last name⟩ may contain only letters. Line may contain leading or trailing spaces.

PROCEDURE DisplayName
      (Name: NameRecord)   IN: Name to be displayed.

PURPOSE/GOAL STATE: Display Name in the form:

⟨last name⟩,⟨first name⟩_⟨initial⟩.

where the underscores indicate required spaces. No other spaces should be displayed. The display should use *write* to display the name at the end of the current output line, without ending the line.

□□□**7.6**
A CASE STUDY: OPERATIONS ON AN INVENTORY LIST

In Section 6.8 we used records, arrays, and strings in choosing a representation for the inventory list of jeans in stock for a clothing store. Let's use that representation again to see how to design and code various operations on such inventory lists. Figure 7.8 shows the final representation chosen in Section 6.8.

```
DEFINED CONSTANTS

MAXINVENTORY = 2000          Maximum number of jeans in stock.


DATA TYPES

MonthRange = 1..12
DayRange = 1..31
YearRange = 1900..2100

Date =
    RECORD
            Month: MonthRange
            Day: DayRange
            Year: YearRange
    END

WaistRange = 22..48          Waist size in inches.
LengthRange = 20..40         Inseam length in inches.
JeansColor = (BLUE, BLACK, BROWN, WHITE)
BrandName = STRING [25]

Jeans =                      Description of one pair of jeans.
    RECORD
            Waist: WaistRange
            Length: LengthRange
            Retail: Real                Price in dollars/cents.
            Wholesale: Real             Price in dollars/cents.
            Color : JeansColor
            InStock: Date               Date shipment received.
            Brand: BrandName
    END

JeansList = ARRAY [1..MAXINVENTORY] OF Jeans
ListLength = 0..MAXINVENTORY

JeansInventory =                  Inventory for one store.
    RECORD
            Stock: JeansList      All the jeans in stock.
            Count: Listlength     Number of jeans in stock.
    END


DATA OBJECTS

MallStore: JeansInventory         Stock at the mall store.
```

FIGURE 7.8 Representation of the Jeans Inventory List for the Mall Store (from Section 6.8)

For these examples, let's design the following operations on JeansInventory lists:

PROCEDURE TotalValue

(List: JeansInventory	IN: Stock at one store.
TotalWholesale: Real	OUT: Total wholesale value of jeans in stock.
TotalRetail: Real)	OUT: Total retail value of jeans in stock.

PURPOSE/GOAL STATE: Compute the sum of the wholesale and retail values of all the jeans in List, and store in TotalWholesale and TotalRetail.

FUNCTION CountBrandStock

(List: JeansInventory	IN
DesiredBrand: BrandName)	IN

FUNCTION VALUE: Integer   Count of jeans of given brand.

PURPOSE: Count the number of jeans of brand DesiredBrand in List.

As expected, both subprograms require a loop that checks the description of each pair of jeans in the inventory list. The design for the subprogram bodies might be:

PROCEDURE Totalvalue

(List: JeansInventory	IN: Stock at one store.
TotalWholesale: Real	OUT: Total wholesale value of jeans in stock.
TotalRetail: Real)	OUT: Total retail value of jeans in stock.

PURPOSE/GOAL STATE: Compute the sum of the wholesale and retail values of all the jeans in List, and store in TotalWholesale and TotalRetail.

ALGORITHM

Step 1. ACTIONS:

```
TotalWholesale := 0
TotalRetail := 0

FOR I := 1 TO List.Count DO
    BEGIN
        TotalWholesale :=
            TotalWholesale + List.Stock[I].Wholesale
        TotalRetail :=
            TotalRetail + List.Stock[I].Retail
    END
```

DATA OBJECTS

I: Integer   FOR loop subscript variable.

FUNCTION CountBrandStock

    (List: JeansInventory   IN
    DesiredBrand: BrandName)   IN

FUNCTION VALUE: Integer   Count of jeans of given brand.

PURPOSE: Count and return the number of jeans of brand DesiredBrand in List.

ALGORITHM

Step 1. ACTIONS:

```
JeansCount := 0
FOR I := 1 TO List.Count DO
   BEGIN
      IF List.Stock[I].Brand = DesiredBrand THEN
          JeansCount := JeansCount + 1
   END
FUNCTION VALUE := JeansCount
```

DATA OBJECTS

JeansCount: Integer   Running count.
I: Integer   FOR loop subscript variable.

EXERCISES

7.13 Given the representation for the JeansInventory list used in the examples above, design, code in Pascal, and test the following subprograms:

a. PROCEDURE FindJeans
    (List: JeansInventory   IN
    Waist: WaistRange   IN: Desired waist size.
    Length: LengthRange   IN: Desired length.
    Color: JeansColor)   IN: Desired color.

PURPOSE/GOAL STATE: For each pair of jeans in List that have the given Waist, Length, and Color, display complete information about that pair of jeans (display all fields) in a readable format. If no jeans match the description, display "No matching jeans in stock."

b. FUNCTION CountReceived
    (List: JeansInventory   IN
    InStockDate: Date)   IN

FUNCTION VALUE: Integer

PURPOSE: Return a count of the number of jeans in List whose "in stock" date is the same as or comes after the given InStockDate.

c. PROCEDURE DeleteFromStock

    (List: JeansInventory   IN/OUT
     Waist: WaistRange   IN
     Length: LengthRange   IN
     Color: JeansColor   IN
     Brand: BrandName)   IN

PURPOSE/GOAL STATE: Find the first pair of jeans in List whose waist, length, color, and brand match those given as parameters. Then delete that pair of jeans from List. List must still be a valid JeansInventory list after the deletion (no holes allowed in the list). If no jeans in List match the description, do nothing.

□

HINT: After the deletion is made, some other jeans record must be copied into the resulting hole in the list. The order of the jeans records in the list does not matter, so *any* other jeans record could be copied. Of course, copying another jeans record into the hole caused by the first deletion means that the other jeans record must be *deleted* from its original position. Choose the other jeans record so that the second deletion does not lead to additional deletions. And don't forget to consider the possibility that the list may be empty or contain only one pair of jeans.

□□□ **7.7**
HAND TRACING EXECUTION OF A PROCEDURE OR FUNCTION

A useful skill when debugging a program is to be able to trace by hand through the execution of a particular subprogram call, to understand exactly the new program state after the call is executed, given that you know the state before the call. To understand the effect of the call, you need to recreate on paper the initial local state of the called subprogram, immediately after parameter transmission is complete, and then trace the sequence of state changes caused by the actions of the subprogram body.

The final local state of a procedure will show what changes the procedure has made to the values of its IN/OUT and OUT parameters. The final local state of a function will show what function value has been stored, to be returned to the caller. Remember that the final local state of a subprogram is thrown away when execution of the subprogram body is complete, except for the value of a function or changes in the values of IN/OUT and OUT parameters (Pascal VAR parameters).

□□

Hand Tracing a Simple Subprogram Call

First, let's look at tracing subprogram calls that do not involve records, arrays, or strings as parameters—only simple parameters containing a single value. To hand trace such a subprogram call, take a piece of paper and follow these steps:

1. *Subprogram call.* Write the subprogram call to be traced on the first line, exactly as it appears in the program.

2. *Actual parameters.* On the line(s) below the call, write down the actual parameters, as follows:

   a. VALUE parameters: If an actual parameter is a VALUE parameter, write down the *value* of the actual parameter expression when the subprogram is called.

   b. VAR parameters: If an actual parameter is a VAR parameter, write down the entire *state* of that data object when the subprogram is called.

3. *Local state heading.* Now write a heading for the trace of the local state of the subprogram, with a column labeled with each of the formal parameter names and each of the local variable names. For each formal parameter, also show whether the parameter is a Pascal VAR or VALUE parameter. If the subprogram is a function, also include a column labeled FUNCTION VALUE, to represent the "hidden" location where the function value is stored. The leftmost column should be labeled ACTION.

4. *Initial local state.* On the first line below the heading, in the ACTION column, write "Initial local state" and place a ?? as the value of each local variable, and, for functions, the function value.

5. *Parameter transmission.* The key step is to properly transmit the parameters. In the second line, in the ACTION column, write "After parameter transmission." Then under each of the columns labeled with formal parameter names, do the following:

   a. If the parameter is a VALUE parameter, then simply write the *value* of the corresponding actual parameter from (2) into the position under the formal parameter name.

   b. If the parameter is a VAR parameter, then *write the name of the actual parameter data object and its value* where you would ordinarily write just the value of the formal parameter, immediately below the ?? in the first line of that column. The name of the actual parameter shows that the formal parameter "points to" that actual parameter, so that any change in the value of the formal parameter represents a change in that actual parameter's value.

6. *Actions.* Now execute the actions of the subprogram body, hand tracing the effect of each action as described in Chapter 4. When an action assigns a new value to a formal parameter, show the new value in the column under that formal parameter name, just as for a local variable. In a function body, when a function value assignment is made, show the new value in the FUNCTION VALUE column. After the last action in the subprogram body has been traced, the last line shows the final local state.

7. *Caller's new state or function value.* Now add a final line to the trace showing the new state of the caller, after the call is complete. On this line, show exactly the same actual parameter data objects shown before the call, but replace the value before the call with the final value shown for the corresponding formal parameter in the local state. If tracing a function call, then this line should be labeled FUNCTION VALUE RETURNED, and should show the final value in the local state column labeled FUNCTION VALUE.

1. Consider the following procedure:

```
PROCEDURE SwapReals
       (VAR X: Real;          {IN/OUT}
        VAR Y: Real);         {IN/OUT}
    {PURPOSE/GOAL STATE: Interchange the values of X and Y}
VAR
       Temp: Real;       {temporary storage variable}
BEGIN
       Temp := X;
       X := Y;
       Y := Temp;
END;   {procedure SwapReals}
```

Suppose you want to hand trace the call in the following segment:

```
A := 1.1;
B := 2.2;
SwapReals (A, B);
```

Following the steps outlined above gives the trace:

Call Being Traced:

```
SwapReals (A, B);
```

Actual Parameters at Time of the Call:

A: 1.1   B: 2.2

Trace of Changes in Local State:

ACTION	X(VAR)	Y(VAR)	TEMP
Initial local state:	??	??	??
After parameter transmission:	A/1.1	B/2.2	??
Temp := X	1.1	2.2	1.1
X := Y	2.2	2.2	1.1
Y := Temp	2.2	1.1	1.1

New State of Caller:

A: | 2.2 | B: | 1.1 |

2. Consider the function AbsAverage from Section 7.2:

```
FUNCTION AbsAverage
      (X: Real;            {IN: first value to average}
       Y: Real)           {IN: second value to average}
        : Real;           {The average}
      {PURPOSE: Compute and return the average of the
      absolute values of X and Y.}
  BEGIN
      AbsAverage := (abs (X) + abs (Y)) / 2;
  END;   {function AbsAverage}
```

Suppose you want to hand trace the call in the following segment:

```
A := 12.0;
C := AbsAverage (A + 2, -4.0);
```

Following the steps outlined above gives the trace:

Call Being Traced:

```
AbsAverage (A + 2, -4.0)
```

Actual Parameters at Time of the Call:

Value of first parameter: | 14.0 |

Value of second parameter: | -4.0 |

Trace of Changes in Local State:

ACTION	X(VALUE)	Y(VALUE)	FUNCTION VALUE
Initial local state:	??	??	??
After parameter transmission:	14.0	−4.0	??
AbsAverage := . . .	14.0	−4.0	9.0

Function Value Returned: | 9.0 |

For a VAR parameter, the actual parameter data object might be an array element or a field of a record. In such a case, follow exactly the same rules. However, if an array element has a subscript expression, you must *evaluate the subscript expression* and use the literal subscript value that results in the trace. Remember that an array element or record field is treated within the subprogram just as though it were a simple data object of the element or field type.

EXAMPLE

Using the same SwapReals procedure shown above, suppose you want to trace the following call:

```
T[2] := 10.0;
S := 5.5;
I := 2;
SwapReals (T[I], S);
```

Following the steps outlined above gives the trace:

Call Being Traced:

```
SwapReals (T[2], S); - note that the subscript expression
                       "I" has been evaluated already.
```

Actual Parameters at Time of the Call:

T[2]: | 10.0 | S: | 5.5 |

Trace of Changes in Local State:

ACTION	X(VAR)	Y(VAR)	TEMP
Initial local state:	??	??	??
After parameter transmission:	T[2]/10.0	S/5.5	??
Temp := X	10.0	5.5	10.0
X := Y	5.5	5.5	10.0
Y := Temp	5.5	10.0	10.0

New State of Caller:

T[2]: | 5.5 | S: | 10.0 |

Hand Tracing with Data Structures as Parameters

Hand tracing when one or several parameters are data structures such as arrays, records, or strings, is complicated by the multiple values stored in each data structure. Obviously you cannot hope to have a column for each element of an array, field of a record, or character position in a string.

For handling data structures in the trace itself, make the following changes in the way that you write down the trace:

1. Begin in the same way, by writing down the call and the actual parameters. Write down the state of each array, record, or string parameter at the time of the call.

2. Use the same heading for the trace table for the local state. In particular, just have a single column for each formal parameter or local variable that is an array, record, or string type.

3. In the "After parameter transmission" line, for each formal parameter data structure that is an array, record, or string:

a. VAR parameters: Write "pointer to ⟨actual parameter name⟩."

b. VALUE parameters: Write "copy of ⟨actual parameter name⟩."

In this way, you never have to write the entire data structure as part of the local state.

4. As you execute the actions of the subprogram and a change is made in a value stored in a data structure parameter:

a. ARRAYS: write only the subscript of the element and its new value.

b. RECORDS: write only the name of the field and its new value.

c. STRINGS: write the *entire new string* after the modification.

5. To find the current value of an array element or record field, scan up the appropriate column to find the last value assigned to that element or field. If no new value has been assigned, then use the original value from the "ACTUAL PARAME-TERS" part.

6. In the final line, where you show the new state of each actual parameter after the subprogram has been executed, you will have to scan the appropriate column to find the last value assigned to each array element or record field by the subprogram.

EXAMPLE

In order to show all three types of data structure in a single short example, we use a procedure that does nothing useful. Suppose that the types and data objects are defined:

DATA TYPES

ArrayType = ARRAY [1..5] OF Real

```
RecordType =
      RECORD
            FieldA: Integer
            FieldB: Real
            FieldC: Boolean
      END
StringType = STRING [20]
```

DATA OBJECTS

ATest: ArrayType	Example array parameter.
RTest: RecordType	Example record parameter.
STest: StringType	Example string parameter.

and the procedure to be traced, in (partial) pseudo-code:

PROCEDURE Example

(A: ArrayType	IN/OUT
R: RecordType	IN—VALUE parameter.
S: StringType)	IN/OUT

ALGORITHM

ACTIONS:

```
I := 2
A [I] := 3.0
R.FieldA := 12
CALL Delete (S, 6, 9)
A [I+1] := 17.2
A [2] := A [I+1]  −  5.0
A [5] := R.FieldB
R.FieldC := TRUE
S := Concat (S, ' + Eggs')
```

DATA OBJECTS

I: Integer   Subscript value.

Now let's hand trace the following call:

Call Being Traced:

CALL Example (ATest, RTest, STest)

Actual Parameters at Time of the Call:

STEST: ['Green Eggs and Ham']

ATest[1]:	1.1	RTest.FieldA:	10	
" [2]:	2.2	" .FieldB:	22.2	
" [3]:	3.3	" .FieldC:	FALSE	
" [4]:	4.4			
" [5]:	5.5			

Trace of Changes in Local State:

ACTION	A(VAR)	R(VALUE)	S(VAR)	I
Initial local state:	??	??	??	??
After parameter transmission:	pointer to ATest	copy of RTest	pointer to STest	??
I := 2				2
A [I] := 3.0	[2]: 3.0			2
R.FieldA := 12		.FieldA: 12		2
CALL Delete (S, 6, 9)			'Green Ham'	2
A [I+1] := 17.2	[3]: 17.2			2
A [2] := A [I+1] − 5.0	[2]: 12.2			2
A [5] := R.FieldB	[5]: 22.2			2
R.FieldC := TRUE		.FieldC: TRUE		2
S := Concat (S, ' + Eggs')			'Green Ham + Eggs'	2

New State of Caller:

STEST: ['Green Ham + Eggs']

ATEST[1]:	1.1
" [2]:	12.2
" [3]:	17.2
" [4]:	4.4
" [5]:	22.2

RTest: *No change* (VALUE parameter)

■

In choosing the actual parameters for a call that you want to trace, limit the complexity of the data structure parameters as much as possible. Choose arrays with only a few elements and short strings for a hand trace if you can.

□ □

Hand Tracing FOR Loops

The heading of a FOR loop is a single line, but execution of the FOR loop involves two pairs of actions that need to be represented separately in the hand trace. We call these actions FOR-START and FOR-NEXT. Each involves an assignment to the ⟨subscript variable⟩, followed by a loop exit test that compares the current value of the subscript variable with the ⟨last subscript⟩ value given in the FOR loop heading:

   a.   FOR-START: —when the FOR is reached the first time.

   ACTIONS:

   ⟨subscript variable⟩ := ⟨first subscript⟩
   (⟨subscript variable⟩ > ⟨last subscript⟩) = TRUE or FALSE

   b.   FOR-NEXT: —after each execution of the loop body.

   ACTIONS:

   ⟨subscript variable⟩ := ⟨subscript variable⟩ + 1
   (⟨subscript variable⟩ > ⟨last subscript⟩) = TRUE or FALSE

In the ACTION column of a hand trace, when you reach the start of a FOR loop, write FOR-START and the pair of actions. If the test gives FALSE, then execute the loop body actions. Then write FOR-NEXT and the pair of actions. Repeat until the test evaluates to TRUE. Then continue with the actions that follow the FOR loop.

The goal of hand tracing is to understand what happens when the loop is executed, without being overwhelmed by the tedious complexity of executing the individual actions. When hand tracing a FOR loop within a subprogram body, choose the subscript range so that you only trace a few repetitions of the loop, in order to limit the complexity of the hand trace.

EXAMPLE   Let's hand trace a call of the FindBestWeek procedure in Section 7.4. Here are the relevant definitions. For the hand trace, let's limit the array to three elements and the loop to three repetitions by using a defined constant:

DEFINED CONSTANTS

NUMWEEKS = 3

DATA TYPES

Week: 1..NUMWEEKS
WeeklySalesList = ARRAY [Week] OF Real

PROCEDURE FindBestWeek

(Sales: WeeklySalesList	IN: Sales for the year.
BestWeek: Week	OUT: Number of best week.
BestSales: Real)	OUT: Sales in best week.

PURPOSE: Find the week with the largest total sales. If several weeks tie, use the week latest in the year.

GOAL STATE: Store the number of the best week in BestWeek and the sales for that week in BestSales.

ALGORITHM

Step 1. PURPOSE: Assume the first week is the best week, and then compare all later weeks against the first week.

GOAL STATE: Set BestWeek and BestSales to the last best week in the year.

ACTIONS:

BestSales := Sales [1]
BestWeek := 1

FOR I := 2 TO NUMWEEKS DO
   BEGIN
      IF Sales [I] > = BestSales THEN
         BestSales := Sales [I]
         BestWeek := I
   END

DATA OBJECTS

I: Integer   FOR loop subscript variable.

Suppose you want to hand trace the call:

Call Being Traced:

CALL FindBestWeek (SList, BWeek, BSales)

Actual Parameters at Time of the Call:

SLIST[1]:	10.0	BWEEK:	??	BSALES:	??
" [2]:	20.0				
" [3]:	15.0				

Trace of Changes in Local State:

ACTION	SALES(VAR)	BESTWEEK(VAR)	BESTSALES(VAR)	I
Initial local state:	??	??	??	??
After parameter transmission:	pointer to SList	BWeek/??	BSales/??	??
BestSales := Sales [1]		??	10.0	??
BestWeek := 1		1	10.0	??
FOR-START: I := 2		1	10.0	2
(I > NUMWEEKS) = FALSE				
IF (Sales [I] > = BestSales) = TRUE				
BestSales := Sales [I]		1	20.0	2
BestWeek := I		2	20.0	2
FOR-NEXT: I := I + 1		2	20.0	3
(I > NUMWEEKS) = FALSE				
IF (Sales [I] >= BestSales) = FALSE				
FOR-NEXT: I := I + 1		2	20.0	4
(I > NUMWEEKS) = TRUE				

New State of Caller:

BWEEK: | 2 |

BSALES: | 20.0 |

SLIST: *Unchanged*

EXERCISES

7.14 Hand trace the function ComputePartialYearSales of Section 7.4, for the call:

$$Y := ComputePartialYearSales (SList, 2, 5)$$

Assume that the value of each element of SList equals its subscript (Slist[1] = 1.0, SList[2] = 2.0, etc.).

7.15 Hand trace the procedure BuildDate of Section 7.5, for the call:

$$CALL \ BuildDate \ (InLine, OutDate)$$

Assume that InLine contains the string:

$$\texttt{'\_\_\_21\_\_May\_\_1988\_\_'}$$

where the underscores represent spaces.

□□□ 7.8
SUBPROGRAM HIERARCHIES AND PROGRAM STRUCTURE CHARTS

Most larger programs are organized into a *hierarchy of subprograms*. The main procedure forms the top level of the hierarchy. Subprogram calls in the main procedure define the subprograms that form the second level of the hierarchy. Each of these subprograms may call other subprograms, which form the third level in the hierarchy, and so forth. The hierarchy is not a strict one—a lower level subprogram might be called from subprograms at several higher levels. "Recursive" subprogram calls (Chapter 12) even allow a subprogram to call itself or to call another subprogram above it in the hierarchy.

□□
Program Structure Charts

A larger program may have several dozen or even hundreds of subprograms. In pseudo-code, you write each subprogram heading on the SUBPROGRAMS list as you identify the need for it. Then, in the final Pascal code the subprogram definitions are placed, in a somewhat arbitrary order, after the TYPE section of the main program. This organization makes it difficult for the reader of a program to determine the subprogram hierarchy simply by looking at the Pascal code itself.

A program *structure chart* is a diagram, as shown in Figure 7.9, that shows how the subprograms in the program are *logically* organized into the hierarchy defined by the calling structure of the program. At the top of the structure chart is a box that represents the main procedure. Below it are the subprograms that are called directly by the main procedure, each represented by a box. Arrows connect the main procedure to each subprogram it calls. Below the second level subprograms are boxes that represent the third level subprograms (subprograms called by the second level subprograms), and so forth.

This graphical representation provides important information to the person who is trying to understand how a Pascal program is organized. A structure chart should be part of the documentation for any program that has more than a few subprograms.

□□
Building a Structure Chart

You can draw the structure chart for a program as you design it by adding a box to the chart as you specify each new subprogram and by adding an arrow to the chart as you write each subprogram call. To draw a structure chart for an existing program, draw a box for the main procedure as the top level of the chart. Then scan the body of the main procedure looking for calls on procedures and functions. Draw a box for each called subprogram, with an arrow directed to it from the main procedure box. If there are several calls on the same subprogram in the main procedure, just draw one arrow. This completes the second level of the chart. Now repeat the process for each second level subprogram—scan its body for subprogram calls and draw boxes and arrows for any new subprograms encountered.

FIGURE 7.9 A Structure Chart for a Pascal Program

Suppose the program skeleton (subprograms and subprogram calls) is:
PROGRAM Example (INPUT, OUTPUT);

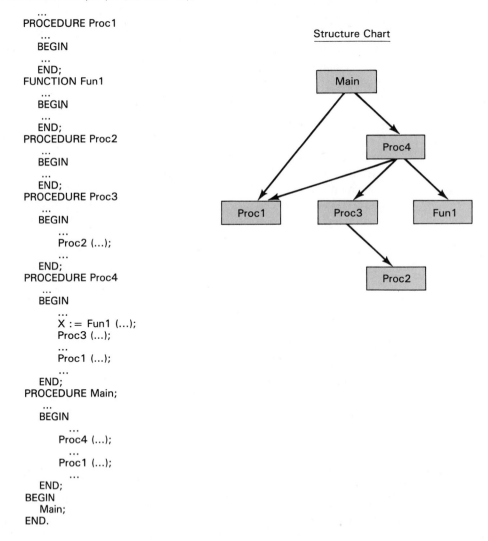

```
    ...
PROCEDURE Proc1
    ...
  BEGIN
    ...
  END;
FUNCTION Fun1
    ...
  BEGIN
    ...
  END;
PROCEDURE Proc2
    ...
  BEGIN
    ...
  END;
PROCEDURE Proc3
    ...
  BEGIN
    ...
     Proc2 (...);
    ...
  END;
PROCEDURE Proc4
    ...
  BEGIN
    ...
     X := Fun1 (...);
     Proc3 (...);
    ...
     Proc1 (...);
    ...
  END;
PROCEDURE Main;
    ...
  BEGIN
    ...
     Proc4 (...);
    ...
     Proc1 (...);
    ...
  END;
BEGIN
  Main;
END.
```

Structure Chart

If there is already a box for a subprogram when you encounter a call on it, just draw an arrow to the existing box. In the final structure chart, there should be only one box for each subprogram and at most one arrow connecting any pair of boxes.

After you have a rough diagram of the structure chart, you may want to reorganize it so that all arrows point down the page, by moving some boxes to a lower level. For example, in Figure 7.9, subprogram Proc1 is shown at the third level in the chart even though it is called from the main procedure, due to the fact that Proc1 is also called by Proc4, which is itself a second level procedure.

EXERCISES

7.16 For each of the following program skeletons, draw the structure chart for the program:

a.
```
PROGRAM Example2 (INPUT, OUTPUT);

       . . .
    FUNCTION Fun1
       . . .
    BEGIN
          . . .
    END;
    PROCEDURE Proc1
       . . .
    BEGIN
          . . .
    END;
    PROCEDURE Proc2
       . . .
    BEGIN
          . . .
       Z := W + Fun1 (...);
       Proc1 (...);
          . . .
       Proc1 (...);
          . . .
    END;
    PROCEDURE Main;
       . . .
    BEGIN
          . . .
       Proc1 (...);
       Proc2 (...);
          . . .
    END;
BEGIN
    Main;
END.
```

b. PROGRAM Example3 (INPUT, OUTPUT);
```
        . . .
    PROCEDURE Proc1
        . . .
      BEGIN
          . . .
      END;
    PROCEDURE Proc2
        . . .
      BEGIN
            . . .
          Proc1 (...);
            . . .
      END;
    PROCEDURE Proc3
        . . .
      BEGIN
            . . .
      END;
    PROCEDURE Proc4
        . . .
      BEGIN
            . . .
          Proc2 (...);
            . . .
          Proc3 (...);
            . . .
      END;
    PROCEDURE Proc5
        . . .
      BEGIN
            . . .
          Proc3 (...);
          Proc2 (...);
          Proc4 (...);
            . . .
      END;
    PROCEDURE Main;
        . . .
      BEGIN
            . . .
          Proc5 (...);
            . . .
          Proc2 (...);
            . . .
          Proc3 (...);
            . . .
      END;
    BEGIN
      Main;
    END.
```

□ □ □ **7.9**
TESTING SUBPROGRAMS

Testing and debugging of a Pascal program is made easier when the program is divided properly into subprograms. The testing strategy to use is called *incremental testing*. You first test individual subprograms and groups of subprograms. You build up in "increments" of one or a few subprograms to larger parts of the program. When each of the major parts has been tested, you follow with testing of the complete program.

Incremental testing allows you to find and correct errors more quickly than the alternative strategy of testing the entire program as a unit from the beginning, called *big bang testing* (see the box). By focusing your tests on a few subprograms at a time, an error detected during testing can be immediately traced to a bug in a small part of the overall program.

In incremental testing, two testing techniques are important: the use of *test drivers* and *stubs*. Let's look first at these two techniques and then return to the development of incremental testing strategies.

□ □
Test Driver Programs

To test a subprogram by itself, separately from the rest of the program, you can build a program that exists only to test the subprogram (or a group of subprograms). This testing program is called a *test driver* (or simply *driver*).

The test driver program usually takes the form:

1. The main procedure has a single purpose: call the subprogram being tested one or more times with test data values as actual parameters.

2. In the main procedure, variables are declared (of the proper data types) to serve as actual parameters in a call of the subprogram being tested.

3. A set of test data values is assigned to the variables that represent the IN and IN/OUT actual parameters. (Alternatively, the test values may be read in and stored in these actual parameter variables.)

4. Before the call, in the main procedure the test values are displayed to show exactly the program state when the subprogram is called.

5. The subprogram is called, using the declared variables as actual parameters.

6. The resulting values of the OUT and IN/OUT actual parameters are displayed to show the new program state after the call. The values of the IN parameters may also be redisplayed to show that they have not been changed by the subprogram.

The driver may call the subprogram several times with different test data values for the IN and IN/OUT parameters. The programmer then inspects the displayed output from a run of the driver to determine if the subprogram produces the correct results for the test input values.

A test driver involves a simple application of the *Cardinal Rule of Debugging* from Chapter 4. The "before" and "after" states that you need to pin down an error in the subprogram are just the states of the test driver before and after the call of the subprogram. Because the driver displays the contents of both states, it is easy to check whether both states are correct. If you detect a bug, then you know that one of the control paths through the subprogram body contains the error.

EXAMPLE   Vic has written a procedure IntegerDivide whose specification is:

PROCEDURE IntegerDivide

(Dividend: Integer	IN
Divisor: Integer	IN
Quotient: Integer	OUT
Remainder: Integer)	OUT

PURPOSE/GOAL STATE: Compute integer Quotient and Remainder of Dividend/Divisor.

Vic is testing the IntegerDivide procedure. His test driver looks like the following. Because it is only used for testing, Vic does not include many comments in the test driver:

```
PROGRAM TestDriver (INPUT, OUTPUT);
  . . .
PROCEDURE IntegerDivide
    . . .
    BEGIN                          ⎫  coded version of
    . . .                          ⎬  procedure to be
    . . .                          ⎪  tested
    END;   {procedure IntegerDivide} ⎭
```

```
PROCEDURE Main;
    VAR
        A, B, C, D: Integer;
        Again: Char;
    BEGIN
        Again := 'y';
        WHILE Again = 'y' DO
          BEGIN
            writeln
              ('Type the dividend and divisor (integers)';
            readln (A, B);

              {Display the state before the call}
            writeln ('Actual parameters before call: ', A, B);

            IntegerDivide (A, B, C, D);

              {Display the state after the call}
            writeln
              ('Actual parameters after call: ', A, B, C, D);

            write ('Another test? (y/n)');
            readln (Again);
          END;
    END;
BEGIN
      Main;
END.
```

He compiles and runs the TestDriver program, entering test values and observing the results of the call of the procedure being tested, until he is satisfied that it is working correctly. ■

Stubs

A second important testing technique is the use of *stubs*. A stub is simply a subprogram with a heading in its correct form (matching that given in the SUBPROGRAMS list) but with a body that does nothing except print a message when it is called during testing, such as:

```
BEGIN
    writeln ('STUB PROCEDURE ⟨name⟩ HAS BEEN CALLED');
    writeln ('PARAMETERS ARE: X = ', ⟨X⟩, ...);
END;
```

You use a stub during testing when you want to test one subprogram before you have implemented the body of one of the subprograms that it calls. You can do the testing if you are willing to write a stub subprogram for each unimplemented lower level subprogram called by the subprogram being tested. This testing situation often arises when you have some relatively unimportant subprograms that you want to design and code last, after you have a running version of the main parts of the program.

By using stubs for missing subprograms, you can write a test driver for the subprogram you want to test (including any complete lower level subprograms that you have already tested). The stubs allow the whole test program to be compiled. During testing you usually choose test values that do not lead to a call of a stub subprogram. If you do call a stub, it is only to be sure that the stub is called at the right time and with the right parameters. The stub does no computation, so after the stub is called, you usually have to end that particular test run.

EXAMPLE Vic is writing a test driver to test a procedure ComputeValues that he has written as part of a larger program. ComputeValues contains a call on another procedure HandleOddSituation that is only called when a rare situation arises during the actions of ComputeValues:

```
PROCEDURE ComputeValues (...)
    ...
   BEGIN
      ...
    IF ...test for rare situation... THEN
         HandleOddSituation (...)
    ELSE
      ...
   END;
```

Vic wants to test ComputeValues, but he does not want to stop to design and code the HandleOddSituation procedure. He just uses a stub for HandleOddSituation:

```
PROGRAM TestDriver (...)
    ...

PROCEDURE HandleOddSituation
      ...   —usual procedure heading
   BEGIN
       {STUB PROCEDURE—replace later}
     writeln ('STUB HandleOddSituation HAS BEEN CALLED');
   END;
```

```
PROCEDURE ComputeValues
    . . .
  BEGIN
      . . .
    IF ...test for rare situation... THEN
          HandleOddSituation (...)
    ELSE
      . . .
  END;

PROCEDURE MAIN;
    . . .
  BEGIN
      . . .    —body of test driver
  END;

BEGIN
    Main;
END.
```

Testing Strategies: Bottom Up and Top Down

The concepts of test drivers and stubs allow you many possible incremental testing strategies for a program that has a number of subprograms. To plan your testing strategy, look at the *structure chart* for the program being tested.

□

Bottom Up Testing. Suppose you want to test each subprogram individually, by using a test driver but without using stubs. Which subprograms should you test first? Obviously, you should start with the subprograms at the *bottom* of the structure chart —the subprograms that do not call any other subprograms. You test these first. When you are sure they are working correctly, you move to the next level of subprograms higher in the structure chart—subprograms that call only subprograms that you have already tested. You can now safely include the tested subprograms in the test of the untested subprogram, and expect the test run to fail only if the untested subprogram fails. This strategy of working from the bottom of the structure chart toward the top is called *bottom-up testing*.

Suppose that instead of testing from the bottom up, you begin testing a subprogram in the middle of the structure chart, where the subprogram being tested calls other subprograms which have not yet been tested. During a test run, errors in the untested subprograms may cause the subprogram you are testing to fail, even if it is correct itself. You will find it hard to locate a bug in such a situation. Bottom-up testing avoids this difficulty.

EXAMPLE   Suppose your program has the structure chart:

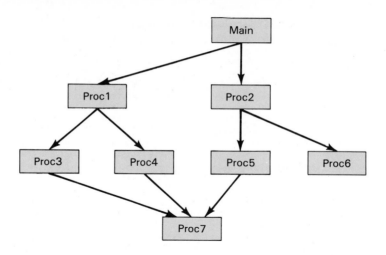

A bottom up testing strategy would test Proc7 and Proc6 individually first. Then Proc3, Proc4, and Proc5 would be tested individually, using the tested version of Proc7. Proc1 and Proc2 could then be tested individually, using the tested versions of the other subprograms. Main would be tested last, using tested versions of all subprograms. ■

□

Top Down Testing.   An alternative testing strategy is to begin at the *top* of the program's structure chart, and write and test the main procedure and one or a few top level subprograms first, with stubs for the remaining subprograms. You then work your way down, implementing one or a few more of the lower level subprograms, replacing the stubs by the completed subprograms, and testing the more complete group. This strategy is termed *top down testing*. With top down testing, you do not need to write special test driver programs.

Commonly, testing a large program involves some combination of top down and bottom up testing. The particular testing strategy that is simplest depends on the structure of the particular program. You try to test groups of subprograms that form natural sub-units of the overall program. Often you want to implement and test the most important parts of the program first, while leaving the less important subprograms as stubs initially.

□ □

Gathering Debugging Information

When testing subprograms or groups of subprograms, you usually want to gather detailed information about the actions that are taking place during program execution. Here are some common ways of gathering useful debugging information during testing:

1. *Automatic tracing facilities.* Many Pascal systems provide automatic tracing facilities that can be used during subprogram testing. Typically the automatic trace displays a message each time a subprogram is called and when it completes its execution, possibly with information about the parameters in the call.

   2. *Entry and exit messages.* If automatic tracing facilities are not available, you can produce your own trace of subprogram execution by using debug WRITE statements. As the first action in a subprogram, say SUB1, display a debug line:

```
BEGINNING SUB1
```

and at the end, as the final action, display

```
LEAVING SUB1
```

These displays allow you to trace the flow of control and determine exactly which subprograms have been called, in what order.

   3. *Display IN values on entry.* Extend the entry message to include displaying the values of the IN and IN/OUT parameters of the subprogram. For example, in a procedure SUB1 with formal parameters A and B, display the entry message:

```
BEGINNING SUB1,  A = xxxx,  B = yyyy
```

These displays allow you to ensure that the correct IN and IN/OUT parameter values are received.

   4. *Display OUT values after return to the caller.* Immediately after the call of the subprogram is complete, display the new values of the OUT and IN/OUT actual parameters. For example:

```
ON RETURN FROM SUB1,  C = xxxx,  D = yyyy
```

These displays allow you to determine if the OUT values are being correctly computed and received by the caller.

   5. *Use a "snapshot" procedure.* A *snapshot procedure* is a procedure that you write to display a "snapshot" of all or part of the program's data state at the time it is called. The snapshot procedure does nothing but display the values of its parameters. Where the program state contains several complex data structures, the snapshot procedure allows you to easily display the contents of these data structures at many points during program execution, simply by inserting a call on the snapshot procedure wherever desired. All the complex WRITE statements are hidden in the snapshot procedure.

EXAMPLE   Suppose you are testing a program that uses a JeansInventory list, as defined in Figure 7.8. The JeansInventory is a data structure consisting of a list of varying length, in which each list element is a record describing a pair of jeans. In testing such a program, it would be useful to have a snapshot procedure that would display the contents of a JeansInventory list. The snapshot procedure might look like this, coded in Pascal:

```
PROCEDURE SnapJeansList
    (VAR List: JeansInventory);    {IN}

   VAR
      I: Integer;              {FOR loop index}
   BEGIN
      writeln ('   SNAPSHOT of Jeans Inventory List'
      writeln;

      FOR I := 1 TO List.Count DO
        BEGIN
           writeln ('Entry ', I, ':');
           writeln (' Waist = ', List.Stock[I].Waist:1,
                   ' Length = ', List.Stock[I].Length:1,
                   ' Retail = ', List.Stock[I].Retail:1,
                   ' Wholesale = ', List.Stock[I].Wholesale:1);
           writeln (' Brand = ', List.Stock[I].Brand:1,
                   ' Color = ', ord (List.Stock[I].Color):1);
           writeln (' In stock date: ',
                       List.Stock[I].InStock.Month:1, '/',
                       List.Stock[I].InStock.Day:1, '/',
                       List.Stock[I].InStock.Year:1);
        END;

      writeln ('   END OF SNAPSHOT');
      writeln;
   END;  {procedure SnapJeansList}
```

Note that the Color field is displayed as an integer, using the *ord* predefined function, rather than as the name of the color in the enumeration, because most Pascal systems do not allow values of enumerated types to be displayed directly. ■

Notice how the snapshot procedure in the example hides the complicated WRITE statements needed to display a data structure like a JeansInventory list. Whenever a program uses a complicated data structure, consider writing a snapshot procedure for it to simplify looking at its contents during program testing.

EXERCISES

7.17 For each subprogram coded in Exercise 7.13, write a test driver and test the subprogram with an appropriate range of test parameters. Use a snapshot procedure like that given above to check the state of the jeans inventory list before and after each call.

□□□ 7.10
PROGRAM PROTOTYPES

Sometimes the requirements that a program must meet are vague or incomplete when you begin the design of a program. The users of the new program may have only a partial understanding of exactly what they want the program to be able to do. You, as the programmer, may find that you need to construct a *prototype* of the program first to meet part of the requirements, as they are understood at the start of the project. You get the prototype running, and then allow the prospective users to try it out to see what additional requirements it should meet, or how the existing requirements might be improved. Gradually, over several cycles of improvements, you modify the program and its requirements specification until you find the right program to fit the users' needs.

By designing a program from the top down and making careful use of abstractions such as data types and subprograms, you can create a prototype program that is easy to expand into a more complete program as you better understand the program's requirements. *Stubs,* in particular, are central to the coding of a prototype. In the prototype, you want a Pascal program that you can compile and execute, but one in which you may not have designed and coded many of the subprograms. By using stubs for the missing subprograms, you allow a running prototype to be built, and still make it easy to later modify the prototype to meet additional or modified requirements based on suggestions by the users.

In many situations, a prototype is focused on the *interactive dialogue* between the program and the user. The initial requirements specify how the dialogue might be organized. A prototype program is constructed that implements the dialogue as specified, but often without the full computations required in the complete program. Thus the user gets to try out the prototype to see if it allows him to request the computations he desires, but the actual results computed by the prototype may not be correct.

Often the user finds that the dialogue implemented by the prototype is incomplete or difficult to use. Changes are made in the requirements, and the prototype is modified to implement the improved dialogue. Ultimately, when the user is satisfied with the dialogue, then the computational subprograms are fully implemented, so that correct results are produced.

□□
Advantages of Prototypes

To summarize the advantages of constructing a prototype during the design and coding of a program:

1. Vague or incomplete requirements may be filled in by the user based on experience with the prototype, thus avoiding construction of a program based on "guessing" at parts of the requirements.

2. A running prototype allows incremental top down testing of the system as stubs are filled in, without the need to construct special test drivers.

Disadvantages of Prototypes

Prototypes also have disadvantages:

1. Building a prototype is a tempting way to avoid the task of carefully specifying program requirements. "Let's get a prototype running and see how we like it" is characteristic of the hacker's approach to programming. You have to put almost as much effort into specifying requirements and designing the program for a prototype as for the complete program. Using a prototype is simply an admission that you are unable to fill in some parts of the requirements at the beginning.

2. As the requirements change, the design of a prototype may be hard to modify in certain ways. You may have to throw away parts of the prototype and re-design them, causing you extra work.

3. Modifying an existing program may introduce new bugs in parts that used to work correctly, unless the modifications are carefully made. You may find that you have to do more testing and debugging as a prototype is extended to the full program than if you had designed and coded all the parts of the program at one time.

□□□ **7.11**
PROGRAM IT WITH STYLE!

Here are some style tips to make your programs more readable and understandable to another person:

1. *White space and indentation.* When a Pascal program contains many subprograms, it is essential that you use white space and indentation to set off the heading, local variable declarations, and body of each subprogram. In general, use at least one blank line before and after each subprogram definition, and indent the parameter list in the heading, the local variable declarations in the VAR section, and the statements in the body. The examples in this chapter show an acceptable style.

2. *The end comment.* The "end comment"

```
END;     {procedure ⟨name⟩}
```

or

```
END;     {function ⟨name⟩}
```

at the end of the body of a subprogram named ⟨name⟩ helps the reader to easily find the start and end of each subprogram definition.

3. *Formal parameters on separate lines*. Writing each formal parameter name, its data type, its IN/OUT specification, and its purpose on a separate line in the subprogram heading makes this crucial information easy to read and understand. We have used this style throughout this chapter.

□□□ 7.12
PSEUDO-CODE AND PASCAL SUMMARY

The new elements introduced in this chapter are the pseudo-code and Pascal for procedures, functions, and the FOR loop.

□□

General Pseudo-code for Subprogram Bodies

Our pseudo-code for subprogram headings was introduced in Chapter 5. To write the body of a subprogram in pseudo-code, write an ALGORITHM part and a DATA OBJECTS list. Place any new data types, operations, or defined constants on the global DATA TYPES, SUBPROGRAMS, and DEFINED CONSTANTS lists, as appropriate.

□□

Function Value Return in Pseudo-code and Pascal

In pseudo-code, within the body of a function, use a *function value assignment:*

FUNCTION VALUE := ⟨expression⟩

to indicate that the value of ⟨expression⟩ is to be assigned to the "hidden" function value location in the local state of a function. The final value assigned to this hidden location is returned as the value of the function when execution of the body is complete.

In Pascal, the function value assignment is coded as an assignment to the *name of the function*:

```
⟨function-name⟩ := ⟨expression⟩
```

□□

Coding Procedures in Pascal

⟨PROCEDURE definition⟩ ::=

```
PROCEDURE ⟨procedure name⟩
    ({[VAR] ⟨formal parameter name⟩: ⟨data type⟩;  ⟨purpose⟩}
     [VAR] ⟨formal parameter name⟩: ⟨data type⟩);  ⟨purpose⟩
⟨purpose/goal state/preconditions⟩
```

```
        [VAR
            ⟨local variable declarations⟩]
        BEGIN
            ⟨statements⟩
        END;    ⟨end comment⟩
```

WHERE
        ⟨procedure name⟩ ::= Pascal identifier.
        ⟨formal parameter name⟩ ::= Pascal identifier.
        ⟨data type⟩ ::= Data type of the formal parameter.
        ⟨purpose⟩ ::=
            A Pascal comment giving the IN, OUT, or IN/OUT classification
            and the purpose of the parameter.
        ⟨purpose/goal state/preconditions⟩ ::=
            A Pascal comment giving the PURPOSE, GOAL STATE, and
            PRECONDITIONS, from the pseudo-code.
        ⟨local variable declarations⟩ ::=
            The Pascal form of the DATA OBJECTS list from the
            pseudo-code, just as for the main procedure.
        ⟨statements⟩ ::=
            The Pascal form of the ALGORITHM part from the pseudo-
            code, just as for the main procedure.
        ⟨end comment⟩ ::= A Pascal comment of the form:
                {procedure ⟨procedure name⟩}
            used to make the end of a procedure definition easily visible to a
            reader of the program.

□

Notes:

1. Use VAR in the procedure heading before the name of each OUT and IN/OUT parameter. Also use VAR before the name of any parameter of a data structure type—array, record, or string. Omit the VAR before the name of an IN parameter of a simple type.

2. If there are no local data objects on the DATA OBJECTS list, omit the entire list of ⟨local variable declarations⟩, including the preceding VAR.

□□

Coding Functions in Pascal

FUNCTION definition ::=

```
FUNCTION ⟨function-name⟩
    ({ [VAR] ⟨formal parameter name⟩: ⟨data type⟩;     ⟨purpose⟩}
     [VAR[ ⟨formal parameter name⟩: ⟨data type⟩))     ⟨purpose⟩
```

```
      :  ⟨data type of value returned⟩;      ⟨result returned⟩
   ⟨purpose/preconditions⟩
[VAR
    ⟨local variable declarations⟩]
BEGIN
    ⟨statements⟩
END;   ⟨end comment⟩
```

WHERE

⟨function name⟩ ::= Pascal identifier.

⟨formal parameter name⟩ ::= Pascal identifier.

⟨data type⟩ ::= Data type of the formal parameter.

⟨purpose⟩ ::=
   A Pascal comment giving the IN classification and the purpose of
   the parameter.

⟨data type of value returned⟩ ::= Integer, Real, Char, Boolean,
   or the name of a subrange or enumerated type.

⟨result returned⟩ ::=
   Pascal comment describing the result returned by the function,
   from the pseudo-code.

⟨purpose/preconditions⟩ ::=
   A Pascal comment giving the PURPOSE and PRECONDITIONS,
   if any, from the pseudo-code.

⟨local variable declarations⟩ ::=
   The Pascal form of the DATA OBJECTS list from the
   pseudo-code, just as for a procedure.

⟨statements⟩ ::=
   The Pascal form of the ALGORITHM from the pseudo-code, just
   as for a procedure.

⟨end comment⟩ ::= A Pascal comment of the form:
         {function ⟨function name⟩}
   used to make the end of a function definition easily visible to a
   reader of the program.

□
Notes:

1. Notice the punctuation of the heading: the closing right parenthesis of the formal
   parameter list is *not* followed by a semicolon; instead the next line begins with a colon
   and a semicolon follows the data type of the result.

2. Use VAR in the heading before the name of a formal parameter of an array, record, or
   string type, to avoid having the actual parameter copied each time the function is
   called.

3. If there are no local data objects on the DATA OBJECTS list, omit the entire list of
   ⟨local variable declarations⟩, including the preceding VAR.

□ □

The FOR Loop

⟨FOR loop⟩ ::=

> FOR ⟨subscript variable⟩ := ⟨first subscript⟩ TO ⟨last subscript⟩ DO
>> BEGIN
>>> ⟨loop body actions⟩
>> END;

> **WHERE**
>> ⟨subscript variable⟩ ::=
>>> A Pascal identifier, the name of the data object to be used to store the current subscript value on each iteration of the loop. The names I, J, and K are often used for subscript variables in Pascal FOR loops.
>> ⟨first subscript⟩ ::=
>>> An ⟨expression⟩ whose value is the first subscript value to be assigned to ⟨subscript variable⟩, before the first execution of the actions in the loop body.
>> ⟨last subscript⟩ ::=
>>> An ⟨expression⟩ whose value is the last subscript value to be assigned to ⟨subscript variable⟩, before the last execution of the actions in the loop body.
>> ⟨loop body actions⟩ ::=
>>> A list of actions to be taken each time the loop is repeated.

□

Meaning of a FOR loop.   The steps in executing a FOR loop are:

1. Execute the ASSIGN action:

    ⟨subscript variable⟩ := ⟨first subscript⟩

2. Test if it is time to stop repeating the loop:

    IF ⟨subscript variable⟩ > ⟨last subscript⟩
        THEN execution of the FOR loop is complete.

3. Execute the ⟨loop body actions⟩.
4. Add one to the value of ⟨subscript variable⟩.
5. Repeat these steps again from step 2.

REVIEW QUESTIONS

7.1 In pseudo-code, what are the two main parts of the *body* of a subprogram?

7.2 What is contained in the *local state* of a procedure? Of a function?

7.3 What happens to the local state of a subprogram when execution of the subprogram body is complete?

7.4 Explain how *VALUE parameters* are transmitted to a Pascal subprogram. Explain how *VAR parameters* are transmitted.

7.5 If a formal parameter is a VALUE parameter, what is allowed as the corresponding *actual parameter* in a call of the subprogram? What if the formal parameter is a VAR parameter?

7.6 How do the Pascal categories of VALUE parameter and VAR parameter correspond to the pseudo-code categories of IN, OUT, and IN/OUT parameter?

7.7 When an *assignment* of a new value is made to a formal parameter within the body of a subprogram, what is the effect on the value of the corresponding actual parameter for a VAR parameter? For a VALUE parameter?

7.8 Suppose you test a procedure and it appears to be working properly, except that one of the OUT or IN/OUT actual parameters does not seem to be getting its new value from the procedure when it is executed. What *Pascal error* is the most common cause of this bug?

7.9 Explain the Pascal rule governing the *order* in which subprogram definitions must appear within the program.

7.10 Explain how to designate within a function body the particular value that is to be returned as the *value of the function*, in pseudo-code and in Pascal.

7.11 What happens when an array, record, or string is transmitted as a VALUE parameter to a subprogram? Why is it a good rule to transmit all data structures as VAR parameters, even for IN parameters?

7.12 Show how to use a *FOR loop* to process all the elements of an array.

7.13 Give the FOR loop pattern used to *display* all the elements of an array A with subscript range 1..N, displaying K elements per line.

7.14 What question should you ask to decide whether a particular loop that processes the elements of an array should be written as a *WHILE loop* or a *FOR loop*?

7.15 Show how to *hand trace* the execution of a call of a procedure or function.

7.16 Show how to hand trace the execution of a FOR loop.

7.17 What is a program *structure chart*? Explain how to determine the structure chart of a Pascal program, given a listing of the program.

7.18 What is *incremental testing*?

7.19 What is *big bang testing*? Why is big bang testing a poor testing strategy?

7.20 What is a *test driver* program? What is the purpose of a test driver?

7.21 What is a *stub*? What is the purpose of a stub?

7.22 What is *bottom up testing*? What is *top down testing*? How are test drivers and stubs used in bottom up and top down testing?

7.23 What is a *snapshot procedure*? How does a snapshot procedure simplify testing when a program uses complex data structures?

7.24 Explain how you might design, code, and test a program as a *prototype* first. How are stubs used in coding a prototype? How do you get from the prototype to a finished program?

7.25 Explain the type of situation in which building a prototype to meet part of the program's requirements might be the best first step before designing the complete program.

7.26 List two advantages and three disadvantages of building a program prototype before the finished program.

■ ■ ■
PROGRAMMING PROBLEMS

7.1 For each of the programming problems 5.1 through 5.4 at the end of Chapter 5, complete the design of the program by choosing an appropriate representation for each data type and a design for the body of each subprogram that you defined. Then code the entire program in Pascal, test it, and debug it.

7.2 *Counting Characters.* Design, code, and test a program that counts the number of occurrences of each letter (upper- and lower-case), digit, and punctuation mark in a sequence of lines of text typed by the user. After the user has typed in his text, the program should display a table showing each character and the number of times that it occurred in the text.

7.3 *Inventory Control.* Design, code, and test a *prototype* of a program to maintain an inventory list of the jeans in stock for a clothing store. The program should provide a menu that allows the user to choose various actions to perform on an inventory list, including at least:

- *Enter* information about new jeans received into the list.
- *Save* a list permanently (in a file).
- *Restore* a saved list (from a file).
- *Report* on the jeans currently in stock.
- *Delete* a pair of jeans from the list.
- *Clear* all the entries out of a list, leaving an empty list.

Other useful operations can be added to the menu, such as some of those used as examples in this chapter. The program should allow the user to make a choice from the menu. The program performs the indicated action, asking the user for additional information as required, and then displays the menu again. The cycle repeats until the user chooses the "quit" option.

The *save* and *restore* operations should be represented by *stubs*. These operations need to use data files, which are not discussed in this book until Chapter 11. Thus the program is a prototype of the full program. Obviously no real user would want to have to reenter the entire inventory list each time the program is used (as will be required by your prototype, without *save* and *restore*). But you can still design, code, and test the rest of the program.

7.4 *Tic-Tac-Toe: Computer vs. Human.* Design, code, and test a program to play the game of tic-tac-toe, pitting the computer against a human player. Tic-tac-toe is the familiar children's game, where the two players alternately enter X's and O's in the squares of the "board," drawn like this:

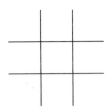

When one player gets three of his symbols in a row, that player wins. If all squares are filled and no player has won, the game is a draw.

The program should have two major parts. One part, the *strategy routine,* should be responsible for choosing the move for the program. The second part, the *game manager,* should be responsible for managing the board by asking the user and the strategy routine, alternately, for their move. Before and after each user move, the game manager should display the board. The game manager is also responsible for deciding if a move is legal. After each move the game manager should check for a win, and if so, then announce the end of the game and the winner. The user should be allowed to abort play of any game instead of choosing a move (for example, if the user sees the game must be a draw eventually). Finally the game manager should allow the user to play a sequence of games against the machine, with the game manager keeping track of the score.

Begin with a *strategy routine* that chooses the program's move in a simple "dumb" way—any legal move will do. Use this simple strategy routine while you test the rest of the program. The program may always lose, but during this testing, you do not really care. Then, when the entire program is working correctly, design and code a "smarter" strategy routine to replace the original one. The "smartest" strategy routine can guarantee that the program never loses—every game is either a draw or the program wins.

7.5 *Tic-Tac-Toe: Computer vs. Computer.* Modify the game manager part of the tic-tac-toe program of 7.4 above so that two strategy routines, prepared by two different programmers can play each other. The user only chooses how many games to play and watches the display of each move chosen, but does not participate in choosing the moves. To slow the play to speeds that a human can watch, have the game manager ask the user to type RETURN each time the board is displayed, to indicate that play should resume.

7.6 *Airport Simulation.* The airport in Charlottesville, Virginia has only one runway, so all air traffic must compete to take-off and land on this runway. Air traffic has been increasing in recent years, and the runway is now used almost constantly. Sometimes planes must wait in a queue to take-off or circle in a "holding pattern" queue before landing. Suppose that you have been employed by the airport management to construct a computer *simulation* of the activity at this airport during a typical day. The goal of the simulation program is as follows:

Input: As input, the simulation program needs this information from the user:

- Starting hour for the simulation, e.g., 4 a.m.
- Number of hours to simulate, e.g., 18 hours.
- For each hour during this period:
    - Estimated number of planes that leave the gates and want to take-off during the hour, e.g., 5 planes in hour 1, 12 in hour 2, and so forth.
    - Estimated number of planes that arrive and want to land during the hour.

■ A time interval, K minutes, that indicates how often to display information about the results of the simulation; e.g., K = 10 means display results at the end of every 10 simulated "minutes."

Output: As output, the simulation program displays a table (or, better yet, a bar graph) showing at the end of each K minutes during the hours being simulated, how many planes were queued waiting to take-off and how many were in the holding pattern waiting to land. Optionally you may show other statistics about the activities, such as the average waiting time to take-off or land during each hour.

The airport management wants to use your program to study what is likely to happen as air traffic continues to increase from its present levels. They want to input various estimates of future traffic levels and then look at the output of the program to see how long the take-off and landing queues become.

Like most computer simulations, your program must make some simplifying assumptions:

1. At any airport, take-offs and landings must be spaced apart for safety and to allow the turbulence caused by one plane's engines to dissipate before the next plane uses the runway. For this simulation, you may use two integer defined constants, TAKEOFFWAIT and LANDINGWAIT, that show how many minutes the runway is tied up during a take-off and landing, respectively, before the runway can be used again (from the time the control tower gives permission to one plane for a take-off or landing until the tower can give permission to the next plane.) Initially, use TAKEOFFWAIT = 2 and LANDINGWAIT = 3. The airport management wants to experiment with the effect of changes in these constants, because the new larger airliners may cause more turbulence and thus may force these waits to be increased for safety.

2. Different types of aircraft take different amounts of time to take-off and land. For this simulation, you may assume that all aircraft take off and land in the same amount of time (given by the constants TAKEOFFWAIT and LANDINGWAIT).

3. Your simulation need take no account of the *order* in which particular planes leave the gate or arrive in the holding pattern. All that the program tracks are the *number* of planes in each queue at any given time.

4. Your simulation may assume that planes arrive immediately in the take-off queue as soon as they leave the gate.

5. Your simulation may assume that the arrivals of planes in the take-off queue or the holding pattern queue are evenly spaced throughout the hour, to the closest minute. For example, if 11 planes arrive in hour 4 during the simulated "day," then you may assume that the first plane arrives in minute 5 of the hour, the second plane in minute 10, and the 11th plane in minute 55 (and no planes arrive during the last five minutes of the hour).

6. Assume also that *landings* always have priority over *take-offs*. Thus, all planes in the holding pattern must land before any plane can take-off.

The simulation program should keep track of the changes in the two queues at the end of each *minute* of the simulated time period (even though the results are only displayed for K minute intervals). At the end of each minute, the program should check to see if another plane should enter the take-off or landing queues and if a plane can leave one or the other queue due to the runway being free. Begin the simulation at minute zero of hour 1, with all queues empty and the runway free. Then cycle through each minute of each hour during the simulated period, displaying the current status of the queues every K minutes.

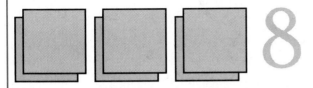

8

Analyzing Programs

CHAPTER GOALS

When you have mastered the content of this chapter you should be able to:

- Explain why skill in *analyzing programs* is an important part of programming.
- Distinguish three types of analysis: *control flow* analysis, *data flow* analysis, and *precondition/postcondition* analysis.
- Use *control flow analysis* to determine the possible *control paths* between any two points in a program and to determine the *path condition* for executing a particular control path.
- Use *data flow analysis* to identify the IN and OUT data objects of an action or program segment.
- Use *data flow analysis* to identify where a particular value is defined, used, and lost within a program segment.
- Draw a *control flow diagram (flowchart)* to describe the control paths and a *data flow diagram* to show the data flow in a program segment.
- Use control flow and data flow analysis to determine how a particular result is computed in a program, to find various kinds of errors, and to determine path conditions.
- Use *precondition/postcondition analysis* to find preconditions and to determine if an action may fail when executed.
- Explain how program *modifications* can introduce new errors in unmodified parts of a program.
- State the *Principle of Safe Modification*.
- Use analysis skills to check that modifications are safe and do not introduce new errors.

With the basic programming elements of Chapters 3 and 4 and the abstractions of Chapters 5, 6, and 7, we have all the elements needed to begin constructing larger programs. This is a good time to pause and look at how to *analyze* a program that uses the programming concepts of Chapters 3–7. Some ground work for program analysis has already been prepared—in Chapter 3, we learned some basic elements of *control flow analysis* and in Chapters 4 and 5, we studied how to identify the *preconditions* of an operation. *Hand tracing,* in Chapters 3 and 7, is also a form of program analysis. Learning how to analyze a program is not a traditional topic in a first computer science course. But analysis skills and methods are the key to being able to construct programs that are correct and reliable. Let's begin with the "why's" of program analysis.

WHY ANALYSIS SKILLS?

Think of a program as an assembly line, where the results of the information processing task are being assembled into a whole. The data objects in the program carry the various data values that are combined to make the final results. The actions and subprograms are like the workers that put the various pieces and sub-assemblies together into the final whole.

Program analysis is concerned with how the parts of a program are *interconnected*—how one action affects later actions or how one data value is defined by one action and then used by later actions. We want to understand how the parts of a program fit together in order to determine if these interconnections are correct.

In analysis we assume that the program structure is already established, and that we are given the pseudo-code for the algorithm or a listing of the coded program. Then we look to analyze and understand what will take place when the algorithm or program is executed—the sequence of actions executed and the changes in the program state that occur during a single run or during all possible runs of the program.

□□
Murphy's Law of Programming

The reasons why analysis skills are valuable in programming may be summarized in a few words: they can save you *time* and *energy,* and possibly *embarrassment, money,* and *grief.*

398   □ Chap. 8 *Analyzing Programs*

Remember *Murphy's Law?*

> **□ Murphy's Law**
>
> Whatever can go wrong, will go wrong!

A Murphy's Law for programs might read:

> **□ Murphy's Law of Programming**
>
> Whatever can still go wrong with a program, after it has been tested and put into use, will go wrong—and always at the most embarrassing or dangerous possible moment!

Put another way, if your "working" program still has a hidden error in it, then, by Murphy's Law, that error seemingly will always show up when your instructor or boss tries your program for the first time, when you are showing your program off to a group of friends, or, in the worst case, when someone is depending on your program for their life or livelihood. Program analysis is aimed at finding the hidden errors in a program, so that Murphy's Law won't find anything that can go wrong.

□ □
Using Analysis Skills

Hidden errors in programs that seem to be "working" are a problem for every programmer. Such errors may be introduced at any stage during the development of a program—in the initial design, during the refinement of some part of the design, during the coding of the design into Pascal, or when the program is modified.

COMPUTER HORROR STORIES: THE BUG HEARD 'ROUND THE WORLD

One program that received extensive testing and analysis before it was put into use was the software that controls the computers in the U.S. Space Shuttle. The computers were made quintuply redundant—five separate computers each making the same calculations and comparing their answers. The software (hundreds of thousands of lines of program) was subjected to thousands of hours of testing and analysis.

Everything seemed to be ready for a flawless first launch back in 1981. The world was watching on television as the countdown proceeded down to the final minutes. Then, as the five computers were fired up and the software started through its initialization sequence to synchronize the timing of the five computers—a *bug*! Murphy's Law! The countdown stopped. A twenty-four hour delay followed while the software team tracked down the bug. Embarrassing! And very expensive! One of the leaders of the project later termed this "the bug heard 'round the world."

Here are some of the ways that analysis skills can be valuable in these various stages:

1. *Verifying that an algorithm or program is correct*. After you have designed a program, but before you code it into Pascal, you would like to know if it is correct—that is, if it satisfies the program requirements. If your algorithm contains any logic errors, you would like to know it *before* you start coding. Analysis skills will help you check each part of the program thoroughly. Your goal: make it run correctly, without any logic errors, the *first time* that it is executed.

2. *Testing and debugging quickly*. Suppose that you are testing your program, and despite your best efforts to make it right the first time, you detect an error. You know that finding the elusive "bug" can take hours or days of your precious time. Analysis skills will help you pinpoint bugs *quickly*. Analysis skills will also help you decide *how* to test so that your tests are thorough and accurate while using the fewest test runs.

3. *Making modifications safely*. If your algorithm or Pascal program must be modified, analysis skills allow you to check that a modification has been made safely, without introducing new errors.

Modifications are made to a program for several reasons:

- *Completing a prototype*. Often a program is first constructed as a "prototype," as discussed in the previous chapter, by using stubs for some of the subprograms. The program is coded into a partially complete but working version, and then it is progressively modified to fill out the missing details.
- *Repairing errors*. When testing or later use of a program uncovers an error, modifications will be required to repair the error.
- *Enhancements to satisfy changed requirements*. Often the original program requirements are changed, to add features that make the program more useful or to modify existing capabilities of the program. New requirements mean that the program must be modified.

Modifications often involve a set of coordinated changes to several different parts of the program. It is easy to overlook how one change affects the surrounding parts of the program. You may insert the correct new statements but fail to notice that a preceding or following statement is affected by the change and no longer will work correctly.

□ □
Basic Analysis Methods

In analyzing programs, we use three basic analysis methods:

1. *Control flow analysis*. We analyze the program to determine the possible *control paths* and the conditions that cause each path to be taken during program ex-

ecution. Control flow analysis tells us the possible sequences in which actions might occur and, thus, which earlier actions might affect each particular later action.

2. *Data flow analysis.* We also analyze the program to determine, for each control path, how the *data values* flow from earlier actions to later ones. For each data value that is stored in a data object, we want to determine where that value is *defined,* where it is *used,* and at what point is it *lost.* We also want to know which actions and data objects participate in defining the value.

Data flow analysis also tells us how an action is connected to particular data objects and values in the data state—which data objects carry values "in" to be used in the action and which data objects carry values "out" to be used in later actions. Data flow analysis thus allows us to determine how the program state is changing as actions are taken and where particular data values are available to be used by particular actions.

3. *Precondition/postcondition analysis.* Individual actions are also connected to the data state through *preconditions*—properties that must be true of the data values used in the action if the action is to work correctly. Preconditions tell us how one action relies on earlier actions to correctly prepare the data values that it uses. A *postcondition* is a property of the data values produced by an action that serves as a *guarantee* that later actions can rely upon. Precondition/postcondition analysis (*pre/post analysis*) thus allows us to determine both the requirements that later actions in a program make on earlier actions and the guarantees that earlier actions can provide to later actions.

□ □

Analyzing Subprograms and Program Segments

Each of these types of analysis can be applied to an entire algorithm or Pascal program, or to smaller parts. Analyzing an entire program as a whole is usually far too complicated. Instead you break the program into "segments," analyze the segments individually, and then analyze groups of segments together, until you have built an analysis of the whole program. A "segment" might be:

- A single step of the algorithm, composed of a short sequence of actions or Pascal statements, such as a step that includes a loop or conditional action,
- A sequence of steps within a single procedure or function,
- A single procedure or function, or
- A group of procedures and functions that operate on a single type of data object.

□□□ **8.2**
CONTROL FLOW ANALYSIS REVISITED

Before learning about data flow analysis and pre/post analysis, let's review and sharpen some control flow analysis concepts that were first discussed back in Chapter 3, in light of the new program elements of Chapters 5–7.

Remember that control flow analysis involves asking two basic questions about a program segment:

1. *Control paths.* What are the *possible control paths* through this segment? That is, what are the possible sequences in which the actions in this segment might be executed?

2. *Path conditions.* Under what conditions will a particular path be followed during program execution? What values in the data state at the start of execution of the segment will cause a particular path to be chosen for execution? We term these conditions the *path conditions* for the control path.

□ □
Elements of a Control Path

A control path in a program consists of one of the possible sequences in which the actions and tests can be executed when the program is run. To write down a description of a control path, you write down the following elements, in the sequence executed or evaluated:

1. Each DISPLAY, READ, ASSIGN, and CALL action encountered along the path.

2. For an IF, write down the *test* and its outcome (TRUE or FALSE). If there are additional "ELSE IF" cases, write down each test whose outcome is FALSE, until you reach the first test whose outcome is TRUE. Follow the first TRUE test with the actions for that alternative.

3. For a WHILE loop, write down the *test* and its outcome. If the outcome is TRUE, then follow with the actions inside the loop and write the WHILE test again. Continue until the WHILE test gives FALSE.

4. For a FOR loop that appears in the program as:

```
FOR ⟨subscript variable⟩ := ⟨first value⟩ TO ⟨last value⟩ DO
    BEGIN
            ⟨actions in body⟩
    END
```

write the loop as you would in a hand trace, using the FOR-START and FOR-NEXT parts, as discussed in Chapter 7:

FOR-START: —when the FOR is reached the first time.
ACTIONS:

⟨subscript variable⟩ := ⟨first value⟩
(⟨subscript variable⟩ > ⟨last value⟩) = TRUE or FALSE

FOR-NEXT: —after each execution of the loop body.

ACTIONS:

⟨subscript variable⟩ := ⟨subscript variable⟩ + 1
(⟨subscript variable⟩ > ⟨last value⟩) = TRUE or FALSE

If the test evaluates to FALSE, then follow with the actions in the loop body and repeat the FOR-NEXT actions, continuing until the FOR-NEXT test returns TRUE.

EXAMPLES

1. What are the possible control paths through this segment?

READ: Sales
IF Sales > 0 THEN
        Total := Total + Sales
DISPLAY: "The total is ⟨Total⟩"

The paths are:

Path 1: READ: Sales
IF (Sales > 0) = TRUE
Total := Total + Sales
DISPLAY: "The total is ⟨Total⟩"

Path 2: READ: Sales
IF (Sales > 0) = FALSE
DISPLAY: "The total is ⟨Total⟩"

2. What are the possible control paths through this segment?

READ: Sales
WHILE Sales > 0 DO
        Total := Total + Sales
        READ: Sales
DISPLAY: "The total is ⟨Total⟩"

The paths are:

Path 1: READ: Sales
WHILE (Sales > 0) = FALSE
DISPLAY: "The total is ⟨Total⟩"

Path 2: READ: Sales
WHILE (Sales > 0) = TRUE
Total := Total + Sales;

READ: Sales
WHILE (Sales > 0) = FALSE
DISPLAY: "The total is ⟨Total⟩"

Path 3:   READ: Sales
           WHILE (Sales > 0) = TRUE
           Total := Total + Sales;

           READ: Sales
           WHILE (Sales > 0) = TRUE
           Total := Total + Sales;

           READ: Sales
           WHILE (Sales > 0) = FALSE
           DISPLAY: "The total is ⟨Total⟩"

and continue with paths that repeat the loop body any given number of times.

3.   What are the possible control paths through this segment?

READ: SalesCount
FOR I := 1 TO SalesCount DO
   BEGIN
      READ: SalesList [I]
   END
DISPLAY: "Sales list has ⟨SalesCount⟩ entries."

The paths are:

Path 1:   READ: SalesCount
           FOR-START: I := 1
                     (I > SalesCount) = TRUE
           DISPLAY: "Sales list has ⟨SalesCount⟩ entries."

Path 2:   READ: SalesCount
           FOR-START: I := 1
                     (I > SalesCount) = FALSE
           READ: SalesList [I]
           FOR-NEXT: I := I + 1
                     (I > SalesCount) = TRUE
           DISPLAY: "Sales list has ⟨SalesCount⟩ entries."

Path 3:   READ: SalesCount
           FOR-START: I := 1
                     (I > Salescount) = FALSE
           READ: SalesList [I]

FOR-NEXT: I := I + 1
            (I > SalesCount) = FALSE
READ: SalesList [I]
FOR-NEXT: I := I + 1
            (I > SalesCount) = TRUE
DISPLAY: "Sales list has ⟨SalesCount⟩ entries."

and continue with paths that repeat the loop body for any given value of SalesCount.
∎

Procedure and Function Calls

When a control path includes a procedure or function call, it is tempting to follow the control flow into the body of the procedure or function, and include the actions in the subprogram body in the control path. We have a simple rule for this situation: *don't*! Don't include actions in the body of a subprogram as part of a control path in a *caller* of that subprogram.

The reason for not following a control path into a subprogram is simple: the subprogram represents an abstract operation, whose internal workings are not part of an analysis of what the *caller* is doing. The caller's action should be based only on what the subprogram *heading* specifies, not on the details of how that subprogram's body works. Later we may change how the subprogram body works, and we do not want to have to analyze again each call of the subprogram to see if we have introduced an error.

Of course, if it appears that the subprogram is not working correctly by not producing the results specified in its heading, then we can analyze the subprogram body. But we treat this as a separate analysis problem: does the subprogram body do what its heading says? This separate analysis is independent of any particular call of the subprogram.

□ □
Describing a Control Path

Suppose you want to describe a particular control path to a friend, where you are both looking at the program written in pseudo-code or at a listing of a coded program. Rather than writing down the actions in the control path, as we did in the examples above, you simply want a way to describe the path in just enough detail so that your friend can find it in the written pseudo-code or listing.

Let's assume that the actions or statements are numbered for easy reference, so that you can refer to "the statement at line 10," for example. To describe a control path, you need to describe the path through each straight-line, branching and looping segment.

1. *Straight-line segments*. If a part of the control path is a straight-line segment (no IF's or loops), then all the actions in the segment are part of the control

path. You can simply say that *"the straight-line segment that begins at line ⟨number⟩ is part of the path."* Often you do not need to mention such a segment explicitly at all because it is obvious that it must be executed whenever execution reaches the start of the segment.

2. *Conditional (IF) segments.* Think of an IF segment as consisting of a sequence of *cases*—first case, second case, and so forth—each beginning with a test. The ELSE case of an IF corresponds to the path in which all the tests in the IF return a FALSE value. We term this the *default case*—the case executed when the tests choose none of the previous cases. If the IF has no ELSE case, then the default case is a "NO ACTION" case.

To describe a control path through an IF, just mention the line where the IF begins and which case is part of the path, for example *"in the IF that begins at line 20 the second case is part of the path."* The test for this case must have been TRUE, and the tests for all preceding cases must have been FALSE in order for the case to have been executed, so naming the case is enough to allow someone to determine exactly the control path (given the pseudo-code or listing). If you say *"the default case is part of the path"* then *all* the tests in the IF must have returned FALSE when the IF was executed.

If the actions for the case chosen in an IF form a straight-line segment, then no further description of the path is needed. If the actions for that case form a branching or looping segment themselves, then you have to describe the path *within* the actions for that case.

EXAMPLES

1. Let's describe all the control paths through the segment used in the example above:

```
1   READ: Sales
2   IF Sales > 0 THEN
3        Total := Total + Sales
4   DISPLAY: "The total is ⟨Total⟩"
```

Path 1: Begin at line 1 and include the first case of the IF at line 2.

Path 2: Begin at line 1 and include the default case of the IF at line 2.

2. Describe the possible control paths through this segment:

```
1   READ: Sales
2   IF   Sales > 0 THEN
3            Gain := Gain + Sales
4            GainCount := GainCount + 1
5   ELSE IF Sales < 0 THEN
6            IF NegSalesOK THEN
7                 Loss := Loss + Sales
8                 LossCount := LossCount + 1
```

```
 9   ELSE
10         DISPLAY: "Zero value entered; value ignored."
11   DISPLAY: "The total is ⟨Total⟩"
```

Path 1: Begin at line 1 and include the first case of the IF at line 2.

Path 2: Begin at line 1 and include the second case of the IF at line 2. Within this case include the first case of the IF at line 6.

Path 3: Begin at line 1 and include the second case of the IF at line 2. Within this case include the default case of the IF at line 6.

Path 4: Begin at line 1 and include the default case of the IF at line 2. ∎

3. *Loop segments.* To describe a control path through a loop, we use the term *iteration:*

□ **Iteration**

An *iteration* of a loop is one repetition of the body of the loop.

An iteration is also called a *trip* through the loop (as in "one trip," "two trips," and so forth). To describe a path through a loop, specify where the loop begins and the number of iterations included in the path—zero iterations, one iteration, etc. For example, you might say *"in the loop that begins at line 30, the path contains three iterations."*

If the loop body is a straight-line segment, then no further description of the loop path is needed, but if the loop body is itself a branching or looping segment, then the control path through the body must be specified *for each iteration*.

EXAMPLES

1. Describe the control paths through this segment:

```
1   READ: Sales
2   WHILE Sales > 0 DO
3         Total := Total + Sales;
4         READ: Sales
5   DISPLAY: "The total is ⟨Total⟩"
```

Path 1: Start at line 1 and include zero iterations of the loop at line 2.

Path 2: Start at line 1 and include one iteration of the loop at line 2.

Path 3: Start at line 1 and include 2 iterations of the loop at line 2.

and so forth, for any given number of iterations.

2. Describe the control paths through this segment:

```
1   MaxSales := 0
2   READ: Sales
3   WHILE Sales > 0 DO
4           IF Sales > MaxSales THEN
5                   MaxSales := Sales
6           READ: Sales
7   DISPLAY: "The total is ⟨Total⟩"
```

Path 1: Start at line 1 and include zero iterations of the loop at line 3.

Path 2: Start at line 1 and include one iteration of the loop at line 3. In the IF at line 4, include the first case.

Path 3: Start at line 1 and include one iteration of the loop at line 3. In the IF at line 4, include the default case.

Path 4: Start at line 1 and include two iterations of the loop at line 3. Within the loop body include the following paths:

- ITERATION 1: First case of the IF at line 4.
- ITERATION 2: First case of the IF at line 4.

Path 5: Start at line 1 and include two iterations of the loop at line 3. Within the loop body include the following paths:

- ITERATION 1: First case of the IF at line 4.
- ITERATION 2: Default case of the IF at line 4.

Path 6: Start at line 1 and include two iterations of the loop at line 3. Within the loop body include the following paths:

- ITERATION 1: Default case of the IF at line 4.
- ITERATION 2: First case of the IF at line 4.

Path 7: Start at line 1 and include two iterations of the loop at line 3. Within the loop body include the following paths:

- ITERATION 1: Default case of the IF at line 4.
- ITERATION 2: Default case of the IF at line 4.

and continue for any given number of iterations, remembering to include both paths through the loop body on each iteration.

3. Describe the control paths through this segment:

```
1   FOR I := 1 TO 12 DO
2       BEGIN
3           READ: SalesList [I]
4       END
5   DISPLAY: "All monthly sales have been input."
```

There is only one control path:

Path 1: Begin at line 1 and include 12 iterations of the loop at line 1. ■

In example 2, notice that an IF within the loop body *doubles* the number of possible paths through the loop.

□ □

Paths Between Two Points in a Subprogram Body

During program analysis, you often need to describe the possible control paths between an execution of one action or statement and an execution of a second action or statement within the same subprogram body. For example, you may be testing a subprogram and have two debug WRITE statements inserted to display the program state in the subprogram being tested. When the first WRITE is executed, the values displayed are correct. When the second is executed, the values displayed are incorrect. By the *Cardinal Rule of Debugging* you want to find the possible control paths that might have led from the first WRITE to the second.

Sometimes the two actions are actually two different executions of the *same action or statement*. For example, the debug WRITE executed during the first iteration of a loop may display correct values and the same WRITE executed on the second iteration may show bad values.

To describe the control path between two actions, first identify the starting action and the ending action by line number. If either is within a loop body, also specify the iteration number. Then trace out all the possible control paths from the first action to the second, using the rules above to describe the paths.

EXAMPLES

1. In this segment, what are the possible paths from the action in line 3 to that in line 6?

```
1   READ: Sales
2   IF Sales > 0 THEN
```

```
3        Total := Total + Sales
4   IF Bonus > 0 THEN
5        Total := Total + Bonus
6   DISPLAY: "The total is ⟨Total⟩"
```

There are two possible paths:

Path 1:   Begin at line 3 and include the first case of the IF at line 4.

Path 2:   Begin at line 3 and include the default case of the IF at line 4.

    2.   In this segment, what are the possible paths from the action in line 4 at the end of the first iteration of the loop body to the action at line 5?

```
1   READ: Sales
2   WHILE Sales > 0 DO
3        Total := Total + Sales;
4        READ: Sales
5   DISPLAY: "The total is ⟨Total⟩"
```

Path 1:   Begin at line 4 and immediately exit the loop to line 5.

Path 2:   Begin at line 4, include a second iteration of the loop, and exit to line 5.

Path 3:   Begin at line 4, include iterations 2 and 3 of the loop, and exit to line 5.

and continue with paths that include any desired number of iterations of the loop. ∎

SPAGHETTI CODE AND THE GOTO STATEMENT

The number of different possible control paths between two points in a program has a lot to do with how complicated the program is to analyze (and verify, debug, or modify). A program or subprogram that has many complicated control paths is known as *spaghetti code*—trying to understand its control paths is like trying to follow the individual strands of spaghetti through a bowl full of it.

Most programming languages (Pascal included) provide some way that a statement can be *labeled.* In Pascal you can write a statement label as an integer before the statement:

    ⟨integer⟩ : ⟨statement⟩

as, for example:

    20: Total := Total + Gallons;

The language then also provides a GOTO statement:

```
GOTO ⟨statement label⟩
```

as, for example:

```
GOTO 20
```

A GOTO statement can be used at any point during program execution to transfer control from the point where the GOTO is executed to the labeled statement, so that execution continues from the labeled statement. For example, instead of writing an IF statement as:

```
IF ⟨test⟩ THEN
   BEGIN
      ⟨action-A⟩
   END
ELSE
   BEGIN
      ⟨action-B⟩
   END;
⟨later-action⟩
```

you could use a GOTO statement to construct exactly the same set of control paths (but make the control paths much more confusing):

```
IF ⟨test⟩ THEN
   BEGIN
      ⟨action-A⟩
      GOTO 20
   END
⟨action-B⟩
20: ⟨later-action⟩
```

In the early days of computing, GOTO statements were the primary way of constructing control paths in a program. Unfortunately, programs coded with GOTO statements are usually difficult to analyze because it is so hard to find all the possible control paths. For example, if you see any action that is labeled, such as the action above:

```
   . . .
20:   ⟨later-action⟩
   . . .
```

then the program could contain many GOTO 20 statements at different points that would cause a control path to lead from the GOTO to the statement labeled 20. Using GOTO statements it is very easy to construct spaghetti code. As a result, most programmers now avoid the use of GOTO statements entirely (and this book adopts the same attitude).

□ □

Control Flow Diagrams (Flow Charts)

We sometimes use diagrams to show the possible control paths through a segment of a program. Such diagrams are called *control flow diagrams* or *flow charts*. In a control flow diagram, each ASSIGN, DISPLAY, READ, or CALL action is placed within a rectangular box with one arrow leading in and one arrow leading out:

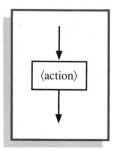

The test in each IF, WHILE, or FOR is placed within a diamond shaped box with one arrow leading in and two arrows labeled TRUE and FALSE leading out:

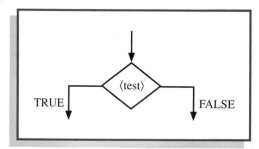

The arrows are then connected to indicate the possible control paths from one action to the next. To show the start and end of a path, oval boxes labeled BEGIN and END are used:

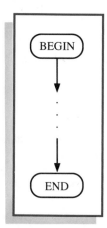

412   □ Chap. 8 *Analyzing Programs*

Sometimes a control flow diagram provides a useful alternative way to describe the possible control paths through a segment. Each path begins at the BEGIN box and follows the arrows through the other boxes until the END box is reached. Figure 8.1 shows control flow diagrams for typical segments.

□ □
Path Conditions

Suppose you have identified the possible control paths in a subprogram body. The next question is: "Under what conditions will each of these paths be taken during program execution?" That is, what values of the IN and IN/OUT parameters at the start of execution of the subprogram will lead to a particular control path being taken? We term such a condition a *path condition*.

FIGURE 8-1   Control Flow Diagrams Show Control Paths

CONTROL FLOW DIAGRAM

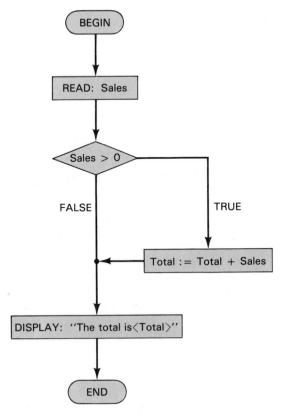

<u>SEGMENT</u>

```
MaxSales := 0
READ: Sales
WHILE Sales > 0 DO
        IF Sales > MaxSales THEN
            MaxSales := Sales
      READ: Sales
DISPLAY: "The largest is⟨MaxSales⟩"
```

<u>CONTROL FLOW DIAGRAM</u>

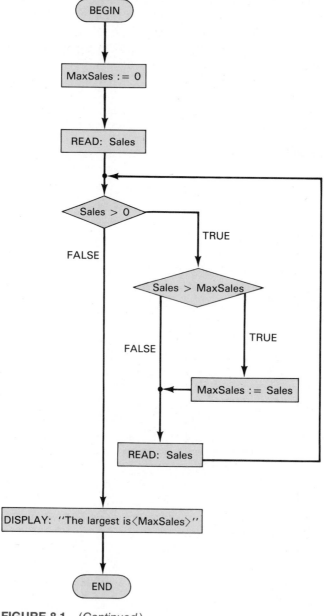

FIGURE 8.1 *(Continued)*

□ **Path Condition**

A *path condition* for a particular control path in a program segment is a *test* (a Boolean-valued expression) describing the properties of the data state at the start of execution of the segment that will cause execution to follow that path through the segment. That is, if the path condition is TRUE at the start of execution of the segment, then execution will follow that control path, and if FALSE, then some other path will be followed.

Figure 8.2 illustrates the path condition concept. If you know the path condition associated with each of the possible control paths in a subprogram, then you can look at the values of the IN and IN/OUT parameters of the subprogram and determine which execution path will be followed. You can also use the path conditions to choose test data that will force execution to follow a particular control path during a test run.

An important check to make on a program that involves several paths is to check the path conditions for the various paths, to see if each path is executed in exactly the correct situations.

CHANGING ATTITUDES TOWARD FLOW CHARTS

In the early days of programming, most programs were designed by using flow charts instead of pseudo-code to represent the actions and control paths. The flow chart was used in coding the final program in somewhat the same way that we have been coding the ALGORITHM part of a pseudo-code design into Pascal. However, whenever an arrow in the flow chart could not be coded directly as part of a statement in the language, the target statement for the arrow would be labeled and a GOTO statement would be used to represent the arrow in the coded program. Too often, the resulting program became an excellent example of "spaghetti code," even if its original design had been well thought out.

As programming languages developed better control statements, such as the Pascal IF, WHILE, and FOR statements, it became unnecessary to use GOTO statements to code a good program design. However, designs expressed as flow charts still often included control paths that were hard to code without using GOTO statements. And flow charts seemed to encourage logic errors due to the ease with which extra control paths could be included in a design. Some programmers started to refer to flow charts as *flaw charts* because of the likelihood of logic errors.

In contrast, pseudo-code ensured that a design could be coded without the use of GOTO's and usually with fewer errors. As a result, flow charts have been largely replaced by pseudo-code for program design.

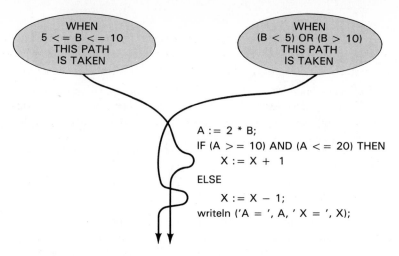

FIGURE 8-2 A Path Condition Tells When a Control Path will be Executed.

EXAMPLE

Lynne is verifying the correctness of her procedure:

```
PROCEDURE MaxOfThree
      (VAR A: Real;          {IN}
       VAR B: Real;          {IN}
       VAR C: Real;          {IN}
       VAR Max: Real);       {OUT}

       {PURPOSE/GOAL STATE: Determine the largest of A, B,
       and C and assign the largest value to Max}

BEGIN
     IF A > B THEN
       BEGIN
           IF A > C THEN
             BEGIN
                 Max := A;
             END
           ELSE
             BEGIN
                 Max := C;
             END;
       END
     ELSE IF B > C THEN
       BEGIN
           Max := B;
       END
     ELSE
       BEGIN
           Max := C;
       END;
END;
```

Lynne begins checking the four possible control paths, looking at the path condition and the assignment to Max for each one. She is particularly worried about default paths and the paths taken when some or all of the values in A, B, and C are equal.

Path 1: (A > B) = TRUE (A > C) = TRUE, which gives a path condition: (A > B) AND (A > C), and the action is: Max := A. OK!

Path 2: (A > B) = TRUE (A > C) = FALSE, which gives a path condition: (A > B) AND (A < = C), and the action is: Max := C. OK!

Path 3: (A > B) = FALSE (B > C) = TRUE, which gives a path condition: (A < = B) AND (B > C), and the action is: Max := B. OK!

Path 4: (A > B) = FALSE (B > C) = FALSE, which gives a path condition: (A < = B) AND (B < = C), and the action is: Max := C. OK!

All the paths look ok. She concludes that her procedure should work correctly in all cases. ■

□ □

Paths That Can Never Be Executed

Suppose that a path condition for a particular control path could never be TRUE in any program state. We say that such a path condition is a *contradiction:*

> □ **Contradiction**
>
> A Boolean-valued expression is a *contradiction* if it can never return TRUE for any program state.

EXAMPLES

1. This expression is a contradiction:

$$(A > 0) \; AND \; (A < 0)$$

because it never gives a TRUE value, regardless of the value of A.

2. This expression is a contradiction if B is declared to be in the subrange 1..100:

$$B = 0$$ ■

If the path condition for some path can never be TRUE, then the control path *can never be executed,* regardless of the values of the data objects when the path begins execution. Thus the "possible path" is actually an "impossible path" when its path condition is considered.

EXAMPLES   **1. Q:** What is the path condition for the path that includes the first case of both IF's in the following segment?

```
IF A > 0 THEN
   BEGIN
      ACount := ACount + 1;
   END;
IF A < 0 THEN
   BEGIN
      ACount := ACount - 1;
   END;
```

A: The path condition is:

$$(A > 0) \text{ AND } (A < 0)$$

which is a contradiction. That path can never be executed.

2. Q: Why is it impossible for a control path to include just one iteration of this loop?

```
Count := 1;
WHILE Count <= 2 DO
   BEGIN
      READ (Sales);
      Total := Total + Sales;
      Count := Count + 1;
   END;
```

A: The path condition for a single iteration is:

$$(1 <= 2) \text{ AND } (2 > 2)$$

which is a contradiction. The path can never be executed. ∎

When analyzing the control paths in a program, watch out for paths that can never be executed. What may appear to be a bug in the program may actually lie on a control path that can never be executed. If you cannot determine from the path condition for a path that the path can never be executed, you have to assume that it can—that is, you have to assume that there are some possible values of the data objects that will lead to execution of that control path. However, it is often obvious, after a simple analysis, that a particular path can never be executed. Once you know a path can never be executed, then you do not have to analyze it further.

EXERCISES

8.1 For the following segment:

```
1     IF Sales > Total[1] THEN
2        BEGIN
3           Total[1] := Sales;
4        END
5     ELSE IF Sales < Total[2] THEN
6        BEGIN
7           Total[2] := Sales;
8        END;
9     IF Sales = Total[1] THEN
10       BEGIN
11          Total[1] := 2 * Sales;
12       END;
```

a. List each of the possible control paths through the segment.
b. Give the path condition for each path listed in (a).
c. List the paths in (a) that can never be executed, if any, and explain why.
d. Draw a control flow diagram of the segment.

8.2 Assume that no subscript range error occurs during execution of the following loop:

```
1     MaxSales := 0;
2     I := 0;
3     WHILE Sales[I] > 0 DO
4        BEGIN
5           IF Sales[I] > MaxSales THEN
6              BEGIN
7                 MaxSales := Sales[I];
8              END;
9           I := I + 1;
10       END
11    writeln ('The largest sales = ', MaxSales);
```

a. List all the possible control paths through the segment that do not include more than two iterations of the loop.
b. Give the path condition for each path listed in (a).

c. List the paths in (a) that can never be executed, if any.

d. Draw a control flow diagram of the segment.

8.3 Assume that no subscript range error occurs during execution of the following loop:

```
1    LastSale := 3;
2    MaxSales := 0;
3    FOR J := 2 TO LastSale DO
4      BEGIN
5         IF Sales[J] > MaxSales THEN
6            BEGIN
7               MaxSales := Sales[J];
8            END;
9      END;
10   writeln ('The largest sales = ', MaxSales);
```

a. List all the possible control paths through the segment that do not include more than two iterations of the loop.

b. Give the path condition for each path listed in (a).

c. List the paths in (a) that can never be executed, if any.

d. Draw a control flow diagram of the segment.

□□□ **8.3**
DATA FLOW ANALYSIS: BASIC CONCEPTS

Data flow analysis is concerned with identifying where data values are defined and used in a program segment. Let's begin with single actions and then look at larger segments.

□□
IN and OUT Data Objects of Single Actions

In a procedure heading, each formal parameter is classified as to whether it carries a data value (or values) IN to the procedure, OUT of the procedure, or both IN and OUT. The same IN and OUT classification can be applied to the data objects used in any single READ, WRITE, CALL, or ASSIGN action. Figure 8.3 shows how the data objects used in an ASSIGN action would be classified. In data flow analysis, we say that an action *uses* the values of its IN data objects and *defines* the new values of its OUT data objects each time it is executed. The original values of the OUT data objects are *lost* when the action is executed.

Identifying the IN and OUT data objects of any READ, DISPLAY, ASSIGN, or CALL action is straightforward if only simple data objects are involved (no arrays, records, or strings):

1. *READ action.* Every simple data object named in a READ action is an OUT data object of the action (because the READ defines a new value for each data object). There are no IN data objects.

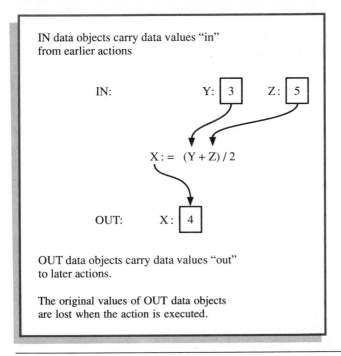

IN data objects carry data values "in" from earlier actions

IN: Y: [3]   Z: [5]

X := (Y + Z) / 2

OUT: X: [4]

OUT data objects carry data values "out" to later actions.

The original values of OUT data objects are lost when the action is executed.

FIGURE 8-3 IN and OUT Data Objects in an ASSIGN Action

2. *DISPLAY action.* Every simple data object named in a DISPLAY action is an IN data object of the action (because the DISPLAY uses the value of the object but does not change it). There are no OUT data objects.

CAUTION: Note the confusing aspect of the IN and OUT data objects of READ and DISPLAY actions. A READ action reads values in (from the keyboard), but it has only OUT data objects; conversely, a DISPLAY action sends values out (to be displayed), but it has only IN data objects.

3. *ASSIGN action.* The simple data object named on the left-hand side of the ":=" is the only OUT data object. Every simple data object used on the right-hand side is an IN data object, including data objects that appear as parameters in function calls.

4. *CALL action.* Each actual parameter in a procedure CALL action gets the same classification as the corresponding formal parameter in the procedure heading. For example, if the first formal parameter is an IN/OUT parameter according to the procedure heading, then the first actual parameter is an IN/OUT data object of the CALL action. Be careful to use only the *sequence* of formal and actual parameters to establish the correspondence, not the names of the parameters.

For an IN formal parameter, the corresponding actual parameter might be an expression containing several data object names. Each of these data objects is classified as an IN data object of the call.

1. **Q:** List the IN and OUT variables for each statement in the following Pascal segment:

```
1    readln (X, Y);
2    A := sqrt(X);
3    B := A + 10;
4    C := B / A;
5    writeln ('The quotient is ', C);
6    A := sqrt(Y) + 2*Z;
7    D := A - 10;
8    writeln ('The results are ', D, A);
```

A: Here is a table of the IN and OUT variables of each statement:

Line	IN Variables	OUT Variables
1	none	X, Y
2	X	A
3	A	B
4	A, B	C
5	C	none
6	Y, Z	A
7	A	D
8	A, D	none

2. **Q:** Given the partial procedure heading:

```
PROCEDURE FindMaxMin
        (Value1: Real;              {IN}
         Value2: Real;              {IN}
         VAR Count: Integer         {IN/OUT}
         VAR Min: Real;             {OUT}
         VAR Max: Real);            {OUT}
```

what are the IN and OUT variables of these two CALL statements?

```
1    FindMaxMin (A, B, C, D, E);
2    FindMaxMin (X + B, sqrt(2*U + W), Ct, NewMin, NewMax);
```

A: From the procedure heading, we know the classification of actual parameters in any call of FindMaxMin will be the same:

```
FindMaxMin (IN, IN, IN/OUT, OUT, OUT);
```

Thus, the actual parameters in the CALL statements would be classified:

Line	IN Variables	OUT Variables	IN/OUT Variables
1	A, B	D, E	C
2	X, B, U, W	NewMin, NewMax	Ct

Identifying the IN and OUT data objects of a single action tells you which data objects are involved in the execution of that action. A data object that is neither IN nor OUT for a particular action cannot affect or be affected by what happens when that action is executed.

Records as IN and OUT Data Objects

Individual fields of a record data object are themselves data objects (of the data type of the field). Sometimes an action may use or define all the fields of a record at once. For example, if TodaysDate and YesterdaysDate are data objects of a record type Date, then the ASSIGN action:

$$TodaysDate := YesterdaysDate$$

uses all the fields of YesterdaysDate and *defines* all the fields of TodaysDate. Thus we would classify for this action:

IN: YesterdaysDate
OUT: TodaysDate

However, another action may use or define only *some* of the fields of a record. For example, in the assignment:

$$TodaysDate.Day := YesterdaysDate.Day + 1$$

we would classify:

IN: YesterdaysDate.Day
OUT: TodaysDate.Day

Arrays as IN and OUT Data Objects

Individual elements of an array are themselves data objects (of the element type of the array). However, the subscript used to designate a particular array element may be either given explicitly, as in the assignment:

$$A[7] := B[2]$$

or it may be given implicitly, using an expression, as in the assignment:

$$A [I] := B [J]$$

What are the IN and OUT data objects of these assignments? In the first, we easily identify:

IN: B[2]   OUT: A[7]

However, in the second, the question is complicated by the fact that I is an IN data object and its value determines which element of array A is assigned a new value, and similarly for J and B.

In data flow analysis, if an explicit subscript is given for an array element, then we can classify that single element as IN or OUT, just as for a field of a record. However, if we cannot tell exactly which element of an array is being used or defined in an action, we take a cautious attitude:

1.   If an element of an array is an IN data object, but we cannot tell which array element because an expression is used as a subscript, then we classify the *entire array* as an IN data object, to indicate that *at least one of the array elements* is used in the action. For example in the assignment:

$$A [I] := B [J]$$

we would classify the entire array B as an IN data object because we know some element of B is used, but we do not know which one.

2.   If an element of an array is an OUT data object, but we cannot tell which array element because an expression is used as a subscript, then we classify the *entire array* as an IN/OUT data object, to indicate that *at least one of the array elements* has a new value defined in the action, and *at least one* of the array elements does NOT have a new value defined (i.e., some of the array elements retain their old values.) For example, in the assignment:

$$A [I] := B [J]$$

we would classify the entire array A as an IN/OUT data object because we know that at least one element of A is assigned a new value and, assuming A has at least two elements, some element of A is *not* assigned a new value.

The third rule to remember about array elements is:

3.   In the *subscript expression* that designates an array element, all the data objects used in the expression are IN data objects of the overall action, regardless of

whether the array element itself is an IN or an OUT object of the action. For example in the assignment:

$$A [I] := B [J]$$

we would classify both I and J as IN data objects.

Q: What are the In and Out data objects of the following actions?

1. `readln (Employee.Age, WeeklyTotal [3]);`

A: OUT: Employee.Age, WeeklyTotal [3]

2. `read (MonthlyTotal [ThisMonth]);`

A: IN: ThisMonth
   IN/OUT: MonthlyTotal

3. `writeln ('Month ', Date.Month, ' Sales = ', Sales);`

A: IN: Date.Month, Sales

4. `write ('The weekly total is ', ListOfTotals [Week]);`

A: IN: ListOfTotals, Week

5. `Homework.Average := (Max + Min) / Homework.Count;`

A: IN: Max, Min, Homework.Count
   OUT: Homework.Average

6. `Positives[3] := Positives[3] + NewPos;`

A: IN: NewPos
   IN/OUT: Positives[3]

7. `Grades[I] := ExamGrade;`

A: In: I, ExamGrade

　　In/Out: Grades

8. Given the heading for procedure FindMaxMin in the example above, consider the call:

```
FindMaxMin (S[12], T[I], Rec.F, U[2], V[J + K]);
```

A: The formal parameters are classified:

　　FindMaxMin (In, In, In/Out, Out, Out);

so the actual parameters are classified:

　　In: S[12], T, I, J, K
　　In/Out: Rec.F, V
　　Out: U[2]

Strings as In and Out Data Objects

Seldom does an action use or define just a single character position in a string. Usually a substring or the entire string is involved in the operation. Thus, we classify a string data object always as a whole, rather than considering individual character positions within the string as individual Char type data objects.

　　If any character or substring is used in an action, the entire string is classified as an In data object. If the *entire string value* is replaced by a new value, then it is an Out data object. And if the current string value is modified, for example, by an *insert* or *delete* operation, then the string is an IN/OUT data object.

Connecting Uses and Definitions of Data Values

Now consider a sequence of actions in a program. In the analysis of the data flow among these actions, we are interested in answering three questions (see Figure 8.4):

　　1. *Which actions might define an IN value of a given action?* If an action, Action2, *uses* a value, say from IN data object X, then, to answer this question about Action2 and X, we trace *backward* through the actions that precede Action2 in the control paths through the segment and find which earlier actions might have *defined* the value of X that is used in Action2. Because different control paths might have defined the value of X differently, we have to consider all the possible control paths

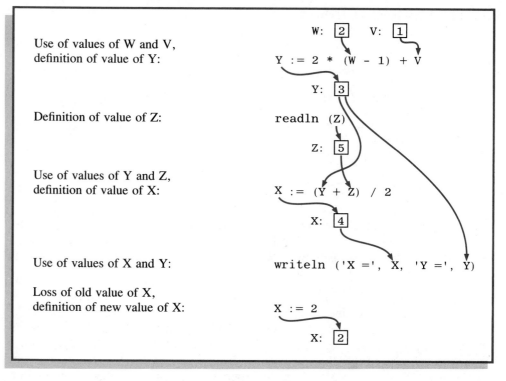

Use of values of W and V, definition of value of Y:

Definition of value of Z:

Use of values of Y and Z, definition of value of X:

Use of values of X and Y:

Loss of old value of X, definition of new value of X:

```
W: 2    V: 1

Y := 2 * (W - 1) + V

Y: 3

readln (Z)

Z: 5

X := (Y + Z) / 2

X: 4

writeln ('X =', X, 'Y =', Y)

X := 2

X: 2
```

FIGURE 8-4 Data Flow Analysis Connects "Definitions" with "Uses" of Data Values

that lead to Action2. On each path, the first action (moving backward along the path) with X as an OUT data object is the action that defines the value used in Action2.

EXAMPLES

1. **Q:** Given the segment:

```
1    readln (X, Y);
2    A := sqrt(X);
3    B := A + 10;
4    C := B / A;
5    writeln ('The quotient is ', C);
6    A := sqrt(Y);
7    D := A - 10;
8    writeln ('The results are ', D, A);
```

Which statement defines the value of A that is used in line 8?

A: Tracing back along the control path from line 8, line 6 contains the first statement that has A as an OUT variable. Thus the assignment in line 6 defines the value of A used in line 8.

2. **Q:** Given the segment:

```
1    Max := C;
2    IF A > B THEN
3      BEGIN
4          Max := A;
5      END
6    ELSE IF B > C THEN
7      BEGIN
8          Max := B;
9      END;
10   D := Max + 1;
```

Which statement defines the value of Max that is used in line 10?

A: The value of Max used in line 10 is defined either in line 1, 4, or 8, depending upon the control path executed. ■

2. *Which actions might cause an OUT value of a given action to be lost?* If one action, Action1, defines a new value for a data object, say OUT data object Y, then, to answer this question about Action1 and Y, we trace *forward* along the possible control paths starting at Action1 and find if some later action in each path stores a new value in Y, so that the value defined by Action1 is lost. Any later action that has Y as an OUT data object causes the original value defined by Action1 to be lost.

EXAMPLE

1. **Q:** Given the segment:

```
1    readln (X, Y);
2    A := sqrt(X);
3    B := A+10;
4    C := B / A;
5    writeln ('The quotient is ', C);
6    A := sqrt(Y);
7    D := A - 10;
8    writeln ('The results are ', D, A);
```

Find the statement where the value of A defined in line 2 is lost.

A: Tracing forward from line 2, the statement in line 6 is the first statement reached that has A as an OUT variable. The value of A defined in statement 2 is lost when statement 6 is executed.

2. **Q:** Given the segment:

```
1    Max := C;
2    IF A > B THEN
3      BEGIN
```

```
4            Max := A;
5        END
6    ELSE IF B > C THEN
7        BEGIN
8            Max := B;
9        END;
10   D := Max + 1;
```

Find the statement where the value of Max defined in line 1 is lost.

A: The value of Max defined in line 1 is lost at line 4 or line 8 on some control paths. However, on one path the value defined in line 1 is never lost; it becomes the OUT value of Max for the segment. ∎

3. *Which actions might use an OUT value of a given action?* If an action, Action1, *defines* a new value for a data object, say OUT data object Y, then, to answer this question about Action1 and Y, we trace *forward* along the possible control paths starting at Action1 and find every later action that *uses* the new value of Y defined by execution of Action1. Each path is followed until the value of Y defined by Action1 is lost on that path or the path ends. A later action with Y as an IN data object is using the value defined by Action1. In this analysis, be sure to include any uses of Y in the tests of IF and WHILE actions and in the headings of FOR loops.

EXAMPLE

1. Q: Given the segment:

```
1    readln (X, Y);
2    A := sqrt(X);
3    B := A + 10;
4    C := B / A;
5    writeln ('The quotient is ', C);
6    A := sqrt(Y);
7    D := A - 10;
8    writeln ('The results are ', D, A);
```

Which statements use the value of A that is defined by the assignment in line 2?

A: Tracing forward from line 2 to and including the statement in line 6, where that value of A is lost, A is an IN variable in lines 3 and 4. Thus, these are the only statements that use the value of A defined in line 2.

2. Q: Given the segment:

```
1    readln (A, B, C);
2    IF A > B THEN
3        BEGIN
4            Max := A;
5        END
```

```
6    ELSE IF B > C THEN
7       BEGIN
8          Max := B;
9       END;
10   writeln (A, B, C, Max);
```

Which statements use the value of B that is defined by the READ statement in line 1?

A: The value of B defined in line 1 is used in the test in line 2 and the statement in line 10 on every control path and is used in lines 6 and 8 on some control paths. ■

□ □

Data Flow Analysis in Loops

Analyzing data flow in a loop is straightforward if you remember three things:

1. *Include the exit test.* Do not forget to include the data objects that appear in the loop exit test in your analysis.
2. *Include the zero-trip path.* Do not forget to consider the path in which the loop body is never executed at all.
3. *Inside the loop body, look "before" to the previous iteration and "after" to the next iteration, as well as "in" the current iteration.* If you are analyzing data flow forward along a control path, at the end of the loop body do not forget the path that leads back through the loop body again on the next iteration. Similarly, when tracing backward along a control path, do not forget the path that goes back around the loop from the beginning of the loop body on the previous iteration.

EXAMPLE   Given the loop segment:

```
1    I := M;
2    NotFound := TRUE;

3    WHILE NotFound AND (I <= N) DO
4       BEGIN
5          NotFound := A[I] <> 0;
6          I := I + 1;
7       END;
```

Q: Which statements might define the value of I used in line 5?

A: On the first iteration, I is defined in line 1 (tracing backward from line 5 to the start of the segment). On every later iteration, I is defined in line 6 in the previous iteration (tracing back around the loop body).

Q: Where is the value of I defined in line 6 lost?

A: On the last iteration, the value of I is not lost in this segment (tracing forward out of the loop body). On all other iterations, the value defined in line 6 is lost at line 6 in the next iteration (tracing to the end of the loop body and then starting again from the start of the loop body).

Q: Identify all the uses of the value of I defined in line 6.

A: On the last iteration, the value of I is used only in the exit test in line 3 (tracing forward out of the loop body). On all other iterations, the value defined in line 6 is used in the exit test on line 3 and in lines 5 and 6 on the next iteration. ■

□ □
IN and OUT Data Objects of an Action Segment

The concepts of data flow analysis may be applied to identify the IN and OUT data objects of any action segment, such as the body of a procedure. Just as for single program actions, the IN data objects of an action segment are those data objects that carry data values "in" to be used in the segment. The OUT data objects carry new data values "out" of the segment. Any values the OUT data objects contained before the segment was executed are lost.

Identifying the OUT data objects of a segment is easy: any OUT data object of any action *within* the segment is an OUT data object of the *entire segment*. That is, once an action in the segment defines a new value for a data object, that data object's original value has been lost, and the newly defined value, or some other new value defined later in the segment for the same data object, is carried out of the segment by the data object.

IN data objects are more difficult to identify. An IN data object is one that is *used* on some control path through the segment *before its value is defined on that same control path*.

EXAMPLES

1. In the straight-line segment:

```
1    Temp := X;
2    X := Y;
3    Y := Temp;
```

the IN and OUT variables are:

IN: X	— used in line 1 before being defined.
Y	— used in line 2 before being defined.
OUT: Temp	— new value defined in line 1.
X	— new value defined in line 2.
Y	— new value defined in line 3.

Temp is not an IN variable, because its use in line 3 is preceded by its definition in line 1 on the only control path.

2. In the conditional segment:

```
1    Max := C;
2    IF A > B THEN
3      BEGIN
4          Max := A;
5      END
6    ELSE IF B > C THEN
7      BEGIN
8          Max := B;
9      END;
10   D := Max + 1;
```

the IN and OUT variables are:

IN: A — used in lines 2 and 4; not defined in segment.

B — used in lines 2, 6, 8; not defined in segment.

C — used in lines 1 and 6; not defined in segment.

OUT: Max — new value defined in lines 1, 4, and 8.

D — new value defined in line 10.

3. In the loop segment:

```
1    I := M;
2    Total := 0;
3    WHILE I <= N DO
4      BEGIN
5          Total := Total + Sales[I];
6          I := I + 1;
7      END;

8    Average := Total / (N-M+1);
```

the IN and OUT variables are:

IN: M — used in lines 1 and 8; not defined in segment.

N — used in lines 3 and 8; not defined in segment.

Sales — used in line 5; not defined in segment.

OUT: I — defined in lines 1 and 6.

Total — defined in lines 2 and 5.

Average — defined in line 8.

Flow Through Values and IN/OUT Data Objects

To say that a particular data object is an OUT object for a segment (but not also an IN object) says that the object is *always* given a new value whenever the segment is executed. If the OUT data object is an array, record, or string, then it says that *every element, field, or character position* is given a new value. Thus, whatever values were originally stored in the data object are *lost* whenever the segment is executed.

Now consider this segment:

```
IF A > 0 THEN
    Max := A
```

Is Max an OUT data object of the segment? There are two control paths through the segment and on only one is Max assigned a new value. On the other, the original value of Max "flows through" unchanged. Max must be classified as an IN/OUT data object because sometimes its original value (the value coming "in") flows through to become its "out" value and sometimes its original value is lost and a new value is assigned. It is exactly as if we had written:

```
IF A > 0 THEN
    Max := A
ELSE
    Max := Max
```

"Flow-through" values affect how we classify data objects in a segment (see Figure 8.5):

□ **Flow Through Value**

A *flow through value* is a data value stored in an OUT data object when a segment begins execution that *may* remain unchanged when the segment is executed.

A flow through value always makes an OUT data object into an IN/OUT object for the segment.

When a segment defines new values for some, but not all, of the elements of an array or of the fields of a record, then the values in the unchanged elements or fields become flow through values, and the entire array or record becomes an IN/OUT data object. Similarly, if a simple data object, such as Max above, has a new value defined on some, but not all, control paths through a segment, then that simple data object becomes an IN/OUT data object of the segment.

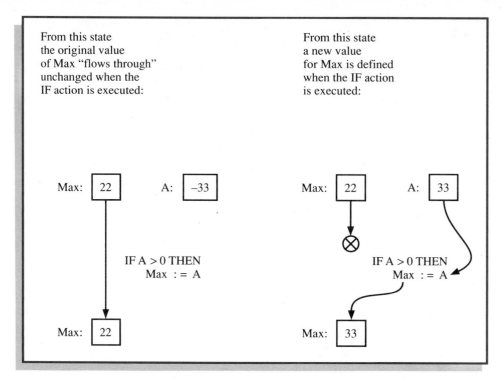

From this state
the original value
of Max "flows through"
unchanged when the
IF action is executed:

From this state
a new value
for Max is defined
when the IF action
is executed:

Max: | 22 | A: | −33 |

Max: | 22 | A: | 33 |

IF A > 0 THEN
    Max : = A

IF A > 0 THEN
    Max : = A

Max: | 22 |

Max: | 33 |

FIGURE 8-5   A "Flow Through" Value May Flow Through a Segment Unchanged

EXAMPLES   Given the FOR loop:

```
FOR I := 1 TO 100 DO
  BEGIN
    A [I] := 0;
  END;
```

Q: Is array A an IN, OUT, or IN/OUT variable of this segment?

A: If array A has subscript range 1..100, then A is an OUT variable because *all* of its elements have a new value defined in the loop. Otherwise A is an IN/OUT variable because the old values of some of the elements flow through the loop unchanged and new values for some elements are defined in the loop. ◼

Flow through values are a common cause of program bugs. For example, suppose a segment is supposed to initialize a variable and, by mistake, the variable is assigned an initial value on every control path but one. On that one path, the variable remains uninitialized; its unpredictable value becomes a flow through value. During testing, all the paths would test correctly except the one with the flow through value. If test data never caused that one path to be taken, the error would never be discovered during testing (and Murphy's Law of Programming would take over from there).

□ □
Data Flow Diagrams

A *data flow diagram* is a diagram that shows how the actions in a control path are connected by the flow of data. Each action is represented by a "bubble" (square bubbles for READ and DISPLAY actions; round bubbles for ASSIGN and CALL actions). The bubbles are connected by arrows showing the flow of data values in and out of each action. The arrows are labeled with data object names to show the IN and OUT data objects of each action.

EXAMPLE   For the segment:

```
1    readln (X, Y);
2    A := sqrt(X);
3    B := A + 10;
4    C := B / A;
5    writeln ('The quotient is ', C);
6    A := sqrt(Y);
7    D := A - 10;
8    writeln ('The results are ', D, A);
```

The data flow diagram is shown in Figure 8.6, using line numbers to label the bubbles.   ■

A data flow diagram shows the flow of data between actions, independently of how the actions happen to be placed in sequence within the program. From the data flow diagram it is easy to see which actions *must* be in sequence and which can be

---

FIGURE 8-6 A Data Flow Diagram for a Straight-line Segment

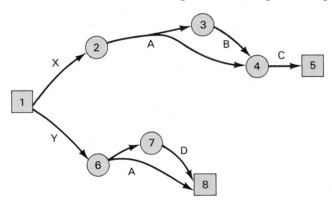

done in another order. For example, from the data flow diagram it is easy to see that actions 2, 3, 4, and 5 must be done in sequence, and actions 6, 7, and 8 must also be done in sequence, but neither sequence uses any values defined by an action in the other sequence.

A data flow diagram is the data flow analogue of a control flow diagram for showing the possible paths of control flow. However, each control path may have a different flow of data, so a separate data flow diagram is required for each control path, in general.

EXERCISES

8.4   Given the Pascal type definitions:

```
TYPE
   Status = (OK, PROBATION, SUSPENDED);
   Name = STRING [20];
   List = ARRAY [1..100] OF Integer;
   Date = RECORD
               Month: Integer;
               Day: Integer;
               Year: Integer;
           END;
```

and the variable declarations:

```
VAR
    Total: Integer;
    I: Integer;
    StudentStatus: Status;
    StudentName: Name;
    GradesList: List;
    NewDate: Date;
    StartDate: Date;
```

List the IN and OUT variables for each of the following Pascal statements:
   a.   StartDate.Day := Total + 2;
   b.   readln (StartDate.Year, GradesList[I]);
   c.   StudentStatus := succ (StudentStatus);
   d.   StudentName := 'Florida_Joe';
   e.   GradesList[2] := StartDate.Year + Total;
   f.   StartDate := NewDate;
   g.   writeln ('Total = ', Total, 'Grade = ', GradesList[I]);

8.5   Procedure ChooseMove has the heading:

```
                                         {IN/OUT}
    PROCEDURE ChooseMove                 {IN}
          (VAR Board: GameBoard;         {OUT}
               Player: Integer;
          VAR Move: Integer);
```

Show the IN, OUT, and IN/OUT classifications of the actual parameters in each of the following calls:

a.   ChooseMove (B, P, M);

b.   ChooseMove (Board, Player[2], Move [CurrentMove]);

8.6   Given the straight-line segment:

```
1    read (A, B, C);
2    D := D + A;
3    E := (A + B + C) / D;
4    B := 2 * B;
5    C := A + B + C;
6    writeln (B, D, C, E);
7    D := sqrt (C);
8    F := A + B + C + D + E;
```

a.   For each of the following uses of a value, give the line number of the statement that defines that value:

B in line 3.
B in line 4.
B in line 8.
C in line 7.
C in line 3.

b.   For each of the following definitions of a value, list the line numbers of statements that use that value:

A in line 1.
B in line 1.
C in line 1.
D in line 2.
C in line 5.

c.   For each of the following definitions of a value, give the line number of the statement where the value is lost, if any:

A in line 1.
C in line 1.
D in line 2.
C in line 5.

d.   Find the IN, OUT, and IN/OUT variables of the segment.

e.   Draw a data flow diagram of the segment.

8.7   Given the following straight-line segment:

```
1    readln (A, B, C);
2    S := A + B + C;
3    T1 := A >= B;
4    S := S / 2;
5    T2 := B >= C;
6    SA := S - A;
7    T3 := A >= C;
8    SB := S - B;
9    T4 := B > A;
10   SC := S - C;
11   MaxA := T1 AND T3;
12   P := 2 * S;
13   writeln ('Sides = ', A, B, C, ' Perimeter = ', P);
14   MaxB := T2 AND NOT T1;
15   B := S * SA * SB * SC;
16   MaxC := NOT T2 AND NOT T3;
17   C := sqrt (B);
18   writeln ('Is A the largest? ', MaxA);
19   writeln ('Is B the largest? ', MaxB);
20   writeln ('Is C the largest? ', MaxC);
21   writeln ('Area = ', C);
```

a. For each of the following uses of a value, give the line number of the statement that defines that value:

B in line 13.

MaxA in line 18.

B in line 17.

B in line 9.

S in line 15.

b. For each of the following definitions of a value, list the line numbers of statements that use that value:

S in line 2.

SC in line 10.

T2 in line 5.

B in line 1.

c. For each of the following definitions of a value, give the line number of the statement where the value is lost, if any:

B in line 1.

C in line 1.

SA in line 6.

d. List the IN, OUT, and IN/OUT variables of the segment.

e. Draw a data flow diagram of the segment.

8.8 List the IN and OUT variables of each of the following segments:

a.
```
readln (A);
X := A + 2;
Y := X * 13;
Z := C;
```

b. read (A,B,C);
      D := 2;
      E := (A + B + C) / D;
c. B := 2 * B;
      C := A + B + C;
      writeln (B,D,C,E);
d. D := sqrt (C);
      C := D * D;
      B := sin (0.5);
      F := A + B + C + D + E;
e. read (C);
      IF A > 0 THEN
        BEGIN
          Max := C + 1;
        END
      ELSE IF B > 0 THEN
        BEGIN
        Max := C - 1;
        END;
      D := Max + 1;

8.9 Given the segment:

```
1    X := C + B;
2    C := 2 * C
3    IF C > X THEN
         BEGIN
4            X := A - 2;
         END
5    ELSE IF X > C THEN
         BEGIN
6            C := B - 2;
         END
     ELSE         .
         BEGIN
7            X := X / B;
8            D := C + 1;
         END;
9    writeln (C, D, X);
```

a. For each of the following uses of a value, list the line numbers of the statements that define that value along some control path through the segment:

C in line 9.
D in line 9.
X in line 9.
X in line 5.
X in line 3.
C in line 8.

b. For each of the following definitions of a value, list the line numbers of the lines where that value is used in the segment on some control path:

C in line 2.
C in line 6.
D in line 8.
X in line 1.
X in line 4.
X in line 7.

c. List the IN, OUT, and IN/OUT variables of the segment.

8.10 Given the loop segment:

```
1   I := M;
2   NotFound := TRUE;
3   WHILE NotFound AND (I <= N) DO
        BEGIN
4           IF A[I] = 0 THEN
                BEGIN
5                   NotFound := FALSE;
                END
            ELSE
                BEGIN
6                   I := I + 1;
                END;
        END;
7   IF NotFound THEN
        BEGIN
8           ZeroPointer := 0;
        END
    ELSE
        BEGIN
9           ZeroPointer := I;
        END;
```

a. For each of the following uses of a value, list the line numbers of the statements that define that value along some control path through the segment:

I in line 3.
I in line 6.
I in line 9.
NotFound in line 3.
NotFound in line 7.

b. For each of the following definitions of a value, list the line numbers of the lines where that value is used in the segment on some control path:

I in line 1.
I in line 6.
NotFound in line 2.
NotFound in line 5.

c. List the IN, OUT, and IN/OUT variables of the segment.

8.11 Hacker Jack coded each of the following procedure declarations, but he forgot to include the IN, OUT, and IN/OUT classifications for the formal parameters. Determine the correct classification for each formal parameter based on how the parameter is used in the procedure body:

a. PROCEDURE ComputeAverages
```
    (VAR A: Real;
     VAR B: Real;
     VAR C: Real);
  BEGIN
    B := (A + C) / 2;
    A := (A + B) / 2;
  END;
```
b. PROCEDURE ReadWrite
```
    (VAR X: Char;
     VAR Y: Char);
  BEGIN
    readln (X, Y);
    writeln (X, Y);
  END;
```
c. PROCEDURE CallDown
```
    (VAR U: Real;
     VAR V: Real;
     VAR W: Real;
     VAR Z: Integer);
  BEGIN
    U := W - 1;
    ComputeValues (V, Z, W);
    U := U + W;
  END;
```

where ComputeValues has formal parameters classified as:

```
ComputeValues (IN, OUT, OUT)
```

d. PROCEDURE SetDate
```
    (VAR Day: Integer;
     VAR Month: Integer;
     VAR Year: Integer;
     VAR D: Date);
  BEGIN
    D.Month := Month;
    D.Day := Day;
    D.Year := Year;
  END;
```

where Date is declared as a record with three fields named Month, Day, and Year.

e. PROCEDURE SetDate as in (d) above, but where Date is a record with four fields named Month, Day, Year, and LeapYear.

□□□ 8.4
USING ANALYSIS: HOW IS A RESULT COMPUTED?

Let's put these control flow and data flow analysis methods to work to answer a basic question that arises in understanding and debugging a program: *how is a particular result computed by the program?* Suppose that you see on your display screen a result that has been computed incorrectly. You have a program listing at hand. How do you determine, out of all the actions and data objects in the program, which were involved in computing that particular result?

The answer can be found through application of (1) *control flow analysis* to find the control paths that lead to the DISPLAY action that displays the incorrect result and (2) *data flow analysis* to find the actions and data objects that participate in computing the value displayed. An error might be caused by:

- The *wrong control path* being chosen for execution, or
- The *wrong computation* being performed on that control path.

In this section, let's assume that you know the correct control path is being executed, and you want to analyze just the computation along that particular control path. In the next section, we look at how to use analysis to check the choice of control path.

□□
Finding the Actions and Data Objects that Participate

Given a particular control path, suppose that you want to determine how a particular result is computed on that path. More specifically, suppose your goal is:

- To identify (by marking in the listing) each action in the segment that participates in computing the result, and
- To identify which of the IN data objects of these actions are actually IN data objects for the entire computation of the result—data objects that bring data values "in" at the beginning of the computation.

The analysis here involves tracing backward along each control path to identify "chains" that connect *uses* of data values with their *definitions*, moving from the display of the final (incorrect) value to its definition as an OUT value of some earlier action, and then from the IN values used in that action to their definitions as the OUT values of still earlier actions, and so forth. The steps in making this analysis are:

1. Start with the action where the value is *used* and find the earlier action that *defines* that value (for the given control path). Mark this earlier action to show that it participates in computing the result value. Make a list of the IN data objects of this marked action. Each of these data objects also participates by providing a data value that is used in computing the final result.

2. For each of the IN data objects on the list, start at the marked action and trace back through the control path to find the earlier action that *defines* the value of that data object on the path. Mark that action as participating and make a list of the IN data objects of that action.

3. Continue to trace back from each action that is marked as participating to find the earlier actions that define the IN values of that action. The backtracing process continues until you reach either an IN data object for the whole path (its value is not defined earlier in the path), or a READ, ASSIGN, or CALL action that has no IN data objects.

Once you have marked the actions and data objects that participate in computing a particular result, you can focus your attention only on those actions and data objects to verify or check the computation of the result. You know that any unmarked actions and data objects in the control path are not participating in computing this particular result. If the computation of this particular result is wrong, then the error must be in one of the marked actions or in the value of one of the IN data objects that is used.

EXAMPLE

Pat Programmer has a job as a "programming consultant" for the introductory programming course at BSU (Big State University). Freshman Fred is a typical beginning programming student who comes to the programming consultant for help in debugging his program. Let's listen in (see Figure 8.7):

Fred: "I'm trying to debug this procedure body. It's just a straight-line segment, but I can't seem to find the error. My program is displaying 7 for the value of X when I know it should be 5. But I looked at the WRITE statement and it is displaying the value of X correctly, and then I looked at the assignment where X is computed, and it seems to be ok. What could be the cause of the error?"

Pat: "You stopped your data flow analysis too soon. You've traced from the use of X in the WRITE statement back to the definition of X in the assignment. Let's keep tracing further back, following the data flow along the control path. The assignment to X is:

```
X := (U + V) / 2;
```

So the computation of X uses the values of U and V. Where are these values defined? Trace back to the statements that define the values of U and V."

Fred: "OK, U is defined here:

```
readln (U, Z);
```

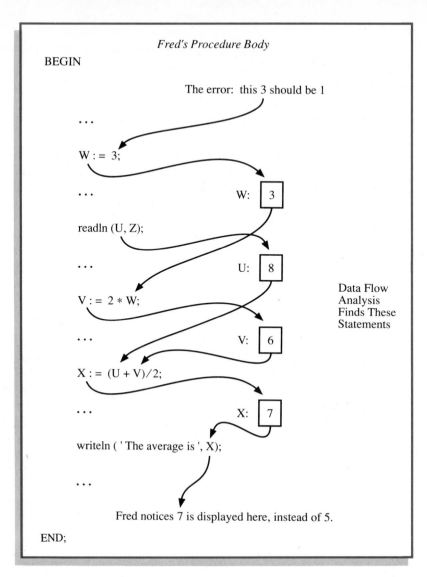

FIGURE 8-7 Use Data Flow Analysis to Find the Statements that Participate in Computing an Output Value

and V here:"

```
V := 2 * W;
```

Pat: "Don't stop yet: Find the definition of the value of W that is used in the assignment to V."

Fred: "W is initialized way back at the beginning of the procedure, with the statement:"

```
W := 3;
```

Pat: "The error must be in one of these statements, or you must have read in the wrong data value for U."

Fred spots the error: "Wait—there's the bug! I meant to initialize W to 1, not 3." ■

□ □
Hand Tracing the Computation of a Value

Often it is useful to hand trace the marked actions in order to check the correctness of the computation. You choose particular values for the IN data objects of the computation, and then trace through the marked actions, executing each action with the test values, and keeping track of each new value defined on a sheet of paper. Because only a few actions and data objects usually participate in computing a single result, you typically have only a few actions and data objects to worry about. The hand tracing is much simpler than when you try to trace all the actions and data objects in a segment.

□ □
Using Back Substitution to Verify the Computation of a Mathematical Formula

Suppose that you find only ASSIGN actions participate in computing a particular result. That is, for a particular control path and OUT value of the path, you have marked the actions that participate and no READ or CALL actions appear. Then you can use a process called *back substitution* to construct a mathematical formula that represents how the OUT value is computed.

Back substitution is the process of substituting for a data object name, say X, that appears in the right-hand side of one ASSIGN action, the *expression* that appears on the right-hand side of an earlier ASSIGN action that defines the value for X. For example, if the value of A is defined by the assignment:

```
A := B + 2 * C;
```

and you find that the values of B and C are defined by the earlier assignments:

```
B := 12;
C := 5 * D + F;
```

then you can substitute 12 for B and 5*D + F for C, to determine that A is computed by the formula:

```
A := (12) + 2 * (5*D + F)
  := 12 + 10*D + 2*F
```

To build the mathematical formula desired, you continue the process of back substitution until the only data object names remaining in the formula are IN data objects of the entire segment. For example, you might substitute for D and F, in the formula above, the expressions that define their values in some earlier assignments. Once you have the formula, you can compare it against the mathematical formula that represents the computation you wanted to perform, and see if the two formulas are the same.

EXAMPLE Fred is trying to verify that his program computes a particular result correctly:

> **Fred:** "The value of Root1 at this point should be the root of the equation, computed by using the quadratic formula:

$$\text{Root1} := \frac{-B + \sqrt{B^2 - 4AC}}{2A}$$

In writing the program, I broke this big formula up into several parts and computed each part in a separate assignment. So B*B − 4*A*C is computed in one place, 2*A in another, and so forth. I thought I might use these partial results to simplify the computation of the other root of the equation. Now I'm not so sure I have computed the formula correctly. How do I check?"

> **Pat:** "First, use data flow analysis to find all the statements that participate in computing the value of Root1."

Fred traces the data flow and finds the statements:

```
read (A, B, C);
. . .
BSquared := B * B;
. . .
Discrim := BSquared - 4*A*C;
. . .
Numerator := sqrt(Discrim) - B;
. . .
Factor := 1 / (A * 2);
. . .
Root1 := Numerator * Factor;
```

> **Pat:** "I see why you are confused by this computation! But if you use back substitution to find the formula computed by the assignment statements in this control path, you should be able to tell exactly what you are computing in terms of the values of A, B, and C that are read in the first statement."

Fred starts working, making the substitutions one at a time in several steps:

1. Substitute for "Numerator" in the final assignment:

   Root1 := (sqrt(Discrim) − B) * Factor

2. Substitute for "Factor" in (1):

$$\text{Root1} := (\text{sqrt(Discrim)} - B) * (1 / (A * 2))$$

3. Substitute for "Discrim" in (2):

$$\text{Root1} := (\text{sqrt(BSquared} - 4*A*C) - B) * (1 / (A * 2))$$

4. Substitute for "BSquared" in (3):

$$\text{Root1} := (\text{sqrt(B} * B - 4*A*C) - B) * (1 / (A * 2))$$

Pat: "Now rearrange this formula using the rules of algebra to see if it is equivalent to the original."

Fred rearranges (4) to get:

$$\text{Root1} := (-B + \text{sqrt(B*B} - 4*A*C)) / (2 * A)$$

Fred: "Looks like the right formula to me!"   ■

□ □

Finding Errors Caused by Uninitialized Data Objects

Suppose a control path leads to an action that uses an *uninitialized data object*. That is, there is an action that *uses* the value of a data object before the value of that data object has ever been *defined* on that control path. One common cause of such errors is a simple typing mistake: inadvertently typing another variable name instead of the correct one.

Uninitialized data object errors are often difficult to track down. Because the data object's value has not yet been defined, its value is unpredictable and may change from run to run of the program. On one test run the program may appear to work correctly, but a later test run using *exactly the same input data* may fail or give different results.

If a subprogram is incorrectly computing a particular result and you suspect that it may be due to an uninitialized data object error, then you can use your analysis skills to find the error quickly:

1. Determine the control path that is being executed when the error occurs, all the way back to the beginning of the subprogram body that is being analyzed.

2. Determine the actions on that control path that participate in computing the incorrect result.

3. Determine the IN data objects of the computation of the result, if any.

You have found an uninitialized data object error if *an IN data object of the path is not an IN (or IN/OUT) parameter of the subprogram.* Now to find the action causing the error, find all the *uses* of that IN value in actions that participate in computing the result.

Freshman Fred is back at the consultant's table. Let's listen.

> **Fred:** "The first time I ran this program it displayed 27 as the value for K, but when I ran it again with the same test data, it printed some crazy, huge value for K. The WRITE statement looks ok, and the assignment that computes the value of K is also ok. What could be going on—maybe the computer is broken?"
>
> **Pat:** "It sounds like you might be using an uninitialized variable somewhere in the computation of K. Uninitialized variables have unpredictable values, and the value may be different on each run. Data flow analysis is needed. Let's trace back through the statements that participate in computing the value of K."

Fred traces back through the control paths, finding all the statements that participate. He comes across one suspicious statement:

```
Q := 2*(Q + 1);
```

Fred knows that Q is a local variable in the subprogram. He traces back to the beginning of the subprogram body, and there is no statement that defines Q before this one.

> **Pat:** "What is the value of Q at the start of execution of this statement? Because Q is a local variable that has not been given an initial value before this statement, Q's value is unpredictable."
>
> **Fred:** "Oh no!! I meant to write: Q := 2*(P+1). Just a typographic error when I originally entered the program—but it took me three hours of debugging to find it!"

EXERCISES

8.12 Given the segment:

```
1    read (A, B);
2    D := D + A;
3    E := (A+B+C) / D;
4    B := 2*B;
5    C := A + B + C;
6    writeln (B, D, C, E);
7    D := sqrt (D);
8    F := C + D;
```

Identify the statements and variables that participate in computing each of the following values. Also list the IN variables for each computation:

   a. The value of E displayed in line 6.

   b. The value of F computed in line 8.

8.13 Assume the following procedures have formal parameters classified as follows:

```
PROCEDURE Proc1 (IN, IN, IN/OUT, IN/OUT)
PROCEDURE Proc2 (IN, OUT, OUT)
PROCEDURE Proc3 (IN/OUT, OUT)
PROCEDURE Proc4 (IN, IN, OUT)
```

Given the segment:

```
1    read (A,B,C);
2    D := (A+B+C) DIV 3;
3    Count := A + 1;
4    Next := B + Count - 1;
5    Total := 2 * D + A;
6    Proc2 (Total, Count, Next);
7    writeln (Count, Next, Total);
```

Identify the statements and variables that participate in computing each of the following values:

   a. The value of Total used in line 7.

   b. The value of Count used in line 7.

   c. The value of Next used in line 7.

8.14 Assume the same procedure definitions as in Exercise 8.13. Given the segment:

```
1    read (A,B,C);
2    D := (A+B+C) DIV 3;
3    Proc3 (A, D);
4    Count := A + 1;
5    Next := B + Count - 1;
6    Proc1 (Next, D, A, B);
7    Total := 2 * D + A;
8    Proc4 (Total, Count, Next);
9    writeln (Count, Next, Total);
```

Identify the statements and variables that participate in computing each of the following values:

   a. The value of Total used in line 9.

   b. The value of Count used in line 9.

   c. The value of Next used in line 9.

8.15 Given the segment:

```
1    X := C + B;
2    C := 2 * C

3    IF C > X THEN
        BEGIN
4            X := A - 2;
        END
5    ELSE IF X > C THEN
        BEGIN
6            C := B - 2;
        END
    ELSE
        BEGIN
7            X := X / B;
8            D := C + 1;
        END;
9    writeln (C, D, X);
```

Identify the statements and variables in this segment that participate in computing each of the following values. Also list the IN variables for each computation:

a. The value of C displayed in line 9, when the control path includes the second case of the IF at line 3.

b. The value of C displayed in line 9, when the control path includes the third case of the IF at line 3.

c. The value of X displayed in line 9, when the control path includes the third case of the IF at line 3.

d. The value of X displayed in line 9, when the control path includes the first case of the IF at line 3.

8.16 Given the loop segment:

```
1    I := M;
2    NotFound := TRUE;

3    WHILE NotFound AND (I <= N) DO
        BEGIN
4            IF A[I] = 0 THEN
                BEGIN
5                    NotFound := FALSE;
                END
            ELSE
                BEGIN
6                    I := I + 1;
                END;
        END;
```

```
7      IF NotFound THEN
           BEGIN
8              ZeroPointer := 0;
           END
       ELSE
           BEGIN
9              ZeroPointer := I;
           END;
```

Identify the statements and variables that participate in computing each of the following values. Also list the IN variables for each computation:

    a.   The value of ZeroPointer defined in line 9, when the control path includes one iteration of the loop at line 3, and the first case of the IF in the loop body.

    b.   The value of ZeroPointer defined in line 9, when the control path includes two iterations of the loop at line 3. On the first iteration, the second case of the IF in the loop body is executed and on the second iteration the first case is executed.

    c.   The value of NotFound used in line 7, when the control path includes one iteration of the loop at line 3, and the first case of the IF in the loop body.

    8.17   Stuart Stanford claims that he can swap the values of two Integer variables, A and B, without using a temporary storage variable, by the assignment segment:

```
A := A + B;
B := A - B;
A := A - B;
```

Stated precisely, he claims that:

$$A_{OUT} = B_{IN}$$

and

$$B_{OUT} = A_{IN}$$

Use data flow analysis to prove or disprove his claim.

    8.18   Do the following segments correctly implement their PURPOSE/GOAL STATE specifications? If not, correct them.

    a.   {PURPOSE/GOAL STATE: Compute RetailPrice =
WholesalePrice plus a markup percentage, defined by
constant MARKUP, and add in the sales tax at a 4 percent
rate. }

```
Temp1 := WholesalePrice + MARKUP * WholesalePrice;
Temp2 := Temp1 + 0.4 * Temp1;
RetailPrice := Temp2;
```

b. {PURPOSE/GOAL STATE: Compute the weighted average, ExamAverage, of the 3 exam scores in variables Exam1, Exam2, and Exam3. Weigh Exam1 and Exam3 equally, but give Exam2 twice the weight of each of the other exams. }

```
Temp1 := Exam1 + Exam3;
ExamAverage := (Temp1 + Exam2) DIV 2;
```

8.19   In the segment:

```
1    A := B + 1;
2    D := 2;
3    E := (A+B+C) DIV D;
4    B := 2*B;
5    C := A+B+C;
6    writeln(B,D,C,E);
7    G := sqrt(C);
8    F := A+B+C+G+E;
```

Determine whether the following OUT values are correctly computed from the IN values B and C:

a.   Is G = square root of $3*B + C + 1$?

b.   Is E = the integer part of $(2*B + C + 1)/2$?

8.20   Hacker Jack has written some confusing code again. Even he can't figure it out. His segment is:

```
1     readln (A, B, C);
2     S := A + B + C;
3     T1 := A >= B;
4     S := S / 2;
5     T2 := B >= C;
6     SA := S - A;
7     T3 := A >= C;
8     SB := S - B;
9     T4 := B > A;
10    SC := S - C;
11    MaxA := T1 AND T3;
12    P := 2 * S;
13    writeln ('Sides = ', A, B, C, ' Perimeter = ', P);
14    MaxB := T2 AND NOT T1;
15    B := S * SA * SB * SC;
```

```
16   MaxC := NOT T2 AND NOT T3;
17   C := sqrt (B);
18   writeln ('Is A the largest? ', MaxA);
19   writeln ('Is B the largest? ', MaxB);
20   writeln ('Is C the largest? ', MaxC);
21   writeln ('Area = ', C);
```

See if you can answer his questions. If he is wrong, tell him why:

a. "I meant to display in line 13 the perimeter of a triangle with sides A, B, and C, computed using the formula Perimeter = A + B + C. Did I get this right?"

b. "I meant to compute the area of the same triangle and display it in line 21, by using the formula:

$$\text{Area} = \text{square root of } (S(S - A)(S - B)(S - C))$$

$$\text{where } S = (A + B + C)/2$$

Did I get this right?"

c. "I meant to have MaxA, MaxB, and MaxC compute the answer to the question of which side of the triangle was the longest, and print the answer in lines 18–20. Did I get this right?"

8.21 This procedure has no IN or IN/OUT parameters. During testing, it appears that the body uses an uninitialized variable. Is this true? If so, which line contains the error? The procedure body is:

```
     BEGIN
1        read (A,B,C);
2        Av := (A+B+C) DIV 3;
3        Ct := A + 1;
4        Tl := 2 * Nt + A;
5        Nt := B + Ct - 1;
6        writeln(Av, Ct, Nt, Tl)
     END;
```

□□□ **8.5**
USING ANALYSIS: HOW IS THE CONTROL PATH CHOSEN?

Analysis skills can be used to solve a different kind of problem: determining how a particular control path is chosen for execution. Suppose you are debugging your program and you observe that the *wrong statements* are being executed. For example, you might see the output from one debug WRITE displayed when running a test case that should never cause that debug WRITE to be executed. There must be an error in the part of the program that chooses the control path, and you can use your analysis skills to find it quickly.

How is a Control Path Chosen?

The particular control path, of all those possible, that is chosen for execution is determined by the results of the *tests* that appear in conditional actions (IF's) and loops (WHILE and FOR). Without conditionals and loops there would be only one possible control path.

To determine how the control path is chosen that leads to the execution of a particular action (like a debug WRITE), follow these steps:

1. Trace backward from the action to find the *possible control paths* leading to that action.
2. Identify the *tests* used in those control paths as part of the execution of IF, WHILE, FOR-START and FOR-NEXT actions.
3. For each data value used in one of these tests, use your analysis skills to find the *actions that participate* and the *data objects that participate* in defining that value along the control paths leading up to the test.

The methods are those used in the last section to identify the actions and data objects that participate in computing an output result. If there is an error in how the control path is chosen for execution, it must be in one of the actions identified by your analysis, or one of the IN data objects of the segment must have contained an incorrect value at the start of execution of the segment.

EXAMPLE   Given the loop segment:

```
1    I := M;
2    NotFound := TRUE;

3    WHILE NotFound AND (I <= N) DO
        BEGIN
4          IF A[I] = 0 THEN
              BEGIN
5                NotFound := FALSE;
              END
           ELSE
              BEGIN
6                I := I + 1;
              END;
        END;

7    IF NotFound THEN
        BEGIN
8          ZeroPointer := 0;
        END
     ELSE
        BEGIN
9          ZeroPointer := I;
        END;
```

Q: Which statements and variables participate in determining the control path that leads to execution of the assignment in line 9?

A: Tracing backward along the control paths from line 9, the IF test in line 7 and the WHILE test in line 3 determine the control path. When the path leads through the loop body, the IF test in line 4 also determines the path. The variables used in these tests are:

- Line 7: NotFound, which is defined in line 2 or line 5 using only literal TRUE/FALSE values.
- Line 3: NotFound, with the same definitions as for line 7. I, which is defined in line 1 or line 6. Line 1 uses the value of IN variable M.
  N, which is an IN variable of the segment.
- Line 4: A, which is an IN variable of the segment.
  I, which is defined as for line 3.

Therefore the control path leading to line 9 is determined by the actions in lines 1, 2, 5, and 6, the tests in lines 3, 4, and 7, and the values of IN variables M, N, and A when the segment begins execution. ■

□□
Identifying Path Conditions

A second use of analysis is to determine the path conditions for a control path— what values of the IN data objects at the start of execution of the path will cause that particular control path to be chosen for execution? This analysis is similar to that used to express the computation of a result as a mathematical formula:

1. Identify the actions that participate in determining the control path, as described above.
2. If all the actions are ASSIGN actions, then use *back substitution* to express each of the values used in a test as a mathematical formula that includes only IN data objects.
3. Write the path condition by taking each of the tests used to determine the path (and their TRUE/FALSE result) and substitute the right mathematical formula for each value used in each test. Then put the Boolean operation AND between each pair of tests. The result is a Boolean-valued expression for the path condition, expressed using only the IN data objects of the path.

EXAMPLE   Given the segment:

```
1    X := C + B;
2    C := 2 * C

3    IF C > X THEN
         BEGIN
4            X := A - 2;
         END
5    ELSE IF X > C THEN
         BEGIN
```

```
6              C := B - 2;
          END
        ELSE
          BEGIN
7              X := X / B;
8              D := C + 1;
          END;
9     writeln (C, D, X);
```

Q: What is the path condition for the path that leads to the assignment in line 6?

A: The path is determined by the tests at line 3 and line 5. Each test uses variables X and C, whose values are defined in lines 1 and 2, using the IN values of variables B and C. The tests and their results in this path are:

$$(C > X) = \text{FALSE}$$
$$(X > C) = \text{TRUE}$$

Substituting for (C+B) for X and (2*C) for C, as defined in lines 1 and 2, and placing AND between the tests gives the path condition:

$$((2*C) > (C+B)) = \text{FALSE}$$
$$\text{AND } ((C+B) > (2*C)) = \text{TRUE}$$

which can be simplified using the rules of algebra to give the path condition:

$$C+B > 2*C \qquad \blacksquare$$

EXERCISES

8.22 Given the following loop:

```
1     Q := 0;
2     R := A;
3     WHILE R >= B DO
          BEGIN
4              Q := Q + 1;
5              R := R - B;
          END;
```

a. Which statements and variables participate in determining the control path through the loop?

b. Which variables are IN variables for the choice of control path?

c. Determine the path conditions for zero, one, and two iterations of the loop, stated using only the IN variables identified in (b). (three paths)

8.23 Given the loop segment:

```
1    I := M;
2    NotFound := TRUE;

3    WHILE NotFound AND (I <= N) DO
         BEGIN
4          NotFound := A[I] <> 0;
5          I := I + 1;
         END;

6    IF NotFound THEN
         BEGIN
7          ZeroPointer := 0;
         END
8    ELSE
         BEGIN
9          ZeroPointer := I;
         END;
```

a. Which tests, statements, and variables participate in determining whether the statement in line 7 is executed?

b. Which variables are IN variables for the choice of this control path?

c. Determine the path conditions for zero and one iteration of the loop, stated using only the IN variables of the segment. (two paths)

□□□ 8.6
PRECONDITIONS AND THE MOST DANGEROUS MOMENT IN PROGRAMMING

Now let's return to an idea that we have met several times in previous chapters, the idea of a "precondition" of an action. When an action is executed, the program state contains certain data values. If an action depends on those values having certain properties if it is to execute its task correctly, we say the action has a *precondition*.

Because preconditions describe properties of the program state, they are a form of *assertion* about the program state. In particular, they describe properties of the IN data objects of the action.

□ **Precondition**

A *precondition* of an action is an assertion stating a property of the values of the IN data objects of the action that *must be true when the action begins execution* if the action is to work correctly.

Writing Preconditions

In writing down a precondition for a segment, it is often helpful to use IN as a subscript on the names of data objects (or variables) in the precondition, to make it clear that we are asserting a required property of the IN data objects *at the start of execution of the segment*.

EXAMPLE The statement:

```
PercentA := (A / Total) * 100
```

has:

PRECONDITION: Total$_{\text{IN}} <> 0$

because the statement would fail due to a division by zero if executed in a state where its IN variable Total contains zero. ■

The Most Dangerous Moment in Programming

You are merrily designing your program, or perhaps you have already reached the coding stage, and you are about to include an action that may *sometimes fail*. That is, there are some possible values for the IN data objects of the action that would cause the action to fail. The action has a *precondition*, whether you know it or not.

You have reached the *most dangerous moment in programming!* You are about to introduce a potential bug into your program, and a bug of the worst possible kind—a bug that will cause the program to *fail sometimes, for some input data*. It will not fail all the time, so that you are sure to catch the error during program testing, but will just fail *sometimes,* so that you may not catch the error during testing unless you just happen to choose the right test input data.

Even worse, the "failure" may not be of an obvious sort when it occurs. Rather than causing the program to CRASH (which would be an obvious failure) the action may simply fail to compute correct results. We term such results *garbage results* because they are useless to any later actions that try to use them. Garbage results may cause later actions to fail in unexpected ways.

Once you have become aware of the situation, what should you do at this "dangerous moment?" The first step is to identify and write down the precondition for the action, so that you know precisely what must be true of the program state for the action to be guaranteed to work correctly. This precondition is like a red warning flag (see Figure 8.8) that says *"Danger here! This action makes assumptions about the program state that may or may not be true."*

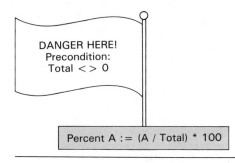

FIGURE 8-8 A Precondition is Like a Red Warning Flag

DANGER HERE!
Precondition:
Total < > 0

Percent A := (A / Total) * 100

The second step is to ensure that the assumptions stated in the precondition are *always true* whenever the action is executed. The next section describes how this can be done.

□ □

How Can an Action Fail?

As you design each action in a program, the action should be inspected to see if it requires a precondition. That is, you look at each action to see if it could fail if one or more of its IN data objects contained the wrong values.

In the previous chapters, we have already seen several reasons why an action may have a precondition:

1. *A basic Pascal arithmetic operation or predefined function may restrict the range of values allowed in one or more IN variables.* The most obvious form of failure is simply failure of a basic Pascal action, such as:

a. An attempt to *divide by zero* (/, DIV, MOD) or to apply MOD to a negative right-hand argument.

b. An attempt to take the *square root of a negative number*.

c. An attempt to add or multiply Integer values whose sum or product will exceed MAXINT.

If one of these operations is executed when its precondition has been violated, your Pascal system may detect the error, display a run-time error message, and terminate execution of the program without ever completing the action. In other cases, your Pascal system will simply perform the action incorrectly, producing incorrect results without any warning.

In all of these cases, one or more of the values used in the action must be restricted in the range of allowed values. The precondition states this range restriction.

EXAMPLES

1. ACTION:

T := sqrt (B*B − 4*A*C)

Possible failure: Attempt to find the square root of a negative number.

Failure result: Execution terminates with run-time error message.

PRECONDITION: $B_{IN}*B_{IN} >= 4*A_{IN}*C_{IN}$

2. **Assume:** Total and Sales are type Integer.

ACTION:

Total := Total + Sales

Possible failure: Sum of Total plus Sales may exceed MAXINT.

Failure result: New value of Total is "garbage."

PRECONDITION: $Total_{IN} + Sales_{IN} <= MAXINT$ ■

2. *A subscript expression may require that a data value be within a restricted range.* An attempt to refer to an array element with a *subscript range error* (too large or too small for the subscript range declared for the array) will cause the action to fail.

A failure of this sort may sometimes be detected by the Pascal system and a run-time error message displayed, or the action may simply be performed incorrectly and no warning given.

EXAMPLE

■ **Assume:** Array Table has subscript range 1..100.

ACTION:

Table [I] := 2*X

■ **Possible failure:** I may be outside the range 1..100.

■ **Failure result:** Execution is terminated with a "subscript range error" message, or execution continues with the assignment having made the contents of a "random" memory location into "garbage."

PRECONDITION: $1 <= I_{IN} <= 100$ ■

3. *An assignment to a subrange variable may require that the right-hand side expression compute a value within a restricted range.* The attempt to assign a value out of range to a variable of a subrange type (a value that is outside of the defined subrange) will cause the assignment to fail.

This failure may sometimes be detected by the Pascal system and a run-time error message displayed, or the action may simply be performed incorrectly and no warning given.

■ **Assume:** Variable ExamGrade is of a subrange type, range 0..100.

ACTION:

ExamGrade := ExamGrade + 10

■ **Possible failure:** The sum may exceed 100.

■ **Failure result:** Execution is terminated with a "subrange violation" error message, or execution continues with variable ExamGrade containing a "garbage" value outside its declared subrange.

PRECONDITION: $ExamGrade_{IN} <= 90$ ■

4. *An action may compute a result using a formula that only works "in some cases" (for some values of the IN variables).*
Errors of this sort are never detected by the Pascal system. The programmer is entirely responsible.

■ **Assume:** StartDate is a record with fields Month, Day, and Year representing a valid date.

ACTION:

StartDate.Day := StartDate.Day + 1

■ **Possible failure:** The new value of the Day field may be past the last day of the month.

■ **Failure result:** StartDate no longer contains a valid date; the date is now a "garbage" date.

PRECONDITION: $StartDate.Day_{IN}$ is not the last day of the month stored in StartDate.Month.   ■

5. *A procedure or function may fail to work correctly for certain values of its IN and IN/OUT parameters.* If a subprogram fails to work correctly for certain values of its parameters, its heading should include the appropriate precondition. Then every call on that subprogram must provide actual parameters that satisfy the precondition.
If the precondition is not satisfied by the actual parameters when the call is made, then some action within the procedure body may fail, causing execution of the procedure to terminate with a run-time error message. Alternatively, the procedure may simply produce "garbage" results or enter an "infinite" loop that never terminates at all.

■ **Assume:**   Procedure FindEntry has the partial heading:

PROCEDURE FindEntry
        (KeyValue: Real   IN
         Table: IdTable   IN
         I: Position)   OUT

PURPOSE/GOAL STATE: ...

PRECONDITION: KeyValue must be an entry in Table.

ACTION:
        CALL FindEntry (NewVal, BigTable, Posn)

■ **Possible failure:**   NewValue is not an entry in BigTable.

■ **Failure result:**   Unknown; depends on how the procedure body happens to be coded. Possibilities: After the call Posn contains a "garbage" value, or FindEntry enters an infinite loop and continues to search Table "forever" looking for NewVal.

PRECONDITION: NewVal is an entry in BigTable.   ■

This list is not complete, but it shows some of the most common situations where an action might fail if the values of the IN variables of the action happened to have the wrong properties.

EXERCISES

8.24   In each of the following situations, describe the way the action might fail. Then determine a precondition that would guarantee the action would not fail:

a.   *Assume:* All variables of type Real.

ACTION:

Root1 := N + D/(2*A)

b.   *Assume:* Ch of type Char; Digit of subrange 0..9.

ACTION:

Digit := ord (Ch) − ord ('0')

c.   *Assume:* Array Table has subscript range 1..100.

ACTION:

Table [I+1] := Table [J−2]

d.   *Assume:* All variables of type Real.

ACTION:

Hypotenuse := sqrt (Side1*Side1 + Side2*Side2)

e. *Assume:* The partial function heading is:

FUNCTION Average3
    (A: Integer
    B: Integer
    C: Integer)

FUNCTION VALUE: Integer

PURPOSE: ...

PRECONDITION: All parameters must be non-negative.

ACTION:

X := Average3 (U+V, K−1, 23)

8.25   READ actions, WRITE actions, and "initialize" actions that use simple variables would seldom need preconditions. Explain why.

8.26   Our description of preconditions as indicating "danger" may seem funny—in all the programs so far the only "danger" in a program failure was that the programmer might be embarrassed. But computer programs are increasingly being used in systems where a failure might really be dangerous to the people using the system. Describe some possible consequences of a program failure in each of the following situations:

a.   Your university is adding an upper deck to its football stadium. The amount of steel reinforcement needed to suspend the deck between concrete pillars is being computed by a program you designed.

b.   An airline determines the amount of jet fuel needed for flights from London to Tokyo using a computer program you designed.

c.   In a new line of automobiles introduced by a major manufacturer, all changes in the speed of a car when under "cruise control" are determined by a program you designed.

8.27   A program failure can have financial consequences also. Describe two situations where you, your parents, or your friends have depended on a computer program whose failure might possibly have cost you or them a lot of money.

□□□ **8.7**
GUARDS, POSTCONDITIONS, AND PRE/POST ANALYSIS

Preconditions on an action represent a danger point because the action depends on properties of the program state that may not always be true. Your goal is to try to construct the program so that you *know* the preconditions of each action will be true whenever that action is executed.

In fact, if you stop to look at the design of some of the subprogram bodies in the preceding chapters, you will find many examples of actions with preconditions. But in almost every case you will also be able to convince yourself that there is no cause for concern—because the program design guarantees that each action can never be executed unless its precondition is satisfied.

□ □
Guarding an Action

Suppose that you spot an action with a precondition, but that action is preceded by an IF, WHILE, or FOR loop test that checks to see if the precondition is satisfied. If the precondition is not satisfied, then the test causes execution to flow down another control path, avoiding the action with the precondition. We say that such a test *guards* the action with the precondition.

When a test guards an action with a precondition and provides an alternative control path when the precondition is not satisfied, then the overall IF, WHILE, or FOR segment usually does not have a precondition, even though one of its constituent actions does.

EXAMPLES

1. In the segment:

```
IF Total <> 0 THEN
  BEGIN
     PercentA := (A / Total) * 100;
  END
ELSE
  BEGIN
     PercentA := 0;
  END;
```

the first assignment to PercentA has the precondition:

PRECONDITION: $Total_{IN} <> 0$

which is exactly the test made in the IF statement that precedes the assignment. Thus the IF test serves to guard the assignment with the precondition. Note that, although the assignment has a precondition, the entire IF segment, taken as a whole *has no precondition*—it will always work correctly for any possible values of its IN variables, Total and A.

2. A FOR loop often provides a guard against subscript range errors. For example, suppose an array A has a subscript range 1..100. Then the FOR loop:

```
FOR I := 1 TO 100 DO
  BEGIN
     A [I] := 0;
  END;
```

guards the assignment to A[I]. The assignment:

```
A [I] := 0;
```

has the precondition:

PRECONDITION: $1 <= I_{IN} <= 100$

but the entire FOR loop requires no precondition.

A guard provides one method to guarantee that a precondition of an action is satisfied. A guard works by forcing execution away from a "dangerous" action, down another control path, when the precondition is violated. Thus a guard uses *control flow* to guarantee a precondition.

□ □

Postconditions and Pre/Post Analysis

Another way to guarantee a precondition of an action involves the use of *data flow analysis* and *postconditions*. We call this method *precondition/postcondition analysis* (or *pre/post analysis,* for short).

In pre/post analysis, we are *not* modifying the program; we are simply *reasoning about the computation of certain results*. In particular, we are reasoning about how the IN values are computed for an action with a precondition. The goal of this reasoning is to try to prove that the precondition *must always be true* whenever the action is reached during execution.

Postconditions are the new element in pre/post analysis. A postcondition for an action represents a *guarantee* about a property of the values of its OUT variables that later actions can count on. More precisely:

□ **Postcondition**

A *postcondition* for an action is an assertion that describes a property that *must be true* of the values of the OUT data objects (or variables) of the action *after* the action has been executed, provided that the action begins execution in a state that satisfies all of its preconditions.

Along with this definition, we need to define a new way that an action can *fail:*

□ **Failure of an Action with a Postcondition**

An action with a postcondition *fails to execute correctly,* starting from a state where its preconditions are true, if the values of its OUT data objects do not satisfy the postcondition when its execution is complete.

Writing Postconditions

A postcondition is an assertion written in the same form as a precondition, with "POSTCONDITION" replacing "PRECONDITION." A postcondition describes properties of OUT variables of the action so the subscript $_{OUT}$ is sometimes used for clarity.

EXAMPLES

1. For the action:

$$Average := (abs\ (X) + abs\ (Y)) / 2$$

we might guarantee:

POSTCONDITION: $Average_{OUT} > = 0$

2. For the action:

$$Total := Total + Sales$$

we might guarantee:

POSTCONDITION: $Total_{OUT} < MAXINT$ ∎

The Pre/Post Analysis Method

We use postconditions as a way of "passing the buck" from an action with a precondition on its IN data objects to the earlier actions that *defined the values* of its IN data objects. This "passing the buck" is the basis for reasoning about whether earlier actions in a control path can guarantee the precondition of a later action in the same control path.

The basic method involved in pre/post analysis is this: To ensure that a precondition on action B is always true, you trace the data flow back to each earlier action A that defines one of the data values that B uses. You attach a postcondition on action A that requires action A to define the values of its OUT data objects so that they meet the preconditions for the IN data objects of action B. If you do this for every possible action that might define the IN values used by B (looking at all the possible control paths), then you know that action B is safe—its precondition is now guaranteed to be satisfied, regardless of the execution path.

But you cannot usually stop with one step of pre/post analysis. You have only "passed the buck" to the earlier actions. Placing a postcondition on an earlier action may cause that action to fail in a new way. Hence it may now need a *precondition*, where it did not need one before. Thus another step of pre/post analysis may be needed to reason about this new precondition. You backtrace again to find where the IN variables of the earlier action are computed and attach a postcondition on these actions to guarantee the new precondition, and so forth.

Ultimately you want to "reason your way" back to reach statements that, even with new postconditions, will never fail— so they need no preconditions. And your chain of pre/post analysis then ends in success.

Suppose that the last action in a straight-line segment is:

$$PercentA := (A\ /\ Total)\ *\ 100;$$

which has the precondition:

PRECONDITION: $Total_{IN} <> 0$

To ensure the precondition is always satisfied, trace back down the execution path to find the action that *defines* the value of Total. Suppose this action is:

$$Total := A + B + C;$$

You put the postcondition on this action:

POSTCONDITION: $Total_{OUT} <> 0$

You have just "passed the buck" to the earlier action. Now the later action can never fail. Its precondition is always guaranteed to be true because the postcondition on the earlier action now guarantees it.

The catch is that the earlier action now will fail if the sum of $A+B+C$ happens to be zero. This action, with its new postcondition, now must have a precondition itself:

PRECONDITION: $A_{IN} + B_{IN} + C_{IN} <> 0$

The new precondition means that you must repeat your pre/post analysis from this earlier action. Suppose you proceed to trace the data flow back one step further, to find where the values of A, B, and C are defined. Let's suppose that you reach the prompt-and-read segment:

```
writeln ('Type three positive numbers.');
readln (A, B, C);
```

```
WHILE  (A <= 0)  OR  (B <= 0)  OR  (C <= 0)  DO
   BEGIN
     writeln ('Try again: all three numbers must be positive!');
     readln (A, B, C);
   END;
```

You attach the postcondition:

$$\text{POSTCONDITION: } A_{OUT} + B_{OUT} + C_{OUT} <> 0$$

to this segment. This postcondition guarantees that the later assignment to Total can never fail due to the sum being zero.

But now you see that the test in the WHILE loop already ensures that this postcondition must always be satisfied when the loop is complete. Success! Without changing the program at all, you have just used pre/post analysis to verify that the precondition, $Total_{IN} <> 0$, on the original action must always be satisfied. ∎

By using pre/post analysis to reason backward through a program's actions, you can try to determine if each precondition on an action is always satisfied. If your algorithm has been designed well, you should find that most preconditions are guaranteed to be satisfied. However, do not be surprised to find situations where you "can't be sure" because of the complexity of a particular control path. And, of course, you also hope to use this analysis to discover any hidden logic errors that might have entered your design.

□ □
Repairing Errors Discovered During Pre/Post Analysis

What if you find a precondition that is *not* guaranteed to be satisfied whenever the action is taken? Then you have identified a true *danger point*, where the program could fail. Or you may simply reach a point where you cannot be sure about a particular precondition—you have traced back as far as you can in the time available, and you still cannot be sure the precondition is always true. What should you do?

Several options need to be considered:

1. *Guard the action*. As discussed above, a guard with an alternative action may be the simplest protection.

2. *Redesign the action*. Often a precondition that cannot be guaranteed is a sign that your design of the action is wrong. The precondition says that there are cases that your action does not handle correctly, perhaps because you did not think about them during the design phase. You may need to rethink the whole action, and then redesign and recode that part of the program.

3. *Redesign the data representation*. A precondition that cannot be guaranteed may also be a sign that you have chosen the data representation poorly, perhaps because you want to represent some cases in the data that cannot be conveniently handled using the representation you have chosen. You may need to rethink the representation of one or more of your data objects, and then redesign and recode that part of the program. For example, you may find that you cannot be sure that the sum or product of Integer variables does not exceed MAXINT during a computation. To be safe, you might want to change the data types of the variables to Real so that a larger range of values can be safely used.

4. *"Fail gracefully."* Sometimes you may determine that the precondition defines a situation where you actually want the program to fail. For example, in a procedure that is to insert a new entry into a table, you might have the precondition "the table must have at least one more unused entry"—so that you have a place to make the insertion. But if the table is full, then what can the program do about it? A good approach is to make the program "fail gracefully" by displaying an error message such as:

TABLE ⟨table name⟩ IS FULL.   EXECUTION MUST TERMINATE.

and then take an action that forces program termination (such as calling the *Halt* procedure provided by most Pascal systems).

By failing gracefully, you insure that the program fails immediately and with an explanation rather than simply continuing to compute with "garbage" data values. For example, in the case of the full table, the solution to the problem may be to increase the size of the table (perhaps by changing the subscript range on an array). But such a change requires modifying the source program and recompiling it. So "failing gracefully" may be the best solution if the table ever does become full during program execution.

5. *Return a "failure" flag.* When working within a subprogram, a variation on the "fail gracefully" approach is to change the subprogram heading to include an additional parameter which can be used to signal to the caller that the subprogram has failed. This parameter might be a simple Boolean flag that signals "success" as TRUE or "failure" as FALSE. If there is more than one way that the subprogram might fail, you might define an enumerated type that names the various possible outcomes, including all potential causes of failure, such as:

OutcomeType = (TABLEFULL, BADENTRY, DUPLICATEENTRY, SUCCESS)

If a subprogram returns a success/failure flag, then the *caller* becomes responsible for checking the flag before using any other results of the subprogram. If the subprogram has failed, the caller might take an alternative action or itself "fail gracefully."

EXAMPLE

Suppose that a procedure InsertInTable has the heading:

PROCEDURE InsertInTable
　　　(Table: TableType　　　　IN/OUT
　　　NewEntry: EntryType)　　IN

PURPOSE/GOAL STATE: Insert NewEntry in Table.

In checking the procedure body, you discover that the actions will fail if the table happens to be full when the procedure is called. But the caller cannot be expected to check whether the table is full before making the call. Instead you modify the procedure heading to add a third parameter, a Boolean "success/failure" flag:

PROCEDURE InsertInTable
    (Table: TableType   IN/OUT
     NewEntry: EntryType   IN
     IsSuccessful: Boolean)   OUT

PURPOSE/GOAL STATE: Insert NewEntry in Table and set IsSuccessful = TRUE. If the table is already full, then make no change in Table and set IsSuccessful = FALSE. ■

EXERCISES

8.28 For each of the following segments, identify the precondition for the segment. Then provide a suitable guard and alternative control path so that the modified segment requires no precondition:

a. Assume array T has subscript range 1..500.

```
FOR I := 1 TO K DO
  BEGIN
    T[I] := 0;
  END;
```

b. Assume Ch of type Char, Digit of subrange 0..9.

```
Digit := ord (Ch) - ord ('0');
```

c. Assume all variables of type Integer.

```
Quotient := I DIV J;
Remainder := I MOD J;
```

d. Assume all variables of type Real.

```
Root1 := (-B + sqrt (B*B - 4*A*C)) / (2*A);
```

8.29 For each of the following program segments and given preconditions for an action, use pre/post analysis to determine if the precondition is always satisfied whenever the action is executed. Show any postconditions and new preconditions that arise during the pre/post analysis.

    a.   In the segment:

```
1    A := A*A;
2    D := D + A;
3    E := (A+B+C) / D;
4    B := 2*A;
5    C := A + B;
6    writeln (B, D, C, E);
7    D := sqrt (C);
8    F := A + B + C + D + E;
```

Assume line 7 has:

        PRECONDITION: $C_{IN} >= 0$.

    b.   In the segment:

```
1    IF B > 0 THEN
        BEGIN
2            X := B + 1;
        END
     ELSE
        BEGIN
3            X := 0;
        END;
4    C := 2 * X;
5    IF A > X THEN
        BEGIN
6            X := A - 2;
        END
7    ELSE IF X > A THEN
        BEGIN
8            C := B - 2;
        END
     ELSE
        BEGIN
9            B := C - 2;
10           X := X / B;
        END;
```

Assume line 10 has:

        PRECONDITION: $B_{IN} <> 0$.

USING ANALYSIS: IS THIS MODIFICATION SAFE?

Whenever you modify a program, either to complete a partially complete "prototype," correct an error, or enhance the program to meet new requirements, you have the potential to introduce new errors in parts of the program that had previously been correct. Many of these errors are the result of inadvertently changing the control flow or the data flow in the modified segment, so that either:

1. The path conditions for executing a path are changed,
2. The computation of some later result is changed, or
3. The precondition on some later action is no longer guaranteed to be satisfied.

We term a modification *safe* if it does not *inadvertently* change the control flow or data flow of the program.

Let's suppose that you are making one or more of the following kinds of modifications to your program:

- Change an existing action.
- Insert a new action.
- Delete an existing action.
- Move an action to an earlier or later point in a control path.
- Insert or delete control paths.
- Modify the tests that choose the control path.

And let's suppose that your modifications "in the small," taken in isolation from the surrounding parts of the program, are correct. That is, you have correctly coded any new statements you are inserting, and you have correctly made the desired changes in any statements that you are modifying. Obviously, if you make an error in changing the parts of the program that you want to change, then you have also introduced a bug, but that kind of error is much easier to spot and correct.

The errors that we are concerned with here are more difficult to find because they appear in actions *that you have not modified and that used to be correct*. So they are not errors that you are likely to notice easily without doing some analysis.

□ □
Two Classes of Safe Modifications

Remember that actions are connected to each other through their IN and OUT data objects and through the "flow" of data from an OUT object of one action that is used as an IN object of a later action in the same control path. If a modification introduces an error in some other part of the program, it must be due to something about the IN and OUT data objects that you used in the modification. Let's look at two *safe* situations first:

1. *No OUT data objects.* Modifications that only *use* the values of existing data objects are always safe. For example, if you want to insert this debug WRITE to display some values:

```
writeln ('DEBUG values, Total = ', Total, 'Count = ', Count);
```

you know the insertion is safe without any checking because this action only uses the IN data objects, Total and Count. Similarly, if you want to delete an action that has no OUT data objects, or move such an action to a new position, the modification is always safe. Thus you can safely insert or delete debug WRITE actions at any point in a program, or you can safely call a snapshot procedure to display a more complicated data object like an array or record, provided that the procedure has no OUT or IN/OUT parameters.

2. *New OUT data objects.* A second form of modification is also safe—a modification that introduces one or more *new data objects* (newly added to the declarations part) and that then uses only those data objects as OUT data objects in new or modified actions. Because existing actions are not using these new data objects, modifications that define and use the values of the new objects but that do not change the values of any existing data objects are always safe.

EXAMPLE

Dave's procedure contains the following loop to read and sum a sequence of fillup amounts, continuing until the user types a zero value:

```
Total := 0;
readln (Gallons);

WHILE Gallons <> 0 DO
   BEGIN
      Total := Total + Gallons;
      readln (Gallons);
   END;
```

Dave wants to modify the segment so that it also computes the average of the fillup values. For this modification he introduces two new variables, FillupCount and FillupAverage:

```
VAR
      FillupCount: Integer;
      FillupAverage: Real;
```

and three new actions to initialize and increment the counter variable and then compute the average:

```
Total := 0;
FillupCount := 0;
readln (Gallons);

WHILE Gallons <> 0 DO
  BEGIN
     Total := Total + Gallons;
     FillupCount := FillupCount + 1;
     readln (Gallons);
  END;

IF FillupCount <> 0 THEN
  BEGIN
     FillupAverage := Total / FillupCount;
```

Because the only OUT variables of the new actions are the new variables Fillup-Count and FillupAverage, Dave knows the modifications are safe—they cannot affect the correctness of the original loop or the correctness of any later actions. ■

□ □
Potentially Unsafe Modifications

The third situation is the one to watch out for: a modification that changes how the value of an *existing data object* is defined. Such modifications change the data flow and are always potentially unsafe. For example, if you insert a new statement that assigns a value to an old data object, or delete a READ or assignment statement, or move to a new position a procedure call that has an OUT parameter, you are changing the existing patterns of data flow in the program. Analysis skills are useful for checking such modifications.

EXAMPLE
Hacker Jack needs to make the same modification to the READ loop as Dave made in the example above. He introduces a new variable, FillupAverage, to store the computed average. But instead of introducing a new variable to store the count, Hacker Jack decides he can just *reuse an existing variable,* OldCount, that he had used earlier in the same procedure for another purpose. His modification looks correct; it matches Dave's version exactly except for using OldCount in place of Dave's FillupCount:

```
Total := 0;
OldCount := 0;
readln (Gallons);

WHILE Gallons <> 0 DO
  BEGIN
     Total := Total + Gallons;
     OldCount := OldCount + 1;
     readln (Gallons);
  END;

IF OldCount <> 0 THEN
  BEGIN
     FillupAverage := Total / OldCount;
```

But when he tests the modified procedure, several results that used to be computed correctly are no longer correct. What has happened?

Jack's modification has interrupted the data flow in the original program. Jack failed to notice that there were two *uses* of data object OldCount on the control path *after* the point where he made his changes. Figure 8.9 shows the problem.

Notice that Jack would not have noticed the errors caused by his modifications unless he checked all the *uses* of OldCount that followed his modifications, on every control path. ■

As the example illustrates, if a modification changes the value of an existing data object, say data object X (so that X is an OUT data object of the new actions), then the change *interrupts* the data flow from the definition of the value of X that precedes the change to any use of the value of X that follows the change, *on every control path affected by the change*.

□ □
The Principle of Safe Modification

Here is the general rule for checking modifications:

□ **Principle of Safe Modification**

To check if a modification is safe:

1. Find all the existing data objects (not newly declared) whose values are *defined* by the modified actions (including by inserted or deleted actions).

2. Find all *uses* of the values of those data objects in actions or tests that *follow* the point of the change on any control path. Each use that you identify may *sometimes* get a different value in the modified program than it got in the original program, because the action that defines that value on at least one control path has been changed.

3. Check each of the uses identified in 2 to see if the value defined by the modification is the value that should be used there. Also check any precondition on an action that uses the new value to be sure that it is still satisfied whenever the action is executed.

Notice the *sometimes* in this principle. Because there may be several control paths leading to a later use of a value, that later use may *sometimes* (on some control paths) get the same value it got in the unmodified program, and *sometimes* it may get the value defined by the modifications. Thus when testing the modified program, if your modifications have introduced a bug, you may *sometimes* fail to find it (and Murphy's Law will take over from there).

Whenever you check that a modification is safe, you have to check control paths from the point of modification all the way to the end of the subprogram body where the change is made (or until the modified value is lost).

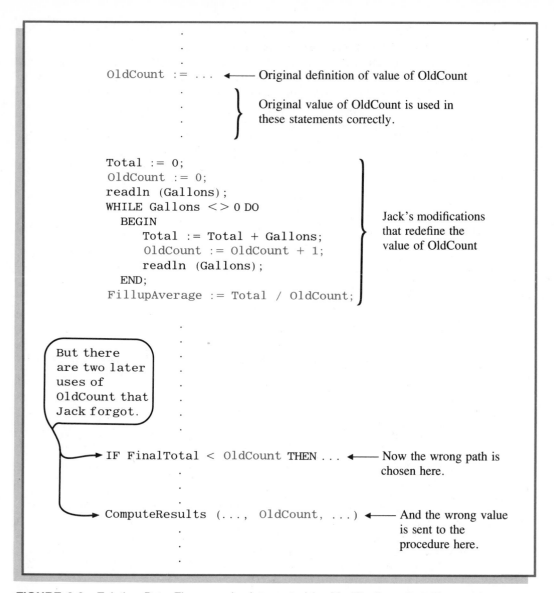

```
         .
         .
         .
    OldCount := ...  ◄──── Original definition of value of OldCount
         .
         .                    Original value of OldCount is used in
         .                }   these statements correctly.
         .
    Total := 0;
    OldCount := 0;
    readln (Gallons);
    WHILE Gallons <> 0 DO
      BEGIN                           Jack's modifications
        Total := Total + Gallons;     that redefine the
        OldCount := OldCount + 1;      value of OldCount
        readln (Gallons);
      END;
    FillupAverage := Total / OldCount;
         .
         .
         .
  But there
  are two later
  uses of
  OldCount that
  Jack forgot.
         .
         .
    IF FinalTotal < OldCount THEN ...  ◄──── Now the wrong path is
         .                                   chosen here.
         .
    ComputeResults (..., OldCount, ...)  ◄──── And the wrong value
         .                                     is sent to the
         .                                     procedure here.
         .
```

FIGURE 8-9 Existing Data Flow may be Interrupted by Modifications that Change the Values of Existing Data Objects

□ □

Avoid Reusing Old Variables

Hacker Jack, in the example above, introduced new errors by failing to check all the control paths. But he could have saved himself a lot of trouble if he had followed a simpler principle:

Jack did not have to use the existing variable OldCount as part of his modification, but he thought it would be easier to reuse the old variable than to declare a new one. Then he spent several hours finding and repairing the bugs that his modification introduced!

□ □

Using Safe Modification: Deleting a Statement

Let's look at a few typical examples of use of the Principle of Safe Modification. Deleting a statement requires only that you check for any later uses of the OUT variables of the statement being deleted:

EXAMPLE: *Deleting an Unnecessary Statement*

We are back at the consultant's table with Fred and Pat:

> *Fred:* "I've made several changes in my program during debugging, and now I'd like to clean it up before I turn it in to be graded. This assignment statement here looks like it can be deleted, but I'm not quite sure:

```
        .
        .
        .
X := Max - Y;
        .
        .
        .
```

> How can I check whether it is safe to delete this statement?"

> *Pat:* "Just use data flow analysis to determine if any later statement *uses* the value of X defined by this statement. You just need to check statements along each control path until you reach a statement that redefines the value of X. If the original value of X is never used, the assignment statement can be deleted safely."

Fred follows the control path forward and finds the READ statement:

```
        .
        .
        .
X := Max - Y;
        .
        .
        .
readln (U, V, W, X);
        .
        .
```

The READ redefines the value of X. He has found no statement that uses X before this statement is reached, so he concludes that it is safe to delete the original statement. ■

□ □
Using Safe Modification: Inserting a Statement

Inserting a statement requires an analysis of control paths both before and after the point of the insertion:

□ **Rule of Safe Insertion**

A statement may be safely inserted at a particular point in the program if:

1. The values of all its IN variables are *defined* at that point, on every control path, and
2. There are no later *uses* of its OUT variables, on any control path, unless the later use is intended to receive the new value defined by the inserted statement.

EXAMPLE: *Inserting a New Statement*

Fred: "I need to insert this assignment statement that I forgot (see Figure 8.10):

```
Average := (X + Y) / 2;
```

But I'm not quite sure if I can safely insert it at this point. Is there an easy way to find out?"

Pat: "Sure. First, look at whether the values of the IN variables, X and Y, are defined at that point."

Fred: "OK there. I've already read in the values for X and Y in an earlier READ statement."

Fred: Can I insert the statement "Average := (X+Y)/2" safely at the point indicated below?

```
        .
        .
        .

IF  (...)  THEN
   BEGIN
       readln  (X,  Y);
   END
ELSE
   BEGIN
       X  :=  0;
       Y  :=  0;
   END;
```

The values of IN variables X and Y are defined in this segment, on every control path.

```
        .
        .
        .
```

◀——— insertion point

Insertion point lies on every control path.

```
        .
        .
        .

W  :=  2  *  U  +  Average;
```

```
        .
        .
        .

IF Average  >=  0  THEN ...
```

Three later uses of the new value of Average, and no later uses of the old value of Average

```
        .
        .
        .

writeln ('Average  =  ', Average);
```

```
        .
        .
        .
```

FIGURE 8-10   Use Data Flow Analysis to Insert a Statement Safely

Pat: "Wait a minute—be sure you check *all the possible control paths.*"

Fred: "Well, you're right. One control path skips the READ statement, but in that case X and Y are assigned zero values, which would be the correct values for computing the average in that case."

Pat: "All right. Now check the control paths *leaving* the point of the insertion. Are there any uses of the OUT variable, Average, after the insertion?"

Fred: "Well, sure—why would I compute the average if I didn't use it! I see three places where the value of Average is used later."

Pat: "Take each use in turn and ask: Do I want to use the new value of Average at this point, or the old value (the value used before the insertion was made)?"

Fred: "OK there—I intend for all three uses of Average to get the new value."

Pat: "What about preconditions on any of those actions that use the new value of Average? Are they still guaranteed?"

Fred: "No preconditions here, so that's ok."

Pat: "One last check. Is there any control path that will bypass the newly inserted statement and still lead to one of the three later uses of Average?"

Fred: "OK there. I'm inserting at a point that is on every control path. Everybody gets the new value of Average."

Pat: "Everything checks out. It looks safe to make the mod." ∎

□ □

Using Safe Modification: Moving a Statement in One Control Path

Moving a statement to a new position is straightforward if only a single control path is affected. Let's suppose that you want to move a particular statement backward along the control path, so that it is executed earlier. The rule is:

> □ **Rule of Safe Backward Movement (One Control Path)**
>
> A statement may be safely moved backward along a control path to any earlier point until a statement is reached that either:
>
> 1. *Defines* the value of an IN variable of the statement, or
> 2. *Uses or defines* the value of an OUT variable of the statement.

EXAMPLE: *Moving a Statement to an Earlier Position*

Fred: "This procedure would be a lot easier to read if I could move this particular statement up closer to the start of the procedure body. Here is the statement:

$$\text{Total} := A + B + C;$$

What do I have to check to decide whether it can be moved safely? And how far up can I move it?"

Pat: "How many control paths contain this statement?"

Fred: "Only one—the procedure body is a straight-line segment."

Pat: "Then it is pretty easy to move it safely. You just need to trace *backward* along the control path from this statement until you come to:

    a. A statement that *uses* or *defines* the *old value* of the OUT variable, Total, or

    b. A statement that *defines* the value of one of the IN variables, A, B, or C.

"You can safely move it back to immediately follow that statement, or anywhere in between."

Fred's analysis identifies the statements shown in Figure 8.11 and he finds the "safe area" shown. ■

□□

Using Safe Modification: "Factoring" a Statement From Several Control Paths

Our final example involves moving a statement to a new position where several control paths are involved. Typically, this situation arises when you notice that the same statement appears in all the cases of an IF statement and it could be "factored" out—deleted from each case and just written once preceding the IF. Another similar situation is when a statement in a loop body is repeating exactly the same computation on each iteration and could be moved out to precede the loop where it would just be executed once.

In either situation, the rule for safe modification is like that for a single control path, but with all control paths considered. Let's just look at the rule for "factoring" a statement out of an IF:

□ **Rule of Safe Factoring of a Statement From An IF**

If *all* the cases of an IF conditional contain an identical statement, then the statement may safely be deleted from each case of the IF and inserted immediately before the entire IF, provided that:

1. The statement could safely be moved to be the *first statement in each case* of the IF, and

2. No OUT variable of the statement appears in any *test* used in the IF.

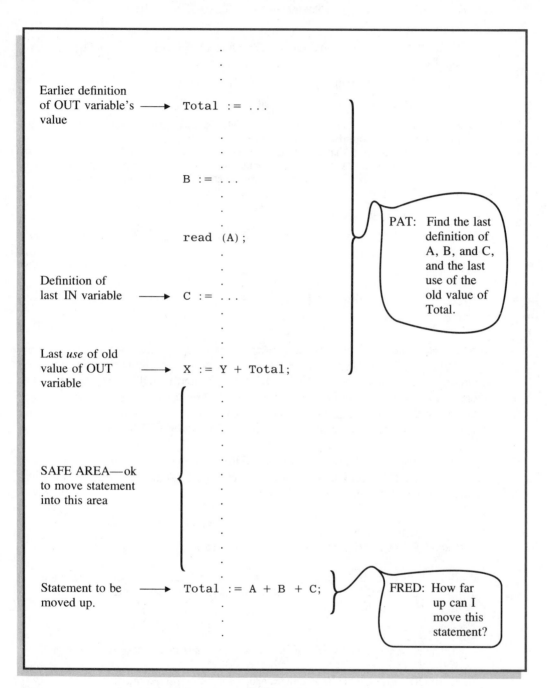

FIGURE 8-11 Use Analysis to Move a Statement Safely

Fred is looking at the statement "Total := Total + X" in each case of his IF statement:

```
IF X > 0 THEN
   BEGIN
      PosCount := PosCount + 1;
      Total := Total + X;
   END
ELSE
   BEGIN
      NegCount := NegCount + 1;
      Total := Total + X;
   END;
```

Fred: "The assignment 'Total := Total + X' appears in each case of this IF. Is it safe to 'factor' out this assignment and write the IF in the form:"

```
Total := Total + X;
IF X > 0 THEN
   BEGIN
      PosCount := PosCount + 1;
   END
ELSE
   BEGIN
      NegCount := NegCount + 1;
   END;
```

Pat: "First you need to check if you could safely move that assignment to the beginning of each case."

Fred: "You mean, would this form be ok?

```
IF X > 0 THEN
   BEGIN
      Total := Total + X;
      PosCount := PosCount + 1;
   END
ELSE
   BEGIN
      Total := Total + X;
      NegCount := NegCount + 1;
   END;
```

Sure—the value of Total could be computed first in both cases."

Pat: "OK, then just check if the OUT variable, Total, is used in any of the tests in the IF."

Fred: "No problem; there is only one test and it doesn't use Total."

Pat: "Then you are safe to make the change. But here's a question for you. Could you factor out that assignment in this form of the IF?"

```
IF  X > 0  THEN
   BEGIN
      PosCount := PosCount + 1;
      Total := Total + X;
   END
ELSE IF  X < 0  THEN
   BEGIN
      NegCount := NegCount + 1;
      Total := Total + X;
   END;
```

Fred: "Sure—you've got the same situation."

Pat: "Got you that time—there's one control path now that doesn't execute that assignment!"

Fred: "Give me a break! That's the default case path where X = 0, so inserting the assignment on that path wouldn't change the value of Total anyway."

Pat: "Not the same situation—you had to make a more complicated analysis to figure out that the change was safe in my version of that IF. The basic rule for safe factoring applies only when the statement being factored appears on *all control paths* through the IF." ∎

EXERCISES

8.30 Assume that procedure Proc3 has parameters classified: Proc3(IN, OUT). Determine which, if any, of the statements in the body of this procedure can be safely deleted:

```
PROCEDURE Proc2
      (A: Real;                {IN}
       VAR Total: Real;        {OUT}
       VAR Count: Integer);    {OUT}

   {PURPOSE/GOAL STATE: Compute values for Total and Count}

VAR
   B: Integer;
   C: Integer;
   D: Integer;
   Next: Integer;
```

```
         BEGIN
1            read (B,C);
2            D := (A+B+C) DIV 3;
3            Count := A + 1;
4            Next := B + C - 1;
5            Total := 2 * D + A;
6            Proc3 (Total, Count);
         END;
```

8.31 Assume that the parameters of procedure ComputeValues are classified: ComputeValues(IN, OUT). Can the statement "X := X + 1" be factored out of each action in the following conditional and placed immediately before the conditional? Why or why not?

```
IF Z > 2*X + Y THEN
  BEGIN
      ComputeValues (Z, Y);
      X := X + 1;
  END
ELSE
    BEGIN
      Z := 2*Z + Y;
      X := X + 1;
      ComputeValues (X, Y);
    END;
```

8.32 Can the statement "Largest := A[Maxposn]" be factored out of each action in the following conditional and placed immediately before the conditional? Why or why not?

```
IF A[2] > A[3]  THEN
  BEGIN
      IF A[2] > A[1]  THEN
        BEGIN
            MaxPosn := 2;
        END
      ELSE
        BEGIN
            MaxPosn := 1;
        END;
      Largest := A[Maxposn];
  END
ELSE IF A[3] > A[1]  THEN
    BEGIN
      MaxPosn := 3;
      Largest := A[Maxposn];
    END
```

```
ELSE
  BEGIN
     MaxPosn := 1;
    `Largest := A[Maxposn];
  END;
```

8.33   Hacker Jack has some more questions about his code segment:

```
1    readln (A, B, C);
2    S := A + B + C;
3    T1 := A >= B;
4    S := S / 2;
5    T2 := B >= C;
6    SA := S - A;
7    T3 := A >= C;
8    SB := S - B;
9    T4 := B > A;
10   SC := S - C;
11   MaxA := T1 AND T3;
12   P := 2 * S;
13   writeln ('Sides = ', A, B, C, ' Perimeter = ', P);
14   MaxB := T2 AND NOT T1;
15   B := S * SA * SB * SC;
16   MaxC := NOT T2 AND NOT T3;
17   C := sqrt (B);
18   writeln ('Is A the largest? ', MaxA);
19   writeln ('Is B the largest? ', MaxB);
20   writeln ('Is C the largest? ', MaxC);
21   writeln ('Area = ', C);
```

See if you can answer Jack's questions:
   a.   Tell me if it's safe to:
Delete the statement in line 11? Why ?
Delete the statement in line 10? Why?
Delete the statement in line 9? Why?
   b.   What is the line number of the earliest line to which I could safely move each of the following statements:
The statement in line 12?
The statement in line 14?
The statement in line 15?
   c.   I want to delete line 14 and insert a new definition of MaxB:

```
MaxB := T2 AND T4;
```

What are the numbers of the lines that bracket the area where it would be safe to insert this statement?

d. I want to add one to A before I display it in line 13. What are the numbers of the lines that bracket the area where it would be safe to insert this statement? I don't want to change the computation of any of the other values.

8.34 For each of the following pairs of segments, determine if their execution order can be reversed without changing the result of the computation (that is, can Seg1 be executed either before Seg2 or after Seg2 without changing the results?). Explain why or why not.

a. Seg1:
```
A := 2;
C := P + X;
D := 2*B + C;
```

Seg2:
```
P := sqrt (X);
Q := X + Y;
R := Y / 2;
```

b. Seg1:
```
P := 2;
C := P + X;
D := 2*B + C;
```

Seg2:
```
P := sqrt (X);
Q := X + Y;
R := Y / 2;
```

c. Seg1:
```
A := 2;
B := 3;
C := X + A;
D := 2*B + C;
```

Seg2:
```
P := sqrt (X);
Q := X + Y;
R := Y / 2;
```

8.35 State a *Rule for Safe Forward Movement* for one control path that gives the conditions to check in order to safely move a statement *forward* along a single control path so that it is executed later. Then apply your rule to answer the following questions about the statements in Hacker Jack's segment above (Exercise 8.33):

a. Can I safely move line 5 forward to immediately precede line 16? Why or why not?

b. Can I safely move line 6 forward to immediately precede line 15? Why or why not?

c. Can I safely move all the assignment statements that participate in computing the value of MaxA displayed in line 18 forward so that they immediately precede line 18? (Keeping them in the same sequence, of course.) Why or why not?

8.36 State a *Rule for Safe Factoring of a Statement Out of a Loop* that gives the conditions to check in order to safely move a statement from the body of a WHILE loop to a position immediately preceding the entire loop. Then use your rule to answer the following question:

Is it safe to factor the statement in line 3 out of the body of the following loop and place it immediately before the loop? Why or why not?

```
1    WHILE X > 0 DO
        BEGIN
2           Total := Total + X;
3           Next := 2 * Y;
4           X := X DIV 2;
        END;
```

□□□ 8.9
NEW STRATEGIES FOR TESTING AND DEBUGGING

The analysis methods discussed in this chapter provide powerful tools for checking the correctness of a program. They also suggest how you might improve your strategy for testing and debugging a program. Here are some new guidelines:

1. *Use analysis skills and limit the amount of debug output that the program displays.* Analysis methods are useful for finding errors quickly. If you know which segment of code to analyze, you can usually find an error more quickly using analysis than using additional test runs and additional debug WRITE statements. But you cannot analyze the whole program—you have to limit your analysis to a reasonably small segment. Thus your strategy in using debug WRITE statements should be to display just enough information with just enough frequency so that you know the values of the key data objects at the end of execution of each major segment of the program. Then let your analysis skills do the rest. It is easier than sorting through mountains of debug output.

2. *Use debug WRITE's to display the control path.* Analysis is made much easier if you know the control path that was followed during execution. Remember that an error can cause execution to follow the wrong control path, and following the wrong path can cause other results to be computed incorrectly. If you do not know the control path taken, then you have to analyze all possible control paths to find the error. So plan your debug WRITE's (or automatic program tracing, if available) so that you can always determine from the debug output exactly what control path was executed. Do not forget to include the number of loop iterations executed in each loop.

3. *Use path conditions to guide the choice of test data for path testing.* Path testing is a good testing strategy—choose test data that "exercises" each of the control paths (limiting the number of iterations of each loop, of course). We discussed this strategy back in Chapter 4. Now you can use your analysis skills to find the path condition for a path in a subprogram body that you want to test, and the path condition tells you immediately what range of test data values can be used to exercise that path.

4. *Use a DEBUGGING flag to allow easy retesting after modification.* Instead of taking your debug WRITE statements out of the program once you have completed testing it, use a debugging flag (as discussed in Chapter 5) and guard each debug WRITE with a conditional:

```
IF DEBUGGING THEN
      ... debug WRITE statements ...
```

Then when you modify the program, it is easy to retest it, simply by changing the defined value of DEBUGGING from FALSE to TRUE and recompiling the program.

5. *Test preconditions within your debugging segments.* Modifications to a program can invalidate the pre/post analysis that you used when you decided that a statement with a precondition did not need to be guarded. You can include a test of a precondition as part of your debug WRITE code if you use the DEBUGGING flag discussed in 4.

EXAMPLE

Suppose your program includes the assignment:

```
Average := Total / Count;
```

which has:

PRECONDITION: $Count_{IN} <> 0$

You use pre/post analysis to determine that Count can never be zero on any program path, so you do not need to guard the assignment. However, what if a modification at some earlier point in the program changes the way Count is computed? Then your pre/post analysis may no longer be valid.

To allow the precondition to be checked automatically when testing after a modification, include a test of the precondition immediately before the assignment:

```
IF DEBUGGING AND ⟨precondition is FALSE⟩ THEN
      ⟨display an error message⟩
```

For example, immediately before the assignment to Average, you might include:

```
IF DEBUGGING AND (Count = 0) THEN
    BEGIN
        DISPLAY:    "ERROR in procedure ⟨name⟩;
                     Precondition violated;
                     Count = 0 when Average is computed."
    END
```

EXERCISES

8.37 Given the conditional segment:

```
IF A[2] > A[3] THEN
  BEGIN
    IF A[2] > A[1] THEN
      BEGIN
        MaxPosn := 2;
      END
    ELSE
      BEGIN
        MaxPosn := 1;
      END;
    Largest := A[Maxposn];
  END
ELSE IF A[3] > A[1] THEN
  BEGIN
    MaxPosn := 3;
    Largest := A[Maxposn];
  END
ELSE
  BEGIN
    MaxPosn := 1;
    Largest := A[Maxposn];
  END;
```

a. Write the path conditions for each control path in the conditional, and then make a list of the (literal) test data values you would choose to test each path exactly once.

b. You are allowed to insert a single debug WRITE *immediately after* the entire conditional segment. Of the five values used or defined in the segment, Largest, Maxposn, A[1], A[2], and A[3], you want to display the *fewest values* that will allow you to decide *exactly which control path was executed* in the conditional. Which values would you choose to display?

■ ■ ■
REVIEW QUESTIONS

8.1 Explain why skill in *analyzing programs* is an important part of programming. Name three stages during the construction of a program where program analysis is needed.

8.2 List the *three basic types* of program analysis discussed in this chapter.

8.3 List and explain briefly the two basic questions asked in *control flow analysis*.

8.4 For each of the different types of actions in a program segment, what is included about that action when you write down the elements of a *control path* through the segment?

8.5   If a control path includes a *subprogram call,* does it also include the statements in the body of the called subprogram? Why or why not?

8.6   What is an *iteration?*

8.7   Explain how to *describe a control path* without writing down the elements of the path, given a program listing.

8.8   What is *spaghetti code?*

8.9   What is a *statement label?* What is a *GOTO statement?* How are these two program elements related to spaghetti code?

8.10   Explain how to use a *control flow diagram* or *flow chart* to diagram the control paths through a segment.

8.11   How are *flow charts* related to *spaghetti code?*

8.12   What is a *path condition* for a control path through a program segment?

8.13   When is a path condition a *contradiction?* What does this indicate about the control path?

8.14   Explain how to determine the IN, OUT, and IN/OUT data objects of an AS-SIGN, DISPLAY, READ, or CALL action. Include simple data objects, records, arrays, and strings.

8.15   When an action refers to an array element designated by a *subscript expression,* such as "A[I]", give three rules for determining how to classify A and I as IN, OUT, or IN/OUT.

8.16   Given a program segment and an action that *uses* a data value, explain how to determine all the places where that value might be *defined*.

8.17   Given a program segment and an action that *defines* a data value, explain how to determine all the places where that value might be *lost*.

8.18   Given a program segment and an action that *defines* a data value, explain how to determine all the places where that value might be *used*.

8.19   What is a *flow-through value* in a program segment?

8.20   How do you determine the IN, OUT, and IN/OUT data objects of a *program segment?* Include both loops and conditionals.

8.21   Explain how to construct a *data-flow diagram* of a straight-line segment. What does a data-flow diagram tell you about the *sequence* in which the actions must be executed?

8.22   Describe how to determine the actions and data objects that participate in *computing a particular result* of a segment.

8.23   What is *back substitution?* When can back substitution be used to construct a *mathematical formula* describing how a particular result is computed in a segment?

8.24   How can you use data flow and control flow analysis to find errors due to *uninitialized* data objects?

8.25   Describe how to identify the actions and data objects that participate in *determining the control path* executed in a segment.

8.26   Explain how to use *back substitution* to determine a *path condition* for a control path.

8.27   What is a *precondition* of an action?

8.28   Why is an action with a precondition a *potential source of error* in a program?

8.29   Name and briefly explain at least one way that each of the basic statement types might *fail*: ASSIGN, DISPLAY, READ, CALL, IF, WHILE, and FOR.

8.30   What is a *guard* for an action with a precondition?

8.31   What is a *postcondition* for an action? How can a postcondition cause an action to *fail* in a new way?

8.32   Explain how to use *pre/post analysis* to determine whether the precondition of an action can be *guaranteed* to be satisfied whenever the action is executed.

8.33   Name and briefly explain five *modification options* to consider when you find an action with a *precondition* that cannot be guaranteed true in all cases.

8.34   What is a *safe modification* to a program segment?

8.35   Name and briefly explain two types of modification that are *always safe*.

8.36   Explain how to identify a *potentially unsafe* modification.

8.37   The *Principle of Safe Modification* states what you need to check to determine if a potentially unsafe modification is safe. What are those checks?

8.38   Why is it a mistake to *reuse an old variable for a new purpose* when modifying a program?

8.39   Describe what you should check to ensure safety when making each of the following types of modifications in a program:
Delete a statement.
Insert a statement.
Move a statement backward to an earlier point in one control path.
Factor a statement out of all cases of an IF.

8.40   Briefly explain four new *strategies for testing and debugging* that are related to use of program analysis skills.

■ ■ ■
PROGRAMMING PROBLEMS

"Cleanroom" program development is a phrase coined by Harlan Mills to describe software that is developed in an environment with one peculiar property: *The programmers are not allowed to do ANY testing of the program they develop.* The program development team designs the program, codes it, analyzes it, and verifies its correctness using the best methods that they have available. But they never are allowed to actually run the program and test it. When they are sure it will work correctly, flawlessly, from the first time it is run, they hand it out of their "cleanroom" to the testing team—the group that actually tests the program.

"Cleanroom" program development puts your analysis skills to the ultimate test— finding *every error* in the design and coding of a program by using analysis alone, rather than testing combined with analysis. The goal is to have a program that runs correctly from the first time it is ever executed.

Try your hand at "cleanroom" program development with the following problems. You are allowed to enter the program and compile it to check for syntax errors, but you are not allowed to execute any part of the program. When designing the program, use all the methods we have discussed, especially stating the requirements carefully first and making use of abstractions to control the complexity of the task. And analyze and verify each part of the program separately before you put the parts together in the final program.

When you are finished, give the program to your instructor or a friend, with the claim: *This program is guaranteed to run correctly*—test it as much as you like, you will not be able to break it!

8.1 *Counting Characters.* Do programming problem 7.2 (Counting characters) from the end of Chapter 7 as a "cleanroom" problem.

8.2 *Binary to Decimal Conversion.* As a "cleanroom" problem, write a program that will read in a binary number as a sequence of bits (zeros and ones) and compute and display the equivalent decimal value. The binary number represents a positive integer value. Allow the user to type any sequence of zeros and ones, up to some maximum, such as 16 bits. For example, the dialogue might be:

> *Program:* Type a binary number of 16 or fewer bits.
> *User:* 011101
> *Program:* 011101 in binary = 29 in decimal

If you do not remember how to convert between numbers in two different number bases, such as base 2 (binary) and base 10 (decimal), look up the algorithm in an elementary mathematics text before you begin.

8.3 *Grades Statistics.* As a "cleanroom" problem, write a program that will allow the user to enter a list of positive integers representing the grades of students on an exam. Each number is in the range from zero to 99. There are at most 500 numbers entered. A negative value ends the list entered. The program should compute and display:

- The highest grade and lowest grade in the list.
- The average of the grades.
- The number of grades that are in each ten point range, 90-99, 80-89, 70-79, and so forth.
- The grade that appears *most frequently* in the list.

8.4 *Extracting a Number Hidden in a Secret Message.* In the spy world, messages often contain hidden numbers. The trick is to send a seemingly ordinary message but include the digits of the number in the correct order spread throughout the message. For example, to send the telephone number 503-973-2009, you might hide the digits in this message:

"Having a wonderful time. It's 50 degrees today and the wind is blowing at 39 miles an hour. Yesterday it got up to 73. There are about 200 people here on a tour, packed into 9 buses. What a crowd! See you next week. Love. J."

As a "cleanroom" problem, write a program that will read a message that the user types and extract the hidden number. After the user has typed the complete message, the program should display the hidden number. Limit the number to a maximum of twenty digits.

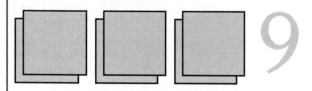

More About Conditionals

CHAPTER GOALS

When you have mastered the content of this chapter you should be able to:

- Design and code *conditional actions* that have many different cases and sub-cases, using IF and CASE statements.
- Determine if the cases in a conditional action are *mutually exclusive* or *nonexclusive.*
- Determine if a set of tests is *mutually exclusive* and *exhaustive.*
- Design the *default case* of a conditional action.
- Determine the *path conditions* for each control path in a complex conditional.
- Use the rules of *negation* and *De Morgan's Laws* to simplify a path condition.
- Identify *redundant tests.*
- Explain the *punctuation rules* for Pascal, including the use of *compound statements* and *empty statements.*

A *conditional action* is an action that chooses among two or more alternative ways to accomplish its result. In this chapter we advance from the simple IF conditional actions of the previous chapters to more complex conditional actions that may have many different cases, some of which may include nested sub-cases. In a larger program, you often find that such complex conditional actions are required. Using good design principles will simplify their design, coding, and analysis.

In Pascal, a conditional action would usually be coded with one or more IF statements. Pascal also provides a CASE statement that allows certain kinds of conditional actions to be coded more easily. We begin by looking at these various forms of conditional action, in pseudo-code and in Pascal.

□□□ **9.1**
CONDITIONAL ACTIONS: IF AND CASE

The IF form of conditional action is familiar from the preceding chapters, but let's look more deeply at this seemingly simple construct. The general form in pseudo-code is (Pascal only adds semicolons and BEGIN-END pairs):

```
IF ⟨test-1⟩ THEN
      ⟨actions to take if test-1 returns TRUE⟩
ELSE IF ⟨test-2⟩ THEN
      ⟨actions to take if test-2 returns TRUE⟩
   …
ELSE
      ⟨default case - actions to take if no test returns TRUE⟩
```

Remember that you can include as many tests and action lists as you want in a single IF. The final default case can be omitted entirely.

Several things are important about this conditional statement:

1. *The cases are "mutually exclusive," meaning that only one set of actions is chosen for execution.* Regardless of the tests used, each time an IF is executed, only one set of actions (one case) is chosen for execution. We say that the cases are *mutually exclusive*.

2. *The order of the cases can make a difference in the choice of actions taken.* The tests are evaluated in sequence, and the first test that returns a TRUE result leads to the actions taken. When an IF is executed, several of the tests may actually give a TRUE result for the program state, but the only action taken is that associated with the *first* test that returns TRUE. In such a situation, reordering the cases in the IF will make a difference in the choice of actions.

3. *The final ELSE case is the "default" case—the actions are taken only if no test returns TRUE.* The default case has no test associated with it, so it is the case taken "as a last resort." If the default case is omitted, then there are no actions taken when no test returns TRUE, and execution of the conditional action has no effect on the program state.

4. *Any case can have "sub-cases."* The actions for one case may include another IF that breaks that case into *sub-cases*. For example:

```
IF ⟨test-1⟩ THEN
        IF ⟨sub-case-test⟩ THEN
                ⟨actions for first sub-case of first case⟩
        ELSE
                ⟨actions for default sub-case of first case⟩
ELSE IF ⟨test-2⟩ THEN
        ⟨actions for second case⟩
ELSE IF ⟨test-3⟩ THEN
        ...
```

Because of the possibility of multiple cases and sub-cases, complex IF conditional statements may have many control paths and may be difficult to design and analyze correctly.

□ □

The CASE Statement in Pseudo-code

Now let's look at a new form of conditional action—the Pascal CASE statement. The CASE statement does not express any conditional actions that cannot be expressed as IF actions, but it does allow a common form of conditional action to be expressed more easily. Our pseudo-code for a CASE conditional action is similar to the Pascal CASE statement:

```
⟨CASE-conditional-action⟩ ::=
        CASE ⟨test-expression⟩ OF
            ⟨value-list⟩:
                    ⟨action-list⟩
            {⟨value-list⟩:
                    ⟨action-list⟩}
            [ELSE
                ⟨default-case-actions⟩]
        END
    WHERE
        ⟨test-expression⟩ ::=
            A data object name or Pascal expression whose value is to be used to
            determine which ⟨action-list⟩ to execute. The data object is usually of
            an enumerated or subrange type.
```

⟨value-list⟩ ::= ⟨data-value⟩ {, ⟨data-value⟩}
⟨data-value⟩ ::=
    A literal value or the name of a defined constant (not a Real value or string).
⟨action-list⟩ ::=
    A list of actions to be executed, or "NO ACTION" if no action is needed for this case.
⟨default-case-actions⟩ ::=
    Actions to be executed if the value of the test expression does not match any value in one of the value lists.

□

Meaning: When a CASE statement is executed, the following steps are taken:

1. The ⟨test-expression⟩ is evaluated to give a value, K.

2. The ⟨value-list⟩ that contains the value K is found and the actions in the ⟨action-list⟩ associated with that ⟨value-list⟩ are executed. If the value K does not appear in any value-list, then the ⟨default-case-actions⟩ are executed.

3. Execution continues with the actions following the end of the CASE.

EXAMPLE   The pseudo-code CASE action:

```
CASE Today.Month OF
    1:
        ⟨actions for Month field = January⟩
    2, 12:
        ⟨actions for Month field = February or December⟩
    3, 4, 5, 6, 7, 8, 9, 10, 11:
        ⟨actions for Month field = March–November⟩
    ELSE
        ⟨actions for an invalid Month field value⟩
END
```

has the same meaning as the IF:

```
IF Today.Month = 1 THEN
    ⟨actions for Month field = January⟩
ELSE IF (Today.Month = 2) OR (Today.Month = 12) THEN
    ⟨actions for Month field = February or December⟩
ELSE IF (Today.Month >= 3) AND (Today.Month <= 11) THEN
    ⟨actions for Month field = March–November⟩
ELSE
    ⟨actions for an invalid Month field value⟩
```

■

    As the example shows, the CASE form of conditional action provides a convenient alternative to a long sequence of IF...ELSE IF... tests.

□ □
The Pascal CASE Statement

The Pascal CASE statement matches our pseudo-code, with three exceptions:

1. In Pascal, insert BEGIN-END pairs around each list of actions and a semicolon after each END.
2. If an action list is "NO ACTION" then only the semicolon is written in the Pascal code.
3. In standard Pascal, there is no ELSE clause in a CASE statement to handle the "default case", where no value in any value list matches the value of the test expression.

In standard Pascal, the default case is treated as an error. Some Pascal systems may terminate program execution; others may simply ignore the default case and execute no action at all for the CASE statement. However, many Pascal systems provide the ELSE clause as an extension to the standard Pascal CASE statement. Check your local *Pascal User's Manual* before writing a CASE with an ELSE clause.

If your system does not provide the ELSE option, you can write the default case by using an IF that guards the CASE statement:

```
IF NOT ⟨test for the default case⟩ THEN
  BEGIN
    CASE ... OF
      ...              --CASE statement without the ELSE
    END;
  END
ELSE
  BEGIN
    ⟨default case actions⟩
  END
```

EXAMPLE   Judy's pseudo-code contains the CASE conditional:

```
CASE LetterGrade OF
  'A':
        ⟨actions for an A grade⟩
  'B':
        ⟨actions for a B grade⟩
  'C':
        NO ACTION
  'D', 'F':
        ⟨actions for a D or F grade⟩
  ELSE
      DISPLAY: "ERROR: Invalid letter grade."
END
```

Judy uses a standard Pascal system that does not provide an ELSE clause option. Thus, in coding her CASE in Pascal she guards the CASE with an IF:

```
IF LetterGrade IN ['A'..'D', 'F'] THEN
  BEGIN
    CASE LetterGrade OF
      'A':
        BEGIN
            ⟨actions for an A grade⟩
        END;

      'B':
        BEGIN
            ⟨actions for a B grade⟩
        END;

      'C':     ;     {NO ACTION}

      'D', 'F':
        BEGIN
            ⟨actions for a D or F grade⟩
        END;
    END;
  END
ELSE
  BEGIN
    writeln ('ERROR: Invalid letter grade.');
  END;
```

EXERCISES

9.1 Express each of the following IF pseudo-code actions as a CASE pseudo-code action. Then code the CASE action as a Pascal CASE statement. Assume a standard Pascal system that does not provide an ELSE option.

a. Suppose a data object, Clock, is of type ClockStatus, defined as:

ClockStatus = (OFF, CLOCKON, RADIOON, TAPEON, ALARM1SET, ALARM2SET)

The IF is:

IF Clock = CLOCKON THEN
    ⟨action-1⟩

ELSE IF (Clock = ALARM1SET) OR (Clock = ALARM2SET) THEN
    ⟨action-2⟩

```
        ELSE IF (Clock = OFF) THEN
                ⟨action-3⟩

    ELSE
            ⟨action-4⟩
```

b. Suppose data object InputChar is of type Char and the IF is:

```
IF (InputChar = '+') OR (InputChar = '−') THEN
        ⟨action-1⟩
ELSE IF (InputChar = '*') OR (InputChar = '/') THEN
        ⟨action-2⟩
ELSE IF InputChar = '%' THEN
        ⟨action-3⟩
ELSE
        ⟨action-4⟩
```

c. Suppose data object GameScore is of subrange type ScoreRange, defined as:

$$ScoreRange = -5..5$$

The IF is:

```
IF (GameScore > 1) AND (GameScore < 5) THEN
        ⟨action-1⟩
ELSE IF (GameScore < 0) AND (GameScore > −5) THEN
        ⟨action-2⟩
ELSE IF GameScore = 5 THEN
        ⟨action-3⟩
ELSE
        ⟨action-1⟩
```

□□□ 9.2
DESIGNING THE STRUCTURE OF A CONDITIONAL ACTION

Suppose your program requires a complex conditional action that has many cases and sub-cases. To design such a conditional, you need a step-by-step plan of attack. Remember our standard approach: DEFINE, then REFINE.

□ □
A Design Plan

A good plan of attack is to begin by making a table of the cases that have to be considered. This is the DEFINE step. For each case, give it an informal name (or number), describe how you test for that case, and tell what action needs to be taken:

CASE	TEST	ACTION
⟨case name⟩	⟨how to test for it⟩	⟨what to do if you find it⟩
⟨case name⟩	⟨how to test for it⟩	⟨what to do if … ⟩
…	…	…

At this early stage, do not worry about the order in which you write down the cases or the details of the tests and actions; those decisions can come later, as the REFINE step. You want the big picture first.

For the actions, consider the possibility that some cases may require no action. If so, simply write NO ACTION in that spot. Also you may find that two cases need the same action. If so, write SAME ACTION AS CASE ⟨case name⟩ for the action of one of the cases.

□ □
Default Case

Complete your table of cases by considering the *default case*. The last line of your table should always be:

DEFAULT CASE   ⟨actions for default case⟩

Notice that there is no ⟨test⟩ for the default case.

For the default case, consider three possibilities:

1. *No default case.* If the cases you listed exhaust all the possibilities, then the default case should never happen. Write the DEFAULT CASE line with an ERROR action:

DEFAULT CASE   ERROR: This case should never happen.

2. *No action in the default case.* If you want to take an action only in the cases you have listed and take no action otherwise, then the default case line should be:

DEFAULT CASE   NO ACTION

3. *A case that covers "all cases not mentioned above."* If your table includes all the "special cases," and in every other case you want to take the same action, then that action should be the default case action:

DEFAULT CASE ⟨action for all cases not listed above⟩

EXAMPLE

Roger is writing a program to keep track of the inventory of books at the college bookstore. The store sets their markup as a percentage of a book's base price, based on the type of book:

BOOK TYPE	MARKUP
Text–Used	15%
Text–New	20%
Reference	30%
General	35%
Magazine	40%

At one point, Roger's program needs to compute the markup for a book given its type. His initial design just sketches out the cases to be considered, based on the preceding table:

CASE	TEST	ACTION
Text–Used	??	Markup := 15
Text–New	??	Markup := 20
Reference	??	Markup := 30
General	??	Markup := 35
Magazine	??	Markup := 40
DEFAULT CASE		ERROR: Unexpected book type.

The TEST column is not filled in because Roger is not yet sure of the data representation to be used for a book. ■

☐ ☐
Sub-cases

Before you leave the DEFINE stage, explore the actions for each case to determine if one or more of the cases will itself split into sub-cases. If so, it is simplest if you also list the sub-cases in the table, so that you can see what is involved in each:

CASE	TEST	ACTION
⟨case name⟩	⟨how to test for it⟩	SUB-CASES AS LISTED BELOW
⟨sub-case-1⟩	⟨sub-case-1 test⟩	⟨sub-case-1 action⟩
⟨sub-case-2⟩	⟨sub-case-2 test⟩	⟨sub-case-2 action⟩
⟨second case⟩	⟨how to test for it⟩	⟨what to do...⟩
...	...	...
DEFAULT CASE		⟨default case action⟩

EXAMPLE

The bookstore decides to use a different markup for textbooks depending on whether the book is hardcover or softcover:

BOOK TYPE	MARKUP
Text–Used	
Soft-cover	10%
Hard-cover	15%
Text–New	
Soft-cover	15%
Hard-cover	20%

Roger's design now becomes:

CASE	TEST	ACTION
Text–Used	??	SUBCASES BELOW
Soft-cover	??	Markup := 10
Hard-cover	??	Markup := 15
Text–New	??	SUBCASES BELOW
Soft-cover	??	Markup := 15
Hard-cover	??	Markup := 20
Reference	??	Markup := 30
General	??	Markup := 35
Magazine	??	Markup := 40
DEFAULT CASE		ERROR: Unexpected book type.

What you have done at this point is to use the table to sketch out the various control paths that the conditional action must include. Each case and sub-case represents a different control path.

□ □
Mutually Exclusive and Nonexclusive Cases

Once you have sketched out the design of a complex conditional to see exactly what cases need to be treated, you need to ask a key question: are the cases *mutually exclusive* or *nonexclusive*? The answer determines whether you need only a single IF or CASE action to express the conditional in pseudo-code, or whether several IF's or CASES's will be required. The distinction is this:

□ **Mutually Exclusive Cases**

The cases are *mutually exclusive* if *exactly one case* should be chosen for execution each time the conditional action is executed.

□ **Nonexclusive Cases**

The cases are *nonexclusive* if *as many as apply* (all those cases where the test returns TRUE) should be chosen for execution each time the conditional action is executed. Possibly no cases, possibly one or several cases, or possibly all cases might be executed.

EXAMPLES

Assigning letter grades based on exam scores is an example of a conditional with *mutually exclusive cases*. Only one of the actions is taken for a given value of Score:

CASE	TEST	ACTION
A	Score >= 90	Grade := 'A'
B	80 <= Score < 90	Grade := 'B'
C	70 <= Score < 80	Grade := 'C'
D	60 <= Score < 70	Grade := 'D'
F	Score < 60	Grade := 'F'
DEFAULT CASE		ERROR: Should never get here.

Giving extra credit for several optional homework assignments is an example of a conditional with *nonexclusive cases*. In the following conditional, the student may get extra credit points for each of three possible extra credit assignments, allowing zero to fifteen total extra credit points:

CASE	TEST	ACTION
#1	ExtraCredit1 = COMPLETE	Score := Score + 3
#2	ExtraCredit2 = COMPLETE	Score := Score + 7
#3	ExtraCredit3 = COMPLETE	Score := Score + 5
DEFAULT CASE		NO ACTION

Sometimes, at an early stage of design, you may find that you have a mix of cases—several nonexclusive groups of mutually exclusive cases. In such a situation, separate each group of mutually exclusive cases into a different table before you go any further. Never mix exclusive and nonexclusive cases in the same table.

EXAMPLE

Professor Reynolds likes complicated grading schemes. In one class he gives four exams and three extra credit assignments. If a student takes all four exams, they are averaged to get his final grade, but if only three are taken, then the three are averaged. If only two are taken, then the student must take a makeup exam. One or no exams taken means the student is dropped from the course. The extra credit problems are worth 2, 4, and 6 points, respectively, on the final grade.

As a first try at putting this grading scheme into a program, you might write the cases:

CASE	TEST	ACTION
4exams	ExamCount = 4	Average all exam scores.
3exams	ExamCount = 3	Drop zero score, average rest.
2exams	ExamCount = 2	Set NeedsMakeup flag.
Drop	ExamCount = 0 or 1	Set MustDrop flag.
Extra1	ExtraCredit1 = COMPLETE	Add 2 to score.
Extra2	ExtraCredit2 = COMPLETE	Add 4 to score.
Extra3	ExtraCredit3 = COMPLETE	Add 6 to score.
DEFAULT CASE		NO ACTION

However, the first four cases are mutually exclusive with each other and the last three are nonexclusive with each other and with the first four. Thus, there really are four separate conditionals involved, each with its own default action:

CASE	TEST	ACTION
4exams	ExamCount = 4	Average all exam scores.
3exams	ExamCount = 3	Drop zero score, average rest.
2exams	ExamCount = 2	Set NeedsMakeup flag.
Drop	ExamCount = 0 or 1	Set MustDrop flag.
DEFAULT CASE		ERROR: Should never happen.

CASE	TEST	ACTION
Extra1	ExtraCredit1 = COMPLETE	Add 2 to score.
DEFAULT CASE		NO ACTION

CASE	TEST	ACTION
Extra2	ExtraCredit2 = COMPLETE	Add 4 to score.
DEFAULT CASE		NO ACTION

CASE	TEST	ACTION
Extra3	ExtraCredit3 = COMPLETE	Add 6 to score.
DEFAULT CASE		NO ACTION

□ □

Choosing the Pseudo-code Form of a Conditional Action

A conditional with mutually exclusive cases is represented in pseudo-code as a CASE action or as a single IF with an ELSE IF part for each additional case, as shown in Figure 9.1. A conditional with nonexclusive cases requires a sequence of separate IF actions with no ELSE IF or ELSE parts, as shown in Figure 9.2.

In Figures 9.1 and 9.2 notice the difference in control paths between the two forms of conditional. With mutually exclusive cases, each path leads only through the actions for a single case. With nonexclusive cases, some paths go through the actions for one case and some go through the actions for several cases. One path leads through no cases and one leads through all the actions for every case.

□ □

When to Use CASE?

When you have a list of mutually exclusive cases, you can use the CASE form of conditional when all the tests involve comparing the value of a single variable or expression against various literal values, defined constants, or small ranges of values. And the values must be values of an *ordinal type* (Integer, Char, Boolean, subrange, or enumeration), not Real or String values. Otherwise you have to use the IF...ELSE IF... form of conditional.

EXAMPLE   This conditional can be written as a CASE action:

CASE	TEST	ACTION
4exams	ExamCount = 4	Average all exam scores.
3exams	ExamCount = 3	Drop zero score, average rest.
2exams	ExamCount = 2	Set NeedsMakeup flag.
Drop	ExamCount = 0 or 1	Set MustDrop flag.

in the form:

```
CASE ExamCount OF
    4:
         Average all exam scores.
```

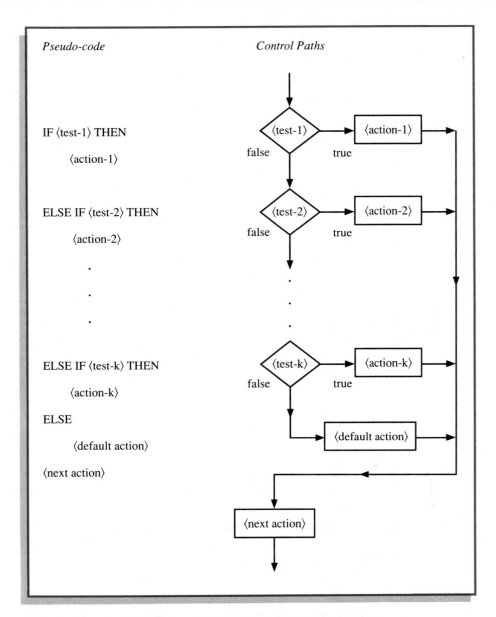

Pseudo-code   Control Paths

IF ⟨test-1⟩ THEN

    ⟨action-1⟩

ELSE IF ⟨test-2⟩ THEN

    ⟨action-2⟩

.

.

.

ELSE IF ⟨test-k⟩ THEN

    ⟨action-k⟩

ELSE

    ⟨default action⟩

⟨next action⟩

FIGURE 9-1 Conditional Action with Mutually Exclusive Cases

    3:
        Drop zero score, average the rest.
    2:
        Set NeedsMakeup flag.
    0, 1:
        Set MustDrop flag.
  END

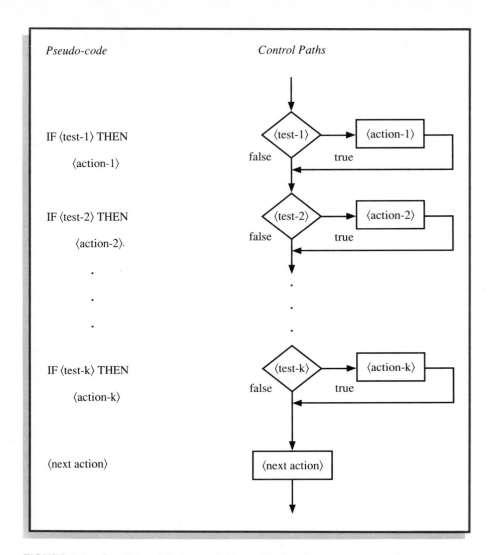

FIGURE 9-2 Conditional Action with Nonexclusive Cases

However, below is a similar conditional that must be written as an IF because the tests for the "4+exams" and "Drop" cases are not in the CASE form:

CASE	TEST	ACTION
4+exams	ExamCount > 3	Average all exam scores.
3exams	ExamCount $= 3$	Drop zero score, average rest.
2exams	ExamCount $= 2$	Set NeedsMakeup flag.
Drop	ExamCount < 2	Set MustDrop flag.

□ □
How Many Paths in a Conditional Action?

In general, the more control paths a program has, the harder it is to understand, analyze, and test. It is easy to calculate the *number of different possible paths* in the different kinds of conditional actions:

1. *Mutually exclusive cases (CASE and IF...ELSE IF...).* In these conditionals, the number of possible control paths is the *sum* of the number of paths through the actions for each separate case. In the simplest situation, if each alternative action is a straight-line segment, then:

Number of control paths = Total number of cases.

If an alternative itself has several sub-cases, then each sub-case adds another path to the overall conditional.

EXAMPLE

In this conditional, the cases are mutually exclusive:

CASE	TEST	ACTION
A	Score >= 90	Grade := 'A'
B	80 <= Score < 90	Grade := 'B'
C	70 <= Score < 80	Grade := 'C'
D	60 <= Score < 70	Grade := 'D'
F	Score < 60	Grade := 'F'
DEFAULT CASE		Set InvalidGrade flag.

There are six cases and each action is a straight-line segment, so there are six possible control paths through the conditional. ■

2. *Nonexclusive cases (sequence of separate IF's or CASE's).* In these conditionals, the number of control paths is the *product* of the number of paths through the actions for each separate IF or CASE. For example, if you have three IF's in sequence and each has two possible paths, then the overall sequence has $2 \times 2 \times 2 = 8$ possible control paths. Adding one more IF with two paths to the sequence will *double* the total number of paths

EXAMPLE

In this conditional the cases are nonexclusive:

CASE	TEST	ACTION
#1	ExtraCredit1 = COMPLETE	Score := Score + 3
#2	ExtraCredit2 = COMPLETE	Score := Score + 7
#3	ExtraCredit3 = COMPLETE	Score := Score + 5
DEFAULT CASE		NO ACTION

THE IF...IF... ERROR

Beginning programmers often make this mistake: Given a conditional action with several mutually exclusive cases, they code it as several separate IF statements in Pascal. As a result, their code has extra control paths, but *the extra paths can never be executed.* The result: confusing "spaghetti code"!

For example, given the cases:

CASE	TEST	ACTION
Pos	X > 0	Sales := Sales + X
Neg	X < 0	Losses := Losses + X
DEFAULT		NO ACTION

the beginner might use the pseudo-code segment:

```
IF X > 0 THEN
   Sales := Sales + X
IF X < 0 THEN
   Losses := Losses + X
```

instead of the correct segment:

```
IF X > 0 THEN
   Sales := Sales + X
ELSE IF X < 0 THEN
   Losses := Losses + X
```

The first IF...IF... segment has four control paths, one of which can never be executed because its path condition is the contradiction (X > 0) AND (X < 0). The second IF...ELSE IF... segment has only the three required control paths.

---

so it would be coded as three separate IF...THEN... statements, each with two paths. The total number of control paths through the three conditionals would be $2 \times 2 \times 2 = 8$. ■

EXERCISES

9.2 For each of the following situations, identify whether the *cases* described are mutually exclusive or nonexclusive:

a. If Number is a prime number, add one to Primes. If not a prime, add one to NonPrimes.

b. If Number is a multiple of 5, add one to FivesCount, if Number is a multiple of seven, add one to SevensCount, and if it is a multiple of nine, add one to NinesCount.

c. If the employee has medical insurance, life insurance, or disability insurance, subtract the appropriate deductions from the GrossPay amount (three separate deductions).

d. If the equation has two roots, compute and store them in Root1 and Root2. If it has only one root, compute and store it in Root1; if it has no roots, set flag RootStatus to NOROOTS.

9.3 For each of the following subprogram headings, design the subprogram body, using an appropriate conditional action:

a. PROCEDURE AdvanceDate
(D: Date)   IN/OUT

PURPOSE/GOAL STATE: Advance date D to next day in sequence.

PRECONDITION: D is not the date Dec. 31, 1999.

The Date type is a record with Integer fields Month, Day, and Year, and the Year is in the subrange 1900..1999.

b. FUNCTION ComputePay
(Hours: Integer   IN: hours worked.
Rate: Real   IN: pay per hour.
Seniority: Integer)   IN: total months employed.

FUNCTION VALUE: Real   Payroll amount.

PURPOSE: Compute and return the employee's weekly pay amount.

Pay is computed according to the rule: Pay the regular rate for up to 40 hours work. Pay 150 percent of the regular rate for overtime above 40 hours. However, employees can earn no overtime pay until they have been employed at least six months.

c. FUNCTION ComputeTax
(Income: Integer)   IN: Income amount in $.

FUNCTION VALUE: Integer   OUT: Tax in $.

PURPOSE: Compute and return the tax owed on Income.

The tax is computed according to the formula:

Tax = 2% of Income	if Income $<=$ \$3000
= \$60 + 3% of (Income over \$3000)	if 3000 $<$ Income $<=$ 5000
= \$120 + 5% of (Income over \$5000)	if 5000 $<$ Income $<=$ 14000
= \$570 + 5.75% of (Income over \$14,000)	if Income $>$ 14000

d. PROCEDURE CheckForWin
   (Moves: MoveArray)   IN: moves to be checked.

   FUNCTION VALUE: WinStatus   Result of check.

   PURPOSE: Check if the three moves in Moves are a WIN, LOSE, DRAW, or CONTINUE for a player in a game of tic-tac-toe, where the player is making the X moves.

The types are defined:

DATA TYPES

Move = (X, OH, BLANK)
MoveArray = ARRAY [1..3] of Move
WinStatus = (WIN, LOSE, DRAW, CONTINUE)

and the rule in tic-tac-toe is:

- All three moves are X → WIN for player
- All three moves are OH → LOSE for player
- At least one BLANK move → CONTINUE to play
- Otherwise → DRAW

Note that this procedure checks only one row, column, or diagonal of the tic-tac-toe board, not the entire board.

9.4 Here are three versions of the same conditional action, written by Nancy, Fred, and Lynne. Nancy's version is:

```
IF (Char1 = '=') AND (Char2 = ' ') THEN
    Operation := EQUAL

ELSE IF (Char1 = '<') AND (Char2 = '>') THEN
    Operation := NOTEQUAL

ELSE IF (Char1 = '<') AND (Char2 = '=') THEN
    Operation := LESSEQ

ELSE IF (Char1 = '<') AND (Char2 = ' ') THEN
    Operation := LESSTHAN

ELSE IF (Char1 = '>') AND (Char2 = '=') THEN
    Operation := GREATEREQ

ELSE IF (Char1 = '>') AND (Char2 = ' ') THEN
    Operation := GREATERTHAN

ELSE
    BadCharFlag := TRUE
```

Fred's version uses sub-cases:

```
IF (Char1 = '=') AND (Char2 = ' ') THEN
    Operation := EQUAL

ELSE IF Char1 = '<' THEN
   BEGIN
      IF Char2 = '>' THEN
          Operation := NOTEQUAL
      ELSE IF Char2 = '=' THEN
          Operation := LESSEQ
      ELSE IF Char2 = ' ' THEN
          Operation := LESSTHAN
   END

ELSE IF Char1 = '>' THEN
   BEGIN
      IF Char2 = '=' THEN
          Operation := GREATEREQ
      ELSE IF Char2 = ' ' THEN
          Operation := GREATERTHAN
   END

ELSE
    BadCharFlag := TRUE
```

Lynne's version uses nonexclusive cases and sub-cases:

```
IF (Char1 = '=') AND (Char2 = ' ') THEN
    Operation := EQUAL

IF Char1 = '<' THEN
    IF Char2 = '>' THEN
        Operation := NOTEQUAL
    ELSE IF Char2 = '=' THEN
        Operation := LESSEQ
    ELSE IF Char2 = ' ' THEN
        Operation := LESSTHAN

IF Char1 = '>' THEN
   BEGIN
      IF Char2 = '=' THEN
          Operation := GREATEREQ
      ELSE IF Char2 = ' ' THEN
          Operation := GREATERTHAN
   END
ELSE
    BadCharFlag := TRUE
```

a. Although the action is the same, the number of control paths differs greatly. Without trying to understand the actions in detail, use the formulas in this section to determine the number of control paths in each version. Count all paths (including the default case), without considering whether a path can ever be executed.

b. Assuming that Nancy's version is correct, determine if the other two versions always give the same results as Nancy's version. If you find any control paths where the actions differ from Nancy's, show the path condition for the erroneous path and the erroneous action taken.

DESIGNING TESTS TO DISCRIMINATE THE CASES

The *tests* that are used to discriminate among the various cases in a conditional involve some important design decisions. Let's suppose that you have completed your initial design of the table of cases in your conditional and that the cases are *mutually exclusive*. We want to focus attention now on the tests in your table:

Case	Test	Action
...	...	...
...	...	...
DEFAULT CASE		...

A test for a particular case is a *Boolean-valued expression,* which might be any one of the following:

1. *Relational tests.* The relational tests, =, < >, >, >=, <, and <= are the most common.

2. *Range tests.* A test for a value lying within a certain range combines two relational tests with AND, for example:

```
IF  (X >= 0)  AND  (X <= 100)  THEN ...
```

3. *Value IN a set of values.* A test for a value being one of a set of literal values might be written using the IN test of Pascal, for example:

```
IF GameResult IN [WIN, LOSE, DRAW] THEN ...
```

4. *Calls on Boolean-valued functions.* A function subprogram that returns a Boolean value might be called directly in a test. For example:

```
IF IsLastDayOfMonth (TodaysDate) THEN ...
```

5. *Combinations with AND, OR, NOT.* More complex tests may be formed by combining simpler tests with the Boolean operations AND, OR, and NOT.

Regardless of the particular tests used in a conditional, there are two questions to ask about the set of tests chosen: are they *mutually exclusive* and are they *exhaustive*? Let's look at these two questions separately.

□ □
Mutually Exclusive and Nonexclusive Tests

Suppose you use two tests in a conditional, and you know that if the first test is TRUE in a given state, then the second must be FALSE, and if the second is TRUE then the first must be FALSE. Such tests are said to be *mutually exclusive:*

□ **Mutually Exclusive Tests**

A set of tests is *mutually exclusive* if, for any given program state, *no more than one of them can return TRUE* for that state.

□ **Nonexclusive Tests**

A set of tests is *nonexclusive* if, for some program state, *more than one can return TRUE* for that state.

For example, these tests are mutually exclusive:

$$A < 0$$
$$A = 0$$
$$A > 0$$

because for any value of A, at most one of them can return TRUE. These tests are also mutually exclusive:

$$A > B$$
$$A < B$$

because for any values of A and B, at most one of them can be TRUE (and possibly neither, if A = B.) On the other hand, these tests are nonexclusive:

$$A <= B$$
$$A >= B$$

because in a state where A = B both tests return TRUE.

Do not confuse the distinction between *tests* that are mutually exclusive and *cases* that are mutually exclusive. To say that the *cases* are mutually exclusive means that we want at most one set of *actions* taken out of those for the possible cases. The IF...ELSE IF... pattern in pseudo-code guarantees that we get mutually exclusive *cases* even if the *tests* are nonexclusive.

Mutually exclusive tests have an important property: given a program state, you can evaluate mutually exclusive tests *in any order* without changing which test first returns a TRUE result. With nonexclusive tests, the *order of evaluation* is important: given a program state, in one order of evaluation one test may be the first to return TRUE, and with another order of evaluation a different test may be the first to return TRUE.

Remember that the cases in your initial design table for a conditional have been written down in whatever order you happened to think of them—the order in which the cases appear in the table is unimportant. But suppose you check the tests used in the design table for a conditional with mutually exclusive cases, and you find that the tests are *nonexclusive*. Immediately you know two things about the design:

1. The tests chosen do *not* actually discriminate the cases completely—sometimes two or more of the tests will return TRUE for the same program state. In such a situation, the table does not specify which action should be taken.

2. If you write an IF...ELSE IF... conditional from the design in the table, the *order* in which the cases are written in the IF will matter. Different orders of the cases will give IF's with different meanings in the states where two or more tests return TRUE.

EXAMPLE

1. Nancy's conditional uses mutually exclusive tests:

CASE	TEST	ACTION
Less	A < B	⟨action-1⟩
Greater	A > B	⟨action-2⟩
Equal	A = B	⟨action-3⟩

When writing the IF pseudo-code, she can write the cases in any convenient order:

```
IF A < B THEN
      ⟨action-1⟩
ELSE IF A > B THEN
      ⟨action-2⟩
ELSE IF A = B THEN
      ⟨action-3⟩
```

or equivalently:

```
IF A > B THEN
        ⟨action-2⟩
ELSE IF A = B THEN
        ⟨action-3⟩
ELSE IF A < B THEN
        ⟨action-1⟩
```

2. Hacker Jack's conditional uses nonexclusive tests:

CASE	TEST	ACTION
Less	A < B	⟨action-1⟩
Not-eq	A <> B	⟨action-2⟩
Equal	A = B	⟨action-3⟩

Jack writes his pseudo-code this way to get a conditional equivalent to Nancy's:

```
IF A < B THEN
        ⟨action-1⟩
ELSE IF A <> B THEN
        ⟨action-2⟩
ELSE IF A = B THEN
        ⟨action-3⟩
```

Notice that if A < B, then both the first and second tests return TRUE. Reordering the cases in this conditional can change the meaning of the IF. For example, if Jack wrote the cases in this order:

```
IF A <> B THEN
        ⟨action-2⟩
ELSE IF A < B THEN
        ⟨action-1⟩
ELSE IF A = B THEN
        ⟨action-3⟩
```

then ⟨action-1⟩ will never be executed because the test sequence leads to ⟨action-2⟩ when A < B instead of to ⟨action-1⟩. ■

Mutually exclusive tests have two other advantages after you have coded the conditional in Pascal:

1. The *path condition* for a case is just the *test for that case*. If the tests are nonexclusive, then the path condition is determined by the entire sequence of tests that precede the case in question.

EXAMPLE

In Nancy's conditional above, the path condition for each case is just the test for that case: A > B for one path, A < B for another, and A = B for the third. The path conditions are unchanged if she reorders the cases in the IF.

In Hacker Jack's conditional, the path conditions depend on the order in which Jack writes the cases in the IF. In his first version, the path condition leading to ⟨action-1⟩ is A < B, but in Jack's second version, the path condition leading to that action is (A = B) AND (A < B), which is a contradiction. ∎

2. Mutually exclusive tests make the conditional *easy to modify* without introducing errors. Because the order of the cases makes no difference if mutually exclusive tests are used, you can insert new cases or delete existing cases without affecting the other cases in the conditional (except where a new case requires a change in the test for an old case).

EXAMPLE

Suppose Nancy wants to introduce a new case when A = B + 1. Nancy needs only change the test for the current case A > B to be A > B + 1, and then she can insert the new case between any two of the existing cases. ∎

□ □

Exhaustive Tests

Now let's consider the second question about a set of tests. Suppose that you have a set of tests in your conditional, and you know that, for any given program state, *at least one of the tests must be TRUE*. We say the tests "exhaust all the possible cases," or, more simply, the tests form an *exhaustive set:*

□ **Exhaustive Set of Tests**

A set of tests is an *exhaustive set* if, for any given program state, *at least one of them must return TRUE.*

For example, the set of tests:

A > 0
A = 0
A < 0

is an exhaustive set because for any value of A, at least one must be true. The set:

> A >= B
> A <= B

is also an exhaustive set, because for any values of A and B, at least one test must be true (and possibly both, if A = B). However, the set:

> A > 0
> A = 0

is not exhaustive if the value of A can ever be negative, because in such a state neither test returns TRUE.

In many situations, you cannot decide if a set of tests is exhaustive without knowing the *data types* of the variables involved in the tests, because you need to know if *all the possible values* of each variable have been included in the tests. For example, the set:

> A >= 1
> A = 0

is exhaustive if A is declared to be in the subrange 0..100. But if A is type Integer, then A could be negative, so the set is not exhaustive. If A is type Real, then the set is not exhaustive because A might have a value between zero and one or be negative.

An exhaustive set of tests guarantees that no *default action* is required in a conditional. Thus, if a conditional uses an exhaustive set of tests, the last line of the design table will always be:

CASE	TEST	ACTION
...	...	...
...	...	...
DEFAULT CASE		ERROR: Not possible.

When a conditional has a default case, you usually need to know the path conditions for that case—in what situations can the default case actions be executed? Using an exhaustive set of tests makes the answer simple: *It should never happen!*

EXAMPLE

These two conditionals represent the same action. Example (a) uses an exhaustive set of tests; (b) does not:

a.   IF A < B THEN
            ⟨action-1⟩

       ELSE IF A > B THEN
            ⟨action-2⟩

       ELSE IF A = B THEN
            ⟨action-3⟩

b.   IF A < B THEN
          ⟨action-1⟩

      ELSE IF A > B THEN
          ⟨action-2⟩

      ELSE
          ⟨action-3⟩

In reading conditional (b), notice that you have to think for a minute to decide when ⟨action-3⟩ might be executed. Conditional (a) leaves no doubt about when ⟨action-3⟩ is taken.

□ □
Redundant Tests

When a sequence of tests has been coded in an IF, the tests are evaluated in sequence, and the *first* test that returns TRUE leads to the action taken. Because the order of the tests is significant, you often find that some parts of some of the tests are *redundant:*

> □ **Redundant Test**
>
> In an ordered sequence of tests, a later test is *redundant* if its value (TRUE or FALSE) can always be determined by knowing the result of one or more of the earlier tests.

EXAMPLE

Redundant tests often appear in a sequence of tests for a value to be within certain ranges. For example, here is a conditional using mutually exclusive and exhaustive tests:

      IF Score >= 90 THEN
          ⟨action-1⟩

      ELSE IF (Score >= 80) AND (Score < 90) THEN
          ⟨action-2⟩

      ELSE IF (Score >= 70) AND (Score < 80) THEN
          ⟨action-3⟩

      ELSE IF (Score >= 60) AND (Score < 70) THEN
          ⟨action-4⟩

      ELSE IF Score < 60 THEN
          ⟨action-5⟩

      ELSE
          ⟨ERROR: Should never get here.⟩

In this conditional, the tests following AND in cases 2–4 ("Score < 90", "Score < 80", "Score < 70") and the test "Score < 60" in case 5 are redundant because you know from the test in the preceding case that each redundant test must always be TRUE whenever execution reaches it. ■

Redundant tests waste execution time—you are repeating a test whose outcome is already known. Thus, they make the program less efficient. The question in coding a conditional is: Should the redundant tests be deleted in order to get a more efficient program? For example, is this a better way to code the above conditional, because it is more efficient?

```
IF Score >= 90 THEN
      ⟨action-1⟩

ELSE IF Score >= 80 THEN
      ⟨action-2⟩

ELSE IF Score >= 70 THEN
      ⟨action-3⟩

ELSE IF Score >= 60 THEN
      ⟨action-4⟩

ELSE
      ⟨action-5⟩
```

Notice that in this conditional we have lost both design goals discussed above: the tests are *neither mutually exclusive nor exhaustive*. In general, to avoid redundant tests, you must rely on the *order* of the tests in the conditional and use a default case for the final case (with no test).

□ □
Should Redundant Cases Be Deleted When Coding an IF?

Old programming hands would almost surely tell you to delete any redundant tests in a conditional. But is it a good thing to do? Let's look at the pros and cons of deleting the redundant tests:

□
Pros.   Deleting the redundant tests has the following advantages:

1. Execution of the IF statement is more efficient, and
2. The statement is shorter, so there is less to write (and get wrong).

□
Cons.   Deleting the redundant tests has the following disadvantages:

1. The tests are no longer mutually exclusive, so you cannot reorder the cases, insert new cases, or delete cases as easily, and

2. The tests are no longer exhaustive so you cannot easily tell when the default action is taken.

In summary, deleting the redundant tests makes the conditional more efficient but harder to understand, analyze, and modify. Unless efficiency is a central issue in your program, it is better to retain the redundant tests in the final conditional. We discuss program efficiency in more detail in Chapter 14.

If you do delete the redundant tests in the Pascal code, leave them in as comments, to aid the reader. For example, write the conditional above:

```
IF  Score >= 90 THEN
       ⟨action-1⟩

ELSE  IF  Score >= 80  THEN          {AND Score < 90}
       ⟨action-2⟩

ELSE  IF  Score >= 70  THEN          {AND Score < 80}
       ⟨action-3⟩

ELSE  IF  Score >= 60  THEN          {AND Score < 70}
       ⟨action-4⟩

ELSE                                 {Score < 60}
       ⟨action-5⟩
```

EXERCISES

9.5   For each of the following sets of tests, determine if the tests are *mutually exclusive* or *nonexclusive:*
  a.   (X >= 10) AND (X <= 20)
          (X >= 20) AND (X <= 25)
  b.   Q = 1
          Q = 2
          Q < 1
          Q > 2
  c.   Status IN [OFF, DISCONNECTED]
          Status IN [ON, READY]
          Status IN [BROKEN, DISCONNECTED]
  d.   (X >= 0) AND (Y < 0)
          (X > 0) AND (Y > 0)
          (X <= 0) AND (Y = 0)
          (X = 0) AND (Y > 0)
          (X < 0) AND (Y > 0)

9.6   Given each of the following sets of tests and the data types of the variables involved, determine if the tests are an *exhaustive set:*
  a.   The tests in 9.5a if X is of type subrange 10..25.
  b.   The tests in 9.5b if Q has type Real.

c. The tests in 9.5b if Q has type Integer.

d. The tests in 9.5c if Status is of enumerated type StatusType defined as:

StatusType = (ON, OFF, BROKEN, READY, DISCONNECTED);

e. The tests in 9.5c if Status is of an enumerated type StatusType defined as:

StatusType = (ON, OFF, BROKEN, READY, DISCONNECTED, INUSE);

f. The tests in 9.5d if X and Y are type Real.

□□□ **9.4**
ANALYSIS: PATH CONDITIONS IN CONDITIONALS

Analysis of conditional actions, for checking correctness, for testing and debugging, or for modification, often requires determination of path conditions for one or more of the paths through the conditional. You find yourself asking the question: Now how exactly is that particular case chosen for execution? The answer, of course, is what we call the path condition for that case.

In a CASE statement, the path conditions are always obvious because the test expression is compared against literal values that are explicitly shown. Thus, we concentrate on IF statements.

□□
Path Conditions for IF's with Mutually Exclusive Tests

We have already noted the ease of finding path conditions in a conditional where the cases are distinguished by mutually exclusive tests: *the test itself is the path condition.*

EXAMPLE

In the following conditional, under what conditions will the final grade, Final, be a 'C'?

```
IF Score >= 90 THEN
    Final := 'A'

ELSE IF (Score >= 80) AND (Score < 90) THEN
    Final := 'B'

ELSE IF (Score >= 60) AND (Score < 80) THEN
    Final := 'C'

ELSE IF Score < 60 THEN
    Final := 'F'

ELSE
    ERROR: Impossible case.
```

Because the tests are mutually exclusive, the path condition is just the test for the third case:

$$(Score >= 60) \text{ AND } (Score < 80) \qquad \blacksquare$$

□ □
The Negation of a Test

Given a test, there is always another test, called its *negation,* that gives exactly the opposite result: for any state where the first test returns TRUE, its negation returns FALSE, and for any state where the first test returns FALSE, its negation returns TRUE.

In programming, any test can be turned into its negation simply by putting it in parentheses and placing the Boolean operation NOT before it. For example, the negation of the test "X > Y" can be written "NOT (X > Y)".

Each relational test has another test that is its natural negation:

$=$ is the negation of $<>$, and vice versa

$<$ is the negation of $>=$, and vice versa

$>$ is the negation of $<=$, and vice versa

For example, the negation of the test "X > Y" can also be written "X <= Y".

When the possible values of a variable are of type Char, an enumerated type, or a subrange type, then the negation of a test on the value of that variable is a test that returns TRUE for all the possible values of that variable where the original test returned FALSE. For example, if variable GameStatus is of type Status, defined as:

Status = (WIN, LOSE, DRAW, UNDECIDED)

then the negation of the test:

GameStatus IN [WIN, LOSE]

is the test:

NOT (GameStatus IN [WIN, LOSE])

or

GameStatus IN [DRAW, UNDECIDED]

Path Conditions for IF's with Nonexclusive Tests

We use negations of tests in path conditions for IF's where the tests are nonexclusive. Suppose you have such an IF, and you need the path condition for a particular case. To find the path condition, first, make a list of all the tests that *precede* the case of interest in the IF, and end the list with the test for the case of interest. Then change all but the last test into its negation (because these tests must have been FALSE in order for execution to reach the case of interest). Finally, put AND between each pair of tests in the list (because all the negations and the last test must be TRUE to reach the case of interest).

EXAMPLE

In the following conditional, under what conditions will the final grade, Final, be a 'C'?

```
IF Score >= 90 THEN
        Final := 'A'
ELSE IF Score >= 80 THEN
        Final := 'B'
ELSE IF Score >= 60 THEN
        Final := 'C'
ELSE
        Final := 'F'
```

The tests are nonexclusive, so first find the case of interest—the third case here. Then list the tests down to the third case:

```
(Score >= 90)
(Score >= 80)
(Score >= 60)
```

Negate the first two tests and put AND between each pair. The path condition is:

```
        (Score < 90)
AND (Score < 80)
AND (Score >= 60)
```

The first test is obviously redundant, so we get (as you probably saw immediately for this simple example) that the path condition is:

$$(Score < 80) \text{ AND } (Score >= 60)$$

■

The Path Condition for the Default Case

The path condition for the default case is often of interest: exactly what conditions will lead execution to the default case instead of to one of the other cases? Of course, if you have used an exhaustive set of tests, then the path condition should be a contradiction, but you might still like to check.

You can determine this path condition by simply treating the default case as you would the last case of an IF with nonexclusive tests. Take a list of all the tests for the other cases, change each test into its negation, and put AND between each pair of negations.

EXAMPLE

Q: What values of X and Y will cause the default action to be taken in the following conditional?

```
IF X > 0 THEN
      ⟨action-1⟩
ELSE IF Y < 0 THEN
      ⟨action-2⟩
ELSE
      ⟨action-3⟩
```

A: The default action is taken when both the tests in the first and second cases return FALSE, written as the AND of the negations of the two tests:

$$NOT(X > 0) AND NOT(Y < 0)$$

which can be simplified to give the path condition for the default case:

$$(X <= 0) \quad AND \quad (Y >= 0)$$

De Morgan's Laws

The path condition for the default case often involves a rather complex mix of AND, OR, and NOT operations. Two rules (named *De Morgan's laws* after their discoverer) provide a way to simplify such conditions:

> □ **De Morgan's Laws**
>
> *Law 1:* The Boolean-valued expression:
>
> NOT (⟨test-1⟩ AND ⟨test-2⟩ AND ... AND ⟨test-k⟩)

is equivalent to:

$$(NOT \ \langle test\text{-}1 \rangle) \ OR \ (NOT \ \langle test\text{-}2 \rangle) \ OR \ ... \ OR \ (NOT \ \langle test\text{-}k \rangle)$$

Law 2: The Boolean-valued expression:

$$NOT \ ((\langle test\text{-}1 \rangle \ OR \ \langle test\text{-}2 \rangle \ OR \ ... \ OR \ \langle test\text{-}k \rangle)$$

is equivalent to:

$$(NOT \ \langle test\text{-}1 \rangle) \ AND \ (NOT \ \langle test\text{-}2 \rangle) \ AND \ ... \ AND \ (NOT \ \langle test\text{-}k \rangle)$$

DeMorgan's laws allow you to change a NOT that applies to the AND or OR of some tests into a NOT on the individual tests themselves and thus simplify a complex path condition.

EXAMPLE

The negation of the test:

$$(X > 0) \quad AND \quad (Y > 0) \quad AND \quad (X > Y)$$

is the test:

$$NOT \quad ((X > 0) \quad AND \quad (Y > 0) \quad AND \quad (X > Y))$$

that De Morgan's laws tell us is equivalent to:

$$NOT(X > 0) \ OR \ NOT(Y > 0) \ OR \ NOT(X > Y)$$

and each simple negation can be replaced by its equivalent to get the more readable form:

$$(X <= 0) \quad OR \quad (Y <= 0) \quad OR \quad (X <= Y) \qquad \blacksquare$$

EXERCISES

9.7 Write the negation of each of the following tests in two ways, using NOT and without using NOT:

a. $X > (Max + 2)$

b. $(Z = 0) \ AND \ (Y > X)$

c. Status IN [ON, READY]

where Status is of enumerated type StatusType defined as:

StatusType = (ON, OFF, BROKEN, READY, DISCONNECTED);

d. (Grade $>=$ 80) AND (Grade $<=$ 90)

e. Employed = FALSE

9.8 What values of X and Y will cause the default action to be taken in the following conditional? Assume X and Y are type Integer. Your answer should be the path condition. Write the path condition in two forms, using NOT and without using NOT:

```
IF (X > Y) AND (Y > 0) THEN
    ⟨action-1⟩
ELSE IF X = 0 THEN
    ⟨action-2⟩
ELSE IF Y = 0 THEN
    ⟨action-3⟩
ELSE
    ⟨default action⟩
```

9.9 Give the path condition for each of the cases in the following conditional, including the default case. Assume all variables are of type Real.

```
IF (A > B) AND (A > C) THEN
    ⟨action-1⟩
ELSE IF (B > A) AND (B > C) THEN
    ⟨action-2⟩
ELSE IF (C > B) AND (C > A) THEN
    ⟨action-3⟩
ELSE
    ⟨default action⟩
```

9.10 Hacker Jack wrote the following conditional with the intent of treating each of the following cases:

Value of Char1	Value of Char2	Assigned Value of Operation
=	space	EQUAL
<	>	NOTEQUAL
<	space	LESSTHAN
<	=	LESSEQ
>	space	GREATERTHAN
>	=	GREATEREQ
Any other	Any other	ERROR: display message

Check the path conditions for each of the paths and see if Jack got it right this time. If you spot an error, list the path condition for the path that contains the error.

```
IF Char1 = '=' THEN
    BEGIN
        IF Char2 = ' ' THEN
            Operation := EQUAL
    END

ELSE IF Char1 = '<' THEN
    BEGIN
        IF Char2 = '>' THEN
            Operation := NOTEQUAL
        ELSE IF Char2 = '=' THEN
            Operation := EQUAL
        ELSE IF Char2 = ' ' THEN
            Operation := LESSTHAN
    END

ELSE IF Char1 = '>' THEN
    BEGIN
        IF Char2 = '=' THEN
            Operation := GREATEREQ
        ELSE IF Char2 = ' ' THEN
            Operation := GREATERTHAN
    END

ELSE
        DISPLAY: "ERROR: Not a valid operation."
```

9.11 Redesign Jack's conditional in 9.10 to get rid of the subcases. Use a set of mutually exclusive tests. Write the path condition for the default case to see if you have correctly treated "all the other cases."

9.12 Julia has written a conditional that determines the cooking method for various kinds of vegetables:

```
IF Leafy AND Crisp THEN
    Method := STEAM

ELSE IF NOT Crisp THEN
    BEGIN
        IF Soft AND Yellow THEN
            Method := BOIL

        ELSE IF (NOT Soft) AND (NOT Yellow) THEN
            Method := ROAST

        ELSE IF Soft AND (NOT Yellow) THEN
            Method := SAUTE
    END

ELSE IF Crisp AND (NOT Leafy) THEN
    Method := FRY
```

a. Determine the number of possible control paths in this conditional.
b. Write the path condition for each path.

PASCAL PUNCTUATION RULES

Our pseudo-code matches the Pascal IF and CASE statements closely, so coding conditionals from pseudo-code is straightforward. However, up to this point we have been using a set of simplified Pascal syntax and punctuation rules for both loops and conditionals. This is a good time to develop a more complete picture of the rules of Pascal syntax and punctuation, and then look at the consequences of these rules.

□□
Basic Semicolon Rules

The rules for placing semicolons in Pascal are simple in principle but confusing in practice. The basic rules are these:

□ **Basic Rules of Semicolons**

Statements. Use a semicolon to *separate two statements.*
Declarations. Use a semicolon to *terminate each declaration* (anything in CONST, TYPE, or VAR sections and procedure and function definitions).

The rule for declarations causes little problem, but the rule for statements is confusing because you cannot punctuate the end of one statement correctly without knowing what comes after it.

□□
Compound Statements

In Pascal, any sequence of statements that is enclosed within BEGIN...END is termed a *compound statement*. For purposes of punctuation, a compound statement is a *single Pascal statement*. For example, these two assignments when enclosed by BEGIN...END form a single Pascal compound statement:

```
BEGIN
    X := X + 1;
    Y := Y + 10;
END
```

□□
Empty Statements

An *empty statement* consists of no characters—nothing is written. The empty statement is a valid Pascal statement and may be written anywhere that a statement is required. The catch is: *an empty statement must be separated by a semicolon from any statement that comes before or after it*.

□□ Pascal Syntax for IF, CASE, WHILE, and FOR

For simplicity of punctuation, we have been including BEGIN...END pairs in IF, CASE, WHILE, and FOR statements whenever a list of statements representing a list of actions is needed. But the actual Pascal syntax in each case is that *any single statement* may appear where we have used BEGIN...END. Thus the basic syntax for these statements is:

IF: IF ⟨test⟩ THEN
      ⟨single statement⟩
{ELSE IF ⟨test⟩ THEN
      ⟨single statement⟩}
[ELSE
      ⟨single statement⟩]

CASE: CASE ⟨expression⟩ OF
    {⟨value list⟩:
      ⟨single statement⟩; }
    ⟨value list⟩:
      ⟨single statement⟩
  END

WHILE: WHILE ⟨test⟩ DO
     ⟨single statement⟩

FOR: FOR ⟨variable⟩ := ⟨first value⟩ TO ⟨last value⟩ DO
     ⟨single statement⟩

Notice that the IF, WHILE, and FOR statements include no semicolons, and the CASE requires a semicolon only to separate the statement for the action in one case from a following value list. In these statements, our use of BEGIN...END simply makes each ⟨single statement⟩ into a compound statement—perfectly legal but more restrictive than required by Pascal.

□□ The "Dangling ELSE" Problem

The fact that the ELSE part of an IF is optional leads to an occasional problem, called the *dangling ELSE*. The problem arises when the two forms of IF are combined in a single statement, so that you see this:

```
IF ⟨test-1⟩ THEN
    IF ⟨test-2⟩ THEN
        ⟨statement-A⟩
ELSE
    ⟨statement-B⟩
```

or this:

```
IF ⟨test-1⟩ THEN
    IF ⟨test-2⟩ THEN
        ⟨statement-A⟩
    ELSE
        ⟨statement-B⟩
```

The indentation shows what you intend: In the first form, ⟨statement-B⟩ is the ELSE part of IF ⟨test-1⟩ THEN... and in the second it is the ELSE part of IF ⟨test-2⟩ THEN....

Unfortunately, indentation means nothing "officially" in Pascal, so these forms are indistinguishable to the Pascal compiler. The ELSE part here is termed a "dangling ELSE" because it could be paired with either the first "IF ⟨test-1⟩ THEN..." or the second "IF ⟨test-2⟩ THEN...".

The Pascal compiler solves the dangling ELSE problem by always pairing the dangling ELSE clause with the *last unmatched IF ⟨test⟩ THEN...* So, to the compiler, either form above means that the ELSE is matched with "IF ⟨test-2⟩ THEN...".

The dangling ELSE is only a problem when combining two IF's, one with an ELSE and another without the ELSE. If both IF's have an ELSE or both do not, there is no difficulty.

□ □
Consequences of the Pascal Syntax and Punctuation Rules

The individual rules about semicolons, compound statements, empty statements, and the dangling ELSE are not complicated, but when combined they cause lots of confusion. Here are the main consequences to look out for in your program:

1. *BEGIN-END pairs can sometimes be omitted.* BEGIN-END is never required within an IF, CASE, WHILE, or FOR statement if the action within the BE-GIN-END is a single Pascal statement.

EXAMPLE

Both these forms are valid in Pascal and mean the same thing:

```
IF A > B THEN
    X := X + 1
ELSE
    Y := Y + 1
```

or, using our standard coding rules:

```
IF A > B THEN
   BEGIN
      X := X + 1;
   END
ELSE
   BEGIN
      Y := Y + 1;
   END
```

2. *Semicolon is optional immediately before END.* Any statement that immediately precedes an END does not need a semicolon to separate it from the "next" statement—because there is no next statement before the END. However, you can write a terminating semicolon on the statement, and then "officially" in Pascal there is an empty statement between the semicolon and the END, which makes the semicolon all right.

EXAMPLE

In our example above, the semicolons could be omitted:

```
IF A > B THEN
   BEGIN
      X := X + 1
   END
ELSE
   BEGIN
      Y := Y + 1
   END
```

3. *A semicolon may never appear at the end of a statement immediately before ELSE.* Before END is ok; before ELSE—never!

EXAMPLE

Suppose you write this IF:

```
IF A > B THEN
   Count := Count + 1;        {The semicolon is INVALID here.}
ELSE
   . . .
```

There is no statement following the assignment and before the ELSE, so the semicolon does not separate two statements and thus it is illegal—the compiler will complain. You cannot claim that there is an "empty statement" after the semicolon here because then there would be two statements between THEN and ELSE, and only one is allowed. So you have to put in BEGIN...END to make the pair into a compound statement if you want to leave the semicolon:

```
IF ⟨test⟩ THEN
   BEGIN
      Count := Count + 1;  {empty statement is here}
   END
ELSE
   ...
```

4. *Inserting new statements is tricky if BEGIN-END pairs are omitted.* If you leave out the BEGIN-END pairs and then later have to insert a statement at that point, you also must insert BEGIN-END and possibly also insert a semicolon at the end of the existing statement.

EXAMPLE

This looks like a nice clean way to write this conditional:

```
IF A > B THEN
      X := X + 1
ELSE
      Y := Y + 1
```

but if you later decide you want to insert a debug WRITE to display the value of X after the assignment in the first case, then you have to (a) insert BEGIN-END around both statements to make the pair into a single compound statement and (b) put the terminating semicolon on the end of the assignment to separate it from the WRITE statement, so the result would be:

```
IF A > B THEN
   BEGIN
      X := X + 1;                {This semicolon is not optional}
      writeln ('DEBUG: X = ', X); {This semicolon is optional}
   END
ELSE
   Y := Y + 1
```

If you had started out with our "standard" form:

```
IF A > B THEN
   BEGIN
      X := X + 1;
   END
ELSE
   BEGIN
      Y := Y + 1;
   END
```

then inserting the debug WRITE requires no other changes.

5. *Use a BEGIN-END around a single IF statement to fix a "dangling ELSE."* Without the BEGIN-END pairs, you may find you have a dangling ELSE. To fix it, insert a BEGIN-END pair.

EXAMPLE

In this conditional, the ELSE is dangling and the compiler pairs it with ⟨test-2⟩:

```
IF ⟨test-1⟩ THEN
    IF ⟨test-2⟩ THEN
        ⟨statement-A⟩
ELSE
    ⟨statement-B⟩
```

To get the ELSE matched with ⟨test-1⟩ you have to make the nested IF into a compound statement:

```
IF ⟨test-1⟩ THEN
    BEGIN
        IF ⟨test-2⟩ THEN
            ⟨statement-A⟩
    END
ELSE
    ⟨statement-B⟩
```

6. *To code a NO ACTION, use an empty statement.* If you want to do nothing for one of the possible cases in an IF or CASE, you just use an *empty statement* as the action—that is, you write nothing (except the terminating semicolon if required).

EXAMPLE

Suppose your pseudo-code for a CASE looks like this:

```
CASE StudentYear OF
    1:    Add 1 to ClassCount [1]
    2:    Add 1 to ClassCount [2]
    3:    Add 1 to ClassCount [3]
    4:    Add 1 to ClassCount [4]
          CALL CheckSeniorStatus (StudentID, Status)
    5:    NO ACTION
    6:    CALL CheckGraduateStatus (StudentID, Status)
END
```

Coded in Pascal, you might write:

```
CASE StudentYear OF
    1: ClassCount [1] := ClassCount [1] + 1;
    2: ClassCount [2] := ClassCount [2] + 1;
    3: ClassCount [3] := ClassCount [3] + 1;
    4: BEGIN
          ClassCount [4] := ClassCount [4] + 1;
          CheckSeniorStatus (StudentId, Status);
       END;
    5: ;      {NO ACTION}
    6: CheckGraduateStatus (StudentID, Status);
END
```

As you can see, the consequences of the full Pascal syntax and punctuation rules for IF, CASE, WHILE, and FOR statements are confusing. They often lead to frustrating errors when you originally code or later modify a section of your program. For that reason, you may find it simpler to stay with our original simplified rules:

1. Always use BEGIN-END pairs in each part of IF, CASE, WHILE, and FOR statements.
2. Terminate every statement with a semicolon, regardless of what follows it. Do *not* treat BEGIN-END (a Pascal compound statement) as a statement itself.

Your Pascal program will use more lines on the page (because of the extra BEGIN-END lines), but it will be easier to code correctly originally and *much easier to modify safely* later.

EXERCISES

9.13 Identify and correct the syntax errors in the following conditionals. Assume that the indentation indicates the programmer's intent.

```
a.  IF X > 0 THEN
            IF Y < 0 THEN
                    X := X + 1;
    ELSE IF X = 0 THEN
            Y := 0;
b.  IF A = B THEN
            X := X + 1;
            Y := Y + 1
    ELSE IF A > B THEN
            IF X = 0 THEN
                    Y := Y + 1
```

9.14   Code into Pascal each of the subprograms designed in Exercise 9.3 and test each of them using a test driver.

□□□**9.6**
PROGRAM IT WITH STYLE!

Some style rules to remember when coding conditional actions:

1.   *Ordering of cases.* Assuming that your tests are mutually exclusive, then choose an order for the cases that makes the conditional easy to read. Two rules of thumb are (a) place the *most likely cases first* and (b) among equally likely cases, place the *simpler cases first.*

2.   *IF spacing and indentation.* In an IF, place each IF ⟨test⟩ THEN, ELSE IF ⟨test⟩ THEN, and ELSE on a separate line, aligned vertically down the page. Indent the actions relative to the start of the IF, ELSE IF, or ELSE lines, and align the actions vertically (same indentation for each action). We have used this style in all the IF examples of this chapter.

3.   *CASE spacing and indentation.* In a CASE indent the value lists slightly from the CASE...OF and END lines. Align the start of the value lists. Unless a value list is very short, place each value list on a separate line, with the actions indented below. Align the actions vertically, using the same indentation for each action. We have used this style in all the CASE examples of this chapter.

4.   *Deleted redundant tests.* If you choose to delete redundant tests in an IF during coding, as discussed in Section 9.3, then be sure to keep the deleted test as a comment so the reader will be aware of it. The comment is particularly important for a deleted test on the final case which turns it into the default case. Section 9.3 shows an example of this style.

□□□ **9.7**
PSEUDO-CODE AND PASCAL SUMMARY

The pseudo-code and Pascal syntax for IF are familiar from preceding chapters.

□ □
Pseudo-code for CASE

```
⟨CASE-conditional-action⟩ ::=
    CASE ⟨test-expression⟩ OF
        ⟨value-list⟩:
                ⟨action-list⟩
        {⟨value-list⟩:
                ⟨action-list⟩}
        [ELSE
            ⟨default-case-actions⟩]
    END
```

WHERE

⟨test-expression⟩ ::=

A data object name or Pascal expression whose value is to be used to determine which ⟨action-list⟩ to execute. The data object is usually of an enumerated or subrange type.

⟨value-list⟩ ::= ⟨data-value⟩ {, ⟨data-value⟩}

⟨data-value⟩ ::=

A literal value or the name of a defined constant (not a Real value or string).

⟨action-list⟩ ::=

A list of actions to be executed, or "NO ACTION" if no action is needed for this case.

⟨default-case-actions⟩ ::=

Actions to be executed if the value of the test expression does not match any value in one of the value lists.

□

Meaning: When a CASE statement is executed, the following steps are taken:

1. The ⟨test-expression⟩ is evaluated to give a value, K.
2. The ⟨value-list⟩ that contains the value K is found and the actions in the ⟨action-list⟩ associated with that ⟨value-list⟩ are executed. If the value K does not appear in any value-list, then the ⟨default-case-actions⟩ are executed.
3. Execution continues with the actions following the end of the CASE.

□ □

The Pascal CASE Statement

The Pascal CASE statement matches our pseudo-code, with three exceptions:

1. In Pascal, insert BEGIN-END pairs around each list of actions and a semicolon after each END.
2. If an action list is "NO ACTION" then only the semicolon is written in the Pascal code.
3. In standard Pascal, there is no ELSE clause in a CASE statement to handle the "default case", where no value in any value list matches the value of the test expression.

In standard Pascal, the default case is treated as an error. Some Pascal systems may terminate program execution; others may simply ignore the default case and execute no action at all. However, many Pascal systems provide the ELSE clause as an extension. Check your local *Pascal User's Manual*.

□ □

Semicolon Rules

1. Use a semicolon to *separate two statements*.
2. Use a semicolon to *terminate each declaration*.
3. Never put a semicolon *immediately before ELSE*.

See Section 9.5 for the detailed Pascal punctuation rules.

REVIEW QUESTIONS

9.1 Show the general form of IF and CASE conditional actions in pseudo-code.

9.2 Explain what happens when an IF is executed; when a CASE is executed.

9.3 Give the general form of a *design table* for designing a complex conditional action.

9.4 What is a *default case*? List three options to consider for the ACTION part of a default case.

9.5 What is a *sub-case*? How would you show subcases in a design table for a conditional?

9.6 Explain the difference between a conditional with *mutually exclusive cases* and one with *nonexclusive cases*.

9.7 Show the form of IF appropriate for a conditional with *mutually exclusive cases*. Show the form appropriate for *nonexclusive cases*.

9.8 Does a CASE conditional have mutually exclusive or nonexclusive cases?

9.9 Explain how to determine the *number of control paths* in a conditional with mutually exclusive cases. With nonexclusive cases.

9.10 What types of *tests* are allowed in a Pascal IF? In a Pascal CASE?

9.11 When is a set of tests *mutually exclusive*? *Nonexclusive*?

9.12 For a given program state, what difference does the *order of evaluation* of a set of mutually exclusive tests make? Of a set of nonexclusive tests?

9.13 What two things are wrong with a design table that uses *nonexclusive tests* to discriminate *mutually exclusive cases*? Name two other advantages of using mutually exclusive tests.

9.14 When is a set of tests *exhaustive?* How do the *data types* of the variables involved affect whether a set of tests is exhaustive?

9.15 What effect does an exhaustive set of tests have on the *possible control paths* in a conditional?

9.16 When is a test *redundant* in a sequence of tests?

9.17 Give two advantages and two disadvantages of *deleting redundant tests* in an IF.

9.18 What is the *negation* of a test?

9.19 Show two ways to form the negation of an expression involving a *relational test* such as "<".

9.20 How would you determine the *path condition* for executing one of the cases in an IF, given that the tests used are *mutually exclusive*? If the tests are *nonexclusive*?

9.21 How would you determine the path condition for the *default case* in an IF?

9.22 Show how to use *De Morgan's Laws* to simplify the negation of a test involving AND or OR.

9.23 List the Pascal rules for punctuation with *semicolons*.

9.24 What is a Pascal *compound statement*? What is a Pascal *empty statement*?

9.25 What is the *dangling ELSE* problem in coding IF statements in Pascal? When does this problem occur? What do you do to ensure that a dangling ELSE does not change the intended meaning of an IF?

9.26 When can a BEGIN-END pair be *omitted* from an IF, CASE, WHILE, or FOR statement in Pascal?

9.27 State one advantage and one disadvantage of omitting BEGIN-END pairs where they are optional.

9.28 A semicolon is *optional* immediately before the reserved word _____, but a semicolon may *never appear* immediately before the reserved word _____ in Pascal.

9.29 How do you code the pseudo-code action "NO ACTION" in a Pascal IF or CASE?

■ ■ ■
PROGRAMMING PROBLEMS

9.1 *The Fringe Benefits Package.* When BSU (Big State U.) hires a new employee, that person has to choose the various fringe benefits desired. There are quite a few options, each with a price tag that is taken as a deduction from the employee's gross monthly pay. Currently the list of choices is as follows:

a. *Health insurance options.* Option A costs $95.25 per month; option B costs $53.75; option C costs $27.50.

b. *Disability insurance options.* Option X is paid by BSU, no charge to the employee; option Y costs $5.25 per month if the employee makes less than $2000/mo. and costs $7.50 if the employee's salary is $2000/mo. or more.

c. *Life insurance options.* The employee can choose the amount of coverage (in increments of $1000), from zero to $100,000. The cost is $1.10/mo. for each $1000 of life insurance coverage if the employee is under age 50 and $1.80/mo. if age 50 or over.

d. *Parking permit.* A Class E permit costs $15/mo. Class F costs $5/mo. No charge for a class D (distant) permit.

e. *Charity contribution.* A gift to a designated charity can be deducted directly from the paycheck. The contribution can be any amount per month that the employee specifies. This deduction is always stated as a percentage of gross pay (for example, one percent per month).

BSU has found that new employees often choose so many expensive options that their net pay each month after deductions is too low, and they come back after getting their first month's paycheck and change to a less expensive set of options, which causes the payroll office much extra paperwork. To avoid the problem, they want a computer program that will allow the employee to try out various choices and observe their effect on his net pay at the time he is being hired.

Design, code, and test a "benefits options" program for BSU. Assume the new employee sits at the terminal and runs your program. The program should collect the information needed about options choices, gross monthly pay, age, and so forth, and then display the total cost of the options chosen, and the resulting net pay amount.

The program should also deduct national, state, and local taxes in determining the net pay amount. For simplicity, assume that the total of all these taxes amounts to 25 percent of the gross monthly pay if the pay is less than $3000/mo. and 35 percent if the pay is $3000/mo. or more.

9.2 *Classifying a Poker Hand.* Beginning poker players often find it hard to remember how to classify the cards in a five-card poker hand. In poker you use an ordinary deck of cards, with the cards in each suit ranked in the order 2, 3, ..., 10, Jack, Queen, King, Ace. The four suits are the usual ones: hearts, diamonds, clubs, and spades. The five-card hand dealt in most poker games is classified as follows, from the best hand to the worst:

- *Royal flush.* 10, Jack, Queen, King, Ace in the same suit.
- *Straight flush.* Five cards in a sequence from the same suit but not including an Ace.
- *Four of a kind.* Four cards of the same rank and one unmatched.
- *Full house.* Three cards of one rank and two of another (three of a kind and a pair).
- *Flush.* Five cards of the same suit, but not in sequence.
- *Straight.* Five cards in sequence, but not in the same suit.
- *Three of a kind.* Three cards of the same rank and two unmatched.
- *Two pair.* Two cards of the same rank, two of another rank, and one unmatched.
- *A pair.* Two cards of the same rank and three unmatched.
- *High card.* Highest card of five unmatched.

Write the requirements for a program that will read a list of the cards in a five-card hand, as typed by the user, and then display the best classification for the hand (based on the list above). Design a convenient input representation for cards as part of the requirements. Then design, code, and test a program to meet your requirements.

9.3 *The Monkey Language.* The syntax of the *monkey* language is quite simple, yet only monkeys can speak it without making mistakes. The syntax of the language is given by the following BNF specification:

⟨sentence⟩ ::=
    ⟨word⟩ {⟨space⟩ ⟨word⟩}.
WHERE
    ⟨word⟩ ::= ⟨syllable⟩ {⟨syllable⟩ ⟨syllable⟩}
    ⟨syllable⟩ ::= ⟨plosive⟩
                 ¦ ⟨plosive⟩ ⟨stop⟩
                 ¦ a ⟨plosive⟩
                 ¦ a ⟨stop⟩
    ⟨plosive⟩ ::= ⟨stop⟩ a
    ⟨stop⟩ ::= b ¦ d
    ⟨space⟩ ::= A space character.

From the BNF, you can see that a sentence in *monkey* consists of a sequence of the letters *a*, *b*, and *d* in certain restricted patterns, and separated by spaces into words. For example, these are actual sentences in *monkey:*

    aba_dab.
    abada_aba_da.

But this is not:

    abab_da.

Design, code, and test a program that will read a sequence of characters, ending in a period, as the user types them in. The sequence is supposed to have been typed by a monkey. Your program's task is to check whether it really is a sentence in *monkey,* or if the user is actually unable to write *monkey* correctly (and thus obviously is a secret agent masquerading as a monkey). Limit the user's input to 80 characters.

9.4 *Turing Machine Simulator.* In Chapter 1, we described the logical "machine" called a *Turing Machine,* which can be "programmed" to perform an information processing task. The key elements of the Turing machine are its *tape,* a sequence of squares each of which contains a single character (similar to an ARRAY [...] OF Char in Pascal) and its *program,* which is simply a table showing what action the Turing machine should take, given its *current instruction number* and the character positioned under its *read/write head* on the tape. Review the description of the Turing machine in Chapter 1.

It is useful to have a program that can *simulate* the actions of a Turing machine, given its program and the initial contents of its tape. Write the requirements for such a program. The program should allow the user to specify the program for the Turing machine, the initial contents of the tape, and the number of the first instruction to be executed. Then the program should "simulate" the actions of the Turing machine as it executes the given program. The program should display the contents of the tape after each instruction of the program is executed, along with the number of the current instruction and the position of the read/write head in the tape. Thus the user should see on the screen a trace of the execution of the Turing machine program.

Design, code, and test a program to meet the requirements that you have specified. As one of your test cases, use the example Turing machine program from Chapter 1. You will have to limit the length of the Turing Machine's tape. If the read/write head tries to move beyond the end of the tape, the program should display an error message and halt.

9.5 *Hand Calculator Program.* It is often convenient to have a program that provides the services of a hand calculator, allowing the user to enter numbers, store them, and perform basic arithmetic operations on them. This program is an extremely simple version of a "calculator." The requirements are as follows:

a. The user is given ten *registers,* named R0 to R9, each of which can store a single Real number. Each register initially contains the value zero.

b. The user may enter a sequence of commands. Each command must have one of the forms (Ri, Rj, and Rk are register names):

```
Rk := ⟨real number literal⟩ ⟨EOLN⟩
```

MEANING: Store the number in register Rk, and display the number stored.

```
Rk := Ri ⟨op⟩ Rj ⟨EOLN⟩
         where ⟨op⟩ is one of +, -, *, or /
```

MEANING: Apply the operation to the numbers stored in registers Ri and Rj and store the result in register Rk. Also display the result.

```
D ⟨EOLN⟩
```

MEANING: Display the contents of all ten registers.

> Q ⟨EOLN⟩

MEANING: Quit.

For example, if you wanted to calculate the value of the expression:

$$2 * 375.1 + 7.189$$

You might see the following dialogue:

```
Program:    CALCULATOR RUNNING
            TYPE COMMAND SEQUENCE:
User:       R0 := 2
Program:    2
User:       R1 := 375.1
Program:    375.1
User:       R6 := 7.189
Program:    7.189
User:       R9 := R0 * R1
Program:    750.2
User:       R0 := R9 + R6
Program:    757.389
User:       D
Program:    R0:  757.389
            R1:  375.1
            R2:  0
            R3:  0
            R4:  0
            R5:  0
            R6:  7.189
            R7:  0
            R8:  0
            R9:  750.2
User:       Q
Program:    CALCULATOR QUITTING
```

Design the calculator program, code the program in Pascal, and test it thoroughly.

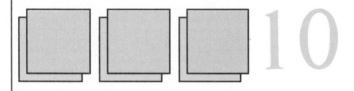

10

More About Loops

CHAPTER GOALS

When you have mastered the content of this chapter, you should be able to:

- Design and code a complex loop, using WHILE, FOR, and REPEAT statements.
- Identify the parts of a loop that form the *loop control.*
- Decide whether a loop should be *count controlled, event controlled,* or *count and event controlled.*
- Design a loop by using a *loop invariant.*
- Describe the *"Loop Designer's Dilemma"* and what to do about it.
- Explain why a loop must make *progress toward termination.*
- Analyze *control flow* and *data flow* during loop execution.
- Identify common *loop design errors.*
- Use the *"Seven Step Loop Check"* to check the correctness of a loop design.

A loop in a program allows us to repeat a given action or sequence of actions over and over, perhaps dozens, hundreds, or thousands of times. Loops allow us to put the enormous processing speed of a computer to good use. Loops also allow us to write programs that are more concise when actions need to be repeated more than once.

□□□ 10.1
THE PASCAL LOOP STATEMENTS: FOR, WHILE, AND REPEAT

Let's begin with a look at the Pascal loop statements—FOR, WHILE, and REPEAT. FOR and WHILE loops are already familiar, and REPEAT is just a variation on the WHILE loop.

□□
The Pascal FOR Statement

Although we have been using the FOR loop only to code an action that is repeated for each element of an array, the FOR loop is also useful for coding other loops. Instead of the *subscript variable* (usually "I") used with arrays, we term the variable in a general FOR loop the *index variable* of the loop. The general FOR loop has two forms:

⟨FOR-loop⟩ ::=

```
    FOR ⟨index-variable⟩ := ⟨first-value⟩ TO ⟨last-value⟩ DO
        ⟨loop-body⟩
  | FOR ⟨index-variable⟩ := ⟨last-value⟩ DOWNTO ⟨first-value⟩ DO
        ⟨loop-body⟩
```

WHERE
⟨index-variable⟩ ::=
    A Pascal identifier naming a simple variable of Integer, Char,
    subrange, or enumerated type. The variable must be a *local variable*
    of the subprogram in which the loop appears.
⟨first-value⟩ ::=
    A Pascal expression giving the smallest value for which the loop body
    should be executed (using the ordering defined for the data type of
    ⟨index-variable⟩.)

⟨last-value⟩ ::=
> A Pascal expression giving the largest value for which the loop body should be executed.

⟨loop-body⟩ ::=
> A single Pascal statement, usually a compound statement enclosed in BEGIN-END.

□

Meaning: The meaning of the TO form is:

1. Evaluate the ⟨first-value⟩ and ⟨last-value⟩ expressions.
2. Assign the value of the ⟨first-value⟩ expression to the ⟨index-variable⟩.
3. Test if the value of ⟨index-variable⟩ is greater than the value of the ⟨last-value⟩ expression (from step 1).
4. If the result of the test is TRUE, then exit the loop and go on to the statement that follows the loop.
5. If the result of the test is FALSE, then
   a. Execute the ⟨loop-body⟩.
   b. Assign:

   > ⟨index-variable⟩ := *succ* (⟨index-variable⟩)

   c. Repeat these same steps from step 3.

The DOWNTO form works in a similar way, except that the ⟨index-variable⟩ begins with the ⟨last-value⟩ and counts down to the ⟨first-value⟩, using the *pred* function to find the "next" value. When the value of the ⟨index-variable⟩ is less than the ⟨last-value⟩ execution of the loop is complete.

Notice that the general Pascal FOR loop allows index variables of type Char or an enumerated type. The *succ* and *pred* functions define the "next" value in the index sequence for a TO and DOWNTO loop, respectively. For example, if TestChar is a Char variable, then you might write:

```
FOR TestChar := 'A' TO 'Z' DO
    ... loop body ...
```

which would execute the loop body 26 times, once for each character in the range from 'A' to 'Z'. Remember that for Integer and subrange types, *succ* and *pred* simply add one and subtract one, respectively.

A few points to remember about the FOR loop:

1. *The ⟨index-variable⟩ cannot be assigned a new value within the loop body.* The ⟨index-variable⟩ can only be used as an IN variable in the loop body; no definition of a new value for this variable within the loop is allowed.
2. *The ⟨first-value⟩ and ⟨last-value⟩ expressions are evaluated only once, at the time the loop is entered.* The same ⟨last-value⟩ (in the TO form) or ⟨first-value⟩ (in the DOWNTO form) is used each time the test for exiting the loop is made. If you assign a

new value in the loop body to one of the variables in the ⟨first-value⟩ or ⟨last-value⟩ expressions, it does *not* affect when the loop exit occurs, because the ⟨first-value⟩ or ⟨last-value⟩ expression is never evaluated a second time.

3. *The loop body may never be executed at all.* The test for exiting the loop is made before the first execution of the loop body. If the ⟨first-value⟩ is greater than the ⟨last-value⟩ then the loop body is never executed.

4. *The value of the ⟨index-variable⟩ is unpredictable after the loop execution is complete.* After execution of the loop is complete, the ⟨index-variable⟩ is considered "uninitialized" if used in any later statements.

5. *DOWNTO is a single word, not two.*

EXAMPLE *Examples of General FOR Loops*

1. {PURPOSE/GOAL STATE: Sum the integers from 1 to N and store the result in Sum}

```
Sum := 0;
FOR Value := 1 TO N DO
     Sum := Sum + Value;
```

2. {PURPOSE/GOAL STATE: Display a "count-down" sequence, starting at 10 and ending with 2, 1, GO!}

```
FOR Count := 10 DOWNTO 1 DO
     writeln (Count);
writeln ('GO!');
```

3. {PURPOSE/GOAL STATE: Display an "encoding table" showing each lower-case letter replaced by its predecessor in the alphabet. 'a' should be encoded as 'z'.}

```
writeln ('LETTER TO ENCODE':20, 'ENCODED LETTER':20);
writeln ('a':15, 'z':20);
FOR Letter := 'b' TO 'z' DO
     writeln (Letter:15, pred (Letter):20);
```

□ □

The Pascal WHILE Statement

The WHILE loop is familiar from the previous chapters:

⟨WHILE-loop⟩ ::=

```
WHILE ⟨test⟩ DO
     ⟨loop-body⟩
```

WHERE
⟨test⟩ ::= Any Boolean-valued expression.
⟨loop-body⟩ ::=
     Any *single* Pascal statement, usually a compound statement enclosed in BEGIN-END.

□

Meaning:

1. Evaluate the ⟨test⟩.
2. If ⟨test⟩ = FALSE, exit the loop.
3. If ⟨test⟩ = TRUE, execute the ⟨loop-body⟩ and repeat these same steps from 1.

A few points to remember:

1. *The loop body may never be executed at all.* If the ⟨test⟩ is FALSE on entry to the loop then the loop body is not executed.
2. *The loop may repeat "forever."* The loop body is executed repeatedly until the ⟨test⟩ = FALSE. If it never is FALSE, the loop becomes an *infinite loop* that repeats "forever."

□ □

The Pascal REPEAT Statement

The REPEAT loop is just a variation on the WHILE loop. Its general form in Pascal is:

⟨REPEAT-loop⟩ ::=

    REPEAT
       ⟨loop-body-sequence-of-statements⟩
    UNTIL ⟨test⟩

       WHERE
          ⟨test⟩ ::= Any Boolean-valued expression.
          ⟨loop-body-sequence-of-statements⟩ ::=
               Any sequence of one or more Pascal statements.

□

Meaning:

1. Execute the ⟨loop-body-sequence-of-statements⟩.
2. Evaluate the ⟨test⟩.
3. If ⟨test⟩ = TRUE, then exit the loop and go on to the statement that follows the loop.
4. If ⟨test⟩ = FALSE repeat these same steps from 1.

EXAMPLES

1.
```
    {PURPOSE/GOAL STATE: Call the PlayGame procedure
     repeatedly until the user says to quit}
REPEAT
   PlayGame (...);
   write ('Want to play again?  (y/n)');
   readln (Response);
UNTIL Response = 'n';
```

2.　{PURPOSE/GOAL STATE: Search the array GradesList
　　[1..LastEntry] to find the first 'A' grade. Store the
　　subscript of that element in FirstA. If no A is found,
　　store zero in FirstA}

```
FirstA := 0;
Found := FALSE;
I := 1;
REPEAT
    IF GradesList [I] = 'A' THEN
      BEGIN
         Found := TRUE;
         FirstA := I;
      END
    I := I + 1;
UNTIL (I > LastEntry) OR Found;
```

Differences Between REPEAT and WHILE Loops

REPEAT and WHILE loops are almost the same. Here are the three differences to remember:

1. The body of a REPEAT loop is *always executed at least once;* the body of a WHILE loop *may never be executed at all.*
2. The test in a REPEAT loop tests whether to *exit* the loop—a TRUE result means *exit the loop.* The test in a WHILE loop tests whether to *continue* the loop—a TRUE result means *continue to execute the loop one more time.*
3. If the body of a WHILE loop contains more than one statement, you must use BEGIN-END to make a compound statement. The body of a REPEAT loop never needs a surrounding BEGIN-END.

Choosing between WHILE and REPEAT

Because a WHILE loop puts the loop exit test first, it is usually easier to read. Consider it your "standard" loop statement, as we have done in the previous chapters. Use the REPEAT only when the action represented:

1. Will *always* have to be done at least once, and
2. The test for stopping the repetition is naturally phrased as an "exit when this event happens" test.

EXAMPLE　The "continue until the user says to quit" loop is usually more understandable as a REPEAT loop. For example the loop above:

```
{PURPOSE/GOAL STATE: Call the PlayGame procedure
repeatedly until the user says to quit}
```

```
REPEAT
   PlayGame (...);
   write ('Want to play again?  (y/n)');
   readln (Response);
UNTIL Response = 'n';
```

is easier to understand than the equivalent WHILE loop:

```
         {PURPOSE/GOAL STATE: Call the PlayGame procedure
          repeatedly until the user says to quit}
Response := 'y';
WHILE Response <> 'n' DO
   BEGIN
      PlayGame (...);
      write ('Want to play again?  (y/n)');
      readln (Response);
   END;
```

□ □

Changing FOR Loops and REPEAT Loops into WHILE Loops

A useful skill is to be able to quickly transform a loop written as a FOR or REPEAT into an equivalent WHILE loop. Often you need to make such a transformation before making modifications to a loop.

□

FOR into WHILE.   Suppose the FOR loop is:

```
FOR I := ⟨first-value⟩ TO ⟨last-value⟩ DO
    ⟨loop-body⟩
```

The equivalent WHILE loop is:

```
I := ⟨first-value⟩;
WHILE I <= ⟨last-value⟩ DO
   BEGIN
      ⟨loop-body⟩
      I := succ (I);
   END
```

provided that the loop body does not change the value of any variable used in the ⟨last-value⟩ expression. If this condition is violated, then to safely get an equivalent WHILE loop you have to declare a new variable, say LastValue, and write the WHILE loop as:

```
I := ⟨first-value⟩;
LastValue := ⟨last-value⟩;

WHILE I <= LastValue DO
    BEGIN
       ⟨loop-body⟩
       I := succ (I);
    END
```

The new variable LastValue is needed to save the ⟨last-value⟩ so that it cannot be changed by any action in ⟨loop-body⟩. A similar transformation can be used to change other forms of the FOR loop into equivalent WHILE loops.

□

REPEAT into WHILE.   To change a REPEAT into a WHILE:

1. Negate the exit test of the REPEAT to get the test in the WHILE,
2. Enclose the loop body in BEGIN...END if it has more than one statement, and
3. Before entering the WHILE loop, assign values to the variables used in the new test so that the test gives TRUE when the loop is entered.

The REPEAT:

```
REPEAT
    ⟨loop-body⟩
UNTIL ⟨test⟩
```

is changed to the equivalent WHILE:

```
⟨assign values to make "NOT ⟨test⟩" give TRUE⟩
WHILE NOT ⟨test⟩ DO
    BEGIN
       ⟨loop-body⟩
    END
```

Instead of writing "NOT ⟨test⟩" in the WHILE loop, you can use the "natural" negations of tests like "<" as discussed in the previous chapter, for example, replacing "<" by ">=". Use DeMorgan's Laws to simplify the result, if needed.

A typical example is a REPEAT loop that tests a flag variable:

```
REPEAT
    ⟨loop-body⟩
UNTIL Flag
```

where the value of Flag is defined in the loop body. The equivalent WHILE loop is
then:

```
Flag := FALSE;
WHILE NOT Flag DO
    BEGIN
        ⟨loop-body⟩
    END
```

EXERCISES

10.1 Transform each of the following FOR loops into an equivalent WHILE
loop:

a. FOR I := 1 TO LastEntry DO
            Total := Total + A [I]

b. FOR I := M DOWNTO N DO
            Product := Product * I

c. FOR J := 2 TO LastGrade DO
            IF Grade [J] > Max THEN
                BEGIN
                    Max := Grade [J];
                    MaxIndex := J;
                END

d. FOR I := A TO B DO
            BEGIN
                ComputeValues (A, B);
                B := B + 1;
            END

10.2 Transform each of the following REPEAT loops into an equivalent
WHILE loop:

a. REPEAT
            X := X - 1;
        UNTIL X <= Y

b. REPEAT
            writeln;
            Count := Count + 1;
        UNTIL Count > SpaceCount

c. REPEAT
            ComputeResults (A, B, Flag);
        UNTIL Flag <> CONTINUE

d. Done := FALSE;
        REPEAT
            IF X > Y THEN
                Done := TRUE
            ELSE
                X := 2 * X;
        UNTIL Done

e.
```
REPEAT
    Quotient := Quotient + 1;
    Remainder := Remainder - B;
UNTIL Remainder < B
```

□□□ **10.2**
BASIC LOOP DESIGN CONCEPTS

An action represented by a loop has several parts. Let's look at the general form of what we will call a *loop segment,* the sequence of program statements that represents the whole action that includes the loop. The *loop body* is the part of the overall action to be repeated as the loop executes. We also include as part of a loop segment an optional *startup segment* that contains actions to be taken before entering the loop body the first time, such as the definition of initial values for some of the data objects used in the loop body or loop exit test.

EXAMPLE

Most of our examples in the previous section contain startup segments. For example, consider this loop segment:

```
{PURPOSE/GOAL STATE: Search the array GradesList
[1..LastEntry] to find the first 'A' grade.  Store the
subscript of that element in FirstA.  If no A is found,
store zero in FirstA}
FirstA := 0;
Found := FALSE;                          STARTUP SEGMENT
I := 1;

REPEAT
    IF GradesList [I] = 'A' THEN
        BEGIN
            Found := TRUE;               LOOP BODY
            FirstA := I;
        END;
    I := I + 1;
UNTIL (I > LastEntry) OR Found;
```

□□
The Loop Control

Terminating the execution of the loop body after the correct number of iterations is the function of the *loop control.* The loop control has three parts:

1. *Exit test.* An *exit test* is required to determine whether to repeat the execution of the loop body or to exit the loop. This test is a Boolean-valued TRUE/FALSE test. To simplify discussion, we label the two possible values of the exit test *exit the loop* and *continue the loop* rather than TRUE/FALSE because of the difference in the Pascal WHILE and REPEAT loops—in a WHILE, a TRUE value means "continue the loop" while in a REPEAT, a TRUE value means "exit the loop."

2. *Initialization of the values of the data objects used in the exit test.* Before entering the loop, some of the data objects used in the exit test must usually be assigned initial values in the startup segment.

3. *Update of the values of the data objects used to control loop exit.* Each time the loop body is repeated, at least one of the data objects used in the exit test or used to choose the execution path through the loop body must have a new value defined. We think of these actions as "updating" the values of these data objects in order to "make progress toward termination" of the loop.

In a FOR loop, you see these parts of the loop control explicitly in the first line of the loop. However, in WHILE and REPEAT loops, only the exit test is included explicitly in the WHILE or REPEAT loop syntax. The initialization appears in the startup segment before the loop and the update of loop control data objects appears as part of the loop body, as shown in Figure 10.1.

FIGURE 10-1 Loop Control Elements in FOR and WHILE Loops

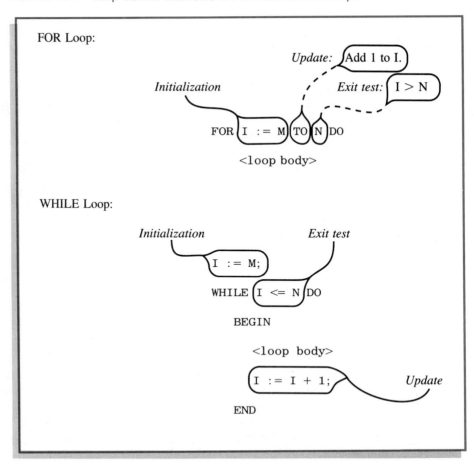

Infinite Loops and "Progress Toward Termination"

An essential ingredient in the loop control is the idea of *progress toward termination* of the loop. Each time the loop body is executed, some action must be taken that brings the loop "closer" to termination. This can only happen in one of two ways:

1. The value of at least one of the data objects used in the loop exit test might be modified during this iteration, or
2. The value of at least one of the data objects used to choose the *control path* within the loop body on the *next loop iteration* might be modified during this iteration.

When a loop body contains an IF or another "nested" loop, *each control path* through the body must make progress toward termination in one of these two ways.

EXAMPLE

In this loop:

```
Done := FALSE;
REPEAT
    IF X > Y THEN
        Done := TRUE
    ELSE
        X := 2 * X
UNTIL Done
```

there are two paths through the loop body. The first case of the IF makes progress toward termination by assigning a new value to the flag variable Done. Done is tested in the loop exit test. The second case of the IF makes progress toward termination by assigning a new value to variable X. X is used on the next iteration to choose the control path through the loop body. ∎

In a FOR loop, progress toward termination is guaranteed because the loop index variable is always automatically incremented or decremented after each iteration. However, in a WHILE or REPEAT loop it is the programmer's responsibility to design the loop body so that "progress toward termination" is made on each control path.

An *infinite loop* is a loop that continues to repeat "forever." At the end of each iteration its exit test always evaluates to "continue the loop." Once a loop executes a control path through the loop body that makes no progress toward termination, that loop becomes an infinite loop. At the end of the iteration, the loop exit test will again return the same result, "continue the loop," which will send execution through the body again on the same control path. But again no progress toward termination will be made, so the exit test will again return "continue the loop," and so on, "forever."

Nancy forgot to include the "update" of the subscript variable, "I := I+1", when she wrote this loop to search an array:

```
{PURPOSE/GOAL STATE: Search the array GradesList
[1..LastEntry] to find the first 'A' grade.  Store the
subscript of that element in FirstA.  If no A is found,
store zero in FirstA}
FirstA := 0;
Found := FALSE;
I := 1;
REPEAT
   IF GradesList [I] = 'A' THEN
      BEGIN
         Found := TRUE;
         FirstA := I;
      END
UNTIL (I > LastEntry) OR Found;
```

As a result, on one control path through the loop body no progress toward termination is made. The loop becomes an infinite loop unless GradesList[1] just happens to be an 'A'. ■

□ □

Types of Loop Control

While we can classify loops according to the Pascal loop statement used (FOR, WHILE or REPEAT), a more basic classification is based on the distinction between *count controlled* and *event controlled* loops:

1. *Count controlled loops.* In a *count controlled* loop, the loop control takes the form of an index variable which "counts" through some specified range, such as in most of the preceding examples. If counting is done in steps of one or minus one, then the loop is usually coded as a Pascal FOR loop, but a WHILE or REPEAT loop must be used for counting by 2's or some other "step size."

EXAMPLE Joe wants a loop that sums the even integers from 2 to 100. He needs a count controlled loop in which the index variable counts by 2's. In Pascal he uses the count controlled WHILE loop:

```
{PURPOSE/GOAL STATE: Sum the integers from 2 to 100 and
store the sum in Total.}
Total := 0;
Count := 2;
WHILE Count <= 100 DO
   BEGIN
      Total := Total + Count;
      Count := Count + 2;
   END;
```
■

2. *Event controlled loops*. In an *event controlled loop* the loop control tests one or more of the OUT or IN/OUT variables of the loop body for an "event" (represented by the result of the test indicating "exit the loop"). You think of the loop as "keep repeating the loop body until the event occurs." Event controlled loops are always coded as WHILE or REPEAT loops.

EXAMPLE

A game playing program repeats a loop that plays one game on each iteration, until the user answers "no" to the question "Want to play again?" The loop control repeats the loop until the "no" event occurs:

```
      {PURPOSE/GOAL STATE: Call the PlayGame procedure
      repeatedly until the user says to quit}
REPEAT
   PlayGame (...);
   write ('Want to play again? (y/n)');
   readln (Response);
UNTIL Response = 'n';
```

3. *Count and event controlled loops*. A *count and event controlled* loop is a combination of count and event controlled loop forms: the "count" represents a *bound on the number of iterations* of the loop while waiting for the "event" to occur. If the event never occurs before the count reaches the bound, then the loop exits anyway. You can think of this as the "three strikes and you're out" loop—three strikes is the *count,* a hit is the *event*. These loops are always coded as WHILE or REPEAT loops. In a REPEAT loop of this type the loop exit test usually has the form:

"Has event happened?" OR "Has count been exceeded"?

In a WHILE loop, the exit test will usually be:

"Has event not happened?" AND "Has count not been exceeded?"

EXAMPLE

```
      {PURPOSE/GOAL STATE: Call procedure BatterUp until the
      result is a HIT or three times the result is a STRIKE.}
Strikes := 0;
REPEAT
   BatterUp (..., Result);
   IF Result = STRIKE THEN
      Strikes := Strikes + 1;
UNTIL (Result = HIT) OR (Strikes >= 3);
```

The equivalent WHILE loop would be:

```
Strikes := 0;
Result := STRIKE;      {any initial value <> HIT}
WHILE (Result <> HIT) AND (Strikes < 3) DO
   BEGIN
      BatterUp (..., Result);
      IF Result = STRIKE THEN
         Strikes := Strikes + 1;
   END;
```

Nested Loops

In a *nested* loop, the loop body itself contains a loop. The *inner loop* has its own loop control, separate from the loop control of the *outer loop*. Each loop may be count controlled, event controlled, or count and event controlled.

EXAMPLE: *Selection Sort*

One way to *sort* the values stored in an array into numerical order uses an algorithm called a *selection sort*. Begin by finding (selecting) the smallest value in the array. Put it in the first position by swapping it with the value currently in the first position. Find the smallest remaining value and swap it into the second position, and so forth. To find the smallest remaining value on each iteration, scan all the remaining unsorted values in the array.

A selection sort uses two nested loops. Both are count controlled. The outer loop counts from 1 to the next to the last array entry, say using a subscript variable I. I represents the array element that will be filled next (with the next smallest value). The inner loop counts from $I+1$ to the end of the array, for instance using subscript variable J. J represents the element whose value is about to be checked to see if it is the smallest value remaining in the unsorted part of the array.

The coded loop might look like this:

```
{PURPOSE/GOAL STATE: Sort the values in array Table
[1..LastEntry] into increasing numerical order}

FOR I := 1 TO LastEntry-1 DO
   BEGIN   {begin outer loop}

            {PURPOSE/GOAL STATE: Find the subscript of the
            smallest remaining value in the unsorted part of
            the array, and store it in SmallestPosn}

      SmallestPosn := I;
      FOR J := I+1 TO LastEntry DO
         BEGIN   {begin inner loop}
            IF Table [J] < Table [SmallestPosn] THEN
               SmallestPosn := J;
         END;    {end inner loop}

            {PURPOSE/GOAL STATE: Swap the smallest remaining
            value into the Ith position in the array}

      SmallestValue := Table [SmallestPosn];
      Table [SmallestPosn] := Table [I];
      Table [I] := SmallestValue;
   END;   {end outer loop}
```

Nested Loop (bracket spanning the inner FOR J loop)

Important Program States During Loop Execution

Let's take a look at the key *program states* that exist during execution of a loop. Figure 10.2 shows where these states occur. These states are:

1. *Loop entry state.* The *loop entry state* is the state immediately after the startup segment has been executed but before the loop exit test has been made the first time (in WHILE and FOR loops). In a FOR loop, the loop entry state occurs *after* the index variable has been assigned its initial value.

The loop entry state is important because it is the state that exists when the loop body begins its execution the first time, and in WHILE and FOR loops it represents the state that determines whether the loop body is skipped entirely.

2. *Loop exit state.* The second important state is the state at the time the loop is exited, immediately before the execution of whatever action follows the loop. This state usually corresponds to the GOAL STATE of the overall loop segment.

FIGURE 10-2 Important States During Loop Execution

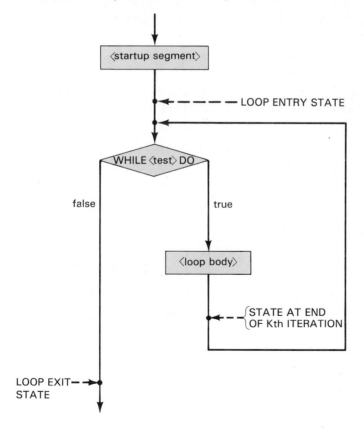

In a FOR loop, the *value of the index variable* is not defined in the loop exit state. (Its value is unpredictable.) If a FOR or WHILE loop takes the "zero trip" path and skips execution of the loop body, then the loop entry state is also the loop exit state.

3. *State at the end of the Kth Iteration.* The other important states occur at the same point during each iteration, at the *end of the execution of the loop body,* just before the exit test is made (in a FOR loop, we use the state *after* the index variable's value has been incremented or decremented). We call these states the *state at the end of the Kth iteration.* Thus, there is an important state at the end of the first iteration, another at the end of the second iteration, and so forth.

The state at the end of the Kth iteration is important because it is the state that determines whether the loop will be exited or repeated again. If the loop is exited, then it represents the loop exit state (except that the value of the index variable in a FOR loop is still defined before loop exit). If the loop is repeated, it represents the state in which the loop body begins execution on the next iteration.

□ □

Loop Invariants

In designing and analyzing loops, we often need to describe the *state at the end of the Kth iteration.* Such a description is termed a *loop invariant:*

> □ **Loop Invariant**
>
> A *loop invariant* is an assertion that describes the *program state* at the *end of the Kth iteration of a loop,* for any positive integer value K.

A loop invariant describes a property of the program state that must be true at the end of each iteration. Think of it as describing how much of the work of the loop has been completed at the end of the Kth iteration.

The term *invariant* is used because we are describing a property of the program state that is constant or unchanging as the loop body is executed repeatedly. Of course, the values stored in our data objects are changing as the loop is executed, so the loop invariant describes *how the values defined and used in the loop body are related to each other and to the number, K, of repetitions of the loop body that have been executed.*

Choosing a loop invariant is the important first step in designing complex loops. We see the details in the next section.

□ □

Writing a Loop Invariant

For writing loop invariants, we use the form:

```
KTH ITERATION: ...loop invariant...
```

to clarify for the reader that the state at the end of a *typical iteration* is being described. Because the loop invariant describes the state at the end of execution of the loop body, it appears in the pseudo-code program design following the last action in the loop body. In Pascal, we include the loop invariant as a comment at the end of the loop body.

EXAMPLE *Examples of Loop Invariants*

1. {PURPOSE/GOAL STATE: Sum the integers from 1 to N and store the result in Sum}

   ```
   Sum := 0;
   FOR Value := 1 TO N DO
      BEGIN
         Sum := Sum + Value;

         {KTH ITERATION: Sum = sum of the first K integers. }
      END;
   ```

2. {PURPOSE/GOAL STATE: Display an "encoding table" showing each lower-case letter replaced by its predecessor in the alphabet. 'a' should be encoded as 'z'. }

   ```
   writeln ('LETTER TO ENCODE':20, 'ENCODED LETTER':20);
   writeln ('a':15, 'z':20);
   FOR Letter := 'b' TO 'z' DO
      BEGIN
         writeln (Letter:15, pred (Letter):20);

         {KTH ITERATION: The K+1st line of the table has been displayed}
      END;
   ```

3. {PURPOSE/GOAL STATE: Search the array GradesList [1..LastEntry] to find the first 'A' grade. Store the subscript of that element in FirstA. If no A is found, store zero in FirstA}

   ```
   FirstA := 0;
   Found := FALSE;
   I := 1;
   REPEAT
      IF GradesList [I] = 'A' THEN
         BEGIN
            Found := TRUE;
            FirstA := I;
         END
      I := I + 1;

      {KTH ITERATION: The first K elements of GradesList
       have been tested, and I = K+1. If the Kth element
       is the first 'A', then FOUND = TRUE and FirstA = K. }

   UNTIL (I > LastEntry) OR Found;                              ■
   ```

EXERCISES

10.3 Identify the three parts of the loop control in each of the following loops, and name the type of loop control being used (count controlled, event controlled, or count and event controlled):

a.
```
A := -5;
REPEAT
    writeln (...);
    A := A + 3;
UNTIL A > 5
```

b.
```
FOR J := 2 TO LastGrade DO
    IF Grade [J] > Max THEN
        BEGIN
            Max := Grade [J];
            MaxIndex := J
        END
```

c.
```
Done := FALSE;
REPEAT
    IF X > Y THEN
        Done := TRUE
    ELSE
        X := 2 * X
UNTIL Done
```

d.
```
ZeroFound := FALSE;
I := 1;
WHILE (NOT ZeroFound) AND (I <= N) DO
    IF A[I] = 0 THEN
        BEGIN
            ZeroFound := TRUE;
            ZeroPosn := I;
        END
    ELSE
        I := I + 1;
```

e.
```
readln (A, B);
Quotient := 0;
Remainder := A;
REPEAT
    Quotient := Quotient + 1;
    Remainder := Remainder - B;
UNTIL Remainder < B
```

☐☐☐ **10.3**
DESIGNING AND CODING LOOPS

Complex loops are often among the most difficult parts of a program to design and code correctly. Let's look at the basic principles first. In the following sections we illustrate how the principles are used in common loop patterns.

Steps in Loop Design

Designing a complex loop is best approached in several steps:

☐

Step 1. Design a *loop invariant* that describes the program state you want to reach at the end of the Kth iteration (a "typical" iteration).

☐

Step 2. Design the *loop control*—count controlled, event controlled, or count and event controlled. Design the exit test, initialization, and update parts of the loop control, to allow you to exit the loop after the desired number of iterations, when the desired "event" occurs, or both.

☐

Step 3. Design a *loop body* that allows you to reach the program state described by the loop invariant. The actions in the loop body must make the loop invariant true at the end of each iteration. To get into and through the first iteration correctly, you may also need to design some *startup actions,* such as initializing variables to be used in the loop.

☐

Step 4. Verify the *correctness* of the loop design to be sure that all the parts work together properly.

Designing a Loop Invariant

Starting with the loop invariant is useful because it forces you to think about the program state that you are trying to reach at the end of each iteration. This state becomes the goal state when you design the loop body and startup actions.

To design the loop invariant, think of what you want the "state of affairs" to be at the end of each iteration of the loop body. Each iteration represents one step in the overall action represented by the loop, so look first at the statement of the overall action to see what "one step" might be. Some typical "steps" on which to base a loop invariant might be:

- The next element of the array has been tested and the flag variable set to the result of the test.
- The next data value has been read and stored in the next element of the array.
- The next value has been computed and added to the total.

From the idea of what "one step" should be, think about what the "state of affairs" should be after "K steps." Describe the state of the variables involved after K steps have been completed. For example, using the "steps" above, you might design the loop invariants:

- KTH ITERATION: The first K elements of the array have been tested and the flag variable contains the result of the test on the Kth element.
- KTH ITERATION: K data values have been read and stored in the first K elements of the array.
- KTH ITERATION: Total contains the sum of the first K computed data values.

Notice how the loop invariant captures the cumulative effect of the K repetitions of the single step made in one iteration. To check the loop invariant, try it out in your head for the first few values of K: Is that what I want accomplished after one iteration? After two iterations? After three?

□ □

Choosing the Type of Loop Control

The next step in design is to choose the type of loop control—how will you get the loop to stop? Again, look at the statement of the action that the loop represents. You will usually see a phrase that indicates how the number of iterations should be controlled. Typical examples:

- "Repeat the procedure call for each month of the fiscal year." (*Count controlled* loop: count from 1 to 12.)
- "Read data values until a zero value is read." (*Event controlled* loop: exit when a zero is read.)
- "Search the elements of the array until the first nonzero value is found, if any." (*Count and event controlled* loop: exit when a nonzero value is found or the end of the array is reached.)

□ □

Designing Count Controlled Loops

For designing count controlled loops in pseudo-code, use a Pascal style FOR loop header:

```
FOR ⟨index-variable⟩ := ⟨first-value⟩ TO ⟨last-value⟩ DO
        BEGIN
                ⟨loop body⟩
        END
```

If the *step size,* the value to be added to the index variable after each iteration, is other than 1, then add the phrase to the loop header:

```
STEP ⟨step-size⟩
```

to specify what the step size should be. For example, to step through the range from 0 to 1 in steps of 1/4 (step size = 0.25), write:

```
        FOR H := 0 TO 1 STEP 0.25 DO
                ⟨loop body⟩
```

To step from a larger value down to a smaller value, use a negative step size:

```
        FOR I := 10 TO 0 STEP −2 DO
                ⟨loop body⟩
```

or use the Pascal "DOWNTO" when the step size is −1. Also be sure to add the index variable to your DATA OBJECTS list.

Note that you can only use "STEP ⟨value⟩" in *pseudo-code,* not in Pascal. In Pascal, a count-controlled loop with a step size other than one or minus one must be coded as a WHILE or REPEAT loop.

EXAMPLE   Suppose that you want to display every even-numbered element in an array TableValues [1..100]. Your design might be:

PURPOSE/GOAL STATE: Display a table of the even numbered
elements of TableValues [1..100].

ACTIONS:

DISPLAY: "Entry Number   Value in Table"

```
FOR Entry := 2 TO 100 STEP 2 DO
        DISPLAY: "⟨Entry⟩        ⟨TableValues [Entry]⟩"
```

KTH ITERATION: Even numbered entries 2 to 2*K of the table have been displayed.   ■

□ □
Designing Event Controlled Loops

The term "event" means "some property of the values of the variables in the program state." Thus an "event" is anything that can be tested in the exit test of a WHILE or REPEAT loop. Some typical events:

- Finding a value with some desired property while searching through the elements of an array, such as the first nonzero value in an array.
- Finding that a flag variable has been set to TRUE after execution of the loop body.
- Finding that the user has typed "no" in response to the question "do you want to continue?"

A distinguishing characteristic of an event controlled loop is that you do not know before executing the loop how many iterations will be required. You simply begin executing the loop, and after each iteration you test whether the event has occurred (and if it never occurs, you have an infinite loop).

To design this type of loop control, identify the "event" that causes exit of the loop, and design an exit test for this event. Then determine the initialization and update actions required to be sure that each iteration makes "progress toward termination" by defining new values for one or more of the variables that appear in the exit test. In pseudo-code, always use a WHILE or REPEAT loop.

EXAMPLE   Suppose that you want to call a procedure ComputeNextValue which returns two OUT values: a data value and a flag. You want to repeatedly call the procedure and add the computed value to Total until a FALSE flag value is returned, indicating that no further values can be computed. Your design might be:

> PURPOSE/GOAL STATE: Compute and sum a sequence of values, using ComputeNextValue to compute each value. Stop when ComputeNextValue returns a FALSE flag value.
>
> ACTIONS:
>
> Total := 0
> CALL ComputeNextValue (. . . , Value, Flag)
>
> WHILE Flag = TRUE DO
>   BEGIN
>   Total := Total + Value
>   CALL ComputeNextValue (. . . , Value, Flag)
>
>   KTH ITERATION: Total contains sum of first K values;
>   Flag = FALSE if Value does not contain the next value.
>
>   END   ■

□ □

Designing Count and Event Controlled Loops

This loop is a simple combination of count controlled and event controlled loop structures. To design such a loop, use a *count controlled WHILE loop* as your basic pattern (not a FOR loop), counting from 1 to the iteration bound:

> ⟨index-variable⟩ := 1
> WHILE ⟨index-variable⟩ <= ⟨iteration-bound⟩ DO
>   ⟨loop body actions⟩
>   ⟨index-variable⟩ := ⟨index-variable⟩ + 1

Now add the loop control for the event:

> ⟨initialize variables involved in the event test⟩
> ⟨index-variable⟩ := 1
> WHILE (⟨index-variable⟩ <= ⟨iteration-bound⟩)
>   AND (NOT ⟨event-test⟩) DO
>   ⟨loop body actions⟩
>   ⟨update variables involved in the event test⟩
>   ⟨index-variable⟩ := ⟨index-variable⟩ + 1

In many cases this form of loop must also be followed by an IF statement that takes different actions to complete the overall segment, depending on which condition caused exit of the loop:

IF ⟨event-test⟩ THEN   —repeat the event test
    ⟨actions required if event occurred⟩
ELSE
    ⟨actions required if iteration bound exceeded⟩

EXAMPLE

PURPOSE/GOAL STATE: Repeatedly call procedure PlayOneGame to play a game. Continue until the user wants to quit or five games have been played.

ACTIONS:

GameCount := 0
Response := 'y'   — initialize to ensure loop entry

WHILE (Response = 'y') AND (GameCount < 5) DO
    BEGIN
        CALL PlayOneGame (...)
        DISPLAY: "Do you want to play again? (y/n)"
        READ: Response
        GameCount:= GameCount + 1

         KTH ITERATION: PlayOneGame has been called K times;
         GameCount = K and Response = 'y' if user wants to play again.
    END

IF Response <> 'y' THEN
        DISPLAY: "Thanks for playing!"
ELSE
        DISPLAY: "Sorry, five games is my limit today." ∎

□ □

Loop Control May Require Separate Variables and Statements

The loop control is often the most confusing part of the loop for beginners. The parts of the loop control—initialization, update, exit test—may actually form a separate "action within an action" in the loop. In some loops the loop control requires additional variables and statements just to determine when to exit the loop. In other computations, the loop control is a natural part of the larger loop action, so that no separate computation is needed to determine when to exit the loop.

A common loop design error is to try to use some part of the main loop computation as the loop control, when it actually is much easier to introduce a new variable and statements solely for loop control. In particular, whenever you are designing a count controlled loop, and you have a variable in the loop body that is being used for some sort of counting, it is tempting to try to use that variable as the index variable for the loop control. Be careful!

EXAMPLE Suppose your goal is: "sum the first 20 *odd* integers, starting at 101." Here the action of the loop requires that you generate a sequence of integers, starting at 101 and counting by 2's. The loop control requires that you count each iteration until you have completed 20 of them. The loop invariant might be:

> KTH ITERATION: Sum contains the sum of the sequence of K odd integers starting at 101. Number contains the next odd integer in the sequence.

It is tempting to try to use variable Number as the loop control variable, and exit when Number reaches the 21st odd integer. The resulting loop might be:

```
Sum := 0;
Number := 101;                    {start at 101}
WHILE Number <= 139 DO
   BEGIN
      Sum := Sum + Number;
      Number := Number + 2;       {count by 2's}
   END
```

In this version, variable Number is used in the loop exit test, as part of the loop control, and it is also used in the loop action. This version is easy to get wrong because the exit test requires that you determine while writing the loop that 139 is the twentieth odd number after 101.

A simpler design treats the loop control as a separate "count to 20" computation, and uses another computation, "count by 2's from 101," to generate the integers to be summed. This version might be:

```
Sum := 0;
Number := 101;                    {start at 101}
FOR I := 1 TO 20 DO
   BEGIN
      Sum := Sum + Number;
      Number := Number + 2;       {count by 2's}
   END
```

In this loop, variable I is used for the separate loop control, counting from 1 to 20. Variable Number is used for the loop action, counting by 2's from 101, but it is not part of the loop control. Here there is no doubt that the loop makes exactly 20 iterations. ∎

□ □
The Loop Designer's Dilemma

After you have the design for the loop control, fill in the rest of the loop body design, using the loop invariant to guide your choice of the actions needed in the loop body and startup segment. There is one potential trouble spot in many loop designs. We call this the *Loop Designer's Dilemma*. Let's see how the dilemma arises. Freshman Fred has just encountered it, and has come to our consultant, Pat Programmer, for help:

FRED ENCOUNTERS THE LOOP DESIGNER'S DILEMMA

Fred: "I'm trying to design this simple loop:

> PURPOSE/GOAL STATE: Sum the squares of the first 20 integers and store the result in Total.

My instructor has added the restriction: use a WHILE loop. My loop invariant is:

> KTH ITERATION: Count = K and Total = sum of the first K integers.

Clearly this is a count controlled loop. I'm using Count as the index variable for counting from 1 to 20.

"From this invariant, I tried to design the loop body. My first attempt was this:

```
Total := 0
Count := 1
WHILE Count <= 20 DO
    Count := Count + 1
    Total := Total + Count * Count
```

In checking the design I discovered an error on the first iteration: Count = 2 the first time Count * Count is added to Total. I decided the initialization was wrong; Count should start at 0. My next design was:

```
Total := 0
Count := 0
WHILE Count <= 20 DO
    Count := Count + 1
    Total := Total + Count * Count
```

Now Count = 1 on the first iteration as desired, but there is a new error: the loop exit test is off by one—there is an extra iteration at the end. On the last iteration, Count = 21 when Count * Count is added to Total; it should only be 20. I tried a third time. This time I changed the exit test to exit one iteration earlier:

```
Total := 0
Count := 0
WHILE Count <= 19 DO
    Count := Count + 1
    Total := Total + Count * Count
```

Now I've got a loop that works, but it took me three tries, and I still don't like the way the loop control seems to count from 0 to 19 rather than from 1 to 20."

Pat: "You're right—it works, but the design is confusing. You just got caught in the 'loop designer's dilemma'."

Pat shows Fred a better way to code this loop; she just reverses the steps in the loop body so that Count is incremented *at the end of the loop body rather than at the beginning:*

```
Total := 0
Count := 1
WHILE Count <= 20 DO
    Total := Total + Count * Count
    Count := Count + 1
```

Fred: "I thought about doing that, but now on the last iteration Count gets incremented and then the new value of Count is never added to Total—that seems sort of inefficient. Why execute that extra wasted step?"

Pat: "True, incrementing Count on the last iteration may be wasted effort. That is why the choice is a dilemma—both alternatives seem to have shortcomings. There doesn't seem to be any right answer."

Let's generalize from Fred's dilemma. When you look at the body of most loops you notice that there are two parts:

1. *Prepare*. Statements that "prepare" for the action of the Kth iteration. These statements increment counters (like Fred's "Count := Count+1"), read new data values, or take other actions to collect the right data values for the Kth iteration.
2. *Perform*. Statements that "perform" the action of the Kth iteration. These actions use the prepared data values to perform the desired action and produce the important results (like Fred's "Total := Total + Count*Count").

You, as a beginning loop designer, would like to make the loop body:

■ Prepare for the action of this iteration, and then
■ Perform the action of this iteration.

but, like Fred, you will find that this approach almost never works. Concisely stated:

THE LOOP DESIGNER'S DILEMMA

In a loop you could either:

1. Prepare for the action of the Kth iteration *at the start of the Kth iteration,* or
2. Prepare for the action of the Kth iteration *at the end of the previous iteration* and prepare for the first iteration in the *startup segment.*

Although 1 seems like the natural choice, 2 is actually the best choice in most loops.

There are two reasons why option 2 turns out to be the best choice:

1. *The first iteration usually requires special preparation.* The "prepare" actions for the first iteration are usually different from those needed for later iterations. Naturally these go into the startup segment (like Fred's "Count := 1"). But if the first thing in the loop body is the "prepare" actions for another iteration, then the initial values are changed again before the "perform" action in the loop body is reached (so Fred's first attempt ended up with Count = 2 when his "perform" action was reached). Actions in the startup segment that prepare for the first loop iteration are said to be *priming the loop.*

2. *The loop exit test usually needs to be made after the "prepare" actions but before the "perform" actions.* Part of the "prepare" actions usually involves the update part of the loop control—updating variables used in the exit test. Usually the exit test is stated as "is another iteration needed using the prepared values?" So you want to make the exit test after you have "prepared" for the next iteration, not before. Fred wanted an exit test "exit when Count exceeds 20" rather than "exit when Count exceeds 19," but his loop body prepared the next value of K after the exit test was made, so he had an "off-by-one" error if he tested for K > 20.

This part of the loop designer's dilemma is sometimes called the *loop-and-a-half problem,* because you want to make the exit test after executing "half" the loop body—after you have "prepared" for the action but before you have "performed" it.

Because option 2 is usually the best solution to this dilemma, you find that each of our loop types has a characteristic form (as already seen in many previous examples). A WHILE loop looks like this:

⟨startup segment: prepare for the first iteration⟩
WHILE ⟨exit test⟩ DO
    BEGIN
        ⟨perform the actions for the Kth iteration⟩
        ⟨prepare for the next iteration⟩
    END

Thus the loop body *begins* with the action desired and *ends* with the preparation for the *next iteration*. REPEAT and FOR loops usually require the same treatment:

⟨startup segment: prepare for the first iteration⟩
REPEAT
    ⟨perform the actions for the Kth iteration⟩
    ⟨prepare for the next iteration⟩
UNTIL ⟨exit test⟩

and:

⟨startup segment: prepare for the first iteration⟩
FOR ⟨index-variable⟩ := ⟨first-value⟩ TO ⟨last-value⟩ DO

```
              BEGIN
                      ⟨perform the actions for the Kth iteration⟩
                      ⟨prepare for the next iteration⟩
              END
```

FOR loops, however, often need no separate "prepare" actions if only the index variable is involved because they are specified directly in the FOR loop header.

The loop invariant also needs to reflect this program state at the end of the loop body. At the end of the Kth iteration the loop should have:

1. Performed the action required for the Kth iteration, *and*
2. Prepared the new data values needed for the exit test and the next iteration.

EXAMPLE   Suppose your loop segment is specified as:

> PURPOSE/GOAL STATE: Read and sum data values until a negative or zero value is read. Store the sum of the positive values in Total.

You expect the loop body to be:

- Read a value   — prepare
- Add the value to Total   — perform

but you have to *test* the new value *before* you add it to Total, so your loop design becomes:

```
              Total := 0
              READ: Value                — prepare for first iteration
              WHILE Value > 0 DO
                      Total := Total + Value     — perform
                      READ: Value            — prepare for next iteration

                      KTH ITERATION: Total = sum of first K positive values read, and
                      Value contains the next value read.                              ■
```

□ □

Coding Loops

If your loop has been designed in pseudo-code as a WHILE or REPEAT loop, then coding the loop is straightforward. For any loop, be sure to include the loop invariant as a comment at the end of the loop body in the Pascal code.

If you have used the FOR loop pseudo-code for design of a count controlled loop, then you can code the loop directly using the Pascal FOR statement only if the "step size" is 1 or -1. Otherwise, code the loop as a WHILE loop, using the count controlled WHILE loop pattern:

```
                COUNT CONTROLLED WHILE LOOP PATTERN


        ⟨index-variable⟩ := ⟨first-value⟩;
        WHILE ⟨index-variable⟩ <= ⟨final-value⟩ DO
          BEGIN
            ⟨loop body⟩;
            ⟨index-variable⟩ := ⟨index-variable⟩ + ⟨step-size⟩
              {KTH ITERATION: ...loop invariant... }
          END


  Be sure to write the update of the index variable as the last statement in the loop
  body. If the step size is negative, use a ">=" exit test instead of the "<=" test.
```

Although a count controlled loop could be coded as a REPEAT loop, it is best to use the standard WHILE loop pattern to avoid confusion.

EXERCISES

10.4 For each of the following PURPOSE/GOAL STATE specifications, design an appropriate loop invariant and loop segment:

a. PURPOSE/GOAL STATE: Sum the squares of the odd integers between 20 and 50 and store the sum in SumSquares.

b. PURPOSE/GOAL STATE: Real array ValueList [1..1000] contains at least one negative value. Find the *last* array element with a negative value and store the value in LastNegative.

c. PURPOSE/GOAL STATE: Real array ValueList [1..1000] *may* contain some negative values. Find the *last* array element with a negative value and store the value in LastNegative. If there are no negative values, store zero in LastNegative.

d. PURPOSE/GOAL STATE: Compute the average of the grades in Integer array GradesList [1..LastEntry] and store the result in ClassAverage.

e. PURPOSE/GOAL STATE: Ask the user to type a loan amount, read it in and store it in LoanAmount. Allowed range: $100-10,000. If outside of range, ask the user to reenter it correctly. Repeat until a correct value is entered.

f. PURPOSE/GOAL STATE: Count the number of values in Real array Table[1..2000] that exceed the value of Threshold. Store the count in OverCount.

10.5 Suppose you have two enumerated types defined:

```
TYPE
    PitchResult = (HIT, STRIKE, BALL);
    BatterResult = (HITIT, STRIKEOUT, WALKED);
```

and a procedure that "simulates" the result of a single pitch:

```
PROCEDURE NextPitch
        (Result: PitchResult)   {OUT: result of pitch}
```

Assume variable NewBatter is of type BatterResult. Design and code the following loop segment. Use as many additional variables as you wish:

> PURPOSE/GOAL STATE: Call NextPitch repeatedly until either Result = HIT, three times Result = STRIKE (a "strikeout"), or four times Result = BALL (a "walk"). Assign NewBatter the appropriate result value.

□□□ 10.4
ANALYZING AND VERIFYING LOOP DESIGNS

After the design of any complex loop is complete, a careful analysis of the design is important to verify that the loop will work correctly. The loop control is the most common source of errors.

□□
Common Errors in Loop Control Design

Here are some common errors to watch out for in designing the loop control:

1. *Infinite loop.* An error in design of the loop control can lead to an infinite loop—a loop where the exit test never gives the result "exit the loop." The three most common reasons for an infinite loop:

a. *No "progress toward termination" on some execution path.* A loop can repeat forever if one of the control paths through the loop body fails to include an update of the loop exit variables or of the variables that determine the choice of control path in the loop body, as discussed in Section 10.2.

b. *Exit test for equality of two Integer values.* WHILE and REPEAT exit tests should always use the tests $<$, $>$, $<=$, or $>=$ on Integer values, rather than the tests $=$ or $<>$. Otherwise, an initial value outside the expected range can cause an infinite loop.

For example, Hacker Jack wrote the loop:

```
I := M
REPEAT
        ⟨loop body⟩
        I := I + 1
UNTIL I = N + 1
```

His intent was to write a count controlled loop with I counting from M to N, but if M happens to be greater than N when the loop is entered the first time, then the exit test, "I = N+1", never becomes true and the loop repeats forever. The correct exit test is "UNTIL I > N", which returns TRUE if M > N on loop entry.

c. *Equality test on two Real values.* When testing Real values for equality, round off errors during the computation of the values may cause computed Real values to be slightly different from their true values. The = or <> test will not work correctly for such values, and the loop may repeat forever.

For example, the following loop should exit after ten iterations, but it will repeat forever on most Pascal systems (all variables of Real type):

```
H := 0;
WHILE H <> 1 DO
   BEGIN
      ⟨loop body⟩
      H := H + 0.1;
   END
```

Because 0.1 cannot be precisely represented as a binary number in a computer, each time 0.1 is added to H, the result will be slightly imprecise, and after 10 iterations, H will be almost equal to 10 (maybe H = 9.999999999 or 10.00000001). But because it is not exactly 10, the equality test always gives FALSE, and the loop continues forever.

This problem, however, is not solved by simply replacing = or <> tests by <, >, <=, or >=. Instead, you have to write the test to check whether the two values are "almost equal," to within some "tolerance." The tolerance is some value close to zero, such as 0.0001, which indicates how close the two values have to be to each other before they are considered equal. (When working with very large numbers, the tolerance may have to be larger; if the numbers are very small, the tolerance may have to be smaller.)

You then write the test for equality by comparing whether the difference of the two values is less than the tolerance (using the absolute value of the difference):

$$\text{abs } (\langle value1 \rangle - \langle value \rangle) < \langle tolerance \rangle$$

For example, the loop above might be written correctly as:

```
H := 0;
WHILE abs (H - 1.0) < 0.0001 DO      {exit if H = 1}
   BEGIN
      ⟨loop body⟩
      H := H + 0.1;
   END
```

2. *Off by one errors.* As common as an infinite loop, but less obvious during testing, is a loop that is "off by one" in the number of iterations. Either the loop exits one iteration too early, or it runs through one iteration too many. The cause may be an exit test that uses < instead of <=, or vice versa, or an incorrect initialization. For example, because he initialized variable Count to zero instead of one, Hacker Jack had an off by one error in this count controlled loop. The loop was supposed to make exactly 20 iterations but it actually makes 21:

```
Total := 0
Count := 0
WHILE Count <= 20 DO
        Count := Count + 1
        Total := Total + Count*Count
```

3. *Zero trip errors.* Another common error is to forget to consider the zero trip path during the design of WHILE and FOR loops. Often variables whose values are defined within the loop body are not properly defined in the zero trip case, leading to attempts to use uninitialized variables or to use old values of variables that would have been replaced by new values if the loop body had been executed. For example, this loop appears to always set the Flag variable to show whether a zero value is found in the part of the array A [M..N]:

```
FOR I := M TO N DO
    BEGIN
        IF A[I] = 0 THEN
                Flag := TRUE
        ELSE
                Flag := FALSE
    END
```

However, if $M > N$ on entry to the loop, then the zero trip path is executed, and no value is assigned to Flag. Flag remains uninitialized or retains its old value. Any later action that uses the value of Flag will get that old value, not a value defined in the FOR loop.

4. *Exit test failure due to a subscript range error.* When an exit test in a WHILE or REPEAT loop uses the operations AND or OR to combine two simpler tests, both simpler tests may be evaluated on each iteration, even if the first test already shows that the loop should exit. A common error is to assume that if the first test says "exit the loop," then the second test will never be evaluated. For example, if you are searching an array A[1..500] for the first zero value, you might want to write:

```
I := 1;
WHILE (I <= 500) AND (A[I] <> 0) DO
    I := I + 1;
```

If the array contains no zero value, then on the last iteration I is assigned 501, and both exit tests may be evaluated. The first test says "exit" but the second test, "A[I]

"<> 0" fails due to a subscript range error. Such a loop must be written by using a flag variable, such as "NotFound" in this version:

```
I := 1;
NotFound := TRUE;
WHILE (I <= 500) AND NotFound DO
   BEGIN
      IF A[I] = 0 THEN
          NotFound := FALSE
      ELSE
          I := I + 1;
   END
```

□ □

Verifying a Loop Design: The "Seven Step Loop Check"

After design of a loop is complete, careful checking of the design is essential. We recommend the following *Seven Step Loop Check,* which first checks the loop body against the loop invariant, and then checks the loop control. The loop invariant plays a major role in several steps of this check, so be sure your invariant is correct before you start.

□

Verifying the Loop Body.   To check the loop body against the loop invariant, proceed as follows:

1. *Check that the loop invariant is true at the end of the first iteration.* Follow execution through the startup segment and through the loop body the first time. Check that the computation on this control path will make the loop invariant true at the end of the first iteration.

2. *Check that if the loop invariant is true at the end of the Kth iteration, and the exit test says to "continue the loop," then it will also be true at the end of the next iteration.* Follow execution from the end of one iteration back through the exit test and the loop body to the end of the next iteration. Assume that the loop invariant is true at the end of one iteration and check that it must then be true at the end of the following iteration.

3. *Check that if the loop invariant is true at the end of the Kth iteration, and the exit test says to "exit the loop," then the GOAL STATE for the entire loop segment will have been reached.* Follow execution from the end of one iteration through the exit test and out of the loop. Assume that the loop invariant is true at the end of the iteration and check that the GOAL STATE for the entire segment is then reached after loop exit.

4. *Check the zero trip case, if allowed.* In FOR and WHILE loops, follow execution through the startup segment and the exit test and see if the GOAL STATE for the entire segment is reached if the test returns "exit the loop."

□

Verifying the Loop Control.   Make a separate check of the loop control, in three steps:

5. *Check the "exit/continue" decision before the first entry into the loop (FOR and WHILE loops only).* Follow the computation through the startup segment to the loop entry state and the first execution of the exit test. Check that, for the values in the loop entry state, whenever the test says "exit the loop" before you ever enter it, you want the zero trip path—no execution of the loop body. Also check that whenever the test says "enter the loop" you indeed want to enter the loop.

6. Check the "exit/continue" decision after the Kth iteration. Assume that the loop invariant is true at the end of the Kth iteration. Check that if the exit test says "exit the loop" when the computation is in this state, you *always* want to exit the loop. Also check that if the exit test says "continue the loop" when the computation is in this state, you *always* want to repeat the loop again.

7. *Check progress toward termination on each path through the loop body.* Assume that the loop invariant is true of the program state at the end of the Kth iteration and the exit test says "continue the loop." Check that each path through the loop body makes "progress toward termination," as discussed above.

EXAMPLE   Fred is making a quick check of his final loop design (after Pat modified it):

PURPOSE/GOAL STATE: Sum the squares of the integers from 1 to 20 and store the sum in Total.

ACTIONS:

Total := 0
Count := 1
WHILE Count < = 20 DO
    Total := Total + Count*Count
    Count := Count + 1

KTH ITERATION: At the end of the Kth iteration, Total contains the sum of the squares of the first K positive integers and Count = K+1.

Fred mentally runs through the "Seven Step Loop Check":

1. *First iteration.* Is the loop invariant true at the end of the first iteration? *Checking:* At the end of that iteration, Total = 0 + 1*1 and Count = 2, which matches the loop invariant when K=1. OK!

2. *Next iteration.* Assume that at the end of the Kth iteration, Total = sum of squares of first K integers and Count = K+1. Is the loop invariant still true after the next iteration? *Checking:* New value of Total = old value of Total + (K+1)*(K+1) and Count = (K+1)+1. So after the (K+1)st iteration, Total = sum of squares of first K+1 integers and Count = K+2. OK!

3. *Loop exit*. Suppose that, at the end of the Kth iteration, Total = sum of squares of first K integers, Count = K+1, and Count > 20 for the first time. Then the loop is exited with Total = the value specified as the GOAL STATE for the segment. OK!

4. *Zero trip*. It can't happen here because Count = 1 in the loop entry state.

5. *First exit/continue decision*. On loop entry, Count = 1, so the test "Count <= 20" is always TRUE. Thus the loop is always entered. OK!

6. *Kth iteration exit/continue decision*. Suppose the loop invariant is true at the end of the Kth iteration, so Count = K+1. If the exit test "Count <= 20" gives FALSE, then Count > 20 and the loop should always be exited. If Count <= 20, then the loop should always be continued through another iteration. OK!

7. *Progress toward termination*. On each iteration, the action "Count := Count + 1" will always be executed, so the value of Count is closer to 20 and the loop has made progress toward termination. OK! ■

Because there are many things that can go wrong with the design of a loop, verifying each loop you write is important. Of course many loops fall into simple standard patterns that can be checked quickly. However, when you are designing a complicated loop, running through the "Seven Step Loop Check" will help you find most errors before you get to the coding stage.

□ □
Loops and Mathematical Induction

You may have been introduced to the concept of *mathematical induction* in a mathematics course as a way of proving a mathematical theorem. If so, you may also have noticed the similarity between that idea and the way we go about verifying that a loop is correct.

Briefly stated, mathematical induction works as follows. Suppose that you want to show some mathematical formula is true for every positive integer, K. You can prove the formula is true by mathematical induction using only two steps:

1. Prove the formula is true for K=1.
2. Assume the formula is true for some arbitrary value, K $\geq$ 1, and show the formula also must then be true for the next value, K+1.

These two steps are almost identical to the first two steps in verifying the correctness of a loop:

1. Check that the loop invariant is true after the first iteration.
2. Assume the loop invariant is true after K iterations, and verify that it also must then be true after K+1 iterations.

These two steps prove by mathematical induction that the loop invariant must be true at the end of the Kth iteration, for any value of K $\geq$ 1. (The rest of the loop verification steps show that the loop exits correctly, which is not an issue in most mathematical proofs.)

□ □

Determining the Iteration Count and Index Value

One distinctive characteristic of a count controlled loop is that you can tell, without executing the loop, how many iterations the loop will make. Suppose the loop design has the pseudo-code heading:

FOR ⟨var⟩ := ⟨first value⟩ TO ⟨last value⟩ STEP ⟨step size⟩ DO

The iteration count is given by the formula:

$$\text{Iteration count} = \frac{\langle \text{last value} \rangle - \langle \text{first value} \rangle}{\langle \text{step size} \rangle} + 1$$

where you take the integer part of the division and ignore any remainder. A zero or negative iteration count indicates the zero trip case: the loop body will never be executed.

Another useful formula gives you the value of the loop index variable on the Kth iteration:

$$\text{Index variable value during Kth iteration} =$$
$$\langle \text{first value} \rangle + (K - 1) * \langle \text{step size} \rangle$$

EXAMPLES

1. Given the loop:

   FOR I := 2 TO N STEP 2 DO
      ⟨loop body⟩

   Q: How many iterations will the loop make?

   A: Number of iterations = $(N - 2)/2 + 1 = N/2$.

   Q: What will be the value of I on the 5th iteration?

   A: Value of I on 5th iteration = $2 + (5 - 1) * 2 = 10$

2. Given the loop:

   FOR J := 200 TO 101 STEP −1 DO
      ⟨loop body⟩

Q: How many iterations will the loop make?

A: $(101 - 200)/-1 + 1 = -99/-1 + 1 = 100$ iterations.

Q: What is the value of J on the 75th iteration?

A: $200 + (75 - 1) * (-1) = 200 - 74 = 126$ ■

EXERCISES

10.6   Identify the loop control error in each of the following loop segments:

a.   PURPOSE/GOAL STATE: Display the squares of the integers from 1 to 20.

ACTIONS:

```
Count := 0
REPEAT
    Count := Count + 1
    Square := Count * Count
    DISPLAY: "⟨Square⟩"
UNTIL Count > 20
```

b.   PURPOSE/GOAL STATE: Find the largest and smallest grades in array Grades [1..100]. Store the largest in MaxGrade and the smallest in MinGrade.

ACTIONS:

```
MaxGrade := Grades [100]
MinGrade := Grades [100]
Posn := 99
WHILE Posn  > = 1 DO
    BEGIN
        IF Grades [Posn] > MaxGrade THEN
          BEGIN
              MaxGrade := Grades [Posn]
              Posn := Posn − 1
          END
        ELSE IF Grades [Posn] < MinGrade THEN
          BEGIN
              MinGrade := Grades [Posn]
              Posn := Posn − 1
          END
    END
```

c.   PURPOSE/GOAL STATE: Find the position of the first zero value in part of array A[1..500]. Start the search at element M and continue through element N. Store the subscript of the first zero element in ZeroPosn. Set flag ZeroFound = TRUE if a zero is found; FALSE otherwise.

ACTIONS:

```
ZeroFound := FALSE
I := M
WHILE (NOT ZeroFound) AND (I <> N+1) DO
    BEGIN
        IF A[I] = 0 THEN
                ZeroFound := TRUE
                ZeroPosn := I
        ELSE
                I := I + 1
    END
```

10.7 Apply the *seven step loop check* to each of the loops that you designed in Exercises 10.4 and 10.5. For each loop, list the seven steps and describe what you are checking in that step for that particular loop.

10.8 For each of the following count controlled loop segments, give a formula for computing the *total number of iterations* the loop will make. Use only literal values or IN variables of the segment in the formula. Also, give a formula for computing the *value of the index variable at the start of the Kth iteration,* using only K, literal values, and IN variables of the segment.

a. N := M*M
FOR I:= M TO N DO
⟨loop body⟩

b. Start := 2
Stop := Start + 1
FOR H := Start TO Stop STEP 0.25 DO
⟨loop body⟩

c. Big := Last + 5
Small := Last − 5
FOR Count := Big TO Small STEP −2 DO
⟨loop body⟩

□ □ □ **10.5**
PROGRAM IT WITH STYLE!

Good style in loops is largely a result of good design. A simple, easy to understand loop design does more than anything else to make the loop understandable to someone reading the program.

□ □
Comments

Good comments are important in making a loop understandable to the reader. Here are some guidelines for commenting loops:

1. *Give the PURPOSE and GOAL STATE of the loop segment as a unit, including the startup segment.* The entire action represented by the loop should be described in a comment that *precedes the startup segment*. Avoid comments that separately describe the startup segment, unless it is especially complicated. You want the reader to understand the entire loop action as a unit, not as separate segments.

2. *Include the loop invariant as a comment*. The loop invariant is the single most important piece of information about what the loop body is doing as it is repeatedly executed, so include it as a comment. Our preferred form for this comment is:

```
{KTH ITERATION: ... loop invariant ...}
```

to suggest to the reader that the comment describes the state that results after the Kth iteration of the loop.

□ □
Indentation and Spacing

Indent the statements in the body of the loop from the loop heading, but do not indent the startup segment. Unless the startup segment is very short, a blank line between the startup segment and the loop itself helps to make it easy to see where the loop begins and ends. We have used this style in the examples of this chapter.

□ □ □ **10.6**
PASCAL AND PSEUDO-CODE SUMMARY

In pseudo-code, we use loop forms that follow the Pascal loop syntax closely. Only the Pascal syntax is shown here.

□ □
The Pascal FOR Loop

The Pascal FOR loop has two forms:

⟨FOR-loop⟩ ::=

```
    FOR ⟨index-variable⟩ := ⟨first-value⟩ TO ⟨last-value⟩ DO
        ⟨loop-body⟩
|   FOR ⟨index-variable⟩ := ⟨last-value⟩ DOWNTO ⟨first-value⟩ DO
        ⟨loop-body⟩
```

> **WHERE**
> ⟨index-variable⟩ ::=
> A Pascal identifier naming a simple variable of Integer, Char, subrange, or enumerated type. The variable must be a local variable of the subprogram in which the loop appears.
> ⟨first-value⟩ ::=
> The smallest value for which the loop body should be executed (using the ordering defined for the data type of ⟨index-variable⟩).

$\langle$last-value$\rangle$ ::=
    The largest value for which the loop body should be executed.
$\langle$loop-body$\rangle$ ::=
    A single Pascal statement, usually a compound statement enclosed in
    BEGIN-END.

□ □

Facts to Remember About the FOR Loop

1. The $\langle$index-variable$\rangle$ cannot be assigned a new value within the loop body.
2. The $\langle$first-value$\rangle$ and $\langle$last-value$\rangle$ expressions are evaluated only once, at the time the loop is entered.
3. The loop body may never be executed at all.
4. The value of the $\langle$index-variable$\rangle$ is unpredictable after the loop execution is complete.
5. DOWNTO is a single word, not two.

□ □

The Pascal WHILE Loop

$\langle$WHILE-loop$\rangle$ ::=

```
WHILE ⟨test⟩ DO
      ⟨loop-body⟩
```

WHERE
    $\langle$test$\rangle$ ::= Any Boolean-valued expression.
    $\langle$loop-body$\rangle$ ::=
        Any single Pascal statement, usually a compound statement enclosed
        in BEGIN-END.

□ □

The Pascal REPEAT Loop

$\langle$REPEAT-loop$\rangle$ ::=

```
REPEAT
      ⟨loop-body-sequence-of-statements⟩
UNTIL ⟨test⟩
```

WHERE
    $\langle$test$\rangle$ ::= Any Boolean-valued expression.
    $\langle$loop-body-sequence-of-statements$\rangle$ ::=
        Any sequence of one or more Pascal statements.

□ □
Differences Between REPEAT and WHILE Loops

1. The body of a REPEAT loop is *always executed at least once;* the body of a WHILE loop *may never be executed at all.*

2. The test in a REPEAT loop tests whether to *exit* the loop—a TRUE result means *exit the loop.* The test in a WHILE loop tests whether to *continue* to execute the loop—a TRUE result means *continue the loop.*

3. If the body of a WHILE loop contains more than one statement, you must use BEGIN-END to make a compound statement. The body of a REPEAT loop never needs BEGIN-END.

■ ■ ■
REVIEW QUESTIONS

10.1 Give the general form of the Pascal *FOR loop* and explain its meaning when executed.

10.2 Give the form of a Pascal *REPEAT loop* and explain its meaning when executed.

10.3 List three important *differences* between the WHILE and REPEAT loops.

10.4 Describe how to *change* a FOR loop into a WHILE loop; a REPEAT loop into a WHILE loop.

10.5 What is a *startup segment* for a loop?

10.6 Name and explain briefly the three parts of the *loop control.* Show where each part appears in a WHILE loop. In a FOR loop. In a REPEAT loop.

10.7 Explain the concept of *progress toward termination* in a loop.

10.8 Distinguish between three types of loop control: *count controlled, event controlled,* and *count and event controlled.* Give an example of each type of loop control.

10.9 What is a *nested loop?*

10.10 What is the *zero trip path* through a loop?

10.11 What is the *loop entry state* for a loop? What is the *state at the end of the Kth iteration?* What is the *exit state?*

10.12 What is a *loop invariant* for a loop?

10.13 What *four steps* are involved in designing a complex loop?

10.14 How is a *loop invariant* related to the GOAL STATE for a loop body?

10.15 In a count controlled loop, what are the elements of the loop control that should be specified in the *pseudo-code FOR loop header?*

10.16 What is a *step size* in a count controlled loop? What two step sizes in pseudo-code can be coded directly as Pascal FOR loops? If a pseudo-code FOR loop uses a step-size other than one of these, how is it coded in Pascal?

10.17 What is an *event* in an event controlled loop? How is the event related to the *exit test* that appears in a WHILE or REPEAT loop?

10.18 In a *count and event controlled* loop, what is the purpose of the *count?* In pseudo-code, is this loop form written using a FOR loop or a WHILE/REPEAT loop?

10.19 Explain why sometimes the *loop control* requires a separate set of actions and data objects in a loop, and sometimes it does not.

10.20 What is the *"loop designer's dilemma"*? What are the *two causes* of this dilemma in loop design?

10.21 What is *priming the loop*? Why does it solve part of the loop designer's dilemma?

10.22 Why do most loop bodies end by *preparing for the next iteration,* even though the loop may exit without another iteration?

10.23 List and briefly explain *three common causes of an infinite loop*.

10.24 What is an *off by one* error?

10.25 What is a *zero trip* error?

10.26 What is a common reason for a *subscript range error* during a loop *exit test*?

10.27 List and briefly explain the steps in the *Seven Step Loop Check*.

10.28 How is verifying the correctness of a loop by using the Seven Step Loop Check related to the concept of *mathematical induction* used to prove theorems in mathematics?

10.29 In a count controlled loop, give the formula for determining the *iteration count* of the loop. Give the formula for determining the *value of the index variable* during the Kth iteration.

10.30 What is the most important *comment* to include when coding a *loop body* in Pascal?

■ ■ ■
PROGRAMMING PROBLEMS

10.1 *Determining a "Round Robin" Tournament Schedule.* Charley is in charge of setting up the schedule of games for a volleyball tournament. There are eight teams entered. The tournament is to be a "round robin" tournament, in which each team plays each of the other seven teams exactly once. The gym has four volleyball courts, so every team will play at the same time on one of the courts. Charley wants a computer program to automate this task. The program is required to compute and display a table that shows the schedule of games for each court, like this:

	COURT 1	COURT 2	COURT 3	COURT 4
Round 1	1 plays 2	3 plays 4	5 plays 6	7 plays 8
Round 2	1 plays 3	2 plays 4	5 plays 7	6 plays 8
.	.	.	.	.
.	.	.	.	.

a. Design, code, and test a program to perform this task for an eight team tournament.

b. Generalize your algorithm to a program that can compute the tournament schedule for any even number of teams in the range 2–50.

10.2 *LISP Parentheses Counter.* In the LISP (LISt Processing) programming language, both programs and data are written as lists enclosed in parentheses. Lists may contain sublists, also enclosed in parentheses, which may contain sublists, and so forth. A typical LISP list might look like this:

(A (((B C) D) (E F G (H I)))

Getting the parentheses properly matched is a problem in LISP programming. One useful tool is a program that matches parentheses in a LISP expression and displays a count that shows how the parentheses are paired, with the outermost parentheses pair numbered zero, the next level numbered one, and so forth. For example, the expression above would be marked:

```
(A ( ( (B C) D) (E F G (H I) ) )
 0   1 2 3    3 2 2      3   3 2 1
```

which shows immediately that there is an unmatched parenthesis in this list. Design, code, and test a program that allows the user to type in any list composed of parentheses and identifiers and that displays the list with a parenthesis count underneath, as shown in the example. Restrict the input expression to one line of input (maximum of 80 characters). The program should identify and display error messages in two cases:

- When the end of the list is reached and at least one parenthesis is unmatched.
- When the number of right parentheses exceeds the number of left parentheses at any point in the input string (so that the count would become negative).

10.3 *Finding Prime Numbers Using the "Sieve of Eratosthenes."* Computers are useful for *searching* through large sets of data values for values that possess certain properties. Often the speed of a computer makes a search algorithm practical in a computer program that would not be practical for a person to use by hand. A simple algorithm that is practical due to the speed of the computer is termed a *brute force* algorithm.

In mathematics, an old problem is to find all the *prime numbers* in a given range, where a prime number is a positive integer that cannot be divided evenly by any positive integer except 1 and the number itself. Thus, for example, 13 is a prime number but 15 is not, because 15 can be evenly divided by 3 (with no remainder).

A brute force algorithm for finding all the prime numbers that are less than some maximum value is one suggested by the Greek astronomer Eratosthenes in about 200 B.C., now called the *Sieve of Eratosthenes*. The idea is to start with *all* the integers from 2 to the given maximum and then progressively "sieve out" non-primes, until all that remains are the prime numbers.

To begin, you simply write down all the integers from 2 to the maximum, for example, all the integers from 2 to 5000. The number 2 is a prime, so you leave 2 in the list and strike out all the multiples of 2 because they cannot be primes (one stroke of the sieve). Then you advance to 3. You leave 3 in the list and strike out all multiples of 3 (a second stroke of the sieve). Now you advance to the next number that remains in the list, which happens to be 5 (because 4 is a multiple of two, so it has been sieved out already). The next number remaining is always a prime, so you leave it in and strike out all its multiples. Keep going until you reach the *square root of the largest number in the range,* in our example, the integer part of *sqrt* (5000). Remaining in your list are all the prime numbers that are less than the specified maximum. Of course, this algorithm is very tedious to use by hand, but it is well-suited to a computer.

Write a program that uses this brute force algorithm to determine all the primes less than a given maximum, where the user is allowed to specify the maximum. Use an array for the list. You will have to restrict the size of the maximum due to the limited size of the array, so be sure to check the user's input so that you won't have any subscript range errors. The program should display: (a) a count of the number of primes in the specified range, and (b) a list of all the primes in the range.

RESTRICTION: Use the sieve algorithm without any "improvements" or "short cuts." Begin by (partially) filling the array with *all* the integers from 2 to the specified maximum. Then repeatedly scan the list to "sieve" out non-primes, as described above. You can delete a non-prime by setting the array entry to zero.

10.4 *List operations.* Mary Dee's job requires that she work with long lists of numbers—positive and negative integers. Often she has two or three lists that she is working with at one time, and sometimes as many as five lists, each of which may contain up to fifty or sixty numbers. She wants a computer program that will give her some help. As she describes her requirements, she wants a program that will allow her to do the following:

- Enter a list of integers, with no more than 100 entries.
- Work with up to five lists at a time, entering each one separately.
- Remove duplicate entries from each list as it is entered (so that no two list entries are the same).
- Display a list.
- Sort a list into decreasing sequence.
- Insert a new entry into a list, leaving the list sorted if it has already been sorted.
- Form a new list representing the *union, intersection,* or *difference* of two existing sorted lists.
- Test if two lists contain exactly the same entries.
- Test if one list is contained in another list (all the entries of the first are also entries in the second).

The *union* of two lists is a list that contains *all* the entries that appear on either list (but no duplicate entries). The *intersection* is a list that contains all the entries that appear on *both* lists. The *difference* is a list that contains all the entries on the first list that do *not* also appear in the second list.

Write a description of the detailed requirements for a program to meet Mary Dee's needs. Then design, code, and test the program.

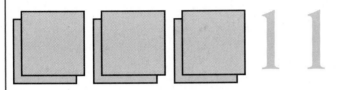

Using Data Files

CHAPTER GOALS

When you have mastered the content of this chapter you should be able to:

- Define the concept of a *data file*.
- Explain the difference between *batch processing* and *interactive* programs in their use of data files.
- Distinguish between *text files* and *nontext files*.
- Explain the concepts of *file status* and *file position*.
- Specify the *format* of a data file.
- Declare and use data files for *input and output* in pseudo-code and Pascal programs.
- Use common *read loop patterns* to read data from a data file.

Many computer programs are used to process large amounts of data—larger than can be entered conveniently by a user directly on a terminal keyboard or than can be displayed conveniently on a display screen. Such programs use *data files* instead of the user's terminal as the target for READ and WRITE operations. Data values are read from a data file, processed, and the results are written back on another data file.

□□□ **11.1**
BATCH PROCESSING AND INTERACTIVE PROGRAMS

All of our programs so far have been *interactive* programs—they interact directly with the user at a terminal. When the program requires input data values, the user must type them on the terminal keyboard. Results are displayed on the terminal screen. Interactive programs have several disadvantages. For reading data, three major problems are:

1. If there is a lot of input data, the user must do a lot of typing.
2. If the user makes a mistake in the typing, the error may cause the program to crash or "fail gracefully" with an error message. The program must be run again and all the input values retyped.
3. Each time the program is run, the input values must be typed again.

For writing data, there are also three major disadvantages:

1. If there is a lot of output data displayed, it may scroll off of the screen before the user can read it.
2. Displayed output data cannot be studied at leisure away from the computer terminal.
3. Displayed output data cannot be saved and used later as input data for another program.

A *batch processing* program is a program that does not interact with the user at the terminal. Instead it reads all its input data from one or more data files and writes all its results on other data files. This approach has several advantages when reading data:

1. If the program reads in many data values, it is more convenient to prepare a separate data file before the program is run, and then let the program read the data from the file. The two most common ways of preparing an input data file are:

a. By using an editor program to enter the data and store it in the input data file. Errors are easy to correct using the editor program, and large numbers of data values are more easily entered.

b. By running another program that creates the input data file as one of its output files.

2. If someone else is preparing the input data for the program then that person does not have to be present when the program is run. For example, in a programming course the instructor may prepare a data file that contains the input data that each student's program is to process.

3. If you run the program repeatedly with the same or similar data values, you only have to prepare the input data file once and then, if necessary, edit it before each run. Input data files can be saved indefinitely and reused with no additional effort on the user's part.

It also has advantages when writing data:

1. Output data files can be saved and printed, to be studied at leisure away from the computer (for example, the output from debug WRITE statements might be sent to a data file for this reason.)

2. Output data files can serve as the input data files for other programs, or the same program on a later run.

3. A data file can serve as a *scratch file* to store a large quantity of data temporarily during execution of a program. An early part of the program writes the data into the scratch file, and a later part of the same program reads and processes the data.

When an input data file is used by a program, the file already exists when you run the program. The program simply reads the data values from the data file, just as if the user had typed them in directly. However, when reading from a data file, no "prompt" is needed before a READ statement. The READ statements simply take the input values from the data file in the order they appear in the file.

□ □

Interactive Programs that Use Data Files

The term *batch processing program* usually refers to a program that *only* uses data files, making no use of the user's terminal. Thus a batch processing program can be run without the user sitting at a terminal while it executes.

An interactive program can also make use of data files, so that it mixes input and output to the user's terminal and to data files. A common situation is the following: you are writing a program whose major output is to be a printed report, but which also needs to display messages on the user's terminal as it runs. For the output that represents the printed report, you use a data file, say a file named REPORT. When the user runs your program, the program displays its messages on the terminal screen (for example, prompting the user for input values or telling the user if an error is detected). When the program has finished execution, there will be a new file named REPORT in the user's file directory. The user can then use an operating system command to send file REPORT to a printer to be printed. Figure 11.1 illustrates this situation.

□□
A Program May Use Many Data Files

Large programs often use several data files. A Pascal compiler program is a good example. Your source program file serves as the "input data file" for the compiler. The compiler writes its "results" in the object program file, and it may use a third file to write a listing of the source program, with error messages. If you use various options that the compiler program provides, you might find the compiler writing information in additional output data files. The compiler may also use a "scratch file" while it is running, where it writes data temporarily at one point during execution and then, at a later point, reads the data back in for further processing.

FIGURE 11-1   Sending Output to a Data File

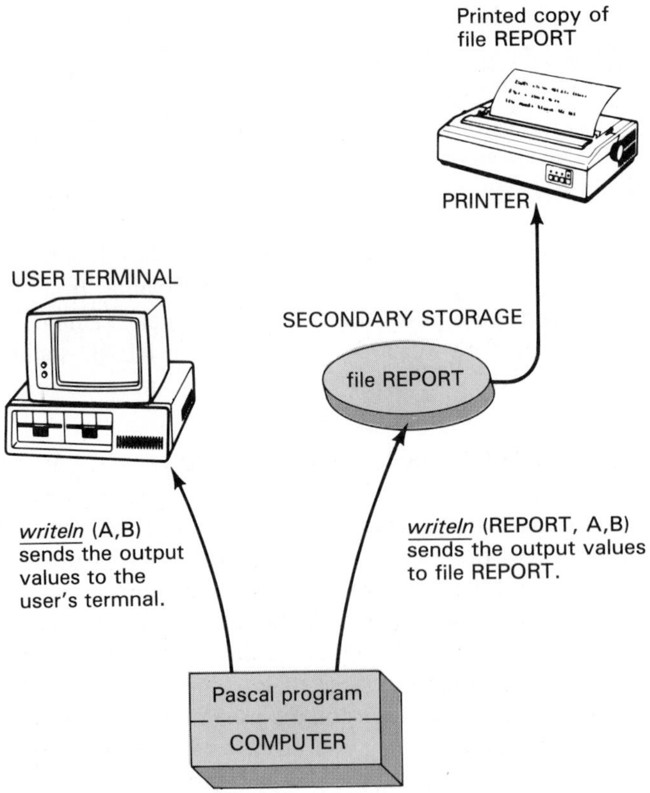

A *data file* is any file within the computer system that contains data to be processed by some program. Thus *any file* in a computer system can serve as a data file. For our Pascal programs, data files may contain values of any of the data types used in the program—Integer, Real, Char, Boolean, or a type that you have defined. Because data files are just ordinary files within a computer system, they are saved indefinitely and can be reused as often as required. Data files are not lost when a particular run of a program ends.

Data files come in two varieties:

1. *Text files.* A *text file* is a file that contains data values in *character form,* that is, each value is represented as a sequence of characters within the file. For example, the integer value 27 would be represented as a sequence of the characters '2' and '7'. A text file can be printed on a printer or displayed on a terminal. It can be created with an editor program by typing in data values on the keyboard in the same way that you create a source program file.

2. *Nontext files.* A *nontext file* (sometimes called a *binary file*) is a file that contains data values in their *binary form,* as they are stored in the computer's memory. In a nontext file, an integer value like 27 might be stored as the 32-bit integer:

00000000000000000000000000011011

instead of as the characters '2' and '7'. A nontext file can store copies of the values from large data objects like arrays and records. For example, a nontext file might contain all the employee records for a large business.

Nontext files are files that can only be read and written by programs. They are not for direct human inspection. So you cannot print a nontext file on a printer or create one with an editor program. Nontext files are used as scratch files in large programs and for output files that are intended to be processed later by other programs. For example, a nontext file of the employee records for a business might be created initially by one program and then "updated" by a second program at the end of each month. A third program might be used to create a printable report (stored in a text file) from the nontext file.

Nontext files are a good subject for a second or later computer science course, but they would take us too far afield here. We focus our attention on text files in this book.

Text File Organization

A text file is organized as follows:

1. The file contains a *sequence of characters,* just as might be displayed on the terminal screen or typed on a keyboard.
2. The characters in the file are divided into *lines,* each terminated with the special non-printing *end of line* character, designated ⟨EOLN⟩.
3. The ⟨EOLN⟩ terminating the last line of the file is followed by a special *end of file* marker, designated ⟨EOF⟩.

Both ⟨EOLN⟩ and ⟨EOF⟩ are inserted automatically by WRITE operations as the file is created.

A file that contains no data values is termed an *empty file.* Such a file contains only the terminating ⟨EOF⟩.

EXAMPLE

A text file that contains a first line with the integers 5, 10, 15, and 20 and a second line with the real numbers 2.22 and 3.33 might appear as the following sequence of characters:

```
5____10_15__20___⟨EOLN⟩__2.22___3.33⟨EOLN⟩⟨EOF⟩
```

□ □
File Status and File Position

There are two new concepts related to the use of data files by a program, the *status* and the *position* of the file. Both the status and the position of a data file can change during execution of a program.

When a program uses a data file, the program begins execution with the file status = *closed,* meaning that the file is not available to be the target of a READ or WRITE operation. Before the file can be used, its status must be changed to one of *open for reading* or *open for writing.* The status of a file determines whether READ or WRITE operations can be executed with that file as the target.

The *position* of a data file only becomes important when the file status = *open for reading.* Think of a data file as having an *input cursor,* just like the cursor on a terminal display screen. When the file status is changed to *open for reading,* the input cursor is positioned on the first character of data in the file. Each time a READ operation is executed on the file, the input cursor advances past the data values read and is left positioned at the first character following the last data value read. The position of the input cursor in the file is termed the *position of the file* (see Figure 11.2). When a READ operation advances the input cursor past the last character in the file then the file is said to be positioned at the *end of file mark.*

A data file whose status is *open for writing* also has a file position, but that position is always at the end of file mark. Each WRITE operation writes its output data

---

The ↑ shows the position of the file.

File position when the file is first opened:

```
5____10_15__20___<EOLN>__2.22___3.33<EOLN> <EOF>
↑
```

File position after execution of the first readln:

```
5____10_15__20___<EOLN>_2.22___3.33<EOLN> <EOF>
                            ↑
```

File position when at the end of file mark:

```
5____10_15__20___<EOLN>__2.22___3.33<EOLN> <EOF>
                                            ↑
```

FIGURE 11-2   The "Position" of a File

---

at that file position, extending the file. After the WRITE, the file is again positioned at the end of file mark, following the newly written data.

□ □
The "State" of a Data File

To understand the program state for a program that uses data files, you need to know the *state of each data file,* which is determined by:

1. *File contents.* What data the file contains—the number of lines and the format and content of each.
2. *File status.* Whether the file is *open for reading, open for writing,* or *closed.*
3. *File position, if the file is open for reading.*

□ □
The Two Names of a Data File

A data file is known to the operating system by one name, its *external file name.* The external file name is the name that appears in the *directory* where the file can be found. If you use an editor program to create the data file, then this is the file name used with the editor.

Inside a Pascal program, while the file is actually being read or written, the file is known by another name, its *internal file name.* The internal file name is the *Pascal identifier* used to refer to the file within the program.

The distinction between these two names is like that between an *actual parameter name* and a *formal parameter name* in a subprogram. The external file name is like the actual parameter name; the internal file name is like the formal parameter name.

All the operations on a data file within a program use the internal file name. However, before the file can be opened for reading or writing, a connection must be established between the internal file name and the external name of the actual file to be used.

Unfortunately, the way that this connection is established varies widely among Pascal systems. Two common methods are:

1. *Special procedure call.* Some Pascal systems require that the program call a special procedure to "connect" the two file names, such as the call:

```
connect (⟨internal file name⟩, '⟨external file name⟩')
```

The internal file name is a Pascal identifier, while the external file name is given as a character string. Of course, the procedure name may not be named *connect*; other common names are *attach* or *assign*.

2. *"Actual parameters" when the program is run.* Other Pascal systems allow you to specify the external file names as though they were actual parameters when an object program is run. For example, if the file containing your object program is named ReportProg and the program reads data from one file and writes results on another, then to run it using data files with the external names MYINPUT and MYOUTPUT, you might use the operating system command:

```
RUN ReportProg (MYINPUT, MYOUTPUT)
```

With this method, no action *inside* the program is required.

Before using data files, check your local *Pascal User's Manual* for the details of how to make the connection between the two names of a file in your Pascal system.

□ □
The Predefined Data Type "Text"

Because a data file is used to store data values, it is a data object, and thus it has a *data type*. The data type of a text file is given by the predefined type "Text", which means "FILE OF Char." If all data files are text files (as in this book), then it is unnecessary to define any new data types for files. Just declare each individual data file as type "Text".

Predefined Operations on Text Files

The operations on Text files in standard Pascal include the following:

1. *read* and *readln:* the same READ operations used to read data from the terminal keyboard.
2. *write* and *writeln:* the same WRITE operations used to display data on the terminal screen.
3. *reset:* a procedure that changes the status of a file to *open for reading* and that positions the file at its first character.
4. *rewrite:* a procedure that creates a new empty file, whose status is *open for writing*.
5. *eof:* a function that tests whether a file is positioned at the *end of file mark,* ⟨EOF⟩.
6. *eoln:* a function that tests whether a file is positioned at an ⟨EOLN⟩.

Most Pascal systems extend this basic set to include additional useful operations on Text files, such as a *close* operation to change a file's status to *closed* or a *seek* operation to position a file at a particular character within the file. Check your local *Pascal User's Manual*.

File Operations Ask the Operating System for Help

The operating system is in overall control of the file system of a computer. An individual Pascal program must ask the operating system for help when performing any operation on a file. For example, when a program wishes to create a new file to receive its output results, the Pascal system makes a request to the operating system to create the file and set its status to *open for writing*. While the operating system is providing this help, it also enters the name of the new file into your local directory, so that after execution of the Pascal program is complete you find the newly created file is still accessible to you.

The Predefined Files: INPUT and OUTPUT

For simplicity in the standard definition of Pascal, the user's terminal is considered to actually consist of two predefined Text files named INPUT and OUTPUT. Whenever a *read* or *readln* operation is executed and no "target" file name is specified, the operation reads data from "file INPUT," which is the terminal keyboard. Whenever a *write* or *writeln* operation is executed and no target file name is specified, the operation writes the data to "file OUTPUT," which is the terminal display screen. Thus the *default file name* for any READ operation is file INPUT and for any WRITE operation is file OUTPUT. Files INPUT and OUTPUT are *predefined files* in every Pascal program and they are always *open for reading* and *open for writing,* respectively.

Redirecting READ and WRITE Operations

Most Pascal systems provide a way for a program to connect the file names INPUT and OUTPUT to actual data files *for a particular run of the program,* so that they no longer refer to the user's terminal. We say that ordinary READ or WRITE operations are *redirected* to a data file instead of to the user's terminal for that run of the program. Thus, a program that is ordinarily run as an interactive program may be turned into a batch processing program for a particular run. The details of redirecting READ and WRITE operations are not part of standard Pascal. You will have to consult your local *Pascal User's Manual* or operating system manual.

EXERCISES

11.1 Find out the following details about the use of data files on your Pascal system:

a. Determine how to *connect* an external file name with the internal name used in a Pascal program.

b. Determine what additional *operations on data files* are provided by your Pascal system, beyond the standard operations listed above.

c. Determine how to *redirect* READ and WRITE operations so that they use data files instead of the user's terminal.

□□□ **11.3**
REQUIREMENTS: SPECIFYING A DATA FILE FORMAT

Programs that work with data files often have strict requirements about the formats of those data files. In a typical situation, you might be hired to write a program to compute the payroll for a small business. The information needed to compute the payroll might already be stored in an "employee data file," a file used by several existing programs. Your program must read the data in the file, in whatever format happens to be used for that file. You don't get to choose—the format of the file becomes part of the *requirements* for your program.

For an output data file, you also may find that the format of the file is a fixed part of the requirements for your program—because an existing program is expecting to use your output file as its input file, in the specified format.

□ □
Specifying a Text File Format

BNF may be used to describe the format of a file. To specify a file format, describe:

1. The sequence of data values in the file, and what each value represents.
2. How the data values are organized: the number of lines, the data values on each line, and the way that each value is separated from the next (e.g., spaces, punctuation).

EXAMPLE

Suppose you have a data file that contains all the information from a particular course offered at your school. Suppose the "course file" contains a first line with the course number and the semester and year the course was taught. The second line contains the number of students enrolled in the course. Each following line gives information about one student: the student's id number, homework average, two exam scores, and final grade. This file format might be described:

FORMAT OF FILE COURSEFILE

⟨COURSEFILE file⟩ ::=
    ⟨course number⟩ ⟨semester⟩ ⟨year⟩⟨EOLN⟩
    ⟨number of students⟩⟨EOLN⟩
    {⟨student-id⟩ ⟨homework⟩ ⟨exam1⟩ ⟨exam2⟩ ⟨final⟩⟨EOLN⟩}
    ⟨EOF⟩

WHERE
    ⟨course number⟩ ::=
        Five-digit integer, the assigned course number.
    ⟨semester⟩ ::=
        Single digit: 1 = Fall, 2 = Spring, 3 = Summer
    ⟨year⟩ ::=
        Positive integer, the year the course was given.
    ⟨number of students⟩ ::=
        Positive integer, number of students enrolled.
    ⟨student-id⟩ ::=
        Nine-digit student id number.
    ⟨homework⟩ ::=
        Real number in range 0..100, the student's homework average.
    ⟨exam1⟩ ::=
        Integer in range 0..100, score on first exam.
    ⟨exam2⟩ ::=
        Integer in range 0..120, score on second exam.
    ⟨final⟩ ::=
        Real number in range 0..120, final average in the course.
    Data values on each line are separated by one or more spaces.

■

EXERCISES

11.2 Design and specify a data file format for each of the following situations:

    a. A data file that contains the high and low temperatures for each day in a particular year. Include the year for which the measurements were made.

    b. A data file that contains the scores of all the basketball games played by your school's team in the last ten years. Include the opponent, final score, and date played for each game.

    c. The inventory number, brief description, number in stock, wholesale price, and retail price for each textbook sold in a college bookstore.

11.3 (Chess players only) Design and specify a file format for a data file that contains the complete sequence of moves in a chess game (such as you might find in a chess book).

□□□ 11.4
DECLARING TEXT FILES: THE GLOBAL DATA OBJECTS LIST

Within a program that uses data files, you declare each file as type Text, just as though it were an ordinary data object. However, in our programs each data file is considered *global* to the entire program, rather than *local* to a single subprogram. That is, within the program, *any subprogram* may read data from a data file or write data to a data file, simply by using the name of the file in a READ or WRITE operation. The file does *not* have to be transmitted as a parameter to a subprogram that performs an operation on it.

This is the first time that we have needed "global" data objects, but it is not the last—other types of global data objects will be used in the upcoming chapters. In pseudo-code, we keep a list of these global data objects, separate from the DATA OBJECTS lists that are local to each subprogram. The form of this list matches that for the local lists:

⟨GLOBAL DATA OBJECTS list⟩ ::=

> **GLOBAL DATA OBJECTS**
> ⟨object-name⟩: ⟨data-type⟩   ⟨purpose⟩
> {⟨object-name⟩: ⟨data-type⟩   ⟨purpose⟩}
>
> **WHERE**
>   ⟨object-name⟩ ::= A Pascal identifier.
>   ⟨data-type⟩ ::= Any defined data type.
>   ⟨purpose⟩ ::= Purpose of the data object.

For a text file, the ⟨object-name⟩ is just the internal file name. The ⟨data-type⟩ is Text. The ⟨purpose⟩ describes whether the file is used for *input* or *output* of data, and the sort of data it contains.

EXAMPLE   **GLOBAL DATA OBJECTS**

> COURSEFILE: Text   Input file of course and grades data.
> REPORT: Text   Output file for report.   ■

□□

Coding the GLOBAL DATA OBJECTS List in Pascal

The GLOBAL DATA OBJECTS list is coded as a VAR section that follows the TYPE section at the beginning of the Pascal program, immediately before the first subprogram definition. This VAR section has the same form as the VAR section within a subprogram.

In most Pascal systems, each internal file name must also be listed in the PROGRAM line at the start of the program:

```
PROGRAM ⟨program-name⟩ (INPUT, OUTPUT, ⟨file-name⟩, ...);
```

EXAMPLE The GLOBAL DATA OBJECTS list in the example above might be coded in Pascal:

```
PROGRAM ⟨name⟩ (INPUT, OUTPUT, COURSEFILE, REPORT);

    CONST
        . . .

    TYPE
        . . .

    VAR
        COURSEFILE: Text;      {Input file of course and grades data}
        REPORT: Text;          {Output file for report}

    PROCEDURE ...
        . . .                               -- procedures and functions

BEGIN
    . . .
END.
```

■

□ □

Files as Parameters to Subprograms

A file name may be an actual parameter in a subprogram call. The corresponding formal parameter is declared as type Text. In Pascal, a file formal parameter must always be a VAR parameter.

EXERCISES

11.4 For each data file described in Exercises 11.2 and 11.3, write a GLOBAL DATA OBJECTS list in pseudo-code and a Pascal VAR section appropriate to declare the file within a Pascal program that uses it.

□ □ □ **11.5**
SENDING OUTPUT TO A TEXT FILE

Writing output data to a text file is similar to displaying output data on the terminal screen. The same WRITE statements may be used for either purpose, simply by specifying the name of the "target" data file in the WRITE statement. Let's look first at the design of an algorithm that uses an output data file and then at the Pascal coding details.

□ □

Design: Steps in Using an Output Data File

In pseudo-code, a program that uses an output data file needs to include the following new actions:

1. *"Connect" the internal Pascal file name and the external file name.* The connection between the internal file name and the external file name must be established. For this text, we use the pseudo-code action:

CONNECT (⟨internal file name⟩, '⟨external file name⟩')

The CONNECT action must be executed before the file is opened. If no file with the specified external file name currently exists, the CONNECT action creates an *empty file* with the specified name.

2. *Open the file for writing.* Before the connected file can be used as the target of a WRITE operation, its status must be set to *open for writing.* We use the pseudo-code action:

OPEN FOR WRITING: ⟨internal file name⟩

CAUTION: If you have connected the Pascal file name to a file that already exists in your directory, then executing an OPEN FOR WRITING operation will *destroy the existing contents of the file.* That is, after the OPEN FOR WRITING is executed, the file will exist as an *empty file,* whose status is *open for writing,* regardless of its contents and status before the OPEN operation.

3. *Use WRITE TO FILE actions to send data to the file.* In pseudo-code, use the syntax:

WRITE TO ⟨internal file name⟩:
⟨description of lines to be written to the file, just as for a DISPLAY action⟩

As many WRITE TO FILE actions as needed may be used. These actions may appear wherever a DISPLAY action might appear. WRITE TO FILE and DISPLAY actions may be intermixed if the program is an interactive program that is using a data file.

4. *Close the output file, if required.* In most Pascal systems, the status of each data file is automatically changed to *closed* when the program terminates. However, some Pascal systems require that the program call a special CLOSE procedure to

change the file status to *closed* before the program terminates, after the last WRITE TO FILE operation. Our pseudo-code action is:

CLOSE: ⟨internal file name⟩

EXAMPLE   Let's design a procedure to write data to a COURSEFILE, where the format of a COURSEFILE is specified in the example of Section 11.3. Without repeating the details, the format in BNF is:

FORMAT OF **COURSEFILE** FILE

⟨COURSEFILE file⟩ ::=
     ⟨course number⟩ ⟨semester⟩ ⟨year⟩⟨EOLN⟩
     ⟨number of students⟩⟨EOLN⟩
     {⟨student-id⟩ ⟨homework⟩ ⟨exam1⟩ ⟨exam2⟩ ⟨final⟩⟨EOLN⟩}
     ⟨EOF⟩

Suppose that inside the program, the data for a particular course is represented as a record data object, defined in pseudo-code as follows:

DEFINED CONSTANTS

MAXSTUDENTS = ?   Maximum course enrollment allowed.

DATA TYPES

StudentInfo =
  RECORD
     ID: Integer   Student identification number.
     Homework: Real   Homework average, range 0..100.
     Exam1: Integer   First exam grade, range 0..100.
     Exam2: Integer   Second exam grade, range 0..120.
     Final: Real   Final course average, range 0..120.
  END

GradesList = ARRAY [1..MAXSTUDENTS] OF StudentInfo
SemesterRange = 1..3
EnrollmentRange = 1..MAXSTUDENTS

CourseData =
  RECORD
     CourseID: Integer   Unique course identification.
     Semester: SemesterRange   When course was offered.
     Year: Integer   Year offered.
     Enrollment: EnrollmentRange Number of students graded.
     Grades: GradesList   Grades for each student.
  END

Your goal is to design the following procedure:

PROCEDURE WriteGradesFile

(Course: CourseData   IN: Data to be written to file.
COURSEFILE: Text)   OUT: File to receive data.

PURPOSE/GOAL STATE: Write out all the data values in Course to file COURSEFILE, using the file format specified in the program requirements.

PRECONDITION: Parameter COURSEFILE is already connected to an external file name.

In pseudo-code, your design might be:

ALGORITHM

Step 1. PURPOSE/GOAL STATE: Open COURSEFILE and write out the first two lines of heading data.

ACTIONS:

OPEN FOR WRITING: COURSEFILE
WRITE TO COURSEFILE:

"⟨Course.CourseID⟩ ⟨Course.Semester⟩ ⟨Course.Year⟩"
"⟨Course.Enrollment⟩"

Step 2. PURPOSE/GOAL STATE: Write out one line of data for each enrolled student.

ACTIONS:

```
FOR I := 1 TO Course.Enrollment DO
    BEGIN
        WRITE TO COURSEFILE: (in a single output line)
        "⟨Course.Grades[I].ID⟩
         ⟨Course.Grades[I].Homework⟩
         ⟨Course.Grades[I].Exam1⟩
         ⟨Course.Grades[I].Exam2⟩
         ⟨Course.Grades[I].Final⟩"
    END
```

Step 3. ACTIONS:
CLOSE: COURSEFILE

DATA OBJECTS

I: EnrollmentRange   FOR loop subscript variable.

□ □
Coding a Program that Writes a Data File

Coding the new actions in Pascal is straightforward.

□

CONNECT and CLOSE.   CONNECT and CLOSE are not part of standard Pascal. You need to check your local *Pascal User's Manual* for the details of coding these actions in your system. Some systems may not require any Pascal action.

□

OPEN FOR WRITING.   The OPEN FOR WRITING operation in Pascal is coded as a call on the predefined procedure *rewrite:*

```
rewrite (⟨internal file name⟩);
```

□

WRITE TO FILE.   Each WRITE TO FILE operation is coded in Pascal as a *write* or *writeln* statement. To specify that you want the data written to a text file rather than displayed, you simply put the *internal file name* as the first parameter in the statement, before the list of data items to be written:

```
writeln (⟨file-name⟩, ...list of output items...);
```

or

```
write (⟨file-name⟩, ...list of output items...);
```

For example, to write a line of output to file REPORT:

```
writeln (REPORT, 'The total is ', Total);
```

The difference between *write* and *writeln* is the same as when writing to the terminal display. Both *write* and *writeln* continue writing the listed output items until all the values have been written. No ⟨EOLN⟩ to mark a line boundary is inserted if *write* is used. *Writeln* inserts an ⟨EOLN⟩ immediately after the last item written.

EXAMPLE   Coding the WriteGradesFile procedure above in Pascal:

```
PROCEDURE WriteGradesFile

   (VAR Course: CourseData;     {IN: Data to be written to file}
    VAR COURSEFILE: Text);      {OUT: File to receive data}
```

```
{PURPOSE/GOAL STATE: Write out all the data values in Course
to file COURSEFILE, using the file format specified in the
program requirements.}

{PRECONDITION: Parameter COURSEFILE is already connected to
an external file name.}

VAR
   I: EnrollmentRange;            {FOR loop subscript variable}
BEGIN
       {PURPOSE/GOAL STATE: Open COURSEFILE and write out the
       first two lines of heading data.}

     rewrite (COURSEFILE);
     writeln (COURSEFILE, Course.CourseID, Course.Semester, Course.Year);
     writeln (COURSEFILE, Course.Enrollment);

        {PURPOSE/GOAL STATE: Write out one line of data for
        each enrolled student.}

     FOR I := 1 TO Course.Enrollment DO
        BEGIN
           writeln (COURSEFILE, Course.Grades[I].ID,
              Course.Grades[I].Homework, Course.Grades[I].Exam1,
              Course.Grades[I].Exam2, Course.Grades[I].Final);
        END;

     close (COURSEFILE);   {if required by Pascal system}

   END;   {procedure WriteGradesFile}
```

EXERCISES

11.5 For each data file format specified in Exercise 11.2, design a representation for the same data in a Pascal program, using appropriate arrays, records, and strings. Then design and code a Pascal procedure that writes the data values from the program data structures to a data file in the specified file format.

□□□11.6
READING DATA VALUES FROM A TEXT FILE

Reading data from a text file is similar to reading data from the terminal keyboard. The same READ statements may be used for either purpose, simply by specifying the name of the "target" data file in the READ statement.

Design: Steps in Reading Data from a Data File

In pseudo-code, the basic actions for reading a file are similar to those for writing a file:

1. *"Connect" the internal file name and the external file name.* The connection between the internal file name and the external file name must be established, just as when writing to a file. For this text, we use the pseudo-code action:

CONNECT (⟨internal file name⟩, '⟨external file name⟩')

The CONNECT action must be executed before the file is opened.

2. *Open the file for reading.* After the connection to the input file is established, the file status must be set to *open for reading*. This operation also positions the file at its first character. We use the pseudo-code action:

OPEN FOR READING: ⟨internal file name⟩

3. *Use READ FROM FILE actions to read data values from the file.* In pseudo-code, use the syntax:

READ FROM ⟨internal file name⟩: ⟨list of data objects to receive the data values⟩

As many READ FROM FILE actions as needed may be used. These actions may appear wherever an ordinary READ action (from the terminal keyboard) might appear. The data values are read from the file starting at the current file position, and the file position is advanced to the first character following the last data value read.

4. *Close the input file, if required.* If your Pascal system requires that an input file be closed after the last READ FROM FILE operation, use the pseudo-code action:

CLOSE: ⟨internal file name⟩

EXAMPLE Suppose we use the course grades data structure again from the example above. At the start of a program that works with course grades data, we might want to fill a data object of type CourseData with the data values stored in a data file. The program would then be able to insert or delete student entries, or modify the values in a student's grade record. At the end of the program, the WriteGradesFile procedure could be used to write out the data to a second data file, so that all the data values were saved. On a later run of the same program, we could read the new data file in, process the values, and write them out again.

Our object here is to design the procedure, ReadGradesFile, that reads in the data values and stores the values in a CourseData data object. The heading for ReadGradesFile might be:

PROCEDURE ReadGradesFile

| (COURSEFILE: Text | IN: File containing data to be read. |
| Course: CourseData) | OUT: Data object to receive data read. |

PURPOSE/GOAL STATE: Read the data values in COURSEFILE and store them in the appropriate fields of Course. The file format is specified in the program requirements.

PRECONDITION: Parameter COURSEFILE is already connected to an external file name.

In pseudo-code, your design might be the following. Notice how the actions in this procedure mirror the actions used to write the data file in procedure WriteGradesFile above.

ALGORITHM

Step 1. PURPOSE/GOAL STATE: Open COURSEFILE and read the first two lines of heading data.

ACTIONS:

```
OPEN FOR READING: COURSEFILE
READ FROM COURSEFILE:
    ⟨Course.CourseID⟩ ⟨Course.Semester⟩ ⟨Course.Year⟩
READ FROM COURSEFILE:
    ⟨Course.Enrollment⟩
```

Step 2. PURPOSE/GOAL STATE: Read one line of data for each enrolled student.

ACTIONS:

```
FOR I := 1 TO Course.Enrollment DO
    BEGIN
        READ FROM COURSEFILE: (from a single line)
            ⟨Course.Grades[I].ID⟩
            ⟨Course.Grades[I].Homework⟩
            ⟨Course.Grades[I].Exam1⟩
            ⟨Course.Grades[I].Exam2⟩
            ⟨Course.Grades[I].Final⟩
    END
```

Step 3. ACTIONS:

> CLOSE: COURSEFILE

□ □

Coding a Program that Reads from a Data File

Coding the new actions in Pascal is straightforward.

□

CONNECT and CLOSE.   CONNECT and CLOSE are not part of standard Pascal. You need to check your local *Pascal User's Manual* for the details of coding these actions in your system. Some systems may not require any Pascal action.

□

OPEN FOR READING.   The OPEN FOR READING operation in Pascal is coded as a call on the predefined procedure *reset:*

> ```
> reset (⟨internal file name⟩);
> ```

Executing this procedure call changes the file status to *open for reading* and positions the file at its first character.

□

READ FROM FILE.   Each READ FROM FILE operation is coded in Pascal as a *read* or *readln* statement. To specify that you want the data read from a text file rather than from the terminal keyboard, put the *internal file name* as the first parameter in the statement.

> ```
> readln (⟨file-name⟩, ...list of variable names...);
> ```

or

> ```
> read (⟨file-name⟩, ...list of variable names...);
> ```

For example:

> ```
> readln (DATAFILE, AccountNumber, InputAmount);
> ```

The READ FROM FILE actions must match the file format exactly, so that data values are read in the sequence that they appear on the file.

Each line boundary, indicated by ⟨EOLN⟩, is read as though it were a single space character. If numbers are being read, then an ⟨EOLN⟩ serves as a space to separate two numbers. If Char data values are being read, then the ⟨EOLN⟩ is read as a space character.

A *read* action continues until data values have been read for each variable in the *read* statement. The file is left positioned at the first character following the end of the last data value read. A *readln* does the same, but after the last data value is read, the file position is advanced to the first character after the next ⟨EOLN⟩. Executing the statement:

```
readln (⟨file name⟩);
```

with no list of variables, simply advances the position of the file to the first character following the next ⟨EOLN⟩. Figure 11.3 illustrates the effect of various READ statements on the state of an input data file INDATA.

□ □
Data Values in a File Must be Read in Sequence

You cannot "backspace" the input cursor in Pascal. Once a data value has been read from an input file, the file is positioned at some point past that data value. You can only read that data value a second time if you execute a second *reset* statement for the file, which moves the input cursor all the way back to the first character in the file. After a *reset*, you would have to read all the data values in the file over again from the beginning.

As you can see, it ordinarily is not a good idea to plan to read the same data value more than once from a file. Design your program so that it reads each data value in a data file in sequence. If a particular value is needed several times during the execution of the program, just read it into a variable and leave the variable unchanged until you have completely finished using that data value.

□ □
Testing for ⟨EOLN⟩ or ⟨EOF⟩

Two predefined Pascal functions allow a program to test whether a file is positioned at an ⟨EOLN⟩ character, marking the end of an input line, or at the ⟨EOF⟩ mark:

eoln (⟨file name⟩)	returns TRUE if the file is positioned at an ⟨EOLN⟩ character; FALSE otherwise.
eof (⟨file name⟩)	returns TRUE if the file is positioned at the ⟨EOF⟩ mark; FALSE otherwise.

These functions are useful to control loops that read data values from files. Some common loop patterns using *eof* and *eoln* are discussed in the next section.

Suppose the initial state of file INDATA is:

File status: *open for reading*.
File contents and position: ___5__10__15__20<EOLN>
                 ↑
           _____2.22___3.33<EOLN>
           <EOF>

READ Segment Executed	**Resulting File State**

Data Types:

```
X, Y, Z, W: Integer
U, V: Real
```

```
read (INDATA, X, Y, Z);
```
                                 ___5__10__15__20<EOLN>
                                              ↑
                                 _____2.22___3.33<EOLN>
                                 <EOF>

```
readln (INDATA, X, Y, Z);
```
    ___5__10__15__20<EOLN>
    _____2.22___3.33<EOLN>
    ↑
    <EOF>

```
read (INDATA, X, Y, Z);
read (INDATA, W, U);
```
    ___5__10__15__20<EOLN>
    _____2.22___3.33<EOLN>
                ↑
    <EOF>

```
readln (INDATA, X);
read (INDATA, U);
```
    ___5__10__15__20<EOLN>
    _____2.22___3.33<EOLN>
         ↑
    <EOF>

```
readln (INDATA, X, Y, Z, W, U);
```
    ___5__10__15__20<EOLN>
    _____2.22___3.33<EOLN>
    <EOF>
    ↑

FIGURE 11-3 Examples of Execution of READ Statements

EXERCISES

11.6 Code the ReadGradesFile procedure in Pascal. The pseudo-code design is given in the example above.

11.7 Design and code a Pascal program to read in fifty Real numbers from a file INDATA and write the numbers and their sum and average out to a file OUTDATA. Ten numbers appear on each input line.

□□□ 11.7
READ LOOP PATTERNS FOR DATA FILES

A *read loop* is a loop that reads a sequence of values from an input data file and processes each value or stores it in an array as it is read. The problem with a read loop is designing the *loop control:* how do you know when the last data value has been read from the file? Two common alternatives are these:

1. *Have a count of how many values to read.* If you know how many values to read, based on the value of an integer variable or constant, you can use a count controlled FOR loop to read the values. The count might be read first from the data file, or it might be a value computed within the program.

EXAMPLE

PURPOSE/GOAL STATE: From file INFILE, read in the number of months and store it in NumMonths. Then read one sales amount for each month. Sum the sales amounts; store in Total.

ACTIONS:

```
READ FROM INFILE: NumMonths
Total := 0
FOR I := 1 TO NumMonths DO
    BEGIN
        READ FROM INFILE: SalesAmount
        Total := Total + SalesAmount
            KTH ITERATION: Total = sum of first K sales amounts.
    END
```

PASCAL CODE:

```
{PURPOSE/GOAL STATE: From file INFILE, read in the
number of months and store it in NumMonths.  Then read
one sales amount for each month.  Sum the sales
amounts; store in Total.}
read (INFILE, NumMonths);
Total := 0;
FOR I := 1 TO NumMonths DO
```

```
BEGIN
    read (INFILE, SalesAmount);
    Total := Total + SalesAmount;

        {KTH ITERATION: Total = sum of first K sales amounts}
END;
```

2. *Read until you read a "sentinel" value.* A *sentinel value* is a value used to indicate the end of a sequence of data values in a data file. If numbers are being read, the sentinel is often a zero or negative number that indicates the end of a sequence of numbers. If Char data values are being read, then the sentinel may be a punctuation mark or a space that marks the end of a sequence of characters.

If the last data value is followed by a sentinel value, you can use an event controlled loop to read the values, where the "event" is reading the sentinel value. The sentinel value must be of the *same data type* as the values being read because it will be read and stored in the same variable as a regular data value before the loop exit test discovers that it is the sentinel value.

EXAMPLE

PURPOSE/GOAL STATE: From file INFILE, read sales amounts until a negative value (the sentinel) is read. Sum the sales amounts; store in Total. The sentinel is not considered a sales amount.

ACTIONS:

```
Total := 0
READ FROM INFILE: SalesAmount
WHILE SalesAmount >= 0 DO    — test for sentinel value
    BEGIN
        Total := Total + SalesAmount
        READ FROM INFILE: SalesAmount

        KTH ITERATION: Total = sum of first K data values;
        SalesAmount contains the (K+1)st value read.
    END
```

PASCAL CODE:

```
    {PURPOSE/GOAL STATE: From file INFILE, read sales
    amounts until a negative value (the sentinel) is read.
    Sum the sales amounts; store in Total.  The sentinel is
    not considered a sales amount.}
Total := 0;
read (INFILE, SalesAmount);
WHILE SalesAmount >= 0 DO       {test for sentinel value}
    BEGIN
        Total := Total + SalesAmount;
        read (INFILE, SalesAmount);
```

```
                        {KTH ITERATION: Total = sum of first K data
                        values; SalesAmount contains the (K+1)st value
                        read}
          END;                                                              ■
```

□ □

Loops Controlled by the Pascal EOF Function

Suppose that the program is reading a data file containing numbers (Real or Integer) and execution has reached a loop that must read *all* the remaining data values in the file. For such a loop, you can use an event controlled read loop, where the event is when the predefined function *eof* signals that the ⟨EOF⟩ mark has been reached.

When reading Real or Integer values and using *eof* to test for ⟨EOF⟩, you must read an *entire line* of data (or multiple lines) on each loop iteration, ending with a *readln*. This is due to a quirk of Pascal: *read* ignores line boundaries and simply scans through lines until it finds the next number in the input file. The last number in the file is always followed by an ⟨EOLN⟩ character, so *eof* does not give a result of TRUE when the *last number* has been read, only when the *last line* has been read. If you execute *read* after the last number has been read, you get a run-time error message "ATTEMPT TO READ PAST END OF FILE" and execution terminates.

To read to the ⟨EOF⟩ mark, use an event controlled loop, where the event is "*eof* (⟨file-name⟩) = TRUE". (If values are being stored in an array, use a count and event controlled loop, with the count being bounded by the size of the array.)

EXAMPLE   File TEMPDATA contains temperature values taken from a series of readings in a scientific experiment. The Real values are stored three per line in the file.

PURPOSE/GOAL STATE: Read all the temperature values, compute the average, and store the average in Average.

ACTIONS:

```
Count := 0
Total := 0
WHILE NOT eof(TEMPDATA) DO
    BEGIN
        READ FROM TEMPDATA: Temp1, Temp2, Temp3
        Total := Total + Temp1 + Temp2 + Temp3
        Count := Count + 3

            KTH ITERATION: K lines of data have been read.
            Total contains sum of all values read; Count contains count of
            values read (3 values/line).
    END
Average := Total / Count
```

PASCAL CODE:

```
                {PURPOSE/GOAL STATE: Read all the temperature values,
                compute the average, and store the average in Average.}
```

```
Count := 0;
Total := 0;

WHILE NOT eof (TEMPDATA) DO
   BEGIN
      readln (TEMPDATA, Temp1, Temp2, Temp3);
      Total := Total + Temp1 + Temp2 + Temp3;
      Count := Count + 3;
            {KTH ITERATION: K lines of data have been read.
             Total contains sum of all values read; Count
             contains count of values read (3 values/line)}
   END;

Average := Total / Count;                                       ▪
```

□ □
Reading a Line of Character Data

If the data is being read from a data file in character form (as a string of characters), you often want to read an entire line of data at a time. To read a single line of data, you usually have two choices:

1. *STRING read.* Read the line as a single character string into a STRING data object. The STRING data object must have a declared length at least as long as the line to be read. The read operation will read the entire line of characters and set the length of the string data object equal to the number of characters in the line. This approach does not use a loop; the entire string is read in a single read operation. *Caution:* STRING data types and this form of read operation are *not* standard Pascal.

2. *Read Char values until an ⟨EOLN⟩ is reached.* Alternatively, you can use a read loop that reads one character at a time. To terminate the loop, use the predefined function *eoln* to test for the end of line character, ⟨EOLN⟩, which can serve as a sentinel value. This approach is the best way to read a line of character data in standard Pascal. (Real and Integer values cannot be read this way because the *read* and *readln* operations ignore ⟨EOLN⟩'s while reading numbers, except that *readln* looks at the ⟨EOLN⟩ *after* the last number read.)

EXAMPLE   Suppose array InputLine is declared to be type "ARRAY [1..MAXLINE] of Char," where MAXLINE is a defined constant.

PURPOSE/GOAL STATE: From file INDATA, read characters to the end of the current input line and store the characters in InputLine. Also store the number of characters read in variable LineLength. If the line has more than MAXLINE characters, ignore the remainder of the line.

ACTIONS:

LineLength := 0
WHILE (NOT eoln (INDATA)) AND (LineLength < MAXLINE) DO

```
      BEGIN
          LineLength := LineLength + 1
          READ FROM INDATA: InputLine [LineLength]

                KTH ITERATION: LineLength = K and InputLine
                [1..LineLength] contains first K characters of the input line.
      END
```

PASCAL CODE:

```
          {PURPOSE/GOAL STATE: From file INDATA, read characters
          to the end of the current input line and store the
          characters in InputLine.  Also store the number of
          characters read in variable LineLength.  If the line
          has more than MAXLINE characters, ignore the remainder
          of the line.}
      LineLength := 0;
      WHILE (NOT eoln (INDATA)) AND (LineLength < MAXLINE) DO
        BEGIN
          LineLength := LineLength + 1;
          read (INDATA, InputLine [LineLength]);

                {KTH ITERATION: LineLength = K and
                InputLine [1..LineLength] contains first K
                characters of the input line.}
      END;
```

EXERCISES

11.8 For each of the following situations, design an appropriate read loop. Then code the loop in Pascal.

a. PURPOSE/GOAL STATE: From file TEXTIN read a sequence of characters representing a sentence. The sentence is terminated by the first period, question mark, or exclamation point. Store the sentence, including the terminating punctuation mark, in variable NextSentence. NextSentence is of type STRING[200]. The sentence is known to have fewer than 200 characters.

b. PURPOSE/GOAL STATE: From file NEWDATA read a sequence of integer values representing employee hours worked. Store the values in the elements of array Hours [1..MAXVALUES]. Stop when the array is full or when the end of file mark is reached. Each line in NEWDATA contains one data value.

c. PURPOSE/GOAL STATE: From file ESSAY read one line of text, terminated by the end of line character. Store the characters of the line in the elements of array TextLine, where TextLine is of type ARRAY [1..100] of Char. Store the number of characters in the line in variable LineLength. Each line in ESSAY has fewer than 100 characters.

PSEUDO-CODE AND PASCAL SUMMARY

Here is a brief summary of the new pseudo-code and Pascal elements introduced in this chapter. Be sure to check the *User's Manual* for your Pascal system to determine if there are local variations in the way that files are accessed and used.

□ □
Declaring Data Files

In pseudo-code, include each data file name on a GLOBAL DATA OBJECTS list, using the predefined type Text:

⟨GLOBAL DATA OBJECTS list⟩ ::=

> GLOBAL DATA OBJECTS

> ⟨file name⟩: Text⟨purpose⟩
> {⟨file name⟩: Text⟨purpose⟩}
> **WHERE**
> > ⟨file name⟩ ::= A Pascal identifier.
> > ⟨purpose⟩ ::=
> > > Whether the file is used for input or output and the type of data it contains.

□ □
Declaring Data Files in Pascal

Include the internal name of the file in the PROGRAM line:

```
PROGRAM ⟨program-name⟩ (INPUT, OUTPUT, ⟨file-name⟩, ...);
```

Code the GLOBAL DATA OBJECTS list as a VAR section that immediately follows the TYPE section of the program:

```
VAR
    ⟨file-name⟩: Text;          {purpose}
    ...
```

□ □
To Write Data Values to a File Other than OUTPUT

In pseudo-code, a program that uses an output data file would need to include the following new actions:

1. *"Connect" the internal Pascal file name and the external file name*. Use the pseudo-code action:

$$\text{CONNECT } (\langle\text{internal file name}\rangle, \text{ '}\langle\text{external file name}\rangle\text{')}$$

The CONNECT action must be executed before the file is opened.

2. *Open the file for writing*. Use the pseudo-code action:

$$\text{OPEN FOR WRITING: } \langle\text{internal file name}\rangle$$

3. *Use WRITE TO FILE actions to send data to the file*. In pseudo-code:

$$\text{WRITE TO } \langle\text{internal file name}\rangle\text{:}$$
$$\langle\text{description of lines to be written to the file, just as for a DISPLAY action}\rangle$$

4. *Close the output file, if required*. In pseudo-code:

$$\text{CLOSE: } \langle\text{internal file name}\rangle$$

□ □

Coding a Program that Writes a Data File

□

CONNECT and CLOSE.   CONNECT and CLOSE are not part of standard Pascal. Check your local *Pascal User's Manual*. Some systems may not require any Pascal action.

□

OPEN FOR WRITING.   Use a call on the predefined procedure *rewrite:*

```
rewrite (⟨internal file name⟩);
```

□

WRITE TO FILE.   Each WRITE TO FILE operation is coded in Pascal as a *write* or *writeln* statement. Put the *internal file name* as the first parameter in the statement, before the list of data items to be written:

```
writeln (⟨file-name⟩, ...list of output items...);
```

or

```
write (⟨file-name⟩, ...list of output items...);
```

To Read Data Values from a File Other than INPUT

In pseudo-code, a program that uses an input data file would need to include the following new actions:

1. *"Connect" the internal Pascal file name and the external file name.* Use the pseudo-code action:

   CONNECT (⟨internal file name⟩, '⟨external file name⟩')

   The CONNECT action must be executed before the file is opened.

2. *Open the file for reading.* Use the pseudo-code action:

   OPEN FOR READING: ⟨internal file name⟩

3. *Use READ FROM FILE actions to read data from the file.* In pseudo-code:

   READ FROM ⟨internal file name⟩:
      ⟨list of data objects to receive the values read⟩

4. *Close the output file, if required.* In pseudo-code:

   CLOSE: ⟨internal file name⟩

Coding a Program that Reads a Data File

□
CONNECT and CLOSE.   CONNECT and CLOSE are not part of standard Pascal. Check your local *Pascal User's Manual.*

□
OPEN FOR READING.   Use a call on the predefined procedure *reset:*

          reset (⟨internal file name⟩);

□
READ FROM FILE.   Each READ FROM FILE operation is coded in Pascal as a *read* or *readln* statement. Put the *internal file name* as the first parameter in the statement, before the list of data objects that receive the values read:

          readln (⟨file-name⟩, ...list of data objects...);

or

          read (⟨file-name⟩, ...list of data objects...);

11.1   How does a *batch processing* program differ from an *interactive* program?

11.2   Give three advantages of batch processing programs over interactive programs when *reading* data and three advantages when *writing* data.

11.3   What is a *data file?*

11.4   What is the difference between a *text file* and a *nontext file?*

11.5   Explain how a text file is organized, including the use of ⟨EOLN⟩ and ⟨EOF⟩.

11.6   What is an *empty file?*

11.7   What is the *status* of a file? What are the three possible status designations for a Pascal text file?

11.8   What is the *position* of a text file? The position only matters when the file has which status?

11.9   To specify the *state* of a data file during execution of a Pascal program, what information about the file would be included?

11.10   Distinguish between the *external name* and the *internal name* of a data file.

11.11   What are two methods used in different Pascal systems to *connect* the internal name of a file to a particular external file?

11.12   What is the effect of reading data from the predefined file INPUT? Of writing data to the predefined file OUTPUT?

11.13   Why are *data file formats* often given as part of the *requirements* of a program?

11.14   When using *BNF* to specify the format of a file, what information do you specify with BNF?

11.15   Explain how to define a text file in pseudo-code and in a Pascal program.

11.16   List and briefly explain the four steps used in pseudo-code that are related to *writing data* to a data file. Tell how each step is *coded in Pascal*.

11.17   List and briefly explain the four steps used in pseudo-code that are related to *reading data* from a data file. Tell how each step is *coded in Pascal*.

11.18   What is the purpose of the predefined function *eoln*? Of the predefined function *eof?*

11.19   What is a *sentinel value* in a data file?

11.20   Explain the *loop pattern* used to read data values from a file when you know how many values to read before you enter the loop.

11.21   Explain *two possible loop patterns* for reading *numbers* from a data file if you do not know how many values to read before entering the loop.

11.22   Explain two ways to read *exactly one line* of character data from a data file.

PROGRAMMING PROBLEMS

11.1 *Weekly Temperature Report*. Design, code, and test a program that reads a file of *daily* high and low temperature values, as specified in Exercise 11.2(a), and that writes a report on file REPORT showing the average high and low temperatures for each *week* of the year.

11.2 *Word and Line Count*. A useful utility program is one that counts the number of words and lines in a file that contains lines of text, such as a file that contains a paper, report, or abstract that you have written. The program should read all the lines in the file and display the counts. For example:

```
WORD  COUNT:   1249
LINE  COUNT:    152
```

Design, code, and test a program to perform this task.

11.3 *Displaying the Moves in a Chess Game*. (Chess players only) Design, code, and test a program that reads a file of chess moves, as specified in Exercise 11.3, and that displays a diagram of a chess board showing the board position after each move. The program should pause after each board position is displayed and ask the user to type a RETURN before the next position is displayed.

11.4 *Student Grades File Maintenance*. Design, code, and test a program for maintaining a "student grades" file, using the examples given in this chapter of the data file format, the CourseData data type representation, and the ReadGradesFile and WriteGradesFile procedures as a basis. The program should display a "menu" of options for the user to choose, such as:

- Read in the contents of a student grades file.
- Modify an existing student entry.
- Insert a new student entry.
- Delete a student entry.
- Change the heading information (course number, semester, year).
- Display a listing of all or part of the course data.
- Quit and write out the course data to a student grades file.

The user should be allowed to repeatedly select actions from this menu, until the "quit" action is selected.

11.5 *Completing the Jeans Inventory Control Prototype*. Programming Problem 7.3 at the end of Chapter 7 involved the construction of a prototype of an inventory control program. The program allowed the user to build and modify an inventory list of the jeans in stock for a clothing store. Two operations in that program were left as stubs, to be filled in later, after data files were discussed in this chapter. The two operations are:

- *Save* an inventory list permanently (in a file).
- *Restore* a saved list (from a file).

Complete the prototype constructed in problem 7.3:

1. Define an appropriate file format for storing the data values in a jeans inventory list.
2. Design, code, and test procedures to implement the Save and Restore operations, to replace the stubs used in the original program.
3. Test the completed program, with the new operations.

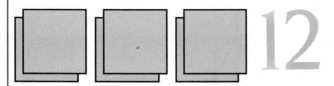

12

Recursion

CHAPTER GOALS

When you have mastered the content of this chapter you should be able to:

- Explain how a *recursive algorithm* is organized.
- Design a *recursive subprogram* and code it in Pascal.
- Explain how a recursive subprogram makes *progress toward termination.*
- Distinguish between *direct recursion* and *indirect recursion.*
- Decide when to use the Pascal *FORWARD declaration.*
- Explain what happens when a recursive subprogram is executed, including the possibility of *run-time stack overflow.*
- Explain how to *analyze* and *verify* the correctness of a recursive subprogram.
- Contrast *recursion* and *loops* as ways of causing repeated execution of a particular sequence of actions.

In computer science, the word *recursion* (from "recur"—"occur again") has a special meaning:

> ☐ **Recursion**
>
> *Recursion* is the process of solving a problem by dividing its solution into two or more simpler subproblems, at least one of which is *a simpler version of the original problem*.

The phrase "simpler version of the original problem" means that the subproblem has the *same form* as the original problem, but the data objects involved are smaller or simpler in some way. For example, if the original problem involves performing an operation on an array, the subproblem may involve performing the same operation on a smaller part of the array, or if the original problem involves determining some property of a large integer value, the subproblem may involve determining the same property of a smaller integer value.

In a program, recursion appears in an interesting way. You see a procedure or function that *calls itself* as part of its own action, but the call uses actual parameters that represent the simpler data objects of the subproblem.

Recursion is one of the most fundamental concepts in programming. Recursion is an alternative to *looping* whenever an action needs to be repeated. But more importantly, it provides a different "mind set" when you are thinking about how to design an algorithm to automate an information processing task.

Analyzing recursive procedures and functions involves an interesting mix of the skills of the previous chapters. We use skills in analyzing conditionals and subprogram calls, and we also need the concept of "progress toward termination" that was important in analyzing loops.

☐☐☐ 12.1
RECURSIVE ALGORITHMS AND SUBPROGRAMS

A *recursive algorithm* is an algorithm in which one of the actions *sometimes* involves *applying the same algorithm to a simpler version of the original problem or task*. Recursive algorithms arise naturally in the design of subprograms to represent certain kinds of operations.

A recursive algorithm has a characteristic structure. It takes the task to be performed (as specified by the parameters of the procedure or function) and uses a *conditional action* to split the task into several cases. The cases fall into two general categories:

1. *Base cases.* Cases in which the task can be performed directly, without recursion. The base cases are the "easy cases."
2. *Recursive cases.* Cases in which the task can be split into two or more subtasks, and at least one of the subtasks can be performed by *applying the same algorithm* (calling the same procedure or function). The recursive cases are the "hard cases."

Recursive algorithms often are shorter and simpler than alternative algorithms for the same task. In fact, a recursive algorithm may sometimes seem like a magic solution to a complicated task—the algorithm never seems to actually *do* anything, but it still accomplishes the task!

In the following examples, we show recursive algorithms for two simple tasks—tasks that could be done as easily (and far more efficiently) with a loop. The real power of recursion comes in more complex situations, particularly when the data structures involved are more complicated than simple arrays. However, these simple examples will give you a chance to become familiar with the basic concept of recursion. Study the following examples closely before you go on.

EXAMPLES

1. Suppose you want a function that computes the sum of the integers in a given range, from M to N. The function heading is:

> FUNCTION FindSumOfRange
>   (M: Integer   IN: Start of range.
>   N: Integer)   IN: End of range.
>   FUNCTION VALUE: Integer
>   PURPOSE: Return the sum of the integers in the range M to N.
>   PRECONDITION: M <= N

You could use a loop, but instead you use a recursive algorithm. Your design of the function body might be:

ALGORITHM

Step 1. RECURSIVE ALGORITHM: If there is only one number in the range, then return that number as the sum; if there are two or more numbers in the range, then the sum is found by adding the first number to the sum of the remaining numbers.

ACTIONS:

```
IF M = N THEN                          — base case
   FUNCTION VALUE := M
ELSE                                   — recursive case
   FUNCTION VALUE := M + FindSumOfRange (M+1, N)
```

Coded in Pascal, the function would look like this:

```
FUNCTION FindSumOfRange

   (M: Integer;              {IN: Start of range.}
    N: Integer)             {IN: End of range.}
     : Integer;             {Function value: sum of range.}

   {PURPOSE: Return the sum of the integers in the range M to N.}
   {PRECONDITION: M <= N}

BEGIN
           {RECURSIVE ALGORITHM: If there is only one number in
           the range, then that is the sum; if there are two or
           more numbers in the range, then the sum is found by
           adding the first number to the sum of the remaining
           numbers.}

   IF M = N THEN
     BEGIN
        FindSumOfRange := M;
     END
   ELSE
     BEGIN
        FindSumOfRange := M + FindSumOfRange (M+1, N);
     END;
END;   {function FindSumOfRange}
```

Discussion: Notice how the IF splits the problem into two cases, a base case and a recursive case. The base case is easy because there is only one number in the range, so the answer is immediate. In the recursive case, the function is called "recursively" to solve the simpler subproblem of summing a range that contains one fewer number than the original problem, using the recursive function call:

```
FindSumOfRange (M+1, N)
```

Note that in the subproblem defined by the actual parameters, the range begins at $M+1$, where the original range began at M. Given the sum that results from solving the subproblem, the answer to the original problem is easily derived by simply adding in the number, M, that was not in the subproblem.

If another subprogram executed the call:

```
Sum := FindSumOfRange (2, 5);
```

that action would begin a "chain" of recursive calls in which the computation might be diagrammed as:

```
FindSumOfRange (2, 5)
     =    2  + FindSumOfRange (3, 5)
                   =    3 + FindSumOfRange (4, 5)
                                 =    4 + FindSumOfRange (5, 5)
                                               =   5
                                 =    9
                   =    12
     =    14
```

Notice how the chain of recursive calls grows until the base case is finally reached, and then the chain "unwinds" as each recursive call completes its computation and sends its result to its caller. Ultimately the chain unwinds back to the original call, which returns the correct result, 14, to the caller.

2. Suppose you want a function to count the number of zero grades in all or part of a GradesList, declared as an array with subscript range [1..500]. Your function heading is:

FUNCTION CountZeros

(List: GradesList   IN
 Start: Integer   IN: place to start counting.
 End: Integer)   IN: place to end counting.

FUNCTION VALUE: Integer   Count of zero grades.

PURPOSE: Return a count of the zero grades in array List [Start..End]. If Start > End, return a zero count.

You could use a loop, but you decide to use a recursive algorithm. Your design might be:

ALGORITHM

Step 1. RECURSIVE ALGORITHM: If there are no elements in the part of the array to be counted, then the count must be zero. If there is at least one element and it is zero, then get the count for the remaining elements and add one to it. Finally, if there is at least one element and it is not zero, then just get the count for the remaining elements.

ACTIONS:

IF Start > End THEN — base case
    FUNCTION VALUE := 0
ELSE IF List [Start] = 0 THEN
    FUNCTION VALUE := — recursive case
        CountZeros (List, Start+1, End) + 1
    ELSE — first element not zero
        FUNCTION VALUE := — recursive case
        CountZeros (List, Start+1, End)

Discussion: This algorithm has one base case and two recursive cases. The base case is trivial—there are no elements to check for zeros. The two recursive cases are distinguished by whether the first element in the range is zero or not. Here the "simpler subproblem" is defined as an array in which one fewer element is to be considered by the recursive call, by changing the beginning of the subscript range to "Start+1" in the call.

Suppose another subprogram wanted to call CountZeros to count the zeros in an array Grades [1..500], by using the call:

```
ZeroCount := CountZeros (Grades, 1, 500);
```

Assume that array Grades happens to contain alternating zero and nonzero elements, so Grades[1] = 0, Grades[2] <> 0, and so forth. The execution of this call would lead to a chain of 500 recursive calls, that might be (partially) diagrammed as follows:

```
CountZeros (Grades, 1, 500)
    = CountZeros (Grades, 2, 500) + 1
        = CountZeros (Grades, 3, 500)
            = CountZeros (Grades, 4, 500) + 1
                = CountZeros (Grades, 5, 500)
                    . . .
                        = CountZeros (Grades, 500, 500) + 1
                            = CountZeros (Grades, 501, 500)
                            = 0
                        = 1
                    . . .
                = 248
            = 249
        = 249
    = 250
```

Here again you see the characteristic chain of recursive calls that grows until the parameters in a call finally reach the base case, and then the chain unwinds as each recursive call is able to complete its computation and return its result to its caller. ∎

Notice how, in each subprogram, the base cases are extremely simple. In Find-SumOfRange, the base case is when the range consists of a single number. In CountZeros, the base case is when there are *no* array elements to be checked. These trivial base cases are typical of recursive algorithms.

Recursive Calls and Recursive Subprograms

Recursion in programming is always connected with the *calls* of procedures and functions. A *recursive call* is a call of a subprogram that occurs *during the execution of another call of the same subprogram*. A subprogram that makes a recursive call is termed a *recursive subprogram*.

A subprogram may be *directly recursive,* by including a call on itself within its own subprogram body. The examples above are all directly recursive subprograms. A subprogram may also be *indirectly recursive,* by calling another subprogram, which may call another, and so forth, until ultimately there is a call of the original subprogram.

In the structure chart for a program that uses recursion, you will see that the box for a directly recursive subprogram has an arrow that loops back to itself. An indirect recursion appears as a path that loops back from a lower level in the structure chart to a higher level, as shown in Figure 12.1.

In Figure 12.1, notice that the three procedures Proc1, Proc3, and Proc5, are each indirectly recursive. That is, starting from any one of the three procedures there is a chain of calls that leads back to that same procedure. For example, starting at Proc5, Proc5 may call Proc1, which may call Proc3, which may make a recursive call on Proc5. In general, when one subprogram is indirectly recursive, through a chain of subprogram calls that ultimately leads to a recursive call, then every subprogram in the chain is indirectly recursive, through the same chain of calls. We say the subprograms in the chain are *mutually recursive*. Thus, in Figure 12.1, Proc1, Proc3, and Proc5 are mutually recursive.

Execution of a Recursive Subprogram

Although it may appear that there is some special trick involved in execution of a recursive subprogram, recursion actually requires nothing beyond the mechanisms of ordinary subprogram execution: a local state for the called subprogram is created, parameters are transmitted, the subprogram body is executed, and the local state is thrown away when execution is complete. If the recursive subprogram is a function, then the function value is returned to the caller before the local state is thrown away.

An example will help to clarify how the execution of a recursive subprogram works.

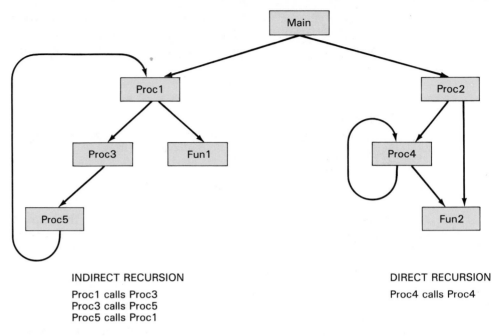

INDIRECT RECURSION

Proc1 calls Proc3
Proc3 calls Proc5
Proc5 calls Proc1

DIRECT RECURSION

Proc4 calls Proc4

FIGURE 12.1 Typical Structure Chart for a Program that Uses Recursion

EXAMPLE *Computing Factorials Recursively*

Definitions of mathematical functions are sometimes given as *recursive definitions*. The "factorial of a positive integer N," written "N!" is a common example. "N!" is informally defined as "the product of the first N positive integers." You probably have seen this definition written recursively as:

$$
\begin{aligned}
N! &= 1 & \text{if } N = 1 \\
&= N * (N-1)! & \text{if } N > 1
\end{aligned}
$$

Such a recursive definition can be coded directly as a Pascal function:

```
FUNCTION Factorial
     (N: Integer)              {IN: value parameter}
     : Integer;               {Function value = N!}
   {PURPOSE: Returns the value N!}

   BEGIN
      IF N = 1 THEN                {base case}
         Factorial := 1
      ELSE                        {recursive case}
         Factorial := N * Factorial (N-1);
   END;
```

Notice the recursive call on Factorial in the last assignment in the function body.

Let's trace the execution of a typical call of this recursive function. Suppose another subprogram executes the assignment:

$$X := Factorial(4);$$

Here are the steps that occur when this assignment statement is executed (the steps are outlined in Figure 12.2):

1. *Partially evaluate Factorial(4)*. The Factorial function is called with actual parameter "4". A local state is created for this execution of Factorial, and the formal parameter, N, is assigned "4" as its initial value, so the local state is:

N: | 4 | FUNCTION VALUE: | ?? |

FIGURE 12.2   Recursive Execution of "X := Factorial (4)"

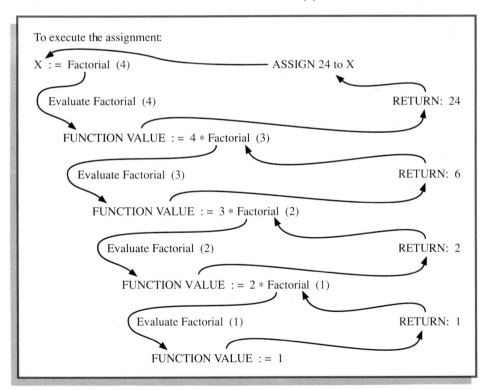

The body of the function definition is executed. From this initial state, the control path is:

```
(N = 1) = FALSE
Factorial := N * Factorial (N-1)
```

On this path, the expression "N * Factorial (N−1)" must be evaluated to get the function value. Because N has the value 4 in the local state, the expression evaluation is "4 * Factorial (3)". This expression involves a recursive function call, Factorial(3). We evaluate this function call *exactly like we would any other function call*—don't be confused by it being a recursive call; nothing different happens when it is executed. Note that we have not completed the first execution of the Factorial function—we have just paused to execute the second function call, and then later we will continue and complete the first execution of Factorial.

2. *Partially evaluate Factorial(3).* A new local state for this call of Factorial is created, with a new location for formal parameter N:

N: | 3 | FUNCTION VALUE: | ?? |

The body of the function definition is executed (again), using this local state. *Important:* This formal parameter N is entirely separate from the parameter N in step 1 above—its value is stored in a separate storage location in the computer's memory. During this execution of the function body, the control path is again:

```
(N = 1) = FALSE
Factorial := N * Factorial (N-1)
```

which leads to the evaluation of the expression "3 * Factorial(2)". Again the recursive function call must be evaluated. Note that here also we have not completed the execution of the Factorial function—we have just paused to execute the recursive function call, and later we will continue with this execution of Factorial.

3. *Partially evaluate Factorial(2).* The body of the function definition is executed a third time, with a new local state:

N: | 2 | FUNCTION VALUE: | ?? |

This state leads to the control path:

```
(N = 1) = FALSE
Factorial := N * Factorial (N-1)
```

and evaluation of the expression "2 * Factorial(1)".

4. *Completely evaluate Factorial(1).* The body of the function definition is executed a fourth time, with a new local state:

N: [1]   FUNCTION VALUE: [??]

Finally the test "N = 1" returns true, so we have the base case in the recursive algorithm. Execution takes the control path:

```
(N = 1)  =  TRUE
Factorial := 1
```

This time execution of the function body is complete, and the final local state is:

N: [1]   FUNCTION VALUE: [1]

We exit the *fourth execution* of the function, and return a value of 1 as the value of Factorial(1). This value, of course, is returned to the caller, which happens to be the third execution of Factorial that began in step 3.

5. *Complete Factorial(2).* Now that we have the value of Factorial(1), we can complete the evaluation of "2 * Factorial(1)" that began in step 3. The result is 2 * 1 = 2, which is assigned as the function value. Execution of the body is complete, and the final local state is:

N: [2]   FUNCTION VALUE: [2]

The value 2 is returned as the function value to the caller.

6. *Complete Factorial(3).* Continuing in the same way, we complete the evaluation of "3 * Factorial(2)" that began in step 2, giving 3 * 2 = 6, and a final local state of:

N: [3]   FUNCTION VALUE: [6]

The value 6 is returned as the function value to the caller.

7. *Complete Factorial(4).* Finally back in the original call on the function, we can complete the evaluation of "4 * Factorial(3)" that began in step 1, giving 4 * 6 = 24, and a final local state of:

N: [4]   FUNCTION VALUE: [24]

The value 24 is returned to the original caller as the function value.

8. *Complete the execution of the original assignment statement.* Finally we have the value 24 for "Factorial(4)", so we can complete the assignment:

```
X := Factorial(4);
```

by assigning 24 as the new value of X. ∎

In this example, you see in more detail the characteristic way that a recursive algorithm "grows" a chain of recursive subprogram calls, leaving each call unfinished, until finally a call reaches a base case. Then the recursive calls are completed, in the *reverse order* of their initiation. The last recursive call is completed first, then the next to the last, and so forth. The original call that began the whole process is the last call to be completed.

□ □
Circularity and "Progress Toward Termination" in Recursion

A problem for beginners in understanding recursion is the seeming *circularity* of a recursive algorithm. If the algorithm for a procedure A is recursive, then it looks suspiciously like you are saying "the way you perform action A is to do action A." Isn't this a circular definition of the action?

Recursive algorithms can indeed be circular. For example, suppose you define a procedure ComputeValue as:

```
PROCEDURE ComputeValue

    (X: Real;        {IN}
    VAR Y: Real);    {OUT}

  {PURPOSE/GOAL STATE: ...}
BEGIN
    ComputeValue (X, Y);              {recursive call}
END;
```

which says exactly: to perform ComputeValue on parameters X and Y just perform ComputeValue on parameters X and Y. What could be more circular!

This procedure definition is valid in Pascal. It can be included in a program, and procedure ComputeValue can be called from another subprogram. And the result is, as you might expect, an *infinite recursion* (the recursive analog of an infinite loop). Suppose the main program calls procedure ComputeValue. Then Compute-Value calls itself recursively, which leads to a second recursive call on Compute-Value, which leads to a third, which leads to a fourth, and so forth. Ultimately the infinite recursion causes the program to CRASH (a detailed explanation of the CRASH is given in Section 12.4.)

A recursive algorithm requires the same concept of "progress toward termination" that you find in a loop. Just as each time around a loop you need to make progress toward termination of the loop (or the loop will repeat "forever"), so also each time you make a recursive call you need to make progress toward termination of the chain of recursive calls.

The characteristic structure of a recursive algorithm comes from the need to make progress toward termination of the recursion:

1. You always test for the base cases first (these tests are like the exit test in a loop), and
2. You never make a recursive call with the values of the actual parameters identical to the *initial values* of the formal parameters when the subprogram began execution—the actual parameters in the recursive call must always make *progress toward one of the base cases*.

EXAMPLES Let's look at our earlier example of recursive function FindSumOfRange and see how it makes "progress toward termination" on each recursive call. The recursive call appears in the body of the function as:

FUNCTION VALUE := M + FindSumOfRange (M+1, N)

Initially, M <= N and the base case tests for "M = N", so adding one to M on each recursive call brings the value of formal parameter M closer to being equal to the value of formal parameter N each time the procedure is called again. ∎

EXERCISES

12.1 For the CountZeros function given at the beginning of this section, explain how it makes "progress toward termination" on each recursive call.

12.2 Show the *local state* of the subprogram at the *beginning* and *end* of execution of the subprogram body for the original call and each recursive call during execution of the following actions. (The subprogram definitions are given in the examples at the start of this section.)

a. `Total := FindSumOfRange (8, 12);`

b. Suppose array Grades of type GradesList contains:

Grades[3]: 2   Grades[4]: 0   Grades[5]: 0

Grades[6]: -4   Grades[7]: 0

The action is:

`Zeros := CountZeros (Grades, 3, 7);`

□□□ 12.2
DESIGNING RECURSIVE SUBPROGRAMS

Directly recursive procedures and functions have a characteristic design structure:

1. The subprogram body is usually an IF statement that treats several cases.
2. The first cases treated are the base cases—the cases that can be solved immediately, without a recursive call.
3. The last cases, the recursive cases, include a recursive call with parameters that are "closer" to one of the base cases.

One important design rule to remember: *You almost never use a loop around a recursive call.* The IF conditional and the recursive calls *replace* the loop that would ordinarily be required. Of course, you can use a loop for some other purpose in the subprogram body. Just remember that a recursive call itself provides repetition of the code in the recursive subprogram's body; no loop is needed to get this repetition.

EXAMPLE *Dave's Recursive Array Search*

Dave needs a procedure that searches an array. The specification is:

PROCEDURE FindZero
    (A: RealArray   IN: array to be searched.
    M: Integer   IN: subscript of first element.
    N: Integer   IN: subscript of last element.
    Posn: Integer   OUT: subscript of first zero.
    Found: Boolean)   OUT: TRUE if zero element found.

PURPOSE/GOAL STATE: Search A[M..N] for a zero element. If found, set Posn = subscript of the first zero element and set Found = TRUE. If not found, set Found = FALSE.

PRECONDITION: M <= N

First Dave sits down to design the body of the FindZero procedure by using a loop. But he gets confused by the loop structure—there is a flag to be set and two exit tests and so forth. Dave knows that recursive algorithms are sometimes simpler than looping algorithms, so he thinks about how a recursive algorithm for FindZero might look.

First he thinks "what are the bases cases—what array would be trivial to search?" His answer: "An array with *one element*! If the element is zero, I've got my result, and if it is nonzero, then I've still got my result."

Then he thinks "If the array has more than one element, then what rule could I use to break it into sub-arrays that could each be searched recursively?" His answer: "Let's keep it simple—break the array into the *first element* and *all the rest*. If the first element is zero, then I've got my result, and otherwise I just make a recursive call on the FindZero procedure to check the rest of the array.

Dave writes down the algorithm design:

ALGORITHM

Step 1. RECURSIVE ALGORITHM: Test the first element. If it is zero, set Found = TRUE and Posn = M. If it is nonzero and the array has only one element, return FALSE. Otherwise, use a recursive call to check the rest of the array.

ACTIONS:

```
IF A[M] = 0 THEN
    Posn := M
    Found := TRUE

ELSE IF M = N THEN      {AND A[M] <> 0}
    Found := FALSE

ELSE        {IF (A[M] <> 0) AND (M < N)}
    CALL FindZero (A, M+1, N, Posn, Found)
```

"Thinking recursively can sure make programming easy sometimes," says Dave as he grabs his fishing pole and takes the afternoon off. ■

□ □
Design Tips for Recursive Algorithms

Here are a few things to think about in trying to design a recursive algorithm:

1. *First find the base cases.* Look for the "trivial" cases first—like Dave's one element array.

2. *Look for the recursive subproblem within the whole problem.* Try to divide the whole problem into parts so that each of the parts is either trivial (a base case) or has the same form as the original problem (but is simpler). Dave divided the array search into two parts, the "first element" and "all the rest." The "all the rest" part had the same form as the original problem, but the part of the array to be searched was smaller.

3. *Define the procedure or function heading so that it allows you to state any one of the subproblems.* The parameters to the recursive procedure or function should be chosen so that the original problem *or any of the subproblems,* including the base cases, can be represented by a call to the procedure or function.

Dave's procedure had parameters M and N that specified the starting and the ending point of the search. By choosing M and N appropriately, he could use the same FindZero procedure to search the whole array or any part of it, including "searching" an array of a single element.

Sometimes, if the original procedure heading is inappropriate for stating the recursive subproblems for your algorithm, you may need to define another auxiliary subprogram that allows the recursion to be stated more easily.

EXAMPLE   Suppose Dave is part of a programming team. The team has already chosen the heading for the FindZero procedure, as follows:

PROCEDURE FindZero

(A: RealArray	IN: array to be searched.
Posn: Integer	OUT: subscript of first zero.
Found: Boolean)	OUT: TRUE if zero element found.

PURPOSE/GOAL STATE: Search A[1..MAXSIZE] for a zero element. If found, set Posn = subscript of zero element and set Found = TRUE. If not found, set Found = FALSE.

Unlike Dave's version of FindZero, this version does not allow specification of which elements of the array to search. The entire array is always searched. Dave cannot use this version of FindZero in a recursive algorithm because he has no way of choosing the parameters in the recursive call so that each call makes progress toward termination.

Dave still has an easy solution. He simply renames his version of FindZero. He chooses the name FindZeroInRange, and he changes the recursive call in the body of his procedure so that it calls FindZeroInRange instead of FindZero. Now he designs the team's version of FindZero as:

PROCEDURE FindZero

(A: RealArray	IN: array to be searched.
Posn: Integer	OUT: subscript of first zero.
Found: Boolean)	OUT: TRUE if zero element found.

PURPOSE/GOAL STATE: Search A[1..MAXSIZE] for a zero element. If found, set Posn = subscript of zero element and set Found = TRUE. If not found, set Found = FALSE.

ALGORITHM

Step 1. ACTIONS:

CALL FindZeroInRange (A, 1, MAXSIZE, Posn, Found)

Dave's procedure FindZeroInRange is an "auxiliary" procedure used only in the recursive algorithm for FindZero. ■

EXERCISES

12.3 Design and code a recursive version of each of the following subprograms:

a. FUNCTION ProductOfOdds

(M: Integer	IN
N: Integer)	IN

FUNCTION VALUE: Integer

PURPOSE: Return the product of the *odd* integers in the range M to N. If M > N, return zero.

PRECONDITION: M and N are both odd integers.

b. FUNCTION CountAboveThreshold

(List: ListOfReals	IN: List of values to test.
Start: Integer	IN: Start of range to test.
End: Integer	IN: End of range to test.
Threshold: Real)	IN

FUNCTION VALUE: Real   Count of values > Threshold.

PURPOSE: Count the number of values in List [Start..End] that are greater than Threshold.

PRECONDITION: Start <= End

Note: Be sure that every *recursive call* satisfies the precondition.

c. FUNCTION IsAllPositive

(A: ArrayOfReals	IN
M: Integer	IN: Start of range.
N: Integer)	IN: End of range.

FUNCTION VALUE: Boolean

PURPOSE: Return TRUE if all values in A[M..N] are positive; FALSE if any value is zero or negative.

d. PROCEDURE DisplayBlankLines

(Count: Integer)　　　　　IN

PURPOSE/GOAL STATE: Display Count blank lines on the display screen.

e. FUNCTION FindMatchingRightParen

(Formula: StringType　　　IN: String to be scanned.
Left: Integer)　　　　　IN: Left parenthesis position.

FUNCTION VALUE: Integer　　Right parenthesis posn.

PURPOSE: Return the position within Formula of the right parenthesis that matches the left parenthesis in Formula [Left], scanning right across the string in Formula starting at character position Left+1. If there is no matching right parenthesis, return a zero value. CAUTION: Formula may contain any number of other left and right parentheses.

f. PROCEDURE FindMaxMin

(List: ValueList　　　　　IN
LastEntry: Integer　　　IN: subscript of last entry.
Max: Real　　　　　　OUT: the largest value.
Min: Real)　　　　　OUT: the smallest value.

PURPOSE/GOAL STATE: Find the largest and smallest values in List [1..LastEntry] and store in Max and Min, respectively. List is an array of Real elements.

PRECONDITION: LastEntry $>= 1$.

12.4　The *Fibonacci sequence* of integers is formed by taking the two integers 1 and 2 as starting values and producing the next value in the sequence by adding together the two preceding values. Starting with 1 and 2, the next value is $(1+2) = 3$, the next value is $(2+3) = 5$, the next is $(3+5) = 8$, and so forth.

You can continue the sequence from any point if you know two of the adjacent values. For example, if you know that 5 and 8 are two adjacent values in the sequence, then you can continue the sequence to the next value $(5+8) = 13$, and the next $(8+13) = 21$, etc.

The following procedure should display the first N values of the Fibonacci sequence if called with:

CALL Fibonacci (N, 1, 2)

PROCEDURE Fibonacci

(N: Integer	IN: Number of values to display.
Start1: Integer	IN: First starting value.
Start2: Integer)	IN: Second starting value.

PURPOSE/GOAL STATE: Display the next N values of the Fibonacci sequence, given the two adjacent values Start1 and Start2 of the sequence.

PRECONDITION: N >= 2

□□□ 12.3
CODING RECURSIVE SUBPROGRAMS IN PASCAL

Any Pascal procedure or function can be called recursively. If a subprogram is *directly recursive* (calls itself in its own body), then you code it exactly as you would if it were not recursive.

Coding subprograms that are *indirectly recursive* in Pascal introduces a minor problem. The problem lies with the Pascal rule that a subprogram that calls a second subprogram must have its Pascal definition *follow* that of the subprogram it calls. For example, if procedure A calls procedure B, then the definition of A must follow that of B in the Pascal program structure.

The reason for this rule in Pascal is simple to understand. The language is designed so that the Pascal compiler need only scan through the program once, from beginning to end. When it reaches any call on a procedure or function, it needs to have already seen the *heading* for that procedure or function (showing the name, formal parameters, and their data types). The compiler checks to see that the call contains the right number of actual parameters and that they are of the correct data types. If the compiler reaches a call on procedure B before it has seen the heading for procedure B, then it cannot check the correctness of the call. Hence the rule in Pascal about the order of subprogram definitions.

A subprogram that is directly recursive causes the compiler no problem because the recursive call in the body of the subprogram appears after the compiler has already processed the heading for the subprogram. However, indirect recursive calls cannot help but violate this rule. For example, if procedure A calls B, which calls C, and C calls A recursively, then there is no possible ordering of the definitions of A, B, and C in the program that can satisfy this rule. You cannot put A's definition first because it calls B, but B's definition cannot be first because it calls C, and C's definition cannot be first because it calls A.

The solution to this problem in Pascal is to require the programmer to *separate one of the procedure or function headings from its body.* The heading of the chosen subprogram is placed *before the first call* on that subprogram. But the body is placed *after all of the subprograms that it calls*. For example, our procedures A, B, and C could then be placed in the sequence:

- Heading for procedure A
- Procedure C (heading and body)
- Procedure B (heading and body)
- Body for procedure A

This order satisfies the requirement that the heading of each subprogram appear before any call of that subprogram.

□ □
The FORWARD Declaration

The syntax for this arrangement in Pascal is the following. You write the heading for a "separated" subprogram exactly as you would ordinarily, and then simply follow the heading with the key word FORWARD, punctuated as follows:

```
PROCEDURE ⟨name⟩

    (⟨formal parameter list⟩);

  FORWARD;
```

or

```
FUNCTION ⟨name⟩

    (⟨formal parameter list⟩)
    : ⟨function value type⟩;

  FORWARD;
```

The whole is called a *FORWARD declaration*.

To write the body, repeat only PROCEDURE or FUNCTION and the subprogram name. *Pascal does not allow you to repeat the formal parameter list and function value type.* Use the syntax:

```
PROCEDURE ⟨name⟩;

  VAR
      ⟨declarations as usual⟩
```

```
      BEGIN
          ⟨statements as usual⟩
      END;
```

or

```
  FUNCTION ⟨name⟩;

      VAR
          ⟨declarations as usual⟩

      BEGIN
          ⟨statements as usual⟩
      END;
```

Totally omitting the formal parameter list becomes confusing when you want to read and analyze the program because the body is in one place and the declarations of the formal parameters are in another. A good rule whenever you are forced to use the FORWARD declaration is to repeat, as a Pascal comment, the formal parameter list (and function value type) with the body of the subprogram. For example:

```
  PROCEDURE ⟨name⟩;
          {((⟨formal parameter list⟩)}    ← a comment now

      VAR
          ⟨declarations as usual⟩

      BEGIN
          ⟨statements as usual⟩
      END;
```

EXERCISE

12.5   Code each of the subprograms designed in Exercises 12.3 and 12.4 in Pascal.

□□□ **12.4**
ERRORS RELATED TO INFINITE RECURSION

In an infinite recursion, there is a control path through the body of a recursive subprogram that makes no "progress toward termination" of the sequence of recursive calls, so that each recursive call leads to another, which leads to another, and so forth, endlessly. The program execution ultimately CRASHES, and the error message displayed after the crash is peculiar. It usually says something like:

```
STACK/HEAP COLLISION
```

What is a *stack/heap collision*? And how is it related to an infinite recursion?

In our model of program execution, when any procedure or function is called, a new storage area in the computer memory is allocated to store the *local state* of the subprogram (the formal parameters and local variables).

Suppose we have our procedures A, B, and C again, and A is called initially from the main program. When A is called initially, a storage area for its local state is allocated. When B is called by A, another storage area for B's local state is allocated. When B calls C, a storage area for C's local state is allocated. And when C calls A recursively, it is treated as any other call of A: a second storage area for A's local state is allocated (with new locations for the values of the formal parameters and local variables). Figure 12.3 shows this sequence.

This allocation of storage for local states continues until one of the subprograms completes its execution without making another call. Then the local state for the completed subprogram call is "thrown away," and the storage for the local state is made available for reuse (we say it is "freed" for reuse). Allocation and freeing of storage continue throughout the execution of the program, as subprograms are called and as they complete their execution.

To simplify the allocation of these storage areas, the Pascal system reserves a single big block of storage in the computer memory before execution of the main program begins. This block of storage is called the *run-time stack*.

When the main program calls a subprogram, storage for the local state of that subprogram is allocated at one end of the run-time stack. Each subsequent call causes storage to be allocated in the next available part of the run-time stack. Thus the run-time stack always is filled with these local states starting at one end and continuing up to a point. This point is termed the *top of the stack*. After the top of the stack, the rest of the run-time stack area is unused, as shown in Figure 12.4.

When a subprogram completes its execution, its local state is always immediately adjacent to the unused area in the run-time stack, so to "free" its local state, the top of the stack is simply moved back to the end of the preceding local state in the stack, effectively adding the local state of the completed subprogram to the unused area of the stack. Figure 12.5 illustrates this behavior.

□ □
Run-time Stack Overflow

Now it is easy to see what happens when a recursion "runs wild" and becomes an infinite recursion. Each recursive call causes another local state to be allocated in the run-time stack. As these calls continue (and no call is ever completed) the unused storage available in the run-time stack slowly decreases. Ultimately one recursive call *overflows* the run-time stack—there is not enough storage left in the run-time

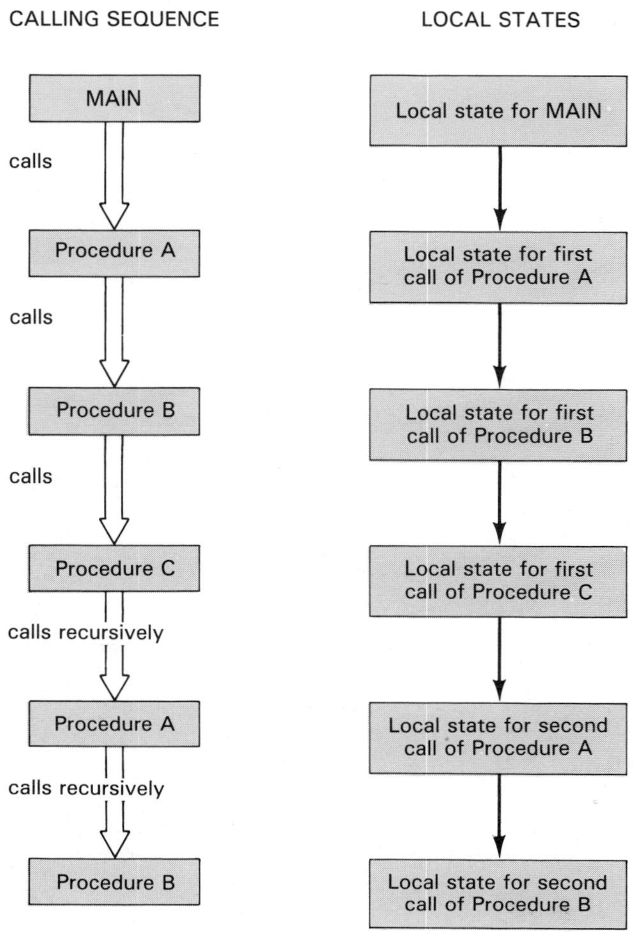

RUN–TIME STACK

| Local state for MAIN |
| Local state for first call of Procedure A |
| Local state for first call of Procedure B |
| Local state for first call of Procedure C |
| Local state for second call of Procedure A |
| Local state for second call of Procedure B |
| Currently unused part of run–time stack area |

Top of the stack

CALLING SEQUENCE

MAIN
calls
Procedure A
calls
Procedure B
calls
Procedure C
calls recursively
Procedure A
calls recursively
Procedure B

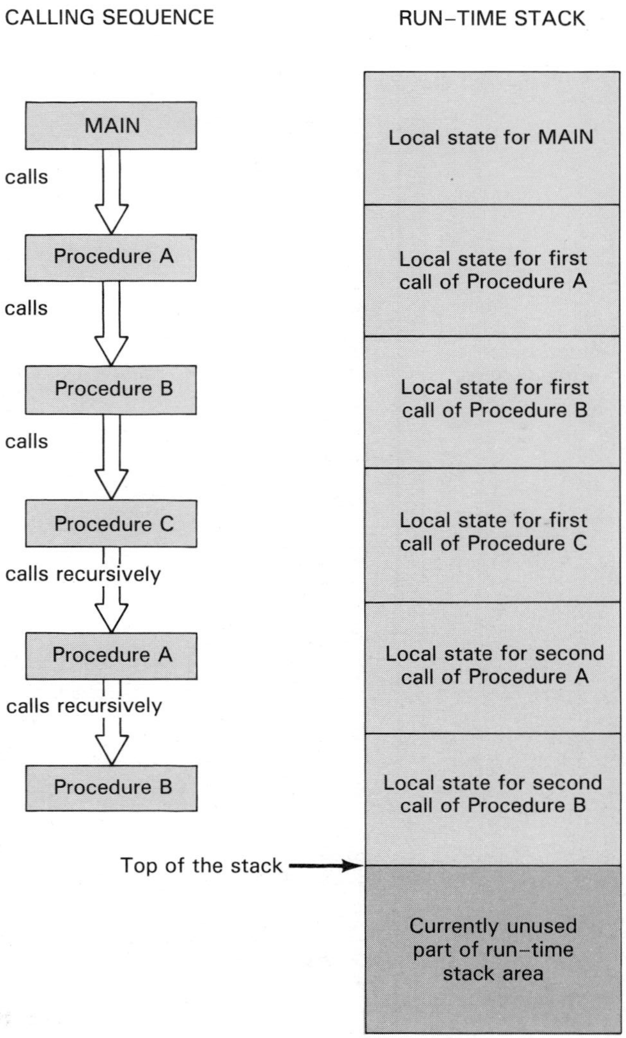

FIGURE 12.4 Local States Allocated in the Pascal Run-time Stack

LOCAL STATES

| Local state for MAIN |
| Local state for first call of Procedure A |
| Local state for first call of Procedure B |
| Local state for first call of Procedure C |
| Local state for second call of Procedure A |
| Local state for second call of Procedure B |

CALLING SEQUENCE

MAIN
calls
Procedure A
calls
Procedure B
calls
Procedure C
calls recursively
Procedure A
calls recursively
Procedure B

FIGURE 12.3 Local States in a Sequence of Recursive Calls

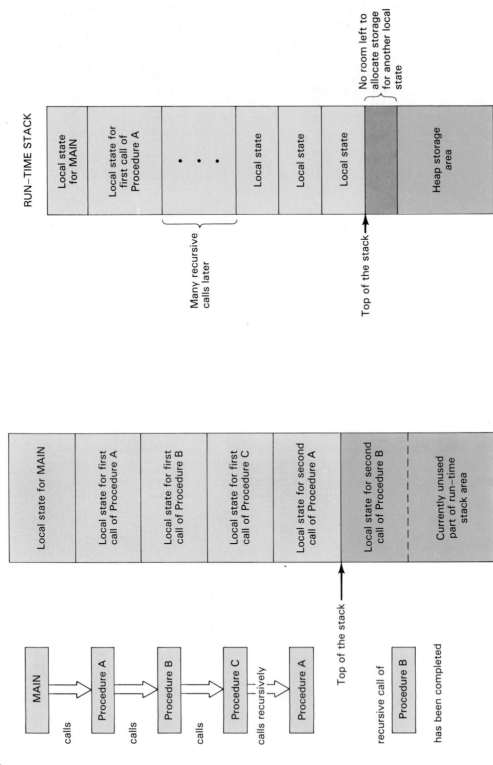

CALLING SEQUENCE

MAIN

calls

Procedure A

calls

Procedure B

calls

Procedure C

calls recursively

Procedure A

Top of the stack

recursive call of

Procedure B

has been completed

RUN–TIME STACK

Local state for MAIN

Local state for first
call of Procedure A

Local state for first
call of Procedure B

Local state for first
call of Procedure C

Local state for second
call of Procedure A

Local state for second
call of Procedure B

Currently unused
part of run–time
stack area

FIGURE 12.5 Run-time Stack After Procedure B completes its execution

RUN–TIME STACK

Local state
for MAIN

Local state for
first call of
Procedure A

Many recursive
calls later

Local state

Local state

Local state

Top of the stack

No room left to
allocate storage
for another local
state

Heap storage
area

FIGURE 12.6 Stack/Heap Collision (Stack "Overflow")

stack to allocate the new local state for the call. At this point, the run-time stack is said to have "collided" with the next storage area, called the *heap* in Pascal, as shown in Figure 12.6. Result: Execution of your program can no longer continue. The Pascal system terminates execution and displays a "helpful" error message such as "STACK/HEAP COLLISION" or "RUN-TIME STACK OVERFLOW."

EXERCISE

12.6   If you are using your own microcomputer, write and run a Pascal program that deliberately enters an infinite recursion. What happens in your Pascal system when the run-time stack overflows its storage area and "collides" with the heap? (Do not try this on a time-shared computer system.)

□□□ **12.5**
ANALYZING RECURSIVE SUBPROGRAMS

The key to analyzing recursive subprograms lies in our old rule for analyzing any subprogram call: *don't try to follow control flow or data flow into the subprogram that is being called*. The rule is particularly important for recursive calls, because if you do follow the control and data into the call, you end up analyzing the same program statements again.

To analyze a recursive subprogram call, treat it as you would any other analysis of a call: look only at the *heading* of the subprogram. *Assume the subprogram works correctly for the recursive call* with the actual parameters given.

Within the body of a recursive subprogram, you can analyze control flow and data flow as you would with any other program segment. Because there are usually no loops, the control paths are usually straightforward to identify and analyze.

□□
Verifying the Correctness of a Recursive Subprogram Body

To check the correctness of your design for the body of a recursive subprogram, do the following:

1.   *Check the base cases*. First check the control path through each base case. Look at the path conditions for taking each path, and look at the actions that compute the results on that path. Is the path chosen for execution in the correct case? Are the expected results computed correctly in that case?

2.   *Check path conditions for the recursive cases*. Next check the path condition for each recursive case. Is each path chosen for execution in the correct case?

3.   *Check the computation in each recursive case, assuming the recursive call works correctly*. For each control path through a recursive case, check the computation of the results on that path. Assume that the recursive call works correctly, as specified by the subprogram heading, just as you would assume that any other subprogram call works correctly without looking at the body of the called subprogram.

4. *Check progress toward termination.* Check that each control path for a recursive case leads to a recursive call in which the *actual parameter values* are "closer" to one of the base cases than were the *formal parameter values* at the start of execution of that control path.

EXAMPLE

Let's check the correctness of Dave's *Recursive Array Search* procedure from Section 12.2. His design is:

PROCEDURE FindZero

(A: RealArray	IN: array to be searched.
M: Integer	IN: subscript of first element.
N: Integer	IN: subscript of last element.
Posn: Integer	OUT: subscript of first zero.
Found: Boolean)	OUT: TRUE if zero element found.

PURPOSE/GOAL STATE: Search A[M..N] for a zero element. If found, set Posn = subscript of zero element and set Found = TRUE. If not found, set Found = FALSE.
PRECONDITION: M <= N

ALGORITHM

Step 1.   RECURSIVE ALGORITHM: Test the first element. If it is zero, set Found = TRUE and Posn = M. If it is nonzero and the array has only one element, return FALSE. Otherwise, use a recursive call to check the rest of the array.

ACTIONS:

```
IF A[M] = 0 THEN
    Posn := M
    Found := TRUE
ELSE IF M = N THEN        {AND A[M] <> 0}
    Found := FALSE
ELSE                      {IF (A[M] <> 0) AND (M < N)}
    CALL FindZero (A, M+1, N, Posn, Found)
```

To verify the correctness, first we check the base cases:

1. *Base cases*. The path condition for the first base case is given by the test: "A[M] = 0". This test returns TRUE when the first array element is zero. The result on this path is to set the Found flag = TRUE and Posn to the subscript of the zero element, as required by the procedure heading. OK!

The path condition for the second base case is given by the test: "(A[M] <> 0) AND (M = N)". This test returns TRUE when the array has only one element to be checked and that element is nonzero. The result of the computation on the path is to set the Found flag = FALSE, as required by the procedure heading. OK!

2. *Path condition for recursive case*. Next we check the path condition for the recursive case. Dave has put a helpful comment that seems to indicate the path condition: "(A[M] <> 0) AND (M < N)". Is Dave right? We can check by using our analysis skills. What is the path condition for the default path in this IF statement? We negate the tests for the two preceding cases and put AND between the negations:

$$NOT \ (M = N) \ AND \ NOT \ (A[M] = 0)$$

which is the same as:

$$M <> N \ AND \ A[M] <> 0$$

It looks like a possible error—Dave's comment didn't include the possibility that this path would be chosen for execution when M > N. But the procedure has a precondition, M <= N, so that rules out a call where M > N. OK!

3. *Check the computation in each recursive case*. The computation in the recursive case is just to call FindZero recursively with the second parameter advanced to M+1 and all the other parameters the same. Because the OUT parameters of the call, Posn and Found, are the OUT parameters of the entire procedure, whatever values these parameters are assigned in the recursive call will remain unchanged when FindZero terminates its own execution after the recursive call. So, if the recursive call finds a zero in the part of the array A[M+1..N] that zero will be located by Posn and Found will be set to TRUE. If no zero is found in A[M+1..N] then Found will be FALSE. The path condition guarantees that we will never make the recursive call unless we know A[M] <> 0, so that would be the right computation to make. OK!

4. *Check progress toward termination*. There is only one control path that leads to a recursive call, and the actual parameters in the call are the same as the formal parameters at the start of execution of the procedure body, with one exception: M has been replaced by M+1. But because the path condition guarantees that

$M < N$, we know that $M+1$ is closer to N. Thus, the part of the array to be searched is one element smaller and we are closer to one of the base cases. OK! ■

□ □

Recursion and Mathematical Induction

In Chapter 10, we saw how verifying a loop by using a loop invariant was related to the concept of *mathematical induction* that is used to prove theorems in mathematics. Verifying a recursive subprogram is also related to proofs that use mathematical induction.

Recall that you use mathematical induction to prove that some mathematical theorem holds for every positive integer value, K, by proving:

1. The theorem is true for $K = 1$.
2. If you assume the theorem is true for some arbitrary value of $K >= 1$, then you can show that the theorem is also true for $K+1$.

In verifying a loop, we take the integer K to be the number of iterations of the loop. First we show that the loop body is correct for one iteration. Then we assume that it is correct for K iterations and show that it must also be correct for $K+1$ iterations.

In verifying a recursive subprogram, we take the integer K to be the *length of the chain of calls (including recursive calls) on the subprogram*. First we look at the case where $K = 1$: there is one (original) call of the subprogram, but no recursive calls are made. These are the base cases that we verify to be correct first.

Next we assume that the subprogram is correct whenever it is called with parameters that lead to a chain of recursive calls that include no more than K calls (including the original call), for some arbitrary value of $K >= 1$. This is what we are doing when we assume, during verification of a path that contains a recursive call, that the recursive call works correctly if the actual parameters are "closer" to one of the base cases. "Closer" means that the chain of recursive calls required to get to the base case is shorter.

Based on this assumption, we show that each path that contains a recursive call is correct. Thus, we show that if we assume the subprogram does work correctly for a chain of K recursive calls, it will also work correctly for a chain of $K+1$ calls. By mathematical induction, the subprogram must work for any possible chain of recursive calls, no matter how long the chain.

EXERCISE

12.7 Use the methods of this section to verify the correctness of the recursive subprograms designed in Exercises 12.3 and 12.4.

□□□ 12.6
TESTING RECURSIVE SUBPROGRAMS

The easiest way to test a recursive subprogram is to use a test driver program to make the initial call on the subprogram. As the chain of recursive calls is made, you want to use debug WRITE statements to display the sequence of calls and returns and to display the values of the parameters in the initial and final local state for each call.

To display this information, use debug WRITE statements at two key points:

1. At the start of the subprogram body, display the values of the IN and IN/OUT parameters.
2. Before leaving the subprogram body, display the values of the OUT and IN/OUT parameters (for a recursive procedure) or the function value (for a function).

□□□ 12.7
RECURSION AND LOOPS

When designing an algorithm for the body of a procedure or function, you often have a choice between an iterative algorithm based on a loop or a recursive algorithm. Which is better? Let's look more closely at the two, considering both similarities and differences.

□□
Similarities

1. *Both provide repetition*. Both loops and recursion provide a way to execute repeatedly a group of statements. In a loop, the loop body is executed repeatedly; in a recursive subprogram, the subprogram body is executed repeatedly.

2. *Both require exit tests and "progress toward termination" to end the repetition*. In recursion, the "exit tests" are the tests for the base cases, and "progress toward termination" is seen in the choice of actual parameters in each recursive call, which must move closer to one of the base cases. An error in these parts of either an iterative or a recursive algorithm can cause an "infinite repetition."

□□
Differences

1. *A loop can be used without representing the action as a subprogram; recursion requires that the action be represented as a subprogram*. A loop is more convenient for simple actions, when an additional subprogram would make the overall program more complex.

2. *A loop executes at the same "level of abstraction" as its surrounding statements; a recursion "descends a level" with each recursive call*. The loop struc-

ture appears more complex in part because there is no abstraction—the loop with its body, exit test, and so forth appears "in-line" with the neighboring statements. The recursive subprogram appears simpler because it is based on reuse of the same "abstract operation" by applying it to a simpler problem.

3. *A loop can exit immediately to the next following statement; a recursion must "unwind the calling chain" before it can exit to the following statement.* Exit from a loop is immediate as soon as one of the exit tests is satisfied, but in a recursion the execution of a base case (the recursive analog of the loop exit test) appears at the very deepest point in the chain of recursive calls. To get back to the point of the original call, you have to "unwind" the calling chain, exiting each level of recursive call to the one above, until you are back at the "top level." Only when the original call is completed can execution continue to the next following statement.

4. *A loop reuses the same data objects on each iteration; a recursion gets a new set of local data objects on each recursive call.* In a loop, the same data objects are used over and over to store different values on each successive iteration. In a recursion, each recursive call has its own local state where values can be saved, and the data objects used in previous levels of recursion are not reused at lower levels.

5. *Recursion is less efficient in use of memory and computer time than looping.* Each recursive call requires that a new local state for the recursive subprogram be allocated in the run-time stack. Then actual parameters must be transmitted and stored and the subprogram body executed. Finally the storage for the local state must be freed for reuse, and control returned to the caller. Each of these steps takes time, and extra storage is required for the local state. In a loop, none of these steps are required. We say that recursion is less *efficient* than looping as a way to repeat an action.

The last reason, *efficiency,* is the primary reason to use a loop for most actions instead of recursion. In most Pascal systems, the practical limit on the "depth" of a chain of recursive calls is usually a few *thousand;* that is, a few thousand repetitions of an action by using recursion would usually come close to an overflow of the run-time stack. On the other hand, there is usually no practical limit on the number of repetitions of a loop—tens of thousands of iterations of a loop would not be unusual. And each execution of a loop iteration is much more efficient than each execution of a recursive call, in general.

□□□ **12.8**
PROGRAM IT WITH STYLE!

Two types of Pascal comments help to make a recursive subprogram more readable:

1. As part of the PURPOSE comment, include "RECURSIVE!" to show the reader that the particular subprogram uses a recursive algorithm.

2. When you use the FORWARD heading for an indirectly recursive subprogram, *repeat the formal parameter list and function value type* as a comment when you later write the separate subprogram body.

□□□ **12.9**
PASCAL SUMMARY

The only new Pascal or pseudo-code element introduced in this chapter is the Pascal FORWARD declaration.

□□

The FORWARD Declaration

Before any subprogram can be called either its full definition must have appeared or a FORWARD declaration specifying just the subprogram heading must have appeared. The syntax is:

⟨FORWARD-declaration⟩ ::=

```
⟨procedure or function heading⟩;
FORWARD;
```

WHERE

⟨procedure or function heading⟩ ::=
   The heading part of a procedure or function definition (not including the local variable declarations and the body).

The local variable declarations and body of the subprogram must appear later in the program, preceded only by the line:

```
PROCEDURE ⟨name⟩;
```

or

```
FUNCTION ⟨name⟩;
```

■■■
REVIEW QUESTIONS

12.1 What is *recursion*?

12.2 What is a *recursive algorithm*? How is a recursive algorithm usually organized?

12.3 What is a *recursive subprogram call*? What is a *directly recursive* subprogram? What is an *indirectly recursive* subprogram? What is *mutual recursion*?

12.4 How does a recursive algorithm make *progress toward termination*?

12.5 Explain the main steps in designing a recursive subprogram.

12.6 When is a *FORWARD declaration* needed in coding recursive subprograms in Pascal? What is the Pascal rule that makes a FORWARD declaration necessary?

12.7 What is an *infinite recursion*? Explain why an infinite recursion causes a Pascal program to crash.

12.8 What is the *run-time stack*? What is *overflow* of the run-time stack? How is run-time stack overflow related to an infinite recursion?

12.9 Explain how to *verify the correctness* of a recursive algorithm. How are the steps in this verification related to *mathematical induction*?

12.10 Explain *two similarities* and *five differences* between loops and recursion.

12.11 What is the *primary reason* for choosing a looping algorithm instead of a recursive algorithm in most situations?

■ ■ ■
PROGRAMMING PROBLEMS

12.1 *Recursive Palindrome Checker*. A character string that reads the same forward or backward is termed a *palindrome*. To make it more interesting, we ignore spaces, punctuation, quotes and apostrophes. We also ignore the distinction between uppercase and lowercase letters. For example, by this definition, these strings are palindromes:

> 987789
> Madam, I'm Adam!
> Able was I ere I saw Elba.
> (((O(O)O)O))

Design, code, and test a program that will determine whether a string entered by the user is a palindrome. Use a recursive algorithm.

12.2 *Recursive Selection Sorting Algorithm*. In the *selection sort* algorithm for sorting the elements of an array of numbers into increasing order, the algorithm works as follows (we discussed this algorithm back in Chapter 10): First, find the smallest element in the array and swap it with the element in the first position in the array. The first array element is now correct. Then find the smallest remaining element in the unsorted part of the array, and swap it with the element in the second position in the array. The first two array elements are now correctly sorted. Continue, by selecting the smallest remaining element at each step and swapping it with the next element in the unsorted part of the array. Write a program that will read in a list of real numbers, sort them using a recursive version of the selection sort algorithm, and display the sorted list.

12.3 *Recursive LISP Parentheses Counter*. Recursion provides a natural way to perform many kinds of *pattern matching*, where the same pattern might reappear as a subpattern within a larger instance of the pattern. For example, in an expression enclosed in parentheses, a sub-expression may itself be enclosed in parentheses. If your algorithm is looking for matched pairs of parentheses, then a recursive call may be all that is required to match nested pairs of parentheses to any depth. The LISP parentheses counter in Programming Problem 10.2 involved just such a pattern matching problem. Do the LISP parentheses counter problem (10.2) by using a recursive algorithm to handle nested sets of parentheses.

12.4 *The Towers of Hanoi.* The "Towers of Hanoi" is an ancient child's puzzle that appears in a new guise in almost every generation. You've probably played with a plastic version of this puzzle at some point in your early years.

In the puzzle, you are given a board with three short posts. On the first post are some rings of increasing diameter, as shown in Figure 12.7. Your goal is to move all the rings to the third post, leaving them stacked in the same order.

There are only two rules:

a. You may only move one ring at a time, from the top position on any post to the top position on any other post.

b. You may never place a larger ring on top of a smaller ring on any post.

Design, code in Pascal, and test a program to solve the Towers of Hanoi puzzle for up to eight rings. Use a recursive algorithm—each recursive call makes one move.

The user should be asked to enter the number of rings to use at the start of each run. The number of moves required doubles for each additional ring, and 8 rings takes 255 moves. For testing, use 4 rings and 15 moves.

FIGURE 12.7 The Towers of Hanoi Puzzle

STARTING POSITION

GOAL POSITION

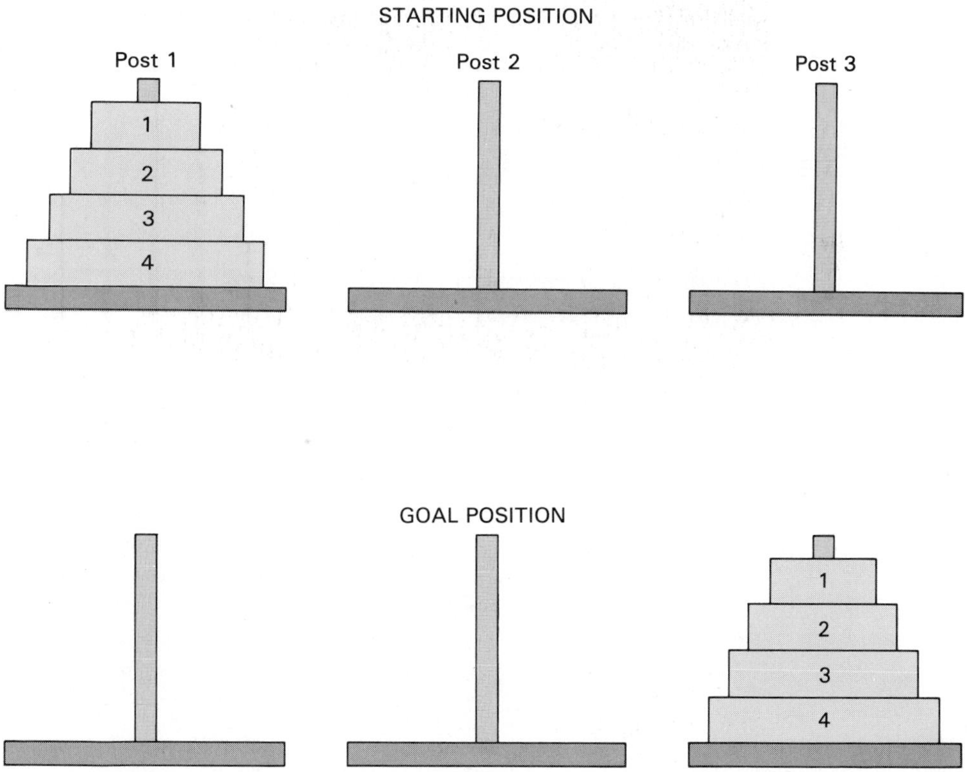

The current state of the posts should be displayed before the first move and after each move is made. The display should have the form (for a four ring puzzle):

```
    POST 1          POST 2          POST 3
      1
      2
      3
      4
---------------   ---------------   ---------------


    POST 1          POST 2          POST 3

      2
      3
      4               1
---------------   ---------------   ---------------


    POST 1          POST 2          POST 3


      3
      4               1               2
---------------   ---------------   ---------------
```

and so forth.

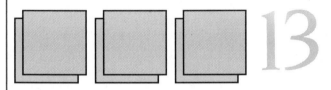

13

Global Data Objects, Abstract Data Types, and Modules

CHAPTER GOALS

When you have mastered the content of this chapter you should be able to:

- Define and use *global data objects* in a Pascal program.
- Explain the basic Pascal *scope rules* for names.
- Describe the advantages and disadvantages of using global data objects.
- Explain how an action becomes *coupled* to the *representation* of a data object.
- Define the concept of an *abstract data type.*
- Explain the importance of *reusable software components.*
- Define the concept of a *module,* and distinguish between the *definition* and the *implementation* of a module.
- Define and use modules to represent reusable software components, including *subprogram libraries* and *abstract data types.*
- Show how to *import* a module into a Pascal program.

Our focus in this chapter is on the way that *data objects, data types,* and *subprograms* are organized in a program. We are looking for ways to control the complexity of a program as it grows to include larger numbers of these elements. Our goal is to limit the ways in which these program elements are connected, so that we can maintain *intellectual control* of the overall program design and organization. Surprisingly, we begin with a concept that can threaten to destroy that control, the concept of a *global data object*. But then we look at the use of *abstract data types* and *modules* to gain better control, including better control of global data objects.

□□□ **13.1**
GLOBAL DATA OBJECTS

To this point, we have limited each subprogram to work only with the data objects in its *local state*—its parameters and local variables. In Pascal and most other programming languages, there is another class of data objects, called *global data objects* or *global variables*. A global data object is accessible to *every subprogram,* simply by using its name as you would a local data object.

The global data objects of a program are data objects separate from the local data objects of any subprogram, as shown in Figure 13.1. Global data objects exist from the beginning of program execution, before the first call of the main procedure. They continue to exist throughout program execution.

The initial state of each global data object is *uninitialized,* meaning the initial value is unpredictable, just as for local data objects. Each time a subprogram *defines* a new value for a global data object (using an assignment or READ), the global data object retains that value until some other subprogram (or possibly the same subprogram at a later point in its execution) defines another value for it. Any subprogram that *uses* the value of a global data object gets whatever value was most recently defined for that global object by any subprogram.

□□

Global Data Objects versus Parameters and Local Data Objects

A global data object may be used to carry a data value IN to a subprogram or to carry a result OUT of the subprogram to be used by other subprograms. Thus, global data objects provide an alternative to parameters as a way of communicating data values from one subprogram to another.

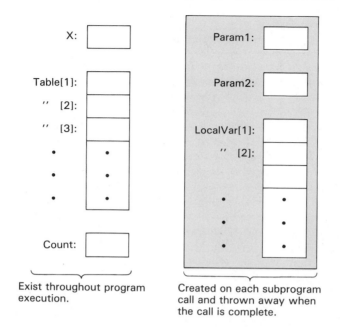

GLOBAL DATA OBJECTS

X:

Table[1]:
" [2]:
" [3]:
•
•
•

Count:

SUBPROGRAM LOCAL STATES

Param1:

Param2:

LocalVar[1]:
" [2]:
•
•
•

Exist throughout program
execution.

Created on each subprogram
call and thrown away when
the call is complete.

FIGURE 13.1 Global Data Objects Exist Throughout Program Execution

If you look at the structure chart for a program, you see the program's organization in terms of which subprograms call each other. Thus, the structure chart
shows the *control flow* between subprograms. Actual parameters and formal parameters provide a way to coordinate *data flow* with those same patterns of control flow.
IN parameters allow data to flow from the caller down to the subprogram being
called. OUT parameters allow data to flow from a subprogram up to its caller. Figure 13.2 shows how parameters allow data to flow among subprograms. Notice how
the data flow follows the patterns of control flow in the structure chart. Data flows
up and down the chart, from higher levels to lower levels and back.

For most purposes, parameters are the most appropriate way to communicate
IN and OUT values to a subprogram. However, sometimes it is desirable to have a
way of communicating data values "across" the structure chart of a program, without
having the data follow the control paths shown in the structure chart. A global data
object can be used for this purpose. Its value can be defined in one subprogram and
that value can be used in another subprogram, without using parameters to communicate the value from the first subprogram up to its caller and ultimately back down
to the second subprogram. Figure 13.2 shows this form of communication.

Global data objects are also an alternative to local data objects in some subprograms. Remember that each time a subprogram is called, a new *local state* is created
for that call which includes new copies of all the subprogram's local data objects.
When the call is complete, the local state is thrown away. Thus, local data objects in

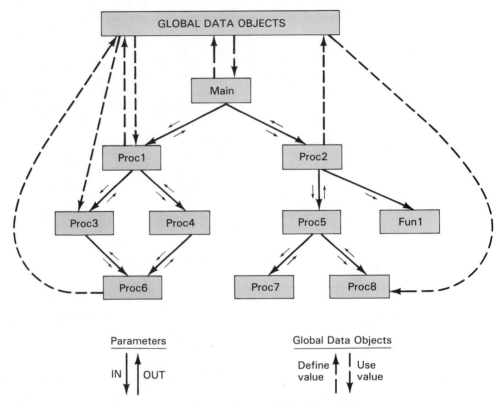

FIGURE 13.2 Data Flow with Parameters and Global Data Objects

a subprogram do not exist between calls, and at the start of each new call all the local data objects are uninitialized again.

Sometimes it is desirable to have a local data object that *retains its value between calls,* so that whatever value it contained at the end of one call is still its value at the start of the next call. Because global data objects continue to exist throughout the execution of the program, they retain their values between calls of any individual subprogram.

A common situation where global data objects are used is one where:

■ The initial value of the global data object is defined in an "initialization" subprogram (possibly the main procedure).

■ Another subprogram then uses that global data object as though it were a local data object, but one that retains its value between calls.

On the first call, the subprogram assumes that the initial value of the global object has been properly set by the initialization subprogram. If the final value of the global data object is important at the end of execution of the program, another subprogram may display the value of the global data object.

Nancy is interested in determining *how many times each subprogram is called* during testing of her program. For example, in procedure MaxMin, she would like to have a local variable, MaxMinCalls, that keeps track of how many times MaxMin is called. At the start of the first call, MaxMinCalls should be zero. During the first call and each subsequent call, MaxMinCalls would be incremented by one. At the end of execution of the entire program, the final value of MaxMinCalls needs to be displayed.

MaxMinCalls acts like a local variable, except that it must retain its value between calls of MaxMin, and it must be initialized in another subprogram and displayed by another subprogram.

Nancy solves the problem by using a global variable for MaxMinCalls:

GLOBAL DATA OBJECTS

MaxMinCalls: Integer   Number of times MaxMin has been called.

At the start of the main procedure, she uses an assignment to initialize MaxMinCalls to zero:

$$\text{MaxMinCalls} := 0$$

At the start of the body of procedure MaxMin, she inserts the statement:

$$\text{MaxMinCalls} := \text{MaxMinCalls} + 1$$

MaxMinCalls is *not* declared as a local variable or as a formal parameter of MaxMin, so it is not part of the local state of the procedure. Thus, each time MaxMin begins execution again, MaxMinCalls will still have the same value that it had at the *end* of the last execution of MaxMin.

At the end of the main procedure, she inserts an action to display the value of MaxMinCalls:

DISPLAY:
"During this run, MaxMin was called ⟨MaxMinCalls⟩ times." ■

□ □
Global Data Objects in Pseudo-code

In pseudo-code, we keep a list of the global data objects in the same form as the list of the local data objects for a subprogram:

⟨GLOBAL DATA OBJECTS list⟩ ::=

GLOBAL DATA OBJECTS

⟨object-name⟩: ⟨data-type⟩   ⟨purpose⟩
{⟨object-name⟩: ⟨data-type⟩   ⟨purpose⟩}
WHERE
> ⟨object-name⟩ ::= A Pascal identifier.
> ⟨data-type⟩ ::= Any defined data type.
> ⟨purpose⟩ ::= Purpose of the data object.

The GLOBAL DATA OBJECTS list tells what data objects *might be used* in any subprogram. Within each subprogram, we need to provide a list of the global data objects that *are used* by that subprogram, either as IN, OUT, or IN/OUT data objects of the subprogram body. Because a global data object connects the subprogram to other parts of the program, we include the list of global data objects as part of the *subprogram heading,* immediately after the list of formal parameters (and function value in a function) and before the PURPOSE and PRECONDITIONS.

Each global variable is specified *exactly as a formal parameter would be specified,* giving its name and data type (as they appear in the GLOBAL DATA OBJECTS list, an IN, OUT, or IN/OUT classification specifying whether the global is used or defined within the subprogram body, and a purpose for the global, using the form:

PROCEDURE or FUNCTION ...
> (... formal parameter list ...)
> GLOBALS:
> > {⟨name⟩: ⟨data type⟩   ⟨classification⟩: ⟨purpose⟩}
> PURPOSE/GOAL STATE: ...
> PRECONDITIONS: ...

WHERE
> ⟨name⟩ ::=
> > The Pascal identifier used to name the object in the GLOBAL DATA OBJECTS list.
> ⟨data type⟩ ::=
> > The data type specified in the GLOBAL DATA OBJECTS list.
> ⟨classification⟩ ::= IN | OUT | IN/OUT
> ⟨purpose⟩ ::= Brief statement of the purpose of the global.

EXAMPLE   Nancy might define the heading for her procedure MaxMin as:

PROCEDURE MaxMin
> (... formal parameter list ...)
> GLOBALS:
> > MaxMinCalls: Integer   IN/OUT: Count of calls of MaxMin.
> PURPOSE/GOAL STATE: ... as usual ...

In a function subprogram, globals may only be used safely as IN data objects, just as a function is restricted to have only IN parameters.

□ □

Global Variables and Scope Rules in Pascal

In a Pascal program, the GLOBAL DATA OBJECTS list is coded as a VAR section that follows the TYPE section, immediately before the first subprogram definition, as shown in Figure 13.3. This VAR section has the same form as the VAR section within a subprogram.

Each variable declared in this VAR section can be used within *every subprogram* that follows. The reason that global variables are visible within every subprogram lies in the *scope rules* of Pascal.

Each *name* used for a global or local variable, formal parameter, data type, defined constant, procedure, or function is defined only within a certain part of the

---

FIGURE 13.3 Scope Rules and Global Variables in Pascal

```
PROGRAM ⟨program name⟩ (...);

CONST
     ⟨list of constant definitions⟩

TYPE
     ⟨list of type definitions⟩

VAR
     ⟨list of variable declarations⟩         -- all these variables
                                              are "global" variables

PROCEDURE ⟨procedure name⟩
          ⟨list of formal parameters⟩
     VAR
          ⟨list of local variables⟩          Any global variable
     BEGIN                                    can be used in any
          ⟨list of statements⟩               subprogram here,
     END;                                     simply by using the
                                              name of the variable
PROCEDURE ...                                 in a statement.
     ... more subprogram declarations ...

BEGIN
     ...
END.
```

overall program. This part is termed the *scope of the definition of the name*. The rules that determine the scope of definition are termed *scope rules:*

□ **Scope Rule**

A *scope rule* is a rule that determines, for a name defined in a program declaration, the other statements or declarations in the program where that definition of the name holds.

Note that scope rules refer to the definition of *names* of variables (and other program elements), not to the definition of *values* of variables.

Global variables are possible in Pascal because of the Pascal scope rules. The actual Pascal rules are rather complex. The key rules are these:

□

Scope Rule 1. The scope of definition of any name defined in the CONST, TYPE, or VAR sections of the *main program* is the entire program following that definition, *including each following subprogram definition,* unless that subprogram uses the same name for a formal parameter or local variable.

□

Scope Rule 2. The scope of definition of any name defined for a formal parameter or local variable *within a subprogram* is the *body of that subprogram.*

Scope Rule 1 is the rule that allows a subprogram to refer to a global variable. If you use a variable name within a subprogram and that name is not declared as a formal parameter or local variable (inadvertently or on purpose), then the Pascal compiler assumes you are referring to a global variable with that name. Figure 13.3 illustrates the situation.

Scope Rule 2 is the rule that ensures that one subprogram cannot access the local variables or parameters of another subprogram. The local state of each subprogram is hidden from all other subprograms (and other calls of the same subprogram). Thus, you can use the same name for a local variable in several different subprograms, with no confusion arising.

The Pascal scope rules have a built-in possibility for error. *By default,* if you forget to declare a formal parameter or local variable in a subprogram, then the compiler *assumes* that you want that subprogram to use a global variable (if there is one with the same name as the formal parameter or the local variable that you forgot to declare).

EXAMPLE

Suppose you have a count controlled WHILE loop in a subprogram that uses a variable named Count, and you forget to declare Count as a local variable in the subprogram. Suppose that you also have a global variable named Count that is used by several other subprograms. When the compiler compiles the subprogram, every reference to "Count" will become a reference to global variable Count.

Suppose that in the body of the WHILE loop, you happen to call one of the subprograms that uses the global variable Count. Then that other subprogram will get the value of Count defined in your WHILE loop, and after each call of the other subprogram, your WHILE loop will see as the value of Count whatever value was assigned to Count by the other subprogram. At this point, you have a very mysterious bug to track down! ■

□ □

Global Data Objects Interfere with Program Analysis

Global data objects are a deceptively simple idea. It appears easier in many situations to use global data objects instead of parameters as a way of making IN values accessible to a subprogram and as a way of receiving OUT values from a subprogram. But, unfortunately, using global data objects can quickly destroy our ability to analyze and understand what a program is doing.

The problem lies in the fact that *global data objects inhibit data flow analysis*. Global data objects act like *hidden parameters* in a subprogram call. Because a global data object is "visible" to every subprogram, its value may be used or defined by any subprogram. As a result, you cannot perform data flow analysis of any segment where a global data object participates in the computation and where there also is *any* subprogram call between a definition and a use of that global data object.

<u>**EXAMPLE**</u>   Suppose that variable A is a global variable. Consider the segment:

```
A := 2;
MaxMin (B, C);
writeln (A, B, C);
```

If the heading for MaxMin mentions no use of any global variables, then a simple data flow analysis should allow you to conclude that A will still have the value 2 when the *writeln* statement is reached, regardless of what computation MaxMin performs.

But suppose that Hacker Jack has written the body of MaxMin as follows:

```
PROCEDURE MaxMin
    (B: Integer;          {IN}
     VAR C: Integer);     {OUT}
BEGIN
    C := B + 1;
    Proc2 (C);
END;
```

So MaxMin calls Proc2. Now suppose that Proc2 happens to change the value of global variable A with the assignment:

```
A := 375;
```

Because of the action of Proc2, your conclusion from data flow analysis is wrong. When the *writeln* statement is reached, the value of A is displayed as 375, not 2. Imagine trying to track down a bug like that! ■

Without accurate data flow analysis, we have a difficult time understanding how a program segment makes a computation, and it is almost impossible to verify that the computation is correct. If a global data object participates in determining the control path chosen in a conditional or loop, then we cannot determine how the control path is chosen. Without data flow analysis, we cannot safely delete a statement, insert a statement, or modify an existing statement.

The term *side effect* captures the negative aspect of using global data objects:

□ **Side Effect**

A subprogram has a *side effect* if it defines a new value for any global data object.

When asked what a particular subprogram does, we might say "Oh that subprogram computes ..., and as a *side effect* it also changes the value of global variable ...." Whenever you hear that a subprogram has a side effect, you are being warned that accurate data flow analysis of the program will be difficult.

□ □
Safe Uses of Global Data Objects

The most important rule about using global data objects is: *never use a global data object as a substitute for a parameter*. To communicate data values among subprograms, try to use a parameter as your first choice. The situations where a global data object is appropriate as an IN or OUT data object in a subprogram have these characteristics:

1. *The data object should not be visible to the caller of the subprogram.* That is, the operation represented by the subprogram would not ordinarily be expected to have such a parameter. For example, Nancy's MaxMinCalls was such a data object. A count of the number of times the subprogram was called is not a natural part of the operation represented by the subprogram. Nancy rightly wanted to keep the count *hidden* from the caller.

2. *The data object needs to be defined or used in several different subprograms that are not directly connected by subprogram calls.* For example, in Nancy's program, only the main procedure and the MaxMin procedure used the global variable MaxMinCalls. MaxMin might have been at the bottom of the structure chart for the program, while the main procedure was at the top. Passing MaxMinCalls as a parameter from Main to MaxMin would have forced an extra parameter to be added to *each subprogram* in the calling chain from Main to MaxMin.

CHANGING ATTITUDES TOWARD GLOBAL VARIABLES

Global variables are best avoided except in carefully controlled circumstances. A program that uses global variables is much more difficult to analyze and modify safely than one that does not use them.

The attitude of avoiding most uses of global variables is a relatively recent one. Earlier in the history of programming, programmers were often encouraged to use global variables extensively. The rationale for this attitude was primarily that it was easier to *write* programs that used mostly (or only) global variables because you did not have to worry with writing lists of actual and formal parameters. You could avoid parameters altogether, or use a few parameters and some global variables in a convenient mix. The scope rules in Pascal are a reflection of this earlier attitude toward global variables, typical of the 1960s and early 1970s.

In some programming languages (early versions of BASIC and COBOL most notably), most procedures used global variables. Sometimes the language did not even allow procedures to have parameters—global variables had to be used.

In the 1980s, attention turned toward designing programs that were easy to *maintain*—meaning "easy to analyze and modify after they have been developed and put into use." Because programs that make extensive use of global variables are hard to analyze and modify, they are hard to maintain. We now see the use of global variables as a poor way to design a program that must be maintained over a long period.

3. *The data object needs to retain its state between the times that it is used by one or more of the subprograms.* For example, in Nancy's program, MaxMinCalls needed to retain its value between each call of procedure MaxMin.

EXERCISE

13.1 Hacker Jack likes to use global variables. Unfortunately, in this program he forgot to declare a local variable in his procedure Swap and the compiler used one of his global variables instead. Without looking at the body of procedure Swap, predict what values should be displayed by the WRITE statement in the main procedure. Then hand trace execution of his program and give the results actually displayed by the WRITE statement:

```
PROGRAM JacksFolly (INPUT, OUTPUT);

VAR
        A:  Integer;
        B:  Integer;
        C:  Integer;
```

```
PROCEDURE Swap
        (VAR X: Integer;          {IN/OUT}
         VAR Y: Integer);         {IN/OUT}

        {PURPOSE/GOAL STATE: Swap the values of X and Y.}

    BEGIN
        B := X;
        X := Y;
        Y := B;
    END;     {procedure Swap}


PROCEDURE Main;
    BEGIN
        A := 5;
        B := 7;
        C := 9;
        Swap (A, B);
        Swap (C, A);
        writeln (A, B, C);
    END;


BEGIN
    Main;
END.
```

□□□ 13.2
ABSTRACT DATA TYPES

Let's review the way that we have approached the definition of data types in the preceding chapters. Our basic design principle is "DEFINE, then REFINE." Applied to the definition of a data type, we first DEFINE only the name of the data type. Then we proceed to DEFINE the headings for various operations (procedures and functions) that work with data objects of that type. Program design continues with the *use* of the data type name in the declaration of particular data objects and with the *use* of the operations to manipulate these data objects in program actions.

Later, we return to choose a particular *representation* for the data type and at the same time we design the *algorithms* to be used in the subprogram bodies to manipulate this representation. This is the REFINE step in our design. Our *Fundamental Principle of Data Representation* ties the choice of the representation for a data type directly to the simplicity of the algorithms that represent the operations.

Once the representation for a data type has been chosen, we have no explicit rule that prevents any action in any subprogram from directly making use of that representation. For example, if we choose the representation of a Date data type to be a record with three fields named Month, Day, and Year, then any action in the program that works with a data object of type Date can directly access any one of these fields. Let's look more closely at this situation.

Coupling an Action to a Data Representation

A major source of complexity in a program comes from the *coupling* between actions in subprogram bodies and the representations of the data objects that they manipulate. This coupling arises whenever an action is based on *how* a data object is represented, rather than just on *what* the data object represents.

Whenever an action uses an individual field of a record variable or an individual element of an array, it becomes coupled to the representation of that data object (see Figure 13.4.) The same coupling occurs when an action uses one of the values of an enumerated type or when an action depends on a particular range for a subrange type. Even knowing whether a particular data object is an Integer or a Real type represents coupling.

To test whether an action is coupled to a particular representation of a data object, ask the question "if I were to change the *definition* of the type of this data object, would I have to change the way this action works?" If the answer is yes, then the two are coupled.

Not every action that uses a data object of a particular data type is coupled to the representation of that object, however. For example, Nancy might write a program that represented a "student grade transcript" as a large record with several fields of type Date. Almost every action that worked with a transcript record might need to read Dates, compare Dates, modify Dates, or display Dates. But these actions would not be coupled to the *representation* of a Date if they worked with Dates only by calling procedures and functions to perform the desired actions on Dates. The operations that are coupled to the representation of a Date are only those that directly reference the Month, Day, and Year fields of the record that represents a Date.

Coupling of actions to a particular data representation means that whenever you change the representation of that data type, you may also have to change the actions that are coupled to that representation. The more coupled actions, the more complicated becomes the change. If you forget to change one of the coupled actions, you leave a bug in the modified program.

Abstract Data Types

The goal of *data abstraction* is to eliminate coupling between the representation of a data type and "outside" subprograms (outside of a small set of basic operations defined on objects of that data type). The actions that are not coupled are only allowed to manipulate data objects of the type by *calling the procedures and functions* that are coupled.

If coupling to outside subprograms is completely eliminated, then the data type becomes an *abstract data type:*

DATA TYPES

DATE =
  RECORD
      Day: Integer
      Month: Integer   } Representation of a Date object.
      Year: Integer
  END

SUBPROGRAMS

FUNCTION DayOf

  (D: Date)

  FUNCTION VALUE: Integer

ALGORITHM

Step 1.   ACTIONS:
              FUNCTION VALUE := (D.Day)   { This reference to a field in the representation of Date D couples the DayOf function to the representation of D.

FUNCTION IsFirstOfMonth

  (D: Date)

  FUNCTION VALUE: Boolean

ALGORITHM

Step 1.   ACTIONS:
              IF DayOf (D) = 1 THEN
                      FUNCTION VALUE := TRUE
              ELSE
                      FUNCTION VALUE := FALSE

} This function is not coupled to the representation of D because it does not refer to a field of the record representing D.

FIGURE 13.4   Coupling Between a Subprogram and a Data Representation

☐ **Abstract Data Type**

An *abstract data type* consists of a data type definition and *all* of the operations (procedures and functions) in the program that are coupled to the representation of that type.

In an abstract data type, the *data type name* and the *headings for the operations* are the *only information* that is made available for use in the rest of the program.

In an abstract data type, we say that the representation of the data type has been *completely hidden* for outside view. Only the subprograms that are part of the abstract data type know how the data type is represented.

EXAMPLE

Hacker Jack has just completed his term project, a large program that is intended to keep track of a calendar of events for the student government of his university. Early in the design of his program he chose the representation for a Date data type, using a Pascal record. Because his program was reading in dates that used three character abbreviations for month names (like JAN, FEB, MAR, . . .), Jack chose the same representation inside the program:

```
TYPE
    MonthAbbrev = STRING [3];
    Date =
        RECORD
            Day: Integer;
            Month: MonthAbbrev;
            Year: Integer;
        END;
```

As he designed and coded the dozen or more subprograms in his program, he routinely wrote code that referred directly to the Month, Day, and Year fields of a Date. And each subprogram that used the Month field assumed that the month was represented as a three character string. When he finished, there were close to 100 references to these fields in various statements in the program. Almost every subprogram referred to one of these fields at some point, so almost every subprogram was coupled to this particular representation of a Date.

Unfortunately, as Jack added each new procedure and function to his program, he increasingly realized that his choice of representation for the month part of a Date had been poor. Although it was easy to read in a Date value, almost every other procedure and function would have been simpler if the month had been represented as an Integer in the range 1–12.

Jack knows that the program would be simpler and the design better (and his grade on the term project higher!) if he changed the definition of the Date data type to represent the month as an integer. But he doesn't do it—almost every part of the program is coupled to the particular representation of Date that he has chosen. To make this seemingly minor change, he would have to check and possibly modify almost every subprogram, and then retest every part. Jack is not happy, but he's stuck with the program as it is.

Nancy is taking the same programming class as Hacker Jack. For her calendar program she has chosen the same representation for dates as Jack, using a record with fields Day, Month, and Year, where Month is a string of three characters. However, Nancy has made a Date into an *abstract data type*. She has allowed only a basic set of subprograms to be coupled to this representation for a Date. She chooses two procedures and three functions:

- PROCEDURE SetDate — Stores a given month, day, and year in a Date data object.
- FUNCTION DayOf — Returns the day part of a Date.
- FUNCTION YearOf — Returns the year part of a Date.
- FUNCTION MonthOf — Returns the month part of a Date, as an integer in the range 1-12.
- PROCEDURE MonthAbbrevOf — Returns the month part of a Date, as a three character string.

Notice that she has two subprograms that return the month part of a date—either as an integer or as a three character string. The underlying choice of representation of the month part of a date is entirely hidden from the rest of the program in Nancy's abstract data type.

These subprograms are the only ones that are coupled to the particular representation of a Date as a Pascal record. The rest of the program is written without any reference to how dates are represented. Whenever a date needs to be created, procedure SetDate is called, whenever the month part of a date is needed, function MonthOf or procedure MonthAbbrevOf is called, and so forth.

As Nancy completes the design of her program, she observes that there is only one call in the rest of the program to procedure MonthAbbrevOf, but there are dozens of calls to function MonthOf. She decides the program would be improved if the month part of a date were represented as an Integer rather than a character string. But her problem in making the modification is much simpler than Jack's because only the Date type definition and the five subprograms might need to be changed. The rest of the program is not coupled to the representation of a Date. She checks and modifies the parts of her Date abstract data type, and quickly has an improved program. ∎

□ □

Data Abstraction, Encapsulation, and Pascal

When a programming language provides mechanisms that support a particular kind of abstraction and information hiding, we say that the language provides *encapsulation* for the abstraction. Pascal provides encapsulation for procedures and functions, because the details of the body of a procedure or function are not *visible* outside, in other subprograms. For example, one procedure cannot directly refer to a local variable of another procedure because the local variables of a procedure are hidden inside the procedure. Similarly, the individual statements in a procedure body are hidden and cannot be used as part of another procedure.

The "encapsulation" of local variables and statements in a subprogram is enforced by the Pascal language, so that the programmer does not have to worry about inadvertently interfering with the action of a procedure through a programming error in another part of the program.

Support by the programming language for definition and encapsulation of abstract data types is desirable for the same reasons. It would be nice to have protection against inadvertently interfering with an abstract data type through a programming error in another part of the program.

However, data types are declared in the TYPE section of a Pascal program, where they are "globally" visible. As a result, *any* Pascal subprogram can refer to the fields of any record data object or to the elements of any array data object. The Pascal language makes no restrictions on which subprograms can be coupled to a particular data representation. Thus, there is no provision in Pascal for encapsulation of abstract data types.

Pascal does not provide support for encapsulation of abstract data types because its definition in the late 1960s came before the introduction of data abstraction concepts into programming, which occurred in the 1970s. Modula-2 and Ada, two important languages from the late 1970s that are based on Pascal, both provide language features for encapsulating abstract data types.

Even in Pascal, however, we can use the concepts of data abstraction. But when we come to *code* an abstract data type in Pascal, we must rely on organizational methods that are not a part of standard Pascal. The concept of a *module* in the next section provides such a method.

EXERCISES

13.2 For each of the following subprograms, determine if the subprogram is coupled to the representation of its parameters. For each parameter, explain why there is or is not coupling:

a. FUNCTION FindZeroLocation

```
    (List: ListType)          {IN}
    : Integer;

{PURPOSE: Find the subscript of the first zero value in
    List [1..500].}
{PRECONDITION: List contains at least one zero value.}

VAR
    I: Integer;               {Loop subscript variable}
```

```
        BEGIN
            I := 1;
            WHILE List [I] <> 0 DO
                I := I + 1;
            FindZeroLocation := I;
        END;    {function FindZeroLocation}
```

b. PROCEDURE ComputeGPA

```
     (Transcript: TranscriptType;      {IN}
      TotalHours: Integer;             {OUT}
      GPA: Real);                      {OUT}
```

{PURPOSE/GOAL STATE: Compute cumulative GPA for student
record in Transcript and store in GPA. Return total
course hours taken in TotalHours.}

```
     VAR
         GradePoints: Real;            {Cumulative grade points}

     BEGIN
         TotalHours := GetTotalHours (Transcript);
         GradePoints := GetTotalGradePoints (Transcript);
         IF TotalHours <> 0 THEN
             GPA := GradePoints / TotalHours
         ELSE
             GPA := 0;
     END;    {procedure Compute GPA}
```

□□□ **13.3**
MODULES: REUSABLE SOFTWARE COMPONENTS

Rather than designing and coding every program "from scratch," choosing every
data representation, and designing every subprogram over again each time you write
a new program, it would be nice to have a way to reuse some of the work that went
into one program in later programs that you develop. The use of "modules" provides
that opportunity.

□ **Module**

A *module* (also termed a *package* or *unit*) is a group of related data types and operations on those data types. Defined constants and data objects that are "global" to the
module may also be included.

  A module has a *definition part,* which contains the part of the module that is
"visible" (available for use) outside the module, and an *implementation part,* which is
the full definition of all the data types, subprograms, constants, and global variables
in the module.

Modules provide an appropriate way to include abstract data types in Pascal programs. They also provide a *safe* way to introduce global data objects and control access to them.

A module is intended to be a *reusable software component*—a piece of software that is larger than a single subprogram but smaller than a complete program and that can be used again and again in constructing different programs. A module is designed, coded, and tested separately from the main part of a program that uses it. Then it is stored in a *separate source program file,* distinct from the file that contains the program using it.

When a program uses one or more of the subprograms, data types, data objects, or constants provided by a module, we say that the program *imports* the module. A larger program may import several modules to provide different types of data objects and operations.

□ □
Two Types of Module

Our modules will be of two main types:

1. *Abstract data types*. Many modules will represent abstract data types, where there is a central data type and a collection of useful operations on data objects of that type. For example, a DateModule might provide a Date data type and a useful collection of functions and procedures to work with dates.

2. *Subprograms with Hidden Global Data Objects*. Most other modules will provide a collection of useful subprograms without any data types. However, in the implementation part, hidden from the user, the subprograms will access one or more global data objects. These global objects will retain data values between calls of the individual subprograms and also provide a way for the subprograms to communicate with each other. For example, a PerformanceMeasurement module might provide a collection of subprograms for collecting information about how many times various parts of a program were executed. A hidden part of the module would be a global data object representing a table of collected performance measurement information. By calling a subprogram in the module, a program could cause data to be entered in the table. By calling another subprogram at the end of a run, a program could cause all the collected data to be displayed. The table and its representation would be entirely hidden within the implementation part of the module.

Sometimes it will be useful to include supportive data types as part of the module, such as a type Month, type Day, and type Year to support the central Date type in the module DateModule. These supporting types may not be abstract types. They often are fully defined subrange or enumerated types. More rarely, a module might provide one or more "visible" global data objects, such as flags, tables, or defined constants.

A New Strategy for Program Development

The concept of a module is the cornerstone of a new strategy for program development: *reuse of existing software components before development of new code*. The goal is to develop a growing *library of modules,* each of which provides some useful collection of data types and operations.

When a new program is to be developed, instead of starting from scratch to develop the program, as in the preceding chapters, you look instead through the library of modules to find the various components that you need. Then you write a main procedure and perhaps a few additional subprograms that are not provided by any existing module. But for most of the work in the program, you simply declare data objects of the types defined by existing modules and then use the operations provided by the modules to manipulate those data objects. If you have an adequate library of modules to start from, the effort required to develop a new program becomes only a fraction of that required to write the same program "from scratch."

As you design a program and you find that no existing module provides the data types or subprograms that you need, you may develop a new module as part of that programming effort. However, because it is defined as a module, you can add it to your library of modules, to be used in the current program and perhaps also to be useful in later programs. Thus the library of available modules is constantly growing.

Advantages of Modules

Modules provide a larger unit of abstraction than we have seen before this point. However, the advantages of modules match closely the advantages of other simpler forms of abstraction, such as subprograms, type definitions, and defined constants, as discussed in Chapter 5:

1. *Information hiding*. A module hides details of the implementation of its parts. This reduces the coupling between the module and other elements of the program. The program becomes easier to understand and analyze.

2. *Reusability*. Modules provide reusable software components.

3. *Replaceability*. Modules allow a particular implementation of a subprogram or data type to be replaced by an improved implementation without change to the rest of the program.

4. *Reliability*. Modules may be tested separately from the rest of the program. Usually they are tested much more thoroughly because they are intended to be reused over and over, and a bug might affect many programs. Because modules reduce coupling between parts of a program, they also make a program easier to analyze and verify.

5. *Hierarchical program organization*. One module may import another module. Thus a module that provides very "high-level" abstractions may rely on simpler modules to provide "lower-level" abstractions. For example, a module that provides an "inventory list" data type (and operations) might be a high-level module. It might import a Date module to define a Date type and operations that would be used as part of the "inventory list" abstraction.

6. *Delayed definition.* A module can be defined and used before its implementation part is completed. That is, another part of the program design can declare data objects of types defined in the module and can call subprograms defined in the module (although of course you cannot compile and execute those parts). If the design of the definition part requires change, the delay in designing the implementation part may save a lot of wasted effort.

7. *Partitioned programming effort.* When a programming team is building a program, the definition parts of new modules can be defined by the group, and then individuals can be assigned the task of implementing and testing each module, separately from the work of developing the main part of the program.

□□□ **13.4**
DESIGNING, CODING, AND USING MODULES

A module consists of a *definition part* and an *implementation part*. The implementation part is familiar. It consists of the complete definitions for the various elements of the module—data types, subprograms, defined constants and global variables. In pseudo-code, these definitions appear exactly as they would in the DATA TYPES, SUBPROGRAMS, DEFINED CONSTANTS, and GLOBAL DATA OBJECTS lists of a complete program. But there is no main procedure or PROGRAM heading line in a module. The BEGIN...END at the end of the program (where the main procedure is called) is also missing.

The definition part is a *selection* of elements from the implementation part, representing those elements that are to be made "visible" to the user of the module. Nothing new is added in the definition part.

Typically the definition part contains:

- The *headings* of the subprograms in the module.
- The *names* of abstract data types provided by the module.

Auxiliary elements to be made visible to the user may also be included in the definition part, such as supporting data types, global variables, or defined constants.

□□
Defining a Module in Pseudo-code

To define a module in pseudo-code, use the syntax:

⟨MODULE-definition⟩ ::=

  MODULE DEFINITION ⟨**module name**⟩
  ⟨definition part⟩

MODULE IMPLEMENTATION ⟨**module-name**⟩

⟨implementation part⟩

WHERE

⟨definition part⟩ ::=

A SUBPROGRAMS list containing subprogram headings.

A DATA TYPES list containing the names of abstract data types and the full definitions of other types.

A DEFINED CONSTANTS list containing the names of defined constants.

A GLOBAL DATA OBJECTS list containing the names and data types of global data objects.

The definition part contains all the elements of the module that are available for use outside the module.

⟨implementation part⟩ ::=

Complete definitions of the various elements of the SUBPROGRAMS, DATA TYPES, DEFINED CONSTANTS, and GLOBAL DATA OBJECTS lists in the definition part, together with any additional subprograms, data types, defined constants, and global data objects that are to be hidden from the user of the module.

EXAMPLE

Let's define a module that provides a Date abstract data type. Suppose we decide to provide the same five operations that Nancy used in her definition of this abstract type:

PROCEDURE SetDate	—Stores a given month, day, and year in a Date data object.
FUNCTION DayOf	—Returns the day part of a Date.
FUNCTION YearOf	—Returns the year part of a Date.
FUNCTION MonthOf	—Returns the month part of a Date, as an integer in the range 1-12.
PROCEDURE MonthAbbrevOf	—Returns the month part of a Date, as a three character string.

The module definition might be:

MODULE DEFINITION DateModule

DATA TYPES

Date = ?	Abstract data type representing a date.
DayRange = 1..31	Allowed range for a day in a date.
YearRange = 1900..2100	Allowed range for a year in a date.
MonthRange = 1..12	Allowed range for a month in a date.
MonthAbbrev = STRING[3]	First three characters in a month name.

SUBPROGRAMS

PROCEDURE SetDate

(Day: DayRange	IN
Month: MonthRange	IN
Year: YearRange	IN
NewDate: Date)	OUT

PURPOSE/GOAL STATE: Stores the given month, day, and year in NewDate.

PRECONDITIONS: The month, day, and year combination must represent a valid date.

FUNCTION DayOf

(GivenDate: Date)   IN

FUNCTION VALUE: DayRange

PURPOSE: Returns the day part of GivenDate.

FUNCTION YearOf

(GivenDate: Date)   IN

FUNCTION VALUE: YearRange

PURPOSE: Returns the year part of GivenDate.

FUNCTION MonthOf

(GivenDate: Date)   IN

FUNCTION VALUE: MonthRange

PURPOSE: Returns the month part of GivenDate, as an integer.

PROCEDURE MONTHABBREVOF

(GIVENDATE: DATE	IN
MONTHSTRING: MONTHABBREV)	OUT

PURPOSE/GOAL STATE: Returns the month part of a Date in MonthString, as a three character abbreviation of the month name.

The module implementation part fills in the details of the representation of a date and of the bodies of the subprograms.

MODULE IMPLEMENTATION **DateModule**

DATA TYPES

Date =	Abstract data type representing a date.
RECORD	Hidden representation.
Day: DayRange	
Month: MonthRange	
Year: YearRange	
END	

DayRange = 1..31	Allowed range for a day in a date.
YearRange = 1900..2100	Allowed range for a year in a date.
MonthRange = 1..12	Allowed range for a month in a date.
MonthAbbrev = STRING[3]	First three characters in a month name.

SUBPROGRAMS

PROCEDURE SetDate

(Day: DayRange	IN
Month: MonthRange	IN
Year: YearRange	IN
NewDate: Date)	OUT

PURPOSE/GOAL STATE: Stores the given month, day, and year in NewDate.

PRECONDITIONS: The month, day, and year combination must represent a valid date.

ALGORITHM

Step 1. ACTIONS:

NewDate.Day := Day
NewDate.Month := Month
NewDate.Year := Year

FUNCTION DayOf

(GivenDate: Date)　　　IN

FUNCTION VALUE: DayRange

PURPOSE: Returns the day part of GivenDate.

ALGORITHM

Step 1. ACTIONS:
FUNCTION VALUE := GivenDate.Day

FUNCTION YearOf

(GivenDate: Date)　　　IN

FUNCTION VALUE: YearRange

PURPOSE: Returns the year part of GivenDate.

ALGORITHM

Step 1. ACTIONS:
FUNCTION VALUE := GivenDate.Year

FUNCTION MonthOf

        (GivenDate: Date)   IN

    FUNCTION VALUE: MonthRange

    PURPOSE: Returns the month part of GivenDate, as an integer.

ALGORITHM

Step 1. ACTIONS:

    FUNCTION VALUE := GivenDate.Month

PROCEDURE MonthAbbrevOf

        (GivenDate: Date   IN
         MonthString: MonthAbbrev)   OUT

    PURPOSE/GOAL STATE: Returns the month part of a Date in MonthString, as a three character abbreviation of the month name.

ALGORITHM

Step 1. ACTIONS:

```
CASE GivenDate.Month OF
    1: MonthString := 'JAN'
    2: MonthString := 'FEB'
    3: MonthString := 'MAR'
    4: MonthString := 'APR'
    5: MonthString := 'MAY'
    6: MonthString := 'JUN'
    7: MonthString := 'JUL'
    8: MonthString := 'AUG'
    9: MonthString := 'SEP'
    10: MonthString := 'OCT'
    11: MonthString := 'NOV'
    12: MonthString := 'DEC'
END
```

Using Modules in Pseudo-code

In pseudo-code, when designing a new program, keep a list of the modules that you want to import into that program:

IMPORTED MODULES

    ⟨module name⟩   ⟨purpose of the module⟩
    {⟨module name⟩   ⟨purpose of the module⟩}

Whenever a module is listed as an IMPORTED MODULE for a program, you can use any element of the definition part of the module within that program, without further definition.

EXAMPLE In a program that imports the Date module:

> **IMPORTED MODULES**
>
> DateModule   Provides the Date type and operations.

Within the main procedure or any other subprogram, you can then define data objects of type Date and call subprograms SetDate, DayOf, MonthOf, MonthAbbrevOf, and YearOf. ∎

□ □
Coding a Module in Pascal

The standard Pascal language provides no direct support for modules. However, we can still make effective use of the module concept.

In order to make it easy to reuse a module in different programs, we store the Pascal code for each module in a *separate source program file*. Let the name of the file be the same as the name of the module. In the file:

1. Enter the *definition part* of the module as a Pascal comment at the beginning of the file.
2. Enter the *implementation part* of the module as Pascal CONST, TYPE and VAR sections (for global variables), just as for a complete Pascal program. Follow these sections with the complete set of subprogram definitions for the module.

EXAMPLE For the Date module, you might use a file named DATEMODULE. The contents of the file would be the coded version of the Date module above:

```
                    {MODULE DEFINITION DateModule
                            DATA TYPES
                    ... copy of the pseudo-code ...
                            SUBPROGRAMS
                    ... copy of the pseudo-code ...}


              {MODULE IMPLEMENTATION DateModule}

      TYPE
         Date =              {Abstract data type representing a date.}
            RECORD                    {Hidden representation.}
```

```
        Day: DayRange;
        Month: MonthRange;
        Year: YearRange;
    END;
    ... Pascal code for other type definitions...
PROCEDURE SetDate
    ... Pascal code ...
FUNCTION DayOf
    ... Pascal code ...
FUNCTION YearOf
    ... Pascal code ...
FUNCTION MonthOf
    ... Pascal code ...
PROCEDURE MonthAbbrevOf
    ... Pascal code ...
```

Importing a Module into a Pascal Program

There are two common ways of importing a module into your program:

- Use *extensions* to standard Pascal provided by your local Pascal system, or
- Use an *editor program* to insert the definitions of imported modules into a program before compiling the program.

Let's look at these alternatives.

Importing a Module by Using an INCLUDE Extension

Many Pascal systems now provide an extension to standard Pascal that allows a module file to be copied into another source program file at a given point. This extension is termed a *file inclusion* feature. You simply put into your source program a statement that says to the compiler: "At this point, copy the entire contents of module file ⟨file name⟩ and place the copy here, just as though it had been entered here originally. Then continue compiling this source program file, starting with the elements of the new module that have just been included." Figure 13.5 illustrates how the file inclusion feature works.

The syntax for writing this file inclusion statement varies with the Pascal system. Often it is simply a special comment of the form:

{$INCLUDE ⟨file name⟩}

or a line that begins with a special character, such as:

#INCLUDE ⟨file-name⟩

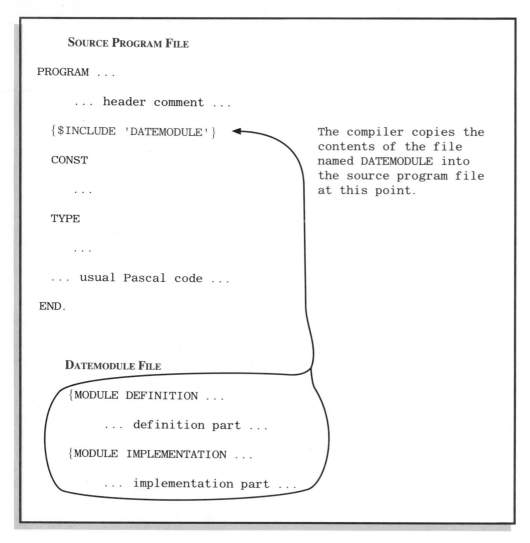

FIGURE 13.5 Using File Inclusion to Import a Module

In a Pascal system that provides a file inclusion feature, the Pascal compiler is set up to recognize the special "file include" comment or statement and to find the named module file and copy the contents of the file into the program.

The compiler has also been set up so that the rules about having just a single CONST, TYPE, and VAR section are relaxed—you can have several of each section (included from different module files), and they can appear before or after procedure and function definitions (from different module files). The rules about the *order* in which subprograms, data types, constants, and global variables are defined have also been relaxed in such a compiler, so that you may call a subprogram *before* the definition of the subprogram has appeared, or you may declare a variable to be of a particular data type, even though that data type is defined in a module that is included at a later point in the program.

EXAMPLE   Nancy wants to import the DateModule into her StudentRecords program. Her Pascal system provides the "file inclusion" extension, so she just inserts the following line immediately before the CONST section in her StudentRecords source program file:

```
{$INCLUDE 'DateModule'}
```

Importing a Module by Using an Editor Program

The second method of importing a module into a Pascal program requires a little more work on your part, but it works for any Pascal system. You use the *editor* to copy the contents of the module file into your program file, placing the various elements in the CONST, TYPE, VAR, and subprogram declaration sections, as appropriate.

EXAMPLE   Nancy's Pascal system does not have an INCLUDE extension, so she imports the DateModule into her StudentRecords program by sitting at a terminal and using the editor to modify her StudentRecords source program file. First she uses the editor to copy the TYPE section from the DateModule file into the TYPE section of her StudentRecords program. She makes sure there is only a single TYPE section in her modified program (deleting the TYPE section header from the DateModule file).

Then she copies the entire set of subprogram definitions from the DateModule file into her StudentRecords program file, inserting the subprograms immediately after the TYPE section and before any of her own subprograms that might call one of the DateModule subprograms.

She checks to see that the result of her editing is a legal Pascal program, and then proceeds with compilation and testing as usual.

Name Conflicts and Naming Conventions

When modules are imported into a program, it often happens that one or more of the *names* (Pascal identifiers) used in a module (for constants, global variables, data types, or subprograms) duplicates a name already in use in the program for some other purpose. Such duplicate names are termed *name conflicts*. For example, if a module uses a variable named InventoryList and the program (or another module) uses a data type named InventoryList, then importing the module causes a name conflict. The name conflict causes the compiler to refuse to compile the program.

In Pascal, the simplest way to avoid name conflicts when importing modules is to use a *naming convention*—a special way of spelling identifiers in order to minimize the possibility of name conflicts. One possible naming convention is to require that all names in a module begin with a three character abbreviation of the module name, preferably using capital letters. For example, in the DateModule, begin each identifier "DAT…".

Such a naming convention reduces the possibility of name conflicts when a module is imported. It also makes it easier to understand, in a program that uses several modules, where a particular identifier is defined within the program—whether it is defined in the program file itself or in an imported module file.

□ □

Examples of Module Definitions

The DateModule example shows a complete module that represents an abstract data type. Let's look at two modules that provide useful subprograms but no abstract data types. Both modules use "hidden" global variables to retain some data values between calls of the subprograms in the module. We use the naming convention described above—each identifier begins with a three character module abbreviation (except for formal parameters and local variables within subprograms).

When global data objects are hidden within a module, they are not listed in the subprogram headings in the *definition part* of the module that the user sees. However, they are included in the subprogram headings in the *implementation part*. Also, the PURPOSE/GOAL STATE in subprogram headings in the definition part omits mention of hidden global data objects. Notice that operations that manipulate hidden global data objects in some cases may require *no parameters*.

EXAMPLE 1: *A Performance Measurement Module*

We mentioned earlier in this chapter that a global variable might be appropriately used to *count the number of times a particular subprogram is called*. Let's extend that idea into a useful module for counting the number of times that any chosen parts of a program are executed. The module will maintain a "hidden" table (global variable) of the form shown in Figure 13.6.

FIGURE 13.6 The Hidden Table of Execution Counts

ENTRY	NAME	COUNT
1	Proc1	5
2	Fun2	127
3	LoopA	2488
4	LoopB	521
5	Proc2	33
.	.	.
.	.	.
.	.	.

Three operations will be provided by the module. We use "PFM" as the naming convention tag for the module:

PROCEDURE PFMInitializeCounts	Initialize the hidden table.
PROCEDURE PFMIncrementCount	Start a new count or increment an existing one.
PROCEDURE PFMDisplayCounts	Display the table of counts.

The definition part for this module in pseudo-code might be as follows.

MODULE DEFINITION Performance Measurement

DATA TYPES

PFMCountName: STRING [10]   An identifying string for a count.

SUBPROGRAMS

PROCEDURE PFMInitializeCounts

- NO PARAMETERS -

PURPOSE/GOAL STATE: Initialize for performance counting.

□

Note: This procedure must be called before any of the other operations in this module are used.

PROCEDURE PFMIncrementCount

(Name: PFMCountName)   IN: The name of the entry to be entered or incremented.

PURPOSE/GOAL STATE: If a previous call with Name has been made, then add one to the count for Name, otherwise enter Name with a count of one.

PROCEDURE PFMDisplayCounts

- NO PARAMETERS -

PURPOSE/GOAL STATE: Display a table of all the performance measurement counts, including the name and count for each part of the program being counted.

For the implementation of the table, we use a list of varying length. The implementation part for the module might be:

MODULE IMPLEMENTATION Performance Measurement

DEFINED CONSTANTS

PFMMAXCOUNTS = 100   Maximum number of table entries.

DATA TYPES

PFMCountName: STRING [10]   An identifying string for a count.

PFMTableEntry =   A table entry.
  RECORD
     Name: PFMCountName   Name provided by user.
     Count: Integer   Number of times executed.
  END

PFMEntryList = ARRAY [1..PFMMAXCOUNTS] OF PFMTableEntry

PFMTableType =   Global count table representation.
  RECORD
     Entries: PFMEntryList   List of table entries.
     Length: Integer   Current length of the list.
  END

GLOBAL DATA OBJECTS

PFMCountTable: PFMTableType   Global count table.

SUBPROGRAMS

PROCEDURE PFMInitializeCounts

     - NO PARAMETERS -

  GLOBALS:
     PFMCountTable: PFMTableType   OUT: Global count table.

  PURPOSE/GOAL STATE: Initialize for performance counting by setting the table length to zero.

□
Note: This procedure must be called before any of the other operations in this module are used.

ALGORITHM

Step 1. ACTIONS:
     PFMCountTable.Length := 0

PROCEDURE PFMIncrementCount

     (Name: PFMCountName)   IN: The name of the entry to be entered or incremented.

  GLOBALS:
     PFMCountTable: PFMTableType   IN/OUT: Global count table.

  PURPOSE/GOAL STATE: If a previous call with Name has been made, then add one to the count for Name in PFMCountTable, otherwise enter Name with a count of one in the table.

ALGORITHM

Step 1. PURPOSE: Search the table for Name.

GOAL STATE: Set Posn = subscript of entry if present. Otherwise set Posn = length of table + 1.

ACTIONS:

```
Posn := 1
NotFound := TRUE
WHILE (Posn <= PFMCountTable.Length) AND NotFound DO
        IF PFMCountTable.Entries [Posn].Name = Name THEN
            NotFound := FALSE
        ELSE
            Posn := Posn + 1
```

Step 2. PURPOSE/GOAL STATE: If not in table and table is not full, make a new entry. If in table, increment count for entry. If table is full, display error message and leave table unchanged.

ACTIONS:

```
IF (Posn = PFMCountTable.Length + 1)
        AND (Posn <= PFMMAXCOUNTS) THEN
    PFMCountTable.Length := Posn
    PFMCountTable.Entries [Posn].Name := Name
    PFMCountTable.Entries .Count := 1
ELSE IF Posn <= PFMCountTable.Length THEN
    PFMCountTable.Entries [Posn].Count :=
        PFMCountTable.Entries [Posn].Count + 1
ELSE
    DISPLAY:
        "ERROR: Count table full; entry ignored."
```

DATA OBJECTS

Posn: Integer	Subscript of table entry.
NotFound: Boolean	Flag for table search.

PROCEDURE PFMDisplayCounts

- NO PARAMETERS -

GLOBALS:

PFMCountTable: PFMTableType   IN: Global count table.

PURPOSE/GOAL STATE: Display a table of all the performance measurement counts, including the name and count for each part of the program being counted.

Step 1. ACTIONS:

DISPLAY: "ENTRY   NAME   COUNT"

FOR I := 1 TO PFMCountTable.Length DO
    DISPLAY: (beneath the headings)
        "⟨I⟩ ⟨PFMCountTable.Entries[I].Name⟩
        ⟨PFMCountTable.Entries[I].Count⟩"   ∎

EXAMPLE 2: *A Random Number Generator Module*

Many programs require a way to generate a sequence of "random" numbers in a given range. That is, each time the program asks for a new "random" number, it receives a number in the given range that appears to have been chosen at random. For example, if the numbers were integers in the range 0 to 100, then a "random" number sequence might be 27, 3, 82, 89, 55, 17, 99, 41, and so forth.

In a computer program, such numbers are ordinarily produced by an abstraction termed a *random number generator*, which might be implemented as a module. The random number generator is programmed to produce a set sequence of "random" numbers, starting from a particular value, called the *seed value*. If the same seed value is used on different runs of the program, then the same sequence of "random" numbers will be produced (making it easier to test the program because the same sequence of random numbers can be guaranteed on each test run).

Because the numbers are not truly chosen at random, the more accurate name is *pseudo-random number generator*—the numbers appear to be chosen at random, but actually they are computed with an algorithm just like any other sequence of data values.

Our random number generator module provides two operations that produce a pseudo-random sequence of Real values in the range from 0 to 1. We use the naming convention that every identifier in the module begins with the module abbreviation "RAN":

MODULE DEFINITION Random Number Generator

SUBPROGRAMS

PROCEDURE RANSetSeed

      (Seed: Real)   IN: New seed value, range 0 to 1.

PURPOSE/GOAL STATE: Initialize for a new random number sequence, beginning with the given seed value. If the given seed is not greater than zero and less than one, a standard seed value is substituted.

FUNCTION RANGetNextRandom

    - NO PARAMETERS -

FUNCTION VALUE: Real

PURPOSE: Return the next "random" number in the current sequence.

The implementation of the module uses a global data object, RANSaveLast-Value to store the last random value returned by RANGetNextRandom.

MODULE IMPLEMENTATION Random Number Generator

DEFINED CONSTANTS

RANSEED = 0.31415821   Well-chosen standard seed value.

GLOBAL DATA OBJECTS

RANSaveLastValue: Real   Last random value generated in the sequence.

SUBPROGRAMS

PROCEDURE RANSetSeed

        (Seed: Real)   IN: New seed value, range 0 to 1.

GLOBALS:
        RANSaveLastValue: Real   OUT: To save the seed.

PURPOSE/GOAL STATE: Initialize for a new random number sequence, beginning with the given seed value. If the given seed is not greater than zero and less than one, a standard seed value is substituted.

ALGORITHM

Step 1. ACTIONS:

    IF (Seed $>=$ 1) OR (Seed $<=$ 0) THEN
        RANSaveLastValue := RANSEED

    ELSE
        RANSaveLastValue := Seed

FUNCTION RANGetNextRandom

           - NO PARAMETERS -

FUNCTION VALUE: Real

GLOBALS:
        RANSaveLastValue: Real   IN/OUT: To save the last
                                number generated.

PURPOSE: Return the next "random" number in the current sequence.

ALGORITHM

Step 1. ACTIONS:

RANSaveLastValue :=
> ... computation to generate next value starting from the current value of RANSaveLastValue ...

FUNCTION VALUE := RANSaveLastValue

□

Note: We omit the details of how to generate the next pseudo-random value in the sequence because an appropriate algorithm is complex and not important to this example. ■

EXERCISE

13.3   Determine what extensions, if any, your Pascal system provides to aid in the definition and importation of modules.

□□□ 13.5
PROGRAM IT WITH STYLE!

When developing modules, two helpful rules of style are:

1. Use a *naming convention* for the identifiers in a module to avoid name conflicts when the module is imported into a Pascal program, and
2. Include the *definition part* of the module in pseudo-code as a *comment* at the beginning of the Pascal module file, so that the user is made aware of which parts of the module are to be "visible" and which are "hidden." Because the Pascal language does not support the difference between visible and hidden parts of a module (all parts are visible according to the rules of Pascal), it is up to the user to use the visible elements of the module only.

□□□ 13.6
PSEUDO-CODE AND PASCAL SUMMARY

The two new elements in this chapter are global data objects and modules.

□□
Global Data Objects

In pseudo-code use a global data objects list:

⟨GLOBAL DATA OBJECTS list⟩ ::=

⟨object-name⟩: ⟨data-type⟩   ⟨purpose⟩
{⟨object-name⟩: ⟨data-type⟩   ⟨purpose⟩}

WHERE

⟨object-name⟩ ::= A Pascal identifier.
⟨data-type⟩ ::= Any defined data type.
⟨purpose⟩ ::= Purpose of the data object.

In Pascal, code the GLOBAL DATA OBJECTS list as a VAR section that immediately follows the TYPE section in the program.

□ □

Subprograms that Use Global Data Objects

In pseudo-code, treat global data objects as though they were "hidden parameters," using the form:

PROCEDURE or FUNCTION ...
     (... formal parameter list ...)
GLOBALS:
     {⟨name⟩: ⟨data type⟩   ⟨classification⟩: ⟨purpose⟩}
PURPOSE/GOAL STATE: ...
PRECONDITIONS: ...

WHERE

⟨name⟩ ::=
     The Pascal identifier used to name the object in the GLOBAL DATA
     OBJECTS list.
⟨data type⟩ ::=
     The data type specified in the GLOBAL DATA OBJECTS list.
⟨classification⟩ ::= IN | OUT | IN/OUT
⟨purpose⟩ ::= Brief statement of the purpose of the global.

□ □

Modules in Pseudo-code

To define a module:

⟨MODULE-definition⟩ ::=

MODULE DEFINITION ⟨module name⟩

⟨definition part⟩

MODULE IMPLEMENTATION ⟨module-name⟩

⟨implementation part⟩

WHERE

⟨definition part⟩ ::=

A SUBPROGRAMS list containing subprogram headings.

A DATA TYPES list containing the names of abstract data types and the full definitions of other types.

A DEFINED CONSTANTS list containing the names of defined constants.

A GLOBAL DATA OBJECTS list containing the names and data types of global data objects.

The definition part contains all the elements of the module that are available for use outside the module.

⟨implementation part⟩ ::=

Complete definitions of the various elements of the SUBPROGRAMS, DATA TYPES, DEFINED CONSTANTS, and GLOBAL DATA OBJECTS lists in the definition part, together with any additional subprograms, data types, defined constants, and global data objects that are to be hidden from the user of the module.

To import a module into a program:

IMPORTED MODULES

| ⟨module name⟩ | ⟨purpose of the module⟩ |
| {⟨module name⟩ | ⟨purpose of the module⟩} |

□ □
Coding a Module in Pascal

1. Put the module code in a separate source program file, named with the module name.
2. Code the definition part of the module as a Pascal comment.
3. Code the implementation part of the module as Pascal CONST, TYPE, and VAR (for global variables) sections and a set of Pascal subprogram definitions.
4. To import a module file into a Pascal program, use an INCLUDE extension or use an editor program to copy each part of the module file into the appropriate place in the source program file.

■ ■ ■
REVIEW QUESTIONS

13.1 What is a *global data object?* How long does a global data object exist during program execution?

13.2 Contrast global data objects and parameters as methods of communicating data values among subprograms.

13.3 What does it mean to say that a global data object *retains its value* between calls of a subprogram?

13.4 What is a *scope rule* in Pascal?

13.5 Explain the Pascal scope rules that apply to global variables and local variables in subprograms.

13.6   What is the major *disadvantage* of using global data objects in a program?

13.7   What is a *side effect* of a subprogram?

13.8   Why should a global variable never be used as a substitute for a parameter?

13.9   Name and explain briefly three characteristics of a situation where a global data object might be effectively used.

13.10   What does it mean to say that a subprogram is *coupled to the representation* of a data object?

13.11   What is an *abstract data type*? What information is *hidden* within an abstract data type?

13.12   What does it mean to say that a programming language provides *encapsulation* for an abstraction?

13.13   Does Pascal provide encapsulation for the bodies of *procedures* and *functions*? Does it provide encapsulation for *abstract data types*? Explain.

13.14   What is a *module*? What are the two main parts of a module?

13.15   Explain the *strategy for program development* that modules are intended to support.

13.16   Name and briefly explain seven *advantages* provided by modules.

13.17   What information is provided in the *definition part* of a module? What information appears in the *implementation part* of the module?

13.18   How is a module coded in Pascal?

13.19   Explain the concept of *importing* a module.

13.20   Describe two ways that a module might be imported into a Pascal program.

13.21   What is a *name conflict*? Why are name conflicts likely to occur when using modules in Pascal?

13.22   What is a *naming convention*? How may a naming convention be used to avoid most name conflicts in a Pascal program that uses modules?

13.23   What is a *random number generator*?

■ ■ ■
PROGRAMMING PROBLEMS

13.1   *Stack Module.* Design, code, and test a module that provides an abstract data type StackOfReals. A *stack* is a data object similar to a list of varying length, but with a restricted set of operations available. The operations on stacks are:

- *Push* a new value onto the top of the stack. (Meaning: insert a new value at the end of the list.)
- *Pop* the top value off the stack. (Meaning: delete the last value from the list.)
- *Get the top value* from the stack. (Meaning: return a copy of the last value in the list.)
- *Test if the stack is empty.* (Meaning: test if the list is empty.)
- *Test if the stack is full.* (Meaning: test if the list has reached its maximum allowed length.)

For this module, we want a StackOfReals abstract data type that provides the above operations for a stack that contains real number values. Use 100 as the maximum number of values allowed in a stack of reals.

13.2 *Queue Module.* Design, code, and test a module that provides an abstract data type QueueOfReals. A *queue* is a data object similar to a stack (Problem 13.1) except that new values are inserted at one end of the queue, termed the *tail* of the queue, and old values are deleted from the other end, termed the *head* of the queue. The operations provided on queues are:

- *Enqueue* a new value at the tail of the queue. (Meaning: insert a new value at the tail end of the list.)
- *Dequeue* the value at the head of the queue. (Meaning: delete the value currently at the head end of the list.)
- *Get the head value* from the queue. (Meaning: return a copy of the value currently at the head end of the queue.)
- *Test if the queue is empty*. (Meaning: test if the queue contains no values.)
- *Test if the queue is full*. (Meaning: test if the queue has reached its maximum allowed length.)

For this module, we want a QueueOfReals abstract data type that provides the above operations for a queue that stores real number values. Use 100 as the maximum number of values allowed in a queue of reals.

13.3 *Word Count Module.* As part of a project to build a program for processing words and sentences, you want a module that provides a simple way to count the frequency of occurrence of various words in the text being processed. The desired operations are:

- *Count a word.* Given a string representing a word, add one to the count for that word. If the word has not been seen before, initialize its count to one.
- *Display word counts.* Display a table of all the words and their frequency counts.

Design, code, and test a WordCount module that provides these two operations.

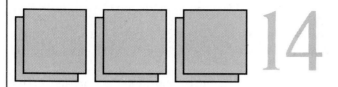

Program Performance
and Algorithm Efficiency

CHAPTER GOALS

When you have mastered the content of this chapter you should be able to:

- Distinguish between the *performance* of a program and the *efficiency* of a particular algorithm or data representation.
- Describe two ways to *measure the performance* of a working program.
- Explain the importance of the *90–10 rule* and the *critical 10 percent* in determining program performance.
- Describe how to *compare the efficiency* of alternative algorithms or data representations.
- Explain the role of the *problem size* in analyzing efficiency.
- Contrast the gains in efficiency realized by *order of* improvements, *constant factor* improvements, and *additive constant* improvements.
- Explain the meaning of the *Big-Oh notation.*
- Compare the efficiency of *linear search* and *binary search* algorithms for looking up entries in unsorted and sorted tables.
- Compare the efficiency of the *selection sort* and *insertion sort* algorithms for sorting the entries of a table.

The design of a program often raises questions of *program performance*. For example, how fast does the program need to run and how much storage is it allowed to use? A related question when designing a particular part of the program is the *efficiency* of that particular data representation or algorithm. For example, how big must that data structure be and how many steps will be required to execute that algorithm?

We use the term *program performance* to refer to a characteristic of the program *as a whole,* while reserving the term *efficiency* to refer to a characteristic of a *part* of the program. The performance of a program is related to the efficiency of its individual parts, but the relationship is more complex than it might appear.

The performance of a program is one of its important characteristics because it affects how costly the program is to use. But there are other characteristics of equal or greater importance that have been our primary focus in the preceding chapters: the *correctness* of the program, the *simplicity* of its design, and the *ease of analysis, testing, and modification*. These characteristics affect the cost of developing the program originally and of maintaining the program over its lifetime.

Improving the performance of a program often makes the program more *complex*. Additional complexity makes the program harder to design, analyze, verify, test, and modify. Thus, to improve the performance of a program, we may have to trade off other desirable characteristics. *Reasonable performance* is always a goal that deserves attention in program design, but *exceptional performance,* bought by increasing the complexity of the program, is not always a good trade-off.

In this chapter we look first at program performance and then at the efficiency of a part of a program. As an important example where efficiency is often a major goal, we investigate the representation of large tables of data and the operations of *searching* and *sorting* large tables.

□□□ 14.1
PROGRAM PERFORMANCE

Program performance is usually measured by the answers to two sets of questions:

1. *Execution speed.* How fast does the program run? Does the speed vary depending on the input data?
2. *Storage use.* How much storage does the program use?

We say that a program has "good performance" if it runs acceptably fast and uses an acceptable amount of storage. If it is too slow or takes too much storage, then it may be necessary to modify it to improve its performance.

PROGRAMS WHERE GOOD PERFORMANCE IS CRITICAL

Although programs written in a first computer science course seldom have requirements for exceptional performance (at the expense of other desirable characteristics), there are many situations in the real world where the performance of a program is a critical issue. For example:

- A program for computing and displaying the position of an airplane on an airport's radar display can take so much time that the position shown on the display is behind the actual position of the aircraft.
- A rocket control program can fail to complete its calculations in time to signal the rocket to make the next course correction.
- A program for preparing a tax return can use so much storage that it cannot be run on the personal computers for which it was designed, without an expensive memory upgrade.
- A Pascal compiler can run so slowly that when an assignment is due in a large programming class and many students are simultaneously trying to compile Pascal programs, the computer system becomes completely overloaded.
- A computer game can take so much time to choose a move that it is no fun to play; you get bored waiting for the computer to respond.

In considering the performance of a program, we are primarily interested in *gross differences* in performance among different versions of the program, not small variations. A few variables, more or less, in two versions of a program will make no noticeable difference in overall storage use, unless the variables are large arrays. A few statements, more or less, in two versions of a program will make no noticeable difference in execution time, unless the statements happen to be in a part of the program that is executed many thousands or millions of times.

To determine the performance of a program, we have two methods available:

- *Measure* the performance of a working version of the program, or
- *Analyze* the expected performance of the algorithms and data representations on which the program is based.

Before we discuss methods for measuring or analyzing performance, let's set the stage by looking at some rules of thumb that govern our approach. These rules are primarily concerned with performance in terms of *execution speed* rather than storage use. They are derived from experience measuring the performance of real programs.

□ □
Some Rules of Thumb about Performance and Efficiency

The beginning programmer often pays far too much attention to the efficiency of each data representation and algorithm in a program, with the result that the program becomes needlessly complicated with little actual effect on performance. Here are several useful rules of thumb to keep in mind when you are trying to improve the performance of a program:

1. *Major performance gains almost always come from a better choice of data representation and algorithm, not from small "tweaks" of an existing design.* Making minor changes to ("tweaking") a data representation or an algorithm in the interest of efficiency is almost always a mistake. If the change *simplifies* the representation or the algorithm then it may be desirable, but desirable because it makes the program easier to understand and modify, not because it makes the program more efficient. Any tweak that makes the representation or the algorithm more *complicated* in the interest of efficiency should be avoided—the loss in other areas is unlikely to be worth a small gain in efficiency. To get major performance improvements, you almost always have to redesign an entire "data abstraction"—a data representation and the operations that use the representation. The discussion of table organization and sorting and searching algorithms in the rest of this chapter illustrates this rule.

2. *The 90–10 Rule.* In most larger programs where performance is an issue, it has been found that only about 5–10 percent of the actions in the program use over 90 percent of the execution time of the program, and the other 90–95 percent of the actions only use less than 10 percent of the execution time. Thus, there is a small set of *critical actions* whose efficiency affects the overall performance of the program, the *critical 10 percent*. This rule of thumb is known as the *90–10 rule:*

□ **The 90–10 Rule**

In most programs more than 90 percent of the execution time is spent executing less than 10 percent of the code. Conversely, more than 90 percent of the code accounts for less than 10 percent of the execution time.

When designing the critical 10 percent of the program, the choice of the best algorithms and data representations can make a substantial difference in execution speed, but when designing the remaining 90 percent of the program, there will be little, if any, improvement in execution speed by using one data representation or algorithm over another.

3. *The "critical 10 percent" of a program is often difficult to determine, even if you designed the program yourself.* Often you cannot determine where the critical 10 percent of a program is without actually building the program and then using special tools to measure the execution speed of parts of the program as it runs. The measurements are used to pinpoint the particular parts of the program that take most of the execution time, and then those parts are examined carefully to see what performance improvements are possible. When a programmer simply makes an "educated guess" about where the critical 10 percent of a program lies, the guess is often wrong. The programmer may spend a lot of time redesigning and recoding a

CHANGING ATTITUDES ABOUT PROGRAM EFFICIENCY

In the early days of computing, in the 1950s and 1960s, computers were scarce and very expensive. Each program needed to be carefully constructed to make the most efficient use of the computer system. In those days, efficiency was an important element in the design of every program.

As computers became more widely available and less expensive, in the 1970s and 1980s, attitudes about program efficiency changed. Although good performance remained a requirement for many programs, we began to understand that concern for efficiency in most parts of a program (outside the critical 10 percent) only increased the complexity of the program, introducing more chance for error without improving performance. And for most programs, if the program were properly designed from the beginning then it would have acceptable performance without any special attention.

Complexity, more than poor performance, became the villain in program design. A program that was overly complicated was likely to be harder to build, harder to test and debug, and far more difficult to modify later than a simpler program. Thus, our attitude today is to strive for designs that are simple and straightforward and that make good use of abstractions. Performance is still important, but it is not the overriding goal that it was in the early days of computing.

part of the program, only to find that the performance of the program changes very little.

4. *The "critical 10 percent" may be in the Pascal system, not in code that you have written.* The critical 10 percent of a program may lie in the Pascal system software used by the program. READ and WRITE operations are particular culprits—a single READ or WRITE operation may take 100 to 1000 times longer to execute than a single ASSIGN action. The performance of a program is often dominated by the time to execute READ and WRITE operations. For example, one large program was measured and was found to spend 75 percent of its time executing a single READ statement that appeared within a loop. Unless you can redesign the program so that it executes fewer READ and WRITE operations (which often is impossible without changing the program's requirements), then you may be unable to improve the program's performance, regardless of how the rest of the program is designed.

Experiments to Measure Program Performance

Suppose you have a working version of a program, but its execution speed fails to meet your requirements. Your question is: *where does this program spend its time?* What subprograms, loops, READ/WRITE operations, or other actions form the critical 10 percent of this program?

The best way to answer this question is to perform some experiments to *measure* where the program spends its time when it is being run with test data that you consider typical of its intended use. There are two ways to obtain these basic performance measurements:

1. *Use a performance measurement tool.* Most computer systems provide one or more software "tools" that can be used to measure the performance of a Pascal program as it runs. These tools typically provide counts of the number of times that different actions in the program are executed. After a run, the measurements are displayed as a graph that shows the counts for each part of the program. The highest "peaks" in the graph are the parts of the program where the most time was spent during that run.

2. *"Instrument" the program yourself.* An alternative is to declare a set of counter variables (usually global variables) and insert your own statements to increment one of the counters each time a particular section of the program is executed, such as a subprogram or a loop iteration. At the end of the test run, you call a subprogram that displays the values of the counter variables. You can also use the *clock function* that is predefined in most Pascal systems to measure the elapsed time of a segment of code, such as a loop or a READ/WRITE operation. This is a crude version of what a performance measurement tool does for you more easily.

□ □
Choosing Test Data

When measuring program performance, the test data used can affect the results. Because different test data values will cause the program to execute different control paths, you must be careful to choose test data that represent a "typical" run of the program, where performance differences would matter. Often this means that the test data cannot be the same that you used during debugging. You may need large quantities of data, typical of that expected during regular use of the program.

□ □
Targeting Performance Measurements

In measuring the execution time of various parts of a program, there are several areas on which to focus attention:

- *Loops.* Within a subprogram body, focus attention on the loops, not on conditional or straight-line segments. Estimate the *number of iterations* for each loop. Focus on event controlled loops that may repeat for a long time before the event occurs and on count controlled loops where the count may get very large.
- *Nested loops.* When one loop contains a second, nested loop, the number of iterations is the *product* of the iterations of each individual loop. Always attend to nested loops.
- *READ/WRITE operations in loops.* Because READ/WRITE operations are always time consuming, focus on loops that contain these operations.
- *Subprogram calls in loops.* A subprogram body often contains a loop. If that subprogram is called within a loop in another subprogram, the effect is the same as a nested loop. Any time-consuming subprogram called within a loop should be a focus of attention.

■ *Recursive subprograms.* Recursion (Chapter 12) is another form of repetition that can be time-consuming. For any recursive subprogram, estimate the *length of the chain of recursive calls*. A long chain of recursive calls can be far more time-consuming than an equivalent number of loop iterations.

In a typical program, you can work your way around the structure chart of the program, examining individual subprograms and estimating their likely effect on program performance. Almost immediately you can usually exclude from further consideration many of the subprograms because:

■ The subprogram body contains no loops (or recursive calls), and
■ The subprogram is only called once or a few times by other subprograms during a typical run.

You are throwing out subprograms that are obviously not in the critical 10 percent. Focus your attention on measuring the performance of the remaining parts of the program.

EXERCISES

14.1   Find out what performance measurement tools are available on your Pascal system and learn to use one of them.

14.2   If you have written a program that has several subprograms and that performs a rather complicated computation:

a.   Try to *guess* where the critical 10 percent of the program lies. Pick out a few actions in the program where you would expect the program to be spending *most of its execution time*.

b.   Try to *measure* where the critical 10 percent of the program lies, either by using a performance measurement tool or by instrumenting the program yourself. How close was your guess to the actual measured critical 10 percent?

□□□ 14.2
ANALYZING EFFICIENCY

Let's shift our focus now to the *algorithms* and *data representations* used in the program. How do you analyze the efficiency of part of a program, before you have a running version of the program? Such an analysis can provide a good measure of the *gross performance* of certain key parts of the program. If you know that the key parts are likely to be in the critical 10 percent, then this analysis can be very helpful.

When you are designing the program, you are particularly interested in *comparing* the efficiency of alternative designs. Will this data representation require a lot more storage than that one? Will this algorithm execute many more operations than that one? The comparisons may help you to choose a design that makes a particular part of the program efficient, and thus that may ultimately contribute to better program performance.

□ □
Time and Space Efficiency

We are concerned with both the *time efficiency* of an algorithm—how fast does it run—and its *space efficiency*—how much storage does it require. In comparing alternative algorithms and data representations, we often find that we can trade time efficiency for space efficiency, or vice versa. That is, we can make the algorithm run faster if we are willing to use more storage space, or we can use less storage space if we are willing to allow the algorithm to take more time.

EXAMPLE Suppose that a lengthy calculation is required to compute an array of data values, which are then used in a part of the program. Later, another lengthy calculation is required to compute a second array of data values that are used in the same part of the program. Ordinarily, we would use two arrays to store the two sets of values. However, if the program ran very fast but used too much storage, and if we never needed both sets of values at the same time, we might choose to use only a single array, and recompute the first set of values if we needed them again after we had already stored the second set in the array. We have traded increased execution time for decreased storage. ■

□ □
The Problem Size, N

In analyzing efficiency, we assume that there is some number N that represents the "size of the problem." In most cases, N is the number of elements in an array that is large enough to store the data values of interest. N might also be the number of input data values being processed or some other measure of "problem size." For this section, consider N as an array size.

Usually, we are interested in differences among algorithms and data representations that only matter when N, the problem size, is "large." In a typical situation, N = 100 or more. For small problems, with N under 100, it will usually be difficult to find differences that noticeably affect program performance. Thus, we concentrate on situations where there is a reasonably large amount of data involved. As our standard example, we use N = 1000. In many situations where performance is a key issue, N will be much larger, in the tens or hundreds of thousands.

EXAMPLE Suppose that you have two algorithms for finding the largest value in a list of N numbers. The first algorithm, the slow one, requires execution of *twice as many actions* as the second, the fast one. Let's suppose that:

■ The fast algorithm uses four operations for each of the N values and the slow algorithm uses eight operations.

■ Each operation takes approximately 1 millisecond (one thousandth of a second, written 1 msec.)

Now suppose you apply both algorithms to arrays of 10 data values, 1000 values, and 10,000 values (N = 10, 1000, 10,000). We estimate the performance:

	Fast Algorithm		Slow Algorithm		
N	*Number of Operations*	*Estimated Execution Time*	*Number of Operations*	*Estimated Execution Time*	*Approximate Time Difference*
10	40	40 msec.	80	80 msec.	<1/10 sec.
1000	4000	4 sec.	8000	8 sec.	4 sec.
10,000	40,000	40 sec.	80,000	80 sec.	40 sec.

For 10 values, the difference in execution speed, less than 1/10 of a second, would not be noticeable to the user (unless the actions were repeated hundreds of times). For 1000 values, the four second difference would be noticeable, but probably not overly annoying. But for 10,000 values, the 40 second difference might make the slow version unacceptable compared to the fast one.

□ □
Three Classes of Performance Improvements

We are interested in distinguishing three classes of performance improvements:

1. *"Order of" improvements.* The most dramatic improvements from one algorithm or data representation to another come when the improved version *gets better as the problem size gets larger*. For example, for N = 100, the new version might be *ten times* better than the old, but for N = 1000, the new version might be a *hundred times* better. Such improvements are termed *order of* improvements.

2. *"Constant factor" improvements.* Far less dramatic, but still important, improvements come when the improved version is a *constant factor* better. For example, the new algorithm might be two times faster or ten times faster than the old. Notice that the *amount of improvement* does not change as the problem size gets larger—it's always two times better or ten times better, regardless of the problem size.

3. *"Additive constant" improvements.* The most minor improvements are those that are *independent of the problem size*. For example, the new version might always take exactly two fewer operations or use five fewer simple variables than the old. Here we are adding or subtracting a constant number of operations or storage locations. Such improvements are termed *additive constant* improvements.

"Order of" Improvements

Suppose you compared two algorithms for searching a telephone directory for a given name:

- *Algorithm 1*. Begin on Page 1, Column 1, and compare each name in the directory against the given name, continuing through the entries in sequence until you find the name you want.
- *Algorithm 2*. Open the directory in the middle, and compare the first name on the page with the given name. If it's the same, quit. If it comes before the given name, take the last half of the directory and repeat the same process. If it comes after the given name, take the first half of the directory and repeat the same process.

Now suppose the directory has 10 entries. Algorithm 1 would take about five steps on the average. Algorithm 2 would average about three. Not much difference.

But if the directory had 10,000 entries (like an average small town telephone book), then Algorithm 1 would take about 5000 steps on the average and Algorithm 2 would average about 13 steps. A dramatic difference!

Algorithm 1 is termed an *order of N* algorithm, written $O(N)$, because the number of steps required is proportional to the problem size, N. If the problem size *doubles*, so that N is twice as large, then Algorithm 1 will require *twice as many steps*.

Algorithm 2 is termed an *order of log N* algorithm, written $O(log_2 N)$, because the number of steps required is proportional to the logarithm (base 2) of N. That is, the number of steps is related to N by the formula:

$$2^{\langle \text{number of steps} \rangle} = N \text{ (approximately)}$$

This formula says that if the problem size *doubles*, Algorithm 2 will only require *one more step*. That is the reason that Algorithm 2 is such a dramatic improvement over Algorithm 1 (and the reason why no one ever uses Algorithm 1 to search a telephone directory!)

There are several *order of* classifications of algorithms that appear frequently and are worth remembering:

- *Order of $log_2 N$, written $O(log_2 N)$*. The number of steps (or the storage used) is related to the problem size by the formula above. Remember the rule: *if the problem size doubles, the algorithm takes one more step* (or the array requires one more element).
- *Order of N, written $O(N)$*. The number of steps or the storage used is directly proportional to the problem size. Remember the rule: *if the problem size doubles, the algorithm takes twice as many steps* (or the array must be twice as large).
- *Order of $N log_2 N$, written $O(N log_2 N)$*. The number of steps or storage used is growing *faster than the problem size*, but not a lot faster. Remember the rule: *if the problem size doubles, the algorithm takes more than twice as many steps, but not a lot more* (or the array must be more than twice as large, but not a lot more).

- *Order of N^2, written $O(N^2)$.* The number of steps or storage used is proportional to the square of the problem size, N∗N. Remember the rule: *if the problem size doubles then the algorithm takes four times as many steps* (or the array requires four times as many elements).

and a final category, the best of all:

- *Constant time or space, written $O(1)$.* The number of steps or storage used does *not* depend on the problem size at all. Remember the rule: *if the problem size doubles, the algorithm still takes the same number of steps* (or the array stays the same size).

The notation that is used for designating these different classifications is sometimes called the *Big-Oh notation* because of its use of a capital O(...) to mean "order of".

To get a better feel for the dramatic differences in speed among algorithms in these different categories, look at Tables 14.1 and 14.2. In Table 14.1, we show the approximate number of operations executed by an algorithm with an efficiency in each of the $\log_2 N$, $N \log_2 N$, and N^2 classes, for various problem sizes. In Table 14.2, we translate these numbers into a form that may be more easily understandable: the approximate length of time you would have to *sit in front of your computer*

TABLE 14.1 "Order of" Differences in Algorithm Operation Counts

Problem Size	Operations Executed by an Algorithm Whose Efficiency Is:		
N	$O(\log_2 N)$	$O(N \log_2 N)$	$O(N^2)$
10	3	30	100
100	6	600	10,000
1000	9	9000	1 million
10,000	13	130,000	100 million
100,000	16	1,600,000	10 billion
1 million	19	19 million	1 trillion

TABLE 14.2 "Order of" Differences in Algorithm Execution Speeds
One operation = approximately 1 millisecond (1000 ops/second)
(FAST means under one second)

N	$O(\log_2 N)$	$O(N)$	$O(N \log_2 N)$	$O(N^2)$
10	FAST	FAST	FAST	FAST
100	FAST	FAST	FAST	10 sec.
1000	FAST	1 sec.	9 sec.	16 min.
10,000	FAST	10 sec.	2 min.	27 hours
100,000	FAST	2 min.	26 min.	4 months
1 million	FAST	16 min.	5 hours	31 years

terminal waiting for an algorithm in the different classes to finish, for the same range of problem sizes and assuming that each operation takes about 1 millisecond.

Notice that on this time scale (1 millisecond/operation) the $O(N^2)$ algorithm is slow even for $N = 100$, and for larger N it rapidly becomes hopelessly slow. However, the $O(N)$ algorithm is still reasonably fast up to $N = 10,000$ and the $O(\log_2 N)$ algorithm is still lightning fast for $N =$ one million.

Our time scale here is actually considerably slower than you might see on most computers. *One microsecond/operation* (1000 times faster) is closer to the speed of most machines today. At these speeds, an $O(N^2)$ algorithm looks considerably better. For example, for $N = 10,000$ it would require a time of less than 2 minutes instead of 27 hours.

□ □

Constant Factor Improvements

The second category of improvements are important when comparing algorithms or data representations *within the same "order of" class*. These differences are stated as "K times better than" (or worse than), where K is some constant multiplier. For example, you might say "Algorithm A is five times better than Algorithm B (regardless of the problem size)" or "Representation 1 takes one-half the storage of Representation 2 (regardless of the problem size)."

Table 14.3 shows how such constant factor improvements might change the speed of an $O(N)$ algorithm. Notice that if the constant factor is large, these performance improvements are substantial for large problem sizes, but less dramatic than *order of* improvements.

□ □

Additive Constant Improvements

When an algorithm is improved by taking out some operations that are only executed once or a few times, or by deleting one or more simple variables, records, or small arrays, then it has been improved by a small constant amount of time or space, independent of the problem size. Such improvements may be worthwhile if they *simplify* the algorithm or data representation, but for large problem sizes they have

TABLE 14.3 Constant Factor Improvements in Algorithm Speed
One operation = approximately 1 millisecond (1000 ops/second)
(FAST means under one second)

N	Original Algorithm	2 times Faster	5 times Faster	10 times Faster	100 times Faster
100	FAST	FAST	FAST	FAST	FAST
1000	1 sec.	FAST	FAST	FAST	FAST
10,000	10 sec.	5 sec.	2 sec.	1 sec.	FAST
100,000	100 sec.	50 sec.	20 sec.	10 sec.	1 sec.
1 million	16+ min.	8+ min.	3+ min.	100 sec.	10 sec.

no major effect on the efficiency of the algorithm or data representation. These are the improvements that usually fall in the category of "tweaking" the program design.

The importance of these small changes is often in another direction. Instead of trying to *decrease* the time or space used by an additive constant, we often try to *increase* the time or space used by a small amount in order to get a *constant factor* or even an *order of* improvement in the overall algorithm. In the next section we see an example of just such a situation when we insert a "sentinel" value in a table (using a constant amount of extra space and time) in order to simplify a search loop. The loop runs two or three times faster after the change (a constant factor improvement), so we have paid a little and gained a lot.

Where to Find Improvements

Order of improvements usually come from a *complete redesign* of a data representation and the operations that use the representation. To get these dramatic improvements you often have to view the problem differently. In the next section, we see one of the simplest cases of such an improvement—changing a table from an *unsorted* to a *sorted* set of entries so that we can search the table using an $O(\log_2 N)$ algorithm instead of an $O(N)$ algorithm.

Constant factor speed improvements usually arise from *taking something out of a loop whose iterations depend on the problem size,* so that there are fewer operations or tests to perform on each iteration. If the original loop used ten operations or tests on each iteration and you can remove half of them, then the loop should run about twice as fast.

Additive constant speed improvements usually arise from deleting operations that are *outside* of a loop that depends on the problem size, such as operations that occur before loop entry or after loop exit.

Average Case and Worst Case Efficiency

Sometimes a given algorithm always executes the same number of operations for a given problem size, regardless of the particular data values used. For example, consider a loop that sums the elements of an array A of size N:

```
Sum := 0
FOR I := 1 TO N DO
    Sum := Sum + A[I]
```

This loop always executes N additions and assignments, regardless of the values in A. Notice that the execution path chosen is determined only by the value of N, not by the values in A.

More commonly, an algorithm will choose a different execution path depending on the particular data values that it is processing. For example, consider this loop to find the first zero element in array A:

```
NotFound := TRUE
I := 1
WHILE (I <= N) AND NotFound DO
        IF A[I] = 0 THEN
                NotFound := FALSE
        ELSE
                I := I + 1
```

Depending on the values in A, the loop may execute only one iteration, two iterations, or in the worst case, N iterations. On the average, we would expect to search about halfway through the array before finding a zero value, executing about N/2 iterations.

When the execution path chosen depends on the particular data values (and not just on the problem size), then the execution time of the algorithm varies. For the same value of N, the algorithm may be very efficient for some data values and very inefficient for others. In such circumstances we focus on two questions:

- *Worst case execution time*. What is the longest that the algorithm might run, if we choose data values that make the algorithm take the *longest possible execution path?*
- *Average execution time*. For the expected range of possible data values, what is the average execution time that we can expect?

Usually we do not care about the *best case* execution time, only the worst case and the average. Notice that if the execution path depends only on the value of N and not on the data values used then the average execution time and the worst case time are always the same.

In general, analysis of an algorithm to predict its average or worst case execution time is difficult. In the next section, we show some simple cases where such analysis is relatively straightforward and produces some useful comparisons. However, even in these cases we must make many simplifying assumptions, such as assuming that all operations take about the same amount of time (so that we can simply count them in order to predict relative execution times). On a particular computer or for particular kinds of data, some of these assumptions may be invalid.

Methods for the careful analysis of different algorithms have been developed rather recently in the history of computer science, beginning in the late 1960s with the work of Donald Knuth. Many common algorithms have now been carefully analyzed, but there are many more that are still poorly understood. And of course new algorithms are being invented all the time.

EXERCISES

14.3 In the following segment:

```
NotFound := TRUE
Posn := 0
I := 1
WHILE (I <= N) AND NotFound DO
```

```
        IF A[I] = 0 THEN
                NotFound := FALSE
                Posn := I
        ELSE
                I := I + 1
```

a. If you delete the variable Posn and both the assignments to Posn, would you expect to get an "order of," a "constant factor" or an "additive constant" improvement in execution time? In storage space?

b. If you delete the exit test "I <= N" would you get an "order of," a "constant factor" or an "additive constant" improvement in execution time?

14.4 What would be the *order of* the execution time of each of the following loop segments:

a. A loop that processes only *every third element* of an array of size N, but applies the same sequence of operations to each element processed.

b. A loop that processes two arrays of size N, and for every element of the first array, it compares that element against every element of the second array.

c. A loop that processes two arrays, one of size N and the other of size $\log_2$ N. For each element of the first array, it multiplies that element with every element of the second array and sums the products.

14.5 For each of the following segments, determine if the number of loop iterations depends on the data values in the array A or only on the value of N:

```
a.    NotFound := TRUE
      Posn := 0
      I := 1
      WHILE I <= N DO
            IF A[I] = 0 THEN
                    NotFound := FALSE
                    Posn := I
            ELSE
                    I := I + 1
```

```
b.    Posn := 0
      I := 1
      WHILE I <= N DO
            IF A[I] = 0 THEN
                    Posn := I
                    I := N + 1
            ELSE
                    I := I + 1
```

□□□ **14.3**
TABLES: REPRESENTATIONS AND OPERATIONS

Many programs organize data into *tables,* just as you would in the real world—tables of sales data, tables of student grade information, tables of weather data, and so forth. A table is distinguished from a *list* of data by the operations that are used. For a table, the most important operation is to *look up* an entry in the table, given a *key* value.

In Chapter 6 we looked at the representation of simple tables by using Pascal arrays in which the *subscripts* represented the key values. The look up operation could then be written:

$$\langle table \rangle \ [\langle key\text{-}value \rangle]$$

to select the entry for a given key value.

Most tables are more complex than this simple representation allows. A familiar example is in the "white pages" of a telephone book. An *entry* consists of a name, address, and telephone number. The *key* value in each entry is the name. The look up operation uses an algorithm that *searches* the table for a given name. The search algorithm relies on the fact that the key values—the names—have been *sorted* into alphabetic order.

In this brief description you see the major elements of the representation and use of a table of data: the table must be represented so that the look up operation can be performed easily and efficiently, which often requires that the table entries be *sorted* so that an efficient *search* algorithm can be used. Thus, we are interested in algorithms for *searching* and *sorting* the entries of a table, given a particular representation for the table.

Searching and sorting algorithms for tables have a long history in computer science. There are dozens of algorithms and table representations, each with different time and space efficiencies and other properties. Because these algorithms are often in the critical 10 percent of large programs, many of them have been carefully analyzed.

□ □

Data Representation for a Table

To allow us to focus on the efficiency of some simple algorithms for searching and sorting a table, we choose a particular data representation for a table in this chapter. We represent a table as a *list of varying length,* as discussed in Chapter 6. We use an array to store the entries of the table. Each entry is a record in which one of the fields is the key value. We use integer key values, but other types of keys would not change the algorithms. The contents of the other fields in an entry are not important for this discussion.

The number N that represents the "problem size" in this situation is the number of entries in the table. Because the number of entries changes as new entries are inserted, we use a defined constant, MAXN, to represent the total number of array elements and use N to represent the current number of table entries at any given time.

In pseudo-code, our table representation would be:

DEFINED CONSTANTS

MAXN = ?   Maximum number of table entries.

DATA TYPES

```
Entry =
    RECORD
        Key: Integer          Key used in look up operation.
        ...                   Any number of other fields.
    END
EntryList = ARRAY [1..MAXN] OF Entry
EntryRange = 0..MAXN

TableType =
    RECORD
        Entries: EntryList    The table itself.
        N: EntryRange         Current number of table entries.
    END
```

In our tables, we insist that there be no two entries with the same key value. Thus, given a key value, the look up operation will always return a single entry in the table, or none at all.

Within this basic representation for tables, we consider only one major option: Are the table entries to be *sorted* so that the key values are ordered, beginning with the entry with the smallest key value and continuing to the Nth entry with the largest key value? The alternative is to leave the entries *unsorted,* so that the key values appear in no particular order.

□ □

Operations on Tables

As with any data type, the operations that are defined on a particular type of table determine what representation will be best for that table in a computer program. For this chapter, we consider only two operations, Search and Insert, each represented by a subprogram:

FUNCTION Search

      (T: TableType   IN: The table to search.
      DesiredKey: Integer)   IN

FUNCTION VALUE: EntryRange   Position of the entry or zero.

PURPOSE: Return the subscript of the entry in table T with the given DesiredKey value. If not in the table, return zero.

PRECONDITION: The table has at least one entry.

PROCEDURE Insert

      (T: TableType   IN/OUT: The table to modify.
      E: Entry)   IN: The entry to insert.

PURPOSE/GOAL STATE: Insert E in table T. If the table is full, display an error message and ignore E.

PRECONDITION: No entry in T has the same key value as E.

Although we only consider the Search and Insert operations here, other operations may be needed for particular kinds of tables. For example:

- *Display*. Display the table entries in ascending or descending order of key values.
- *Delete*. Delete an entry, given its key value.
- *Modify*. Modify an existing entry in some way.
- *Range search*. Find all the entries in the table whose key values fall within some specified range.

These additional operations may affect how the table is best represented.

□ □
Assumptions About the Use of the Operations

Some of our design decisions are based on how often we expect the Search and Insert operations to be used and on what we assume about the relative sequence of the operations. Let's make these assumptions about the program that uses Search and Insert:

- The program builds the table first, using N calls on the Insert procedure.
- The program then uses the Search function exclusively, calling it many more than N times.

□ □ □ **14.4**
UNSORTED TABLES AND LINEAR SEARCH

Let's begin with the *unsorted* table representation, leaving the entries in no particular order of key values. Insert and Search may be represented by straightforward algorithms:

□
Insert.   Because we do not care about the order of the table entries, we can always insert a new entry at the end of the table. Our procedure is:

PROCEDURE Insert

(T: TableType	IN/OUT: The table to modify.
E: Entry)	IN: The entry to insert.

PURPOSE/GOAL STATE: Insert E in table T. If the table is full, display an error message and ignore E.

PRECONDITION: No entry in T has the same key value as E.

ALGORITHM

Step 1.   PURPOSE/GOAL STATE: If the table is not full, increment N and insert E at the Nth position. Otherwise, display an error message and do nothing.

ACTIONS:

```
IF T.N < MAXN THEN
    T.N := T.N + 1
    T.Entries [N] := E        — copies entire entry
ELSE
    DISPLAY: "ERROR: Table full; entry ignored."
```

DATA OBJECTS

- none -

□

Search.   To find an entry with a given key in an unsorted table, we use a *linear search*—begin with the first entry and search through the entries in sequence until we find the desired one or reach the end of the table. The Search procedure might be written:

FUNCTION Search

(T: TableType	IN: The table to search.
DesiredKey: Integer)	IN

FUNCTION VALUE: EntryRange   Position of the entry or zero.

PURPOSE: Return the subscript of the entry in table T with the given DesiredKey value. If not in the table, return zero.

PRECONDITION: The table has at least one entry.

ALGORITHM

Step 1.   PURPOSE/GOAL STATE: Do a linear search through the table entries. If not found, set NotFound = TRUE. Otherwise set NotFound = FALSE and I = position of the entry.

ACTIONS:

```
I := 1
NotFound := TRUE
WHILE (I <= T.N) AND NotFound DO
    IF T.Entries[I].Key = DesiredKey THEN
        NotFound := FALSE
    ELSE
        I := I + 1
```

Step 2.   PURPOSE/GOAL STATE: Test whether the given key matched a key in the table and set the function value appropriately.

ACTIONS:

```
IF NotFound THEN
    FUNCTION VALUE := 0
ELSE
    FUNCTION VALUE := I
```

DATA OBJECTS

NotFound: Boolean   Loop exit flag.
I: Integer   Loop subscript variable.

□ □
Analyzing the Efficiency of the Operations on Unsorted Tables

Our efficiency analysis would proceed as follows:

1. *Insert*. Efficiency (Insert) = O(1).
The insert operation takes the same amount of time to execute, regardless of the size of the table, so it is a constant time operation.

2. *Search*. Efficiency (Search) = O(N).
The WHILE loop in Step 1 is the only part of the algorithm whose execution depends on the problem size, N. The number of loop iterations varies depending on whether the desired key is found in the table, and which entry matches it if so. However, regardless of whether and where the key is found, the speed of the search operation in general depends on the number of entries in the table. If there are twice as many table entries, then we would expect the search operation to take twice as long on the average and in the worst case.

For this Search algorithm, we can be more precise about the number of comparison operations (tests) executed. Notice that checking a single entry takes three tests, to compare the desired key against the key in the entry, to test if we are at the end of the table, and to test the NotFound flag. From this fact, we can determine:

1. *Cost of an unsuccessful search* = 3 * N comparisons always.
If the entry is not in the table, we have to check every entry before we stop. There are N entries and each takes three tests, so the total number of comparisons is 3*N.

2. *Cost of a successful search* = 1.5 * N comparisons on the average.
If the entry is in the table, then we might find it in the first position or in the last position. On the average, we would expect to search about halfway down the table before finding an entry. Checking each entry takes three tests, so the average cost is $1/2 * (3*N) = 1.5*N$.

The cost of step 2 in the linear search algorithm is ignored, as is the cost of the actions in the startup segment for the loop. These actions are only executed once, so they only add a constant amount to the time of the algorithm, regardless of the value of N.

Using a "Sentinel Key"

Let's look at a simple way to improve the search algorithm for this table. The change will speed the algorithm by a *constant factor*. The resulting search algorithm will still be O(N), but it will be approximately *three times as fast* as the original.

The change requires that we make two additions to the algorithm that *slow* the algorithm by a constant amount and that *increase* the storage by a constant amount:

1. First, we add one extra element to the table array by increasing MAXN by one. This extra element, however, *will never be used for a real entry,* so the table will still be able to store the same maximum number of entries. That is, we never allow N to reach the new value of MAXN. Only MAXN-1 entries are now allowed in the table before we declare it full.

2. Before we begin a search, we *insert the desired key* into the *first free entry* in the table. We do this by executing the assignment:

$$T.Entries[T.N+1].Key := DesiredKey$$

The inserted key is termed a *sentinel key*. Our restriction 1 guarantees that there is always a free entry in which to make this insertion even if the table is full. Figure 14.1 shows the idea of a sentinel key.

FIGURE 14.1 Inserting a Sentinel Key Before Starting a Search

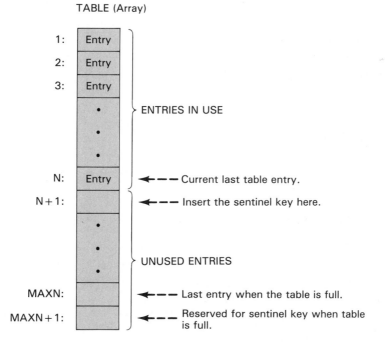

Now we make another simple change in the search algorithm: we *delete the test for the end of the table,* the loop exit test "I <= T.N". We can do this because we know that the search will always terminate either by finding a matching key in a table entry or by finding the sentinel key value that we just inserted.

Deleting the test for the end of the table simplifies the loop considerably because we no longer need the flag variable. The test for the given key may be used directly as the loop exit test. The revised search algorithm is:

ALGORITHM

Step 1. PURPOSE/GOAL STATE: Do a linear search through the entries. Insert a sentinel key first.

ACTIONS:

```
T.Entries[T.N+1].Key := DesiredKey
I := 1
WHILE T.Entries[I].Key <> DesiredKey DO
        I := I + 1
```

Step 2. PURPOSE/GOAL STATE: Test whether the given key matched a key in the table or the sentinel key. Set the function value appropriately.

ACTIONS:

```
IF I = N+1 THEN
    FUNCTION VALUE := 0
ELSE
    FUNCTION VALUE := I
```

□ □
Efficiency of a Search using a Sentinel Key

Let's analyze this new search algorithm. We focus our attention on the WHILE loop. The startup part of Step 1 and all of Step 2 are only executed once, so they change only additive constants of the loop execution time.

The new WHILE loop is substantially faster. Checking each table entry now requires only one comparison operation instead of three, and the loop body contains the same assignment used before. Our conclusion is that the new algorithm should be approximately three times faster:

1. *Cost of an unsuccessful search* = N+1 comparisons always.
2. *Cost of a successful search* = N/2 comparisons on the average.

A nice trade-off! We added a constant increase in storage and a new action in the startup segment for the loop and deleted two tests within the loop itself to gain a threefold speedup of the algorithm.

EXERCISES

14.6 Does it ever matter *which direction* you search an unsorted table? What if you started with the Nth entry and worked back toward the first entry? You could use a zeroth entry to hold the sentinel key.

a. Describe a situation where such a "backward search" might be more efficient on the average than a "forward search."

b. The comparison of backward search and forward search brings out a *hidden assumption* about the frequency of use of the Search operation for *particular key values*. What is the hidden assumption for a situation where forward search is better than backward search? For a situation where the direction of search makes no difference?

□□□ 14.5
SORTED TABLES AND BINARY SEARCH

In the real world, why do we usually prefer that the entries in a table, such as a telephone directory, be *sorted* so that the key values appear in an increasing (or decreasing) sequence? The obvious answer is "because it makes searching the table fast and simple." Let's look at this table representation in more detail.

With a sorted table, the simplest search algorithm is termed *binary search*. The idea behind binary search is to use the ordering of the key entries in the table to speed the search. You begin at the *middle* of the table, and compare the desired key against the middle entry. Based on that comparison, you choose either the first half of the table or the last half (two halves means a "binary" split of the table, hence "binary search"). You then compare the desired key against the middle entry of the chosen half, and split that half into two parts. You continue splitting the table into smaller and smaller parts until you hit the entry you want, or you find the place where the entry would be if it were in the table, but it isn't.

The binary search algorithm is slightly more complicated than the linear search algorithm. You need to keep two variables as "pointers" to the start and end of that part of the table you are currently considering. We call these pointer variables, Left and Right. Initially, we set Left = 1 and Right = N. After the first split of the table, either Left = N/2 + 1 or Right = N/2 − 1, because only half the table remains to be searched. Each time we split the table, we either move Left closer to Right or Right closer to Left, until they meet.

In pseudo-code, the binary search algorithm might be written:

FUNCTION Search

        (T: TableType   IN: The table to search.
        DesiredKey: Integer)   IN

    FUNCTION VALUE: EntryRange)   Position of the entry or zero.

    PURPOSE: Return the subscript of the entry in table T with the given Key value. If not in the table, return zero.

    PRECONDITION: The table has at least one entry.

ALGORITHM

Step 1. PURPOSE/GOAL STATE: Split the table in half and test the key of the middle entry. If not equal to DesiredKey, take the left or right half, depending on whether the middle key is greater or less than DesiredKey. Repeat the process until you find an entry with a key = DesiredKey or there is nothing left to split.

ACTIONS:

```
Left := 1
Right := T.N

REPEAT
    Middle := (Left + Right) DIV 2
    IF DesiredKey < T.Entries[Middle].Key THEN
        Right := Middle − 1
    ELSE
        Left := Middle + 1
UNTIL (DesiredKey = T.Entries[Middle].Key) OR (Left > Right)
```

Step 2. PURPOSE/GOAL STATE: Test if the middle entry on the last split contained the desired key, and set the function value appropriately.

ACTIONS:

```
IF DesiredKey = T.Entries[Middle].Key THEN
    FUNCTION VALUE := Middle
ELSE
    FUNCTION VALUE := 0
```

DATA OBJECTS

Left: Integer	Position of the left end of the part of the table being searched.
Right: Integer	Position of the right end of the part of the table being searched.
Middle: Integer	The middle element of the part of the table being searched.

□ □
Analysis of the Binary Search Algorithm

Binary search is typical of what is termed a *divide and conquer* algorithm. With each loop iteration, we divide the remaining part of the table in half, and completely avoid searching one of the two halves. Thus after one iteration, we throw half the table out and never search it. After the next iteration, we throw out half the remainder = 1/4 of the total table. Then 1/8 on the next iteration, then 1/16, and so forth. We "conquer" the table search problem by dividing the table repeatedly.

TABLE 14.4 Comparing Linear Search and Binary Search (worst case execution paths)

	Iterations for a Linear Search		Iterations for a Binary Search	
Table Size	*If Found*	*If Not Found*	*If Found*	*If Not Found*
10	10	11	4	4
100	100	101	7	7
1000	1000	1001	10	10
10,000	10,000	10,001	14	14
100,000	100,000	100,001	17	17
1,000,000	1,000,000	1,000,001	20	20

Efficiency (Search) = $O(\log_2 N)$ using the binary search algorithm. In binary search, if the table is twice as big, it only adds one more step to the search, which is the basic characteristic of an $O(\log_2 N)$ algorithm.

A more detailed analysis of the binary search algorithm (not detailed here) can give a more precise result. For an unsuccessful search, the algorithm never uses more than $\log_2 N + 1$ iterations of the REPEAT loop. For a successful search, in the worst case it would also require $\log_2 N + 1$ iterations. Table 14.4 shows a "worst case" comparison of binary search and linear search (with a sentinel key).

The comparison of linear search and binary search is not entirely fair—notice that each iteration in binary search takes slightly longer than each iteration of linear search because there are more operations to perform. Regardless, the difference in the *number of iterations* for large values of N is so dramatic that even if each iteration took many more steps, we would still choose binary search over linear search.

EXERCISE

14.7 Determine how a *linear search* algorithm could be improved if the table entries were sorted. Compare the efficiency of this algorithm with:

- Linear search of an unsorted table.
- Binary search of a sorted table.

□□□ 14.6
BUILDING A SORTED TABLE

Clearly there is a dramatic improvement in the efficiency of the search algorithm when the table is sorted. But how much does it cost to sort the table? And how does the Insert operation work if the table must be kept sorted?

The second question is easy to answer because we have assumed that all the table entries are inserted before the first Search operation. This means that the Insert operation may still leave the entries unsorted, as before. Then, before the first Search operation, we call a Sort procedure to sort the table.

The heading for this Sort procedure might be:

PROCEDURE Sort

       (T: TableType)   IN/OUT: Table to be sorted.

      PURPOSE/GOAL STATE: Sort the entries in T so that they appear in T in increasing sequence of key values.

Choosing a good sorting algorithm is now the question. There are dozens of different ways to sort a table. Let's look at two of the simplest ones.

□ □

Selection Sort

In Chapter 10, we used a *selection sort* as an example of a nested loop. In the selection sort algorithm, you begin by finding (selecting) the table entry with the smallest key. You put it in the first position by swapping it with the current first entry. Then you find the entry with the smallest remaining key and swap it into the second position, and so forth. To find the smallest remaining key on each iteration, you have to scan all the remaining unsorted values in the array.

A selection sort uses two nested loops. Both are count controlled. The outer loop counts from 1 to the $N - 1$, the next to the last table entry, say using a subscript variable I. I represents the entry that will be filled next (with the entry with the next smallest key). The inner loop counts from I+1 to N, say using subscript variable J. J represents the entry whose key is about to be checked to see if it is the smallest key remaining in the unsorted part of the table. Figure 14.2 illustrates how a selection sort works.

The selection sort algorithm in pseudo-code might look like this:

PROCEDURE Sort

       (T: TableType)   IN/OUT: Table to be sorted.

      PURPOSE/GOAL STATE: Sort the entries in T so that they appear in T in increasing sequence of key values.

      ALGORITHM

Step 1.   PURPOSE/GOAL STATE: Use a selection sort to sort the entries in T.

      ACTIONS:

        FOR I := 1 TO T.N $-$ 1 DO

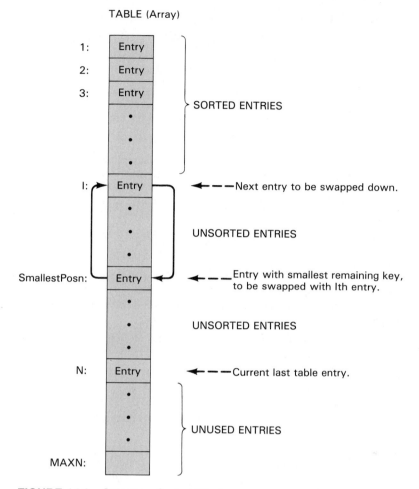

TABLE (Array)

FIGURE 14.2 Selection Sort at Work

Step 1a. PURPOSE/GOAL STATE: Find the subscript of the entry with the smallest remaining key in the unsorted part of the array, and store it in SmallestPosn.

ACTIONS:

```
SmallestPosn := I
FOR J := I+1 TO T.N DO
    IF T.Entries[J].Key < T.Entries[SmallestPosn].Key THEN
        SmallestPosn := J
```

Step 1b. PURPOSE/GOAL STATE: Swap the entry with the smallest remaining key into the Ith position in the array, unless I has the smallest key.

ACTIONS:

IF I <> SmallestPosn THEN
    SmallestEntry := T.Entries[SmallestPosn]
    T.Entries[SmallestPosn] := T.Entries[I]
    T.Entries[I] := SmallestEntry

DATA OBJECTS

I: Integer	Outer loop subscript variable.
J: Integer	Inner loop subscript variable.
SmallestEntry: Entry	Temporary storage during swap.
SmallestPosn: Integer	Subscript of entry with smallest key.

□ □
Analyzing the Efficiency of Selection Sort

First, notice that the number of iterations of both the outer and inner loops depend only on N, the problem size, and not on the particular values in the array being sorted. Immediately we can conclude that the number of iterations is proportional to N∗N, or $O(N^2)$.

In analyzing this sort algorithm, we are concerned with two operations in particular:

- *Comparisons*. The number of times two key values are compared by the algorithm.
- *Moves*. The number of times an entry must be copied from one array element or temporary storage variable to another.

Looking at where these operations appear in the two loops:

□

Comparisons.   The only comparison operation is within the inner loop. Because the inner loop makes $O(N^2)$ iterations, the number of comparisons is the same.

□

Moves.   The move operations occur in the swap in step 1b, with three moves per swap. Because this step is in the outer loop but outside the inner loop, it must be executed N-1 times. So the number of moves is 3∗(N-1), which is O(N).

To summarize our analysis, the selection sort takes $O(N^2)$ comparisons and O(N) moves to sort the array.

□ □
Insertion Sort

Let's look at another straightforward sorting algorithm, the *insertion sort*. Think of the way that you might sort a hand of playing cards into sequence. Compare the first two cards, and reverse their order if needed. Then find where the third card fits among the first two, and insert it in its proper place. Then find where the fourth card fits among the first three, and insert it, and so forth.

Our program version of this algorithm uses an outer loop that moves down the table, taking each entry in turn, starting with the second entry. For each entry, an inner loop moves *backward* through the table (toward the first entry), comparing the key in the chosen entry against the key in each preceding entry. If the preceding entry key is greater than the chosen key, then the preceding entry is moved down one place in the table (leaving a hole immediately before it). If the key of the preceding entry is smaller than the key of the chosen entry, then the chosen entry is moved into the hole that comes immediately after it. Figure 14.3 illustrates how the insertion sort works.

FIGURE 14.3 Insertion Sort at Work

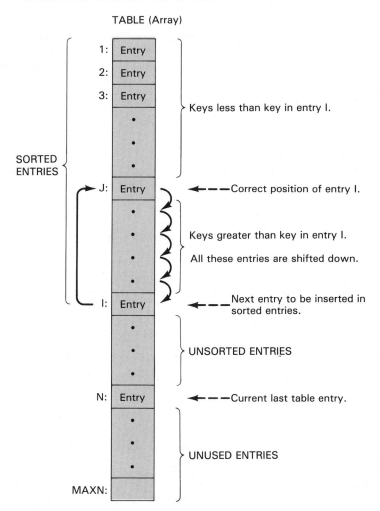

The insertion sort algorithm in pseudo-code might be written:

PROCEDURE Sort

>> (T: TableType)   IN/OUT: Table to be sorted.

>> PURPOSE/GOAL STATE: Sort the entries in T so that they appear in T in increasing sequence of key values.

>> **ALGORITHM**

Step 1.   PURPOSE/GOAL STATE: Use an insertion sort to sort the entries in T.

>> ACTIONS:

>>> FOR I := 2 TO T.N DO

Step 1a.   PURPOSE/GOAL STATE: Save a copy of entry I. Then move entries down in the sorted part of the table until an entry is reached with a key less than that of the Ith entry. Set J = position where entry I should be inserted.

>> ACTIONS:

```
SaveEntry := T.Entries[I]
J := I
NotFound := TRUE
WHILE (J > 1) AND NotFound DO
    IF SaveEntry.Key > T.Entries[J−1].Key THEN
        NotFound := FALSE
    ELSE
        T.Entries[J] := T.Entries[J−1]
        J := J − 1
```

Step 1b.   PURPOSE/GOAL STATE: Insert the copy of entry I into the Jth position in the table, unless I = J.

>> ACTIONS:

```
IF I <> J THEN
    T.Entries[J] := SaveEntry
```

>> **DATA OBJECTS**

I: Integer	Outer loop subscript variable.
J: Integer	Inner loop subscript variable.
SaveEntry: Entry	Temporary storage while shifting.

Analysis of the Efficiency of Insertion Sort

Let's look at the number of comparison and move operations during execution of the insertion sort algorithm. First, notice that the outer FOR loop always executes $N - 1$ iterations, regardless of the table entries. However, the execution path in the inner WHILE loop does depend on the table entries. Thus, there will be a *worst case* and an *average case* to consider, which makes the algorithm considerably harder to analyze.

□

Comparisons. For each table entry, in the worst case, it might have to be compared against all the preceding entries (if it needed to be inserted at the beginning of the table). Thus, the algorithm requires $O(N^2)$ comparisons in the worst case.

□

Moves. In the worst case, which again is when each entry must be inserted at the beginning of the table, each entry in the sorted part of the table will have to be moved on each iteration of the FOR loop, giving $O(N^2)$ moves.

Thus, the insertion sort in the worst case requires both $O(N^2)$ comparisons and $O(N^2)$ moves. And the worst case is when the table initially has its entries in *reverse order* of their final sorted positions—each entry is moved all the way back to the start of the table when it is reached, causing all the intervening entries to be shifted down.

The insertion sort is actually better in many situations than this analysis would suggest. Suppose that the entries in the table are already in sorted order (or almost in sorted order) when the sort operation is executed (because they just happened to be inserted in that order by Insert.) Then the insertion sort is $O(N)$ in comparisons and moves—it makes a single sweep through the table, comparing only the keys on adjacent entries, and moving no entries. In this situation, insertion sort is much faster than selection sort, which always makes $O(N^2)$ comparisons.

Summary of the Analysis

Putting all the various conclusions from our efficiency analysis together, we know that:

1. Binary search is dramatically better than linear search, $O(\log_2 N)$ versus $O(N)$, but binary search requires a sorted table.
2. Sorting the table with either a selection sort or an insertion sort is likely to be costly, unless we know that the entries are inserted initially in approximately sorted order. In general, both sort algorithms require $O(N^2)$ comparisons.
3. Because all the insertions are made before the table must be searched the first time, we can use a constant time, $O(1)$, insertion algorithm.

We see the trade-off in these facts. Is it worth sorting the table in order to speed up the Search operation? We only have to sort the table once. The Search will be performed many times. If the table is large, say with N = 1000, then the search operation will be much more efficient each time. Probably the cost of sorting the table is less than the cost of repeatedly using a much more expensive linear search.

Neither sort algorithm is particularly fast. Is there a better sorting algorithm? The best general sorting algorithm is a divide and conquer algorithm called *quicksort*, whose average execution time is $N \log_2 N$, but it is a more complex, recursive algorithm. We might consider using this algorithm instead of either selection sort or insertion sort.

As you can see, trying to make a part of a program efficient can often involve difficult trade-offs. One operation becomes slower while another becomes faster. Or the algorithms become far more complex (and likely to have errors) in order to gain some efficiency. Or an algorithm that appears to be better based on its worst case efficiency actually turns out to be worse in the average case. The best rule of thumb is: proceed with caution when considering modifications to improve a program's efficiency!

EXERCISES

14.8   The inner loop of the insertion sort might be made more efficient if we could place a *sentinel key* at the beginning of the table, somewhat like we did with the linear search loop, so that it was unnecessary to make a special test for the start of the table each iteration. Determine how to make this change in the insertion sort algorithm, and analyze its effect on the efficiency of the algorithm.

14.9   Suppose that the Insert operation is required to always leave the table *sorted*, so that we can intermix Insert and Search operations. What algorithm would you choose for Insert in that situation? Why?

■ ■ ■
REVIEW QUESTIONS

14.1   What is the *performance* of a program? What two questions are asked when measuring performance?

14.2   What is the difference between the performance of a program and the *efficiency* of one of its parts?

14.3   What is the *90–10 rule?*

14.4   What is the *critical 10 percent* of a program?

14.5   What two rules of thumb suggest that it may often be difficult to find or improve the performance of the critical 10 percent?

14.6   Name and briefly explain two approaches to *measuring* the performance of a program.

14.7   In performance measurement, what program elements should be targeted for particular attention?

14.8 What is the difference between *time efficiency* and *space efficiency* in a subprogram?

14.9 What is meant by the *problem size* in discussing efficiency? How does the problem size affect the importance of analyzing the efficiency of an algorithm or data representation?

14.10 What is the difference between an *order of* improvement in the efficiency of an algorithm or data representation, a *constant factor* improvement, and an *additive constant* improvement?

14.11 Describe briefly what it means for an algorithm or data representation to have an efficiency that is O(1), O(log$_2$ N), O(N), O(N log$_2$ N), and O(N^2).

14.12 Identify the *general type of modification* to an algorithm that might be required to obtain an *order of* efficiency improvement, a constant factor improvement, or an additive constant improvement.

14.13 What is the difference between *worst case* efficiency and *average case* efficiency?

14.14 What is the difference between a *sorted table* and an *unsorted table*?

14.15 Explain the algorithms for *linear search* and *binary search* of a table. Which algorithm requires a sorted table?

14.16 What is a *sentinel key*? What is its purpose in the linear search algorithm?

14.17 Analyze the efficiency of *linear search with a sentinel key* and *binary search* in the worst case, assuming that the desired entry is in the table. Assuming that the desired entry is not in the table.

14.18 Explain the *selection sort* algorithm and analyze the approximate number of compare and move operations required to sort a table of N entries.

14.19 Explain the *insertion sort* algorithm and analyze the approximate number of compare and move operations it requires.

14.20 How do the *particular key values* in the table affect the efficiency of the selection sort? Of the insertion sort?

■ ■ ■
PROGRAMMING PROBLEMS

14.1 *Binary Search for a Root of an Equation*. The binary search algorithm may also be applied in a situation that seems very different from that of searching a sorted array. Consider the problem of finding a root of a "well-behaved" function f(x) in some interval, [P,Q]. Suppose that f(P) < 0 and f(Q) > 0, as shown in Figure 14.4. Because the graph of the function is below the X-axis at the start of the interval and above the X-axis at the end, you know the function must have a root (i.e., must equal zero) at some point between P and Q because the graph has to cross the X-axis at some point in that interval (and possibly at more than one point). How can you find a point where the function value is zero?

Try this version of the binary search algorithm: divide the interval in half and check the function value at the midpoint, P + (Q−P)/2. If f(midpoint) = 0 you have your answer—the root is at the midpoint. If not, then take the interval between P and the midpoint if f(midpoint) > 0 and take the interval between the midpoint and Q if f(midpoint) < 0. You now have an interval half the size of the original interval, but in all other aspects the problem is the same because the function is still below the X-axis at the start of the interval and above

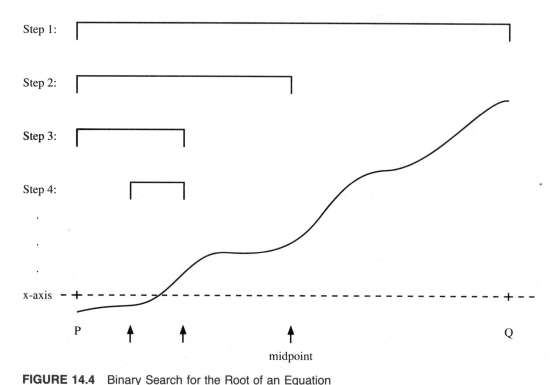

Step 1:

Step 2:

Step 3:

Step 4:

x-axis

P

midpoint

Q

FIGURE 14.4 Binary Search for the Root of an Equation

it at the end. Repeat the search step on this new interval. Do you think this is an O(log$_2$ N) algorithm? Why?

Write a program to apply this binary search algorithm to the problem of finding a root of a cubic equation, $Ax^3 + Bx^2 + Cx + D$. Allow the user to specify the coefficients, A, B, C, and D to be used and the interval [P,Q] to search. Note that there may be no roots of the equation within the interval.

Caution: When testing whether the function value is equal to zero, remember to use the "approximate equality" test as discussed in Chapter 10. Otherwise the algorithm may fail to detect the root when it gets close to it.

14.2 *Sorting an Array of Pointers to Entries.* There are other ways of representing a table that make searching and sorting simpler in various situations. Consider the situation where you want to be able to look up an entry using different key *fields* at different times. For example, suppose you have a table of names and telephone numbers. Sometimes you want to look up a *name* to get the telephone number and sometimes you want to look up a *telephone number* to get the name. If you sort the table on the name field then you can use binary search to find the name, but you would be forced to use a linear search to look up a telephone number.

A solution to this problem is to use a second array that contains the *subscripts* of the entries in the array that represents the table. We think of the subscripts as *pointers* to entries in the main table. Instead of sorting the entries in the original table to represent the sorted order for the second key field, you sort the *pointers* so that they point to the entries in the main table in the correct order. Now you can use a binary search on the table of pointers instead of a linear search on the original table.

If the subscript range for the first table is of subrange type TableRange = 1..MAXN, then this second array is declared to be of type:

ARRAY [TableRange] OF TableRange

In the example of the table of names and telephone numbers, suppose that you sort the original table, Table1, into alphabetical order of names. Then the second array, TableOf-Pointers, contains pointers to the entries in Table1 in the order of their telephone number fields. Suppose Table1 [20] contains the "smallest" telephone number. Then TableOfPointers [1] = 20. If Table1 [7] contains the next smallest telephone number, then TableOfPointers [2] = 7, and so forth.

To assign the smallest telephone number to variable NewNumber, you might use the assignment:

```
NewNumber := Table1 [TableOfPointers[1]].TelephoneNumber;
```

Notice how the telephone number field is selected from Table1, using the subscript value that is retrieved from the table of pointers.

Design, code, and test a program that allows the user to enter a list of names and telephone numbers to form a table. Then allow the user to look up either name or telephone number by using the other item as the key. Use a sorted table and binary search for one key. Use a sorted table of pointers and binary search for the other key.

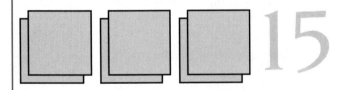

Multidimensional Arrays and Real Numbers

CHAPTER GOALS

When you have mastered the content of this chapter you should be able to:

- Define and use *multidimensional arrays* in a program.
- Decide whether to represent a *table* as an array of records or a two-dimensional array.
- Define operations on two-dimensional arrays.
- Use mathematical notations to define vector and matrix operations in pseudo-code without using loops.
- Explain the properties of real numbers and of arithmetic with real numbers in a computer, including *round off, overflow,* and *underflow* errors.

Arrays with more than one dimension, termed *multidimensional* arrays, are an important data representation in many programs, particularly for computing tasks in scientific and engineering fields. These same types of programs often involve extensive calculations with *real number* data values as well.

□□□ **15.1**
WHAT IS A MULTIDIMENSIONAL ARRAY?

To this point, the arrays that we have been using are *one-dimensional,* meaning that the elements of the array can be visualized as forming a single sequence:

Array [1]
Array [2]
.
.
.
Array [N]

A one-dimensional array has a single subscript range.

A *two-dimensional array* (or *matrix*) can be visualized as a *two-dimensional* grid of elements, formed from rows and columns, as shown in Figure 15.1. In a two-dimensional array, there are two subscript ranges, one numbering the rows and the second numbering the columns.

In describing a two-dimensional array, we often simply refer to the number of rows and columns, using the notation:

⟨rows⟩ × ⟨columns⟩

For example, we might refer to a "10 x 8 matrix M," meaning that M is a two-dimensional array with ten rows and eight columns, as in Figure 15.1. Unless we explicitly mention a different subscript range, we assume that both subscript ranges start at 1.

A *three-dimensional array* can be visualized as forming a cube, such as shown in Figure 15.2, divided into a sequence of *planes,* each consisting of rows and columns. A three-dimensional array has three subscript ranges, numbering the rows,

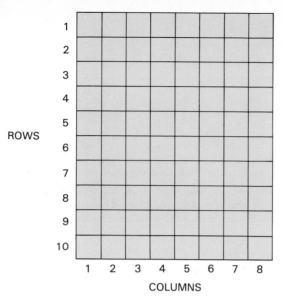

ROWS

COLUMNS

Array M
M is a 10 × 8 array.

FIGURE 15.1 A Two-dimensional Array

FIGURE 15.2 A Three-dimensional Array

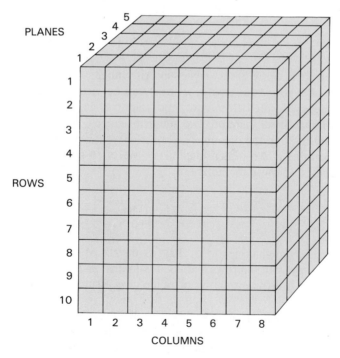

PLANES

ROWS

COLUMNS

Array C
C is a 10 × 8 × 5 array.

the columns, and the planes. To describe the shape of a three-dimensional array, we use the notation:

$$\langle\text{rows}\rangle \times \langle\text{columns}\rangle \times \langle\text{planes}\rangle$$

For example, we might say that "C is a 10 x 8 x 5 array," meaning that C is a three-dimensional array with five planes, each with ten rows and eight columns.

Arrays with more than three dimensions are possible, although rarely used. In general, the term *multidimensional array* is used to refer to any array with more than a single dimension. Notice that the *number of dimensions* of a multidimensional array means the number of *subscript ranges* used in its definition.

In this chapter, we focus our attention on two-dimensional arrays. Once you understand how to use two-dimensional arrays, the extension to arrays with more than two dimensions is straightforward.

□ □

Defining a Two-dimensional Array

A two-dimensional array has two subscript ranges specified in its definition, but otherwise the definition is the same as for an ordinary one-dimensional array. A type definition for a two-dimensional array would have the form:

```
⟨type name⟩ = ARRAY [⟨row-subscripts⟩, ⟨column-subscripts⟩]
                OF ⟨element-type⟩;
```

EXAMPLES

1. To represent a chess board as an 8 x 8 array of "squares":

```
ChessBoard = ARRAY [1..8, 1..8] OF Square;
```

2. To represent a 52 x 7 table of the high temperature in River City for each day of the year, organized so that each row represents a week and the columns represent the days in the week:

```
TemperatureTable = ARRAY [1..52, 1..7] OF Real;
```

3. To represent a table showing the frequency of occurrence of each letter of the alphabet in each page of a text of up to 500 pages. The rows are numbered with the page numbers and the columns are labeled with the letters of the alphabet:

```
CharFrequencyTable = ARRAY [1..500, 'a'..'z'] OF Integer;
```
■

Selecting an Element of a Two-dimensional Array

To select a particular element from a two-dimensional array, you must specify both its row subscript and its column subscript:

⟨array name⟩ [⟨row subscript⟩, ⟨column subscript⟩]

The same rules apply to these subscript expressions as for the one-dimensional case.

EXAMPLE If Board is type ChessBoard and Table is type CharFrequency Table, as defined above, then these are valid statements for selecting elements:

```
Board [1, 8] := NextMove (...);
S := Board [NextMoveRow, 2];
IF Table [Page, Letter] = 1 THEN ...
```

Representing Tables Using Two-dimensional Arrays

A two-dimensional array is often considered as an alternative representation for a *table* of data values. In the preceding chapters, we have used an *array of records* as our primary representation. Let's compare the two.

Suppose we represent a table with 50 rows and three columns as an array of records, using the type definitions:

```
⟨entry⟩ =

    RECORD
        ⟨field1⟩: ⟨type1⟩;
        ⟨field2⟩: ⟨type2⟩;
        ⟨field3⟩: ⟨type3⟩;
    END;

⟨table type⟩ = ARRAY [1..50] OF ⟨entry⟩;
```

The array of records representation gives the table shown in Figure 15.3a.

A similar table of 50 rows and three columns might also be represented as a two-dimensional array, using the type definition:

```
⟨table type⟩ = ARRAY [1..50, 1..3] OF ⟨element type⟩;
```

The two-dimensional array representation gives the table shown in Figure 15.3b.

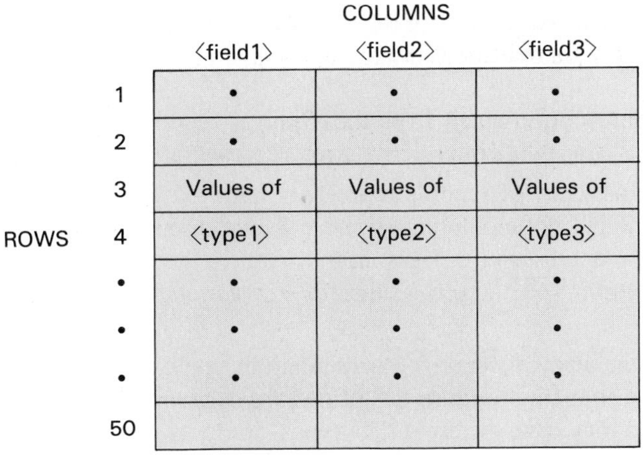

FIGURE 15.3a A Table Represented as an Array of Records

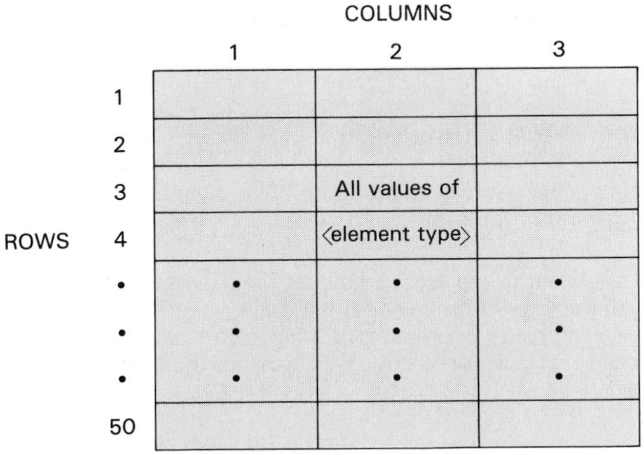

FIGURE 15.3b A Table Represented as a Two-dimensional Array

Although the two representations appear similar, there are several important differences:

1. In the array of records representation, each column can store a *different type of data*. For example, column 1 can store Integer values, column 2 Real values, and column 3 can be some other type. In the two-dimensional array, *every column stores the same type of data*. For example, all values must be integers or all must be reals.

2. In the array of records representation, the *field names* serve as *meaningful column names*. In the two-dimensional array representation, the subscript range used to name the columns is usually less meaningful.

3. In the array of records representation, each row of the table is a *separate record data object*. Thus, an individual row of the table can be used as an actual parameter in a subprogram call or an entire row can be copied into another row with a single assignment statement. In the two-dimensional array representation, the rows are not separate data objects. Only the individual elements can be treated as separate data objects.

These three differences favor the array of records representation for most tables. However, the two-dimensional array representation has advantages of its own:

4. In the array of records representation, you can use a subscript expression to select a row but not a column. Because the columns are named with field names, you cannot use a subscript expression to select the field. In the two-dimensional array representation, you can use a *subscript expression to choose either the row or the column* (or both).

5. In the array of records representation, you cannot use a loop to process every data value in a row because the values are selected with field names rather than subscripts and may have different data types. In the two-dimensional array representation, *a loop can be used to sweep through all the elements in a row* (or a column).

These differences in the two representations make certain types of operations convenient in one representation that are inconvenient in the other. But there is a more fundamental distinction between the two representations:

- In a *two-dimensional array* the values in every row and column should represent the same *type of information*.
- In an *array of records* the values in different columns (different fields of the record) should represent *different types of information*.

EXAMPLES

1. Suppose you want to represent a table of the daily high temperature in River City for each day of the week and for the 52 weeks in a year. Each data value in the table represents the same type of information, a temperature value. A 52 x 7 array would provide a convenient representation, using type Real for the temperature values:

⟨table type⟩ = ARRAY [1..52, 1..7] OF Real;

2. Suppose you want to represent a table of the weekly average high temperature, average low temperature, and precipitation for the 52 weeks of the year. Each data value is a Real number, but the table columns represent different types of information. The best representation here is an array of records:

WeeklyData =

RECORD
  AverageHigh: Real;
  AverageLow: Real;
  Precipitation: Real;
END;

⟨table type⟩ = ARRAY [1..52] OF WeeklyData;

□ □ Coding Two-dimensional Arrays in Pascal

In Pascal, two-dimensional arrays (and multidimensional arrays in general) follow the same rules for definition and use as one-dimensional arrays. You simply include the second subscript range in the type definition and the second subscript expression when you select an element, as in the preceding examples.

□ □ Storage Use in Multidimensional Arrays

The number of elements in a multidimensional array is the *product* of the number of elements in each dimension (each subscript range.) Even small subscript ranges can lead to arrays that require large amounts of storage. For example, a 20 x 200 array has 4000 elements. A 10 x 50 x 50 array has 25,000 elements.

EXERCISES

15.1   For each of the following situations, determine whether an array of records or a two-dimensional array would be a more appropriate representation (based only on the type of information to be stored in the table, not on the operations required):

a.   A table of the height, weight, and age of every student in a class.

b.   A game board for the game of checkers.

c.   A *digitized picture,* where the picture is divided into a large number of points in regular rows and columns. Each number in the table represents the darkness/lightness of the picture at that point, on a scale of 0–8.

d.   A table of the payments on a car loan, where the columns represent the principal and interest for each month during the life of the loan.

□ □ □ 15.2
OPERATIONS ON TWO-DIMENSIONAL ARRAYS

Most operations on two-dimensional arrays involve one of the following:

■ A loop that processes the elements in a particular *row*.

■ A loop that processes the elements in a particular *column*.

■ Two nested loops that process *every element* of the array.

If every element is to be processed, the outer loop will sweep down the rows, one at a time, and the inner loop will sweep across the elements of each row in turn, or conversely, the outer loop will sweep across the columns and the inner loop will sweep down the elements of each column.

Suppose A is a 20 x 30 array of real numbers.

1. To sum the elements in *row* 5 and store the result in Total, you might use the loop:

        Total := 0
        FOR J := 1 TO 30 DO
            Total := Total + A [5,J]

2. To sum the elements in *column* 5 and store the result in Total, you might use the loop:

        Total := 0
        FOR I := 1 TO 20 DO
            Total := Total + A [I,5]

3. To sum *all the elements* and store the result in Total, you might use the nested loops:

        Total := 0
        FOR I := 1 TO 20 DO
            FOR J := 1 TO 30 DO
                Total := Total + A [I,J]   ■

A more complex loop structure arises when the goal is to *process each row* separately in an inner loop, but to use an outer loop to sweep through all the rows so that every row is processed. In this situation, the result of the operation is usually a *one-dimensional array of results.*

EXAMPLE   Suppose A is a 20 x 30 array of Real numbers and V[1..20] is a one-dimensional array. To sum the elements of each row of A and store the result in the element of V with the same subscript as the row, you might use the nested loops:

        FOR I := 1 TO 20 DO
            Total := 0
            FOR J := 1 TO 30 DO
                Total := Total + A[I,J]
            V[I] := Total

Notice that Total is reinitialized to zero at the start of each iteration of the outer loop. An alternative way to write this loop is to use V[I] to accumulate the total for the Ith row:

        FOR I := 1 TO 20 DO
            V[I] := 0
            FOR J := 1 TO 30 DO
                V[I] := V[I] + A[I,J]   ■

Matrix and Vector Operations

In many scientific and engineering programs, most of the data is represented using one- and two-dimensional arrays. Traditionally in these applications areas, one-dimensional arrays are called *vectors* and two-dimensional arrays are called *matrices* (singular, *matrix*).

Operations often process the elements of vectors or rows and columns of matrices and produce results that are stored in other vectors and matrices. Such operations are expressed using a notation that describes how a "typical element," the ijth element for a matrix or the ith element of a vector, is produced from the elements of other arrays. For example, the assignment:

$$A_i := B_i + 3$$

means "each element of vector A is computed by adding three to the corresponding element of vector B." The assignment:

$$D_{ij} := E_{ij} + F_{ij}$$

means "each element of matrix D is assigned the sum of the corresponding elements of matrices E and F. (Of course, all three matrices must have the same subscript ranges.)

This notation is useful in pseudo-code for expressing many operations on vectors and matrices *without using a loop*. When such a pseudo-code operation is translated into Pascal, one or more FOR loops are used. For example, the assignment above to A_i is coded as the Pascal FOR loop (assuming A and B have subscript range 1..N):

```
FOR I := 1 TO N DO
    A[I] := B[I] + 3
```

and the assignment to D_{ij} is coded as the nested loops:

```
FOR I := 1 TO M DO
    FOR J := 1 TO N DO
        D[I,J] := E[I,J] + F[I,J]
```

assuming D, E, and F are M x N matrices.

□ □

The Summation and Product Notations

Mathematical formulas sometimes express the summation of a sequence of data values by using the Greek letter sigma in the notation:

$$\sum_{i=1}^{N} \langle \text{expression involving } i \rangle$$

For example, the assignment:

$$\text{Total} := \sum_{i=1}^{N} A_i$$

means "sum the elements of array A[1..N] and store the result in Total." For products, the notation uses the Greek letter pi:

$$\prod_{i=1}^{N} \quad \langle \text{expression involving } i \rangle$$

For example, the assignment:

$$\text{Product} := \prod_{i=M}^{N} B_i$$

means "multiply the elements of array B[M..N] and store the result in Product."

Both the summation and product notations are useful in pseudo-code for specifying many common operations on vectors and matrices without using FOR loops. The translation into a Pascal FOR loop is straightforward. For example, the assignment to Total above is coded as the loop:

```
Total := 0;
FOR I := 1 TO N DO
      Total := Total + A[I]
```

and the assignment to Product is:

```
Product := 1;
FOR I := M TO N DO
      Product := Product * B[I]
```

If the summation or product appears as part of a more complex expression, the Pascal code will usually require the introduction of a temporary storage variable for collecting the partial sums or products as the loop is executed. After the loop exit, the remainder of the expression is computed, using the value of the temporary storage variable. For example, the pseudo-code assignment:

$$\text{Average} := \left(\sum_{i=1}^{N} B_i \right) / N$$

would be coded in Pascal with a temporary storage variable, say Sum, to collect the sum of the elements of B, as follows:

```
Sum := 0
FOR I := 1 TO N DO
      Sum := Sum + B[I]
Average := Sum / N
```

EXERCISES

15.2 For each of the following assignments in pseudo-code, write an equivalent Pascal FOR loop or two nested FOR loops. Assume that arrays A, B, and C are $M \times N$ matrices, where M and N are defined constants, and U, W, and V are M element vectors.

a. $U_i := V_i + A_{i3}$

b. $Result := 2 * \left(\sum\limits_{j=1}^{N} B_{7j} \right)$

c. $W_i := \left(\prod\limits_{j=1}^{N} C_{ij} \right) / V_i$

d. $V_i := \sum\limits_{j=1}^{N} (B_{ij} + 2)$

15.3 The *matrix transpose* of a $M \times N$ matrix A is the $N \times M$ matrix A^T, defined as:

$$A^T_{ji} = A_{ij}$$

Write a Pascal segment to store in matrix BTranspose the transpose of matrix B, where B is 20×30 and BTranspose is 30×20.

15.4 Translate the following statement into an appropriate mathematical expression (and assignment) using the pi notation: "For each column I in $M \times N$ matrix D, compute the product of the elements in the Ith column and store the product in the Ith element of vector W." Then code an equivalent Pascal segment for the computation.

15.5 Write a Pascal segment to compute the sum of the elements on the diagonal of an $M \times M$ matrix S, defined as:

$$DiagonalSum := \sum\limits_{i=1}^{M} S_{ii}$$

COMPUTING WITH REAL NUMBERS

Let's change our focus now to a different topic: computations that involve data values of type Real. Many scientific and engineering computations involve both multidimensional arrays and real numbers, so the two topics are natural companions in this chapter, although they are not directly related.

In this section, we are concerned with the special types of errors that arise when Real numbers are used in calculations. To this point, we have assumed that arithmetic operations applied to Real values would give correct results. Unfortunately, arithmetic with Real values in a computer is not so simple.

□ □
Approximate Real Numbers

Real numbers in a computer are stored in a form of *scientific notation* called "binary floating point representation." We discussed this representation briefly back in Chapter 2. For our discussion here, however, the details of the hardware representation of real numbers are not important. What we are concerned with are the *effects* of this representation when you compute with Real values in Pascal (or any other programming language).

For this discussion, we can illustrate the effects of the hardware representation by using the Pascal scientific notation. In scientific notation, a number is represented as a *mantissa* and an *exponent*. For example, 2.345×10^3 is a number in decimal scientific notation with a mantissa of 2.345 and an exponent of $+3$. The digits in the mantissa are termed the *significant digits* of the number.

In Pascal scientific notation, you write a real number as:

$$\langle sign \rangle \ \langle mantissa \rangle \ \text{E} \ \langle exponent \rangle$$

where the ⟨mantissa⟩ shows the significant digits in the number and the ⟨exponent⟩ determines the true position of the decimal point in the number. A positive exponent, K, "floats" the decimal point K places to the right, and a negative exponent, $-K$, "floats" the decimal point K places to the left, from wherever the decimal point appears in the ⟨mantissa⟩ (hence the term *floating point* for this type of number representation).

EXAMPLES

1. The number 2.345×10^3 can be written in Pascal scientific notation as:

$$+ \ 2.345 \ \text{E} \ +3$$

Written in ordinary decimal notation, the number is:

$$2345.$$

Notice that the exponent of $+3$ floats the decimal point three places to the right in the mantissa.

2. The number:

$$1.23 \ \text{E} \ -4$$

in Pascal scientific notation represents the number:

$$0.000123$$

Notice that the negative exponent floats the decimal point four places to the left in the mantissa.

The peculiar properties of Real numbers in a computer come primarily from the use of scientific notation, with the mantissa and exponent, and one additional restriction:

In a computer, both mantissa and exponent are represented with a fixed number of digits.

The number of digits in the mantissa and exponent of a real number vary among different types of computers, but within a particular type of computer, each real number will have a prespecified number of digits in its mantissa and a prespecified number in its exponent. For example, the mantissa might always have 24 bits and the exponent eight bits.

We can understand the peculiar properties of computer real numbers by looking at these properties in terms of the Pascal scientific notation, with some restrictions. For these examples, we require:

- The mantissa must have *exactly ten digits* and the exponent must have *exactly three digits*.
- The decimal point is always *at the left end* of the mantissa.
- The *first digit of the mantissa cannot be a zero*, unless the entire number is zero.

EXAMPLES   Some numbers written in our example representation:

NUMBER	AS WRITTEN
23	+ .2300000000 E +002
2,345,678	+ .2345678000 E +007
− 23	− .2300000000 E +002
0	+ .0000000000 E +000
0.2345	+ .2345000000 E +000
0.00002345	+ .2345000000 E −004
−1,234,567,891	− .1234567891 E +010
11,234,567,891	Cannot be represented; more than ten significant digits.

■

□ □
Properties of Computer Real Numbers

Our decimal representation for real numbers has the same sort of characteristics that the binary representation for reals in a computer has. The key properties are these:

1. *There is a largest positive real number and a largest negative real number.* Just as with integers, we have limits on the maximum size of a real number. In our decimal representation, the largest positive real is:

$$+ .9999999999 \text{ E } +999$$

and the largest negative real is:

$$- .9999999999 \text{ E} +999$$

Notice that a *large positive exponent* indicates a large real number, and the sign of the mantissa indicates whether the large number is positive or negative.

2. *Real numbers have a limit on their accuracy.* The limit on the number of significant digits in the mantissa limits the accuracy with which a real number can be represented. For example, in our representation, we can represent the number:

$$21.00000075$$

but not:

$$21.0000007468$$

because the second number has more than ten significant digits. We have to round off the second number to exactly ten digits.

3. *There is a smallest positive real number (closest to zero) and a smallest negative real number.* The smallest positive number in our representation is:

$$+ .100000000 \text{ E} -999$$

and the smallest negative number is:

$$- .100000000 \text{ E} -999$$

Notice that a *large negative exponent* indicates a number that is very close to zero.

□ □
Arithmetic Operations with Real Numbers

Whenever we perform arithmetic operations on real numbers, we need to exercise some care. There are several characteristic types of errors that may occur:

1. *Overflow errors.* Most obviously, the result of an addition, subtraction, or multiplication can exceed the limits on the size of a real number, much like exceeding MAXINT when working with integer values. The limit is exceeded when the *exponent part* of a real number gets too large (in our example, when it exceeds +999). An error of this type is termed an *overflow error*.

2. *Underflow errors.* The result of an arithmetic operation can also be *too close to zero,* so that it is closer to zero than the smallest positive real number (or, on the negative side, closer than the smallest negative real). This limit is exceeded when the *exponent part* of a real number exceeds its negative limit (in our example, when it exceeds -999). An error of this sort is termed an *underflow error.*

3. *Round off errors.* The result of an arithmetic operation can have too many significant digits, meaning that it must be rounded off to the maximum number of digits allowed in the computer (in our example, rounded off to ten digits). The rounding off means that the number is only *approximately correct.* The process of rounding off the number introduces a *round off error,* which is the amount that the rounded value differs from the true value of the number.

Overflow and underflow errors are rare because the exponent part usually allows extremely large numbers and numbers very close to zero to be represented. In our example numbers, the largest exponent is $+999$, meaning that we can represent numbers as large as:

$$1,000,000, \ldots over\ 900\ zeros \ldots , 000,000$$

The smallest exponent is -999, meaning that we can get as close to zero as the number:

$$0.00000 \ldots over\ 900\ zeros \ldots 0001$$

In most computer systems, overflow and underflow errors during arithmetic operations cause a computation to terminate with a run-time error message.

Round off errors, however, are a fundamental fact of computer arithmetic. After each arithmetic operation, the result may be rounded off. The computation continues with the rounded off result. There is no "error" signaled when the rounding off causes some significant digits to be lost.

□ □
The Rules of Algebra May Not Apply Here

Round off errors mean that the precise sequence of arithmetic operations in a formula, such as on the right-hand side of an assignment, can affect the result computed. If you rearrange the formula according to the rules of algebra, the computed result may be slightly different. For example, in algebra the two formulas:

$$A \times (B - C)$$

and

$$(A \times B) - (A \times C)$$

are equivalent. Either version should give exactly the same result, for all possible values of A, B, and C. But in a computer the two formulas may not give the same result. That is, the two assignment statements:

$$Result := A * (B - C);$$

and

$$Result := (A * B) - (A * C);$$

may not assign the same value to Result. The first version involves a subtraction of two real values followed by a multiplication with a third real value. The second version involves two multiplications followed by a subtraction. Each arithmetic operation produces an intermediate result that may be rounded off, which is then combined again in a second arithmetic operation and the result is again rounded off. Because the numbers produced as intermediate results are different, the round off error will be slightly different in each version.

□□

Operating with Large and Small Numbers

One effect of round off errors in computer arithmetic is particularly confusing. If an arithmetic operation is performed with one operand being *very large* and the other operand being *very small* the effect of the operation may be entirely lost due to round off error—the result will be just exactly the larger number. For example, suppose A = 23,000,000 and B = .0046. Then in our example system:

$$A + B = A$$

that is:

$$A + B = 23,000,000.0046$$

which has more than ten significant digits, so the result is rounded to 23,000,000.00 which is just the value of A that we started with.

EXAMPLE Diana, an amateur astronomer, has prepared a program to determine how many years it will be before one of the moons of Mars impacts the planet. It is known that the moon's orbit brings it slightly closer to Mars each year. Her program takes the distance of the moon from Mars at the present time (a large number) and the distance that the moon moves closer to the planet in a single year (a very small number). It enters a loop that repeatedly subtracts the small number from the larger one, to approximate the movement of the moon toward the planet. To her surprise, the loop becomes an infinite loop, and the calculated distance of the moon from Mars never changes.

Why? Round off error! Subtracting the small number from the large one leads to a result with more significant digits than the real number representation on her computer allows. When the result is rounded off, the number computed is exactly the starting distance of the moon from Mars, unchanged by the subtraction. ∎

□ □

Large Losses of Accuracy

In a single arithmetic operation, round off error can make the result slightly inaccurate. However, when a long computation is made using real numbers, such as a sequence of thousands of additions, subtractions, or multiplications, these small errors may accumulate until the effect is an *overwhelming loss of accuracy*. The result may not even be close to the true answer. For example, a computation that should lead to an answer close to zero may in fact produce a result close to 1000.

Almost every scientific or engineering calculation, as well as many calculations in banking, economics, and other areas, involves long sequences of operations on real numbers. In these computations, the potential for round off errors to accumulate and destroy the accuracy of the results is a very real one. One part of the branch of computer science (and mathematics) called *numerical analysis* involves the study of such computations and of the amount of round off error that can accumulate when such computations are performed on computers.

□ □

Testing Equality of Real Numbers

In Chapter 10, we noted that a loop exit test that uses the tests "=" or "<>" to compare real number values is a common cause of an infinite loop. If A and B contain real number values that are the result of a computation, then the test:

$$A = B$$

will usually give FALSE even when the computations of A and B should have given the same values. Round off error is again the culprit. For example, this loop is an infinite loop on most computers:

```
H := 0
WHILE H <> 1.0 DO
        ⟨compute something using H⟩
        H := H + 0.1
```

When 0.1 is added to H on each iteration, round off error (and the fact that the computer representation of 0.1 is slightly inaccurate to begin with) causes the result to be slightly inaccurate. As a result, H never exactly equals 1.0, and the loop continues forever.

The correct test for equality of two real numbers in a program is to test if the numbers are "close enough" to each other to be considered equal, given the limited accuracy of arithmetic on the computer. You choose a *tolerance* which represents "close enough"—a value close to zero such as 0.000001. Then you see if the numbers are within the tolerance of each other. If so, you call them "equal." Because you do not know whether round off error will make one number slightly too large or slightly too small, compared to the other, the test requires that the *absolute value* of the difference of the numbers be compared to the tolerance:

$$\text{abs}\ (\langle\text{first}\rangle\ -\ \langle\text{second}\rangle)\ <\ \langle\text{tolerance}\rangle$$

For example, the exit test in the loop above could be written:

$$\text{WHILE abs}\ (H\ -\ 1.0)\ >\ 0.000001\ \text{DO}\ .\ .\ .$$

□ □

Count Controlled Loops and Real Numbers

In general, using real numbers to control a count controlled loop may lead to problems. For example, the loop above:

```
H := 0
WHILE H <> 1.0 DO
        ⟨compute something using H⟩
        H := H + 0.1
```

is a count controlled loop, where the goal is to use Real variable H to count from 0 to 1 in steps of one-tenth. If you use the correct test for inequality, you get the loop:

```
H := 0
WHILE abs (H − 1.0) > 0.000001 DO
        ⟨compute something using H⟩
        H := H + 0.1
```

This loop may still become an infinite loop if the tolerance used, 0.000001 in this case, is smaller than the round off error that accumulates during the repeated additions of 0.1 to H as the loop iterates. For example, suppose that after 10 iterations, the computed value of H is 1.000002 instead of 1.0 because of round off error. Then the value of H is not within the specified tolerance of 1.0. The exit test says "continue again," and the loop falls into an infinite repetition.

In general, avoid using real values to control a count controlled loop. Instead, use a separate Integer variable for the counting, preferably in a FOR loop. For example, the correct way to code the loop above is:

```
H := 0
FOR I := 1 TO 10 DO
    BEGIN
        ⟨compute something using H⟩
        H := H + 0.1
    END
```

Real variable H is still incremented on each iteration, but it is no longer used as part of the loop control.

EXERCISES

15.6   For your Pascal system, determine the maximum number of significant digits in a Real number.

15.7   Write a test program that adds a very large number and a very small number, where the number of significant digits in the result should cause round off error to erase the effect of the small number on the sum. Display both numbers before the addition and the result after. Can you observe the effect of round off error?

15.8   Write a test program that repeatedly adds 0.1 to the starting value 2.0. Display the sum after every 1000 iterations, continuing for 50,000 iterations total. The result should be exactly 5002. How close is the computed value to the true value?

■ ■ ■
REVIEW QUESTIONS

15.1   What is a *multidimensional* array?

15.2   How do you determine the *number of dimensions* of a multidimensional array?

15.3   How do you *select* a particular element from a two-dimensional array?

15.4   For representing a *table of data* (with rows and columns), give three advantages of an *array of records* representation and two advantages of a *two-dimensional array* representation for the table.

15.5   How do you determine the *total number of elements* in a two- or three-dimensional array?

15.6   What is a *matrix?* What is a *vector?*

15.7   Explain how operations on the elements of matrices and vectors may be described in pseudo-code *without using loops.* Describe how to code such formulas in Pascal.

15.8 Explain the meaning of the *summation* (Greek sigma) and *product* (Greek pi) notations and describe how to code formulas that use these notations into Pascal loops.

15.9 Explain what it means to say that Real numbers in a computer are usually *approximations* to the actual real values.

15.10 Describe *three important properties* that distinguish computer real numbers from the real numbers used in mathematics.

15.11 Explain how arithmetic operations with real numbers in a computer can lead to *overflow* errors, *underflow* errors, and *round off* errors.

15.12 Explain why two versions of the same mathematical formula that are equivalent under the rules of algebra may not produce equivalent results when evaluated in a computer (if Real number values are involved).

15.13 Why is it possible to add a large real number and a small real number in a computer and find that the result equals the large number?

15.14 If a computation involves a long sequence of arithmetic operations with real numbers, is the result always close to the true result (the result if you had made the computation by hand)? Why or why not?

15.15 Explain how to test if two real values are "equal."

15.16 Explain the proper way to write a count controlled loop where the first and last values in the range and the increment on each iteration are all real values.

■ ■ ■
PROGRAMMING PROBLEMS

15.1 *Checking for a Magic Square*. An N × N matrix of integers is a *magic square* if all the rows, columns, and diagonals sum to the same value and each integer value from 1 to N^2 appears exactly once. For example, this is a 5 × 5 magic square because each row, column and diagonal sums to 65 and each of the integers from 1 to 25 appears exactly once:

17	24	1	8	15
23	5	7	14	16
4	6	13	20	22
10	12	19	21	3
11	18	25	2	9

Write a program that will allow the user to enter the values for a magic square of size 10 × 10 or smaller and that will check whether the values do in fact form a magic square.

15.2 *Conway's Game of Life*. An interesting mathematical model of the evolution of a group of simple organisms is the *Game of Life* invented by J.H. Conway. Think of an N × N matrix as composed of cells. Each cell may contain a simple organism or be empty.

Initially, as the first "generation", some of the cells in the center of the matrix contain organisms and the rest are empty. Organisms are born and die depending on the contents of their eight neighboring cells, according to the following rules:

a. If in one generation, an empty cell has exactly three neighboring cells containing organisms, then a new organism is born in that cell in the next generation.

b. If in one generation, an organism has fewer than two neighboring cells containing organisms, then it dies from isolation before the next generation and its cell becomes empty.

c. If in one generation, an organism has more than three neighboring cells containing organisms, then it dies from overcrowding before the next generation and its cell becomes empty.

d. All other organisms survive unchanged to the next generation.

The "game" proceeds by simulating the generations of organisms that are produced by these rules. For example, here are the first several generations produced by starting with the initial generation on the left:

```
  □         □ □     □    □          □       □ □ □
□ □       □ □ □     □        □   □ □    □ □  □   □
  □         □ □     □    □          □       □ □ □

GEN 1     GEN 2    GEN 3         GEN 4       GEN 5
```

Write a program that will "play" Conway's Game of Life. The user should be able to enter the initial placement of organisms. Then the program should display each succeeding generation on the screen. After each generation is displayed, wait for the user to hit RETURN before continuing.

In Conway's definition, the matrix was infinite in all directions. However, for the program, limit the matrix to 20×80, so that it can be displayed on the screen conveniently. Consider any cell outside the matrix as always empty for purposes of determining the next generation of organisms on the border of the array.

15.3 *Computing the Value of an Infinite Series.* Mathematical values are often defined by using an *infinite series*—a sum of an infinite number of terms, where the terms get successively smaller. We say that the terms of the series *converge* to the correct value. To compute the value, you compute each term and add it to the total until the new term becomes smaller than a specified tolerance. For example, you might be asked to compute the value of the infinite series:

$$S = 1/3 + 1/9 + 1/27 + \ldots + 1/3^k + \ldots$$

to within an accuracy of 0.00001, which means that you would compute the successive terms of the series until the value of the next term was less than 0.00001.

Write a program that will allow the user to enter the desired tolerance and that will compute the value of the series above to within that tolerance. The program should report the sum of the terms and the number of terms needed to reach the tolerance. Design the program so that each term is computed within a subprogram, so that the same program can be used to compute the value of any other infinite series simply by replacing the subprogram.

15.4 *Matrix Operations.* Write a program that will provide the following operations on N × N matrices. Use 4 × 4 matrices for testing:

a. Enter values to be stored in an N × N matrix, for up to three matrices at a time.

b. Display the contents of one of the stored matrices.

c. Add the corresponding elements of two N × N matrices to get a new N × N matrix.

d. Sum all the elements of a matrix.

e. Test whether a matrix is *symmetric,* meaning that the element A[I,J] = A[J,I] for all I and J.

f. Test whether a matrix is *upper triangular,* meaning that every element below and to the right of the main diagonal is zero, i.e., A[I,J] = 0 if I > J.

g. Test whether a matrix is *tridiagonal,* meaning that the only nonzero elements are those on the main diagonal or on the diagonals immediately above or below the main diagonal, i.e., A[I,J] = 0 if I is not equal to J, J+1 or J−1.

A

Table of ASCII Character Codes

Keyboard Character	Binary ASCII Code	Integer Equivalent	Keyboard Character	Binary ASCII Code	Integer Equivalent
!	00100001	33	P	01010000	80
"	00100010	34	Q	01010001	81
#	00100011	35	R	01010010	82
$	00100100	36	S	01010011	83
%	00100101	37	T	01010100	84
&	00100110	38	U	01010101	85
'	00100111	39	V	01010110	86
(	00101000	40	W	01010111	87
)	00101001	41	X	01011000	88
*	00101010	42	Y	01011001	89
+	00101011	43	Z	01011010	90
,	00101100	44	[	01011011	91
–	00101101	45	\	01011100	92
.	00101110	46	]	01011101	93
/	00101111	47	^	01011110	94
0	00110000	48		01011111	95
1	00110001	49	`	01100000	96
2	00110010	50	a	01100001	97
3	00110011	51	b	01100010	98
4	00110100	52	c	01100011	99
5	00110101	53	d	01100100	100
6	00110110	54	e	01100101	101
7	00110111	55	f	01100110	102
8	00111000	56	g	01100111	103
9	00111001	57	h	01101000	104
:	00111010	58	i	01101001	105
;	00111011	59	j	01101010	106
<	00111100	60	k	01101011	107
=	00111101	61	l	01101100	108
>	00111110	62	m	01101101	109
?	00111111	63	n	01101110	110
@	01000000	64	o	01101111	111

Keyboard Character	Binary ASCII Code	Integer Equivalent	Keyboard Character	Binary ASCII Code	Integer Equivalent
A	01000001	65	p	01110000	112
B	01000010	66	q	01110001	113
C	01000011	67	r	01110010	114
D	01000100	68	s	01110011	115
E	01000101	69	t	01110100	116
F	01000110	70	u	01110101	117
G	01000111	71	v	01110110	118
H	01001000	72	w	01110111	119
I	01001001	73	x	01111000	120
J	01001010	74	y	01111001	121
K	01001011	75	z	01111010	122
L	01001100	76	{	01111011	123
M	01001101	77	¦	01111100	124
N	01001110	78	}	01111101	125
O	01001111	79	space	01111110	126

□
Notes:

1. The *integer equivalent* column shows the value returned by the predefined function *ord* for the given character value, and it also represents the decimal equivalent of the binary number used as the ASCII code.

2. The remaining ASCII codes represent nonprinting *control characters* and are not included in the table.

B

Other Features of Standard Pascal

Standard Pascal contains a number of features that are sometimes useful but that have not come up in the preceding chapters. Without giving full details, we mention the most important of these features here. References [1,2], as well as many other Pascal texts, provide further information. These additional features are listed in approximate order of importance.

Pointer Types and Dynamic Data Structures

Pascal provides a *pointer* data type and an operation *new* that may be used to create a new variable of a particular type and a pointer to the new variable. Using pointers and the *new* operation, the important class of *dynamic data structures* may be created and manipulated. These are data structures that grow and shrink in size during program execution, as opposed to arrays, records, and strings, whose size is invariant during execution of the program.

Nontext Files

Data values may be written to data files without first being converted to character form. The contents of such files may later be read in by the same or another program. These files are termed *nontext* files or *binary* files. They are discussed briefly in Chapter 11. Nontext files are useful for storing data when the data does not have to be displayed or edited by the user.

Sets and Set Operations

Pascal provides a way of defining data types that represent *sets* of values chosen from an *ordinal* base type, such as a Char, a subrange, or an enumerated type. Most Pascal implementations restrict the size of the base type, often to a rather small range of values.

Variables may be declared to be of set types. When set types are used, some of the basic arithmetic and relational operation symbols are extended to sets as follows:

OPERATION SYMBOL	MEANS
+	Union of two sets.
*	Intersection of two sets.
−	Difference of two sets.
=	Are the sets identical?
<>	Are the sets not identical?
<=	Is set1 a subset of set2?
>=	Is set2 a subset of set1?
IN	Is this value in the set?

□ □
Variant Records

A single record type definition may provide several alternative definitions for the fields of the record, termed *variants* of the record. This feature is useful when the object represented by the record may have different sets of attributes in different cases. For example, in an employee payroll record, you might see variants corresponding to:

- The fields needed to describe a *salaried* employee.
- The fields needed to describe an *hourly* employee.
- The fields needed to describe a *temporary* employee.

□ □
The WITH Statement

The WITH statement provides a shorthand way of writing a sequence of statements that select the fields of a record variable. The syntax is:

⟨WITH statement⟩ ::=

```
WITH ⟨record-variable⟩ DO
     ⟨WITH statement body⟩
```

The ⟨WITH statement body⟩ is any statement or sequence of statements enclosed in BEGIN...END. Inside the body, the fields of the ⟨record-variable⟩ may be selected *without* preceding them with the record variable name and the dot. For example, instead of writing:

```
StudentRecord.Name := NewName;
StudentRecord.Age := StudentRecord.Age + 1;
```

you can write the equivalent:

```
WITH StudentRecord DO
  BEGIN
     Name := NewName;
     Age := Age + 1;
  END;
```

Although WITH statements sometimes make a program slightly easier to code, they usually make the program harder to read.

□ □

Nested Subprogram Definitions

If one subprogram logically forms a part of a second subprogram (and is only called by the second subprogram) then the subprogram definition may be "nested" inside of the definition of the second subprogram. The nested subprogram definition is placed immediately after the VAR section of the second subprogram. The nested subprogram is not visible to any subprogram outside the second subprogram (and may not be called from any outside subprogram).

This feature is sometimes useful when a subprogram uses an auxiliary subprogram (such as in some recursive algorithms). In general, however, nested subprograms make the program harder to read.

□ □

Procedures and Functions as Parameters to Subprograms

The names of procedures and functions may be passed as parameters to other subprograms. The receiving subprogram may then call the *actual parameter* procedure or function by executing a call using the corresponding *formal parameter* name. This mechanism is occasionally useful in providing additional flexibility in the way a subprogram is written. The subprogram executes most of its actions in the usual way, but at a key point it calls a procedure or function to execute some action. That procedure or function is sent in as a parameter and does not have to be specified when the subprogram is written.

□ □

GOTO Statements and Statement Labels

Any Pascal statement may be labeled with an integer label:

$$\langle \text{integer} \rangle: \ \langle \text{statement} \rangle$$

Executing the statement "GOTO ⟨integer⟩" causes the control path to continue with the statement labeled with the designated integer rather than continuing in the ordinary sequence. Labels and GOTO statements are discussed briefly in Chapter 8. Although occasionally useful, their use often leads to "spaghetti code."

REFERENCES

[1] Jensen, K. and N. Wirth, *Pascal User Manual and Report,* 3rd edition, New York: Springer-Verlag, 1985.

[2] Cooper, D., *Standard Pascal: User Reference Manual,* New York: W.W.Norton, 1983.

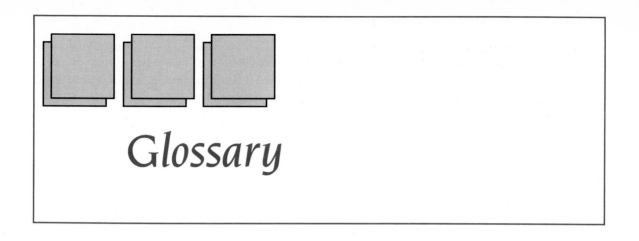

Glossary

Abstract data type   A data type together with all the operations on data objects of that type that make use of information about the representation of the data type.

Abstraction   The process of hiding details in a program, or the result of the process.

Action of a program   A part of a program that can be executed to change the state of the program; in Pascal, a *statement*.

Actual parameter   A data object or data value provided by the caller of a subprogram for use by the called subprogram.

Algorithm   A specification of the sequence of steps required to perform an information processing task and the data objects used in performing each step. Each step must be clearly defined and unambiguous.

Applications program   A computer program that performs an information processing task of interest in a particular area of human activity such as in business, science, or engineering. (As distinguished from programs such as compilers or operating systems that are used in the operation of a computer system.)

Argument   A formal parameter or actual parameter in a function heading or function call.

Arithmetic/logic unit (ALU)   The part of the computer's processor that performs the basic operations of the computer, such as addition, multiplication, and comparison, as requested by the *control unit*.

Arithmetic operation   One of the operations of addition, subtraction, multiplication, or division.

Array data type   A data type composed of a sequence of simpler data objects, called the *elements* of the array; each element may be selected by specifying its *subscript*. The range of possible subscripts is given by a subrange of integers or another ordinal type.

Array variable   A data object of an array data type.

ASCII   American Standard Code for Information Interchange; the most widely used method of encoding character data as sequences of bits for use in a computer system.

Assertion   A statement describing a property or characteristic of one or more states of a program during its execution.

Automatic tracing facility   Special software that provides debugging information about execution of a program without the use of debug WRITE statements within the program itself.

Average case efficiency   The efficiency of an algorithm when operating on "typical" input data (as opposed to *worst case efficiency*).

Back substitution   The process of substituting, for a variable name in one expression, the expression used to define the value of that variable in an assignment statement earlier in the control path.

Backus-Naur Form (BNF) A special notation developed by John Backus and Peter Naur for describing the form (syntax) of one or more lines of text.

Batch processing program A program that reads all its input data from data files and that writes all its results in data files, so that there is no interaction with the user's terminal during program execution (as opposed to an *interactive program*).

Big bang testing Testing a program as a unit, including all its subprograms, without first testing the subprograms separately (as opposed to *incremental testing*).

Big-Oh notation A notation used to describe the efficiency of an algorithm or data representation.

Binary encoding The representation of a piece of information as a sequence of bits.

Binary file See *nontext file*.

Binary search A search algorithm for a sorted table in which the table is split into two halves during each step of the search, with the search continuing in only one of the halves (as opposed to *linear search*).

Bit A binary digit; a zero or one. The basic unit of storage and information transfer in a computer system.

Body of a loop See *loop body*.

Body of a subprogram The actions or statements that are to be executed whenever the subprogram is called.

Boolean In Pascal, a data type with only two possible values, True and False.

Boolean operation An operation whose operands and result are of type Boolean; in Pascal, one of the operations AND, OR, or NOT.

Bottom up testing Testing a program by first testing the subprograms at the lowest level of the subprogram hierarchy, then testing the subprograms that call the lowest level subprograms, and so forth, working from the bottom towards the top of the program's structure chart (as opposed to *top-down testing*).

Branching program A program that contains a conditional action that chooses between one of several possible execution paths.

Bug An error in a program.

Byte A sequence of bits long enough to represent one character of data; usually eight bits, but the number can vary depending on the computer system.

Call of a subprogram An action that causes execution of a subprogram to take place during execution of a program.

Cathode ray tube (CRT) See *display*.

Central processing unit (CPU) See *processor*.

Char In Pascal, a data type that includes all the possible values consisting of a single character of data, such as "A" or "+".

Character string A sequence of character data values.

Coding The activity of constructing a complete computer program from a description of the algorithm to be used.

Command execution The process in which the operating system of a computer executes a command typed by the user.

Comment In Pascal, explanatory text or other information included in a program to aid readability by a person but which is ignored by the compiler.

Compiler A program used to translate a *source program,* written in some programming language, into an *object program* that can be executed by a computer.

Compound statement In Pascal, a sequence of statements enclosed in BEGIN...END that syntactically are treated as a single statement.

Computer A programmable electronic machine for processing information.

Computer science The systematic study of algorithmic processes that describe and transform information: their theory, analysis, design, efficiency, implementation, and application.

Conditional An action that chooses one of several alternative actions to execute each time it is executed; in Pascal, an IF or CASE statement.

Contradiction A Boolean-valued expression that can never return TRUE for any program state; equivalently, a path condition for a path that can never be executed.

Control flow analysis Analysis of a program or algorithm to determine the possible control paths and the conditions under which each path will be executed.

Control flow diagram See *flow chart*.

Control path One possible sequence in which the actions of a subprogram or algorithm may be executed.

Control unit (CU) The part of the computer's processor that controls the sequence in which the instructions of a program are executed.

Count and event controlled loop A loop in which the loop control combines both count controlled and event controlled forms. The count represents a bound on the number of iterations. The loop exits when the event is detected or when the count reaches its limit, whichever occurs first.

Count controlled loop A loop in which the loop control takes the form of a counter variable that counts through some specified range, with the loop exiting when the end of the range is reached.

Counter A data object used for counting in a program; usually of type Integer or a subrange of Integer.

Critical ten percent The actions in a program that account for most of its execution time, which usually amount to less than ten percent of all the actions in the program. See *ninety-ten rule*.

Cursor position The position within a line of input data where the next READ operation will begin reading.

Data abstraction The grouping of a complex set of data items into a single unit, such as a data type represented by an array or record.

Data file A file on which data values are written or a file from which data values are read during execution of a program.

Data flow analysis Analysis of a program segment that is concerned with identifying where particular data values are defined, used, and lost during execution of the segment.

Data flow diagram A diagram that shows how the actions in a control path are connected by their IN and OUT data objects.

Data object A named storage location in a program where one or more data values may be stored.

Data representation See *representation of a data type*.

Data state The collection of all the data objects used by a program and their current contents at a particular point during execution of the program.

Data structure A data object that can store more than one data value at a time, such as an array or record.

Data type An abstraction that defines a set of data values and the organization of those values within a data object. (See also *abstract data type*.)

Data value A single piece of data used in a program, such as a single number or character.

Debug WRITE statement A WRITE statement inserted solely for the purpose of displaying information during testing of a program and not during ordinary use of the program.

Debugging Finding and correcting an error in a program.

Default A specification of what is to be done during program execution in a situation where the program does not explicitly indicate the desired action.

Default case In a conditional action, a case that is to be executed when none of the other cases are chosen for execution.

Defined constant In Pascal, an identifier that represents a literal value, defined in the CONST section of a program.

Dialogue The sequence of interactions between the user and the program that occur as an interactive program is executed, consisting of the prompts and results that the program displays on the terminal screen and the input data that the user types on the keyboard.

Dial-up connection A connection between a terminal and a computer system that is established through a telephone line.

Digitizing The process of encoding a picture, sound, or other piece of information not typed on a keyboard into a sequence of bits.

Directly recursive subprogram A subprogram that contains a call on itself as one of the actions in its own body (as opposed to *indirectly recursive*).

Directory Within the file system of a computer, a list of the files that are part of a particular group of files, containing information about the name, time of creation, and other facts about each file.

Disk drive In a computer system, the device used to store and retrieve bits from a magnetic disk.

Diskette (floppy disk) A small removable magnetic disk.

Display The output part of a terminal; it receives a sequence of bits from the computer, decodes the bits, and displays the appropriate characters or other information on a television-like screen.

Display state The information that is displayed on the terminal display screen at a particular point during execution of a program.

Divide and conquer algorithm An algorithm that works by breaking a problem into two or more major parts that can be solved independently and the results combined.

Documenting a program Providing information in the form of comments within a program or written supplementary documents that make the program understandable to a person.

Dumb terminal A terminal that has no significant processor, memory, or secondary storage of its own and that cannot be used as a computer by itself.

Echo To use a debug WRITE statement to display a data value immediately after it has been read in, in order to check that the value was input correctly.

Editor A program that aids a computer user in entering programs, data, or other text typed on a terminal keyboard into a file in a computer system, or that aids the user in modifying, displaying or printing the contents of an existing file.

Effective procedure A procedure for performing an information processing task that always leads to the desired result in a finite number of steps.

Efficiency of an algorithm The time required to execute the steps of an algorithm or the number and size of the data objects used by the algorithm. See *time efficiency* and *space efficiency*.

Efficient program A program that avoids unnecessary actions and data objects in order to execute more quickly and use less of the computer's memory during its execution.

Electronic mail Software that allows one user to type in a message and send it to another user of the same computer system, or, via a network, to a user of another computer system.

Empty file A data file that contains no data values; usually a file whose status has just been changed to "open for writing."

Empty list A list that contains no entries.

Empty statement In Pascal, a "statement" that consists of no characters, used as a mechanism to allow semicolons to be written at the end of statements where they otherwise would be disallowed.

Encapsulation Information hiding within an abstraction that is supported by features of a programming language, so that the information hiding is guaranteed to be complete (without the use of "coding conventions" by the programmer).

End of file marker (EOF) In Pascal, an indication of the end of a data file, logically represented by a special mark that can be tested by the *eof* function.

End of line character (EOLN) In Pascal, a special character that marks the end of a line of input data or output data in a data file or on the terminal screen.

Enumerated data type A data type whose definition consists of a list of identifiers that serve as the literal values of the type.

Event controlled loop A loop in which the loop control takes the form of a test after each iteration to determine if some "event" has occurred during execution of the loop body. Repetition continues until the "event" is detected by the test and then the loop exits.

Exhaustive tests A set of tests such that at least one must return a TRUE value for any given program state.

Expression In Pascal, a part of a statement that specifies how to compute a single data value.

Extension of a programming language A statement, declaration, or other aspect of a programming language as it is implemented on a particular computer system that is not part of the standard definition of the language.

External file name The name of a file as it is known to the operating system of the computer (as opposed to *internal file name*).

Factoring a statement Removing a statement from within a loop or conditional and placing it before the loop or conditional.

Fetch operation In a computer memory, the process of retrieving a copy of the value stored in a particular word or byte.

Field width In Pascal, a specification of the number of character positions in an output line to allot for a particular output data value.

File A permanent storage area for programs or data in the secondary storage part of a computer system.

File system The storage areas in a computer system that provide permanent storage for user programs and data and the programs that control access to this storage; user pro-

grams and data are stored in individual *files* in the file system.

Final state The state of a program or of one of its subprograms when all the actions in its ALGORITHM part have been completed and it is about to terminate.

Fixed disk A magnetic disk that is permanently housed with its associated disk drive and attached to a computer system (as opposed to a *removable disk*).

Flag A data object or variable used to carry the result of a test from the point where the test is made (where the flag is "set") to the point where the result of the test is needed (where the flag is "tested").

Floppy disk See *diskette*.

Flow chart A diagram showing the control paths through a program segment.

Flow through value A data value that is stored in an OUT data object of a program segment at the beginning of execution of the segment and that may not be lost when the segment is executed.

Formal parameter A local data object within a subprogram whose initial value is determined by the corresponding *actual parameter* provided by the caller; used to transfer data values into the subprogram from the caller and/or to transfer data values back to the caller from the subprogram.

Fraction size In Pascal, a specification of the number of digits to the right of the decimal point to include in an output line for a particular Real data value.

Function subprogram A subprogram that is called during the execution of an expression and whose execution results in a single data value being returned to the caller.

Function value assignment In Pascal, an assignment statement within the body of a function that specifies the value to be returned to the caller as the result of the function's execution.

Giga- A prefix meaning *one billion*.

Global data object (global variable) A data object that is accessible by name within every subprogram of a program. In Pascal, a variable declared in the VAR section of the main program.

Goal state   A description of the program state to be reached at the end of a sequence of program actions.

Guard   A test that is made before an action or program segment is executed and that allows execution of the action or segment only if the test is satisfied; the test usually tests whether a *precondition* of the action or segment is true.

Hacker   1. A person who uses illegal or devious means to make use of a computer system on which he has no authorized account. 2. A programmer who writes programs quickly and somewhat crudely, without proper attention to the requirements, design, or testing of the program (in the same sense that a hack writer writes books quickly and somewhat crudely).

Hand tracing   The process of executing the actions of a program by hand for particular test data values, while keeping track of the program state on a piece of paper. Also known as "playing computer."

Hardware   The physical components of a computer system, such as the processor, memory, secondary storage and input/output devices.

Hard-wired connection   A connection between a terminal and computer system using a direct wire or cable connection (as opposed to a *dial-up* or *network* connection).

Header comment   A comment placed at the beginning of a program or subprogram that identifies the purpose and provides other general information about the program or subprogram.

Heading of a subprogram   The specification of the name and parameters (order and data type of each) of a subprogram.

Hierarchy of subprograms   The logical organization of the subprograms in a program into a hierarchy based on the calls that each subprogram makes on the others. The main procedure is at the top of the hierarchy, the

subprograms it calls are at the second level in the hierarchy, and so forth.

Identifier   In Pascal, a name for a variable, data type, constant, subprogram, or other program element.

Implementation of a programming language   On a computer system, the compiler or interpreter program that makes it possible to execute programs written in the programming language on that computer system.

Importing a module   Making the "visible" elements of a module available for use in another part of a program.

Incremental testing   Testing a program by testing its subprograms separately first and then in ever larger groups until the entire program has been tested.

Indirectly recursive subprogram   A subprogram that does not directly call itself but that initiates a chain of subprogram calls that leads eventually to a recursive call on itself (as opposed to *directly recursive*).

Infinite loop   A loop in which the loop exit test never returns a value that causes exit of the loop, so that the loop body is executed "forever" (until some outside action is taken to terminate it).

Infinite recursion   A chain of recursive calls of a subprogram in which each execution of the subprogram body leads to another recursive call, so that no execution of the body is ever completed.

Information hiding   The process of hiding details within an abstraction, such as the details of a data representation within a data type or the details of actions within a subprogram.

Initial state   The state of a program or of one of its subprograms immediately before the execution of the first action in its ALGORITHM part (in a subprogram, usually after parameter transmission is complete).

Inner loop   A loop that is contained within the body of another loop, the *outer loop*.

Input data   The data that is typed by the user on a terminal keyboard in response to a prompt or that is read from a file during execution of a program.

Input device In a computer system, a device used to transfer programs and data into the computer from the outside world.

Insertion sort An algorithm for sorting the entries in a table that works by inserting the first remaining entry from the unsorted part into its correct place in the sorted part.

Instrument a program To add data objects and actions to a program whose purpose is to provide a measure of the performance of the program, such as a counter that determines the number of times a particular part of the program is executed.

Integer In Pascal, a data type that includes all positive and negative integers that can be used by a program.

Integrated programming environment A programming environment in which the user can easily shift between editing a program, compiling a program, and executing a program, without starting and stopping the editor and compiler programs separately.

Interactive program A program that displays its results on the terminal display screen and that reads its input data from the terminal keyboard as it is executed, so that it interacts directly with the user as it runs (as opposed to a *batch processing program*).

Intermediate state A state that is neither an *initial state* nor a *final state* that occurs during execution of a program or of one of its subprograms.

Internal documentation Written documents or comments within a program that are used to make the internal structure of the program understandable to a person (as opposed to a *user's manual* for the program).

Internal file name The name by which a data file is known inside a program (as opposed to *external file name*).

Interpreter A program that takes a source program and directly executes each of the actions specified by the program, in the proper sequence, without ever translating the program into an object program.

Iteration One repetition of the body of a loop.

Kilo- A prefix meaning *one thousand*.

Linear search An algorithm for searching a table that works by scanning the table entries one by one in the order that they appear in the table (as opposed to *binary search*).

Literal value A data value that is written explicitly as part of the description of a program action in pseudo-code or Pascal, rather than being computed or read in during execution of the program.

Local state In a subprogram, the data state composed only of the parameters and local data objects of the subprogram.

Logic error An error in an algorithm or program that is not a result of a mistake in coding the program (as opposed to *syntax error* or *semantic error*).

Login The process of establishing that a user attempting to access a time-shared computer system has an authorized account on that system.

Logout The process of completing and terminating a session in which a person has made use of a time-shared computer system.

Loop An action that repeats a sequence of simpler actions, the *loop body*, until a test indicates that the repetition should end.

Loop body The sequence of actions that is repeated when a loop is executed.

Loop control The tests and actions in a loop and its startup segment that are concerned with determining when the repetition of the loop body should end.

Loop entry state The program state at the time the body of a loop begins execution for the first time.

Loop exit state The program state at the time of exit from a loop.

Loop invariant An assertion that describes a property of the program state that is true at the end of each iteration of the body of a loop (or at some other designated point in the loop body), regardless of the number of iterations of the loop.

Looping program   A program that contains a loop.

Magnetic disk   In a computer system, a disk shaped secondary storage device with a surface coating that can be easily magnetized.

Magnetic tape   In a computer system, a length of plastic tape used for secondary storage; the tape has a surface coating that can be easily magnetized.

Main procedure   The procedure that controls the overall action of a program; the procedure at the top level of a program's structure chart.

Mainframe   A large computer system capable of handling fifty to several hundred simultaneous users.

Maintenance of a program   Programming activities that occur after a program has been tested and put into regular use, such as correction of residual errors, improvements to the program, and modifications required due to changes in the operating system or other surrounding software.

Matrix   A two-dimensional array.

Mega-   A prefix meaning *one million.*

Memory (main memory)   In a computer system, the storage area for programs and data that are currently in use by the system (as opposed to *secondary storage*).

Memory address   In a computer memory, the number that identifies a particular word or byte within the memory.

Menu   A list of commands or choices displayed on a computer terminal's display screen from which the user chooses the next action for the computer to take.

Micro-   A prefix meaning *one millionth of.*

Microcomputer   The simplest type of computer system; for a single user.

Milli-   A prefix meaning *one thousandth of.*

Minicomputer   A medium-sized computer system capable of handling ten to fifty simultaneous users.

Mips   Millions of instructions executed per second; a measure of computer speed.

Modem   Short for *modulator-demodulator;* a device that allows a computer terminal to use a telephone line to establish a connection with a computer system or computer network.

Modularity   The organization of a program into relatively independent parts, such as subprograms and data types, such that each part may be replaced or modified without affecting more than a few of the other parts.

Module   A group of related data types and operations (subprograms) on those data types, possibly also including defined constants and data objects that are "global" to the operations of the module. Also termed a *package* or *unit.*

Multidimensional array   An array with two or more subscript ranges (dimensions).

Mutually exclusive cases   A set of cases in a conditional action of which at most one is chosen for execution each time the conditional is executed (as opposed to *nonexclusive cases*).

Mutually exclusive tests   A set of tests exactly one of which can return a TRUE value in any given program state (as opposed to *nonexclusive tests*).

Mutually recursive subprograms   A group of subprograms in which there exists a chain of calls, starting at any member of the group and leading through the other members, that ends in a recursive call by one of the other members on the starting subprogram. Each member of the group is *indirectly recursive.*

Name conflict   The inadvertant use of the same name for two separate program elements when the language does not allow that use.

Naming convention   A rule for choosing the names (identifiers) in a program so as to make it impossible or unlikely that a name conflict will occur.

Nano- A prefix meaning *one billionth of*.

Negation of a test A test that always returns a TRUE value when the original test returns FALSE, and vice versa.

Nested loop A loop that appears inside the body of another loop.

Network of computers (computer network) A group of computers connected together using wires or cables in such a way that a user can access any of the individual computers from a terminal connected to the network or to any of the other computers.

Ninety-ten (90–10) rule The rule of thumb that says that most programs spend at least 90 percent of their execution time executing less than 10 percent of the program actions.

Nonexclusive cases A set of cases in a conditional action of which more than one may be chosen for execution each time the conditional is executed (as opposed to *mutually exclusive cases*).

Nonexclusive tests A set of tests in which more than one can return a TRUE value in some program state (as opposed to *mutually exclusive tests*).

Nontext file A data file that contains data values in their binary form, as they are stored in the computer's memory (as opposed to a *text file*). Also termed a *binary file*.

Object program A computer program in a form in which it can be immediately executed by the processor of a computer system; usually the result of the translation performed by a compiler.

Off by one error An error in the control part of a loop that causes the loop to execute one iteration too many or too few in certain situations.

Operand A data value used by an operation in performing its action.

Operating system The program or collection of programs that control and monitor the overall operation of a computer system.

Operation A part of a program action that computes a new data value or that changes

the program state, possibly using some existing data values, its *operands*.

Ordinal data type A data type composed of a sequence of data values in which each value except the last has a well-defined successor and each value except the first has a well-defined predecessor; in Pascal, an enumerated or subrange type or one of the predefined types Integer, Char, or Boolean.

Outer loop A loop whose body contains another loop, termed the *inner loop*.

Output data The results produced by execution of a program and displayed on the terminal screen or stored in a file.

Output device In a computer system, a device used to transfer programs and data from the computer to the outside world.

Output line In Pascal, a single line of text that ends with an end-of-line character (EOLN) and that is written to the terminal display or a data file during execution of a program.

Overflow error An error that occurs when an arithmetic operation (or other operation) produces a numeric result that is too large (in either the positive or negative direction) to be represented in the binary encoding used in the computer system.

Package See *Module*.

Parameter transmission At the time that a subprogram is called, the process of making the connection between the *actual parameters* specified in the subprogram call and the *formal parameters* specified in the subprogram heading.

Partially filled array An array data object in which only some of the elements are ordinarily used when the program is executed.

Path condition Given a particular control path through a program segment, a test that gives a TRUE value at the beginning of execution of the segment if execution will follow that control path when the segment is executed.

Path testing Testing a program by choosing test data that will cause particular control paths within the program to be executed.

Performance of a program The speed of execution of a program, the amount of memory or secondary storage required for its use, or the amount of other computer system resources that are required for its use.

Peripheral device In a computer system, an input/output or secondary storage device housed in a separate cabinet from the computer's processor and memory.

Personal computer See *microcomputer*.

Pico- A prefix meaning *one trillionth of*.

Position of a file The position of the cursor in a file that is open for reading or writing, indicating the next character or data value that will be read from the file or the position where the next data value will be written in the file.

Postcondition An assertion stating a property of the data values produced by execution of an action or program segment that must be true when execution is complete, provided that the action or segment begins execution in a state that satisfies all of its *preconditions*.

Precedence order The order in which the operations within an expression will be chosen for execution if no parentheses are used for grouping the operations.

Precondition An assertion stating a property of the data values used by an action or program segment that must be true when the action or segment begins execution if the action or segment is to work correctly (as opposed to a *postcondition*).

Precondition/postcondition analysis (pre/post analysis) Reasoning about the correctness of a computation by using chains of postconditions and preconditions. Beginning with a precondition of one action, postconditions are attached to earlier actions, which may lead to new preconditions on those actions, and so forth.

Predefined function A function subprogram that is defined as part of a particular Pascal implementation and that may be used in any program without definition inside the program.

Priming a loop Executing actions in the startup segment for a loop that serve to create the correct loop entry state for the first iteration of the loop body.

Private file A file accessible only by a single user, the owner of the file (as opposed to a *public file*).

Problem size In discussing the efficiency of an algorithm or program segment, a rough measure of the number of data items to be processed, such as the size of an input data file or the size of a table or array.

Procedural abstraction The grouping of a complex sequence of actions into a single unit in which details are hidden, such as a procedure or function.

Procedure A subprogram that is called in a separate statement and whose execution changes the state of the caller.

Processor The part of the computer hardware that executes the instructions in a program, also called the *central processing unit (CPU)*.

Program An algorithm for performing an information processing task that has been stated using the notation provided by some programming language.

Programmer A person who engages in programming.

Programming The activity of designing, constructing, testing, or modifying a computer program.

Programming environment The software of the computer system that is used during the process of constructing, compiling, and testing a program, such as editors, compilers, debuggers, and automatic tracing systems.

Programming language A notation for writing programs to be executed by a computer.

Programming method A method used by a programmer to speed the construction or modification of a computer program.

Programming tool A part of the software or hardware of a computer system that automates some part of the task of constructing, testing, or modifying a computer program.

Progress toward termination In a loop, the idea that each repetition of the loop body must include some actions that bring the program state "closer" to a situation where the loop exit test will cause an exit of the loop. In a recursion, the idea that each recursive call of a subprogram must include some change in the actual parameter values that allows the next level of recursion to begin in a state that is "closer" to one of the base cases of the recursion.

Prompt A message displayed by a program on the terminal screen that requests the user to type something on the keyboard.

Prototype A simplified version of a program that satisfies some part of the program's requirements.

Pseudo-code An informal description of the design of a program, written so that each part is in approximate correspondence with a part of the final coded program.

Public file A file that can be accessed by all users of a computer system.

Random access memory (RAM) A computer memory in which any individual word or byte can be used in a fetch/store operation by giving its memory address; the usual form of computer memory.

Range test A test that determines whether a particular data value is within a specified range of possible data values.

Reading data Copying one or more data values into one or more data objects in the computer's memory from a data file or as typed in by the user.

Real In Pascal, a data type that includes all the numbers that may have fractional parts, including zero and all the integers.

Record data type A data type composed of a sequence of named simpler data objects, called the *fields* of the record.

Record variable A data object of a record data type.

Recursion The process of solving a problem by dividing its solution into two or more simpler subproblems, at least one of which is a simpler version of the original problem.

Recursive algorithm An algorithm in which one of the actions sometimes involves applying the same algorithm to a simpler version of the original problem or task.

Recursive call Execution of a call on a subprogram that occurs during the execution of the body of the same subprogram in response to an earlier call.

Recursive subprogram A subprogram that makes a recursive call.

Redundant test In an ordered sequence of tests, a test whose value (TRUE or FALSE) can always be determined by knowing the result of one or more of the tests that precede it in the sequence.

Reference parameter See *VAR parameter.*

Register In a computer's processor, an internal storage area for data or instructions.

Relational operation An operation that compares its two operands and produces a TRUE/FALSE (Boolean) result; in Pascal, one of the operations =, <>, <, >, <=, or >=.

Removable disk A magnetic disk that may be removed from the cabinet that houses a disk drive, for separate storage.

Representation of a data type The details of how the data values in a data object of the data type are organized, including the data types of individual values and their ranges.

Requirements for a program A detailed specification of the information processing task to be performed by a program, including a description of the input data, required processing, and output data for the program, possibly with additional assumptions about the use or performance characteristics of the program.

Reserved word In Pascal, a word such as WHILE, IF, or PROGRAM that is written as a necessary part of a statement, declaration, or other program element; a reserved word cannot be used by the programmer as an identifier.

Right justified Positioning an output data item so that it ends in the rightmost character position of its field within an output line.

Robust program A program that continues to operate or that "fails gracefully" when given incorrect input data, by either detecting the bad input data and requesting a correction or by producing a meaningful error message and terminating execution.

Round off error The loss of precision in the representation of a real number in a computer that occurs because of the limited length (number of digits) in the number representation inside the computer.

Routine A subprogram.

Run time The time during which a program is being executed by a computer.

Run time error message An error message produced by a computer system in response to detection of an error during execution of a program.

Run time stack The storage area in the computer's memory where the local states for subprograms are allocated storage at the time a subprogram call is made.

Run time stack overflow An error that occurs when a subprogram call is made and there is no space left in the run-time stack to allocate storage for the local state of that subprogram. Usually a result of an infinite recursion. In Pascal, also termed a *stack/heap collision*.

Scope rule A rule that determines, for a name defined in a program declaration, the other statements or declarations in the program where that definition of the name holds.

Scratch file A data file used for temporary storage of data during execution of a program. Data values are written on the file at one point during execution of the program and then later the data values are read in and processed again.

Secondary storage In a computer system, the storage area for programs and data that are not currently being used by the system or that are being used infrequently; usually a magnetic disk or magnetic tape.

Selection sort An algorithm for sorting the entries in a table that works by selecting the largest (or smallest) entry remaining in the unsorted part of the table and inserting it at the end of the sorted part.

Semantic error A mistake in the meaning of a coded program statement or declaration, where what is written does not mean what the programmer intended (as opposed to *syntactic error* and *logic error*).

Semantics of a programming language The meaning of the individual statements and declarations of the language.

Sentinel key In a linear search through a table, a copy of the desired key value that is placed at the end of the table in order to guarantee that the search will always succeed, so that no test for the end of the table is needed in the search algorithm.

Sentinel value A value used to indicate the end of a sequence of data values in a data file or in a sequence of values typed by the user.

Side effect A change made by a subprogram in the value of a global data object.

Simple data object (simple variable) A data object that can store only a single data value at a time during program execution, such as a single number or character value.

Size of an array The number of elements in an array.

Snapshot procedure A procedure used during testing and debugging whose purpose is to display the current values of one or more data objects.

Software The programs that are available to be run on a computer to perform various information processing tasks.

Source program A program as written by a programmer, before being compiled into an *object program*.

Space efficiency The number and size of the data objects used by an algorithm or program segment, or the total amount of storage used during program execution.

Spaghetti code A program or subprogram that contains many complicated control paths.

Spreadsheet A program that allows a user to

easily compute and display tables of figures and to easily recompute the tables in order to answer "what if" questions about the data.

Spurious error message   An error message produced by a compiler that suggests that a correct program element is incorrect.

Stack/heap collision   See *run-time stack overflow*.

Standard programming language   A programming language whose syntax and semantics have been completely specified in a written document that has been accepted as the "standard" definition of the language by a government agency or international standards organization.

Startup segment   A sequence of actions immediately preceding a loop whose purpose is to correctly define starting values for data objects used in the loop exit test or loop body.

State of a program   At a particular point during the execution of a program, the collection of all the data objects used by the program and their current contents, the information that is currently displayed on the terminal screen, and the current contents, position, and status of all data files used by the program.

Statement   In Pascal, an action in the body of a subprogram.

Statement label   In Pascal, an integer used to label a statement so that the statement may be named in a "go to" statement.

Status of a file   Whether a data file is open for reading, open for writing, or closed at some point during execution of a program.

Step size   In a count-controlled loop, the amount added to (or subtracted from) the counter variable at the end of each loop iteration.

Stepwise refinement   The process of designing a program by first defining the large steps in the algorithm, and then refining each step to provide more detail, repeating the process at each level of design until all details have been filled in.

Store operation   In a computer memory, the process of changing the settings of the bits in a particular word or byte to represent a particular data value.

Stored program   Instructions for carrying out an information processing task that are stored in the memory of a computer.

Straight-line actions   A sequence of actions that are always executed in the same order, one after the other.

Structure chart   A diagram showing the logical subprogram hierarchy of a program in terms of the calls that individual subprograms make on other subprograms.

Stub   A subprogram whose heading is correct but whose body has not been completely defined; the subprogram can be compiled, but it does not perform the intended action.

Style in programming   Elements of the way a program is coded that have nothing to do with the correctness of the program but that are intended to make the program more understandable to a human reader.

Subprogram   An operation defined within a program; either a procedure or function.

Subrange   A data type defined as a restriction of an existing ordinal data type, such as Integer or Char, to a smaller set of possible values.

Subscript expression   In a program statement, an expression that follows the name of an array variable and that is evaluated to determine the subscript of the array element to be used when the statement is executed.

Subscript range   The range of subscript values that name elements of a particular type of array; specified as part of the definition of an array data type.

Subscript range error   During execution of a statement, evaluation of a subscript expression that gives a subscript value outside of the declared subscript range for an array.

Subscripted variable   In a program statement, an array variable name followed by a subscript expression.

Supercomputer The largest and fastest type of computer system.

Syntactic error (syntax error) A mistake in the form of a coded program declaration or statement, such as an error in spelling, punctuation, or grammar (as opposed to *semantic error* and *logic error*).

Syntax of a programming language The form (spelling, punctuation, grammar) of the statements and declarations of a programming language.

System malfunction A error caused by a failure of the hardware or software of the computer system but not caused by an error in the particular program that is being executed.

Tape drive In a computer system, a device for reading/writing bits on the surface of a magnetic tape.

Tera- A prefix meaning *one trillion*.

Terminal In a computer system, an input/output device with a display screen and keyboard that is used by a person to gain access to the system.

Test An operation that produces a TRUE/FALSE (Boolean) result.

Test driver A program constructed for the sole purpose of testing one or more subprograms that will ultimately form part of a larger program.

Testing a program Execution of a program in order to determine whether it is operating correctly.

Text file A data file that contains data values represented in character form (as opposed to a *nontext file*).

Time efficiency The speed of execution of an algorithm or program segment.

Time-shared computer system A computer system that allows many users to simultaneously access and use the system.

Top-down design The process of designing a program by starting at the top level of the program, with the main procedure, and progressively developing the algorithm steps and data representations at lower levels of detail.

Top-down testing Testing a program by first testing the main procedure and the subprograms at the top levels of the program's structure chart, working down toward the lowest level subprograms, with untested subprograms represented by *stubs* during testing.

Tracing execution Following the sequence of actions taken during execution of a program.

Trip One execution of a loop body; an *iteration*.

Turing machine A simple mathematical "machine" capable of being programmed to carry out an effective procedure.

Turing's thesis The hypothesis that any effective procedure may be represented as a program for a Turing machine.

Two-state device An electronic device that can represent a single bit by being in exactly one of two possible "states" at any time.

Underflow error An error that occurs when an arithmetic operation (or other operation) produces a real number result that is so close to zero that it cannot be represented in the binary encoding used in the computer system.

Uninitialized variable During execution of a program, any variable that has not yet been assigned a value by an action of the program; the value of an uninitialized variable is unpredictable if used in an action.

Unit See *Module*.

User interface The overall characteristics of how a program interacts with its user.

User's manual A written document that describes how to make use of a particular program.

Value parameter In Pascal, a parameter for a subprogram that is transmitted by copying the value (or values in the case of a data structure) of the actual parameter into the formal parameter.

VAR parameter In Pascal, a parameter for a subprogram that is transmitted by storing a pointer to the actual parameter in the storage location of the formal parameter, so that whenever the subprogram uses or defines the value of the formal parameter, the actual parameter is used or defined.

Variable In Pascal, a data object.

Vector An array with a single subscript range; a one-dimensional array.

Verification The activity of checking a program or algorithm for correctness, especially to detect logic errors.

Word In a computer memory, a sequence of bits that can store a single number; usually 2–8 bytes.

Word processor An editor program that is specialized for the creation and modification of documents such as letters, reports, and books.

Workstation A computer system for one or a few users with more computational power and memory than a microcomputer.

Worst case efficiency The efficiency of an algorithm when operating with input data that makes it perform as badly as possible (as opposed to *average case efficiency*).

Writing data Copying data values from one or more data objects in the computer's memory to a data file or to be displayed on the user's terminal screen.

Zero-trip path A control path through a loop that does *not* include the statements in the loop body.

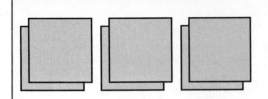

Answers to Selected Exercises

☐☐
Chapter 1

1.1 Change instruction 1 so that if a "." is read then the next instruction is 3. Then insert *Instruction 3:*
If read 0–7, write 2–9, move left, and HALT.
If read 8, write 0, move left, and next instruction = 2.
If read 9, write 1, move left, and next instruction = 2.
If read space, write 2, move left, and HALT.

1.3 Change instruction 1 so that if a space is read, then write a space, move left, and make 2 the next instruction.

☐☐
Chapter 2

2.15 **a.** Two gigabits.   **d.** One milli-inch.
       b. One picometer.   **e.** Three megabucks.
       c. One nanogram.   **f.** One terameter.

2.16 **a.** 0.0000175 seconds.
       b. 12,000,000,000,000 seconds.
       c. 64,000 bits.
       d. 3,000,000,000 bytes.
       e. 0.0000000024 grams.

☐☐
Chapter 3

3.2 ⟨fancy-integer⟩ ::= 0 | ... as given originally ...

3.3 **a.** ⟨date⟩ ::=

             ⟨day⟩/⟨month⟩/⟨year⟩

WHERE

$\langle$day$\rangle$ ::= Integer in the range 1 to 31.
$\langle$month$\rangle$ ::= Integer in the range 1 to 12.
$\langle$year$\rangle$ ::= Integer in the range 1900 to 2100.

d. $\langle$weather report$\rangle$ ::=

TEMP = $\langle$temperature$\rangle$
WIND = $\langle$wind speed$\rangle$ [FROM $\langle$direction$\rangle$]
PRECIP = $\langle$precipitation$\rangle$ [OF $\langle$type of precipitation$\rangle$]
SKY = $\langle$cloud cover$\rangle$

WHERE

$\langle$temperature$\rangle$ ::= Temperature in degrees Celsius.
$\langle$wind speed$\rangle$ ::= Wind speed in miles per hour.
$\langle$direction$\rangle$ ::= N | NE | E | SE | S | SW | W | NW
$\langle$precipitation$\rangle$ ::= Amount of precipitation in inches.
$\langle$type of precipitation$\rangle$ ::= RAIN | SNOW | SLEET
$\langle$cloud cover$\rangle$ ::=
CLEAR | SCATTERED | BROKEN | OVERCAST | FOG

3.4 c.

INPUTS: Length of base.
Height.
Whether figure is a rectangle or a right triangle.
PROCESSING: Compute perimeter.
Compute area.
OUTPUTS: Perimeter and area.
Type of figure.
ASSUMPTIONS: Use at a science fair.

DIALOGUE

PROGRAM: "Welcome to the Science Fair.
This demonstration program computes the perimeter and area of a figure.
You choose whether the figure is a rectangle or a right triangle and give the base and height of the figure. Type R for a rectangle or T for a right triangle:"

USER: $\langle$figure-type$\rangle$

PROGRAM: "Type the length of the base, in centimeters:"

USER: $\langle$length$\rangle$

PROGRAM: "Type the height of the figure, in centimeters:"

USER: $\langle$height$\rangle$

PROGRAM: "For a ⟨figure⟩ of base ⟨length⟩ and height ⟨height⟩:
                AREA = ⟨area⟩ square centimeters.
                PERIMETER = ⟨perimeter⟩ centimeters."

WHERE

⟨figure-type⟩ ::= R | T
⟨length⟩ ::= Positive real number length of the base, in centimeters.
⟨height⟩ ::= Positive real number height, in centimeters.
⟨figure⟩ ::= TRIANGLE | RECTANGLE
⟨area⟩ ::= Computed area of figure, in square centimeters.
⟨perimeter⟩ ::= Computed perimeter of figure, in centimeters.

3.5 DATA OBJECTS

c. Has Insurance: Boolean   TRUE if employee bought insurance.

d. Team1Score: Integer   First team's game score.
   Team2Score: Integer   Second team's game score.

g. FastSnail: Real   Speed of fastest snail in km/hr.

3.6   **a.** Yes, because it describes the relation between the value of X and the values of A, B, and C in a program state.

c. No, because it does not describe a property of any data object in a program state.

3.7   **a.** Total := Grade1 + Grade2
    Average := Total / 2

b. DISPLAY: "Please type two grade values (range 0-100)."
    READ: Grade1, Grade2

c. DISPLAY: "Total = ⟨Total⟩   Average = ⟨Average⟩"

d. IF Grade1 > Grade2 THEN
    FinalGrade := 'A'
  ELSE
    FinalGrade := 'B'

e. IsComplete := Count = 10

g. Total := 0
   READ: Grade
   WHILE Grade <> 0 DO

Total := Total + Grade
READ: Grade

3.8 Yes, you still need an extra data object. A sequence might be: Save := A;
A := B; B := C; C := Save.

3.9 **a.** Total1: 18   Count1: 0   Total2: 20   Count2: 6
    c. Total1: 9   Count1: 5   Total2: 2   Count2: 6

3.10 **c.** Using the requirements specification from 3.4 c:

ALGORITHM

Step 1: PURPOSE/GOAL STATE: Display the greeting messages.

Step 2: PURPOSE: Prompt the user for the type of figure, the base, and the height.
GOAL STATE: Type of figure stored in FigureType, base length stored in
Base, and height in Height.

Step 3: PURPOSE/GOAL STATE: Compute the area and perimeter for the chosen type
of figure and store in Area and Perimeter.

Step 4: PURPOSE/GOAL STATE: Display the figure type, base, length, area, and
perimeter.

3.11 **c.** Using the roughed-in algorithm from 3.10, the complete algorithm is:

Step 1: PURPOSE/GOAL STATE: ... as above ...
ACTIONS:

DISPLAY: "Welcome to the Science Fair."
This demonstration program computes the perimeter and
area of a figure."
You choose whether the figure is a rectangle or a right triangle and give the base and height of the figure."

Step 2: PURPOSE/GOAL STATE: ... as above ...
ACTIONS:

DISPLAY: "Type R for a rectangle or T for a right triangle:"
READ: FigureType
DISPLAY: "Type the length of the base, in centimeters:"
READ: Base
DISPLAY: "Type the height of the figure in centimeters:"
READ: Height

Step 3: PURPOSE/GOAL STATE: ... as above ...

ACTIONS:
    IF FigureType = 'T' THEN
        Area := 1/2 * Base * Height
        Perimeter := Base + Height +
            sqrt (Base * Base + Height * Height)
    ELSE   — Rectangle case
        Area := Base * Height
        Perimeter := 2 * Base + 2 * Height

Step 4: PURPOSE/GOAL STATE: ... as above ...

    ACTIONS:
    IF FigureType = 'T' THEN
        DISPLAY: "For a TRIANGLE of base ⟨Base⟩ and height ⟨Height⟩:"
            ELSE
        DISPLAY: "For a RECTANGLE of base ⟨Base⟩ and height ⟨Height⟩:"
        DISPLAY: "AREA = ⟨Area⟩ square centimeters.
            PERIMETER = ⟨Perimeter⟩ centimeters."

DATA OBJECTS

FigureType: Char	Type of figure.
Base: Real	Base of figure, in centimeters, > 0.
Height: Real	Height of figure, in centimeters, > 0.
Area: Real	Computed area of figure, in centimeters.
Perimeter: Real	Computed perimeter, in centimeters.

3.13 Insert the action between 2.2 and 2.3:

    FillupCount := 0

Insert the action in the loop body in 2.4:

    FillupCount := FillupCount + 1

Insert the action at the end of 4.1:

    DISPLAY: "NUMBER OF FILLUPS = ⟨FillupCount⟩"

3.14 b.   HAND TRACE

Step	Action	Total	Number	Count	Average
INITIAL STATE:		0	7	5	20
1.1	DISPLAY: . . .	0	7	5	20
1.2	Count := . . .	0	7	0	20
2.1	READ: . . .	0	0	0	20
2.2	WHILE . . .	0	0	0	20
3.1	Average := . . .	ERROR: Division by zero.			

FINAL STATE: None, the program crashed!

f. To repair the second error, replace action 3.1 by:

3.1 IF Count <> 0 THEN
     Average := Total / Count
   ELSE
     Average := 0

□ □
Chapter 4

4.1 Valid: May271988. Invalid: 27May1988, 2Timer (cannot begin with a digit), OnProbation?, X-YCoordinate, RosieO'Grady (illegal character).

4.3 **b.** VAR
```
    Size: Integer;        {City size, range 1 to 500
                           square miles.}
    Population: Real;      {City population, range 1 to 30
                           million.}
    AverageIncome: Real;  {Average personal income, range
                           $1000 - $50,000}
```

4.4 **a.** {PURPOSE/GOAL STATE: Set LargestScore to the larger of Score1 or Score2 and set Found = TRUE if Score2 is the larger. Otherwise set Found = FALSE.}

```
    If Score1 < Score2 THEN
       BEGIN
           LargestScore := Score2;
           Found := TRUE;
       END
    ELSE
       BEGIN
           LargestScore := Score1;
           Found := FALSE;
       END;
```

b. {PURPOSE: Sum the integers from 1 to MaxCount. GOAL STATE: Total contains the sum.}

```
    Count := 1;
    Total := 0;
    WHILE Count <= MaxCount DO
       BEGIN
           Total := Total + Count;
           Count := Count + 1;
       END;
```

4.5 **a.** Valid, Real. **e.** Valid, Integer.
d. Invalid. **h.** Valid, Integer.

4.6 **a.** 0 **c.** 1 **e.** 4

4.7 **a.** E := 2 * 2 - ((B + 1) + A); or E := 3 - B - A;
b. Z := 21 * sqrt (U+V) - (U-W);

4.8 **a.** Y := sqrt ((A+B) * (A-B)) / (A*A - 1);

4.9 **b.** IsBit := (Ch = '0') OR (Ch = '1');

4.10 **a.** FALSE **c.** 3 **e.** '7' **g.** '4'

4.12 **a.** *Precondition:* B <> 0
c. *Precondition:* G > 0
e. *Precondition:* A > 0 and B > 0

4.14

```
writeln ('And_the_answer_to_your_question_is_', Answer:1, '!');
```

4.15 **a.** writeln ('Linda''s birthday is ', BirthMonth:1, '/',
                        BirthDay:1, '/', BirthYear:1,'.');
b. writeln ('*':BirthMonth);

4.16 **a.** writeln ('PRINCIPAL':30, 'INTEREST':20);
        writeln (33.3:26, 5.55:20);
        writeln (22.2:26, 4.44:20);
c. writeln (' ':10, 'Jane Roe');
        writeln;
        writeln (' ':10, '109 Dogwood Lane');
        writeln;
        writeln (' ':10, 'River City, Virginia');
d. writeln ('   ¦   ¦   ':45);
        writeln ('   ¦   ¦   ':45);
        writeln ('   ¦   ¦   ':45);
        writeln ('-----+-----+-----':45);
        writeln ('   ¦   ¦   ':45);
        writeln ('   ¦   X ¦   ':45);
        writeln ('   ¦   ¦   ':45);
        writeln ('-----+-----+-----':45);
        writeln ('   ¦   ¦   ':45);
        writeln ('   ¦   ¦   ':45);
        writeln ('   ¦   ¦   ':45);
```

**4.17 c.**

```
write ('Please type your name or initials (3 letters only):');
readln (Initial1, Initial2, Initial3);
writeln 'Hi ', Initial1, Initial2, Initial3, '! Let''s compute!');
```

4.21 The most useful place to use a debug WRITE statement is within the WHILE loop, to check that the Gallons value is read correctly and correctly added to TotalGallons each time. Immediately after the "readln" in the loop body, insert the WRITE statement:

```
writeln ('Gallons = ', Gallons, 'TotalGallons = ', TotalGallons);
```
```

5.1 DEFINED CONSTANTS

    a. TENTHPOWEROFTWO = 1024   2 to the 10th power.
    b. MAXCLASSSIZE = ?   Maximum number of students in a class.
        MAXEXAMGRADES = ?   Maximum number of exam grades.
        MAXHOMEWORKS = ?   Maximum number of homework assignments.

5.2 CONST

```
TENTHPOWEROFTWO = 1024;     {2 to the 10th power. }
MAXCLASSSIZE = 200;         {Maximum number of students
                             in a class. }
MAXEXAMGRADES = 3;          {Maximum number of exam
                             grades. }
MAXHOMEWORKS = 10;          {Maximum number of homework
                             assignments. }
```

5.4 **a.** The natural data types might include:
    BoardPosition
    King
    Queen
    Pawn
    Rook
    b. The natural data types might include:
    Temperature
    WindSpeed
    Precipitation
    BarometricPressure
    CloudCover
    c. The natural data types might include:
    Student
    Course
    FinalGrade
    ExamGradesList
    HomeworkGradesList

5.5 **a.** FUNCTION ComputeGradeAverage

    (Grades: ListOfGrades   IN: Grades to be averaged.
     GradesCount: Integer)   IN: Number of Grades in the list.
    FUNCTION VALUE: Real   Average of grades.

PURPOSE: Compute the average of the grades in the list.
PRECONDITION: GradesCount must be in the range 0 to MAX
    NUMBEROFGRADES.

DATA TYPES

ListOfGrades = ?   List of exam grades.

b. PROCEDURE DisplaySalesGraph
  (MonthlySales: SalesList) IN: Total sales each month.

PURPOSE: Display a graph of the monthly sales for the year.

GOAL STATE: Graph displayed on the terminal screen.

DATA TYPES

SalesList = ? List of monthly sales totals for a year.

d. PROCEDURE FindMaxMinGrades

(Grades: ListOfGrades	IN
GradesCount: Integer	IN: Number of Grades in the list.
HighestGrade: Integer	OUT: Highest grade in the list.
LowestGrade: Integer)	OUT: Lowest grade in the list.

PURPOSE/GOAL STATE: Set HighestGrade = highest grade in list Grades and set LowestGrade = lowest grade in the list.

PRECONDITION: GradesCount must be in the range 0 to MAXNUM-BEROFGRADES.

DATA TYPES

ListOfGrades = ? List of exam grades.

f. PROCEDURE AlphabetizeNamesList
(Names: ListOfNames) IN/OUT

PURPOSE/GOAL STATE: Reorder the names in the Names list into alphabetical order.

DATA TYPES

ListOfNames = ? A list of names.

5.6 **a.** Average := ComputeGradeAverage (CS101List, ClassSize)

> *Valid* if CS101List is of type ListOfGrades and ClassSize is of type Integer.

Average := ComputeGradeAverage (CS101List, −2)

> *Invalid:* Precondition is not satisfied.

b. CALL DisplaySalesGraph (SalesFor1986)

> *Valid* if SalesFor1986 is of type SalesList.

CALL DisplaySalesGraph (SalesFor1986, 12)

> *Invalid:* Wrong number of actual parameters.

d. CALL FindMaxMinGrades (Grades, 200, High, Low)

> *Valid* if Grades is of type ListOfGrades and High and Low are of type Integer.

CALL FindMaxMinGrades (High, Low, Grades, 200)

> *Invalid:* Wrong order of actual parameters.

□ □
Chapter 6

6.1 **b.** "June 19, 1989" (give the actual date) or "The third Wednesday of next month"
 d. "One more than 26" or "XXVII"

6.2 **b.** `WaterTemp = 0..50;`   {Temperature of pond water.}
 d. `Initial = 'A'..'Z';`   {Middle initial.}

6.4 **c.** HomeworkStatus = (COMPLETE, PARTIAL, NOTBEGUN)

6.5 **a.** 0   **c.** DISCONNECTED   **e.** FALSE

6.7 **b.** DATA TYPES

Temperature = $-100..140$
CloudCoverOptions = (CLEAR, SCATTERED, BROKEN, OVERCAST)
PrecipitationOptions = (NONE, RAIN, SNOW, HAIL, SLEET, FOG)
WindSpeed = 0..150
Direction = (N, NE, E, SE, S, SW, W, NW, NOWIND)

WeatherData =
    RECORD
        AirTemp: Temperature
        CloudCover: CloudCoverOptions
        Precipitation: PrecipitationOptions
        Wind: WindSpeed
        WindDirection: Direction
    END

DATA OBJECTS

StartOfRace = WeatherData   Weather at start of the race.
EndOfRace = WeatherData   Weather at end of the race.

Assignments:

StartOfRace.AirTemp := 50;
StartOfRace.CloudCover := CLEAR;
StartOfRace.Precipitation := NONE;
StartOfRace.Wind := 0;
StartOfRace.WindDirection := NOWIND;

6.8   **a.** Data Types

ShortTable = ARRAY [0..6] OF Integer

Data Objects

PowersOfThree: ShortTable   List of the powers of three.

Assignments:

PowersOfThree [0] := 1
PowersOfThree [1] := 3
PowersOfThree [2] := 9
PowersOfThree [3] := 27
PowersOfThree [4] := 81
PowersOfThree [5] := 243
PowersOfThree [6] := 729

6.10 Data Types

     a. MonthLengthRange = 28..31
        MonthLengthTable = ARRAY [1..12] OF MonthLengthRange
     d. ItemChoices = (MILK, EGGS, ...)
        ItemList = ARRAY [1..MAXITEMS] OF ItemChoices
        ItemCount = 0..MAXITEMS
        GroceryList =
            RECORD
                Items: ItemList
                ListLength: ItemCount
            END
     f. ScoreRange = 0..MAXRUNS
        InningsCount = 1..MAXINNINGS
        InningScore =
            RECORD
                Team1: ScoreRange
                Team2: ScoreRange
            END
        InningsScoreList = ARRAY [1..MAXINNINGS] OF InningScore
        GameScore =
            RECORD
                Innings: InningsScoreList
                InningsPlayed: InningsCount
            END

6.11   **a.** Reduce the list length count by one; make no change in the list itself.

6.12   **a.** Data Types

WeekdayName = STRING [9]

DATA OBJECTS

WeekDay: WeekdayName   Name of this day.

Assignments:

WeekDay := 'Monday';

6.13 **a.** This algorithm assumes no leading spaces in Date1; the string in Date1 is left unchanged.

ACTIONS:
    Posn := 1
    Day1 := Copy (Date1, Posn, 2)
    Posn := Posn + 3
    Month1 := Copy (Date1, Posn, 3)
    Posn := Posn + 4
    Year1 := Copy (Date1, Posn, 4)
    DISPLAY: ⟨Month1⟩ ⟨Day1⟩, ⟨Year1⟩ — centered.

6.14 **b.** Markup := MallStore.Stock[2].Retail − MallStore.Stock[2].
              WholeSale

       DISPLAY: "The markup is ⟨Markup⟩."

d. DesiredColor := WHITE
    DesiredWaist := 30
    DesiredLength := 28
    NotFound := TRUE
    I := 1
    WHILE NotFound AND I <= MallStore.Count DO
        IF MallStore.Stock[I].Color = DesiredColor
            AND MallStore.Stock[I].Length = DesiredLength
            AND MallStore.Stock[I].Waist = DesiredWaist THEN
        NotFound := FALSE
        ELSE
            I := I + 1
    IF NotFound THEN

        DISPLAY: "The desired jeans are not in stock."
    ELSE

        DISPLAY: "The desired jeans are available."

□ □
Chapter 7

7.1 The Pascal code is:
    b. PROCEDURE FindMaxMin

```
        (VAR Max: Real;        {IN/OUT}
         VAR Min: Real);       {IN/OUT}
```

{PURPOSE/GOAL STATE: Compare the values of Max and Min and set Max to the larger of the two original values and Min to the smaller.}

```
VAR
    Save: Real;              {Used if a swap is needed.}


BEGIN
    IF Min > Max THEN
        BEGIN
            Save := Max;
            Max := Min;
            Min := Save;
        END;
END;        {procedure FindMaxMin}
```

d. PROCEDURE FindRoot

```
(B: Real;                   {IN}
 C: Real;                   {IN}
 VAR Root: Real;            {OUT: Root of the equa-
                            tion, if any}

 VAR RootExists: Boolean);  {OUT: TRUE if root
                            exists;
                            FALSE if equation has
                            no root}
```

{PURPOSE/GOAL STATE: Find the root of the linear equation B*X + C = 0. Store the root in Root and set RootExists = TRUE. If the equation has no root, set RootExists = FALSE and assign no value to Root.}

{PRECONDITION: The equation has at most one root.}

```
BEGIN
    IF B = 0 THEN
        BEGIN
            RootExists := FALSE;
        END
    ELSE
        BEGIN
            RootExists := TRUE;
            Root : = - C / B;
        END;
END;        {procedure FindRoot}
```

7.3 b. FUNCTION FindArea
```
        (Diameter: Real)      {IN}
         : Real;

        {PURPOSE: Return the Area of the circle with the
        given diameter}.

    CONST
      PI = 3.1416;

    BEGIN
        FindArea := PI * sqr (Diameter / 2);

    END;        {function FindArea}
```

7.4 The Pascal procedure body is:

```
BEGIN
        IF Ch IN ['A'..'Z', 'a'..'z'] THEN
          BEGIN
             ClassifyChar := LETTER;
          END
        ELSE IF Ch IN ['0'..'9'] THEN
          BEGIN
             ClassifyChar := DIGIT;
          END
        ELSE IF Ch = ' ' THEN
          BEGIN
             ClassifyChar := SPACE;
          END
        ELSE IF Ch IN ['(', ')', '[', ']', '{', '}'] THEN
          BEGIN
             ClassifyChar := PAREN;
          END
        ELSE IF Ch IN ['+', '-', '*', '/', '%'] THEN
          BEGIN
             ClassifyChar := ARITH;
          END
        ELSE
          BEGIN
             ClassifyChar := OTHER;
          END;
    END;        {function ClassifyChar}
```

7.6 b. The Pascal code is:

```
PROCEDURE PutOnSale

    (VAR StockJeans: Jeans;          {IN/OUT}
     SalePrice: Real);               {IN}
```

```
              {PURPOSE/GOAL STATE: Change the price field of
              StockJeans to SalePrice. }

       BEGIN
              StockJeans.Price := SalePrice;

       END;          {procedure PutOnSale}
```

7.7 **b.** The Pascal code is:

```
FUNCTION CountBestWeeks

     (VAR Sales: WeeklySalesList)                    {IN}
     : Integer;

       {PURPOSE: Return a count of the number of weeks in
       which sales equal the sales for the best week of the
       year}.

     VAR
       Count: Integer;          {Count of best weeks. }
       BestWeek: Integer:       {Number of best week. }
       BestSales: Real;         {Best week sales. }
       I: Integer;              {FOR loop subscript variable. }

BEGIN

              {PURPOSE/GOAL STATE: Set BestSales to sales in
              best week of year. }

       FindBestWeek (Sales, BestWeek, BestSales);

              {PURPOSE/GOAL STATE: Set Count = number of weeks
              with sales equal to BestSales value. }

       Count := 0;
       FOR I := 1 TO 52 DO
         BEGIN
           IF Sales [I] = BestSales THEN
             BEGIN
                Count := Count + 1;
             END;
         END;

              {PURPOSE/GOAL STATE: Return function value. }


       CountBestWeeks := Count;

       END;          {function CountBestWeeks}
```

7.11 Assume you have a function, StringToInteger, defined as follows:

FUNCTION StringToInteger
  (InString: STRING[10])   IN: Integer in string form.
    FUNCTION VALUE: Integer   The equivalent integer.
PURPOSE: Convert InString to an integer value and return it.

Then the ConvertStringDate procedure might be written:

PROCEDURE ConvertStringDate
  (DateIn: StringDate   IN: Date in Merrell's format.
  DateOut: Date)   OUT: Date in Nancy's format.
PURPOSE/GOAL STATE: Convert DateIn to the equivalent date DateOut, represented as three integers instead of as three strings.

ALGORITHM

Step 1: PURPOSE/GOAL STATE: Convert the day and year fields of DateIn to integers and store in the fields of DateOut.

ACTIONS:
    DateOut.Day := StringToInteger (DateIn.Day)
    DateOut.Year := StringToInteger (DateIn.Year)

Step 2: PURPOSE/GOAL STATE: Compare the month of DateIn against the possible months and assign the correct month value to the month field of DateOut.

ACTIONS:
    IF DateIn.Month = 'January' THEN
        DateOut.Month := 1
    ELSE IF DateIn.Month = 'February' THEN
        DateOut.Month := 2
       ...
    ELSE IF DateIn.Month = 'December' THEN
        DateOut.Month := 12

□ □

Chapter 8

8.1 **a.** *Path 1*: Include for the IF at line 1: the first case.
           For the IF at line 9: the first case.
    Path 2: Include for the IF at line 1: the first case.
           For the IF at line 9: the default case.
    Path 3: Include for the IF at line 1: the second case.
           For the IF at line 9: the first case.
    Path 4: Include for the IF at line 1: the second case.
           For the IF at line 9: the default case.

Path 5: Include for the IF at line 1: the default case.
For the IF at line 9: the first case.

Path 6: Include for the IF at line 1: the default case.
For the IF at line 9: the default case.

b. *Path 1*: Sales > Total[1] AND Sales = Total[1]
(contradiction)

Path 2: Sales > Total[1] AND Sales <> Total[1]

Path 3: Sales = Total[1] AND Sales < Total[2]

Path 4: Sales < Total[2] AND Sales < Total[1]

Path 5: Sales = Total[1] AND Sales >= Total[2]

Path 6: Sales < Total[1] AND Sales >= Total[2]

c. Path 1 can never be executed because its path condition is a contradiction.

8.3 **a.** Because LastSale is always equal to 3 when the loop at line 3 is reached, the loop always executes exactly two iterations. Thus there are only four possible paths that can ever be executed:

Path 1: Include for the loop at line 3: two iterations.
Within the loop body, include for the IF at line 5:
Iteration 1: The first case.
Iteration 2: The first case.

Path 2: Include for the loop at line 3: two iterations.
Within the loop body, include for the IF at line 5:
Iteration 1: The first case.
Iteration 2: The default case.

Path 3: Include for the loop at line 3: two iterations.
Within the loop body, include for the IF at line 5:
Iteration 1: The default case.
Iteration 2: The first case.

Path 4: Include for the loop at line 3: two iterations.
Within the loop body, include for the IF at line 5:
Iteration 1: The default case.
Iteration 2: The default case.

b. *Path 1*: Sales[2] > 0 AND Sales[3] > Sales[2]

Path 2: Sales[2] > 0 AND Sales[3] <= Sales[2]

Path 3: Sales[2] <= 0 AND Sales[3] > 0

Path 4: Sales[2] <= 0 AND Sales[3] <= 0

c. All four paths can be executed for some values of Sales[2] and Sales[3].

8.4 **b.** IN: I   OUT: StartDate.Year   IN/OUT: GradesList

c. IN/OUT: StudentStatus

d. OUT: StudentName

g. IN: Total, I, GradesList

8.5 **b.** IN: Player[2], CurrentMove   OUT: Move   IN/OUT: Board

8.6 **a.**

Value used	Is defined in line
B in line 3	1
B in line 8	4
C in line 7	5

b.

Value defined	Is used in lines
B in line 1	3, 4
D in line 2	3, 6, 8
C in line 5	6, 7, 8

c. *Value defined*   *Is lost in line*
     C in line 1   5
     C in line 5   Never lost in this segment
d. IN/OUT: D   OUT: A, B, C, E, F

8.8   **a.** IN: C   OUT: A, X, Y, Z
     c. IN: A, D, E   IN/OUT: B, C
     e. IN: A, B   OUT: C, D   IN/OUT: Max

8.9   **a.** *Value used*   *Is defined in line*
     D in line 9   8 or IN
     X in line 9   1, 7, 4
     X in line 3   1
     b. *Value defined*   *Is used in lines*
     C in line 2   3, 5, 8, 9
     D in line 8   9
     X in line 4   9
     c. IN: A, B   OUT: X   IN/OUT: C, D

8.10   **a.** *Value used*   *Is defined in line*
     I in line 3   1, 6
     NotFound in line 7   2, 5
     b. *Value defined*   *Is used in lines*
     I in line 6   3, 4, 6, 9
     NotFound in line 5   3, 7
     c. IN: M, A, N   OUT: I, NotFound, ZeroPointer

8.11   **a.** A: IN/OUT   B: OUT   C: IN
     c. U: OUT   V: IN   W: IN/OUT   Z: OUT
     e. Day: IN   Month: IN   Year: IN   D: IN/OUT

8.12   **a.** Statements: 1, 2, 3   Variables: A, B, C, D   IN: C, D

8.13   **a.** Statements: 1, 2, 5   Variables: A, B, C, D
     b. Statements: 1, 2, 5, 6   Variables: Total, A, B, C, D

8.14   **a.** Statements: 1, 3, 4, 5, 6, 7
     Variables: A, B, D, Next, Count

8.15   **a.** Statements: 6   Variables: B   IN: B
     c. Statements: 1, 7   Variables: B, C   IN: B, C

8.16   **a.** Statements: 1, 9   Variables: I, M   IN: M
     c. Statements: 5   Variables: none   IN: none

8.18   **a.** No. Replace MARKUP by (MARKUP/100).

8.19   **a.** Correct

8.20   **a.** Yes

8.22   **a.** Statements: 2, 5   Variables: A, B, R
     b. IN: A, B
     c. Zero iterations: A < B
     One iteration: A >= B AND (A − B) < B
     Two iterations: A >= B AND (A − B) >= B AND (A − 2*B) < B

8.24   **b.** May fail if Ch does not contain a digit character.
     Precondition: Ch IN ['0'..'9']
     d. Cannot fail. The parameter of *sqrt* is always zero or greater.

8.28 **a.** *Precondition*: K <= 500

```
IF K > 500 THEN
  BEGIN
    K := 500;
  END;
FOR ... - as given in text
```

c. *Precondition*: J >= 0

```
IF J < 0 THEN
  BEGIN
    writeln (
      'ERROR: Variable J is negative.  Used -J.');
    J := -J;
  END;
Quotient := ...      - as given in text
Remainder := ...
```

8.29 **a.**

Step 1. Determine that the value of C used in line 7 is defined at line 5. To guarantee the precondition on line 7, attach the following postcondition to line 5:

$$Postcondition: C >= 0$$

Step 2. To guarantee the postcondition at line 5, attach the following precondition to line 5:

$$Precondition: A + B >= 0$$

Step 3. Use back substitution to determine how A and B are computed at line 5:

$$A + B = (A_{IN} * A_{IN}) + 2 * (A_{IN} * A_{IN})$$
$$= 3 * (A_{IN} * A_{IN})$$

But $A_{IN} * A_{IN} >= 0$ for any value of A_{IN}. Thus, $A + B >= 0$ in all cases. We conclude that the precondition at line 5 is always satisfied when line 5 is reached, and so the original precondition at line 7 is always true when line 7 is reached.

8.30 Line 3 can be deleted because the value of Count is never used before it is lost in line 6.

8.33 **a.** No. The value of MaxA is used in line 18.
No. The value of SC is used in line 15.
Yes, unless the value of T4 is needed as an OUT value of the segment. The value of T4 is never used in the segment.
b. The statement in line 13 could be moved to line 5.
The statement in line 14 could be moved to line 6.
The statement in line 15 could be moved to line 14.

c. Insert anywhere after line 9 and before line 19.

d. Insert anywhere after line 9 and before line 13.

8.34 **a.** No. The order of execution matters because P is defined in Seg2 and used in Seg1.

c. Yes. Either order of execution gives the same results because no variable is defined in both segments or defined in one segment and used in the other.

8.36 A *Rule for Safe Factoring of a Statement out of a* WHILE *Loop*:

A statement in a WHILE loop body may be safely deleted from the loop body and placed immediately before the entire loop provided that:

1. The statement could safely be moved to be the first statement within the loop body, and

2. No OUT variable of the statement appears in the exit test of the WHILE loop.

In the given loop, the statement in line 3 can be safely moved to line 2 at the start of the loop body, and OUT variable Next does not appear in the exit test of the loop, so the statement can be safely factored out of the loop.

8.37 **a.** There are four control paths with the path conditions:

Path 1: A[2] > A[3] AND A[2] > A[1]
Path 2: A[2] > A[3] AND A[2] <= A[1]
Path 3: A[2] <= A[3] AND A[3] > A[1]
Path 4: A[2] <= A[3] AND A[3] <= A[1]

Any test data values that satisfy these path conditions will work, for example:

To execute path 1:	A[1] = 1	A[2] = 3	A[3] = 2
To execute path 2:	A[1] = 4	A[2] = 3	A[3] = 2
To execute path 3:	A[1] = 1	A[2] = 3	A[3] = 3
To execute path 4:	A[1] = 3	A[2] = 3	A[3] = 3

b. You could display either the values of A[1], A[2], and A[3] or the values of Maxposn, A[2], and A[3].

□ □
Chapter 9

9.1 **a.** CASE Clock OF

```
CLOCKON:
    ⟨action-1⟩
ALARM1SET, ALARM2SET:
    ⟨action-2⟩
OFF:
    ⟨action-3⟩
ELSE
    ⟨action-4⟩
END;
```

Pascal: CASE Clock OF

```
CLOCKON:
    BEGIN
        ⟨action-1⟩
```

```
        END;
    ALARM1SET,  ALARM2SET:
      BEGIN
          ⟨action-2⟩
      END;
    OFF:
      BEGIN
          ⟨action-3⟩
      END;
    RADIOON,  TAPEON:
      BEGIN
          ⟨action-4⟩
      END;
  END;
```

b.
```
CASE InputChar OF
     '+',  '-':
          ⟨action-1⟩
     '*',  '/':
          ⟨action-2⟩
     '%':
          ⟨action-3⟩
ELSE
     ⟨action-4⟩
END
```

Pascal:
```
IF InputChar IN ['+',  '-',  '*',  '/',  '%'] THEN
  BEGIN
      CASE InputChar OF
           '+',  '-':
             BEGIN
                 ⟨action-1⟩
             END;
           '*',  '/':
             BEGIN
                 ⟨action-2⟩
             END;
           '%':
             BEGIN
                 ⟨action-3⟩
             END;
      END;
  END
ELSE
  BEGIN
      ⟨action-4⟩
  END;
```

9.2 **a.** Mutually exclusive.
   b. Nonexclusive.
   c. Nonexclusive.
   d. Mutually exclusive.

9.3 **c.** FUNCTION ComputeTax
   (Income: Integer)   IN: Income amount in $.
   FUNCTION VALUE: Integer   OUT: Tax in $.
   PURPOSE: Compute and return the tax owed on Income.

ALGORITHM

Step 1:   PURPOSE/GOAL STATE: Distinguish the various cases and compute and return the correct tax amount.

ACTIONS:
   IF   Income $<=$ 3000 THEN
        FUNCTION VALUE := 0.02 $*$ Income

   ELSE IF (Income $>$ 3000) AND (Income $<=$ 5000) THEN
        FUNCTION VALUE := 60 + 0.03 $*$ (Income $-$ 3000)

   ELSE IF (Income $>$ 5000) AND (INCOME $<=$ 14000) THEN
        FUNCTION VALUE := 120 + 0.05 $*$ (INCOME $-$ 5000)

   ELSE IF Income $>$ 14000 THEN
        FUNCTION VALUE := 570 + 0.0575 $*$ (Income $-$ 14000)

9.4 **a.** Nancy's version: 7 paths.
   Fred's version: 9 paths.
   Lynne's version: 40 paths.

9.5 **a.** Nonexclusive.   **b.** Mutually exclusive.
   c. Nonexclusive.   **d.** Mutually exclusive.

9.6 **a.** Exhaustive.   **b.** Not exhaustive.   **c.** Exhaustive.
   d. Exhaustive.   **e.** Not exhaustive.   **f.** Not exhaustive.

9.7 **a.** NOT (X $>$ (Max+2)) *or* X $<=$ (Max+2)
   c. NOT (Status IN [ON, READY])
        or Status IN [OFF, BROKEN, DISCONNECTED]
   e. NOT (Employed = FALSE) *or* Employed

9.9   The tests are mutually exclusive, so the path conditions for the first three cases are just the tests for the cases in the IF. The tests are not exhaustive, so the path condition for the default case is:

   NOT ((A $>$ B) AND (A $>$ C)) AND NOT ((B $>$ A) AND (B $>$ C))
   AND NOT ((C $>$ B) AND (C $>$ A))

which simplifies to:

$$((A <= B) \text{ OR } (A <= C)) \text{ AND } ((B <= A) \text{ OR } (B <= C))$$
$$\text{AND } ((C <= B) \text{ OR } (C <= A))$$

9.10 In the second subcase of the second case, replace EQUAL by LESSEQ in the assignment. Also, in the following cases no assignment is made to Operation and no error message is displayed:

$(Char1 = '=')$ AND $(Char2 <> space)$
$(Char1 = '<')$ AND $(Char2 <> space, '>' \text{ or } '=')$
$(Char1 = '>')$ AND $(Char2 <> space \text{ or } '=')$

9.12 **a.** 7 paths.

b. The tests for the three main cases are mutually exclusive and exhaustive. The tests for the subcases in case 2 are mutually exclusive. Thus the path conditions are:

Case 1: Leafy AND Crisp
Case 2, subcase 1: NOT Crisp AND (Soft AND Yellow)
Case 2, subcase 2: NOT Crisp AND (NOT Soft AND NOT Yellow)
Case 2, subcase 3: NOT Crisp AND (Soft AND NOT Yellow)
Case 2, default case:

NOT Crisp AND NOT (Soft AND Yellow) AND
NOT (NOT Soft AND NOT Yellow) AND
NOT (Soft AND NOT Yellow)

or simplifying:

NOT Crisp AND (NOT Soft OR NOT Yellow) AND (Soft OR Yellow)
AND (NOT Soft OR Yellow))

or simplifying:

NOT Crisp AND NOT Soft AND Yellow

Case 3: Crisp AND NOT Leafy

Default case: Not possible; tests are exhaustive.

9.13 **a.** There is a semicolon before the ELSE and a "dangling ELSE". The simplest correction is:

```
IF X > 0 THEN
   BEGIN
     IF Y < 0 THEN
         X := X + 1;
   END
ELSE IF X = 0 THEN ... as before
```

b. The first case requires a BEGIN-END around the two assignments.

□ □
Chapter 10

10.1 **b.**
```
I := M;
WHILE I >= N DO
```

```
            BEGIN
                Product := Product * I;
            END;  I := I - 1;
    d.  I := A;
        SaveFinalValue := B;
        WHILE I <= SaveFinalValue DO
          BEGIN
              ComputeValues (A, B);
              B := B + 1;
              I := I + 1;
          END;
```

10.2 **b.**
```
        writeln;
        Count := Count + 1;
        WHILE Count <= SpaceCount DO
          BEGIN
              writeln;
              Count := Count + 1;
          END;
```
    c.
```
        ComputeResults (A, B, Flag);
        WHILE Flag = CONTINUE DO
          BEGIN
              ComputeResults (A, B, Flag);
          END;
```
    e.
```
        Quotient := Quotient + 1;
        Remainder := Remainder - B;
        WHILE Remainder >= B DO
          BEGIN
              Quotient := Quotient + 1;
              Remainder := Remainder - B;
          END;
```

10.3 **b.** *Initialization*: J := 2 (in FOR loop header)
      Exit text: J > LastGrade (in FOR loop header)
      Update: J := J + 1 (in FOR loop header)
      Type of loop control: Count controlled.
    c. *Initialization*: Done := FALSE
      Exit test: Done = TRUE
      Update: Done := TRUE
      Type of loop control: Event controlled.
    d. *Initialization*: ZeroFound := FALSE
                I := 1
      Exit test: ZeroFound OR (I > N)
      Update: ZeroFound := TRUE
             I := I + 1
      Type of loop control: Count and event controlled.

10.4 **a.** ACTIONS:
```
        SumSquares := 0
        FOR I := 21 TO 49 STEP 2 DO
```

```
                    BEGIN
                            SumSquares := SumSquares + I*I
                          KTH ITERATION: SumSquares contains the sum of
                          the first K odd integers greater than 20.
                    END
```

b. ACTIONS:

```
                    I := 1000
                    WHILE ValueList [I] >= 0 DO
                          I := I - 1
                          KTH ITERATION: Last K elements of ValueList
                          are not negative and I = subscript of the
                          (K+1)st element from the end.
```

10.6 **a.** Off by one error. Count = 21 on last iteration.
   b. Infinite loop. Posn is not updated on some paths.
   c. Infinite loop if M > N+1 on loop entry.

10.8 **a.** Iteration count = (M*M − M)/1 + 1 = (M−1)*M + 1
   Value of I during the Kth iteration = M + K − 1
   b. Iteration count = (3 − 2)/0.25 + 1 = 5
   Value of H during the Kth iteration = 2 + (K−1)*0.25 = 1.75 + 0.25*K

□ □

Chapter 11

11.2 **a.**   *FORMAT OF FILE DAILYTEMPS*

⟨DAILYTEMPS file⟩ ::=

⟨year⟩⟨EOLN⟩
{⟨day⟩ ⟨high-temp⟩ ⟨low-temp⟩⟨EOLN⟩}
⟨EOF⟩ ::=

WHERE

⟨year⟩ An integer, the year number.
⟨day⟩ ::= An integer day number in the range 1..366.

⟨high-temp⟩ ::=
   An integer giving the high temperature for the specified day,
   in degrees C.

⟨low-temp⟩ ::=
   An integer giving the low temperature for the specified day,
   in degrees C.

11.6

```
PROCEDURE ReadGradesFile

(VAR COURSEFILE: Text;        {IN: File containing data to be
                               read.}
  VAR Course: CourseData);    {OUT: Data object to receive data
                               read.}

  {PURPOSE/GOAL STATE: Read the data values in COURSEFILE and
  store them in the appropriate fields of Course. The file
  format is specified in the program requirements.}

  {PRECONDITION: Parameter COURSEFILE is already connected to
  an external file name.}

  VAR
    I: Integer;              {FOR loop subscript variable.}
BEGIN
      {PURPOSE/GOAL STATE: Open COURSEFILE and read the first
      two lines of heading data into the fields of the Course
      record.}

  reset (COURSEFILE);
  readln (Course.CourseID, Course.Semester, Course.Year);
  readln (Course.Enrollment);

      {PURPOSE/GOAL STATE: Read one line of data for each
      enrolled student into the fields of an element of the
      Course.Grades array.}

  FOR I := 1 TO Course.Enrollment DO
    BEGIN
        readln (Course.Grades[I].ID,
                Course.Grades[I].Homework,
                Course.Grades[I].Exam1,
                Course.Grades[I].Exam2,
                Course.Grades[I].Final);
    END;
END;
```

11.8 b. ACTIONS:

$$I := 1$$

WHILE NOT eof (NEWDATA) AND I <= MAXVALUES DO
   READ FROM INDATA: Hours [I] —use readln
   $$I := I + 1$$

KTH ITERATION: The Kth value has been read
from file INDATA and stored in the Kth
element of Hours. $I = K + 1$.

12.1 On each recursive call, the subscript Start of the array element where counting is started is increased by one while End remains unchanged, so that there is one fewer element to be counted. Thus, on each recursive call, Start is closer to the end of the array and, thus, is closer to the base case where Start > End.

12.2 b.   LOCAL STATE

(The List array remains unchanged on each call)

	At Start of Execution			At End of Execution		
	Start	End	Function Value	Start	End	Function Value
Initial call:	3	7	??	3	7	3
1st recursive call	4	7	??	4	7	3
2nd recursive call	5	7	??	5	7	2
3rd recursive call	6	7	??	6	7	1
4th recursive call	7	7	??	7	7	1
5th recursive call	8	7	??	8	7	0

12.3 b. ALGORITHM

Step 1: PURPOSE/GOAL STATE: Determine Count for List[Start].

ACTIONS:
        IF List[Start] > Threshold THEN
            Count := 1
        ELSE
            Count := 0

Step 2: PURPOSE/GOAL STATE: If only one element is to be checked, return Count as the result. Otherwise use a recursive call to check the remainder of List.

ACTIONS:
        IF Start = End THEN
            FUNCTION VALUE := Count
        ELSE
            FUNCTION VALUE := Count +
                    CountAboveThreshold (List, Start+1, End, Threshold)

d. ALGORITHM

Step 1: ACTIONS:
IF Count > 0 THEN
DISPLAY: One blank line
IF Count > 1 THEN
CALL DisplayBlankLines (Count − 1)

☐☐ Chapter 13

13.1 9   5   7   should be displayed.
9   9   5   is actually displayed.

13.2 **a.** FindZeroLocation is coupled to the representation of parameter List because the subprogram body refers to List [I], so List is assumed to be represented by an array.

b. ComputeGPA is *not* coupled to the representation of any of its parameters, except to assume that parameters TotalHours and GPA are numbers. No representation for parameter Transcript is assumed within this procedure.

☐☐ Chapter 14

14.3 **a.** Constant factor improvement in speed. Additive constant improvement in storage.

b. Constant factor improvement in speed.

14.4 **a.** $O(N)$ **b.** $O(N^2)$ **c.** $O(N \log_2 N)$

14.5 **a.** Depends only on N.
b. Depends on the values in A.

14.6 **a.** Assume that the last values inserted in the table are the ones most frequently looked up. Then backward search is more efficient.

14.7 If the table were sorted, then the linear search algorithm would not have to scan the entire table to determine that a desired entry was not in the table. Instead it could stop the search when it first passed the point in the sorted table where the entry would have appeared. On the average, only $1/2$ the table entries would have to be searched, instead of all the entries. The improvement in the average search time is $1/2 * N$, which is a constant factor improvement in speed. Thus, the linear search of a sorted table is still an $O(N)$ algorithm, as compared to $O(\log_2 N)$ for binary search.

☐☐ Chapter 15

15.1 **a.** Array of records.
b. Two-dimensional array.
c. Two-dimensional array.
d. Array of records.

15.2 **b.**
```
Sum := 0;
FOR J := 1 TO N DO
  BEGIN
    Sum := Sum + B[7, J];
  END;
Result := 2 * Sum;
```

```
    d. FOR I := 1 TO M DO
         BEGIN
             Sum := 0;
             FOR J := 1 TO N DO
                BEGIN
                    Sum := Sum + B[I, J] + 2;
                END;
             V[I] := Sum;
         END;
15.3  FOR I := 1 TO 20 DO
         BEGIN
             FOR J := 1 TO 30 DO
                BEGIN
                    BTranspose [J, I] := B [I, J];
                END;
         END;
```

Index

File inclusion, 683–85
File name:
  external, 595–96
  internal, 595–96
File: (*See also* Data file)
  private, 47
  public, 47
File system, 46–47
Final state, 95
  of a Turing machine, 9
Flag, debugging, 222–23
Flag variable, 163–64
  failure, 469–70
Flow chart, 415
Floating point, 60–61 (*See also* Real number)
Floppy disk. *See* Diskette
Flow chart. *See* Control flow diagram
Flow through value, 433–35
FOR loop, 343–53, 545–47
  and arrays, 343–53
  and hand tracing, 372–74
  Pascal punctuation, 531
Formal parameter, and procedure body, 315–23 (*See also* Parameter)
Format:
  of data file, 598–99
  of output line, 174–80
Formula, and ASSIGN actions, 101–2
Fortran, 56
FORWARD declaration, 642–43
Fraction size specification, 178–80
Function, 102, 232 (*See also* Subprogram)
  body of, 325–28
  call of, 239–42
  on Char values, 165
  heading for, in pseudo-code, 232–33
  in Pascal, 327–28
  predefined, 102, 158–59
  value assignment, 325–28
  value of, 232
Fundamental Principle of Data Representation, 259–60
  and abstract data types, 668

Game of Life, 752–53
Game program, 51
Garbage result, 458
Giga- (prefix), 69
Global data object, 658–67
  attitudes toward, 667
  and data files, 600
  and data flow, 659–60
  and local data objects, 659–61
  and modules, 675
  and parameters, 658–61, 666–67

in Pascal, 663–65
and program analysis, 665–67
in pseudo-code, 661–63
retention of value, 660–61
safe use of, 666–67
and scope rules, 663–65
and side effects, 666
and structure chart, 660
uninitialized, 658
GLOBAL DATA OBJECTS list, 600–601, 661–62
Global variable. *See* Global data object
Goal state, 97–98
  of a procedure, 230–31
GOTO statement, 410–11, 759–60
  and flow charts, 415
Guard, 464–65

Hacker, 45, 77
Hacking, 76–77
Halting problem, 22
Hand tracing, 117–20
  and data structure parameters, 369–72
  disadvantages of, 120
  of FOR loops, 372–74
  and program analysis, 127, 445
  of subprogram execution, 364–74
Hanging program, 194
Hard-wired connection, 43
Hardware:
  basic components, 41
  definition, 13
  organization of, 57–68
  reliability, 57–58
  useful characteristics of, 57
Header comment, 142–43
Heap, 646–47
Hierarchical program structure, 248
  and modules, 676–77
Hierarchy of subprograms. *See* Subprogram hierarchy
Hints for algorithm development, 109–12
Hollerith, Herman, 5
Home computer. *See* Microcomputer
Horror stories:
  The Bug Heard 'Round the World
  Electronic Mail Answered Automatically, 52
  Never Correct Operating System, 35
  Upside Down Space Shuttle, 146

Identifier, 139–40
  choice of, 204–5, 249–50
IF, 103–5, 149, 495–96 (*See also* Conditional action)
  Pascal punctuation, 531
Importing a module, 675, 681–85

IN parameter, 318
IN test, 166–67
IN/OUT analysis:
  of an action, 420–26
  of a segment, 431–35
INCLUDE extension, 683–85
Incremental testing, 379–84
Indentation, 205
Index variable, 545
  value during loop iteration, 580–81
Infinite loop, 555–56
  causes, 574–75
  during testing, 194
Infinite recursion, 634
Infinite series, 753
Informatics, 16
Information hiding, 247–48
  and modules, 676
Information processing machine, 2
Information processing task, 2–3
Information science, 16
Initial state, 94–95
  of a Pascal program, 147
  of a Turing machine, 8
Initial value:
  of an array, 279
  of a record, 273
Input data, 80–81
Input device, 41, 64–65
INPUT file, 597
Insertion, during modification, 478–80
Insertion sort algorithm, 724–27
Instruction, binary representation, 61
Instruction execution cycle, 68
  speed of, 68
  of a Turing machine, 8–9
Instrumentation of a program, 702–3
Integer:
  binary representation of, 60
  conversion to character, 166
  data type, 92
  literal value, 151–52
  range of, 146
Integrated circuit, 14
Integrated programming environment, 50
  and compiler, 190
Intellectual control of a program, 77–78
Interactive dialogue, 80–82, 85–88
Interactive program, 79
  and batch processing, 590–92
Intermediate state, 95
Internal documentation, 203–4
Internal file name, 595–96
Interpreter, 54
Intersection, of lists, 588
Iteration, 407
Iteration count, 580–81

Jacquard, Joseph-Marie, 5

Key value, in a table. *See* Table
Keyboard, 65
Keypunch, 14
Kill a program, 195
Kilo- (prefix), 69
Knuth, Donald, 710

Label on a statement, 759–60
Length:
  of a character string, 294–96, 298
  of a list, 289–91
Library:
  of abstractions, 248
  of modules, 676
Light pen, 65
Limits of computation, 22–23
Line printer, 15
Linear search, 714–18
LISP, 56, 587
List:
  of constant known length, 283–84
    operations on, 284
  of varying length, 289–92
    operations on, 292–93
    and tables, 712
Literal character string, 295–96
  in BNF, 83
Literal data value, 100
  and defined constants, 219
  in Pascal, 151–54
Local state, 317
  and hand tracing, 364–74
Logic, mathematical, 7
Logic error, 117
  correction of, 127
Login, 44
Logout, 44
Loop:
  body of, 553
  bound on iterations, 557
  coding of, 572–73
  control, 553–57
    choice of, 564
    design of, 564–68
    initialization, 554
    types of, 556–57
  count and event controlled, 557
  count controlled, 556
  count controlled WHILE loop, 573
  and data flow analysis, 430
  design concepts, 553–73
  entry state, 559
  errors in design, 574–76
  event controlled, 557
  exit state, 559
  exit test, 553
    errors in, 574–75
  FOR, 343–53, 545–47

FOR and REPEAT into WHILE,
    550–52
index value during iteration,
    580–81
infinite, 555–56
  causes of, 574–75
invariant, 560–61
  design of, 563–64
  and loop verification, 577
iteration count, 580–81
and mathematical induction,
    579–80
and matrix/vector operations,
    739–42
nested, 558
off by one error, 575–76
and performance measurement,
    702–3
priming of, 571
progress toward termination,
    555–56
READ patterns for data files,
    612–16
real numbers in exit test, 749–51
and recursion, 651–52
Seven Step Check, 577–79
startup segment, 553
state at end of Kth iteration, 560
step size, 564–65
steps in design, 563
subscript range error in exit test,
    576–77
WHILE vs. FOR, 352–53
WHILE vs. REPEAT, 549–50
zero trip error, 576
Loop and a half problem, 571
Loop Designer's Dilemma, 568–72
Looping program, 123–24
Lovelace, Ada, 5

Magic square, 752
Magnetic core memory, 14
Magnetic disk, 15
Magnetic tape, 15
Main procedure, 138–39, 323
Mainframe, 71–72
Maintenance of a program, 203–4
Malfunction of computer system,
    201–2
Mathematical formula, in Pascal,
    154–62
Mathematical function. *See* Function
Mathematical induction:
  and loops, 579–80
  and recursion, 650
Mathematics:
  and computer science, 22
  and programming, 21–22
Matrix. *See* Array
Mauchley, John, 12

MAXINT, 146
McCarthy's 91 function, 129–30
Mega- (prefix), 69
Memory, 41
  array in, 279–80
  organization of, 61–63
  random access, 63
  record variable in, 273–74
  size of, 70
Memory address, 62
Memory chip, 14
Menu, 47
Micro- (prefix), 69
Microcomputer, 40, 70, 72
Microprocessor chip, 14
Milli- (prefix), 69
Mills, Harlan, 492
Minicomputer, 71–72
Minsky, Marvin, 23
Mips, 68
MOD operation, 157–58
Modem, 44
Modification:
  analysis of, 472–84
  potentially unsafe, 474–75
  reasons for, 400
  safe, 472–77
Modularity, 249
Modulator-demodulator, 43
Module, 674–92
  and abstract data types, 675
  advantages of, 676–77
  coding in Pascal, 682–83
  definition part, 674, 677–79
  design of, 677–81
  examples of, 686–92
  implementation part, 674, 677–81
  import of, 675, 681–85
  and INCLUDE extension, 683–85
  library of, 676
  and name conflicts, 685–86
  and naming conventions, 685–86
  performance measurement exam-
    ple, 686–90
  pseudo-code for, 677–82
  random number generator example,
    690–92
  and reusable software, 676
  types of, 675
  use of, 681–82
Morse Code, 68
Most Dangerous Moment in Pro-
    gramming, 458
Mouse, 65
Movement, during modification,
    480–84
Multidimensional array. *See* Array
Murphy's Law of Programming, 399
Mutual recursion, 629
Mutually exclusive cases, 504–10
Mutually exclusive tests, 515–18

Name. *See* Identifier
Name conflict, 685–86
Naming convention, 685–86
Nano- (prefix), 69
Naur, Peter, 83
Negation of a test, 524
Nested loop, 558
Nested subprogram, 759
Network:
  of computers, 15, 43–44
  switching, 5–6
Ninety-one function. *See* McCarthy's
    91 function
Ninety-ten (90–10) Rule, 700
Nonexclusive case, 504–10
Nonexclusive test, 515–18
Nontext file, 593, 757
Number:
  integer. *See* Integer
  real. *See* Real number
Numerical analysis, 749
Numerical and symbolic computation, 17

Object. *See* Data object
Object program, 49
Operand, 98
Operating system, 15, 17, 46–47
Operation, 98 (*See also* Subprogram)
  arithmetic, 102
  on an array, 278–79, 343–53
  Boolean, 103, 162–63
  on a character string, 294,
    296–303, 354–59
    summary table, 355
  compare/test, 227
  copy, 100
  counting, 101
  coupling to data representation,
    669–72
  creation, 227
  and data representation, 260
  division, 156–58
  on enumerated data type, 265–66
  fetch in a memory, 63
  precedence of, 159–61
  read, 63
  read/display, 228
  on a record, 273, 329–39
  relational, 103, 162
  retrieval, 227
  store in a memory, 63
  on subrange data type, 263
  swap, 100–101
  test, 102
  types of, 227–28
  update, 227
  write, 63
ORD operation, 165
Order of. *See* Efficiency, *order of*
  improvements

Ordering:
  of character values, 164–65
  of enumerated type values, 266–67
Oughtred, William, 5
Out-of-bounds error. *See* Subscript
    range error
Output data, 80–81
Output device, 41, 65–66
OUTPUT file, 597
Output line, in Pascal, 171
Overflow error, 746–47

Package. *See* Module
Packed array, 302
Parameter:
  actual, 238–40
    in a function, 232
    in a procedure, 229
  correspondence of actual and for-
    mal, 240–41
  and data structures, 340–41
  formal:
    in a function, 232–33
    in a procedure, 229–31
  order of, 250
  subprogram name as, 759
  value, 322–23
  VAR, 321–23
Parameter transmission, 317–23, 326
  and data files, 601
  and hand tracing, 364–74
  IN parameters, 318–19
  IN/OUT and OUT parameters,
    319–20
Partially filled array, 289–90
Pascal, Blaise, 5
Pascal programming language, 56
  coding in, 138
  punctuation rules, 530–36
  scope rules, 663–65
Path condition, 413–19
  analysis of, 454–56
  and conditional actions, 523–27
  and contradiction, 417–19
  for default case, 526–27
  and mutually exclusive tests, 518,
    523–24
  and nonexclusive tests, 525
Path, control. *See* Control path
Path testing, 197–98
Patterns in algorithm design, 111–12
Performance, 698–703 (*See also*
    Efficiency)
  and critical ten percent, 700–701
  measurement of, 701–2
    module for, 686–90
  ninety-ten rule, 700
  rules of thumb, 699–701
  and tweaking, 700, 709
Peripheral device, 70

Personal computer. *See* Microcomputer
Pico- (prefix), 69
Picture:
  binary representation of, 61
  digitized, 739
PL/I, 56
Playing computer. *See* Hand tracing
Plotter, 66
Pointer data type, 757
Portable program, 56
Position of a file, 594
Postcondition, 465–68
Pre/post analysis, 401, 465–70
Precedence of operations, 159–61
Precision of a real number, 147
Precondition, 119, 457–62
  of an expression, 167–69
  and failure of an action, 458–62
  of a function, 232–33
  and a guard, 464–65
  and the "most dangerous moment
    in programming," 458
  of a procedure, 230–31
  of a subprogram, 242
  of a subscript expression, 281–83
Precondition/postcondition analysis,
    401, 465–70
PRED operation, 165
Primary storage. *See* Memory
Prime number, 587
Priming a loop, 571
Principle of Safe Modification, 475
Print field, in Pascal, 174
Printer, 65–66
Private file, 47
Problem size and efficiency, 704–5
Problems:
  airport simulation, 395–96
  automatic teller machine (ATM), 257
  binary search for root of equation,
    729–30
  binary to decimal conversion
    (cleanroom), 493
  board game manager, 257
  Captain Nemo's Message Encoder,
    312
  carpet man, 135
  checkbook balancing, 135
  chess move display, 621
  converting character string to in-
    teger, 214
  Conway's Game of Life, 752–53
  counting characters, 394
  counting characters (cleanroom), 493
  currency exchange, 313
  display a rectangle, 213
  Euclid's GCD algorithm, 135
  extracting number from message
    (cleanroom), 493
  fringe benefits package, 540